Lecture Notes in Computer Science 5014

Commenced Publication in 1973
Founding and Former Series Editors:
Gerhard Goos, Juris Hartmanis, and Jan van Leeuwen

Editorial Board

David Hutchison
　Lancaster University, UK
Takeo Kanade
　Carnegie Mellon University, Pittsburgh, PA, USA
Josef Kittler
　University of Surrey, Guildford, UK
Jon M. Kleinberg
　Cornell University, Ithaca, NY, USA
Alfred Kobsa
　University of California, Irvine, CA, USA
Friedemann Mattern
　ETH Zurich, Switzerland
John C. Mitchell
　Stanford University, CA, USA
Moni Naor
　Weizmann Institute of Science, Rehovot, Israel
Oscar Nierstrasz
　University of Bern, Switzerland
C. Pandu Rangan
　Indian Institute of Technology, Madras, India
Bernhard Steffen
　University of Dortmund, Germany
Madhu Sudan
　Massachusetts Institute of Technology, MA, USA
Demetri Terzopoulos
　University of California, Los Angeles, CA, USA
Doug Tygar
　University of California, Berkeley, CA, USA
Gerhard Weikum
　Max-Planck Institute of Computer Science, Saarbruecken, Germany

Jorge Cuellar   Tom Maibaum
Kaisa Sere (Eds.)

FM 2008:
Formal Methods

15th International Symposium on Formal Methods
Turku, Finland, May 26-30, 2008
Proceedings

 Springer

Volume Editors

Jorge Cuellar
Siemens Corporate Technology
Otto-Hahn-Ring 6
81730 München, Germany
E-mail: jorge.cuellar@siemens.com

Tom Maibaum
McMaster University
Software Quality Research Laboratory
and Department of Computing and Software
1280 Main St West, Hamilton, ON L8S 4K1, Canada
E-mail: tom@maibaum.org

Kaisa Sere
Åbo Akademi University
Department of Information Technology
20520 Turku, Finland
E-mail: kaisa.sere@abo.fi

Library of Congress Control Number: 2008927062

CR Subject Classification (1998): D.2, F.3, D.3, D.1, J.1, K.6, F.4

LNCS Sublibrary: SL 2 – Programming and Software Engineering

ISSN   0302-9743
ISBN-10   3-540-68235-X Springer Berlin Heidelberg New York
ISBN-13   978-3-540-68235-6 Springer Berlin Heidelberg New York

This work is subject to copyright. All rights are reserved, whether the whole or part of the material is concerned, specifically the rights of translation, reprinting, re-use of illustrations, recitation, broadcasting, reproduction on microfilms or in any other way, and storage in data banks. Duplication of this publication or parts thereof is permitted only under the provisions of the German Copyright Law of September 9, 1965, in its current version, and permission for use must always be obtained from Springer. Violations are liable to prosecution under the German Copyright Law.

Springer is a part of Springer Science+Business Media

springer.com

© Springer-Verlag Berlin Heidelberg 2008
Printed in Germany

Typesetting: Camera-ready by author, data conversion by Scientific Publishing Services, Chennai, India
Printed on acid-free paper   SPIN: 12271788   06/3180   5 4 3 2 1 0

Preface

This volume contains the proceedings of Formal Methods 2008, the 15th International Symposium on Formal Methods, organized by Åbo Akademi University, Turku, Finland, during May 26-30, 2008. The series of Formal Methods conferences is supported by FME (Formal Methods Europe), an independent association which aims to stimulate the use of, and the research on, formal methods for system development. The first event in this series was VDM Europe, held in 1987. The scope of the symposium has grown since then, encompassing all aspects of software and hardware that are amenable to formal analysis.

As in previous years, this symposium brought together innovators and practitioners in precise mathematical methods for software development, academic and industrial users as well as researchers, tool developers and vendors. We received 106 submissions from 24 countries, a demonstration of the international nature of the event. Each submission was carefully refereed by at least three reviewers. The Programme Committee finally selected 23 papers for presentation at the symposium after what was sometimes really extensive discussion! We would like to extend our thanks once more to all the members of the Programme Committee and to all the reviewers for their excellent and efficient work. (The names of all involved appear over the page.) Apart from the regular papers, there were five invited talks at the symposium, given by Arvind, Shmuel Katz, Paolo Bresciani, Jay Misra, and Dawson Engler. Arvind and Katz also submitted papers to accompany their talks and these are included in the volume.

The Formal Methods 2008 symposium also included various related events. There were five workshops, coordinated by the Workshop Chair, John Derrick: Formal aspects of virtual organizations, John Fitzgerald and Jeremy Bryans; Overture/VDM++, Peter Gorm Larsen and Shin Sahara; Refinement Workshop, John Derrick; Pilot Projects for the Grand Challenge in Verified Software, Jim Woodcock, and Computational Models for Cell Processes, Ion Petre and Ralph-Johan Back. There were also seven tutorials, coordinated by the Tutorial Chair, Marina Waldén: Computational Systems Biology (full day), Ion Petre and Ralph-Johan Back; Teaching formal methods to students in high school and introductory university courses (full day), Ralph-Johan Back; Event-B and the Rodin Platform (full day), Jean-Raymond Abrial; Why formal verification remains on the fringes of commercial development (full day), Arvind; Formal Methods and Signal Processing (half day), Raymond Boute; Runtime Model Checking of Multithreaded C Programs Using Automated Instrumentation Dynamic Partial Order Reduction and Distributed Checking (half day), Ganesh Gopalakrishnan and Yu Yang; and Formal modelling and analysis of real-time systems using UPPAAL (half day), Paul Pettersson and Wang Yi. There was also an associated Doctoral Symposium, organized by Elena Troubitsyna, that included presentations by doctoral students as well as a Poster and Tool Exhibition, organized by Michael Leuschel.

An Industry Day was organized by the Formal Techniques Industrial Association (ForTIA) in parallel with the first day of the main symposium. The first invited speaker of the symposium, Arvind, was shared between the main programme and that of the Industry Day. This associated event was organized by Peter Gorm Larsen and Sari Leppänen. Five short contributed papers from the Industry Day are included in this volume.

The electronic submission, refereeing and Programme Committee discussions were well supported (almost always!) by EasyChair, developed by Andrei Voronkov at the University of Manchester, UK. Our thanks to him and also to our publisher Springer, in particular to Anna Kramer for helping with the preparation of the proceedings. Pablo Castro worked hard on putting together this volume, ably assisting the editors. Finally, we would like to thank all the speakers, all the sponsors (listed at the end of the Preface), and especially the Organizing Committee for all the hard work necessary for putting on this great event.

May 2008

Jorge Cuellar
Tom Maibaum

Symposium Organization

The Department of Information Technologies at Åbo Akademi University, Turku, Finland together with the Formal Methods Europe association collaborated to the organization of the Formal Methods 2008 symposium. We would like to acknowledge the hard work of the following persons involved in the process of putting on Formal Methods 2008.

Symposium Chairs

General Chair	Kaisa Sere (Åbo Akademi University)
Programme Chairs	Jorge Cuellar (Siemens, Germany)
	Tom Maibaum (McMaster University)
Steering Committee	Dines Bjørner, John Fitzgerald, Marie-Claude Gaudel
	Stefania Gnesi, Ian Hayes, Pamela Zave, Jim Woodcock
Industry Day Chairs	Peter G. Larsen (Eng. College of Aarhus)
	Sari Leppänen (Nokia, Helsinki)
Workshop Chair	John Derrick (Sheffield University)
Tutorial Chair	Marina Waldén (Åbo Akademi University)
Doctoral Symposium Chair	Elena Troubitsyna (Åbo Akademi University)
Tools and Poster Exhibition Chair	Michael Leuschel (University of Düsseldorf)

Organizing Committee at Åbo Akademi University

Kaisa Sere (General Chair)
Marina Waldén (Finances)
Luigia Petre (Coordination)
Tiina Haanila (Secretary)
Magnus Dahlvik (Webmaster)
Johannes Eriksson (Photographer)

Programme Committee

Bernhard K. Aichernig	Technical University of Graz, Austria
Keijiro Araki	Kyushu University, Japan
Alessandro Armando	Genova University, Italy
Ralph-Johan Back	Åbo Akademi University, Turku, Finland
Gilles Barthe	INRIA at Sophia-Antiplois, France

David Basin ETH, Zurich, Switzerland
Frank de Boer CWI Amsterdam, The Netherlands
Ed Brinksma University of Twente, The Netherlands
Dawson Engler Stanford University, USA
Marcelo Frias University of Buenos Aires, Argentina
Dimitra Giannakopoulou RIACS/NASA Ames, USA
Radu Grosu Stony Brook University, USA
Joshua Guttman MITRE Corporation, USA
Constance Heitmeyer NRL, USA
Cliff Jones Newcastle University, UK
Shmuel Katz Technion, Israel
Paddy Krishnan Bond University, Australia
Axel van Lamsweerde Louvain University, Belgium
Rustan Leino Microsoft Research, Redmond, USA
Dominique Méry Nancy University, France
Marius Minea Technical University of Timisoara, Romania
Madhavan Mukund CMI, Chennai Mathematical Institute, India
Cesar Munoz National Institute of Aerospace, USA
Tobias Nipkow Technical University of Munich, Germany
José Nuno Oliveira University of Minho, Portugal
Paritosh K Pandya Tata Institute of Fundamental Research, Mumbai, India
John Rushby SRI, USA
Augusto Sampaio University of Pernambuco, Brazil
Steve Schneider University of Surrey, UK
Emil Sekerinski McMaster University, Canada
Vitaly Shmatikov University of Texas at Austin, USA
Douglas Smith Kestrel, USA
Ketil Stølen SINTEF and University of Oslo, Norway
Andrzej Tarlecki Warsaw University, Poland
Sebastian Uchitel Imperial College, UK and University of Buenos Aires, Argentina
Alan Wassyng McMaster University, Canada
Roel Wieringa Twente University, The Netherlands
Martin Wirsing Ludwig-Maximilians-Universität, Munich, Germany
Pierre Wolper University of Liege, Belgium
Jim Woodcock University of York, UK

External Reviewers

Nazareno Aguirre
Zoe Andrews
Luis Barbosa
Manuel Barbosa
Frédéric Besson

Olivier Bournez
Guillaume Brat
Einar Broch Johnsen
Sean Callanan
Roberto Carbone

Supratik Chakraborty
Tom Chothia
Piotr Chrzastowski-Wachtel
Jacek Chrzaszcz
Dave Cllarke
Ernie Cohen
Pieter Cuijpers
Pedro D'Argenio
Deepak D'Souza
Ernst-Erich Doberkat
Adalberto Farias
David Feitelson
Maria João Frade
Leo Freitas
Juan Galeotti
Mihaela Gheorghiu Bobaru
Alwyn Goodloe
David Gries
Ian Hayes
Kelly Hayhurst
Alexei Iliasov
Ryszard Janicki
Ralph Jeffords
Michael Kaminski
Felix Klaedtke
Beata Konikowska
Wouter Kuijper
Rom Langerak
Sławomir Lasota
Peng Li
Kamal Lodaya
Mass Soldal Lund
Jeffrey Maddalon
Angelika Mader
Jacopo Mantovani
Jelena Marincic
Nicolas Markey
Peter Mehlitz
Larissa Meinicke
Sun Meng
Dominique Mery
Peter Mosses
Wojciech Mostowski
Alexandre Mota
K. Narayan Kumar

Martin Neuhaeusser
Olga Pacheco
Paritosh Pandya
Matthew Parkinson
Ken Pierce
Marta Pietkiewicz-Koutny
Lorenzo Platania
Serena Elisa Ponta
Ivan Porres
Viorel Preoteasa
R. Ramanujam
Rodrigo Ramos
Atle Refsdal
Arend Rensink
Tamara Rezk
Ragnhild Kobro Runde
Benedikt Schmidt
Cristina Seceleanu
Tiberiu Seceleanu
Fredrik Seehusen
Justin Seyster
Radu Siminiceanu
Bjørnar Solhaug
Kim Solin
Jorge Sousa Pinto
Mike Spivey
Christoph Sprenger
Martin Steffen
Meng Sun
S. P. Suresh
Sarah Thompson
Helen Treharne
Edward Turner
Michael Wahler
Freek Wiedijk
Burkhart Wolff
Andreas Wombacher
Jim Woodcock
Huang Xiaowan
Shaofa Yang
Santiago Zanella Beguelin
Artur Zawlocki
Xiangpeng Zhao
Marcelo d'Amorim
Jaco van de Pol
Xu Wang

Sponsors

We gratefully acknowledge the support and sponsorship from the following organizations: NOKIA, TUCS (Turku Centre for Computer Science), Stiftelsen för Åbo Akademi Forskningsinstitut (Foundation of the Åbo Akademi Research Institute), Faculty of Technology at Åbo Akademi University, Federation of Finnish Learned Societies, FORTIA (Formal Techniques Industrial Association), FME (Formal Methods Europe), and Distributed System Design Laboratory.

 Distributed Systems Design Laboratory

Table of Contents

Session 1. Invited Talks

Aspects and Formal Methods 1
    Shmuel Katz

Getting Formal Verification into Design Flow 12
    Arvind, Nirav Dave, and Michael Katelman

Lessons in the Weird and Unexpected: Some Experiences from Checking Large Real Systems 33
    Dawson Engler

Simulation, Orchestration and Logical Clocks 34
    David Kitchen, Evan Powell, and Jayadev Misra

Session 2. Programming Language Analysis

CoVaC: Compiler Validation by Program Analysis of the Cross-Product 35
    Anna Zaks and Amir Pnueli

Lazy Behavioral Subtyping 52
    Johan Dovland, Einar Broch Johnsen, Olaf Owe, and Martin Steffen

Checking Well-Formedness of Pure-Method Specifications 68
    Arsenii Rudich, Ádám Darvas, and Peter Müller

Session 3. Verification

Verifying Dynamic Pointer-Manipulating Threads 84
    Thomas Noll and Stefan Rieger

Proofs and Refutations for Probabilistic Refinement 100
    A.K. McIver, C.C. Morgan, and C. Gonzalia

Assume-Guarantee Verification for Interface Automata 116
    Michael Emmi, Dimitra Giannakopoulou, and Corina S. Păsăreanu

Session 4. Real-Time and Concurrency

Automated Verification of Dense-Time MTL Specifications Via Discrete-Time Approximation 132
    Carlo A. Furia, Matteo Pradella, and Matteo Rossi

A Model Checking Language for Concurrent Value-Passing Systems 148
  Radu Mateescu and Damien Thivolle

Session 5. Grand Chellenge Problems

Verification of Mondex Electronic Purses with KIV: From a Security
Protocol to Verified Code 165
  *Holger Grandy, Markus Bischof, Kurt Stenzel,
  Gerhard Schellhorn, and Wolfgang Reif*

Incremental Development of a Distributed Real-Time Model of a
Cardiac Pacing System Using VDM 181
  Hugo Daniel Macedo, Peter Gorm Larsen, and John Fitzgerald

Session 6. FM Practice

Industrial Use of Formal Methods for a High-Level Security
Evaluation 198
  Boutheina Chetali and Quang-Huy Nguyen

Secret Ninja Formal Methods....................................... 214
  Joseph R. Kiniry and Daniel M. Zimmerman

Specification and Checking of Software Contracts for Conditional
Information Flow 229
  *Torben Amtoft, John Hatcliff, Edwin Rodríguez, Robby,
  Jonathan Hoag, and David Greve*

Session 7. Runtime Moitoring and Analysis

JML Runtime Assertion Checking: Improved Error Reporting and
Efficiency Using Strong Validity 246
  Patrice Chalin and Frédéric Rioux

Provably Correct Runtime Monitoring (Extended Abstract) 262
  Irem Aktug, Mads Dam, and Dilian Gurov

Session 8. Communication

A Schedulerless Semantics of TLM Models Written in SystemC Via
Translation into LOTOS 278
  Olivier Ponsini and Wendelin Serwe

A Rigorous Approach to Networking: TCP, from Implementation to
Protocol to Service 294
  Tom Ridge, Michael Norrish, and Peter Sewell

Session 9. Constraint Analysis

Constraint Prioritization for Efficient Analysis of Declarative Models ... 310
  Engin Uzuncaova and Sarfraz Khurshid

Finding Minimal Unsatisfiable Cores of Declarative Specifications 326
  Emina Torlak, Felix Sheng-Ho Chang, and Daniel Jackson

Precise Interval Analysis vs. Parity Games 342
  Thomas Gawlitza and Helmut Seidl

Session 10. Design

Introducing Objects through Refinement 358
  Tim McComb and Graeme Smith

Masking Faults While Providing Bounded-Time Phased Recovery 374
  Borzoo Bonakdarpour and Sandeep S. Kulkarni

Towards Consistent Specifications of Product Families 390
  Alexander Harhurin and Judith Hartmann

Session 11. Industry Day

Formal Methods for Trustworthy Skies: Building Confidence in the
Security of Aircraft Assets Distribution 406
  *Scott Lintelman, Richard Robinson, Mingyan Li, and
  Krishna Sampigethaya*

An Industrial Case: Pitfalls and Benefits of Applying Formal Methods
to the Development of a Network-Centric RTOS 411
  Eric Verhulst, Gjalt de Jong, and Vitaliy Mezhuyev

Software Engineering with Formal Methods: Experiences with the
Development of a Storm Surge Barrier Control System............... 419
  Klaas Wijbrans, Franc Buve, Robin Rijkers, and Wouter Geurts

Application of a Formal Specification Language in the Development
of the "Mobile FeliCa" IC Chip Firmware for Embedding in Mobile
Phone 425
  Taro Kurita, Miki Chiba, and Yasumasa Nakatsugawa

Safe and Reliable Metro Platform Screen Doors Control/Command
Systems 430
  Thierry Lecomte

Author Index.. 435

Aspects and Formal Methods

Shmuel Katz

Department of Computer Science
The Technion, Haifa 32000, Israel
katz@cs.technion.ac.il

Abstract. Aspects are now commonly used to add functionality that otherwise would cut across the structure of object systems. In this survey, both directions in the connection between aspects and formal methods are examined. On the one hand, the use of aspects to facilitate (general) software verification, and especially model checking, is demonstrated. On the other hand, the new challenges to formal specification and verification posed by aspects are defined, and several existing solutions are described.

Keywords: Aspects, interference, model-checking, detection, specification.

1 Introduction

Aspects are modular units that treat concerns of object-oriented systems that otherwise would crosscut the inheritance hierarchy and classes. They have proven useful for a wide variety of tasks including debugging, logging, adding security or privacy, expressing variants for software product lines, or increasing the flexibility of middleware components.

The approach was first presented in the AspectJ [17] extension of Java, and has been generalized to a variety of languages and aspect-oriented software development techniques (see, for example, [9]). When a concern such as security or logging is encapsulated in an aspect, this aspect contains both the code associated with the concern, called *advice*, and a description of when this advice should run, called a *pointcut descriptor*. The binding of some *base program* with an aspect (or in general, a collection of aspects), is termed *weaving* and yields an *augmented program*. The pointcut descriptor identifies the *joinpoints* in the execution of a program at which the advice should be invoked, either augmenting or replacing code at the joinpoints.

Aspects are distinguished as a software construct in at least two characteristics. First, unlike procedures, they are not activated by "requests" in the base program. The joinpoints where advice is applied are not explicit in the code of the base program–an aspect advice is not "called"— but are defined in the declaration of the aspect itself. Second, the pointcuts that govern the execution of advice are evaluated dynamically. When a pointcut identifies joinpoints, these joinpoints are not static locations in the code; rather, in the most popular and expressive joinpoint models used by aspect-oriented programming languages, joinpoints are well-defined points during the *execution* of a program. Depending on the runtime context of a particular point, such as the methods on the program's stack, or the values currently in certain data fields, the same static code location might match a pointcut at one time, but fail to match it at another. To give the programmer access to these dynamic data, a pointcut may also expose values of program variables or names of objects or methods to the advice.

In this survey, first the use of aspects in formal methods, and in particular to aid in practical verification tools, is demonstrated, for Java Pathfinder. Then the other direction is considered: how formal methods can be used for aspects, including their specification and verification, and analysis of possible interferences among multiple aspects woven to a system. To demonstrate how general principles and well-known techniques of formal methods can be extended and adapted to aspects, I concentrate on examples from my own work that extend and adapt classical assume-guarantee specifications, techniques from model checking, and interference freedom of parallel processes.

2 Aspects for Model Checking

Java PathFinder (JPF) [26] is a model checker [5] that is implemented as a Java virtual machine. That is, JPF executes Java's virtual machine code, but unlike a regular virtual machine, JPF explores all the possible states that the program may reach. As in other software model checkers, the assertions we want to check are inserted into the program at appropriate points, as annotations or comments.

JPF keeps track of every state (the content of the heap and the stack of each thread) the program has visited. When the program reaches a point that may lead to several possible executions (for example when two threads are executing in parallel) JPF reruns the program on all the possible executions. As a result, any assertion we embed in the code will be checked for all the possible executions of the program. This means that if the assertion never triggers an exception then we are sure that the program can never violate the assertion. As an additional benefit, if the assertion is violated then JPF creates a report that consists of the entire history of the execution up to the point of the violation.

There are two problems with the standard use of assertions in formal verification. The first problem is that we have to change the program every time we decide to check for a different property. The second problem is that often a single property cannot be checked in a specific place, but we must distribute assertions at several places in the code.

By using aspects we can solve both problems. We can write a different aspect for each new property and then weave it into the program without having to manually edit it. And by using the appropriate pointcut patterns we can easily distribute the different assertions to their appropriate locations. It also becomes trivial to remove the assertions when we have finished with the verification task. Finally, the connection between the pointcuts — representing where assertions are made — and the advice — representing the assertion itself — is immediate and direct.

Suppose we wish to ensure that every message that contains a password is encrypted when it enters the medium. Rather than inserting assertions in the source program, this requirement is best represented using the following aspect:

```
public aspect AllSentAreEncrypted {

  pointcut sendingMessage(Message m) :
    call(public void Medium.send(Message)) &&
    args(m);

  before(Message m) : sendingMessage(m) {
    if (m.hasPassword())
      assert(encrypted(m.getPassword()));
  }
  private boolean encrypted(String s) { // ... }
}
```

This use of aspects to express assertions and specifications, including pre- and post-conditions or contracts between modules (as seen in [20]) appears already in early examples found on the AspectJ webpage.

2.1 Aspects for Modelling and Abstraction

Beyond their use for specification and annotation, aspects can help to treat abstraction and modularization cleanly. In recent years it has become evident that full post-facto formal verification of implemented software systems is impractical due to the size of the state-space involved. Inductive methods have floundered due to the difficulty in providing appropriate invariants, and model checking has proven unable to directly handle the huge state-space of complex software with asynchronous threads or processes. Thus any attempt to introduce formal methods for general software has to either deal directly with key abstract models, e.g., of individual modules, or provide a methodology for abstracting an implemented system by isolating components for independent analysis and/or reducing the possible values of fields or variables.

Indeed, model checking the entire source code of a production system seems impractical even in principle. Most systems today are distributed — they interact with databases and with clients which may be located in different computers around the world. A typical complete model of the system must include at least the standard library, the server's kernel, the database, and the TCP/IP stack.

In such cases we must replace the subsystem by a more abstract model. This is very similar to the idea of a stub in testing. Rather than testing the system against a live database, we create a mock database object with a fixed set of records.

A related problem is that JPF, like any other model checker, assumes the program is independent from any external environment. That is, it assumes that the program does not take any input and does not emit any output. When such operations exist in the program they are simply ignored by JPF. This assumption is essential for the model checking algorithm to work, but it creates a practical problem when our programs perform I/O.

When a program performs an input operation it takes information from its external environment. The program cannot assume what the exact value of the input will be, instead it is the environment that makes the decision. The usual Java Pathfinder solution is to replace the input operation by a nondeterministic choice operation. A program that uses nondeterministic choice instead of input has the same set of potential behaviors as the original, but is independent of any particular environment and can be model checked. Thus before applying the model checker, a Java fragment:

```
Integer x =
    Integer.getInteger(System.in.readline());
```

would be replaced by a nondeterministic choice:

```
Integer x = Verify.getInt(0,5);
```

This program does not read anything from the outside world. When we run it on a standard virtual machine the operation `Verify.getInt` picks values at random from the range 0..5, simulating the choices made by a user. However, when we run this program on JPF, it will cause the machine to backtrack to the location of `getInt` and rerun the scenario with every possible value from the range 0..5.

Aspects can be used to cleanly treat the needed abstractions and isolation of the system component discussed above, by encapsulating the needed changes into *abstraction aspects*. For example, the client and the server may communicate in real life by establishing a TCP/IP channel between them. However we are not interested in model checking the TCP/IP protocol stack, but rather would like to focus on checking the interaction between the client and the server. We would therefore like to make the assumption that the TCP/IP subsystem is a perfect medium. It never forgets messages, it never rearranges them and it never duplicates them. In order to enforce this assumption on our program we create a simple `Medium` class that consists of two queues, one for sending messages from the client to the server and one for returning messages from the server to the client. We then use an abstraction aspect that replaces the calls to the underlying socket interface with calls to our `Medium` object.

Of course, if we would like to check how our system behaves when the connection is faulty we can change the `Medium` class, perhaps using nondeterministic operations, for example to sometimes drop a message, or replace one message with another and so on. Eventually it is up to us to decide how realistic we would like the model of the environment to be.

For I/O, the abstraction aspects adding nondeterminism can determine which values are to be checked for input, while assertion aspects check whether the intended output values are correct. Consider a system which reads user names and passwords in a getUserInput method, and then checks whether the password is authorized for that user using a database query. An aspect would replace the input with a small domain of user-password pairs, and the database queries with different possible responses.

In short, aspects provide a clean mechanism for expressing specifications, for abstracting away from irrelevant parts of the system, and for reducing the statespace to enable model checking, and should be incorporated into modern software verification tools.

3 Formal Methods for Aspects

Now we turn to the other direction: applying formal methods to systems with aspects. The new issues raised by aspects provide ample ground for innovative use of the conventions and the "bag of tricks" we have developed in formal methods research over many years. I will give several examples that demonstrate how existing principles of formal methods can be adapted to aspect specification and verification. These examples are taken from my own work, with which I am most familiar. In the following section, some other relevant work is briefly surveyed.

3.1 The Quest for Modularity

Clearly, given a base program, a collection of aspects with their pointcut descriptors and advice, and a system for *weaving* together these components to produce a stand-alone augmented program, we can verify properties of this augmented system using standard software verification, either inductive methods or software model checking techniques. For example, AspectJ weaving produces Java bytecode, and this can be used as the input for Java Pathfinder to check properties of the augmented system.

However, the general quest for modular proof techniques is clearly relevant for aspects. It would be preferable if we could employ a modular technique in which an aspect can be considered separately from any base program. Such an approach will allow us to:

- obtain verification results that hold for a particular aspect with any base program from some class of programs, rather than for only one base program in particular;
- use the results to reason about the application of aspects to base programs with multiple evolving state machines describing changing configurations during execution, or to other systems not amenable to model checking; and
- avoid model checking augmented systems, which may be significantly larger than either their base systems or aspects, and whose unknown behavior may resist abstraction.

The second point above relates to object-oriented programs that create new instances of classes (objects) with associated state machine components. Often, the assumption of an aspect about the key properties of those base state machines to which it may be woven can indeed be shown to hold for every possible machine that corresponds to an object configuration of a program. For example, it may involve a so-called *class invariant*, provable by reasoning directly on class declarations, as in [1].

3.2 Specifications of Aspects

In order to separately reason about aspects, the first question to be answered is what should the specification of an aspect include. Aspect advice is a collection of code fragments, to be activated at various states of a base system. It turns out to be valuable to consider aspects as system transformers that given a base system, return an augmented version. Then the specification can have the familiar assume-guarantee form, but not merely involving the points where the aspect applies and when the advice finishes.

Its specification is (a) its *assumption* about any system into which it may be woven, and (b) a *guarantee* about properties of the result of weaving the aspect into any system satisfying the assumption.

The form of the specification is an instance of the *assume-guarantee* paradigm but generalized to relate to global properties of two systems: the one before weaving the aspect, and the one afterwards. The assumption of an aspect can include information on what is expected to be true at join-points, global invariants of the underlying system, or assumed properties of instances of classes or variables that may be bound to various parameters of the aspect when it is woven. The result assertion can include both new properties added by the aspect, and those properties of the basic system that are to be maintained in a system augmented with the aspect. Both parts of aspect specifications can be expressed in linear temporal logic.

An aspect is correct with respect to its assume-guarantee specification if, whenever it is woven (by itself) into a system that satisfies the assumption, the result will satisfy the guarantee. This view of aspect specification and correctness appears in [23], adapting earlier work on superimpositions that also had a similar view of specifications.

Sometimes a classical situation is appropriate, where the assumption relates to the joinpoints and the guarantee to what is true immediately after the advice. For example, if the joinpoints are exactly at the method calls with sensitive information, then the aspect might guarantee that the actual call occurs after encrypting the parameters. In this case, the usual *precondition* and *postcondition* terminology could be used. The assumption is that the joinponts precisely coincide with the sensitive method calls, and the guarantee is that when such method calls are executed in the augmented system, the arguments are encoded. But in other situations a more global assumption and guarantee are needed: for example, to widen a property true only for part of the base system. Consider an assumption that, in the base system, states satisfying predicate B lead to a desired response R, and an aspect that, when woven over such a system, causes *every* execution to eventually reach a state satisfying B (perhaps long after finishing the advice of the aspect) and does not disturb the property assumed about the base. Then the woven system can be guaranteed to always eventually have a desired response R.

3.3 Using LTL Tableaux as Generic Base Programs

An aspect is not a program, and cannot execute on its own. Yet we would like to prove once and for all that an aspect satisfies its specification, i.e., whenever the aspect is woven to a system that satisfies the assumption assertion of the aspect, then the woven system is guaranteed to satisfy the guarantee assertion. To do such a proof modularly, in classic procedure-based systems, we must show that the assumption at the initial state of a procedure or method is enough to prove the guarantee when it completes. Here, as seen above, the assumption is often more global. But consider how LTL model checking is done: a tableau statemachine representing the LTL assertion to be shown is created, the negation is taken by switching the initial states of the tableau, and then the cross product with the system to be checked is considered. If this machine is empty, the desired property holds, and if it is not, a counter example to the desired property is produced.

The proof method suggested in [10] and the MAVEN tool presented there exploit the tableau idea to allow a modular correctness proof for aspects. The basic idea of that work, described for the verification of a single aspect relative to its specification, is that a single model can be generated from the aspect assumption, the pointcut description, and the advice, and used to model check the result assertion. If that model check succeeds, the augmented program resulting from the weaving of the aspect to any underlying system satisfying the aspect assumption is guaranteed to satisfy the result assertion of the aspect.

The single model to be checked is built from the tableau that corresponds to the linear temporal logic assertion of the aspect assumption. This tableau is a generic model for all the systems satisfying the assumption of the aspect, and the state machine fragments that correspond to the advice are woven according to the pointcut descriptions. The tableau contains all the possible behaviors of the base systems into which the aspect can be woven. In other words, for any given underlying system that satisfies the assumption of the aspect, for every computation of this system there is a corresponding computation of the tableau, satisfying the same LTL properties. A generic model is built by weaving the aspect statemachine into the tableau of the aspect's assumption. The guarantee of the aspect is then checked on that model.

In [10] it is shown that if the system S_1 results from weaving the aspect into some appropriate base system, and the system S_2 is the result of weaving the aspect into the tableau, then for every computation of S_1 there exists a corresponding computation of S_2. The properties we check are LTL properties, and an LTL property holds in a system iff each computation of this system, taken alone, satisfies this property. So if there exists a "bad" base system S such that S satisfies the assumption of the aspect, but the resulting assertion of the aspect is violated when it is woven into S, then there exists a "bad" computation in the woven system, violating the guarantee of the aspect. For this bad computation there exists a corresponding bad computation in the (tableau + aspect) state machine. It follows that indeed it is enough to model-check the guarantee of the aspect on the (tableau+aspect) system only.

It then remains to show that a given base system indeed satisfies the assumptions of the aspect, and it can be concluded that the resultant woven system with that aspect satisfies the aspect guarantee, without directly model checking the augmented system.

3.4 Using Interference Freedom Checks for Aspects

The discussion in the previous subsection related to a single aspect. However, when multiple aspects are woven they may interfere with each other. Aspects have been said to (at least potentially) interfere if they have overlapping joinpoints, change the same variables, or mutually influence each others' joinpoints. The most general definition (and the one most familiar to formal methods practitioners) uses the assume-guarantee specifications of aspects described in Section 3.2 to define interference freedom in a way analogous to interference freedom among processes in shared-memory systems [21]. In that classic work, interference freedom among processes is defined in terms of whether independent and local Hoare-logic proofs of correctness for each parallel process are invalidated by operations from other processes.

In [14] interference among a set of aspects that are each correct relative to their assume-guarantee specification is defined as:

Definition 1. it A set $\{A_1,\ldots,A_n\}$ of aspects is *interference-free* if whenever the assumptions $P_1,\ldots,P_n$ hold in a system, the augmented system obtained after weaving the aspects in any order satisfies the guarantees $R_1,\ldots,R_n$.

The individual proofs that each aspect is correct when woven alone (as seen in the previous subsection) correspond to the n local proofs of [21], while interference among aspects deals with the n^2 checks of interference-freedom. A key point, adapted for aspect interference checks in [14], is that the other processes may change the values of shared variables, but there is no interference as long as the independent proofs are not invalidated. The level of interleaving in shared memory systems is much finer than for aspects: every local assertion about memory values can be invalidated by another assignment by a different processor. The fact that aspect advice is only activated at joinpoints means that less stringent conditions can be used, and that modular model checking can be used as a proof component.

Using the noninterference idea, for each pair of aspects A and B in a collection (that satisfy certain restrictions on their form), when A's assumption is true, it should be shown to maintain the assumption and the guarantee of B, and vice versa. These proofs can be done by producing a generic model of both assumptions, and another of A's assumption and B's guarantee, weaving A into each (using the MAVEN system described earlier), and checking the appropriate property (B's assumption in the first case, and its guarantee in the second), and then repeating where the roles of A and B are reversed. Such checks for each pair of aspects are proven sufficient to detect interference or establish interference freedom for any order of application of any collection of aspects in a library.

4 Related Work and Summary

Of course, there are many other works that apply formal methods to aspects. A full description is not feasible, and in any case would quickly become outdated. Thus here I only describe a sampling of existing work, to demonstrate the breadth of work on this subject.

The first to separately model check aspect state machine segments that correspond to advice is [18], where the verification is modular in the sense that base and aspect machines are considered separately. The verification method allows for joinpoints within advice to be matched by a pointcut and themselves advised. The treatment there is for a particular aspect woven directly to a particular base program, checking whether properties which hold for the base program can be extended to the augmented program (using branching-time logic CTL).

In [16], model checking tasks are automatically generated for the augmented system that results from each weaving of an aspect. The approach has the disadvantage of having to treat the augmented system, but offers the benefit that needed annotations and set-up need only be prepared once. That work takes advantage of the Bandera [11] system to generate input to model checking tools directly from Java code.

In [15] a semantic model based on state machines is given, and syntactically identifiable categories of aspects are shown to automatically preserve classes of temporal properties when woven.

Some other works, such as [6] and [24], have an assume-guarantee structure for aspect specification, similar to the specifications suggested here, but model checking is not used.

There is also work on detecting whether the pointcuts of aspects match common joinpoints or overlapping introductions [8,12]. This is important because the semantics of weaving can be ambiguous at such points, and be the source of errors.

Some work has also been done in identifying potential influence by using dataflow techniques showing that one aspect changes (or may change) the value of some field or variable that is used and potentially affects the computation done by the advice of another aspect [22,28]. Slicing techniques for aspects [29,3,25] can also be used for such detection. Since such potential influence is often harmless, false positives can result.

There is also extensive work on formal semantics for aspects, such as [4,7,19,27], applying denotational, structured operational, or functional semantics. The nature of weaving, and possible weaving strategies have been at the center of such investigations. Other work, based on model checking, determines whether the weaving of aspect scenarios is done correctly [13].

One convenient source for papers on formal methods and semantics of aspects is the annual Foundations of Aspect Languages (FOAL) Workshop, associated with the Aspect-Oriented Software Development Conference. The Common Aspect Proof Environment (CAPE) [2], developed as part of the EU AOSD-Europe Network of Excellence, provides Eclipse downloads and an integrated environment of formal methods tools for aspects, including several of the tools mentioned here.

In summary, aspects are an interesting modularity concept, useful in many contexts including within formal methods tools. They raise important issues of modularity, compositionality, specification, and proof that often require new extensions and application of the familiar techniques of formal methods. Such research is ongoing, but far from complete, and provides ample challenges and opportunities for formal analysis and verification methods.

Acknowledgments. This survey describes joint work with David Feitelson, Max Goldman, Emilia Katz, and Marcelo Sihman, and has benefitted from discussions with them. The support of the AOSD-Europe Network of Excellence is also appreciated.

References

1. Abraham, E., de Boer, F.S., de Roever, W.-P., Steffen, M.: An assertion-based proof system for multithreaded java. Theoretical Computer Science 331(2-3), 251–290 (2005)
2. AOSD-Europe. Common Aspect Proof Environment (CAPE) http://www.cs.technion.ac.il/~ssdl/research/cape/
3. Balzarotti, D., D'Ursi, A., Cavallaro, L., Monga, M.: Slicing AspectJ woven code. In: Proc. of Foundations of Aspect Languages Workshop (FOAL 2005) (2005)
4. Bruns, G., Jagadeesan, R., Jeffrey, A., Riely, J.: μABC: A Minimal Aspect Calculus. In: Gardner, P., Yoshida, N. (eds.) CONCUR 2004. LNCS, vol. 3170, pp. 209–224. Springer, Heidelberg (2004)
5. Clarke Jr., E.M., Grumberg, O., Peled, D.A.: Model Checking. MIT Press, Cambridge (1999)
6. Devereux, B.: Compositional reasoning about aspects using alternating-time logic. In: Proc. of Foundations of Aspect Languages Workshop (FOAL 2003) (2003)
7. Djoko, S.D., Douence, R., Fradet, P.: Aspects preserving properties. In: Proc. of PEPM 2008 Workshop (2008)
8. Douence, R., Fradet, P., Sudholt, M.: Composition, reuse, and interaction analysis of stateful aspects. In: Proc. of 3th Intl. Conf. on Aspect-Oriented Software Development (AOSD 2004), pp. 141–150. ACM Press, New York (2004)
9. Filman, R.E., Elrad, T., Clarke, S., Aksit, M.: Aspect-Oriented Software Development. Addison-Wesley, Reading (2005)
10. Goldman, M., Katz, S.: MAVEN: Modular Aspect Verification. In: Grumberg, O., Huth, M. (eds.) TACAS 2007. LNCS, vol. 4424, pp. 308–322. Springer, Heidelberg (2007)
11. Hatcliff, J., Dwyer, M.: Using the Bandera Tool Set to Model-Check Properties of Concurrent Java Software. In: Larsen, K.G., Nielsen, M. (eds.) CONCUR 2001. LNCS, vol. 2154, pp. 39–58. Springer, Heidelberg (2001)
12. Havinga, W., Nagy, I., Bergmans, L., Aksit, M.: A graph-based approach to modeling and detecting composition conflicts related to introductions. In: AOSD 2007: Proc. of 6th international conference on Aspect-oriented software development, pp. 85–95. ACM Press, New York (2007)
13. Katz, E., Katz, S.: Verifying Scenario-Based Aspect Specifications. In: Fitzgerald, J.S., Hayes, I.J., Tarlecki, A. (eds.) FM 2005. LNCS, vol. 3582, pp. 432–447. Springer, Heidelberg (2005)

14. Katz, E., Katz, S.: Incremental analysis of interference among aspects. In: Proc. of 2008 Foundations of Aspect Languages (FOAL) Workshop, ACM Digital Library, New York (2008)
15. Katz, S.: Aspect Categories and Classes of Temporal Properties. In: Rashid, A., Aksit, M. (eds.) Transactions on Aspect-Oriented Software Development I. LNCS, vol. 3880, pp. 106–134. Springer, Heidelberg (2006)
16. Katz, S., Sihman, M.: Aspect Validation Using Model Checking. In: Dershowitz, N. (ed.) Verification: Theory and Practice. LNCS, vol. 2772, pp. 373–394. Springer, Heidelberg (2004)
17. Kiczales, G., Hilsdale, E., Hugunin, J., Kersten, M., Palm, J., Griswold, W.G.: An Overview of AspectJ. In: Knudsen, J.L. (ed.) ECOOP 2001. LNCS, vol. 2072, pp. 327–353. Springer, Heidelberg (2001), http://aspectj.org
18. Krishnamurthi, S., Fisler, K., Greenberg, M.: Verifying aspect advice modularly. In: FSE 2004, pp. 137–146. ACM, New York (2004)
19. Lammel, R.: A semantical approach to method-call interception. In: Proc. of First Intl. Conf. on Aspect-Oriented Software Development (AOSD 2002), pp. 41–55. ACM Press, New York (2002)
20. Meyer, B.: Object-Oriented Software Construction. Prentice-Hall, Englewood Cliffs (1988)
21. Owicki, S., Gries, D.: An axiomatic proof technique for parallel programs. Acta Informatica 6, 319–340 (1976)
22. Rinard, M., Salcianu, A., Bugrara, S.: A classification system and analysis for aspect-oriented programs. In: Proc. of International Conference on Foundations of Software Engineering (FSE 2004) (2004)
23. Sihman, M., Katz, S.: Superimposition and aspect-oriented programming. BCS Computer Journal 46(5), 529–541 (2003)
24. Sipma, H.B.: A formal model for cross-cutting modular transition systems. In: Proc. of Foundations of Aspect Languages Workshop (FOAL 2003) (2003)
25. Storzer, M., Krinke, J.: Interference analysis for aspectj. In: Proc. of Foundations of Aspect Languages Workshop (FOAL 2003) (2003)
26. Visser, W., Havelund, K., Brat, G.P., Park, S., Lerda, F.: Model checking programs. Autom. Softw. Eng. 10(2), 203–232 (2003)
27. Wand, M., Kiczales, G., Dutchyn, C.: A semantics for advice and dynamic join points in aspect-oriented programming. Trans. on Prog. Langs and Systems (TOPLAS) 26(5), 890–910 (2004)
28. Weston, N., Taiani, F., Rashid, A.: Interaction analysis for fault-tolerance in aspect-oriented programming. In: Proc. of 2007 Workshop on Methods, Models, and Tools for Fault Tolerance (2007)
29. Zhao, J.: Slicing aspect-oriented software. In: IEEE International Workshop on Programming Comprehension, pp. 251–260 (2002)

Getting Formal Verification into Design Flow

Arvind[1], Nirav Dave[1], and Michael Katelman[2]

[1] Computer Science and Artificial Intelligence Lab
Massachusetts Institute of Technology, Cambridge, MA 02139, USA
{arvind,ndave}@csail.mit.edu
[2] Department of Computer Science
University of Illinois at Urbana-Champaign, Urbana, IL 61801, USA
katelman@uiuc.edu

Abstract. The ultimate goal of formal methods is to provide assurances about the quality, performance, security, etc. of systems. While formal tools have advanced greatly over the past two decades, widespread proliferation has not yet occurred, and the full impact of formal methods is still to be realized. This paper presents some ideas on how to catalyze the growth of formal techniques in day-to-day engineering practice. We draw on our experience as hardware engineers that want to use, and have tried to use, formal methods in our own designs. The points we make have probably been made before. However we illustrate each one with concrete designs. Our examples support three major themes: (1) correctness depends highly on the application and even a collection of formal methods cannot handle the whole problem; (2) high-level design languages can facilitate the interaction between design and formal methods; and (3) formal method tools should be presented as integrated debugging aids as opposed to one requiring mastering a foreign language or esoteric concepts.

1 Introduction

Over the past few decades, formal techniques have made impressive progress. For example, serious theorems (*e.g.,* relative consistency of AC with ZF) have been mechanically verified [1], and huge improvements in the range and capacity of decision procedures (*e.g.,* linear arithmetic, uninterpreted functions, bit-vectors, SAT solving) have been made [2,3,4,5,6]. In the hardware industry, a number of commercial tools to support formal verification have sprung up [7,8,9,10,11,12]. These improvements in tools and techniques have gotten the attention of both the research community and industry. Formal methods are used within the research community in numerous case studies ranging from security [13] and wireless protocols [14] to processors [15] and cache-coherence protocols [16] to buffer overflows in software [17]. In the industrial setting, ever-increasing system complexity in both hardware and software has fostered interest in formal methods (*e.g.,* [18,19,20,21,22]). Indeed, in the hardware industry, formal methods are even widely employed for certain types of verification tasks. Sadly, despite all of these advances and a receptive climate, formal methods have had no discernable effect on the day-to-day design flow. Both hardware and software designers still reach verification closure primarily through *ad hoc* testing and low-level debugging.

Designers are paid to make efficient systems within some constraints. The constraints may be on performance (*e.g.*, a video codec must process 30 frames per second at 720p), power (*e.g.*, a cell phone may not dissipate more that 3W), cost (*e.g.*, the chip must not cost more than $5) or some other metric like compatibility (*e.g.*, a DSP that must run all existing applications). In addition there are always limited resources and time-to-market pressures. In such an environment, many designers believe (with some justification) that extensive testing is sufficient to reach the corresponding confidence for the economic or social consequences of failure. It is difficult to find cases where a product is shipped only after it passes a full "formal verification".

The current design flows are strongly biased towards *post-design verification*. Of course design engineers are encouraged to perform unit testing but the primary task of verification rests with a verification team that is often two to three times the size of the design team. Good verification teams prepare elaborate test plans and then employ a horde of engineers to actually write and perform the tests. By way of analogy, this is how the automobile industry used to be in the United States until the early 1980's. It employed more and more inspectors to try to avoid shipping defective automobiles. This proved ineffective in developing higher quality automobiles. Then the Japanese industry started focusing on *zero-defect* components which resulted in drastically improved quality.

The aim of this paper is to provide, via a rich set of examples, insights into the problems that designers face and how formal methods may alleviate some of these problems. We are convinced that designers want their designs to be correct, and would use methods and tools that isolate tricky problems quickly. However, a designer is unlikely to employ a tool that is too hard to use or too slow, or provides information that the designer is at best peripherally interested in. Designers are rarely interested in tools that require daunting specifications in some totally unfamiliar form, or which may not be available at the time of design. If the verification of a WiFi protocol block requires, say, axiomatization of the 802.11a standard in PVS, then the specification task itself would overwhelm the design task. Additionally, large formal specifications are at least as hard to debug as large designs and their engineering utility is questionable even when correct.

We make three points in this paper with the goal of stirring a discussion about how to address the gap between day-to-day engineering practice and the unrealized potential of formal methods:

1. *Correctness depends on the application. Different applications require vastly different formal techniques.* Most designs will benefit from both the application of formal methods and testing via executable specifications (see Section 2).
2. *Formal tools must be tied directly to high-level design languages.* There is a great deal of high-level information that needs to be communicated to formal

tools. Much of it is also needed for the design itself. The only practical way to get this information to the tools is by extracting it directly from the design itself; designers are unlikely to restate knowledge in a different notation solely for the sake of verification (see Section 3).
3. *Most formal methods and tools have a post-design bias. Instead they should be presented as debugging aids during the design process.* In the most successful cases, designers are unaware that they are using a formal method. A good design method is much more likely to be used by the designers if it is enforced by the tools (see Section 4).

In this paper we focus only on hardware design, though our observations may apply equally to software. We also do not address the problems of defective tools (*e.g.*, the compiler itself produces incorrect code, ambiguities in the design language). In the hardware industry there is a tendency to merge the testing of the tool and of the design. We feel strongly that these activities should be kept separate. The designer must have a high degree of confidence that the tools are bug-free or the verification task is truly monumental. Also, we do not focus on manufacturing bugs (*e.g.*, stuck-at-zero faults) or the errors introduced by physical design tools. We also ignore the issue of lack of education in formal methods on part of design engineers; we live in an environment (*i.e.*, MIT) where this is not an issue. We focus only on the technical challenges involved in making formal methods fit within an effective design-debug loop. *Our goal is to help the designer produce designs which, if implemented in a totally automatic way using bug-free tools, would have completely satisfied the specification.*

2 What Needs to be Verified: Examples from Hardware

Over the last decade we have designed a variety of complex digital systems. Our verification methodology has been based primarily on testing and occasionally on handwritten proofs for very difficult parts of the design. In our design explorations we've found a number of places where formal verification could have been highly useful. However, in no instance have we found that formal verification would have replaced testing. This is because testing provides a more-than-adequate guarantee for some aspects of the verification task and setting up a testbench is usually significantly easier than a formal verification tool. Nevertheless, there are situations where a designer cannot get sufficient confidence in the correctness of the design even with extraordinary amount of testing.

In this section we illustrate the verification task via a number of examples taken from our own personal experiences and highlight where formal methods could have had significant impact. These examples should also make it obvious to the reader that *proper verification involves domain specific knowledge*.

2.1 Simple Deterministic Designs: *IP Lookup*

The Longest Prefix Match (LPM) function is used in Internet Protocol (IP) packet routers to determine the output port to which an input packet should be

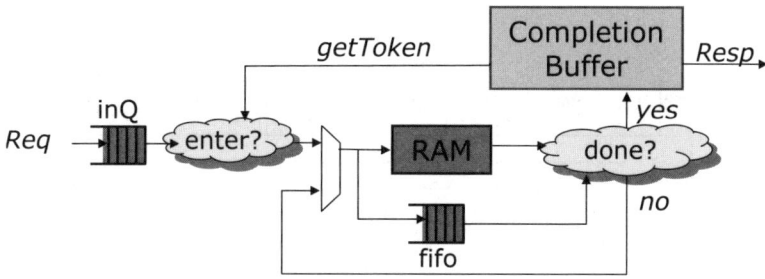

Fig. 1. Circular Pipeline Design

forwarded. It is a requirement that the router maintain the ordering of packets between the same source and destination. For cost and power reasons, the memory size must be kept small. This rules out a flat table implementation which even for IPv4 would need 2^{32} elements. Desigjns often use a tree-structured table which allows one to exploit the similarities in table entries with common prefixes. The lookup procedure essentially reads the table repeatedly using different parts of the IP address. If a result is found, an output is produced, otherwise another read is performed in the part of the table holding the relevant subtree. For most schemes, an IPv4 lookup requires between 1 and 4 memory reads.

One efficient implementation [23] of this lookup functionality is based on a circular pipeline shown in Figure 1. It includes a FIFO of partially served requests, a pipelined memory, and a completion buffer that ensures that outputs are sent out in the correct order.

Writing an operational description of IP Lookup is easy. The functional correctness is deterministic and can be implemented in any sequential language as a single lookup in a flat IP table. Indeed, with a simple executable description and random stimulus generation, we can achieve a high degree of confidence via testing that the design does not produce wrong answers. However, checking other requirements is a different story. Do packets come out in order? Does each packet produce a result packet? One may need to check this if there is a danger of dropped packets because the design cannot keep up with the specified input rate. Is there a dead-cycle, that is, can a new packet enter the system in the cycle when an old packet leaves? All these questions are very important for the designer, and to set up tests to check all these properties is not always easy and often not satisfactory. If one could formally state these properties and easily verify them, most designers would take the time to do so.

2.2 Dealing with Noise: *802.11a*

802.11a is an IEEE standard for wireless communication [24]. The protocol translates raw bits from the Media Access Control (MAC) into Orthogonal Frequency Division Multiplexing (OFDM) symbols comprised of 64 32-bit fixed-width complex numbers. The protocol is designed to operate at different data rates; at

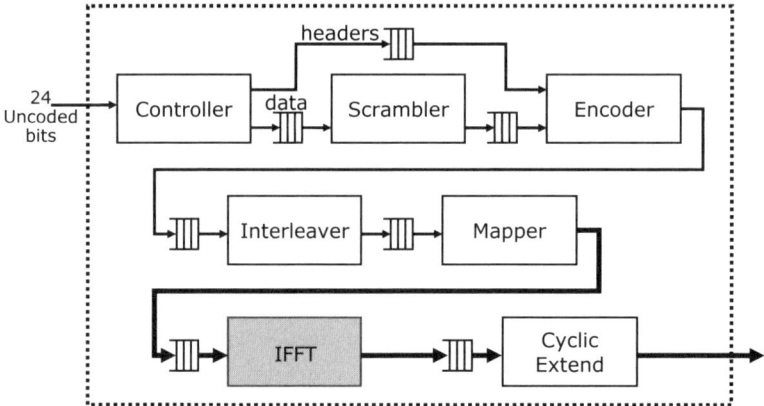

Fig. 2. 802.11a Transmitter Pipeline

higher rates it consumes more input to produce each symbol. Regardless of the rate, to be acceptable an implementation must be able to generate an OFDM symbol every 4 μs.

The 802.11a specification only specifies how data is to be transmitted. This specification is given operationally as a sequence of stream processing functions (see Figure 2). Each of these functions can be viewed in a way that is similar to the IP lookup function and consequently it is easy to translate the 802.11a specs into an executable sequential program. In fact the block structure in the reference is often directly visible in the implementation. Verification can be performed by comparing the test results from the design against the executable specs. For debugging purposes it is not uncommon to instrument the standard executable code to capture the bitstream after each functional block and compare it against the internal bitstreams.

On the receiving side, the input is tightly coupled with the digital-to-analog conversion at the transmitter, the noise properties of the transmission medium, analog-to-digital conversion at the receiver and the phase shift between sender and receiver. We can partition this problem into two subproblems: given a transmitted stream, "can the receiver synchronize its phase to match the transmitter's phase?", and "given a noisy transmitted packet can the receiver successfully reconstruct the original packet?". Since we know the noise models the standard is supposed to correct, we can introduce the correctable noise effects on a transmitted packet (including possible phase shifts) relatively easily.

Currently, to reach sufficient confidence that an 802.11a design is transmitting and receiving data reliably, we take into account two more facts. First, the 802.11a codec was designed to reduce the effect of corner cases, which determined the worst-case behavior. Second, since we can always drop data, not getting all the *exact* behavior in corner cases only reduces the space of noise which can be corrected, slightly degrading performance. Additionally, unlike the IP lookup example, all of the design complexity lies in the data transformations, not the control logic. These points make it so that once we have a system where a few packets are sent and received correctly, our confidence that the design is "good enough" to ship becomes very high. Of course more directed testing can be performed to gain more confidence.

What simple directed testing does not cover, however, is the correctness of fractional-level arithmetic, which is used pervasively in 802.11a. Designers need confidence that their numerical logic works (of course, such an arithmetic library is useful for other designs as well). This task is well suited to formal verification.

It is not uncommon in such designs that one transforms a block from an obviously correct implementation into a higher-performing one. For example, one may transform a large combinational circuit into a folded pipeline to reduce area. These transformations will always need to be correct in the functional sense but may not result in equivalent FSMs. It is possible to describe these transformations in such a way that the functional behavior is abstracted away, *i.e.*, passed in as a parameter. It would be incredibly useful if transformations of this sort were formally verified so that we could do architectural exploration without adding to the testing burden.

2.3 Specification of a Lossy System: *The H.264 Video CODEC*

The H.264 Advanced Video Codec is an ITU standard for encoding and decoding video with a target coding efficiency twice that of H.263 and with comparable quality to H.262 (MPEG2) [25]. H.264 enables PAL (720 × 576) resolution video to be transmitted at 1Mbit/sec. Like other video coding standards, H.264 specifies only how to reconstruct a video from an encoded bitstream, not how a video is encoded. The goal of the encoder designer is to produce as compressed a bitstream as possible without the degrading the user-perceivable quality. Sometimes the encoder also has the constraint of how much computation can be performed because the encoding may have to be done in real time or on a handheld device such as cell phone or camcorder.

Since the encoding is lossy, what does it even mean to correctly encode a video? We could compare the original video with the results of encoding and then decoding the same video, but how does one classify user-perceivable differences? A number of heuristics which approximate user-perceivable differences exist, but these are too crude for verification purposes. Consequently there is no hard or fast rule that the design *must* ensure. (Fortunately, a few errors here and there are unlikely to be catastrophic in this application).

The decoder can be described as a relatively complex dataflow graph as shown in Figure 3. Unlike the 802.11a transmitter which had a significant but still manageable description, the decoding reference for H.264 is 80 thousand lines of C and an English specification that runs into hundreds of pages! Neither of these descriptions is complete: the English is ambiguous in many places and the C code represents only a deterministic representation of the codec. While many rich and complex transformations can be applied on the C code, some arbitrary choices require significant high-level knowledge to find, effectively ruling them out without additional knowledge. Thus, complete understanding of the codec

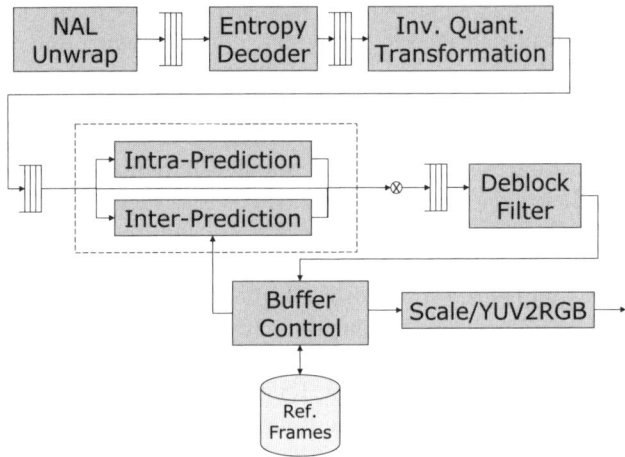

Fig. 3. H.264 Decode Block Level Diagram

requires significant use of both of these specifications in tandem. We believe that H.264 is complex enough that there is virtually no hope of ever directly generating a complete formal specification, especially one that could be ready during the design process.

Given these complications, designers are limited to testing for all but the simplest sub-blocks. For the decoder, we test by taking a good mix of interesting videos, encoding them, and then checking that the output of the reference C code and design match. As with the 802.11 transmitter, by instrumenting the reference code one can also generate internal bitstreams at the output of functional blocks and compare them against the design.

The main use of formal methods in this example, like 802.11, would be restricted to testing arithmetic libraries, correctness of transformations for performance, etc. One could also formally verify some tricky parts of dataflow in the pipeline. For example, one could prove that the inter-prediction block does not read the reference frame before it has been properly constructed. However, in case of such an error the bitstream is unlikely to match with the C reference code and the error would be caught by running a few sample videos.

2.4 Nondeterminism: *Cache Coherence*

Verifying the correctness of a cache coherence protocol for shared memory systems presents a unique challenge. On one hand, there is no ambiguity about a correct answer; each Load is supposed to return a value from a set of possible Store values. On the other hand, both the protocol and its operating environment exhibit nondeterminism, *i.e.*, time dependent behavior. This is also an area where absolute correctness is expected. After all, software systems rely on the perfect behavior of Load-Store instructions on any machine!

Protocols are often described abstractly in tabular form where each line represents a valid transition in the protocols abstract state space. These transitions (or *rules*) are allowed to be applied in any order. Even though many rules can be applied at a time, their behavior is understandable as if the rules were applied one at a time in some order. This representation captures the nondeterminism of both the protocol and its environment accurately. These tabular descriptions are often independent of the number of processors or the size of caches.

Cache coherence protocols present two challenges in verification: how to incorporate nondeterminism in the verification framework and how to state formally the correctness criterion so that it is of use in the verification process. An operational model of a protocol, *i.e.*, an interpreter that applies protocol rules in some deterministic order is of limited use because it explores a very small subset of the nondeterministic state space. Even for cleverly designed tests it is hard to convince oneself that the protocol functions correctly in all cases and enters neither deadlock nor livelock in any circumstance. The verification problem is further exacerbated by the fact that modern protocols tend to be very complex for performance reasons and are understood by very few implementers.

Model checking has proven quite useful in identifying obscure bugs in cache coherence protocols. Indeed, for these reasons cache coherence protocols are well-trodden ground in the formal methods literature (*e.g.*, see [26]). This literature also shows the limitations of model checking if one is looking for an absolute guarantee of correctness for this problem. First, the designer/verifier builds an abstraction of the real design, because the tools cannot handle the real design. Second, the designer looks for a set of invariants, such as "a dirty copy of an address cannot exist in more than one cache", whose proof will guarantee the correctness of the whole protocol. Third, to keep the state space from exploding, model checking is applied to a small machine configuration (*e.g.*, three caches and two unique addresses). The designer has to convince himself that if there is a bug in the protocol it will show up in this small system.

We think all these steps are fraught with problems; there is always a chance of omitting an important detail in the abstraction process. Without a formal proof it is difficult to convince oneself that a set of invariants is sufficient to verify the whole protocol. Finally, one needs to prove, that the correctness of the simple system configuration that was checked implies the correctness of all possible system configurations.

This is one area where model checking coupled with mechanical theorem proving can be very useful in proving the correctness of a protocol. But to be useful in practice, the implementation must be generated automatically from the protocol description that is used in the verification process. We will also report our attempts at mechanical theorem proving of a complex cache coherence protocol in Section 4.

2.5 Simple Specification, Complex Design: *Processors*

Microprocessors encompass many important architectural concepts that occur throughout the wider spectrum of digital logic design. At the same time, "absolute correctness" is what is required of a microprocessor. People are more tolerant of software bugs than a microprocessor which "sort of works". Given the economic importance of microprocessors it is not surprising that microprocessors have pushed verification research and continues to be a rich source of technical problems and proving ground for new verification tools. In addition, the size and complexity of modern microarchitectures has led to a situation where functional verification is a significant contributor to the microprocessor design cycle.

Specifying the correctness of a microprocessor is relatively straightforward: it must respect the semantics of the target instruction set (ISA). Modulo certain complexities (*e.g.*, virtual memory, exceptions) a typical ISA consists of basic arithmetic, memory, and branching instructions that together constitute a simple but extremely expressive programming language. Unlike the previous example of H.264 or 802.11a, this specification can be defined via a simple (one-instruction-at-a-time) processor implementation or some other software ISA interpreter in a straightforward manner. The proof obligation is then that the more complex implementation matches the simpler one. These days microprocessors are often multicore or appear in shared memory systems. Consequently, cache coherence issues discussed in the previous section can be treated as a subset of microprocessor verification problem.

The classic technique for establishing that a particular microarchitecture is a correct implementation of an ISA is to show that its state transitions can be simulated by a much simpler and obviously correct "reference implementation" of the ISA. Since a real implementation has much larger state space than a reference implementation, one has to provide abstraction functions that map the elements of the real implementation to the elements of the reference implementation. Most abstraction functions are based on *flushing* or *killing*. The flushing abstraction [15,27,28,29] returns an ISA state by completing partially executed instructions in the pipeline. In contrast, killing squashes partially executed instructions and returns the system to the ISA state corresponding to the last committed instruction. Processors are really nondeterministic (consider interrupts and shared memory) and when reasoning about nondeterministic behavior, killing has advantages over flushing because there is a unique last instruction, but there can be several possible futures for uncommitted instructions [29].

Intellectually stimulating as these ideas are, their impact on commercial processor development is minimal. The biggest impediment is that none of these ideas are actually applied to a real implementation, *i.e.*, an RTL description from which the gates may be synthesized automatically or semi-automatically. They are applied to an abstraction of the implementation, where the abstraction is motivated as much by what the tool can handle as what needs to be verified.

Nevertheless correct processor design remains one of the most promising areas for formal verification. In addition to test codes (micro-benchmarks) and model checking, mechanical theorem proving would be needed to gain confidence that a processor with caches, TLBs and branch predictor and cache-coherence engine works in all cases.

3 High-Level Design Languages Are a Prerequisite for Incorporating Formal Methods into Design

In the previous section we have shown through examples that domain specific knowledge is essential to formulate a verification plan for a design. Furthermore, formal verification requires some sort of specification or high-level architectural information to state properties to be proven. What we argue in this section is that this sort of information is communicated best as part of the design and hence, *directly* through the design language. This isn't just a vehicle to communicate high-level information to various tools, it is also a way to communicate *to the designer* the results of the checking and to help him understand and fix errors. For example, type checking is most meaningful when the typing system allows for rich type structures defined by the user. The ideal situation occurs when the abilities of the formal analysis engine and the intention of the high-level language concept match, so that the underlying discipline can be *enforced*. The best example of this is again typing, where the intent of the system is to better manage which operations go with which data, and type checking algorithms are able to statically enforce this discipline.

This section is organized around a set of high-level concepts which we feel can improve both design and formal analysis. They do not all neatly fit the ideal case described above, but nevertheless elucidate important areas where language and formal methods should fit together to the betterment of the design process. *No existing language embodies all of these concepts, but several incorporate a subset.*

3.1 Static Type Checking

Type systems are one of the most accepted ideas in software engineering and appear in varying degree of sophistication in almost all languages. Algebraic and record constructors, in particular, allow a designer to design a rich type structure allowing for notions like choice and grouping in user-defined types. For instance, a `Maybe` type groups a data value with a valid bit. This guarantees that the value is accessible only when the bit is true.

The purpose of typing is to avoid operations on improperly structured objects; and when checked it helps designers avoid a large class of mistakes and actually speeds up design. The reason that typing and type checking is successful is because the high-level intent of types is made completely clear *by the language*. Therefore the errors returned by a type check seem natural to the designer and can be addressed quickly. In addition, type information also serves as useful documentation for the designers.

Type correctness is best enforced *statically*, at compile time, and has proved incredibly successful in this role. In fact, static type checking has gotten so pervasive that most engineers do not even consider it to be a formal method; *formal methods are about correctness, type checking is just common sense*. We have seen that other forms of enforcing a type discipline fail to work as well. For example, enforcing type correctness dynamically, as in Scheme or Perl, pinpoints bugs much later in the design process than static type checking. Extra-lingual attempts in Verilog – a language with weak typing – invariably fail, because the typing enforced by the compiler does not match the extra-lingual discipline, and therefore is not checked automatically. Designers cannot be bothered to do hand checking.

3.2 High-Level Parameterization

Often when an engineer starts to design a functional block, a number of similar sub-blocks become apparent. For instance, one can imagine variations of a FIFO with different sizes or different types of data elements. It makes little sense for designers to make each of these variations separately; rather, one should have a design which can be supplied the element type and the size as parameters. Using a modern type system the type of element can be specified polymorphically so that all the attendant FIFO operations accept and return only correct types.

Parameterization allows us to abstract unnecessary details and factor the proof obligation. Parameterization by data type shows that the specifics of the data element are unimportant to verifying the FIFO's behavior. Secondly, parameterization of the FIFO size allows us to make proofs across all FIFO sizes, amortizing verification costs.

In hardware this sort of parameterization is very common and keeping to a small set of stateful building blocks can dramatically help in reducing complexity. It is also likely to result in designs that are highly reusable. However, an important requirement in hardware design is that parameterization should not add extra logic – all the effects of parameterization should disappear when the block is instantiated. This can be accomplished by a compiler via *static elaboration*, a simpler form of *partial evaluation*.

3.3 Modularity

Perhaps the most important high-level abstraction for a designer is modularity. The purpose of modularity is to elucidate high-level functionality through the encapsulation of implementation details. This enhances readability of the code and improves its reuse amongst designers and between projects. Proper modularity also permits the designer to have several different implementations of the same interface. For example, small (*i.e.*, one or two element) FIFOs may be implemented very differently from larger (*i.e.*, several hundred element) FIFOs, but may have the same interface. In addition, modularity may serve as a natural place for formal tools to divide up proof obligations into tractable pieces.

Hardware also presents an opportunity to design a family of modules which may differ only in their concurrency properties. For example, one can imagine several different types of FIFOs for different design situations. For a FIFO to be used in a pipeline, it is necessary that enqueue and dequeue can happen concurrently, and the effect of dequeue should take place before the effect of enqueue. On the other hand for a FIFO to be used in a rate matching buffer, one also needs concurrent enqueue and dequeue but the effect of enqueue to take place before the effect of dequeue. Formal specification of such properties in a FIFOs interface would dramatically benefit the verification process.

Additionally, a system with strong modularity may admit modular refinement, where the designer derives various implementations from an original design serving as a "golden" specification. These derivations come in two types: design-independent transformations which are provable solely based on the language semantics, and design-specific refinements whose correctness depends upon domain-specific knowledge. Both of these changes are clear places where formal methods are useful, especially the provably correct transformations as they give the designer a useful toolbox of easy but powerful design choices he can make. For example, we have shown that using a few pipelining combinators we can effectively take a functional description of FFT expressed as a pure combinational circuit and quickly generate various "folded pipeline" versions [30]. (In a folded pipeline the same "stage logic" is reused across several cycles to implement different pipeline stages). Formally proving that these have the same input-output behavior would mean that showing the correctness of a combinational design (which is straightforward) would imply the correctness of the folded design (which is much more challenging).

Many software languages have strong enough modular interfaces that proper isolation is guaranteed. However, most hardware description languages (*e.g.,* Verilog, VHDL) have modules which serve only as structural abstractions, and do not easily allow one to abstract the behavior across module boundaries. Verilog designers do use modules as abstractions, but because of the complications due to its concrete timings, transferring these abstractions of interfaces to formal tools is quite difficult.

In contrast, modules in Bluespec [31], a language in which we have written all the examples discussed in this paper, require a stronger method-oriented interface which groups related ports into methods. Bluespec semantics is based on Guarded Atomic Actions (*i.e.,* rules), which is the same semantic model that underlies Unity [32]. In Bluespec every method has a notion of being "ready to be applied", and a compiler enforced microprotocol guarantees that a method cannot be applied unless it is ready. This allows the designer to decouple the timings of interactions from different methods, giving them the ability to play with the intra-cycle ordering. A formal tool can gain information about how a circuit can be used because the method calling protocol is uniform and implied by the language semantics, rather than in comments preceding the module definition.

3.4 Unified Language for Design and Specification

"Golden" reference specifications tend to be given in a different language than the one used in implementation. This is because implementation languages often require more details than what people writing the reference model wish to deal with. Ideally, a good high-level language would not only allow one to write good designs but also, when possible, to write reference specifications as well. This may not be possible if the specification is so abstract as to not even be executable. If it is possible then design becomes simply a refinement of the specification. The designer is saved from the major task of manually translating from the reference specification language into the implementation language.

It is important to note that refinement is only natural when moving between the high-level reference and detailed implementation does not involve significant changes in the concurrency or semantic model. For instance, Verilog has two separate "sublanguages": Behavioral Verilog which is generally used for rough-cut behavioral specifications, and Synthesizable Verilog which is used to the represent implementable designs. While these two languages have the same syntax, the simulation semantics of Verilog does not always match the Verilog synthesis semantics. While there may be a way to refine from the initial high-level specification to a synthesizable implementation, the semantic difference significantly hinders such a transformation. SystemC experiences this same problem as well. Its high-level simulation semantics closely resembles OS-thread concurrency, and therefore is a mismatch for the underlying hardware model that it needs to describe. Esterel [22] represents a significant improvement because its semantic model is consistent with synchronous FSMs. These more closely correspond with the eventual hardware implementation. Similarly, Bluespec offers a better basis for formal methods in this regard as its nondeterministic guarded-atomic-action semantics are consistent from high-level specification to implementation.

A key for languages to be able to operate at both levels is to have a large selection of high-level constructs which have solid refinable reference implementations. This can be addressed partially via good standard libraries in a high-level language where commonly used circuits like arithmetic units, register files, FIFOs and memories can be encapsulated and expressed cleanly. This is trickier than what one might expect because, in most hardware descriptions languages module interfaces are time sensitive.

3.5 Handling Nondeterminism

Closely related to the previous point is a language's ability to express and resolve nondeterminism. An important aspect in verification is the ability to express inherent nondeterminism in the correctness specification. A specification of a speculative processor should permit an unspecified number of speculative instructions to be executed before the speculation is resolved. Tthe cache coherence protocol described in Section 2.4 has nondeterminism in the memory access stream, and with the 802.11 specification, there is probabilistic nondeterminism having to do with the transmission medium.

With the exception of Bluespec, hardware design languages do not permit one to express nondeterminism. An oft heard remark about nondeterminism is that it significantly complicates reasoning about systems (See, for example, Berry's comment about the need of determinacy in Esterel [33]). This ignores the fact that nondeterminism can be viewed as an axis of flexibility for implementation purposes. Once we have learned to deal with nondeterminism, to quote Dijkstra [34]: *"[It] is no longer frightening. On the contrary! We shall learn to appreciate it, even as a valuable stepping stone in the design of an ultimately fully deterministic mechanism."*

For example, Bluespec semantics permits nondeterminism in the selection of rules to be executed in a given cycle. The compiler removes this nondeterminism to generate the final hardware in a process called *scheduling*. It has been shown that the compiler can generate efficient hardware automatically, but the user can also provide guidance from the source code if necessary. We can think of a Bluespec design as a nondeterministic specification and the additional information the designer passes to the compiler to choose a good scheduler as implementation details. This flexibility allows designers to explore many different design options easily.

Nondeterminism also results in a simplification of the verification process. For example we have shown how a cache coherence protocol [35] can be specified naturally in Bluespec. The original protocol, after we made sure rules were selected fairly for execution, served immediately as a working implementation. Assuming that the original protocol was correct, this implementation was guaranteed to be correct. The verification task now only requires us to show that further refinements to the design preserve this correctness.

3.6 Property Specification

Property specification is a mechanism through which relatively simple *assertions* can be made about a design. For example, in C the `assert` macro can be used to halt execution when, at a prespecified execution point, the state of the program is determined to be bad. Assertions on the hardware side are used somewhat differently, as *monitors* of the circuit's dynamic behavior over multiple cycles. When behavior satisfying the assertion is witnessed, the event is recorded and reported to the user. Alternatively, a design can be proven to always satisfy the assertion. For example, a typical assertion is that the state of some register never has more than one bit set to 1 (*i.e.*, it is 1-hot encoded).

SystemVerilog [36], a proper extension to Verilog, adds a number of language features to Verilog, including an assertion language, objects, and a more sophisticated type system. The assertion language is a combination of regular expressions and temporal logic. The designer benefits greatly from having Verilog embedded directly within the language for defining assertions. For example, assertions are pervasive across module instances so it is possible to define a one-hot register module. This module can be reused repeatedly in the design and even across designs.

Specification languages have to be limited in their expressivity to make the proof obligations for automatic decision procedures tractable. The BAT system [5] is interesting in the sense that it is geared towards handling bit-level implementations and incorporates sophisticated decision procedures to prove non-trivial assertions about them. In its present form BAT lacks many properties of high-level design languages, but it may be an appropriate compilation target for languages like SystemVerilog or Bluespec.

Even though many decision procedures are totally automatic, in practice, using them requires that we limit the complexity of the assertions as well as the design unit over which they are considered. Given this limitation, there may be room for specialized solvers aimed at common classes of local assertions.

3.7 FSM Equivalence and Automatic Retiming

In the EDA industry we have seen wide adoption of equivalence checking technologies. All of the major EDA vendors supply such tools [8,9,10], which provide some guarantee that low-level transformations on netlists result in functionally equivalent circuitry. These systems allow *retiming* optimizations to be tried without any worries about the correctness of the system has changes. This work has been highly successful for two major reasons. First, the algorithms are effective on real-world designs. Second, the optimizations which are allowed can quickly eke out crucial system performance improvements.

Intel's Integrated Design and Verification (IDV) environment built on the Forte [20] formal verification system is a more cutting-edge example of successful integration of formal methods into the design process. The input to IDV is an executable and synthesizable model expressed in a general-purpose reflected functional language (reFLect). The tool allows the designer to transform the circuit in a way that maintains a sequential refinement relation at every step. The transformation process is used throughout – from high-level algorithmic transformations down to detailed physical placement changes. This allows the tool to catch implementation bugs as soon as they are made. In order to remove specification bugs, the Forte tool also has more sophisticated formal analysis capabilities which require more user intervention. For example, it has been used to verify the correctness of an x86 instruction-length decoder and formally link an x86 floating-point unit with the IEEE specification expressed using real numbers.

3.8 Formalized Testing

Property specification is used for more than just assertions about one-hot registers or constraints on complicated protocols, they are widely used to define *functional coverage goals*. Instead of an assertion firing to indicate a breach of protocol (*e.g.,* a one-hot register has two 1 bits) the satisfaction of a property now indicates greater coverage of the planned test space (*e.g.,* pipeline flush occurred). Coverage-driven testing is becoming very popular with languages such as SystemVerilog [36] that integrate coverage goal specification with the design. Integration of the languages makes the testing goals clearer (similar syntax is used) and simply more convenient.

Coverage goals given in a language such as SystemVerilog advance verification practice by *formalizing* the testplan and removing ambiguity from the English descriptions. This saves time in developing directed test cases, reduces redundant work, and allows tools to automatically manage the testing effort. The management tools that accompany simulators yield essential information for steering the testing effort. Without such tools, it is not even clear when we have exercised a particular behavior. The view into the logic may only be through waveforms, and going through the generated waveform data from even a simple case can be daunting. Techniques also exist for generating test-stimulus through formal methods, most of which rely on having formalized coverage goals to guide the underlying deduction mechanisms.

4 Issues with Incorporating Formal Methods into Design

We have seen the development of a rich variety of formal tools over the last two decades: temporal logic model checkers (*e.g.*, SMV [2], SPIN [37]); theorem provers (*e.g.*, ACL2 [38], PVS [39], Isabelle/HOL [40]); automated decision and semi-decision procedures (*e.g.*, BAT [5], Z3 [4], UCLID [3], Yices [41], Alloy [42]); and other specification languages and tools (*e.g.*, B [43], IOA [44], TIOA [45]). Most tools today can handle much larger problems, have better libraries, and are much more robust than a decade ago. In spite of these advances these tools have at best seen marginal penetration in the design community. The community of users of these tools has not gone far beyond the tool designers, who tend to be highly inclined mathematically.

The only way to use any of these tools is to learn an entirely new system often involving its own mathematical concepts which are divorced from the concepts used in most designs. The barrier to entry is so high that the effort required is almost never justified by the economic gains. We think that there is an obvious way to fix this problem, though it requires a change in the mindset of the formal methods community:

1. *Tools must be invokable from the design language in a seamless manner. This implies that the tools must be able to take unmodified source as input as well as report results in a manner consistent with the language.*
2. *If possible, tools should be entirely automatic requiring no user intervention to facilitate the proof process. Alternatively, if tools require some user guidance, this information must be provided through the design language.*

In this section we demonstrate how the lack of these two characteristics make current methods extremely difficult to integrate into design flows. We do this by considering the possible verifications of two designs described previously using current tools. In one case we focus on a model-checking-based platform, and in the other we consider theorem proving.

4.1 IP Lookup: *Using Model Checkers in Practice*

Consider what the process would be to verify the IP lookup design of Section 2.1 using the SPIN model checker. The design is written in Bluespec, but the SPIN tool accepts Promela as input. The first thing that needs to be done is to convert the Bluespec into Promela. While this could possibly be done *mechanically*, as it stands today the designer must translate by hand. The same is true for most design languages and this is highly undesirable. A manual translation can easily introduce new behaviors into the design, or remove behaviors that existed before translation. Therefore, the translation itself has to be verified, making this approach a non-starter.

After translation, the next barrier that we come up against is specifying the property to be verified. Consider the property that there is a one-to-one correspondence between inputs and output of the IP lookup design. Currently, the designer is expected to be able to represent this in LTL. This is a significant challenge as such logics are a completely foreign way of thinking for most designers. Worse, since we are limited by LTL we cannot even represent the possibly unbounded size of the input-output relation. The designer is left wondering whether this is a result of him not knowing how to express the property, LTL being restrictive, or an actual issue in his design.

Assuming that the property actually can be represented in LTL, it is likely that a direct translation will be completely untenable. That is, given the propositional nature of LTL, the only view into the state is through *unary predicates.* Therefore, if a direct translation of the code is done, then this number will be gigantic. For example, given a 32-bit register, each of the 2^{32} states would need to be encoded separately to get all information out of the design. These numbers quickly become far larger than any model checker can reasonably handle. Alternatively, the designer must abstract away certain states and prove that a much smaller representation preserves the property being checked. For example, with IP lookup a reasonable abstraction would use certain key assumptions about the lookup table (*e.g.,* that a lookup chain in the table is of length 1 to 4). Representing such abstraction naturally in the design language is a challenging open problem..

However, even if we assume some abstraction is done correctly, what happens if SPIN evaluates the correctness property and reports a bug? The designer must now translate this failed path back into something useful to reason about. In this case, the ideal way to express this would be the relevant indexes in the IP lookup and, the inputs questions, and the timings of the rules in the system. Extracting this from the given path is tedious for a designer. Any help in making the data more accessible would pay significant dividends.

For formal methods to work effectively in an engineering design flow, it is important to prevent the user from having to jump through hoops. But how would the designer want to be able to use a formal system? First, the designer wouldn't have to manually translate from the design language (in this example Bluespec). Second, apropos Section 3.4, a correctness specification would also be given as part of the design in some natural dialect of Bluespec. In this case it may involve adding virtual state to represent unique request tags which can be verified to occur in sequential order at output. By informing the system of the invariant that should be maintained, (*i.e.,* packet identifiers leave in sequential order) compilation would either prove or disprove this assertion. If wrong, the system would give an initial state and an understandable sequence of rule firings (a single semantic step in Bluespec) witnessing the failure. This would allow the designer to stay focused on his design in the language to which he is used while incorporating the verification task easily with compilation, a task he must do frequently in design.

4.2 Cache Coherence: *Using Theorem Provers in Practice*

In his dissertation, Xiaowei Shen described an adaptive cache coherence protocol called Cachet [46,47] and proved it correct. This proof was very long and complicated and it was decided that it should be proved mechanically using PVS [16] to guarantee no mistakes were made. The mechanical proof considered a significant subset of the protocol. Despite already having completed a handworked proof of the complete protocol, it took an engineer skilled both in design and formal methods six months of effort to complete, a significant expenditure. Clearly, this amount of effort is much too burdensome for general integration in the design flow. However, it is still worthwhile to consider how this would apply for verifying the implementation.

A full proof of our implementation requires effort just to get an implementation into PVS. One possible approach would be to synthesize the code and then feed it into PVS as one large Boolean next-state function. Of course, the user then has to reason at this horribly tedious level of detail. Alternatively, we could try to axiomatize Verilog or Bluespec semantics directly in PVS, but this adds a layer of indirection in the proof which may complicate things. Ideally the user could express booleans which represented the interesting properties to be verified (e.g., no multiple modified version of an address) directly in the design.

Secondly, even with a good representation of the code in PVS, the proof becomes much more complicated based on the fact that any implementation is bound to involve many system details not elucidated by the protocol. For example, while the abstract proof could assume that all coherence messages are received, in an implementation with finite buffering and various routing logic, this too must be verified. This would be quite difficult to formulate, let alone prove in PVS.

5 Conclusion

Formal methods have come a long way, but for reasons we have outlined in this paper, a large gap remains between current formal methodologies and engineering practice. Except in a few instances, formal methods are not tightly integrated into the design-debug loop. We have argued that for widespread adoption formal methods must be invoked through high-level design languages and must present a semantic model that makes sense to the designer. Incorporation of assertions in SystemVerilog is an example of a good start but its effectiveness is limited. The weak semantics of Verilog, inability to express the full spectrum of interesting correctness properties, and the capacity of current tools all take away from usability.

The range of examples in this paper have shown that even for a single application often more than one formal technique is needed to show correctness. It may not be desirable to try to unify too many concepts into one specification language. For example, should every design language be so powerful that it can express probabilistic correctness? Or, to put this another way, just because someone might develop a system where probabilities are important (e.g., our 802.11 transmitter) should probabilities be in the language? It is a difficult question to answer as it is not clear where one should draw the line. For example, in Bluespec nondeterminism is inherent in the language, but its observability remains latent in the current set of tools. In this case, probabilities are entirely foreign to this model and it is not clear how they will affect the system.

Based on our design experience in Bluespec, we think we can express, programmatically, many assertions that we would like to prove about the design. This may require the introduction of extra state and rules, but semantically it requires no new concepts for the user. If these assertions and associated code are syntactically identifiable in the source then it should be straightforward to eliminate them once the design is deemed to be working correctly. Such a method may provide a continuum between "proof by simulation" and proof by formal means. The real technical challenge is how to place restrictions on this verification code so that the decision or semi-decision procedures have a high chance of success. We plan to pursue this line of research in the future.

Acknowledgments

This paper and much of the examples discussed was done as part of the CSAIL-Nokia collaboration. This work was also supported by NSF grant CCF-0541164. We would like to thank Rishiyur Nikhil, George Harper, Srini Devadas, Daniel Jackson, and Pete Manolios for their generous advice on the penultimate draft of this paper. We are also thankful to Carl Sager for clarifying our understanding of the use of Forte tool inside Intel.

References

1. Paulson, L.C.: The Relative Consistency of the Axiom of Choice Mechanized using Isabelle/ZF. London Mathematical Society Journal of Computation and Mathematics 6 (2003)
2. McMillan, K.L.: Symbolic Model Checking: An Approach to the State Explosion Problem. PhD thesis, Carnegie Mellon University (1992)
3. Bryant, R.E., Lahiri, S.K., Seshia, S.A.: Modeling and Verifying Systems Using a Logic of Counter Arithmetic with Lambda Expressions and Uninterpreted Functions. In: 14th International Conference on Computer Aided Verification (CAV), Copenhagen, Denmark (2002)
4. de Moura, L., Bjorner, N.: Z3: An Efficient SMT Solver. In: 14th International Conference on Tools and Algorithms for the Construction and Analysis of Systems (TACAS), Budapest, Hungary (2008)
5. Manolios, P., Srinivasan, S.K., Vroon, D.: BAT: The Bit-Level Analysis Tool. In: Proceedings of the 19th International Conference on Computer Aided Verification (CAV), Berlin, Germany (2007)
6. Moskewicz, M.W., Madigan, C.F., Zhao, Y., Zhang, L., Malik, S.: Chaff: engineering an efficient SAT solver. In: Proceedings of the 38th conference on Design automation (DAC), Las Vegas, NV (2001)
7. Mentor Graphics Corp.: 0-In® Formal Verification, www.mentor.com/products/fv/abv/0-in_fv/
8. Synopsys, Inc.: Formality® Equivalence Checker, www.synopsys.com/products/verification/

9. Mentor Graphics Corp.: FormalPro^{TM}, www.mentor.com/products/fv/ev/formalpro/
10. Cadence Design Systems, Inc.: Cadence® Encounter® Conformal® Equivalence Checker, www.cadence.com/products/digital_ic/conformal/index.aspx
11. Jasper Design Automation, Inc.: JasperGold® Verification System, www.jasper-da.com/products_jaspergold.htm
12. Cadence Design Systems, Inc.: Incisive® Formal Verifier, www.cadence.com/products/functional_ver/incisive_formal_verifier/index.aspx
13. Meadows, C.: The NRL Protocol Analyzer: An Overview. The Journal of Logic Programming 26(2), 113–131 (1996)
14. Kwiatkowska, M.Z., Norman, G., Sproston, J.: Probabilistic Model Checking of the IEEE 802.11 Wireless Local Area Network Protocol. In: Proceedings of the Second Joint International Workshop on Process Algebra and Probabilistic Methods, Performance Modeling and Verification (PAPM-PROBMIV), Copenhagen, Denmark (2002)
15. Burch, J.R., Dill, D.L.: Automatic Verification of Pipelined Microprocessor Control. In: Proceedings of the 6th International Conference on Computer Aided Verification (CAV), Stanford, CA (1994)
16. Stoy, J.E., Shen, X., Arvind.: Proofs of Correctness of Cache-Coherence Protocols. In: Oliveira, J.N., Zave, P. (eds.) FME 2001. LNCS, vol. 2021, pp. 47–71. Springer, Heidelberg (2001)
17. Flanagan, C., Leino, K.R.M., Lillibridge, M., Nelson, G., Saxe, J.B., Stata, R.: Extended static checking for Java. In: Proceedings of the ACM SIGPLAN 2002 Conference on Programming Language Design and Implementation (PLDI), San Diego, CA (2002)
18. Ball, T., Rajamani, S.K.: The SLAM project: debugging system software via static analysis. In: Proceedings of the 29th ACM SIGPLAN-SIGACT Symposium on Principles of Programming Languages (POPL), Portland, OR (2002)
19. Russinoff, D.M.: A Case Study in Fomal Verification of Register-Transfer Logic with ACL2: The Floating Point Adder of the AMD Athlon^{TM} Processor. In: Proceedings of the Third International Conference on Formal Methods in Computer-Aided Design (FMCAD), Austin, TX (2000)
20. Seger, C.J., Jones, R., O'Leary, J., Melham, T., Aagaard, M., Barrett, C., Syme, D.: An Industrially Effective Environment for Formal Hardware Verification. Computer-Aided Design of Integrated Circuits and Systems, IEEE Transactions on 24(9), 1381–1405 (2005)
21. Cousot, P., Cousot, R., Feret, J., Mauborgne, L., Miné, A., Monniaux, D., Rival, X.: The ASTREÉ Analyzer. In: Proceedings of the 14th European Symposium on Programming (ESOP), Edinburgh, UK (2005)
22. Berry, G.: The Foundations of Esterel, 425–454 (2000)
23. Arvind, N.R.S., Rosenband, D.L., Dave, N.: High-level synthesis: an essential ingredient for designing complex ASICs. In: Proceedings of the IEEE/ACM International Conference on Computer-Aided Design (ICCAD), San Jose, CA (2004)
24. IEEE: IEEE standard 802.11a supplement. Wireless LAN Medium Access Control (MAC) and Physical Layer (PHY) Specifications (1999)
25. International Telecommunication Union: H.264, www.itu.int/rec/T-REC-H.264
26. Joshi, R., Lamport, L., Matthews, J., Tasiran, S., Tuttle, M., Yu, Y.: Checking Cache-Coherence Protocols with TLA+. Form. Methods Syst. Des. 22(2) (2003)
27. Arvind, S.X.: Using Term Rewriting Systems to Design and Verify Processors. IEEE Micro 19(3), 36–46 (1999)

28. Krstić, S., Jones, R.B., O'Leary, J.: Mothers of Pipelines. Electron. Notes Theor. Comput. Sci. 174(8), 7–22 (2007)
29. Manolios, P.: Correctness of Pipelined Machines. In: Johnson, S.D., Hunt Jr., W.A. (eds.) FMCAD 2000. LNCS, vol. 1954, pp. 161–178. Springer, Heidelberg (2000)
30. Dave, N., Pellauer, M., Gerding, S., Arvind.: 802.11a Transmitter: A Case Study in Microarchitectural Exploration. In: Proceedings of Formal Methods and Models for Codesign (MEMOCODE), Napa, CA (2006)
31. Bluespec, Inc. Waltham, MA: Bluespec SystemVerilog Ver. 3.8 Reference Guide (November 2004)
32. Chandy, K.M., Misra, J.: Parallel Program Design: A Foundation. Addison-Wesley, Reading (1988)
33. Berry, G.: The Esterel v5 Language Primer Version v5_91 (2000)
34. Dijkstra, E.W.: A Discipline of Programming. Prentice Hall PTR, Upper Saddle River (1997)
35. Dave, N., Ng, M.C., Arvind.: Automatic Synthesis of Cache-Coherence Protocol Processors Using Bluespec. In: Proc. of Formal Methods and Models for Codesign, Verona, Italy (2005)
36. Dave, N., Ng, M.C., Arvind.: Standard for SystemVerilog: Unified Hardware Design, Specification and Verification Language (IEEE Std. 1800-2007)
37. Holzmann, G.J.: The SPIN MODEL CHECKER: Primer and Reference Manual. Addison-Wesley, Reading (2003)
38. Kaufmann, M., Moore, J.S., Manolios, P.: Computer-Aided Reasoning: An Approach. Kluwer Academic Publishers, Norwell (2000)
39. Owre, S., Rushby, J.M., Rushby, J.M., Shankar, N.: PVS: A Prototype Verification System. In: Proceedings of the 11th International Conference on Automated Deduction (CADE), Saratoga Springs, NY (1992)
40. Nipkow, T., Paulson, L.C., Wenzel, M.: Isabelle/HOL: A Proof Assistant for Higher-Order Logic. Springer-Verlag, London (2002)
41. SRI International: Yices, yices.csl.sri.com/index.shtml
42. Jackson, D.: Alloy: A Lightweight Object Modelling Notation. ACM Trans. Softw. Eng. Methodol. 11(2), 256–290 (2002)
43. Abrial, J.-R.: The B-Book: Assigning Programs to Meanings. Cambridge University Press, New York (1996)
44. Lynch, N.A., Tuttle, M.R.: Hierarchical correctness proofs for distributed algorithms. In: Proceedings of the Sixth Annual ACM Symposium on Principles of Distributed Computing (PODC), Vancouver, British Columbia (1987)
45. Archer, L.M.H.L., Mitra, N., Umeno, S.: Specifying and Proving Properties of Timed I/O Automata in the TIOA Toolkit. In: Proceedings. Fourth ACM and IEEE International Conference on Formal Methods and Models for Co-Design (MEMOCODE), Napa, CA (2006)
46. Shen, X.: Design and Verification of Adaptive Cache Coherence Protocols. PhD thesis, MIT, Cambridge, MA (2000)
47. Shen, X., Rudolph, L., Arvind,: CACHET: An Adaptive Cache Coherence Protocol for Distributed Shared-Memory Systems. In: Proceedings of the 13th ACM SIGARCH International Conference on Supercomputing, IEEE Computer Society, Los Alamitos (1999)

Lessons in the Weird and Unexpected: Some Experiences from Checking Large Real Systems

Dawson Engler

Computer Science and Electrical Engineering
Stanford University,
Engler@csl.stanford.edu

Abstract. This talk will draw on our efforts in using static analysis, model checking, and symbolic execution to find bugs in real code, both in academic and commercial settings. The unifying religion driving all these efforts has been: results matter more than anything. That which works is good, that which does not is not. While this worldview is simple, reality is not. I will discuss some what we learned in struggling with this mismatch.

Simulation, Orchestration and Logical Clocks

David Kitchen, Evan Powell, and Jayadev Misra

University of Texas at Austin
misra@cs.utexas.edu

Abstract. A language in which discrete event simulations can be coded needs to support the features (1) to describe behavior of a single physical process, (2) to describe concurrent ctivities of multiple physical processes, including communication, synchronization and interruption, (3) to account for passage of time, and (4) to record system state at appropriate points and create statistical summaries. Orc, a recent language for orchestration of distributed services, combines these features so that complex simulations can be expressed very succinctly. This talk describes the relevant features of Orc for simulation and illustrates them using a number of realistic examples. Additionally, we show that certain combinatorial problems, such as shortest paths in graphs and many problems in computational geometry, can be cast as simulation problems, and solved very simply in Orc.

CoVaC: Compiler Validation by Program Analysis of the Cross-Product

Anna Zaks and Amir Pnueli[*]

New York University, New York
{ganna,amir}@cs.nyu.edu

Abstract. The paper presents a deductive framework for proving program equivalence and its application to automatic verification of transformations performed by optimizing compilers. To leverage existing program analysis techniques, we reduce the equivalence checking problem to analysis of one system – a cross-product of the two input programs. We show how the approach can be effectively used for checking equivalence of consonant (i.e., structurally similar) programs. Finally, we report on the prototype tool that applies the developed methodology to verify that a compiler optimization run preserves the program semantics. Unlike existing frameworks, CoVaC accommodates absence of compiler annotations and handles most of the classical intraprocedural optimizations such as constant folding, reassociation, common subexpression elimination, code motion, dead code elimination, branch optimizations, and others.

1 Introduction

Compilers, especially optimizing compilers, are quite large applications, which are bound to have bugs. For example, the GCC Bug Database contains over 3 thousand reported bugs some of which may alter the behavior of programs being compiled. This is highly undesirable, especially in safety critical and high-assurance software, where the effort of program correctness verification is extensive. First, the developers manually examine code and test it. Then, numerous verification tools and techniques are applied to verify that the source code satisfies the desired properties. After all the rigorous checks are complete, the program is compiled by an optimizing compiler and released. Clearly, the verification effort should not stop here – it is highly advisable to ensure that the transformations performed by a compiler preserve the semantics of a program.

That is precisely the goal of Translation Validation (TV) [1] – it ensures that optimizing transformations preserve program semantics. In essence, instead of attempting the verification of a given compiler, each compiler run is followed by a validation pass that automatically checks that the target code produced by the compiler is semantically equivalent to the source code. A good question is: "Can this goal be achieved?" The problem of program equivalence is undecidable. However, since the focus is only on compiler optimizations, the number of false

---

[*] This research has been supported in part by a grant from the Microsoft Phoenix Academic Program and the NSF CSR–EHS grant CNS-0720581.

alarms can be drastically minimized or even eliminated, intuitively, due to the fact that we are aware of the analyses used by the optimizing compilers, and since those analyses are mechanical in nature.

In this paper, we present a Compiler Verification by Program Analysis of the Cross-Product framework (CoVaC) – a novel translation validation approach, in which one constructs a *comparison system* – a cross-product of the source and target programs. The input programs are equivalent if and only if the comparison system satisfies a certain specification. This allows us to leverage the existing methods of proving properties of a single program instead of relying on program analysis and proof rules specialized to translation validation, used by the existing frameworks [2,3,4]. CoVaC is not tailored to validation of compiler transformations – it targets program equivalence in general; for example, it can be applied to validation of language-based security properties [5].

The CoVaC framework can be used in various settings, and, while the check for specification conformance is expected to be the same, the construction of the comparison system may diverge. For example, compiler writers may use translation validation for the creation of a self-certifying compiler and, thus, may assume full knowledge of the inner workings of a particular compiler. In this case, the compiler itself may output the comparison system. The second part of this paper pursues the other extreme – it describes a method for automatic generation of the comparison system, and thus, a translation validation algorithm, which accommodates no compiler cooperation. To the best of our knowledge, the existing translation validation frameworks which handle a comparable set of optimizations at least to some degree rely on compiler assistance. The lack of compiler dependency makes it possible to develop a general purpose verification tool that can be used to verify the transformations performed by different compilers. Such tool would be especially useful to compiler users who may have to work with a particular existing compiler. Additionally, this methodology can be of service to compiler developers to facilitate testing of immature compilers.

In order to make the validator of non-cooperative compilers feasible and effective, we currently restrict the set of transformations under consideration to intraprocedural optimizations in which each loop in the target program corresponds to a loop in the source program; we refer to such input systems as *consonant*. Many of the classical compiler optimizations such as constant folding, reassociation, induction variable optimizations, common subexpression elimination, code motion, branch optimizations, register allocation, instruction scheduling, and others fall into this category. These optimizations are usually referred to as structure preserving [2]. Finally, this paper reports on a prototype tool CoVaC that applies the developed framework to verification of optimizing transformations performed by LLVM [6] – an aggressive open-source C and C++ compiler.

In summary, this paper makes the following contributions. First, it presents a novel deductive framework for checking equivalence of infinite state programs. Second, it defines the notion of consonance and shows how the method can be effectively applied to consonant programs. The presented algorithm does not rely on any additional input; thus, it can be used to verify compilations while treating the compiler as a black-box. Due to lack of space, the paper does not contain proofs and only briefly discusses the implementation details. For a full version, the reader is referred to our technical report [7].

The rest of the paper is organized as follows. Section 2 introduces our formal model and defines the notion of correct translation. We describe the general framework for establishing program equivalence in Section 3. Section 4 presents the algorithm for comparison system construction, which requires no compiler cooperation. An example is presented in Section 5; and Section 6 focuses on the experimental results. We discuss the related work and conclude in Section 7.

2 Formal Model and the Notion of Correct Translation

2.1 Transition Graphs

Our model is similar to that presented in [8] for verification of procedural programs.

A program (application) $\mathcal{A}$ consists of $m+1$ procedures: $main$, f_1, ..., f_m, where $main$ represents the main procedure, and f_1, ..., f_m are procedures which may be called from $main$ or from other procedures. We use $f_i(\vec{x};\ \&\vec{z})$ to denote the signature of a procedure. Here, call-by-value parameter passing method is used for $\vec{x}$, and call-by-reference is used for $\vec{z}$. A procedure may return a result by means of $\vec{z}$ variables. We use $\vec{y}$ to denote the typed variables of a procedure. $\vec{y} = (\vec{x};\ \vec{z};\ \vec{w})$, i.e. the variables in $\vec{y}$ are partitioned into $\vec{x}$, $\vec{z}$, and $\vec{w}$, where $\vec{x}$ and $\vec{z}$ are the *input* parameters and $\vec{w}$ denotes the *local* variables.

Each procedure is presented as a *transition graph* $f_i := (\vec{y}, \mathcal{N}_i, \mathcal{E}_i)$ with variables $\vec{y}$, nodes (locations) $\mathcal{N}_i = \{r^i = n_0^i,\ n_1^i,\ n_2^i,\ \ldots,\ n_k^i = t^i\}$ and a set of labeled edges $\mathcal{E}_i$. It must have a distinct root node r^i as its only entry point, a distinct tail node t^i as its only exit point, and every other node must be on a path from r^i to t^i. Nodes of the graph are connected by directed edges labeled by instructions. There are four types of instructions: guarded assignments, procedure calls, reads, and writes. Consider a procedure $f_i(\vec{x};\ \&\vec{z})$ with $\vec{y} = (\vec{x},\ \vec{z},\ \vec{w})$. Let $\vec{u}$ include variables from $\vec{y}$; and $E(\vec{y})$ be a list of expressions over $\vec{y}$.

- A *guarded assignment* is an instruction of the form $c \rightarrow [\vec{u} := E(\vec{y})]$, where guard c is a boolean expression. When the assignment part is empty, we abbreviate the label to a pure condition $c?$.
- *Procedure call* instruction $f_k(E(\vec{y}), \vec{u})$ denotes a call to procedure $f_k(\vec{x}_k;\ \&\vec{z}_k)$, passing input parameters $E(\vec{y})$ by value and $\vec{u}$ by reference.
- *Read* and *write* instructions are denoted by $read(\vec{u})$ and $write(\vec{u})$. They are used to express the interaction of the procedure with the outside world; e.g. I/O instructions.

The implicit guards of read, write, and procedure call instructions always evaluate to *true*. A transition graph is *deterministic* when, for every node n, the guards of all edges departing from n are mutually exclusive. A transition graph is *non-blocking* when, for every node, the disjunction of the guards evaluates to *true*. In this work, we only consider deterministic non-blocking systems.

Transition graphs can be used to model programs written in procedural languages. In order to construct a formal model of a program, we first choose a set of program locations Υ such that:

- At least one location in each loop belongs to Υ.
- For every procedure, both procedure entry and exit belong to Υ.
- The locations before and after read, write, and procedure call belong to Υ.

Each procedure whose implementation is given is represented by a transition graph. We choose the set Υ of a procedure f_i to be the set of nodes for the corresponding transition graph. For every pair of locations n, m in Υ, if there exists a path π from n to m, which does not pass through any other location from Υ, we add edge (n, m) to the graph and label it by the instruction that summarizes the effect of executing the path π.

2.2 States and Computations

We denote by $\vec{d} = (\vec{d^x};\ \vec{d^z};\ \vec{d^w})$ a tuple of values, which represents an interpretation (i.e., an assignment of values) of the procedure variables $\vec{y} = (\vec{x};\ \vec{z};\ \vec{w})$. A *state* of a procedure f is a pair $\langle n; \vec{d}\rangle$ consisting of a node n and a data interpretation $\vec{d}$. A $(\vec{\xi}, \vec{\zeta})$-*computation* of procedure f is a maximal sequence of states and labeled transitions:

$$\sigma : \langle r;\ (\vec{\xi}, \vec{\zeta}, \vec{\top})\rangle \xrightarrow{\lambda_1} \langle n_1;\ \vec{d_1}\rangle \xrightarrow{\lambda_2} \langle n_2;\ \vec{d_2}\rangle \ldots$$

The tuple $\vec{\top}$ denotes uninitialized values. At the first state of the computation, the location is r, the entry location of f; the values of input variables $\vec{x}$ and $\vec{z}$ are set to $\vec{\xi}$ and $\vec{\zeta}$, respectively, and the local variables $\vec{w}$ are not initialized. Labels of the transitions are either labels of edges in the program or the special label *ret*. Each transition must be justified by either an intra-procedural transition, a call transition, or a return transition such that the call and return transitions are *balanced*. See our technical report [7] for the formal definition.

We use $Cmp(f)$ to denote the computations of a transition graph f. We define a set of computations of a procedural program $\mathcal{A}$, denoted $Cmp(\mathcal{A})$, to be the set of computations $Cmp(main)$.

2.3 Correct Translation

In this work, we are only concerned with intraprocedural optimizations, so for simplicity, we are going to assume that the corresponding procedures of $\mathcal{S}$ and $\mathcal{T}$ have the same names; we are going to use a superscript notation to differentiate between the source and target procedures. We define the correctness of translation via equivalence of program behaviors that can be observed by the user. Intuitively, given the same input, both, $\mathcal{S}$ and $\mathcal{T}$, must produce the same output and should either both terminate or generate infinite computations. We also observe the values of input and output parameters of every procedure.

Given a computation, we define V_s – the set of *observable variables* at a state $s = \langle n; d\rangle$, to be the minimal set satisfying the following conditions:

- If s is a state immediately after transition $read(\vec{u})$, $V_s \supseteq \vec{u}$.
- If s is a state immediately before transition $write(\vec{u})$, $V_s \supseteq \vec{u}$.
- If $n = r$ is the entry node of procedure $f(\vec{x}, \&\vec{z})$, $(V_s \supseteq \vec{x}) \wedge (V_s \supseteq \vec{z})$.
- If $n = t$ is the exit node of procedure $f(\vec{x}, \&\vec{z})$, $V_s \supseteq \vec{z}$.

Above, we use $V_s \supseteq \vec{u}$ to denote $V_s \supseteq \{v : v \text{ in } \vec{u}\}$.

We associate *observation function* $\mathcal{O}$ with each program, mapping the source and target states and transition labels into a common domain. The observation function needs to ensure that read and write transitions of the source and target computations match. Formally, given a state $s = \langle n; d \rangle$, an observation function $\mathcal{O}(s)$ is defined as following. Let V_s be the set of observable variables at s. If $V_s = \emptyset$ then $\mathcal{O}(s) = \bot$, else $\mathcal{O}(s) = \vec{d}_{V_s}$. We obtain $\vec{d}_{V_s}$ by restricting $\vec{d}$ only to the values that correspond to the variables in V_s. Given a transition label λ, an observation function $\mathcal{O}(\lambda)$ is defined as follows. If λ is a label of a transition that is a read, a write, a call to procedure g, or a return from g, $\mathcal{O}(\lambda)$ is equal to $read$, $write$, $call_g$, or ret_g, respectively. Otherwise, $\mathcal{O}(\lambda) = \bot$.

An *observation* of a computation σ, denoted $o(\sigma)$, is obtained by applying the observation function $\mathcal{O}$ to each state and each transition label in σ. That is, for $\sigma : s_1 \xrightarrow{\lambda_1} s_2 \xrightarrow{\lambda_2} s_3 \ldots$, we get $o(\sigma) : \mathcal{O}(s_1) \xrightarrow{\mathcal{O}(\lambda_1)} \mathcal{O}(s_2) \xrightarrow{\mathcal{O}(\lambda_2)} \mathcal{O}(s_3) \ldots$.

Definition 1. *Computations σ and σ' are* **stuttering equivalent***, denoted $\sigma \sim_{st} \sigma'$, if their observations $o(\sigma)$, $o(\sigma')$ only differ from each other by finite sequences of pairs $\bot \xrightarrow{\bot}$ or $\xrightarrow{\bot} \bot$.*

Stuttering equivalence is used to ensure that even though the programs may have to execute a different number of instructions to get to an observable state, the difference is always finite. Our assumption is that the user is not time-sensitive so this finite delta cannot be observed. For example, $\beta \sim_{st} \beta'$:

$o(\beta) : \bot \xrightarrow{read} (5, 22) \xrightarrow{\bot} \bot \xrightarrow{\bot} \bot \xrightarrow{\bot} (110) \xrightarrow{write} \bot$

$o(\beta'): \bot \xrightarrow{read} (5, 22) \xrightarrow{\bot} \bot \xrightarrow{\bot} (110) \xrightarrow{write} \bot \xrightarrow{\bot} \bot$

In both computations, first two numbers: 5 and 22, are read; and then, after a finite number of steps, their product: 110, is written out.

Definition 2. *We say that procedure f_T is* **a correct translation** *of procedure f_S if, for every $(\vec{\xi}, \vec{\zeta})$-computation σ_T in $Cmp(f_T)$, there exists a $(\vec{\xi}, \vec{\zeta})$-computation σ_S in $Cmp(f_S)$ such that $\sigma_T \sim_{st} \sigma_S$, and vice versa. Program $\mathcal{T}$ is a correct translation of program $\mathcal{S}$ if $main_T$ is a correct translation of $main_S$.*

3 Equivalence Checking by Program Analysis of the Cross-Product $\mathcal{S} \boxtimes \mathcal{T}$

In this section, we show that the problem of establishing correct translation is equivalent to construction of a cross-product (comparison) system $\mathcal{C} = \mathcal{S} \boxtimes \mathcal{T}$ and checking if $\mathcal{C}$ satisfies a set of correctness conditions. Our framework is general enough for establishing translation correctness of deterministic systems in presence of a wide set of intraprocedural transformations and can be easily extended to cope with interprocedural optimizations as well. Later in the paper, we present application of the method to proving translation of consonant systems. However, the general framework can be used to reason about translation correctness in presence of structure modifying optimizations such as loop transformations [9].

3.1 Comparison Graphs

Assume we are given two programs, $\mathcal{S}$ and $\mathcal{T}$. For each pair of the corresponding source and target procedures, $f^S = (\vec{y}^S, \mathcal{N}^S, \mathcal{E}^S)$ and $f^T = (\vec{y}^T, \mathcal{N}^T, \mathcal{E}^T)$, a graph satisfying the set of rules below is called a *comparison transition graph*, denoted $f = (\vec{y}, \mathcal{N}, \mathcal{E}) = f^S \boxtimes f^T$. f represents a simultaneous execution of f^S and f^T. The collection of comparison graphs for all procedures constitutes the comparison program $\mathcal{C} = \mathcal{S} \boxtimes \mathcal{T}$.

Rule 1. *(Structural Requirement)*

1. *The variables of the comparison graph $\vec{y} = (\vec{x}, \vec{z}, \vec{w})$ are defined as follows: $\vec{x} = \vec{x}^S \circ \vec{x}^T$; $\vec{z} = \vec{z}^S \circ \vec{z}^T$; and $\vec{w} = \vec{w}^S \circ \vec{w}^T$, where $\vec{v} \circ \vec{u}$ denotes concatenation of two vectors.*
2. *Each node of f is a pair of source and target nodes: $\mathcal{N} \subseteq \mathcal{N}^S \times \mathcal{N}^T$. Let r^S, t^S and r^T, t^T denote the exit and entry nodes of f^S and f^T respectively. Then $r = \langle r^S, r^T \rangle$ and $t = \langle t^S, t^T \rangle$ are the entry and exit nodes of f.*
3. *Each edge of the graph $e = (\langle n^S, n^T \rangle, \langle m^S, m^T \rangle) \in \mathcal{E}$, labeled by a pair of instructions $\langle op^S; op^T \rangle$, should be justified by one of the following:*
   - $(n^S, m^S) \in \mathcal{E}^S$ *and it is labeled by* op^S; $(n^T, m^T) \in \mathcal{E}^T$ *and it is labeled by* op^T; *and* op^S *and* op^T *are instructions of the same type (either both reads, writes, assignments, or calls to procedures with the same name).*
   - $(n^S, m^S) \in \mathcal{E}^S$, *labeled by assignment* op^S; $n^T = m^T$; *and* $op^T = \epsilon$.
   - $(n^T, m^T) \in \mathcal{E}^T$, *labeled by assignment* op^T; $n^S = m^S$; *and* $op^S = \epsilon$.

   Where, ϵ stands for assignment true?, which represents an idle transition.

Since the edges of a comparison graph are labeled by the same type instructions, reads and writes of the two systems are performed in sync.

A *composed transition* $\langle n; \vec{d} \rangle \xrightarrow{e^S; e^T} \langle n'; \vec{d'} \rangle$ is interpreted as a sequential composition of the source and target transitions with one exception. Let e^S and e^T be labeled by $read(\vec{u}^S)$ and $read(\vec{u}^T)$. Then, the transition is enabled only if $\vec{d'}_{u^S} = \vec{d'}_{u^T}$, where $\vec{d'}_{u^S}$ and $\vec{d'}_{u^T}$ are obtained from $\vec{d'}$ by restricting it to the values that correspond to the variables $\vec{u}^S$ and $\vec{u}^T$. Thus, we require that the values fed into the source and target reads are equal. Given σ in $Cmp(f)$, we use $\sigma\!\uparrow_S$ to denote a path obtained by projection of σ onto the states and transitions related to procedure f^S.

Rule 2. *There does not exist σ in $Cmp(f)$ such that $\sigma\!\uparrow_S$ or $\sigma\!\uparrow_T$ contains an infinite sequence of ϵ-transitions.*

The following claim follows directly from Rule 1 and Rule 2: $\forall \sigma \in Cmp(f)$: $(\exists \sigma^S \in Cmp(f^S) : \sigma^S \sim_{st} \sigma\!\uparrow_S) \wedge (\exists \sigma^T \in Cmp(f^T) : \sigma^T \sim_{st} \sigma\!\uparrow_T)$; i.e.

every computation of the comparison graph has the corresponding computations in both source and target.

In addition, we should ensure the reverse of the previous claim: the computations of the comparison graph represent all the computations of the input systems. We say that computations of an input system, say $Cmp(f^S)$, are *covered* by $Cmp(f)$ when the following condition holds: $\forall \sigma^S \in Cmp(f^S), \exists \sigma \in Cmp(f) : \sigma^S$ differs from $\sigma \uparrow_S$, by only finite sequences of (padding) ϵ-transitions. The notion of coverage is stronger then stuttering equivalence, so it follows that $\sigma^S \sim_{st} \sigma \uparrow_S$.

Rule 3. *Computations of f^S and computations of f^T are covered by $Cmp(f)$.*

Note that following Rule 3, not all edges of the input graphs have to be in the comparison graph, which allows us to disregard the unreachable states of the input systems. Now as we have defined a comparison graph, let's consider what properties it should satisfy in order to guarantee the correctness of translation.

Definition 3. *A comparison graph $f = f^S \boxtimes f^T$, is a witness of correct translation if for every $((\vec{\xi} \circ \vec{\xi}),(\vec{\zeta} \circ \vec{\zeta}))$-computation of f, its target and source projections have equal observations.* Note, we restrict the computations under consideration to those in which the input parameters are initialized with the same values.

Theorem 1. *Target function f^T is a correct translation of source function f^S if and only if there exists a witness comparison graph $f = f^S \boxtimes f^T$. In addition, if f^T is a correct translation of f^S then every comparison graph $f = f^S \boxtimes f^T$ is a witness of correct translation.* (Refer to [7] for the proof of the theorem.)

Thus, in order to determine the correctness of translation, it is sufficient to construct a comparison graph and check if it is, indeed, a witness. Fig. 1 depicts an example of a witness comparison graph. For example, let σ be the $(\vec{\top};(5,5))$-computation of $f(\&(Y,y)) = f^S(\&Y) \boxtimes f^T(\&y)$ defined by user input 10 then

$$o(\sigma\uparrow_S) = o(\sigma\uparrow_T) = \bot \xrightarrow{\bot} \bot \xrightarrow{read} (10) \xrightarrow{\bot} (300) \xrightarrow{write} \bot$$

```
Y := Y + 12 + 13;      read(X);                 ε;                    write(Y * X);
        ε              read(x)                  y := y + 25           write(y * x)
[0,0] ─────────── [1,0] ─────────── [2,1] ─────────── [2,2] ─────────── [3,3]
```

Fig. 1. A comparison transition graph for $f(\&(Y,y))$. We use capital variables to denote the variables of the source and their lower case counterparts for the target.

3.2 Witness Verification Conditions

Let φ_n be an assertion associated with a node n. An assertion network $\Phi_C = \{\varphi_n : n \in locations\ of\ C\}$ for a program C is said to be **invariant** if for every state $\langle n; \vec{d} \rangle$ occurring in a computation, $d \models \varphi_n$. That is, on every visit of a computation of node n, the data state satisfies the corresponding assertion φ_n.

Suppose a comparison program $\mathcal{C} = \mathcal{S} \boxtimes \mathcal{T}$ and an invariant network have been constructed. The rules presented below can be used to generate Witness Verification Conditions for $\mathcal{C}$. Whenever the verification conditions are valid, all the transition graphs that constitute $\mathcal{C}$ are witnesses of correct translation, so we can apply Theorem 1 to safely conclude that the translation is correct; otherwise, we report that the translation is erroneous.

- For a write edge (n, m) labeled by ($write(\vec{u}^S); write(\vec{u}^T)$):
  $$\varphi_n \rightarrow (\vec{u}^S = \vec{u}^T).$$
- For a call edge $e = (n, m)$ labeled by ($g^S(E^S, \vec{u}^S); g^T(E^T, \vec{u}^T)$), we check that the call arguments are equal:
  $$\varphi_n \rightarrow (E^S = E^T) \wedge (\vec{u}^S = \vec{u}^T)$$
- If n is the exit node of the comparison transition graph $f^S \boxtimes f^T$, where $f^S(\vec{x}^S; \&\vec{z}^S)$ and $f^T(\vec{x}^T; \&\vec{z}^T)$, we check if the values of the variables passed by reference are equal:
  $$\varphi_n \rightarrow (\vec{z}^S = \vec{z}^T).$$

Claim 1. *Let $main^S$ and $main^T$ be the main procedures of $\mathcal{S}$ and $\mathcal{T}$ respectively. A comparison graph $main = main^S \boxtimes main^T$ is a witness of correct translation and, consequently, $\mathcal{S}$ is a correct translation of $\mathcal{T}$ if all the* Witness Verification Conditions *associated with $\mathcal{C}$ are valid.*

Note that since we are checking that the procedure input parameters are equivalent, the invariant generation algorithm can be intraprocedural. Essentially, one can apply an assume-guarantee reasoning, where f is checked to be a witness, assuming that all the callees of a procedure f are witnesses themselves.

The presented conditions do not constitute an inductive proof of translation correctness: it is assumed that the assertions in $\Phi_\mathcal{C}$ are indeed invariants of $\mathcal{C}$. The extra requirement that has to be satisfied in case such a proof is desirable is that the invariant assertion network should be *inductive* [10,7]. The availability of such a proof increases the level of confidence and allows third-party verification. In addition, it is required if one is to employ invariant generation techniques that may introduce *false positives*, such as probabilistic algorithms [11]. Automatic theorem provers such as YICES[12], CVC3[13], can be utilized to independently check the validity of the proof.

The rest of this paper describes a method for comparison system construction. However, generation of program invariants and checking their correctness are essential ingredients for solving a translation validation problem. Here, one of the main advantages of our approach comes into play. Since we have reduced the translation validation problem to analysis of a single system, any existing technique out of a vast body of work on invariant generation can be used. From our experiments, we found that, among others, global value numbering [14] and assertion checking – a static program verification technique based on computation of weakest-precondition [15], are quite effective in this setting. Refer to our technical report [7] for a detailed discussion.

4 Comparison Graph Construction

We have developed a construction algorithm for *consonant* input programs (i.e., structurally similar programs). This restriction allows for effective application of our methodology to verification of optimizing compilers in absence of compiler annotations. The comparison system $\mathcal{C} = \mathcal{S} \boxtimes \mathcal{T}$ is just a collection of all graphs $f = f^S \boxtimes f^T$, where f^S and f^T are the corresponding procedures from $\mathcal{S}$ and $\mathcal{T}$. Thus, it suffices to present a construction algorithm for a procedure f.

4.1 Consonant Transition Graphs

We are going to use a transition graph $f^S = (\vec{y}^S, \mathcal{N}^S, \mathcal{E}^S)$ to define several notions, which apply to both f^S and f^T. Each node of f^S belongs to one of the following categories: read, write, call, branch, unconditional assignment, or exit; denoted rd, wt, cl, br, ua, and tl respectively. Intuitively, the type of a node n depends on the type of the edges outgoing from n. Specifically, we say that a node $n \in \mathcal{N}^S$ is a read node, written $\tau(n^S) = rd$, if $\exists\, (n^S, m^S) \in \mathcal{E}^S$ and (n^S, m^S) is labeled by a read instruction. Similarly, we define write and call nodes; the type of the exit node is tl. The remaining nodes are categorized as either unconditional assignment or branch nodes depending on whether there is more than one assignment edge outgoing from n. The node types are well defined due to the fact that the graphs are deterministic and read, write, and call edges are implicitly conditioned on *true*. Given a transition graph f^S, we define a set of *cut points*, denoted $\mathcal{P}^S$, to be a subset of graph nodes such that $\mathcal{P}^S = \{\, n^S\, :\, n^S \in \mathcal{N}^S \wedge \tau(n^S) \neq ua\, \}$. Adding all branch nodes, not only loop heads, to the cut point set allows us to have different granularity, depending on the choice of the transition graph nodes (see Section 2.1). Finer granularity improves efficiency; but it is not always applicable: the input programs have to be consonant modulo the chosen cut point set. Every computation σ^S defines a corresponding sequence of cut points, which can be obtained from σ^S by first selecting the nodes of each subsequent state and then removing nodes that are not in $\mathcal{P}^S$ from that sequence.

Definition 4. *We say that graphs f^S and f^T are* consonant *if there exists a partial map $\kappa : \mathcal{P}^S \mapsto \mathcal{P}^T$ such that $\forall\, \sigma^S, \sigma^T : \sigma^S \in Cmp(f^S)$, $\sigma^T \in Cmp(f^T)$ the following holds: if σ^S and σ^T are defined by the same input sequence, and $n_0^S, n_1^S, ...$ and $n_0^T, n_1^T, ...$ are the cut point sequences defined by σ^S and σ^T, then $(\kappa(n_i^S) = n_i^T) \wedge (\tau(n_i^S) = \tau(n_i^T))$. Such map is called a* control abstraction.

Our comparison graph construction is going to discover the control abstraction by composing the corresponding nodes. Surprisingly many compiler optimizations preserve consonance of programs. For example, code motion, constant folding, reassociation, common subexpression elimination, dead code elimination, instruction scheduling, branch optimizations all fall into this category. On the other hand, loop reordering transformations such as tiling and interchange are not covered by the method presented below.

4.2 Algorithm Compose

Fig. 2 presents pseudocode for the compose algorithm that iteratively constructs a comparison graph $f = f^S \boxtimes f^T$ for consonant input transition graphs f^S and f^T. We start the construction with a node $n_0 = \langle n_0^S, n_0^T \rangle$, where n_0^S and n_0^T are the entry nodes of f^S and f^T, respectively. The new node n_0 is added to the WorkList, which is our discovery frontier: if a node n is placed into WorkList, it means that, potentially, more edges outgoing from n may be discovered. At each iteration, we remove a node n from the WorkList and apply matchEdges function to construct a list of newly discovered outgoing edges. The end nodes of the edges, denoted n_e, are placed into WorkList. Even though we always discover a new edge, n_e could have been added to f at some previous iteration and may also have successors in f. In that case, all its eventual successors must also be added to WorkList. Intuitively, if a new path leading to a node is added, that node has to be processed again since more outgoing edges could be discovered. The function matchEdges may fail, returning NULL. This happens when we cannot construct a comparison system satisfying the requirements from Section 3.1.

```
//Initialization:
n_0:=CompNode(n_0^S, n_0^T); C.Nodes:={n_0}; C.Edges:={}; WorkList := {n_0};
//Iteration:
while( ! WorkList.isEmpty()) {
    n := WorkList.removeElement();
    MatchList := matchEdges(n,S,T);
    if(MatchList == NULL) ABORT;

    while(! MatchList.isEmpty()){
        e_new := MatchList.removeElement();
        n_e = NewCEdge.toNode();
        C.Nodes.add(n_e);    //unlike the edge, n_e may not be new*
        C.Edges.insert(e_new);
        WorkList.add(n_e);
        WorkList.add(getDescendants(n_e));
    }
}
```

Fig. 2. Algorithm compose that constructs the comparison transition graph $f = f^S \boxtimes f^T$. * Procedure *add* does not add duplicate items to a collection.

Matching the source and target edges (matchEdges): Below is a set of rules used to add new edges to the comparison graph:

- **Matching edges of the same type:** Given a node $\langle n^S, n^T \rangle$, we match the outgoing edges if and only if $\tau(n^S) = \tau(n^T)$.
- **Adding ϵ–transitions:** If $n^S \notin \mathcal{P}^S$ (implying $\tau(n^S) = ua$), we match the source assignment edge with an ϵ–transition on the target. The case of $n^T \notin \mathcal{P}^T$ is handled analogously.

- **Raising error:** If none of the rules are applicable to a node $\langle n^S, n^T \rangle$, matchEdges returns NULL, and the construction of $\mathcal{C}$ is aborted.

We always match read, write, and function call edges if both systems can take such a step. Guarded assignment edges can also be composed with each other; but we require that either both systems are currently at a branch node (or a loop head depending on the desired granularity) or neither. Since the input systems are consonant, this condition allows to align the corresponding source and target cut points. The case when only one of systems has reached a cut point is covered via ϵ–transitions, so that it can wait for the other system to catch up. Note that since ϵ is only composed with unconditional assignments, it is guaranteed that the comparison system does not contain an ϵ–cycle, so the wait always is finite. Finally, we fail when both systems are at cut point nodes n^S, n^T but $\tau(n^S) \neq \tau(n^T)$. For example, one system is ready to read while the other is about to execute a procedure call.

Branch Alignment: Consider the case when $\tau(n^S) = \tau(n^T) = br$. By the first rule of matchEdges, the outgoing edges should be matched. However, there is an obvious efficiency problem with simply taking all possibilities (i.e., cartesian product) when we consider two nodes with multiple outgoing assignment edges. Such straightforward approach may lead to a number of edges in f being quadratic in the number of edges in the input graphs. More importantly, if we mismatch the branches, unreachable nodes could be introduced into the graph, which may lead to further misalignment down the road. In particular, read, write, and function call edges may get out of sync. Consider the example in the figure below. Suppose $C = c$, $X = x$, and $Y = y$. Then f^T is a correct translation of f^S. However, if we compose edges $(0, 1)$ and $(4, 6)$ just relying on the fact that they are both conditional assignments ($\tau(0) = \tau(4) = br$), the algorithm presented so far will raise an error when examining the newly added unreachable node $\langle 1, 6 \rangle$. Thus, there is a need for comprehensive branch matching. One such method is presented below; in addition to resolving the misalignment issue, it usually constructs a comparison graph linear in the size of the input graphs.

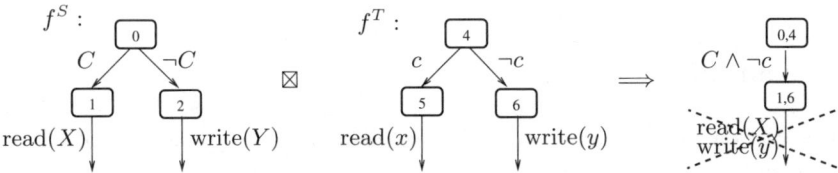

Assume that we have an algorithm $InvGen(f_k)$ that, given a partially constructed graph f_k, obtained after the kth iteration of compose, outputs a *set of invariants* $\{\varphi_n^k : n \in \text{locations of } f_k\}$. We will use these invariants to facilitate the edge matching at iteration $k + 1$ so that the composed edges that would introduce infeasible paths are ruled out. Let $\mathcal{E}_n^S$ represent the set of source edges outgoing from n^S s.t. each edge $e^S \in \mathcal{E}_n^S$ is labeled by $c^S \rightarrow [\vec{u^S} := E^S(\vec{y})]$. Similarly, we define $\mathcal{E}_n^T$.

A pair $(e^S, e^T) \in \mathcal{E}_n^S \times \mathcal{E}_n^T$ is matched if and only if
- it does not yet belong to the comparison graph and
- $(\varphi_n^k \wedge c^S \wedge c^T)$ is satisfiable.

We only want to add an edge if there exists an execution through f_k in which e^S and e^T are enabled simultaneously. An important question to ask is how the decision made using a partially constructed graph f_k relates to the fully constructed graph f. Let φ_n^{fix} be the invariant which can be obtained by running *InvGen* on the fully constructed comparison graph f. Invariant φ_n^k is an underapproximation of φ_n^{fix}, meaning, for some assertion Φ_n^k, $\varphi_n^k = (\varphi_n^{fix} \wedge \Phi_n^k)$.

Lemma 1. *No spurious predictions are possible: if the match (e^S, e^T) is made with φ_n^k, it also complies with φ_n^{fix}.* As a practical consequence, algorithm compose never has to remove any of the previously added edges; thus, it never backtracks. The converse does not hold: we may discover more matches with invariant φ_n^l, where $l : l > k$ is a later iteration of algorithm compose. For this reason, the algorithm adds n_e and its decedents to the WorkList (see Fig. 2).

Theorem 2. *The following are properties of algorithm* compose:

- *Termination:* algorithm compose terminates.
- *Soundness:* if algorithm compose succeeds, the resulting graph $f = f^S \boxtimes f^T$ satisfies all of the requirements presented in Section 3.1.
- *Completeness:* if f^T and f^S are consonant, compose succeeds in construction of a comparison graph $f = f^S \boxtimes f^T$ given a strong enough *InvGen*.

Note that the completeness of the algorithm is conditional on strength of *InvGen* algorithm used for branch matching. As we show in [7], even for consonant graphs the invariant may need to be strong enough to express reachability, which is undecidable for infinite state systems. All hope is not lost: it is usually feasible to construct the invariants sufficient for our particular application – verification of compiler transformations, intuitively, due to the fact that compilers base their decisions on automated reasoning. The proof of the theorem and the discussion on the *InvGen* used in practice can be found in [7].

5 Example

In this section, we present an example that demonstrates application of compose algorithm to comparison system construction along with the generated invariants and Witness Verification Conditions. Consider Fig. 3. The first two graphs depict the *source* transition graph and the *target* obtained from the source after constant copy propagation, if simplification, loop invariant code motion, reassociation, and instruction scheduling. Cut point nodes are denoted by double circles. We use capital letters to denote the source variables and their lowercase counterparts for the target. MEM and mem denote the memory heaps. The procedure first reads in two elements – one is stored in register K and the other one in memory at address A. Then, ten elements of the array, stored starting at address P, are being assigned to. Finally, the first element of the array is printed out. We assume that the addresses of the array elements do not overlap with A.

After the third iteration of the algorithm `compose` (from Section 4), we obtain graph $\mathcal{C}_3$ (Comparison 3), which is constructed as following. On the first iteration, an assignment of the source is matched up with an ϵ-transition on the target. On the second iteration, node $\langle 1, 0 \rangle$ is considered, and since both procedures are ready to execute reads, the composed read edge is added. Next, we examine node $\langle 2, 1 \rangle$. Since only the source procedure has reached a cut point, it waits for the target system to catch up by taking an ϵ-transition. On the fourth iteration, node $\langle 2, 2 \rangle$ is considered for the first time and the algorithm $InvGen(\mathcal{C}_3)$ returns $\varphi^3_{\langle 2,2 \rangle} : (I = i = 1)$, which is used to align the branches of the loop and obtain $\mathcal{C}^4$ (Comparison 4). However, $\varphi^3_{\langle 2,2 \rangle} \wedge (I \geq 10) \wedge (i \geq 10)$ is unsatisfiable. Thus, the matching of the loop exit edges is ruled out by the invariant. At the end of the fourth iteration, node $\langle 2, 2 \rangle$ is added to the `WorkList` again. Notice that $\varphi^3_{\langle 2,2 \rangle}$ does not hold in system $\mathcal{C}^4$ since I and i are updated in the loop, so $InvGen(\mathcal{C}^4)$ widens the invariant, resulting in $\varphi^4_{\langle 2,2 \rangle} : (I = i)$, which allows to match up the loop exit edges ($\varphi^4_{\langle 2,2 \rangle} \wedge (I \geq 10) \wedge (i \geq 10)$ is satisfiable). Finally, we match the write edges and obtain $\mathcal{C} = \mathcal{C}_6$ (Comparison 6).

After the comparison system is constructed, we generate the `Witness Verification Condition` to check that both systems write out the same values (following the rules from Section 3.2):

$$\varphi^{fix}_{\langle 3,3 \rangle} \to (MEM[P] = mem[p]).$$

An *inductive* invariant network for the comparison program is presented below. The validity of the verification condition directly follows from $\varphi^{fix}_{\langle 3,3 \rangle}$.

$$\varphi^{fix}_{\langle 0,0 \rangle} : (MEM = mem) \wedge (A = a) \wedge (P = p) \wedge (A \notin [P..P+9])$$
$$\varphi^{fix}_{\langle 1,0 \rangle} : (I = 1) \wedge (C = 5) \wedge \varphi^{fix}_{\langle 0,0 \rangle}$$
$$\varphi^{fix}_{\langle 2,1 \rangle} : (K = k) \wedge \varphi^{fix}_{\langle 1,0 \rangle}$$
$$\varphi^{fix}_{\langle 2,2 \rangle} : (I = i) \wedge (u = (MEM[A] + C) * K) \wedge (C = 5) \wedge \varphi^{fix}_{\langle 0,0 \rangle}$$
$$\varphi^{fix}_{\langle 3,3 \rangle} : (MEM = mem) \wedge (P = p)$$

$\varphi^{fix}_{\langle 0,0 \rangle}$ asserts our assumptions that at the entry to the programs, the memory heaps of the source and target are the same; the corresponding address variables of the two systems are equal; and the address variable $A(a)$ does not overlap with the addresses of the elements of the source(target) array. The most interesting invariant is $\varphi^{fix}_{\langle 2,2 \rangle}$, which asserts that, after each loop iteration, the source and target heaps stay equivalent. Its validity is ensured by the following facts: the addresses at which memory is updated are equal (due to $I = i \wedge P = p$); the expressions stored at those addresses are equal (since $u = (MEM[A] + C) * K \wedge I = i$); $MEM[A]$ is not altered by the loop (because $A \notin [P..P+10]$).

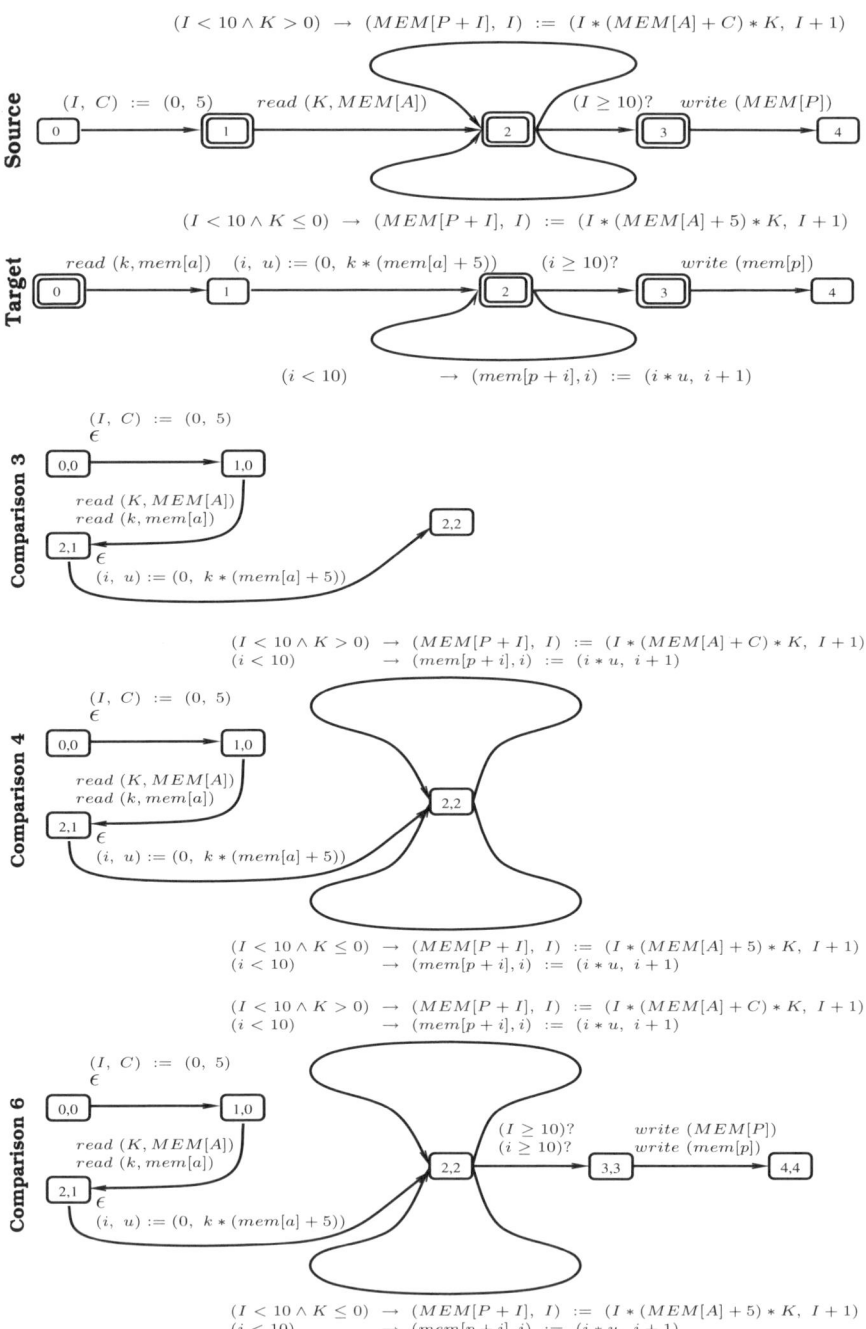

Fig. 3. Source and Target are the input transition graphs: the programs before and after the optimization, respectively. Next, we depict the comparison graphs obtained at the three stages of the comparison graph construction.

6 CoVaC Tool

We have developed a prototype tool CoVaC based on the presented methodology and used it to verify the optimizations performed by LLVM compiler [6]. The tool has been developed in C++ and uses LLVM data structures for program representation and parsing. Its current line count is at approximately 7,000.

One of the main focuses of the tool is balancing precision and efficiency. To achieve this balance, CoVaC generally utilizes a two-phase strategy: first, it applies fast lightweight analyses, and then, resorts to deep and precise analyses. A good illustration of the two-phase approach is expression equivalence checking, which is one of the central subgoals of our framework. We employ a fast but imprecise value numbering algorithm during the first phase. When value numbering is inconclusive, we resort to assertion checking – a static program verification technique based on computation of weakest-precondition [15], which uses CVC3 theorem prover [13] as the backend.

We have tested the tool performance on a set of C programs compiled from the CoVaC feature tests, selected programs from the LLVM test suite, and third party implementation of several algorithms (such as in-place heapsort, binary search, print first N primes, etc.), with the total line count of approximately 1K, which corresponds to 2K lines of LLVM bytecode. On average, when validating highly optimized code: 0.53 optimizations per line, CoVaC spends 1 second per every 61 lines, assuming no compiler collaboration. The most time is spent on calls to assertion checker, which is dispatched once per every 8 lines. The prototype's performance provides a strong evidence that a practical validator can be constructed, especially taking into account that, unlike compiler, the tool is used few times per program's lifetime. The most notable exception is application of the framework to compiler testing. However, in such a case, CoVaC can be called after every optimization path rather than after a complete run, and verification of lightly optimized code is much faster since value numbering is sufficient for resolving most of the equivalence checks.

7 Related Work and Conclusion

Our approach can be seen as application of bisimulation equivalence [16] to translation validation and checking equivalence of infinite state programs. Good examples of existing general translation validation frameworks are [17,9,18], [4], and [3]; all present program analysis and proof rules specialized to program equivalence checking. [17,9,18] and [4] rely on compiler debug information to guide their effort. [3] attempts to eliminate the dependency; however, the compiler annotations are the essential part of its heuristics for branch matching. Even though CoVaC can benefit from compiler annotations in the same way as the existing approaches, it does not require any. [18] focuses on handling interprocedural optimizations; and tools presented in [9] and [4] provide additional rules for loop reordering optimizations (loop interchange, fusion, etc.), which do not preserve consonance. Similar extensions can be incorporated into our general framework; however, their application to non-cooperative compilers is a topic of future research. [19] describes a complete method (no false alarms) for translation validation specialized to register allocation and spilling. For a comprehensive survey on compiler verification in general, refer to [20].

We presented a framework for checking program equivalence based on construction of a cross-product system, which reduces the problem to verification of a single program and allows for utilization of the existing off-the-shelf program analyses and tools. In particular, we have shown how the CoVaC framework can be applied to verification of non-cooperative compilers and used it on practice to validate a wide range of optimizations performed by an aggressive modern compiler, LLVM[6]. Many interesting questions remain. For example, we plan to extend our method to support interprocedural optimizations and explore the ways in which the validator failures can be analyzed and used to pinpoint compilation errors. We are also interested in investigating application of the CoVaC framework to development of a self-certifying compiler and validation of language-based security properties, specifically, checking conformance with information flow policies [5].

References

1. Pnueli, A., Siegel, M., Singerman, E.: Translation Validation. In: Steffen, B. (ed.) ETAPS 1998 and TACAS 1998. LNCS, vol. 1384, pp. 151–166. Springer, Heidelberg (1998)
2. Zuck, L., Pnueli, A., Fang, Y., Goldberg, B.: VOC: A methodology for the translation validation of optimizing compilers. Journal of Universal Computer Science 9(3), 223–247 (2003)
3. Necula, G.C.: Translation validation for an optimizing compiler. In: Programming Language Design and Implementation, pp. 83–95. ACM Press, New York (2000)
4. Rival, X.: Symbolic transfer function-based approaches to certified compilation. In: POPL, pp. 1–13. ACM Press, New York (2004)
5. Barthe, G., D'Argenio, P., Rezk, T.: Secure information flow by self-composition. In: Computer Security Foundations Workshop, p. 100. IEEE Computer Society Press, Los Alamitos (2004)
6. Barthe, G., D'Argenio, P., Rezk, T.: The LLVM Compiler Infrastructure Project, http://llvm.org/, http://llvm.org/, http://llvm.org
7. Zaks, A., Pnueli, A.: CoVaC: Compiler validation by program analysis of the cross-product. Technical report, NYU (2007), http://cs.nyu.edu/acsys/publications.html
8. Pnueli, A.: Verification of procedural programs. In: We Will Show Them! Essays in Honour of Dov Gabbay, vol. 2, pp. 543–590. College Publications (2005)
9. Zuck, L., Pnueli, A., Goldberg, B., Barrett, C., Fang, Y., Hu, Y.: Translation and run-time validation of loop tranformations. Formal Methods in System Design 27(3), 335–360 (2005)
10. Floyd, R.W.: Assigning meanings to programs. In: Symposia in Applied Mathematics, vol. 19, pp. 19–32 (1967)
11. Gulwani, S., Necula, G.: Global value numbering using random interpretation. In: POPL, pp. 342–352. ACM Press, New York (2004)
12. The YICES SMT Solver, http://yices.csl.sri.com

13. CVC3: An Automatic Theorem Prover for Satisfiability Modulo Theories (SMT), http://www.cs.nyu.edu/acsys/cvc3/
14. Simpson, L.T.: Value-Driven Redundancy Elimination. PhD thesis, Rice University (1996)
15. Dijkstra, E.W.: A Discipline of Programming. Prentice-Hall, Englewood Cliffs (1976)
16. Park, D.: Concurrency and automata on infinite sequences. In: 5th GI-Conference on Theoretical Computer Science, pp. 167–183. Springer, Heidelberg (1981)
17. Fang, Y.: Translation Validation of Optimizing Compilers. PhD thesis, New York University (2005)
18. Pnueli, A., Zaks, A.: Validation of interprocedural optimizations. In: 7th International Workshop on Compiler Optimization Meets Compiler Verificaiton (2008)
19. Huang, Y., Childer, B.R., Soffa, M.L.: Catching and identifying bugs in register allocation. In: Static Analysis Symposium, pp. 281–300. Springer, Heidelberg (2006)
20. Dave, M.A.: Compiler verification: a bibliography. SIGSOFT Softw. Eng. Notes 28(6), 2–2 (2003)

Lazy Behavioral Subtyping*

Johan Dovland, Einar Broch Johnsen, Olaf Owe, and Martin Steffen

Dept. of Informatics, University of Oslo, Norway
{johand,einarj,olaf,msteffen}@ifi.uio.no

Abstract. Late binding allows flexible code reuse but complicates formal reasoning significantly, as a method call's receiver class is not statically known. This is especially true when programs are incrementally developed by extending class hierarchies. This paper develops a novel method to reason about late bound method calls. In contrast to traditional behavioral subtyping, reverification is avoided without restricting method overriding to fully behavior-preserving redefinition. The approach ensures that when analyzing the methods of a class, it suffices to consider that class and its superclasses. Thus, the full class hierarchy is not needed, and *incremental* reasoning is supported. We formalize this approach as a calculus which lazily imposes context-dependent subtyping constraints on method definitions. The calculus ensures that all method specifications required by late bound calls remain satisfied when new classes extend a class hierarchy. The calculus does not depend on a specific program logic, but the examples in the paper use a Hoare-style proof system. We show soundness of the analysis method.

1 Introduction

Late binding of method calls is a central feature in object-oriented languages and contributes to flexible code reuse. A class may extend its superclasses with new methods, possibly overriding the existing ones. This flexibility comes at a price: It significantly complicates reasoning about method calls as the binding of a method call to code cannot be statically determined; i.e., the binding at run-time depends on the actual class of the called object. In addition, object-oriented programs are often designed under an *open world assumption*: Class hierarchies are extended over time as subclasses are gradually developed and added. In general, a class hierarchy may be extended with new subclasses in the future, which will lead to new potential bindings for overridden methods.

To control this flexibility, existing reasoning and verification strategies impose restrictions on inheritance and redefinition. One strategy is to ignore openness and assume a "closed world"; i.e., the proof rules assume that the complete inheritance tree is available at reasoning time (e.g., [24]). This severely restricts the applicability of the proof strategy; for example, libraries are designed to be extended. Moreover, the closed world assumption contradicts inheritance as an object-oriented design principle, which is intended to support incremental development and analysis. If the reasoning relies on the world being closed, extending the class hierarchy requires a costly reverification.

---
* This research is partially funded by the EU project IST-33826 CREDO: Modeling and analysis of evolutionary structures for distributed services (http://credo.cwi.nl).

An alternative strategy is to reflect in the verification system that the world is open, but to constrain how methods may be redefined. The general idea is that to avoid reverification, any redefinition of a method through overriding must *preserve* certain properties of the method being redefined. An important part of the properties to be preserved is the method's contract; i.e., the pre- and postconditions for its body. The contract can be seen as a description of the promised behavior of all implementations of the method as part of its interface description, the method's *commitment*. Best known as *behavioral subtyping* (e.g, [20, 2, 19, 25]), this strategy achieves incremental reasoning by limiting the possibilities for code reuse. Once a method has committed to a contract, this commitment may not change in later redefinitions. That is overly restrictive and often violated in practice [26]; e.g., it is not respected by the standard Java library definitions.

This paper relaxes the property preservation restriction of behavioral subtyping, while embracing the open world assumption of incremental program development. The basic idea is as follows: given a method m declared with p and q as the method's pre- and postcondition, there is no need to restrict the behavior of methods overriding m and require that these adhere to that specification. Instead it suffices to preserve the "part" of p and q actually *used to verify* the program at the current stage. Specifically, if m is used in the program in the form of a method call $\{r\}$ $e.m(\ldots)$ $\{s\}$, the pre- and postconditions r and s at that call-site constitute m's *required* behavior and it is those weaker conditions that need to be preserved to avoid reverification. We call the corresponding analysis strategy *lazy behavioral subtyping*. This strategy may serve as a blueprint for integrating a flexible system for program verification of late bound method calls into object-oriented program development and analysis tools environments [5, 6, 7].

The paper formalizes this analysis strategy using an object-oriented kernel language, based on Featherweight Java [15], and using Hoare-style proof outlines. Formalized as a syntax-driven inference system, class analysis is done in the context of a *proof environment* constructed during the analysis. The environment keeps track of the context-dependent requirements on method definitions, derived from late bound calls. The strategy is incremental; for the analysis of a class C, only knowledge of C and its superclasses is needed. We show the soundness of the proposed method.

Paper overview. Sect. 2 introduces the problem of reasoning about late binding, Sect. 3 presents the approach taken in this paper, and Sect. 4 gives the details of the inference system. Related work is discussed in Sect. 5 and Sect. 6 concludes the paper.

2 Late Bound Method Calls

2.1 Syntax for an Object-Oriented Kernel Language

To succinctly explain late binding and our analysis strategy, we use an object-oriented kernel language (Fig. 1) with a standard operational semantics (e.g., [15]) . We assume a functional language of side-effect free expressions e. A program P consists of a list $\overline{L}$ of class definitions, and a method body. A class extends a superclass, which may be Object, with fields $\overline{f}$ and methods $\overline{M}$. To simplify, we let fields have distinct names, methods with the same name have the same signature (i.e., no method overloading), programs be well-typed, and ignore the types of fields and methods. For classes B and

$$P ::= \overline{L}\{t\} \qquad L ::= \text{class } C \text{ extends } C \{\overline{f}\,\overline{M}\}$$
$$M ::= m(\overline{x})\{t\} \qquad t ::= v := \text{new } C() \mid v := e.m(\overline{e}) \mid v := e$$
$$v ::= f \mid \text{return} \qquad \mid \text{skip} \mid \text{if } b \text{ then } t \text{ else } t \text{ fi} \mid t;t$$

Fig. 1. The language syntax, where C and m are class and method names (of types Cid and Mid, respectively). Expressions e include declared fields f, the reserved variables this and return, and Boolean expressions b. Vector notation denotes lists; e.g., a list of expressions is written $\overline{e}$.

```
class C₁ {
   m():(p₁,q₁){⟨t₁⟩}
   n₁():(_,_){...;{r₁} this.m() {s₁};...}
   n₂():(_,_){...;{r₂} this.m() {s₂};...}
}
```

```
class C₂ extends C₁ {           class C₃ extends C₁ {
   m():(p₂,q₂){⟨t₂⟩}                m():(p₃,q₃){⟨t₃⟩}
}                                }
```

Fig. 2. A class hierarchy with proof outlines for overridden methods

$C, B \leq C$ denotes the reflexive and transitive subclass relation derived from class inheritance. If $B \leq C$, we say that B is *below* C and C is *above* B.

A method M takes parameters $\overline{x}$ and contains a statement t, which may be composed. The sequential composition of statements t_1 and t_2 is written $t_1;t_2$. The statement $v := \text{new } C()$ creates a new object of class C with fields instantiated to default values, and assigns the new reference to v. A possible constructor method in the class must be called explicitly. In a method invocation $e.m(\overline{e})$, the object e receives a call to the method m with actual parameters $\overline{e}$. The statement $v := e.m(\overline{e})$ assigns the value of the method activation's return variable to v. (For convenience, we often write $e.m(\overline{e})$ or simply $e.m$ instead of $v := e.m(\overline{e})$.) There are standard statements for skip, conditionals if b then t else t fi, and assignments $v := e$. As usual, this is read only.

Late binding. Or dynamic dispatch is a central concept of object-orientation, already present in Simula [8]. A method call is late bound, or *virtual*, if the method body to be executed is selected at run-time, depending on the callee's actual class. Virtual calls are bound to the first implementation found above the actual class. The mechanism can be illustrated by an object of class C_2 which executes a method n_1 defined in its superclass C_1 and this method issues a call to a method m defined in both classes (see Fig. 2). With late binding, the code selected for execution is associated to the first matching signature for m above C_2; i.e., m of C_2 is selected and not the one in C_1. If n_1, however, were executed in an instance of C_1, the virtual invocation of m would be bound to the definition in C_1. We say that a definition of m is *reachable* from C if there is a class $D \leq C$ such that a call to m will bind to that definition for instances of D. For instance, if m is overridden by D, that declaration is reached from C for instances of D. Thus, for a virtual call there might be several reachable definitions.

$$\text{(Assign)} \ \{q[e/v]\} \ v := e \ \{q\} \qquad \text{(Cond)} \ \frac{\{p \land b\} \ t_1 \ \{q\} \quad \{p \land \neg b\} \ t_2 \ \{q\}}{\{p\} \ \texttt{if } b \texttt{ then } t_1 \texttt{ else } t_2 \texttt{ fi} \ \{q\}}$$

$$\text{(New)} \ \{q[\texttt{new}_C/v]\} \ v := \texttt{new } C() \ \{q\}$$

$$\text{(Skip)} \ \{q\} \ \texttt{skip} \ \{q\}$$

$$\text{(Seq)} \ \frac{\{p\} \ t_1 \ \{r\} \quad \{r\} \ t_2 \ \{q\}}{\{p\} \ t_1; t_2 \ \{q\}} \qquad \text{(Adapt)} \ \frac{p \Rightarrow p_1 \quad \{p_1\} \ t \ \{q_1\} \quad q_1 \Rightarrow q}{\{p\} \ t \ \{q\}}$$

$$\text{(Call)} \ \frac{\forall i \in S. \ \{p_i[\bar{e}/\bar{x}]\} \ body^i_{m(\bar{x})} \ \{q_i\}}{\{\bigwedge_{i \in S}(p_i[\bar{e}/\bar{x}])\} \ v := e.m(\bar{e}) \ \{\bigvee_{i \in S}(q_i[v/\texttt{return}])\}} \quad S = \texttt{implements}(\texttt{classOf}(e), m)$$

Fig. 3. Closed world proof rules. Let `classOf(e)` denote the class of expression e and $p[e/v]$ the substitution of all occurrences of v in p by e [12], extended for object creation following [24]. The function `implements(C,m)` returns all classes where a call to m from class C may be bound.

2.2 Reasoning about Virtual Calls

Apart from the treatment of late bound method calls, our reasoning system for the other statements follows standard proof rules [3, 4] for partial correctness, adapted to the object-oriented setting; in particular, de Boer's technique using sequences in the assertion language addresses the issue of object creation [9]. We present the proof system using Hoare triples $\{p\} \ t \ \{q\}$, where p is the precondition and q is the postcondition to the statement t [12]. The meaning of a triple $\{p\} \ t \ \{q\}$ is standard: if t is executed in a state where p holds and the execution terminates, then q holds after t. The derivation of triples can be done in any suitable program logic. Let PL be such a program logic and let $\vdash_{\text{PL}} \{p\} \ t \ \{q\}$ denote that $\{p\} \ t \ \{q\}$ is derivable in PL. A *proof outline* [23] for a method definition $m(\bar{x})\{t\}$ is an annotated method $m(\bar{x}):(p,q)\{\langle t \rangle\}$ where $\langle t \rangle$ is the method body t annotated with pre- and postconditions to method calls. The derivability $\vdash_{\text{PL}} m(\bar{x}):(p,q)\{\langle t \rangle\}$ of a proof outline is given by $\vdash_{\text{PL}} \{p\} \ \langle t \rangle \ \{q\}$. For $m(\bar{x}):(p,q)\{\langle t \rangle\}$, the pair (p,q) is called the *commitment* of method m. For simplicity, we assume that `return` does not occur in p and that $\bar{x}$ do not occur in q. To prove an assertion, the annotated method body $\langle t \rangle$ may impose *requirements* on methods called within t, expressed by pre- and postconditions to those calls. For a call $\{r\} \ n() \ \{s\}$ in $\langle t \rangle$, (r,s) is the required assertion for n. To ensure that the requirement is valid, every reachable definition of n must be analyzed.

If the proof system assumes a closed world, all classes must be defined before the analysis can begin, as the requirement to a method call is derived from the commitments of all reachable implementations of that method. To simplify the presentation in this paper, we omit further details of the assertion language and the proof system (e.g., ignoring the representation of the program semantics — for details see [24]). The corresponding proof system is given in Fig. 3; the proof rule (Call) captures late binding under a closed world assumption. The following example illustrates the proof system.

Example 1. Consider the class hierarchy of Fig. 2, where the methods are decorated with proof outlines. The specifications of methods n_1 and n_2 play no role in the discussion and are given a wildcard notation $(\_,\_)$. Assume $\vdash_{\text{PL}} m():(p_1,q_1)\{\langle t_1 \rangle\}$, $\vdash_{\text{PL}} m():(p_2,q_2)\{\langle t_2 \rangle\}$, and $\vdash_{\text{PL}} m():(p_3,q_3)\{\langle t_3 \rangle\}$ for the definitions of m in classes C_1,

C_2, and C_3, respectively. Let us initially consider the class hierarchy consisting of C_1 and C_2 and ignore C_3 for the moment. The proof system of Fig. 3 gives the Hoare triple $\{p_1 \wedge p_2\}$this.$m()\{q_1 \vee q_2\}$ for each call to m, i.e., for the calls in the bodies of methods n_1 and n_2 in class C_1. To apply (ADAPT), we get the proof obligations: $r_1 \Rightarrow p_1 \wedge p_2$ and $q_1 \vee q_2 \Rightarrow s_1$ for n_1, and $r_2 \Rightarrow p_1 \wedge p_2$, and $q_1 \vee q_2 \Rightarrow s_2$ for n_2. *Extending* now the class hierarchy with C_3 breaks the closed world assumption and requires to *reverify* the methods n_1 and n_2. With the new Hoare triple $\{p_1 \wedge p_2 \wedge p_3\}$this.$m()\{q_1 \vee q_2 \vee q_3\}$ at every call site, the proof obligations given above for applying (ADAPT) no longer apply.

3 A Lazy Approach to Virtual Calls

This section presents informally the approach to reason about virtual calls which is based on an open world assumption. It supports incremental reasoning about classes and is well-suited for program development, being less restrictive than behavioral subtyping. A formal presentation is given in Sect. 4.

Reconsider class C_1 of Example 1. The proof outlines for n_1 and n_2 require that $\{r_1\}$this.$m()\{s_1\}$ and $\{r_2\}$this.$m()\{s_2\}$ hold in the bodies of n_1 and n_2, respectively. The assertions (r_1, s_1) and (r_2, s_2) may be seen as *requirements* to reachable definitions of m; for m's definition in C_1, both $\{r_1\}$ t_1 $\{s_1\}$ and $\{r_2\}$ t_1 $\{s_2\}$ must hold. However, the proof obligations for method calls have shifted from the call site to the declaration site, which allows incremental reasoning. During the verification of a class only the class and its superclasses need to be considered, subclasses are ignored. If we later analyze subclass C_2 or C_3, the *same requirements* apply to their definition of m. Thus, no reverification of the bodies of n_1 and n_2 is needed when new subclasses are analyzed.

Although C_1 is analyzed independently of C_2 and C_3, its requirements must be considered during subclass analysis. For this purpose, a *proof environment* is constructed while analyzing C_1 recording that C_1 requires both (r_1, s_1) and (r_2, s_2) from m. Subclasses are analyzed in the context of this proof environment, and may in turn extend the proof environment with new requirements, tracking the scope of each requirement. For two independent subclasses, the requirements made by one subclass should not affect the other. Hence, the order of subclass analysis does not influence the assertions to be verified in each class. To avoid reverification, the proof environment also tracks the commitments established for each method definition. The analysis of a requirement to a method definition immediately succeeds if the requirement follows from the previously established commitments of that method.

3.1 Assertions and Assertion Entailment

We consider an assertion language with expressions e constructed as follows:

$$e ::= f \mid z \mid ops(\bar{e}) \mid \texttt{this} \mid \texttt{return}$$

Here, f is a program field, z a logical variable, and ops an operation on abstract data types, ignoring field access. An *assertion* (of type *Assert*) is a pair of Boolean expressions. Let p' denote an expression p with all occurrences of fields f substituted by f', avoiding name capture. We define entailment for assertions and for sets of assertions:

Definition 1 (Entailment). *Let (p,q) and (r,s) be assertions and let $\mathcal{U}$ and $\mathcal{V}$ denote the assertion sets $\{(p_i, q_i) \mid 1 \leq i \leq n\}$ and $\{(r_i, s_i) \mid 1 \leq i \leq m\}$. Entailment is defined by*

1. $(p,q) \twoheadrightarrow (r,s) \triangleq (\forall \bar{z}_1 \,.\, p \Rightarrow q') \Rightarrow (\forall \bar{z}_2 \,.\, r \Rightarrow s')$,
   where $\bar{z}_1$ and $\bar{z}_2$ are the logical variables in (p,q) and (r,s), respectively.
2. $\mathcal{U} \twoheadrightarrow (r,s) \triangleq (\bigwedge_{1 \leq i \leq n}(\forall \bar{z}_i \,.\, p_i \Rightarrow q'_i)) \Rightarrow (\forall \bar{z} \,.\, r \Rightarrow s')$.
3. $\mathcal{U} \twoheadrightarrow \mathcal{V} \triangleq \bigwedge_{1 \leq i \leq m} \mathcal{U} \twoheadrightarrow (r_i, s_i)$.

Note that the relation $\mathcal{U} \twoheadrightarrow (r,s)$ corresponds to classic Hoare-style reasoning to prove $\{r\}\,t\,\{s\}$ from $\{p_i\}\,t\,\{q_i\}$ for all $1 \leq i \leq n$, by means of the adaptation and conjunction rules [3]. Note that entailment is reflexive and transitive, and $\mathcal{V} \subseteq \mathcal{U}$ implies $\mathcal{U} \twoheadrightarrow \mathcal{V}$.

3.2 Class Analysis with a Proof Environment

We now illustrate the role of the proof environments during class analyses through a series of examples. The environment collects method commitments and requirements in two mappings S and R which, given a class name and method identifier, return a set of assertions. The analysis of a class both uses and changes the proof environment.

Propagation of requirements. Method requirements encountered during the analysis of a proof outline in a class C are verified for the known reachable definitions and imposed on future subclasses. If $m(\bar{x}) : (p,q)\{\langle t \rangle\}$ is shown while analyzing C, we extend $S(C,m)$ with (p,q). For each requirement $\{r\}\,n\,\{s\}$ in the proof outline, (r,s) must hold for definitions of n reached by instances of C. Furthermore, $R(C,n)$ is extended with (r,s) as a restriction on future subclass redefinitions of n.

Example 2. Consider the analysis of class C_1 in Fig. 2. The commitment (p_1, q_1) is included in $S(C_1, m)$ and the requirements (r_1, s_1) and (r_2, s_2) are included in $R(C_1, m)$. Both requirements must be verified for the definition of m in C_1, i.e., the definition of m reachable from C_1. Consequently, for each (r_i, s_i), $S(C_1, m) \twoheadrightarrow (r_i, s_i)$ must hold, which follows from $(p_1, q_1) \twoheadrightarrow (r_i, s_i)$.

In the example, the requirements made by n_1 and n_2 follow from the established commitment of m. Generally, the requirements need not follow from the previously shown commitments. It is then necessary to provide a new proof outline for the method.

Example 3. If (r_i, s_i) does not follow from (p_1, q_1) in Example 2, a new proof outline $m : (r_i, s_i)\{\langle t_1 \rangle\}$ must be analyzed similarly to the proof outlines in C_1. The mapping $S(C_1, m)$ is extended by (r_i, s_i), ensuring the desired relation $S(C_1, m) \twoheadrightarrow (r_i, s_i)$.

The analysis strategy must ensure that once a commitment (p,q) is included in $S(C,m)$, it will always hold when the method is executed in an instance of any (future) subclass of C, without reverifying m. In particular, when m is overridden, the *requirements* made by methods in C to m must hold for the new definition of m.

Example 4. Consider class C_2 in Fig. 2, which redefines m. After analysis of the proof outline $m : (p_2, q_2)\{\langle t_2 \rangle\}$, $S(C_2, m)$ is extended with (p_2, q_2). In addition, the superclass requirements $R(C_1, m)$ must hold for the new definition of m to ensure that the commitments of n_1 and n_2 apply for instances of C_2. Hence, $S(C_2, m) \twoheadrightarrow (r_i, s_i)$ must be shown for each $(r_i, s_i) \in R(C_1, m)$, similar to $S(C_1, m) \twoheadrightarrow (r_i, s_i)$ in Example 2.

When a method m is (re)defined in a class C, all superclass invocations of m from instances of C will bind to the new definition. The new definition must therefore support the requirements from all superclasses. Let $R{\uparrow}(C,m)$ denote the union of $R(B,m)$ for all $C \leq B$. For each method m defined in C, it is necessary to ensure the following property:

$$S(C,m) \twoheadrightarrow R{\uparrow}(C,m) \qquad (1)$$

It follows that m must support the requirements from C itself; i.e., $S(C,m) \twoheadrightarrow R(C,m)$.

Context-dependent properties of inherited methods. Let us now consider methods that are inherited but not redefined, say, m is inherited from a superclass of C. In this case, virtual calls to m from instances of C are bound to the first definition of m above C, but virtual calls *by* m are bound *in the context of* C, as C may redefine methods invoked by m. Furthermore, C may impose new requirements on m not proved during the analysis of the superclass, resulting in new proof outlines for m. In the analysis of the new proof outlines, we know that virtual calls are bound from C. It would be unsound to extend the commitment mapping of the superclass, since the new commitments are only part of the subclass context. Instead, we use $S(C,m)$ and $R(C,m)$ for *local commitment and requirement extensions*. These new commitments and requirements only apply in the context of C and not in the context of its superclasses.

Example 5. Let the following class extend the hierarchy of Fig. 2:

```
class C₄ extends C₁ {
    n():(_,_){...;{r₄} this.m() {s₄};...}
}
```

Class C_4 inherits the superclass implementation of m. The analysis of n's proof outline yields $\{r_4\}\ m\ \{s_4\}$ as requirement, which is included in $R(C_4,m)$ and verified for the inherited implementation of m. The verification succeeds if $S(C_1,m) \twoheadrightarrow (r_4,s_4)$. Otherwise, a new proof outline $m:(r_4,s_4)\{\langle t_1\rangle\}$ is analyzed under the assumption that virtual calls are bound in the context of C_4. When analyzed, (r_4,s_4) becomes a commitment of m and it is included in $S(C_4,m)$. This mapping acts as a local extension of $S(C_1,m)$ and contains commitments of m that hold in the subclass context.

Assume that a definition of m in a class A is reachable from C. When analyzing a requirement $\{r\}\ m\ \{s\}$ in C, we can then rely on $S(A,m)$ and the local extensions of this mapping for all classes between A and C. We assume that programs are type-safe and define a function $S{\uparrow}$ recursively as follows: $S{\uparrow}(C,m) \triangleq S(C,m)$ if m is defined in C and $S{\uparrow}(C,m) \triangleq S(C,m) \cup S{\uparrow}(B,m)$ otherwise, where B is the immediate superclass of C. We can now revise Property 1 to account for *inherited methods*:

$$S{\uparrow}(C,m) \twoheadrightarrow R{\uparrow}(C,m) \qquad (2)$$

Thus, each requirement in $R(B,m)$, for some B above C, must follow from the established commitments of m in context C. Especially, for each $(p,q) \in R(C,m)$, (p,q) must either follow from the superclass commitments or from the local extension $S(C,m)$. If (p,q) follows from the local extension $S(C,m)$, we are in the case when a new proof outline has been analyzed in the context of C. Note that Property 2 reduces to Property 1 if m is defined in C.

Analysis of class hierarchies. A class hierarchy is analyzed in a top-down manner, starting with Object and an empty proof environment. Classes are analyzed after their respective superclasses, and each class is analyzed without knowledge of possible subclasses. Methods are specified in terms of proof outlines. For each method $m(\bar{x})\{t\}$ defined in a class C, we analyze each (p,q) occurring either as a specification of m in some proof outline, or as an inherited requirement in $R{\uparrow}(C,m)$. If $S(C,m) \dashrightarrow (p,q)$, no further analysis of (p,q) is needed. Otherwise a proof outline $m(\bar{x}):(p,q)\{\langle t\rangle\}$ needs to be analyzed, after which $S(C,m)$ is extended with (p,q). During the analysis of a proof outline, annotated (internal) calls $\{r\}\,n\,\{s\}$ yield requirements (r,s) on reachable implementations of n. The $R(C,n)$ mapping is therefore extended with (r,s) to ensure that future redefinitions of n will support the requirement. In addition, (r,s) is analyzed with respect to the implementation of n that is reached for instances of C; i.e., the first implementation of n above C. This verification succeeds immediately if $S{\uparrow}(C,n) \dashrightarrow (r,s)$. Otherwise, a proof outline for n is analyzed in the context of C, which again extends $S(C,n)$ by (r,s). Each call statement in this proof outline is analyzed in this manner. For *external* calls $\{r\}\,x.m()\,\{s\}$, where x refers to an object of class C', we require that (r,s) follows from the requirements $R{\uparrow}(C',m)$ of m in C'.

The mapping S reflects the *definition of methods*; each lookup $S(C,m)$ returns a set of commitments for a particular implementation of m. In contrast, the mapping R reflects the *use of methods* and may impose requirements on several implementations.

Lazy behavioral subtyping. Behavioral subtyping in the traditional sense does *not* follow from the analysis. Behavioral subtyping would mean that whenever a method m is redefined in a class C, its new definition must implement all superclass *commitments* for m; i.e., the method would have to satisfy $S(B,m)$ for all B above C. For example, behavioral subtyping would imply that m in both C_2 and C_3 in Fig. 2 must satisfy (p_1,q_1). Instead, the R mapping identifies the requirements imposed by virtual calls. Only these assertions must be supported by overriding methods to ensure that the execution of superclass' code does not have unexpected results. Thus, only the behavior assumed by the virtual call statements is ensured at the subclass level. In this way, requirements are *inherited by need*, resulting in a lazy form of behavioral subtyping.

Example 6. Consider a class defining two methods which increment counters.

```
class A {
  int x = 0; y = 0
  inc() { x := x+1; y := y+1 }
  incX2() { this.inc(); this.inc() }
}
```

Let $(x = z_0, x = z_0 + 2)$ be a commitment of *incX2*, based on a requirement $(x = z_0, x = z_0 + 1)$ to *inc*, included in $R(A, inc)$. If A is later inherited by a class B, B may override *inc*, provided $R(A, inc)$ is supported by the new implementation. The behavior of *incX2* does not depend on other possible commitments in $S(A, inc)$; e.g., $(x = y, x = y)$ and $(y = z_0, y = z_0 + 1)$. In fact, the subclass implementation of *inc* may assign any value to y without breaking the reasoning system.

4 An Assertion Calculus for Program Analysis

The incremental strategy outlined in Sect. 3 is now formalized as a calculus which tracks commitments and requirements for method implementations in an extensible class hierarchy. Given a program, the calculus builds an environment which reflects the class hierarchy and captures method commitments and requirements. This environment forms the context for the analysis of new classes, possibly inheriting already analyzed ones. Proofs of the lemmas can be found in [11].

4.1 The Proof Environment of the Assertion Calculus

A class is represented by a tuple $\langle D, \overline{f}, \overline{M} \rangle$ from which the superclass identifier D, fields $\overline{f}$, and methods $\overline{M}$ are accessible by observer functions *inh*, *att*, and *mtds*, respectively. Let $M.body = t$ for a method $M = m(\overline{x})\{t\}$ (or its proof outline). Class names are assumed to be unique, and method names to be unique within a class. The superclass identifier may be *nil*, representing no superclass (for class Object).

Definition 2 (Proof environments). *A proof environment $\mathcal{E}$ of type Env is a tuple $\langle P_\mathcal{E}, S_\mathcal{E}, R_\mathcal{E} \rangle$, where $P_\mathcal{E} : Cid \to Class$ is a partial mapping and $S_\mathcal{E}, R_\mathcal{E} : Cid \times Mid \to Set[Assert]$ are total mappings.*

In an environment $\mathcal{E}$, $P_\mathcal{E}$ reflects the class structure, $S_\mathcal{E}(C,m)$ the set of commitments for m in C and $R_\mathcal{E}(C,m)$ a set of requirements to m from C. For the *empty environment* $\mathcal{E}_\emptyset$, $P_{\mathcal{E}_\emptyset}(C)$ is undefined and $S_{\mathcal{E}_\emptyset}(C,m) = R_{\mathcal{E}_\emptyset}(C,m) = \emptyset$ for all $C : Cid$ and $m : Mid$. Let $\leq_\mathcal{E} : Cid \times Cid \to Bool$ be the reflexive and transitive subclass relation on $\mathcal{E}$.

Next we define some *auxiliary functions* on proof environments $\mathcal{E}$. Let $\uparrow P_\mathcal{E}(C).att$ denote the fields of C and of its superclasses; i.e., the declared fields accessible from methods in C, including the implicit declaration this : C. Denote by $t' \in t$ that the statement t' is contained in the statement t, and by $C \in \mathcal{E}$ that $P_\mathcal{E}(C)$ is defined. The function $bind_\mathcal{E}(C,m) : Cid \times Mid \to Cid$ returns the first class above C in which the method m is defined. This function will never return *nil* for type correct calls. Let the recursively defined functions $S\uparrow_\mathcal{E}(C,m)$ and $R\uparrow_\mathcal{E}(C,m) : Cid \times Mid \to Set[Assert]$ return all commitments of m both above C and below $bind_\mathcal{E}(C,m)$, and all requirements to m that are made by all classes above C in the proof environment $\mathcal{E}$, respectively. Finally, $body_\mathcal{E}(C,m) : Cid \times Mid \to Stm$ returns the body of m in $bind_\mathcal{E}(C,m)$.

A *sound environment* reflects that previously analyzed classes are correct. If an assertion appears in $S_\mathcal{E}(C,m)$, there must be a verified proof outline M in PL for the corresponding method body. For internal calls $\{r\}\ n\ \{s\}$ in M, (r,s) must be included in $R_\mathcal{E}(C,n)$; i.e., all requirements made by the proof outline are in the R-mapping. For external calls $\{r\}\ x.n\ \{s\}$ in M, where x is of class D, the requirement (r,s) must follow from the requirements of n in the context of D. Note that D may be independent of C; i.e., neither above nor below C. Finally, method commitments must entail the requirements (see Property 2 of Sect. 3.2). Sound environments are defined as follows:

Definition 3 (Sound environments). *A sound environment $\mathcal{E}$ satisfies the following conditions for all $C : Cid$ and $m : Mid$:*

1. $\forall (p,q) \in S_{\mathcal{E}}(C,m) \,.\, \exists \langle body_{\mathcal{E}}(C,m) \rangle \,.\, \vdash_{\text{PL}} m(\bar{x}) : (p,q) \{\langle body_{\mathcal{E}}(C,m) \rangle\}$
   $\wedge \, \forall \{r\}\, n\, \{s\} \in \langle body_{\mathcal{E}}(C,m) \rangle \,.\, R_{\mathcal{E}}(C,n) \twoheadrightarrow (r,s)$
   $\wedge \, \forall \{r\}\, x.n\, \{s\} \in \langle body_{\mathcal{E}}(C,m) \rangle \,.\, \exists D\,.\, ((x:D) \in {\uparrow} P_{\mathcal{E}}(C).att) \Rightarrow R{\uparrow}_{\mathcal{E}}(D,n) \twoheadrightarrow (r,s)$
2. $S{\uparrow}_{\mathcal{E}}(C,m) \twoheadrightarrow R{\uparrow}_{\mathcal{E}}(C,m)$

Note that in this definition, the proof outline required by Condition 1 need not be in C itself, but may be found above C as described by $body_{\mathcal{E}}(C,m)$. Let $\models_C \{p\}\, t\, \{q\}$ denote $\models \{p\}\, t\, \{q\}$ under the assumption that virtual calls in t are bound in the context of C, and let $\models_C m(\bar{x}) : (p,q)\, \{t\}$ be given by $\models_C \{p\}\, t\, \{q\}$. If there are no method calls in t and $\vdash_{\text{PL}} \{p\}\, t\, \{q\}$, then $\models \{p\}\, t\, \{q\}$ follows by the soundness of PL.

Although method redefinitions in a subclass need not respect the commitments of method definitions in superclasses, Lemma 1 below ensures that the commitments of method definitions in superclasses will hold when invoked from a subclass, even if auxiliary methods have been redefined.

Lemma 1. *Given a sound environment $\mathcal{E}$ and a sound program logic* PL. *For all C : Cid, m : Mid, and (p,q) : Assert such that $C \in \mathcal{E}$ and $(p,q) \in S{\uparrow}_{\mathcal{E}}(C,m)$, we have $\models_D m(\bar{x}) : (p,q)\, \{body_{\mathcal{E}}(C,m)\}$ for each $D \leq_{\mathcal{E}} C$.*

In a *minimal* environment $\mathcal{E}$, the mapping $R_{\mathcal{E}}$ only contains requirements that are caused by some proof outline; i.e., there are no superfluous requirements. Minimal environments are defined as follows:

Definition 4 (Minimal Environments). *A sound environment $\mathcal{E}$ is* minimal *iff*

$\forall (r,s) \in R_{\mathcal{E}}(C,n) \,.\, \exists (p,q), m, \langle body_{\mathcal{E}}(C,m) \rangle \,.$
$(p,q) \in S_{\mathcal{E}}(C,m) \wedge \vdash_{\text{PL}} m(\bar{x}) : (p,q) \{\langle body_{\mathcal{E}}(C,m) \rangle\} \wedge \{r\}\, n\, \{s\} \in \langle body_{\mathcal{E}}(C,m) \rangle$

Reverification is avoided by incrementally extending $S_{\mathcal{E}}(C,m)$. If a virtual call requires a verified specification, it is found in $S_{\mathcal{E}}(C,m)$. Thus, the avoidance of reverification can be seen as a dual to the first condition to Def. 3: If $\{p\}\, body_{\mathcal{E}}(C,m)\, \{q\}$ is proved, the commitment (p,q) is added to $S_{\mathcal{E}}(C,m)$.

4.2 The Analysis Operations of the Assertion Calculus

An open program may be extended with new classes, and there may be mutual dependencies between the new classes. For example, a method in a new class C can call a method in another new class D, and a method in D can call a method in C. In such cases, a complete analysis of one class cannot be carried out without consideration of mutually dependent classes. We therefore choose class sets as the granularity of program analysis. A *module* is a set of classes, and a module is *self-contained* with regard to an environment $\mathcal{E}$ if all method calls inside the module can be successfully bound inside that module or to classes represented in $\mathcal{E}$.

In the calculus, judgments have the form $\mathcal{E} \vdash \mathcal{A}$, where $\mathcal{E}$ is the proof environment and $\mathcal{A}$ is a list of *analysis operations* on the class hierarchy. The analysis operations have the following syntax:

$$O ::= \varepsilon \mid analyzeMtds(\overline{M}) \mid verify(m, \overline{R}) \mid analyzeOutline(t) \mid O \cdot O$$
$$S ::= \emptyset \mid L \mid require(C, m, (p,q)) \mid S \cup S$$
$$\mathcal{A} ::= module(\overline{L}) \mid [\langle C : O \rangle\,;\, S] \mid [\varepsilon\,;\, S] \mid \mathcal{A} \cdot module(\overline{L})$$

These analysis operations may be understood as follows. A set $\overline{L}$ of class declarations is analyzed by the module operation $module(\overline{L})$. Classes are assumed to be syntactically well-formed and well-typed. Inside a module, the classes are analyzed in some order, captured by the set S. The operation $\mathtt{class}\ C\ \mathtt{extends}\ D\ \{\overline{f}\,\overline{M}\}$ initiates the analysis of class C. The operation $[\langle C : O \rangle ; S]$ analyzes O in the context of class C before operations in S are considered. Upon completion, the analysis yields a term of the form $[\varepsilon ; S]$. The analysis of a specific class consists of the following operations, all inside the context of that class. The operation $analyzeMtds(\overline{M})$ initiates analysis of the proof outlines $\overline{M}$. The operation $verify(m,\overline{R})$ verifies the set $\overline{R}$ of assertions with respect to the method m. The operation $analyzeOutline(t)$ analyzes the method calls in the statement t. Since the operation only occurs in the context of a class C, virtual calls are bound in this context. The operation $require(D,m,(p,q))$ applies to external calls to ensure that m in D satisfies the requirement (p,q). Requirements are lifted outside the context of the calling class C by this operation, and the verification of requirement (p,q) for m in D is shifted into the set of analysis operations S.

4.3 The Inference Rules of the Assertion Calculus

Class modules are analyzed in sequential order such that each module is self-contained with regard to the already analyzed modules. Program analysis is initiated by $\mathcal{E}_0 \vdash module(\overline{L})$, where $\overline{L}$ is a module that is self-contained with regard to the empty environment. The analysis of a module is carried out by manipulation of the $module(\overline{L})$ operation according to the inference rules below. During module analysis, the proof environment is extended, keeping track of the currently analyzed class hierarchy and the associated method commitments and requirements. When a $module$ operation succeeds, the resulting environment represents a verified class hierarchy. New modules may introduce subclasses of previously analyzed classes, and the calculus is based on an open world assumption as a module may be analyzed in the context of previously analyzed modules and independent of later modules.

There are three different *environment updates*; the loading of a new class L and the extension of the commitment and requirement mappings with an assertion (p,q) for a given method m and class C. These are denoted $extS(C,m,(p,q))$ and $extR(C,m,(p,q))$, respectively. Environment updates are represented by the operator $\oplus : Env \times Update \to Env$, where the first argument is the current proof environment and the second argument is the environment update, defined as follows:

$$\mathcal{E} \oplus \mathtt{class}\ C\ \mathtt{extends}\ D\ \{\overline{f}\,\overline{M}\} = \langle P_{\mathcal{E}}[C \mapsto \langle D,\overline{f},\overline{M}\rangle], S_{\mathcal{E}}, R_{\mathcal{E}}\rangle$$
$$\mathcal{E} \oplus extS(C,m,(p,q)) = \langle P_{\mathcal{E}}, S_{\mathcal{E}}[(C,m) \mapsto S_{\mathcal{E}}(C,m) \cup \{(p,q)\}], R_{\mathcal{E}}\rangle$$
$$\mathcal{E} \oplus extR(C,m,(p,q)) = \langle P_{\mathcal{E}}, S_{\mathcal{E}}, R_{\mathcal{E}}[(C,m) \mapsto R_{\mathcal{E}}(C,m) \cup \{(p,q)\}]\rangle$$

The corresponding *inference rules* are given in Fig. 4. Note that $\mathcal{A}$ represents a list of modules which will be analyzed later, and which may be empty. Rule (NEWMODULE) initiates the analysis of a new module $module(\overline{L})$. The analysis continues by manipulation of the $[\varepsilon ; \overline{L}]$ operation that is generated by this rule. For notational convenience, we let $\overline{L}$ denote both a set and list of classes.

Rule (NEWCLASS) selects a new class from the current module, and initiates analysis of the class in the current proof environment. The premises ensure that a class cannot

$$\frac{\mathcal{E} \vdash [\varepsilon; \overline{L}] \cdot \mathcal{A}}{\mathcal{E} \vdash module(\overline{L}) \cdot \mathcal{A}} \quad \text{(NEWMODULE)}$$

$$\frac{C \notin \mathcal{E} \quad D \neq nil \Rightarrow D \in \mathcal{E}}{\mathcal{E} \oplus (\text{class } C \text{ extends } D \ \{\overline{f} \ \overline{M}\}) \vdash [\langle C: analyzeMtds(\overline{M})\rangle; S] \cdot \mathcal{A}} \quad \text{(NEWCLASS)}$$
$$\frac{}{\mathcal{E} \vdash [\varepsilon; \{\text{class } C \text{ extends } D \ \{\overline{f} \ \overline{M}\}\} \cup S] \cdot \mathcal{A}}$$

$$\frac{\mathcal{E} \vdash [\langle C: verify(m, \{(p,q)\} \cup R{\uparrow}_{\mathcal{E}} \ (P_{\mathcal{E}}(C).inh, m)) \cdot O\rangle; S] \cdot \mathcal{A}}{\mathcal{E} \vdash [\langle C: analyzeMtds(m(\overline{x}) : (p,q)\{\langle t\rangle\}) \cdot O\rangle; S] \cdot \mathcal{A}} \quad \text{(NEWMTD)}$$

$$\frac{S{\uparrow}_{\mathcal{E}} (C, m) \twoheadrightarrow (p,q) \quad \mathcal{E} \vdash [\langle C: O\rangle; S] \cdot \mathcal{A}}{\mathcal{E} \vdash [\langle C: verify(m, (p,q)) \cdot O\rangle; S] \cdot \mathcal{A}} \quad \text{(REQDER)}$$

$$\frac{\vdash_{\text{PL}} m(\overline{x}) : (p,q) \ \{\langle body_{\mathcal{E}}(C,m)\rangle\}}{\mathcal{E} \oplus extS(C,m,(p,q)) \vdash [\langle C: analyzeOutline(\langle body_{\mathcal{E}}(C,m)\rangle) \cdot O\rangle; S] \cdot \mathcal{A}} \quad \text{(REQNOTDER)}$$
$$\overline{\mathcal{E} \vdash [\langle C: verify(m, (p,q)) \cdot O\rangle; S] \cdot \mathcal{A}}$$

$$\frac{\mathcal{E} \oplus extR(C,m,(p,q)) \vdash [\langle C: verify(m,(p,q)) \cdot O\rangle; S] \cdot \mathcal{A}}{\mathcal{E} \vdash [\langle C: analyzeOutline(\{p\} \ m \ \{q\}) \cdot O\rangle; S] \cdot \mathcal{A}} \quad \text{(CALL)}$$

$$\frac{x : D \in {\uparrow} P_{\mathcal{E}}(C).att \quad \mathcal{E} \vdash [\langle C: O\rangle; S \cup \{require(D,m,(p,q))\}] \cdot \mathcal{A}}{\mathcal{E} \vdash [\langle C: analyzeOutline(\{p\} \ x.m \ \{q\}) \cdot O\rangle; S] \cdot \mathcal{A}} \quad \text{(EXTCALL)}$$

$$\frac{C \in \mathcal{E} \quad R{\uparrow}_{\mathcal{E}}(C,m) \twoheadrightarrow (p,q) \quad \mathcal{E} \vdash [\varepsilon; S] \cdot \mathcal{A}}{\mathcal{E} \vdash [\varepsilon; \{require(C,m,(p,q))\} \cup S] \cdot \mathcal{A}} \quad \text{(EXTREQ)}$$

$$\frac{\mathcal{E} \vdash [\varepsilon; S] \cdot \mathcal{A}}{\mathcal{E} \vdash [\langle C: \varepsilon\rangle; S] \cdot \mathcal{A}} \quad \text{(EMPCLASS)} \qquad \frac{\mathcal{E} \vdash \mathcal{A}}{\mathcal{E} \vdash [\varepsilon; \emptyset] \cdot \mathcal{A}} \quad \text{(EMPMODULE)}$$

$$\frac{\mathcal{E} \vdash [\langle C: O\rangle; S] \cdot \mathcal{A}}{\mathcal{E} \vdash [\langle C: verify(m, \emptyset) \cdot O\rangle; S] \cdot \mathcal{A}} \quad \text{(NOREQ)}$$

$$\frac{\mathcal{E} \vdash [\langle C: O\rangle; S] \cdot \mathcal{A}}{\mathcal{E} \vdash [\langle C: analyzeMtds(\emptyset) \cdot O\rangle; S] \cdot \mathcal{A}} \quad \text{(NOMTDS)}$$

$$\frac{\mathcal{E} \vdash [\langle C: O\rangle; S] \cdot \mathcal{A} \quad t \text{ does not contain call statements}}{\mathcal{E} \vdash [\langle C: analyzeOutline(t) \cdot O\rangle; S] \cdot \mathcal{A}} \quad \text{(SKIP)}$$

$$\frac{\mathcal{E} \vdash [\langle C: verify(m, \overline{R_1}) \cdot verify(m, \overline{R_2}) \cdot O\rangle; S] \cdot \mathcal{A}}{\mathcal{E} \vdash [\langle C: verify(m, \overline{R_1} \ \overline{R_2}) \cdot O\rangle; S] \cdot \mathcal{A}} \quad \text{(DECOMPREQ)}$$

$$\frac{\mathcal{E} \vdash [\langle C: analyzeOutline(t_1) \cdot analyzeOutline(t_2) \cdot O\rangle; S] \cdot \mathcal{A}}{\mathcal{E} \vdash [\langle C: analyzeOutline(t_1;t_2) \cdot O\rangle; S] \cdot \mathcal{A}} \quad \text{(DECOMPCALLS)}$$

$$\frac{\mathcal{E} \vdash [\langle C: analyzeMtds(\overline{M_1}) \cdot analyzeMtds(\overline{M_2}) \cdot O\rangle; S] \cdot \mathcal{A}}{\mathcal{E} \vdash [\langle C: analyzeMtds(\overline{M_1} \ \overline{M_2}) \cdot O\rangle; S] \cdot \mathcal{A}} \quad \text{(DECOMPMTDS)}$$

Fig. 4. The inference system, where $\mathcal{A}$ is a (possibly empty) list of analysis operations. To simplify the presentation, we let m denote a method call including actual parameters.

be introduced twice and that the superclass has *already been analyzed*. The class hierarchy is extended with the new class and the analysis continues by traversing the proof outlines by means of the *analyzeMtds* operation. Note that at this point in the analysis, the class has no subclasses in the proof environment. Rule (NEWMTD) generates a set of requirement assertions for a method. The requirement set is constructed from the specified commitment of the method and the superclass requirements to the method.

The rules (REQDER) and (REQNOTDER) address the verification of a particular requirement with respect to a method implementation. If the requirement follows from the commitments of the method, rule (REQDER) proceeds with the remaining analysis operations. Otherwise, a proof of the requirement is needed. As $\langle body_\mathcal{E}(C,m) \rangle$ nondeterministically selects a proof outline, the rule applies to any proof outline for the method available in class C. Remark that (REQNOTDER) is the only rule which extends the S mapping. The considered requirement leads to a new commitment for m with respect to C, and the commitment itself is assumed when analyzing the method body. This captures the standard approach to reasoning about recursive procedure calls [13].

Rule (CALL) analyzes the requirement of a local call occurring in some proof outline. The rule extends the R mapping and generates a *verify* operation which analyzes the requirement with respect to the implementation bound from the current class. The extension of the R mapping ensures that future redefinitions of m must respect the requirement; i.e., the requirement applies whenever future redefinitions are considered by (NEWMTD). Rule (EXTCALL) handles external calls on the form $x.m$ (ignoring field shadowing). The requirement to the external method is removed from the context of the current class and inserted as a *require* operation in S. The class of the callee is found by the declaration of x. Rule (EXTREQ) can first be applied *after* the analysis of the callee class, and the requirement must then follow from the requirements of this class.

Rule (EMPCLASS) concludes the analysis of a class when all analysis operations have succeeded in the context of the class. The analysis of a module is completed by the rule (EMPMODULE). Thus, the analysis of a module is completed after the analysis of all the module classes and external requirements made by these classes have succeeded.

In addition, there are some structural rules. The rules (NOREQ) and (NOMTDS) apply to the empty requirement set and the empty method list, respectively. Rule (SKIP) applies to statements which are irrelevant to this analysis. These rules simply continue the analysis with the remaining analysis operations. Finally, the rules (DECOMPMTDS), (DECOMPREQ), and (DECOMPCALLS) flatten non-empty method lists, requirement sets and statements into separate analysis operations. Note that a proof of $\mathcal{E} \vdash module(\overline{L})$ has exactly one leaf node $\mathcal{E}' \vdash [\varepsilon\,;\emptyset]$; we call $\mathcal{E}'$ the environment resulting from the analysis of $module(\overline{L})$.

Properties of the inference system. Although the individual rules of the inference system do not preserve soundness of the proof environment, the soundness of the proof environment is preserved by the successful analysis of a module. This allows us to prove that the proof system is sound for module analysis.

Theorem 1. *Let $\mathcal{E}$ be a sound environment and $\overline{L}$ a set of class declarations. If a proof of $\mathcal{E} \vdash module(\overline{L})$ has $\mathcal{E}'$ as its resulting proof environment, then $\mathcal{E}'$ is also sound.*

Theorem 2 (Soundness). *If PL is a sound program logic, then the derived proof outline logic combined with the calculus also constitutes a sound proof system.*

Furthermore, the inference system preserves minimality of proof environments; i.e., only requirements needed by some proof outline are recorded in the $R_\mathcal{E}$ mapping.

Lemma 2. *If $\mathcal{E}$ is a minimal environment and $\overline{L}$ is a set of class declarations such that a proof of $\mathcal{E} \vdash module(\overline{L})$ leads to the resulting environment $\mathcal{E}'$, then $\mathcal{E}'$ is also minimal.*

Finally we show that the proof system supports verification reuse in the sense that commitments are remembered.

Lemma 3. *Let $\mathcal{E}$ be an environment $\mathcal{E}$ and $\overline{L}$ a list of class declarations. Whenever a proof outline $m(\overline{x}):(p,q)\{\langle t\rangle\}$ is verified during analysis of some class C in $\overline{L}$, the commitment (p,q) is included in $S_\mathcal{E}(C,m)$.*

5 Related Work

Object-orientation poses several challenges to program logics; e.g., inheritance, late binding, recursive method calls, aliasing, and object creation. In the last years several programming logics have been proposed, addressing various of these challenges. Numerous proof methods, verification condition generators, and validation environments for object-oriented languages have been developed, including [1,22,14,16,6]. In particular, Java has attracted much interest, with advances being made for different (mostly sequential) aspects and sublanguages of that language. In particular, most such formalizations concentrate on closed systems. A recent state-of-the-art survey of challenges and results for proof systems and verification in the field is given in [18], and for an overview of verification tools based on the Java modeling language JML, see [7].

Proof systems especially studying late bound methods have been shown to be sound and complete assuming a closed world [24]. While this is proof-theoretically satisfactory, the closed world assumption is unrealistic in practice and necessitates costly reverification when the class hierarchy is extended (as discussed in Sect. 1). To support object-oriented design, proof systems should be constructed for incremental reasoning. Most prominent in that context are different variations of behavioral subtyping [20, 26, 19]. Virtual methods [25] similarly allow incremental reasoning by committing to certain abstract properties about a method, which must hold for all its implementations. Although sound, the approach does not generally provide complete program logics, as these abstract properties would, in non-trivial cases, be too weak to obtain completeness. Virtual methods furthermore force the developer to commit to specific abstract specifications of method behavior early in the design process. In particular, the verification platforms for *Spec#* [5] and JML [7] rely on versions of behavioral subtyping.

The fragile base class problem emerges when seemingly harmless superclass updates lead to unexpected behavior of subclass instances [21]. Many variations of the problem relate to imprecise specifications and assumptions made in super- or subclasses. By making method requirements and assumptions explicit, our calculus can detect many issues related to the fragile base class problem.

6 Conclusion

This paper presents lazy behavioral subtyping, a novel strategy for reasoning about late bound method calls. The strategy is designed to support incremental reasoning and avoid reverification in an open setting, where class hierarchies can be extended by inheritance. Lazy behavioral subtyping is more flexible than strategies based on traditional behavioral subtyping, while retaining the open world assumption. To focus the presentation, we have abstracted from many object-oriented language features and presented the approach for an object-oriented kernel language supporting single inheritance. This reflects the mainstream object-oriented languages today, such as Java and $C^{\#}$.

We currently integrate lazy behavioral subtyping in a program logic for Creol [17, 10], a language for dynamically reprogrammable active objects, developed in the context of the European project Credo. This integration requires a generalization of the analysis to *multiple inheritance* and concurrent objects, as well as to Creol's mechanism for *class upgrades*. Moreover an adaptation is needed to Creol's type system, which is purely based on interfaces. Interface types provide a clear distinction between internal and external calls. By separating interface level subtyping from class level inheritance, class inheritance can freely exploit code reuse based on lazy behavioral subtyping while still supporting incremental reasoning techniques. This program logic with lazy behavioral subtyping will be part of the programming environment for Creol, based on Eclipse.

Acknowledgment. We are grateful for helpful comments from Wolfgang Ahrendt and the anonymous reviewers of *Formal Methods 2008*.

References

1. Abadi, M., Leino, K.R.M.: A Logic of Object-Oriented Programs. In: Dershowitz, N. (ed.) Verification: Theory and Practice. LNCS, vol. 2772, pp. 11–41. Springer, Heidelberg (2004)
2. America, P.: Designing an object-oriented programming language with behavioural subtyping. In: de Bakker, J.W., de Roever, W.-P., Rozenberg, G. (eds.) Foundations of Object-Oriented Languages, pp. 60–90. Springer, Heidelberg (1991)
3. Apt, K.R.: Ten years of Hoare's logic: A survey — Part I. ACM Transactions on Programming Languages and Systems 3(4), 431–483 (1981)
4. Apt, K.R., Olderog, E.-R.: Verification of Sequential and Concurrent Systems. In: Texts and Monographs in Computer Science, Springer, Heidelberg (1991)
5. Barnett, M., Leino, K.R.M., Schulte, W.: The Spec# Programming System: An Overview. In: Barthe, G., Burdy, L., Huisman, M., Lanet, J.-L., Muntean, T. (eds.) CASSIS 2004. LNCS, vol. 3362, pp. 49–69. Springer, Heidelberg (2005)
6. Beckert, B., Hähnle, R., Schmitt, P.H. (eds.): Verification of Object-Oriented Software. LNCS (LNAI), vol. 4334. Springer, Heidelberg (2007)
7. Burdy, L., Cheon, Y., Cok, D.R., Ernst, M., Kiniry, J., Leavens, G.T., Leino, K.R.M., Poll, E.: An overview of JML tools and applications. In: Arts, T., Fokkink, W. (eds.) *Proceedings of FMICS 2003*. ENTCS, vol. 80, Elsevier, Amsterdam (2003)
8. Dahl, O.-J., Myhrhaug, B., Nygaard, K. (Simula 67) Common Base Language. Technical Report S-2, Norsk Regnesentral (Norwegian Computing Center), Oslo, Norway (May 1968)

9. de Boer, F.S.: A WP-calculus for OO. In: Thomas, W. (ed.) ETAPS 1999 and FOSSACS 1999. LNCS, vol. 1578, pp. 135–149. Springer, Heidelberg (1999)
10. de Boer, F.S., Clarke, D., Johnsen, E.B.: A Complete Guide to the Future. In: De Nicola, R. (ed.) ESOP 2007. LNCS, vol. 4421, pp. 316–330. Springer, Heidelberg (2007)
11. Dovland, J., Johnsen, E.B., Owe, O., Steffen, M.: Lazy behavioral subtyping. Research Report 368, Dept. of Informatics, University of Oslo (November 2007), heim.ifi.uio.no/creol
12. Hoare, C.A.R.: An Axiomatic Basis of Computer Programming. Communications of the ACM 12, 576–580 (1969)
13. Hoare, C.A.R.: Procedures and parameters: An axiomatic approach. In: Engeler, E. (ed.) Symposium On Semantics of Algorithmic Languages. Lecture Notes in Mathematics, vol. 188, pp. 102–116. Springer, Heidelberg (1971)
14. Huisman, M.: Java Program Verification in Higher-Order Logic with PVS and Isabelle. PhD thesis, University of Nijmegen (2001)
15. Igarashi, A., Pierce, B.C., Wadler, P.: Featherweight Java: a minimal core calculus for Java and GJ. ACM Transactions on Programming Languages and Systems 23(3), 396–450 (2001)
16. Jacobs, B., Poll, E.: A Logic for the Java Modeling Language JML. In: Hussmann, H. (ed.) ETAPS 2001 and FASE 2001. LNCS, vol. 2029, pp. 284–299. Springer, Heidelberg (2001)
17. Johnsen, E.B., Owe, O.: An asynchronous communication model for distributed concurrent objects. Software and Systems Modeling 6(1), 35–58 (2007)
18. Leavens, G.T., Leino, K.R.M., Müller, P.: Specification and verification challenges for sequential object-oriented programs. Formal Aspects of Computing 19(2), 159–189 (2007)
19. Leavens, G.T., Naumann, D.A.: Behavioral subtyping, specification inheritance, and modular reasoning. Technical Report 06-20a, Department of Computer Science, Iowa State University, Ames, Iowa (2006)
20. Liskov, B.H., Wing, J.M.: A behavioral notion of subtyping. ACM Transactions on Programming Languages and Systems 16(6), 1811–1841 (1994)
21. Mikhajlov, L., Sekerinski, E.: A Study of the Fragile Base Class Problem. In: Jul, E. (ed.) ECOOP 1998. LNCS, vol. 1445, pp. 355–382. Springer, Heidelberg (1998)
22. von Oheimb, D., Nipkow, T.: Hoare Logic for NanoJava: Auxiliary Variables, Side Effects, and Virtual Methods Revisited. In: Eriksson, L.-H., Lindsay, P.A. (eds.) FME 2002. LNCS, vol. 2391, pp. 89–105. Springer, Heidelberg (2002)
23. Owicki, S., Gries, D.: An axiomatic proof technique for parallel programs I. Acta Informatica 6(4), 319–340 (1976)
24. Pierik, C., de Boer, F.S.: A proof outline logic for object-oriented programming. Theoretical Computer Science 343(3), 413–442 (2005)
25. Poetzsch-Heffter, A., Müller, P.: A programming logic for sequential Java. In: Swierstra, S.D. (ed.) ESOP 1999 and ETAPS 1999. LNCS, vol. 1576, pp. 162–176. Springer, Heidelberg (1999)
26. Soundarajan, N., Fridella, S.: Inheritance: From code reuse to reasoning reuse. In: Devanbu, P., Poulin, J. (eds.) Proc. Fifth International Conference on Software Reuse (ICSR5), pp. 206–215. IEEE Computer Society Press, Los Alamitos (1998)

Checking Well-Formedness of Pure-Method Specifications

Arsenii Rudich[1], Ádám Darvas[1], and Peter Müller[2]

[1] ETH Zurich, Switzerland
{arsenii.rudich,adam.darvas}@inf.ethz.ch
[2] Microsoft Research, USA
mueller@microsoft.com

Abstract. Contract languages such as JML and Spec# specify invariants and pre- and postconditions using side-effect free expressions of the programming language, in particular, pure methods. For such contracts to be meaningful, they must be well-formed: First, they must respect the partiality of operations, for instance, the preconditions of pure methods used in the contract. Second, they must enable a consistent encoding of pure methods in a program logic, which requires that their specifications are satisfiable and that recursive specifications are well-founded.

This paper presents a technique to check well-formedness of contracts. We give proof obligations that are sufficient to guarantee the existence of a model for the specification of pure methods. We improve over earlier work by providing a systematic solution including a soundness result and by supporting more forms of recursive specifications. Our technique has been implemented in the Spec# programming system.

1 Introduction

Contract languages such as the Java Modeling Language (JML) [21] and Spec# [2] specify invariants and pre- and postconditions using side-effect free expressions of the programming language. While contract languages are natural for programmers, they pose various challenges when contracts are encoded in the logic of a program verifier or theorem prover, especially when contracts use pure (side-effect free) methods [13]. This paper addresses two challenges related to pure-method specifications.

The first challenge is how to ensure that a specification is *well-defined*, that is, that all partial operations are applied within their domain. For instance method calls are well-defined only for non-null receivers and when the precondition of the method is satisfied. This challenge can be solved by encoding partial functions as under-specified total functions [15]. However, it has been argued that such an encoding is counter-intuitive for programmers, is not well-suited for runtime assertion checking, and assigns meaning to bogus contracts instead of having them rejected by a verifier [8]. Another solution is the use of 3-valued logic, such as LPF [3]. However, 3-valued logic is typically not supported by the theorem provers that are used in program verifiers. We present a technique based on 2-valued logic to check whether a specification satisfies all partiality constraints. If the check fails, the specification is rejected.

The second challenge is how to ensure that a specification is consistent. In order to reason about contracts that contain pure-method calls, pure methods must be encoded in the logic of the program verifier. This is typically done by introducing an uninterpreted function symbol for each pure method m, whose properties are axiomatized based on m's contract and object invariants [10, 13]. A specification is *consistent* if this axiomatization is free from contradictions. Consistency is crucial for soundness. We present a technique to check consistency by showing that the contracts of pure methods are satisfiable and well-founded if they are recursive. If the consistency check fails, the specification is rejected.

An inconsistent specification of a method m is not necessarily detected during the verification of m's implementation [13]: (1) m might be abstract; (2) partial correctness logics allow one to verify m w.r.t. an unsatisfiable specification if m's implementation does not terminate; (3) any implementation could be trivially verified based on inconsistent axioms stemming from inconsistent pure-method specifications; this is especially true for recursion, when the axiom for m is

```
interface Sequence {
  [Ghost] int Length;

  invariant Length >= 0;
  invariant IsEmpty() ==> Length == 0;
  invariant !IsEmpty() ==> Length == Rest().Length + 1;

  [Pure][Measure=Length] int Count(Object c)
     requires !IsEmpty();
     ensures result >= 0;
     ensures result == (GetFirst() == c ? 1 : 0) +
                       (Rest().IsEmpty() ? 0 : Rest().Count(c));
  [Pure] bool IsEmpty();
  [Pure] Object GetFirst()
     requires !IsEmpty();
  [Pure] Sequence Rest()
     requires !IsEmpty();
     ensures result != null;

  // other methods and specifications omitted
}
```

Fig. 1. Specification of interface Sequence. We use a notation similar to Spec#, which is an extension of C#. The **Pure** attribute marks a method to be side-effect free; pre- and postconditions are attached to methods by **requires** and **ensures** clauses, respectively. Invariants are specified in **invariant** clauses; in postconditions, **result** denotes the return value of methods. User-specified recursion measures are given by the **Measure** attribute. Fields marked with the **Ghost** attribute are specification-only.

needed to verify its implementation. These reasons justify the need for verifying consistency of specifications independently of implementations.

We illustrate these challenges by the interface Sequence in Fig. 1. It contains pure methods to query whether the sequence is empty, and to get the first element and the rest of the sequence. Method Count returns the number of occurrences of its parameter in the sequence. The interface contains the specification-only ghost field Length, which represents the length of the sequence. The interface is equipped with method specifications and invariants specifying Length.

We call a specification *well-formed* if it is well-defined and consistent. The main difficulty in the checking of well-formedness lies in the subtle dependencies between the specification elements. For instance, to be able to show that the expression Rest().Count(c) in Count's postcondition is well-defined, the guarding condition !Rest().IsEmpty(), the precondition of Count, and the contract of Rest are needed. These specification elements together allow one to conclude that the receiver is not null and that the preconditions of Rest and Count are satisfied. That is, we need the specification of (axioms for) some pure methods to prove the well-definedness of other pure methods.

The second challenge is illustrated by the specification of method Count. Consistency requires that there actually is a result value for each call to Count. This would not be the case, for instance, if the first postcondition required **result** to be strictly positive. Since the specification of Count is recursive, proving the existence of a result value relies on the specification of Count. Using this specification is sound since the recursion in Count's specification is well-founded: the first and third invariant, and the precondition of Count guarantee that the sequence is finite, and the guarding condition together with the precondition of Count and the third invariant guarantees that we recurse on a shorter sequence. Again, we have a subtle interaction between specifications: proving the consistency of a pure method makes use of the specification of this method as well as invariants and the specification of the methods mentioned in these invariants.

These examples demonstrate that generating the appropriate proof obligations to check well-formedness is challenging. A useful checker must permit dependencies between specification elements, but prevent circular reasoning.

Approach and Contributions. We show well-formedness of specifications by posing proof obligations to ensure: (1) that partial operations are applied within their domains, (2) the existence of a possible result value for each pure method, and (3) that recursive specifications are well-founded. In order to deal with dependencies between pure methods, we determine a dependency graph, which we process bottom-up. Thereby, one can use the properties of a method m to prove the proof obligations for the methods using m.

To deal with partiality, we interpret specifications in 3-valued logic. However, we want to support standard theorem provers, which typically use 2-valued logic and total functions [22, 14]. Therefore, we express the proof obligations in 2-valued logic by applying the Δ formula transformer [17] to the specification expressions. We proved the following soundness result: If all proof obligations for the pure methods of a program are proved then there is a partial model for the axiomatization of these pure methods. In other words, we guarantee that the partiality constraints are satisfied and the axiomatization is consistent.

Our approach differs from existing solutions for theorem provers [11,22], where consistency is typically enforced by restricting specifications to conservative extensions, but no checks are performed for axioms. Since specifications of pure methods are axiomatic, the approach of conservative extensions is not applicable to contract languages. Moreover, theorem provers require the user to resolve dependencies by ordering the elements of a theory appropriately. We determine this order automatically using a dependency graph.

Our approach improves on existing solutions for program verifiers in three ways. First, it supports (mutually) recursive specifications, whereas in previous work recursive specifications are severely restricted [13,12]. Second, our approach allows us to use the specification of one method to prove well-formedness of another, which is needed in many practical examples. Such dependencies are not discussed in previous work [9,13] and are not supported by program verifiers that perform consistency checks, such as Spec#. Neglecting dependencies leads to the rejection of well-formed specifications. Third, we prove consistency for the axiomatization of pure methods; such a proof is either missing in earlier work [9,12] or only presented for a very restricted setting [13].

For simplicity, we consider pure methods to be strongly-pure. That is, pure methods may not modify the heap in any way. An extension to weakly-pure methods [13], which may allocate and initialize objects, is possible.

Outline. Sec. 2 defines well-formedness of pure-method specifications. We present sufficient proof obligations to guarantee the existence of a model in Sec. 3. We discuss how our technique can be applied with automatic theorem provers in Sec. 4. We summarize related work in Sec. 5 and offer conclusions in Sec. 6.

2 Well-Formedness

In this section, we define the well-formedness criteria for the specifications of pure methods. Even though some criteria such as partiality also apply to non-pure methods, we focus on pure methods in the following.

Preliminaries. We assume a set **Heap** of heaps with the usual properties. For simplicity, we assume that a program consists of exactly one class; a generalization to several classes and subclassing is possible.

Since there is a one-to-one mapping between pure methods and the corresponding uninterpreted function symbols, we can state the well-formedness criteria directly on the function symbols. In particular, we say "the specification of a function f" to abbreviate "the specification of the pure method encoded by function f". We assume a signature with the function symbols $\mathbf{F} := \{f_1, f_2, \ldots, f_n\}$, which correspond to the pure methods of a program.

For simplicity we assume pure methods to have exactly one explicit parameter. Thus, all functions in **F** are ternary with parameters for the heap (h), receiver object (o), and explicit parameter (p). We assume that all formulas and terms are well-typed.

We define a specification of **F** as **Spec** := $\langle$**Pre, Post, INV**$\rangle$, where:

- **Pre** maps each $f_i \in$ **F** to a formula. We denote **Pre**(f_i) as **Pre**$_{f_i}$. Due to the syntactic structure of preconditions, the only free variables in **Pre**$_{f_i}$ are h, o, and p.
- **Post** maps each $f_i \in$ **F** to a formula. We denote **Post**(f_i) as **Post**$_{f_i}$. Due to the syntactic structure of postconditions, the only free variables in **Post**$_{f_i}$ are h, o, p, and the result variable res. Since we assume pure methods to be strongly-pure, one heap variable is enough to capture the heap before and after the method execution.
- **INV** is a set of formulas $\{$**Inv**$_1$, **Inv**$_2$, ..., **Inv**$_m\}$. Due to the syntactic structure of invariants, the only free variables in **Inv**$_i \in$ **INV** are the heap h and the object o to which the invariant is applied.

  We use **SysInv** := $\forall\, o \in h.\, \wedge_{i=1}^{m}$ **Inv**$_i$ to denote the conjunction of all invariants for all allocated objects, where $o \in h$ expresses that a reference o refers to an allocated object in heap h. Note that **SysInv** is an open formula with free variable h.

Structures and Interpretations. To define the interpretation of specifications, we use a structure **M** := $\langle$**Heap, R, I**$\rangle$, where **R** is the set of references and **I** is an interpretation function for the specification of a function $f \in$ **F**: **I**(f) : **Heap** $\times$ **R** $\times$ **R** $\rightarrow$ **R**. This structure can be trivially extended to other sorts like integer or boolean.

For a formula φ, we define the interpretation in total structures $[\varphi]^2_{\mathbf{M}}e$ in the standard way. Here, e is a *variable assignment* that maps the free variables of φ to values. For the interpretation in partial structures $[\varphi]^3_{\mathbf{M}}e$, we follow Berezin et al. [5]: intuitively, the interpretation of a function is defined if and only if the interpretations of all parameters are defined and the vector of parameters belongs to the function domain. The interpretation of logical operators and quantifiers is defined according to Kleene logic [20].

A total interpretation maps a formula to a value in **Bool**$_2$:= $\{\mathbf{T}, \mathbf{F}\}$, while a partial interpretation maps a formula to a value in **Bool**$_3$:= $\{\mathbf{T}, \mathbf{F}, \bot\}$. A partial structure **M** can be extended to a total structure $\hat{\mathbf{M}}$ by defining values of functions outside of their domains by arbitrary values. To check whether or not a value in **Bool**$_3$ is $\bot$ we use the following function:

$$\mathbf{wd} : \mathbf{Bool}_3 \rightarrow \mathbf{Bool}_2$$

$$\mathbf{wd}(x) := \begin{cases} \mathbf{T}, & \text{if } x \in \{\mathbf{T}, \mathbf{F}\} \\ \mathbf{F}, & \text{if } x = \bot \end{cases}$$

Well-Formedness Criteria. A specification **Spec** is well-formed (denoted by $\models$ **Spec**) if there exists a partial model **M** for the specification. A structure **M** is a *partial model* for specification **Spec**, denoted by $\mathbf{M} \models \mathbf{Spec}$, if it satisfies the following four criteria:

1. Invariants are never interpreted as $\bot$, that is, for each $\mathbf{heap} \in \mathbf{Heap}$:

    $\mathbf{wd}([\mathbf{SysInv}]_\mathbf{M}^3 e)$ holds

    where $e := [h \to \mathbf{heap}]$.

2. Preconditions are never interpreted as $\bot$ in heaps that satisfy the invariants of all allocated objects, that is, for each $f \in \mathbf{F}$, $\mathbf{heap} \in \mathbf{Heap}$, $\mathbf{this} \in \mathbf{heap}$, and $\mathbf{par} \in \mathbf{heap}$:

    if $[\mathbf{SysInv}]_\mathbf{M}^3 e$ holds, then $\mathbf{wd}([\mathbf{Pre}_f]_\mathbf{M}^3 e)$ holds

    where $e := [h \to \mathbf{heap}, o \to \mathbf{this}, p \to \mathbf{par}]$.

3. The values of the parameters belong to the domain of the interpretation of function symbols, provided that the heap satisfies the invariants and the precondition holds. That is, for each $f \in \mathbf{F}$, $\mathbf{heap} \in \mathbf{Heap}$, $\mathbf{this} \in \mathbf{heap}$, and $\mathbf{par} \in \mathbf{heap}$:

    if $[\mathbf{SysInv}]_\mathbf{M}^3 e$ and $[\mathbf{Pre}_f]_\mathbf{M}^3 e$ hold,
    then $\langle \mathbf{heap}, \mathbf{this}, \mathbf{par} \rangle \in \mathbf{dom}(\mathbf{I}(f))$ holds

    where $e := [h \to \mathbf{heap}, o \to \mathbf{this}, p \to \mathbf{par}]$.

4. Postconditions are never interpreted as $\bot$ for any result, and the interpretation of function f as result value satisfies the postcondition, provided that the heap satisfies the invariants and the precondition holds. That is, for each $f \in \mathbf{F}$, $\mathbf{heap} \in \mathbf{Heap}$, $\mathbf{this} \in \mathbf{heap}$, and $\mathbf{par} \in \mathbf{heap}$:

    if $[\mathbf{SysInv}]_\mathbf{M}^3 e$ and $[\mathbf{Pre}_f]_\mathbf{M}^3 e$ hold,
    then for each $\mathbf{result} \in \mathbf{heap}$ $\mathbf{wd}([\mathbf{Post}_f]_\mathbf{M}^3 e')$ holds,
    and $[\mathbf{Post}_f]_\mathbf{M}^3 e$ holds

    where $e := [h \to \mathbf{heap}, o \to \mathbf{this}, p \to \mathbf{par}, res \to \mathbf{I}(f)(\mathbf{heap}, \mathbf{this}, \mathbf{par})]$,
    $e' := [h \to \mathbf{heap}, o \to \mathbf{this}, p \to \mathbf{par}, res \to \mathbf{result}]$.

Axiomatization. As motivated in Sec. 1, a verification system needs to extract axioms from the specifications of pure methods. We denote the axiom for function symbol f as $\mathbf{Ax}_f$ and the axioms for all functions as $\mathbf{Ax_{Spec}}$. Formally:

$$\mathbf{Ax}_f := \forall\ h, o \in h, p \in h.\ \mathbf{SysInv} \wedge \mathbf{Pre}_f \Rightarrow \mathbf{Post}_f[f(h,o,p)/res]$$

$$\mathbf{Ax_{Spec}} := \bigwedge_{f \in \mathbf{F}} \mathbf{Ax}_f$$

From well-formedness criterion 4 and $\mathbf{Ax}_f$, we can conclude that if a structure **M** is a partial model for specification **Spec** then it is a model for $\mathbf{Ax_{Spec}}$:

   if $\mathbf{M} \models \mathbf{Spec}$ then $\mathbf{M} \models \mathbf{Ax_{Spec}}$

Consequently, if specification **Spec** is well-formed then the axioms are consistent:

if $\models$ **Spec** then $\models$ **Ax$_{\text{Spec}}$**

Important to note is that this property does not hold in the other direction, that is, if $\models$ **Ax$_{\text{Spec}}$** then $\models$ **Spec** is not necessarily true. For example, consider a method with precondition `1/0 == 1/0` and postcondition `true`. In 2-valued logic, the axiom is trivially consistent, but the specification is not well-formed (criterion 2). This demonstrates that our well-formedness criteria require more than just consistency, namely also satisfaction of partiality constraints.

3 Checking Well-Formedness

In this section, we present sufficient proof obligations that ensure that a specification is well-formed, that is, the existence of a model.

3.1 Partiality

We want our technique to work with first-order logic theorem provers, which are often used in program verifiers. These provers check that a formula holds for all total models. However, we need to check properties of partial models. Therefore, we apply a technique that reduces the 3-valued domain to a 2-valued domain by ensuring that $\bot$ is never encountered. This is a standard technique applied in different tools, for instance, in B [4], CVC Lite [5], and ESC/Java2 [9].

The main idea is to use the formula transformer Δ [17,4], which takes a (possibly open) formula φ and *domain restriction* δ, and produces a new formula φ'. The interpretation of φ' in 2-valued logic is true if and only if the interpretation of φ in 3-valued logic is different from $\bot$. The domain restriction δ is a mapping from a set of function symbols $\mathbf{F}_\delta$ to formulas. δ characterizes the domains of the function symbols of $\mathbf{F}_\delta$. For instance for the division operator, the domain restriction δ requires the divisor to be non-zero. Thus, $\Delta(a/b > 0, \delta) \equiv b \neq 0$.

For lack of space, we do not give the details of the Δ operator and refer the reader to [4]. The most important property for our purpose is the following [5]:

$$\mathbf{M} \models \delta \Rightarrow ([\Delta(\varphi, \delta)]^2_{\mathbf{M}} e = \mathbf{wd}([\varphi]^3_{\mathbf{M}} e)) \tag{1}$$

which captures the intuition of Δ described above. Δ is a syntactical characterization of the semantical operation $\mathbf{wd}$. Thus, using Δ, we can check in 2-valued logic the partiality properties we are interested in.

Property (1) interprets formulas w.r.t. a structure $\mathbf{M}$. This structure with function symbols $\mathbf{F}_\delta$ has to be a model for δ (denoted by $\mathbf{M} \models \delta$), that is:

- The domain formulas are defined, that is, for each $f \in \mathbf{F}_\delta$
  $\mathbf{wd}([\delta(f)]^3_{\mathbf{M}} e)$ holds for all e.
- δ characterizes the domains of function interpretations for $\mathbf{M}$, that is, for each $f \in \mathbf{F}_\delta$ and $\mathbf{val}_1, \ldots, \mathbf{val}_k \in \mathbf{R}$:
  $[\delta(f)]^3_{\mathbf{M}} e$ holds if and only if $\langle \mathbf{val}_1, \ldots, \mathbf{val}_k \rangle \in \mathbf{dom}(\mathbf{I}(f))$
  where $e := [v_1 \rightarrow \mathbf{val}_1, \ldots, v_k \rightarrow \mathbf{val}_k]$ and $\{v_1, \ldots, v_k\}$ are the parameter names of f. (Since methods have only one explicit parameter, $k = 3$.)

3.2 Incremental Construction of Model

In general, showing the existence of a model requires one to prove the existence of all its functions. To be able to work with first-order logic theorem provers, we approximate this second-order property in first-order logic. We generate proof obligations whose validity in 2-valued first-order logic guarantees the existence of a model. However, if we fail to prove them then we do not know whether a model exists or not. That is, the procedure is sound but not complete. However, it works for the practical examples we have considered so far.

The basic idea of our procedure is to construct a model incrementally. We build a dependency graph whose nodes are function symbols and invariants. There is an edge from node a to node b if the specification of function a or the invariant a applies function b. The dependency graph of interface Sequence is presented in Fig. 2.

The dependency graph may be cyclic. However, we disallow cycles that are introduced by preconditions. In other words, a precondition must not be recursive in order to avoid fix-point computation to define the domain of the function. This is not a limitation for practical examples.

We construct the model by traversing the dependency graph bottom-up. We start with the empty specification $\mathbf{Spec}_0 := \langle \emptyset, \emptyset, \emptyset \rangle$, for which we trivially have a model $\mathbf{M}_0$. In each step j, we select a set of nodes $G_j := \{g_1, g_2, \ldots, g_k\}$ such that if there is an edge from g_i to a node n then either n has already been visited in some previous step (i.e., $n \in G_1 \cup \ldots \cup G_{j-1}$) or $n \in G_j$. Moreover, we choose G_j such that it has one of the following forms:

1. G_j contains exactly one invariant $\mathbf{Inv}_l \in \mathbf{INV}$.
2. G_j contains exactly one function symbol $f_l \in \mathbf{F}$ and the specification of f_l is not recursive.
3. G_j is a set of function symbols, and the nodes in G_j form a cycle in the dependency graph, that is, they are specified recursively in terms of each other. G_j may contain only one node in case of direct recursion.

We call the pre- and postconditions and the invariants of G_j the *current specification fragment*, s_j. We extend $\mathbf{Spec}_{j-1}$ with s_j resulting in $\mathbf{Spec}_j$. We impose proof obligations on s_j that guarantee that the model $\mathbf{M}_{j-1}$ for $\mathbf{Spec}_{j-1}$ can be extended to a model $\mathbf{M}_j$ for $\mathbf{Spec}_j$. Since this construction is inductive, we may assume that all specification fragments processed up to step $j-1$ are well-formed.

It is easy to see that an order in which one can traverse the dependency graph always exists. However, the chosen order may influence the success of the model construction. Essentially one should choose an invariant node whenever possible because the invariant provides information that might be useful for later steps.

3.3 Proof Obligations

We now present the proof obligations for the three different kinds of current specification fragments s_j. We refer to the elements of $\mathbf{Spec}_j$ as $\mathbf{Pre}_j$, $\mathbf{Post}_j$, and $\mathbf{INV}_j$. To make the formulas more readable we use the following notations:

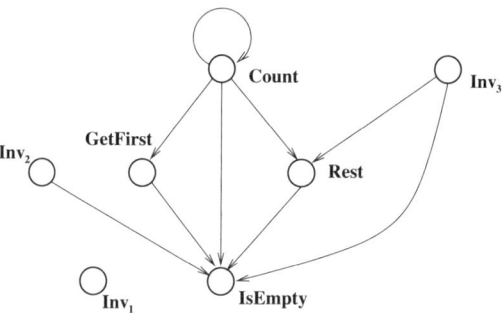

Fig. 2. Dependency graph for interface Sequence

- $\mathbf{SysInv}_j := \forall\, o \in h.\ \bigwedge_{Inv \in \mathbf{INV}_j} Inv$. $\mathbf{SysInv}_j$ is the conjunction of invariants processed up to step j. After the last step z of the construction of the model, we have $\mathbf{SysInv}_z = \mathbf{SysInv}$.
- F_j denotes the set of function symbols whose pre- and postconditions have been processed up to step j: $F_j := \mathbf{dom}(\mathbf{Pre}_j)$, and thus $F_j = \mathbf{dom}(\mathbf{Post}_j)$.
- We denote the axioms for $\mathbf{Spec}_j$ as follows:

$$\mathbf{Ax}_f^j := \forall\, h, o \in h, p \in h.\ \mathbf{SysInv}_j \wedge \mathbf{Pre}_f \Rightarrow \mathbf{Post}_f[f(h,o,p)/res]$$

$$\mathbf{Ax}_{\mathbf{Spec}_j} := \bigwedge_{f \in F_j} \mathbf{Ax}_f^j$$

$\mathbf{Ax}_f^j$ is the definition of the axiom for a function f according to specification $\mathbf{Spec}_j$. Note that the axiom $\mathbf{Ax}_f^j$ may be different for different j since $\mathbf{SysInv}_j$ gets gradually strengthened during the construction of the model. Therefore, the axiom $\mathbf{Ax}_f^j$ becomes gradually weaker. This is an important observation for the soundness of our approach. After the last step z of the construction of the model, we have $\mathbf{Ax}_f^z = \mathbf{Ax}_f$ and $\mathbf{Ax}_{\mathbf{Spec}_z} = \mathbf{Ax}_{\mathbf{Spec}}$.

The following proof obligations are posed on the three different types of specification fragments in step j.

Invariant $\mathbf{Inv}_l$. The invariant $\mathbf{Inv}_l$ must be well-defined for each object, provided the invariants $\mathbf{SysInv}_{j-1}$ hold.

$$\mathbf{Ax}_{\mathbf{Spec}_{j-1}} \Rightarrow \forall\, h.\ (\mathbf{SysInv}_{j-1} \Rightarrow \Delta(\forall\, o \in h.\ \mathbf{Inv}_l, \mathbf{Pre}_{j-1})) \tag{2}$$

Note that we use preconditions $\mathbf{Pre}_{j-1}$ as domain restriction. Although invariants additionally restrict the domain of functions, these restrictions are never violated due to the assumption that $\mathbf{SysInv}_{j-1}$ holds.

Example. We instantiate the proof obligation for a specification fragment from Fig. 1. The corresponding dependency graph is presented in Fig. 2. The traversal of the dependency graph first visits the first invariant since it has no dependencies. The well-definedness of the invariant is trivial. Next, the traversal takes method IsEmpty, which is also processed trivially since the method has no specifications. As third node, the second invariant is picked. For this specification fragment, the following proof obligation is generated.

$\forall\ h.\ ((\forall\ o \in h.\ h[o, Length] \geq 0) \Rightarrow$
$\Delta(\forall\ o \in h.\ IsEmpty(h, o) \Rightarrow h[o, Length] = 0, \{\langle IsEmpty, true\rangle\}))$

where $h[o, f]$ denotes field access with receiver object o and field f in heap h. Note that $\mathbf{Ax_{Spec_2}}$ has been omitted since it is equivalent to true. After the application of the Δ operator, the proof obligation requires one to prove that (1) o is non-null since it is the receiver of a method call and a field access, and that (2) the domain restriction of $IsEmpty$ is not violated. The first property holds since $o \in h$, the second since the domain restriction of $IsEmpty$ is true. □

Pre- and Postcondition of a Single Function f_l. This case requires two proof obligations for the non-recursive pre- and postcondition of f_l, respectively. The first proof obligation checks that the precondition of f_l is defined for all receiver objects and parameters in all heaps in which the invariants hold.

$$\mathbf{Ax_{Spec_{j-1}}} \Rightarrow \forall\ h, o \in h, p \in h.\ (\mathbf{SysInv}_{j-1} \Rightarrow \Delta(\mathbf{Pre}_{f_l}, \mathbf{Pre}_{j-1})) \quad (3)$$

Example. Assume method Rest is selected as fourth specification fragment. The corresponding proof obligation is the following.

$\forall\ h, o \in h.$
$(\ (\forall\ o \in h.\ h[o, Length] \geq 0\ \wedge\ (IsEmpty(h, o) \Rightarrow h[o, Length] = 0)) \Rightarrow$
$\Delta(\neg IsEmpty(h, o), \{\langle IsEmpty, true\rangle\})\ )$

Again, $\mathbf{Ax_{Spec_3}}$ has been omitted since it is equivalent to true. After the application of the Δ operator, the same properties need to be proven as above: o is non-null and the domain restriction of $IsEmpty$ is not violated. □

The second proof obligation checks that the postcondition of f_l is never interpreted as $\bot$ for any result, and that there exists a value which satisfies the postcondition for all receiver objects and parameters that satisfy the precondition in all heaps in which the invariants hold.

$$\mathbf{Ax_{Spec_{j-1}}} \Rightarrow \forall\ h, o \in h, p \in h.\ (\mathbf{SysInv}_{j-1} \wedge \mathbf{Pre}_{f_l} \Rightarrow \quad (4)$$
$$(\forall\ res.\ \Delta(\mathbf{Post}_{f_l}, \mathbf{Pre}_{j-1})) \wedge (\exists\ res.\ \mathbf{Post}_{f_l}))$$

Example. The proof obligation for the postcondition of method Rest is:
$\forall\ h, o \in h.$
$(\ (\forall\ o \in h.\ h[o, Length] \geq 0\ \wedge\ (IsEmpty(h, o) \Rightarrow h[o, Length] = 0))\ \wedge$
$\neg IsEmpty(h, o)$
$\Rightarrow$
$(\forall\ res.\ \Delta(res \neq null, \{\langle IsEmpty, true\rangle\})) \wedge (\exists\ res.\ res \neq null)\ )$

As before, $\mathbf{Ax_{Spec_3}}$ is equivalent to true. The first conjunct is proved trivially since formula $res \neq null$ does not contain any partial operation. To satisfy the second conjunct, we instantiate res with o. □

Pre- and Postconditions of a Set of Recursively-Specified Functions.
This case handles both direct and mutual recursion. That is, we have a set of functions $G_j := \{g_1, g_2, \ldots, g_k\}$ with $k \geq 1$. We assume that for each function g_i in G_j the programmer provides a measure function $\|\cdot\|_{g_i} : \mathbf{Heap} \times \mathbf{R} \times \mathbf{R} \to \mathbb{N}$ using the **Measure** attribute. We assume that there is no recursion via measure functions, that is, the definition of measure function $\|\cdot\|_{g_i}$ may only contain function symbols from $G_1 \cup \ldots \cup G_{j-1}$, but not from G_j.

Since preconditions must not be recursively specified (see Sec. 3.2), the proof obligation for the precondition of each g_i is identical to proof obligation (3) for the non-recursive case.

In order to prove well-formedness of postconditions, we first need to show that user-specified measures are well-defined and non-negative. For a function g_i with measure attribute **Measure**$=\mu_{g_i}$, we introduce a new pure method M_{g_i} with precondition $\mathbf{Pre}_{g_i}$ and postcondition $\mu_{g_i} \geq 0$. The dependency graph is extended with a node for M_{g_i} and an edge from g_i to M_{g_i}. Node M_{g_i} is processed like any other node. This allows measures to rely on invariants and to contain calls to pure methods.

Proof obligation (5) below for postconditions is similar to proof obligation (4), but differs in two ways: First, we have to prove that the recursive specification is well-founded. Since we have already shown that our measure functions yield non-negative numbers, it suffices to show that the measure decreases for each recursive application. We achieve this by using a domain restriction that additionally requires the measure for recursive applications to be lower than the measure *ind* of the function being specified. If the measure *ind* is 0, the domain restriction becomes false, which prevents further recursion. Note that the occurrence of *ind* seems to violate the condition that domain restrictions do not contain free variables other than the parameters of the function whose domain they characterize. However, since *ind* is universally quantified, we may consider *ind* to be a constant for each particular application of the domain restriction. (One could think of the universal quantification as an unbounded conjunction, where *ind* is a constant in each of the conjuncts.)

Second, for the proof of well-formedness of the specification of a function g_i, we may assume the properties of the functions recursively applied in this specification. This is an induction scheme over the measure *ind*, which is expressed by the assumption in lines 4 and 5 of the following proof obligation, which must be shown for each method g_i.

$$\mathbf{Ax}_{\mathbf{Spec}_{j-1}} \Rightarrow$$
$$\forall \, ind \in \mathbb{N}, h, o \in h, p \in h.$$
$$(\mathbf{SysInv}_{j-1} \wedge \mathbf{Pre}_{g_i} \wedge \|\langle h, o, p \rangle\|_{g_i} = ind \,\wedge$$
$$(\bigwedge_{l=1}^{k} \forall \, o' \in h, p' \in h. \; \mathbf{Pre}_{g_l}[o'/o, p'/p] \,\wedge\, \|\langle h, o', p' \rangle\|_{g_l} < ind \Rightarrow \quad (5)$$
$$\mathbf{Post}_{g_l}[o'/o, p'/p, g_l(h, o', p')/res])$$
$$\Rightarrow$$
$$(\forall \, res. \; \Delta(\mathbf{Post}_{g_i}, \mathbf{Pre}_{j-1} \cup \{\langle g_l, \mathbf{Pre}_{g_l} \wedge \|\langle h, o, p \rangle\|_{g_l} < ind \rangle \,|\, l \in 1..k\})) \,\wedge$$
$$(\exists \, res. \; \mathbf{Post}_{g_i}))$$

Example. Since the size of proof obligation (5) for the postcondition of method Count (the only recursive specification in our example) is rather large, we use a considerably smaller example here, namely the factorial function with the following specification.

```
[Pure][Measure=p] int Fact(int p)
  requires p >= 0;
  ensures p == 0 ==> result == 1;
  ensures p > 0 ==> result == Fact(p-1)*p;
```

To simplify the example, we omit the variables for heap h and receiver object o.

First, we need to prove that measure p is well-defined and non-negative. This is trivially proven since the measure does not contain partial operators and the precondition of Fact guarantees that p is non-negative.

Next, we need to show proof obligation (5). For brevity, we only show it for the second postcondition, which is the interesting case containing recursion:

$\forall\ ind \in \mathbb{N}, p.$
$\quad (p \geq 0\ \wedge\ p = ind\ \wedge$
$\quad\ (\forall\ p'.\ p' \geq 0 \wedge p' < ind\ \Rightarrow$
$\quad\quad\quad (p' = 0 \Rightarrow Fact(p') = 1)\ \wedge\ (p' > 0 \Rightarrow Fact(p') = Fact(p'-1) * p'))$
$\quad \Rightarrow$
$\quad (\forall\ res.\ \Delta(p > 0 \Rightarrow res = Fact(p-1) * p, \{\langle Fact,\ p \geq 0 \wedge p < ind \rangle\ \}))\ \wedge$
$\quad (\exists\ res.\ p > 0 \Rightarrow res = Fact(p-1) * p)\ )$

We need to show that the two quantified conjuncts on the right-hand side of the implication hold. Proving that the existential holds is straightforward due to the equality. The other conjunct is more interesting. The only partial operator is $Fact$ and after applying the Δ operator the sub-formula simplifies to:

$\forall\ res.\ p > 0 \Rightarrow p - 1 \geq 0\ \wedge\ p - 1 < ind$

The first conjunct is provable from $p > 0$ and the second from $p = ind$ in the premise of the proof obligation. □

Soundness. The above proof obligations are sufficient to show that a specification is well-formed:

> **Theorem.** If a specification **Spec** does not contain recursive preconditions and all of the above proof obligations for **Spec** hold then **Spec** is well-formed, that is, $\models$ **Spec** holds.

The proof of this theorem runs by induction on the order of specification fragments given by the dependency graph. For each recursive specification fragment, the proof uses a nested induction on the recursion depth ind. Due to lack of space, we refer to [23] for a detailed proof sketch.

Modularity. In general, adding new classes to a program does not invalidate the proofs for the well-formedness criteria of existing methods and invariants.

This is because we assume behavioral subtyping, which ensures that the axiom for an overriding method is weaker than the axiom for the overridden method. Although new classes can introduce cycles in the dependency graph that involve existing methods, proofs remain valid since we introduce new function symbols for overriding methods, which thus do not interfere with existing proofs.

The invariants of additional classes strengthen **SysInv**, which appears as part of the premises of proof obligations; thus, they weaken the proof obligations.

4 Application with Automatic Theorem Provers

The proof obligations presented in the previous section are sufficient to show the well-formedness of a specification. However, they are not well-suited for automatic theorem provers such as Simplify [14] or Z3 for two reasons. First, the proof obligations to ensure consistency for postconditions (proof obligations (4) and (5)) contain existential quantifiers, for which automatic theorem provers often do not find suitable instantiations. Second, the proof obligation for the well-foundedness of recursive specifications (proof obligation (5)) is in general proved by induction on *ind*, but induction is not supported well by automatic theorem provers. In this section, we discuss these issues.

Consistency. Spec# uses four approaches to find witnesses for the satisfiability of a specification, that is, instantiations for the existential quantifiers[1]. First, if a postcondition has the form `result R E`, where R is a reflexive operator and E is an expression that does not contain `result` and recursive calls, then there always exists a possible result value, namely, the value of E [12]. Thus, this part of the proof obligations can be dropped. Second, if a pure method has a body of the form `return E`, where E does not contain a recursive call, then expression E is a likely candidate for a witness. It suffices to use a simplified proof obligation to show that this candidate actually is a witness. Third, for many postconditions, good candidates for witnesses can be inferred by simple heuristics. For instance, for a postcondition `result > E`, one might try `E + 1`. Finally, if the former approaches do not work, Spec# allows programmers to specify witnesses for model fields explicitly. One could use the same approach for pure methods.

Well-Foundedness. Proof obligation (5) in general requires induction. For instance, if function $f(n)$ has a postcondition $(n = 0 \Rightarrow res = 1) \wedge (n > 0 \Rightarrow res = 1/f(n-1))$, one needs to apply induction to prove that f never returns zero. However, induction is needed only if the function is specified recursively *and* the recursive call occurs as an argument to a partial function, as in this example. In our experience, this is not the case for most specifications. For instance, proving proof obligation (5) for the factorial function does not require induction, as we have shown in Sec. 3.3. Therefore, this proof obligation is not a major limitation in practice.

---
[1] Most of these approaches were proposed and implemented by Rustan Leino and Ronald Middelkoop.

5 Related Work

We sketch what three important groups of formal systems do in the areas of consistency and well-definedness checking.

Theorem Provers. Isabelle [22] is an interactive LCF-style theorem proving framework based on a small logical core. Everything on top of the core is supposed to be defined by conservative extensions, which ensures the consistency of the specification. The use of axioms is possible but discouraged since inconsistency may be introduced. Recursion (both direct and mutual) is supported and the well-foundedness of the recursion has to be proven. Isabelle handles partiality by under-specification [15] and requires no well-definedness checks.

PVS [11] is similar to Isabelle with respect to consistency guarantees. The main difference is in the modeling of partial functions. Although PVS also considers functions to be total, predicate subtyping is used to restrict the domain of functions. This makes the type system undecidable leading to Type Correctness Conditions to be proven [24].

Formal Software Development Systems. Z is a formal specification language for computing systems [25]. The work closest to ours is the approach of Hall et al., which shows how a model conjecture can be derived from a Z specification [16]. Partiality is handled by under-specification [26].

The B method [1] is similar to Z but is more focused on the notion of refinement. Satisfiability of the specification has to be proven in each refinement step. B allows users to add axioms whose consistency is not checked. Thus, they may introduce unsoundness. B allows functions to be partial and requires specifications to be well-defined by using the Δ formula transformer [4].

VDM [18] also checks satisfiability of specifications and allows the use of (possibly inconsistent) axioms. VDM uses LPF [3], a 3-valued logic. In contrast to our approach, well-definedness is not proven before the actual proof process, but is proven together with the validity of verification conditions.

Program Verifiers. ESC/Java2 [19] is an automatic extended static checker for Java programs annotated with JML specifications. The tool axiomatizes specifications of pure methods [10]. Consistency of the axiom system is not ensured, which can lead to unsoundness. Recently, well-definedness checks have been added by Chalin [9] but it is not clear how dependencies among specification elements are handled, and no soundness proof is provided.

Jack [7] is a program verifier for JML annotated Java programs. The backend prover of the tool is Coq [6]. The tool axiomatizes pre- and postconditions of pure methods separately. This separation ensures that axioms are only instantiated when a pure-method call occurs in a given verification condition—as opposed to be available to the theorem prover at any time. However, since Jack does not check consistency, unsoundness can still occur by the use of axioms. Jack does not support mutual recursion and does not check well-definedness.

The Spec# program verifier ensures consistency of axioms over pure methods by the approaches described in Sec. 4 and by allowing programmers to declare a static call-order on pure methods. Only a simple form of recursive specifications is supported where the measure is based on the ownership relation. The well-foundedness of this relation can be checked by the compiler without proof obligations [12]. Spec# does not fully check well-definedness of specifications.

Our technique improves on our own earlier work [13] by allowing pure-method calls in invariants, ensuring well-formedness of specifications, supporting mutual recursion, taking dependencies into account, and by precisely defining what the proposed proof obligations guarantee. On the other hand, [13] handles weak-purity which we omitted in this paper for simplicity. However, our work could be extended following the technique described in [13].

6 Conclusion

Well-formedness of specifications is important to meet programmer expectations, to reconcile static and runtime assertion checking, and to ensure soundness of static verification. We presented a new technique to check the well-formedness of specifications. We showed how to incrementally construct a model for the specification, which guarantees that the partiality constraints of operations are respected and that the axiomatization of pure methods is consistent. Our technique can be applied in any verification system, regardless of its contract language, logic, or backend theorem prover. As a proof of concept, we implemented our technique in the Spec# verification system.

As future work, we plan to develop adapted proof obligations that require induction in fewer cases. We expect that this can be done by generating specific proof obligations for each given recursive call, which encode the inductive argument. We also plan to investigate how to conveniently specify measures for methods that traverse object structures.

Acknowledgments. We are grateful to Julien Charles, Farhad Mehta, and Burkhart Wolff for helpful discussions on related work. Thanks also to the anonymous reviewers for their insightful comments. Geraldine von Roten implemented the presented technique in the Spec# system.

This work was funded in part by the Information Society Technologies program of the European Commission, Future and Emerging Technologies under the IST-2005-015905 MOBIUS project.

References

1. Abrial, J.R.: The B Book: Assigning Programs to Meanings. Cambridge University Press, Cambridge (1996)
2. Barnett, M., Leino, K.R.M., Schulte, W.: The Spec# programming system: An overview. In: Barthe, G., Burdy, L., Huisman, M., Lanet, J.-L., Muntean, T. (eds.) CASSIS 2004. LNCS, vol. 3362, pp. 49–69. Springer, Heidelberg (2005)
3. Barringer, H., Cheng, J.H., Jones, C.B.: A logic covering undefinedness in program proofs. Acta Informatica 21, 251–269 (1984)
4. Behm, P., Burdy, L., Meynadier, J.-M.: Well Defined B. In: International B Conference, pp. 29–45. Springer-Verlag, Heidelberg (1998)

5. Berezin, S., Barrett, C., Shikanian, I., Chechik, M., Gurfinkel, A., Dill, D.L.: A practical approach to partial functions in CVC Lite. In: PDPAR (2004)
6. Bertot, Y., Castéran, P.: Interactive Theorem Proving and Program Development. Coq'Art: The Calculus of Inductive Constructions. In: Texts in Theoretical Computer Science, Springer, Heidelberg (2004)
7. Burdy, L., Requet, A., Lanet, J.-L.: Java applet correctness: A developer-oriented approach. In: Araki, K., Gnesi, S., Mandrioli, D. (eds.) FME 2003. LNCS, vol. 2805, pp. 422–439. Springer, Heidelberg (2003)
8. Chalin, P.: Are the logical foundations of verifying compiler prototypes matching user expectations? Formal Aspects of Computing 19(2), 139–158 (2007)
9. Chalin, P.: A sound assertion semantics for the dependable systems evolution verifying compiler. In: ICSE, pp. 23–33. IEEE Computer Society Press, Los Alamitos (2007)
10. Cok, D.: Reasoning with specifications containing method calls and model fields. Journal of Object Technology 4(8), 77–103 (2005)
11. Crow, J., Owre, S., Rushby, J., Shankar, N., Srivas, M.: A Tutorial Introduction to PVS (April 1995)
12. Darvas, Á., Leino, K.R.M.: Practical reasoning about invocations and implementations of pure methods. In: Dwyer, M.B., Lopes, A. (eds.) FASE 2007. LNCS, vol. 4422, pp. 336–351. Springer, Heidelberg (2007)
13. Darvas, Á., Müller, P.: Reasoning About Method Calls in Interface Specifications. Journal of Object Technology (JOT) 5(5), 59–85 (2006)
14. Detlefs, D., Nelson, G., Saxe, J.B.: Simplify: A theorem prover for program checking. Technical Report HPL-2003-148, HP Labs (2003)
15. Gries, D., Schneider, F.B.: Avoiding the undefined by underspecification. In: van Leeuwen, J. (ed.) Computer Science Today. LNCS, vol. 1000, pp. 366–373. Springer, Heidelberg (1995)
16. Hall, J.G., McDermid, J.A., Toyn, I.: Model conjectures for Z specifications. In: 7th International Conference on Putting into Practice Methods and Tools for Information System Design, pp. 41–51 (1995)
17. Hoogewijs, A.: On a formalization of the non-definedness notion. Zeitschrift für Mathematische Logik und Grundlagen der Mathematik 25, 213–217 (1979)
18. Jones, C.B.: Systematic software development using VDM. Prentice-Hall, Englewood Cliffs (1986)
19. Kiniry, J.R., Cok, D.R.: ESC/Java2: Uniting ESC/Java and JML. In: Barthe, G., Burdy, L., Huisman, M., Lanet, J.-L., Muntean, T. (eds.) CASSIS 2004. LNCS, vol. 3362, pp. 108–128. Springer, Heidelberg (2005)
20. Kleene, S.C.: Introduction to Metamathematics. Van Nostrand (1952)
21. Leavens, G.T., Baker, A.L., Ruby, C.: Preliminary design of JML: a behavioral interface specification language for Java. ACM SIGSOFT Software Engineering Notes 31(3), 1–38 (2006)
22. Nipkow, T., Paulson, L.C., Wenzel, M.T.: Isabelle/HOL — A Proof Assistant for Higher-Order Logic. LNCS, vol. 2283. Springer, Heidelberg (2002)
23. Rudich, A., Darvas, Á., Müller, P.: Checking well-formedness of pure-method specifications (Full Paper). Technical Report 588, ETH Zurich (2008)
24. Rushby, J., Owre, S., Shankar, N.: Subtypes for Specifications: Predicate Subtyping in PVS. IEEE Transactions on Software Engineering 24(9), 709–720 (1998)
25. Spivey, J.M.: Understanding Z: a specification language and its formal semantics. Cambridge University Press, Cambridge (1988)
26. Valentine, S.H.: Inconsistency and Undefinedness in Z - A Practical Guide. In: International Conference of Z Users, pp. 233–249. Springer, Heidelberg (1998)

Verifying Dynamic Pointer-Manipulating Threads

Thomas Noll and Stefan Rieger

RWTH Aachen University
Software Modeling and Verification Group
52056 Aachen, Germany
{noll,rieger}@cs.rwth-aachen.de

Abstract. We present a novel approach to the verification of concurrent pointer-manipulating programs with dynamic thread creation and memory allocation as well as destructive updates operating on arbitrary (possibly cyclic) singly-linked data structures. Correctness properties of such programs are expressed by combining a simple pointer logic for specifying heap properties with linear-time (LTL) operators for reasoning about system executions. To automatically solve the corresponding model-checking problem, which is undecidable in general, we abstract from non-interrupted sublists in the heap, resulting in a finite-state representation of the data space. We also show that the control flow of a concurrent program with unbounded thread creation can be characterized by a Petri net, making LTL model checking decidable (though not feasible in practice). In a second abstraction step we also derive a finite-state representation of the control flow, which then allows us to employ standard LTL model checking techniques.

1 Introduction

Techniques for the verification of elementary properties of pointer programs are highly desirable. Programming with pointers is error-prone with potential pitfalls such as dereferencing null pointers and the emergence of memory leaks. So far, the field of pointer analysis has primarily focused on sequential programs. But pointer programming becomes even more vulnerable in a concurrent setting where threads can be dynamically created, and where data structures such as linked lists are shared between several threads.

We present an approach to model checking concurrent programs that operate on singly-linked data structures. It stays within the realm of traditional (linear-time) model checking. This facilitates the usage of standard model checkers for validating temporal properties addressing absence of memory leaks, dereferencing of null pointers, dynamic creation of cells, and simple and position-dependent aliasing.

Our approach is illustrated by considering a simple concurrent programming language that besides the usual control structures offers primitives for thread creation, pointer manipulation, cell creation and destruction, and (guarded) atomic regions that allow to implement concurrency control constructs such as test-and-set primitives, semaphores, and monitors.

The operational semantics of our language is defined in a modular way. The *control-flow semantics* is given by a (finite) Petri net whose places correspond to the control locations of the program. The *heap semantics* is specified by transformation rules which describe the effect of executing single commands.

The combination of both yields a labeled transition system (modeled by a Petri net) which is generally infinite due to the unbounded creation of both control threads and heap cells. Its desirable properties are expressed in a first-order linear-time temporal logic (LTL) that is enriched with assertions on pointer structures such as reachability and freshness of cells, or pointer aliasing.

Since the model-checking problem is generally undecidable in this setting we introduce a first abstraction, which addresses the data space of the program. Our list abstraction exploits a variant of summary nodes [7] to obtain a finite representation of the heap and thus eliminates one potential source of undecidability. In fact, known results then allow us to conclude that the data abstract model-checking problem is decidable even though the underlying transition system is still infinite (see Thm. 5.7). However, its intractability forces us to apply a second abstraction step in which we also derive a finite-state representation of the control flow, which altogether yields a finite transition system. As a result, standard LTL model-checking algorithms can be employed. Both abstractions are obtained in a fully mechanized manner. Moreover they are sound in the sense that they over-approximate the concrete program behavior.

2 Related Work

Related work on the topic of analyzing pointer-manipulating programs can be classified into the following (often overlapping) categories, which mainly focus on sequential programming languages: *predicate abstraction* [1,8,23], *shape analysis* [2,26,27], *regular model checking* [3,5], *dataflow analysis* [21,33,34], *Hoare-style approaches* [6,18], and *separation logic* [22,24]. In summary, many of the characterizing features of our approach are already present in earlier papers: the restriction to singly-linked lists without data fields [1,3,11,16,19,20] which still allows to model many practical applications such as device drivers, the introduction of abstract entities which represent a potentially unbounded number of heap cells (called "summary nodes" in [7]), and the observation that, in this setting, the number of sharing points in heap structures is bounded by the number of program variables [1,4,20].

Pointer analysis in connection with concurrency is only considered in rather few places. Most publications concentrate on specific questions such as aliasing or escape analysis [25,28] or the analysis of safety properties [13,30], or particular applications such as concurrent garbage collection are studied [9,10,29]. To our knowledge, the only pointer logics allowing to specify liveness properties of concurrent systems are ETL [31] and NTL [11]. In contrast to these, however, we avoid the use of temporal operators inside quantification. In this way, involved mechanisms to keep track of the identities of individual heap nodes are not required.

Thus our approach is unique in that it supports concurrent programs with dynamic thread creation, memory allocation, and destructive updates operating on arbitrary (possibly cyclic) linked lists. Moreover it integrates both abstraction and model checking in a fully automated way and supports a linear-time logic in which both safety and liveness properties can be expressed, allowing to use standard LTL model checkers.

3 A List-Manipulating Programming Language

Given sets PV of program variables and $\mathcal{P}$ of thread names, a *dynamic list-manipulating program* (DLMP) π has the form ($v_i, v \in PV$ and $p_j, p \in \mathcal{P}$)

$$\pi = \mathbf{var}\ v_1, ..., v_k;\ \mathbf{proc\ main}(S_0);\ p_1(S_1); ...;\ p_l(S_l)$$

Here each S_i ($0 \leq i \leq l$) is of the form $s_{i1}; ...; s_{ir_i}$ with $s_{ij} \in \text{CMD}$, where CMD is the set of the following commands:

PExp := PExp	pointer assignment	**new**(PExp)	object creation
if BExp **goto** n	conditional jump	**del**(PExp)	object destruction
goto n	unconditional jump	**spawn**(p)	spawn instance of thread p
atc(BExp)	guarded atomic region	**exit**	thread termination
end atc	end of atomic region		

Pointer expressions (PExp) comprise the special constant *nil* denoting an undefined pointer value, a program variable, or the (de)referencing of a program variable. Arbitrary dereferencing depths can be emulated using a sequence of atomic assignments. The *Boolean expressions* (BExp) are standard.

PExp ::= *nil* | v | $*v$ | $\&v$ BExp ::= PExp = PExp | BExp $\wedge$ BExp | $\neg$BExp

Note that we do not allow nesting of atomic regions. In the following we assume for simplicity that π as above is globally given (if not mentioned otherwise).

Fig. 1 shows a DLM-program that simulates a simple server/worker scenario. The server creates new objects in an infinite loop and inserts them into a list. For each object a new worker thread is spawned deleting one object from the list when it is executed. Without imposing fairness constraints this may lead to an infinite number of both objects and threads.

Petri Nets. We use Petri nets to describe the operational semantics of DLMPs.

Definition 3.1. *A Petri net is a tuple* $\mathfrak{P} = (P, T, src, tgt, \ell, m_0)$ *where P is a set of* places, T *a set of* transitions, $src, tgt : T \to 2^P$ *associate each transition with its source and target places,* $\ell : T \to L$ *is a transition* labeling function, *and $m_0 : P \to \mathbb{N}$ the initial marking. A state of $\mathfrak{P}$ is a marking $m : P \to \mathbb{N}$. The set of all markings is denoted by Mark($\mathfrak{P}$).*

Petri nets are high-level representations of (infinite) transition systems whose transitions are characterized by the *token game*. If in a marking m a transition t is enabled, i.e. $m(p) > 0$ for all $p \in src(t)$, and if its firing yields m', we write $m \triangleright_t m'$. $m \triangleright m'$ means that there exists $t \in T$ such that $m \triangleright_t m'$.

Definition 3.2 (Run). Let $\mathfrak{P} = (P, T, src, tgt, \ell, m_0)$ be a Petri net. A run of $\mathfrak{P}$ is a (possibly infinite) sequence of markings $\rho = m_0 m_1 m_2 ... \in Mark(\mathfrak{P})^* \cup Mark(\mathfrak{P})^\omega$ such that $m_i \triangleright m_{i+1}$. The set of all those runs is denoted by $Runs(\mathfrak{P})$.
For $\rho = m_0 m_1 ... \in Runs(\mathfrak{P})$ let $|\rho| \in \mathbb{N} \cup \{\infty\}$ be the length of ρ. We write $\rho[k]$ to denote the suffix starting from the k-th marking, i.e., $m_k m_{k+1}... \in Runs(P, T, src, tgt, \ell, m_k)$ which implies $\rho[k] = \varepsilon$ for $|\rho| \leq k$, and we set $\rho_i := m_i$.

Finally we call a Petri net k-safe if at no time any place holds more than k tokens and bounded if there exists a k for which it is k-safe. Clearly only bounded Petri nets can be represented by finite transition systems.

Concrete Heap Semantics. Defining the semantics of DLM-programs requires a formal model of the heap.

Definition 3.3. A heap configuration is a tuple $H = (N, A, \mu, F)$ with a set of nodes $N \supseteq PV$, a set of abstract nodes $A \subseteq N \setminus PV$, a successor function $\mu : N \to N_{nil}$ (where $N_{nil} := N \cup \{nil\}$), and a set of flags $F \subseteq \text{Flags} := \{err, leak, del\} \cup \{new_n \mid n \in N\} \cup \{spawn_p \mid p \in \mathcal{P}\}$.
$\mathbf{H}$ denotes the set of all heap configurations; $\mathbf{H_\emptyset} \subseteq \mathbf{H}$ the set of all concrete ones (i.e., those with $A = \emptyset$).

The nodes represent both the dynamic objects at runtime and the static program variables (which cannot be deleted). Edges, as formalized by the μ-function, encode the points-to information of a specific program state. The set A of abstract nodes will later be used for our heap abstraction technique (see Sct. 4) and will be empty throughout the current section. Finally the flags give special information about a state, e.g., whether a runtime error or memory leak occurred, a node was created or deleted, or a thread has been spawned.

To delete unreachable nodes that do not influence program semantics a garbage collection mapping denoted by $\downarrow$ is applied. Whenever it removes an unreachable node, it sets the leak flag to indicate a potential memory leak.

```
var x, y;
proc main(
01    new(x);
02    spawn(server); )

server(
11    spawn(worker);
12    atc(tt);
13        y := x;
14        new(x);
15        *x := y;
16    end atc;
17    goto 11; )

worker(
21    atc(x ≠ nil);
22        y := x;
23        x := *x;
24        del(y);
25    end atc; )
```

Fig. 1. Server/Worker

Definition 3.4. Let $H = (N, \emptyset, \mu, F) \in \mathbf{H_\emptyset}$. The semantics of pointer expressions is given by the partial function $[\![\cdot]\!] : \text{PExp} \rightharpoonup N_{nil}$, defined as follows (where $\bot$ denotes the undefined value).[1]

$[\![nil]\!] := nil \qquad [\![v]\!] := \mu(v) \qquad [\![*v]\!] := \mu([\![v]\!]) \qquad [\![\&v]\!] := v$

The semantics of Boolean expressions, $[\![\cdot]\!] : \text{BExp} \rightharpoonup \mathbb{B}$, is standard but strict, i.e., it becomes undefined if at least one subexpression is undefined.

---
[1] The definition implies $\mu(nil) = \bot$ and so $[\![\cdot]\!]$ can indeed yield undefined results.

The effect of executing a program statement is captured by a transition relation which associates the source and target heap configuration with the given statement and an indicator from the set $\{0, 1, \bot\}$. Here 1 denotes the normal execution of a statement or the selection of the then-branch of an **if**-command, 0 only occurs in the else-branch of **if**-statements, and $\bot$ represents the failure of a command (e.g., dereferencing a null-pointer).

Definition 3.5. *The* heap transformation relation, $\to_h \subseteq (\boldsymbol{H_\emptyset} \backslash \{H_{\mathrm{err}}\}) \times \mathrm{CMD} \times \{0, 1, \bot\} \times \boldsymbol{H_\emptyset}$, *is given as follows. Here $H_{\mathrm{err}} := (PV, \emptyset, \{v \mapsto \mathrm{nil} \mid v \in PV\}, \{\mathrm{err}\})$, $H = (N, A, \mu, F) \in \boldsymbol{H_\emptyset} \setminus \{H_{\mathrm{err}}\}$ with $A = \emptyset$, and $f[x/y]$ denotes a function update where y is the new value of x. (We only show some example rules.)*

$$\frac{[\![\alpha]\!] \neq \bot}{H, v := \alpha \xrightarrow{1}_h (N, A, \mu[v/[\![\alpha]\!]], \emptyset)\downarrow} \qquad \frac{[\![\alpha]\!] = \bot}{H, v := \alpha \xrightarrow{\bot}_h H_{\mathrm{err}}}$$

$$\overline{H, \mathbf{new}(v) \xrightarrow{1}_h (N \uplus \{n\}, A, \mu[v/n], \{\mathrm{new}_n\})\downarrow}$$

$$\frac{[\![\alpha]\!] \neq \mathrm{nil}}{H, \mathbf{del}(\alpha) \xrightarrow{1}_h (N \setminus \{[\![\alpha]\!]\}, A, \mu[[\![\alpha]\!]/\bot, \mu^{-1}([\![\alpha]\!])/\mathrm{nil}], \{\mathrm{del}\})\downarrow}$$

$$\frac{[\![b]\!] \neq \bot}{H, \mathbf{if}\ b\ \mathbf{goto}\ n \xrightarrow{[\![b]\!]}_h (N, A, \mu, \emptyset)} \qquad \frac{[\![b]\!] = \bot}{H, \mathbf{if}\ b\ \mathbf{goto}\ n \xrightarrow{\bot}_h H_{\mathrm{err}}}$$

$$\frac{[\![b]\!] = 1}{H, \mathbf{atc}(b) \xrightarrow{1}_h \hat{H}} \qquad \frac{[\![b]\!] = \bot}{H, \mathbf{atc}(b) \xrightarrow{\bot}_h H_{\mathrm{err}}}$$

Note that the heap flags (except err) are only active in the configuration directly following the corresponding event.

As our final goal is to combine the heap and control-flow semantics, we now represent the heap transformation relation by a Petri net. The labels will later be used for synchronizing the two nets.

Definition 3.6. *The* concrete heap semantics *is the (infinite, 1-safe) Petri net $\mathfrak{P}^h := (P, T, src, tgt, \ell, m_0)$ with $P \subseteq \boldsymbol{H_\emptyset}$, $T = \{(H, H', c, x) \mid H, c \xrightarrow{x}_h H')\}$, $src(H, H', c, x) = \{H\}$, $tgt(H, H', c, x) = \{H'\}$, $\ell(H, H', c, x) = (c, x)$, $m_0(H_0) = 1$ for a given $H_0 \in P$ (typically the empty heap), and $m_0(H) = 0$ for $H \neq H_0$.*

Control-Flow Semantics. In the context of concurrency and dynamic threading it does not suffice to only consider the effects of certain statements on the heap; the control flow of the program is also crucial. It can again be modeled by a Petri net.

Definition 3.7. *The* control-flow semantics *of π is given by the Petri net $\mathfrak{P}^c := (P, T, src, tgt, \ell, m_0)$ with $P = \{\mathrm{lock}\} \cup \bigcup_{i=0}^{l} \bigcup_{j=1}^{r_i} \{ij\}$, $\ell : T \to \mathrm{CMD} \times \{0, 1, \bot\}$, $m_0(01) = 1$, $m_0(\mathrm{lock}) = 1$ and $m_0(p) = 0$ for all $p \notin \{01, \mathrm{lock}\}$. For $0 \leq i \leq l$ and $1 \leq j \leq r_i$ let lock_{ij} be the singleton set containing lock if s_{ij} is not inside an atomic region and the empty set otherwise. The transitions $(T, src$ and $tgt)$ are then given as follows:*

s_{ij}	$\ell(t)$	$src(t)$	$tgt(t)$
if b **goto** n	$(s_{ij}, 0)$	$\{ij\} \cup \text{lock}_{ij}$	$\{i(j+1)\} \cup \text{lock}_{ij}$
	$(s_{ij}, 1)$	$\{ij\} \cup \text{lock}_{ij}$	$\{in\} \cup \text{lock}_{ij}$
	$(s_{ij}, \bot)$	$\{ij\} \cup \text{lock}_{ij}$	$\emptyset$
goto n	$(s_{ij}, 1)$	$\{ij\} \cup \text{lock}_{ij}$	$\{in\} \cup \text{lock}_{ij}$
atc(b)	$(s_{ij}, 1)$	$\{ij, \text{lock}\}$	$\{i(j+1)\}$
	$(s_{ij}, \bot)$	$\{ij, \text{lock}\}$	$\emptyset$
end atc	$(s_{ij}, 1)$	$\{ij\}$	$\{i(j+1), \text{lock}\}$
spawn(p_x)	$(s_{ij}, 1)$	$\{ij\} \cup \text{lock}_{ij}$	$\{i(j+1), x1\} \cup \text{lock}_{ij}$
exit	$(s_{ij}, 1)$	$\{ij\} \cup \text{lock}_{ij}$	lock
$\alpha := \alpha'$, **new**(α), **del**(α)	$(s_{ij}, 1)$	$\{ij\} \cup \text{lock}_{ij}$	$\{i(j+1)\} \cup \text{lock}_{ij}$
	$(s_{ij}, \bot)$	$\{ij\} \cup \text{lock}_{ij}$	$\emptyset$

If one of the target places is not in P we omit the corresponding out-edge (e.g. in case of thread termination or a jump out of range).

Example 3.8. The graph in Fig. 2 shows the Petri net modeling the control-flow semantics of the program from Fig. 1. The round nodes represent the places and the rectangles the (labeled) transitions of the net. If there are incoming and outgoing edges to the same place they are drawn as bidirectional arrows. In the initial state there are only tokens in the places 01 and lock.

Concrete DLMP-Semantics. Now that we defined the heap as well as the control flow semantics of our programming language we have to combine both.

Definition 3.9. *Let $\mathfrak{P}^c = (P^c, T^c, src^c, tgt^c, \ell^c, m_0^c)$ be the control flow and $\mathfrak{P}^h = (P^h, T^h, src^c, tgt^c, \ell^h, m_0^h)$ the heap semantics of π. The concrete semantics of π is the Petri net $\mathfrak{P} := \mathfrak{P}^c \otimes \mathfrak{P}^h := (P^c \cup P^h, T, src, tgt, \ell, m_0)$ where*

$T = \{((t^c, t^h) \in T^c \times T^h \mid \ell^c(t^c) = \ell^h(t^h)\}$ $\quad \ell(t^c, t^h) = \ell^c(t^c)$
$src(t^c, t^h) = src(t^c) \cup src(t^h)$
$tgt(t^c, t^h) = tgt(t^c) \cup tgt(t^h)$ $\quad m_0(p) = \begin{cases} m_0^c(p) & \text{if } p \in P^c \\ m_0^h(p) & \text{otherwise} \end{cases}$

As one might suspect the concrete semantics cannot be used as-is in verification techniques since DLM-programs are *Turing complete*[2].

4 Data Abstraction

To tackle the verification problem we use heap abstraction techniques to generate a *data abstract semantics* that over-approximates the behavior of the concrete one, i.e., whose runs cover all concrete ones. In our setting this approach is correct but generally incomplete: although we can conclude from the satisfaction of a

---

[2] DLM-programs can simulate a counter machine (the values of the counters are represented by lists of the corresponding length).

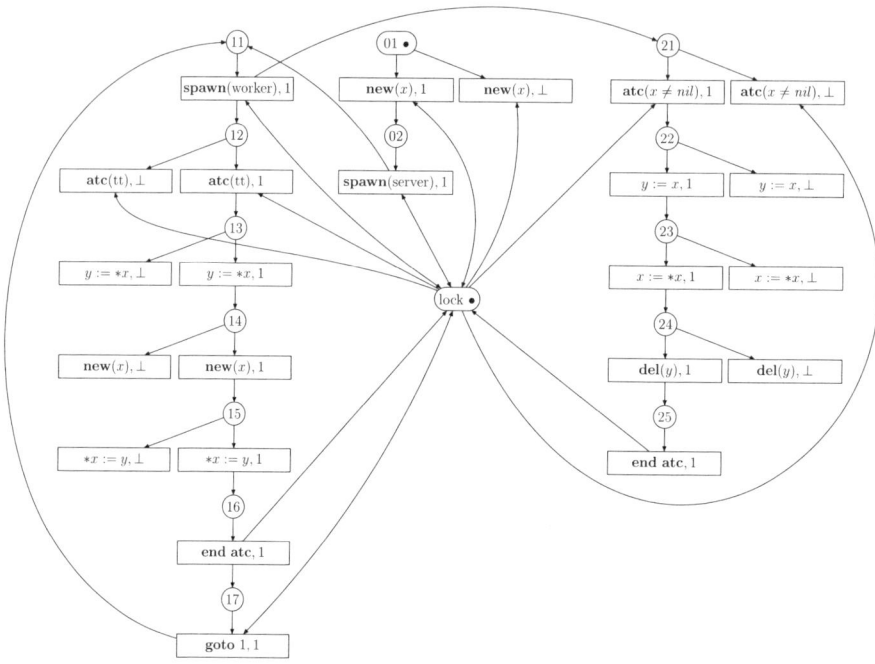

Fig. 2. Control-flow semantics for the server/worker example

property in the abstract state space the validity in the concrete case, the inverse is not possible anymore. Our heap abstraction is parameterized via a global constant $M \in \mathbb{N}$ which allows a systematic refinement. For a given $M > 0$ we set $\mathbb{M} := \{0, 1, ..., M, \star\}$, where $\star$ represents all values greater than M.

Chain Abstraction and Canonical Configurations. For heap abstraction we adopt the idea of *summary nodes*. Summary nodes are not allowed to represent arbitrary structures but only so-called *chains* which are non-interrupted sublists, i.e., list segments where only the head node is allowed to have more than one predecessor. This abstraction technique is well known [7,11,26]. For further details you may also refer to [15].

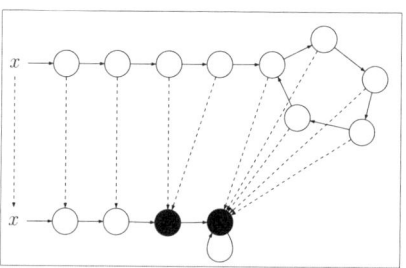

Fig. 3. An Abstraction Morphism

Based on the concept of chains one can define so-called *abstraction morphisms* which are surjective functions of the type $h : N_1 \to N_2$ for $H_i = (N_i, A_i, \mu_i, F_i) \in \mathbf{H}$ that retain the graph structure while collapsing chains of length greater than M to abstract nodes. In Fig. 3 an example is depicted.

We write $H_2 \le H_1$ to denote that there is an abstraction morphism that abstracts H_1 to H_2. In this context we will also write $h(H_1) = H_2$ lifting h to heap configurations. If $|N_1| = |N_2|$, h is an isomorphism. We then write $H_1 \cong H_2$.

Note that a given source configuration can give rise to different abstractions. To obtain a unique canonical representation of a concrete heap configuration we collapse only *maximal* chains and do not abstract nodes that are closer than three μ-steps to a program variable. This yields a concrete expression semantics.

The set of all such canonical configurations is denoted by $\boldsymbol{H}_\natural$. It can be shown that for every concrete heap configuration a unique canonical configuration exists which is related to the former by a morphism $h_\natural$ [15]. We will use it as *abstraction function* in the following. The lower graph in Fig. 3 is a canonical configuration.

Abstract Heap Semantics. Regarding the expression semantics nothing needs to be modified in the data-abstract setting: in a canonical configuration, abstract nodes have a distance greater than two from the variable nodes such that every pointer expression refers to a concrete node. The expression semantics can therefore be chosen identical to the concrete case (Def. 3.4), now interpreted on canonical configurations.

Definition 4.1 (Abstract Heap Transformation Relation). *The abstract heap transformation relation* $\Rightarrow_h \subseteq (\boldsymbol{H}_\natural/_\cong \setminus \{\{H_{\mathrm{err}}\}\}) \times \mathrm{CMD} \times \{0, 1, \bot\} \times \boldsymbol{H}_\natural/_\cong$ *is depicted in Fig. 4 for* $H = (N, A, \mu, F) \in \boldsymbol{H}_\natural$. *We focus on assignments since the other rules are analogous to the concrete case. For simplicity we use representatives of the isomorphism classes.*

In Fig. 4 the semantic rules are visualized by examples. Rules 1 and 2 lead to a potential increase in the distance from variables to abstract nodes: consider an assignment of the form $y := \mathit{nil}$. If y points into a list whose head is referred to by another variable, we possibly increase the distance from that variable to abstract nodes. The assignment therefore potentially yields a non-canonical configuration making a re-abstraction necessary.

In rule 3 there might be the necessity for both concretization and abstraction. The execution of the assignment yields an intermediate configuration which is generally not canonical since the variable v could now be too close to an abstract node. Therefore we have to find a more concrete configuration H' whose abstraction yields the intermediate configuration. There might be more than one solution, thus this rule is nondeterministic (indicated by dashed arrows). After the concretization a re-abstraction is used to obtain the canonical form.

Due to our canonical representation, $\boldsymbol{H}_\natural/_\cong$ is finite and its size depends (linearly) on the number of program variables and the value of the precision constant M^3. This implies the finiteness of the abstract heap semantics but not the boundedness of the data abstract program semantics as defined below.

---

[3] The number of nodes is bounded by $(2M + 3) \cdot |PV|$.

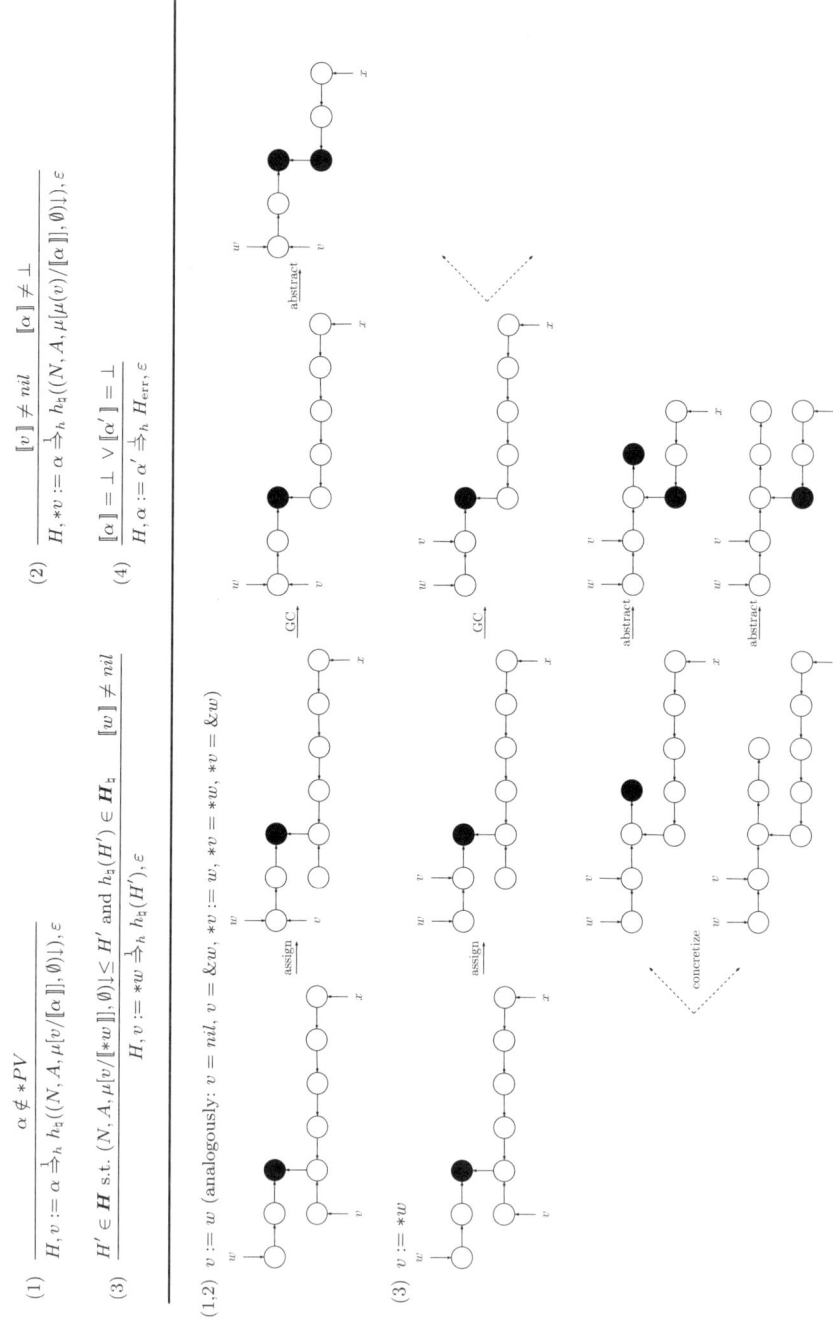

Fig. 4. Abstract rules and exemplary visualization ($M = 2$)

Definition 4.2. *The* abstract heap semantics *is the Petri net* $\mathfrak{P}_\natural^h := (P, T, src, tgt, \ell, m_0)$ *with* $P \subseteq \boldsymbol{H}_\natural/\cong$, $T = \{(K, K', c, x) \mid K, c \xRightarrow{x}_h K'\}$, $\ell(K, K', c, x) = (c, x)$, $src(K, K', c, x) = \{K\}$, $tgt(K, K', c, x) = \{K'\}$ *and* $m_0(K_0) = 1$ *for a* $K_0 \in P$ *(e.g. the empty heap congruence class) and* $m_0(K) = 0$ *for* $K \neq K_0$.

The data abstract program semantics *is given by the Petri net* $\mathfrak{P}_\natural := \mathfrak{P}^c \otimes \mathfrak{P}_\natural^h$ *where* $\otimes$ *is as in Def. 3.9.*

5 A Logic for Pointer Programs

In the previous sections we have defined our programming language and both its concrete and abstract semantics. In this section we will present a logic which allows us to reason about heap configurations and program behavior. In the following LV denotes a set of logical variables with $LV \cap PV = \emptyset$.

Pointer Logic. Pointer Logic deals with single configurations, and can be used to express graph properties as well as to inspect the special heap flags.

Definition 5.1. *We define the set of* Pointer Logic formulae *(PL-formulae) as follows:*

$$\text{NExp} ::= nil \mid v \ (\in PV) \mid x \ (\in LV) \mid *\text{NExp}$$
$$\text{Atomic} ::= \text{tt} \mid \text{ff} \mid f \ (\in \text{Flags}) \mid \text{NExp} = \text{NExp} \mid \text{NExp} \leadsto \text{NExp}$$
$$\text{PL} ::= \text{Atomic} \mid \neg \text{PL} \mid \text{PL} \wedge \text{PL} \mid \exists x : \text{PL}$$

As usual we will use the logical operations $\vee$, $\rightarrow$, and $\forall$ as abbreviations. In contrast to pointer expressions in DLM-programs, the logic supports dereferencing operations of arbitrary depth. The predicate $\leadsto$ expresses the reachability of heap objects, whereas $=$ is true iff both expressions refer to the same object.

Definition 5.2. *Let* $\beta : LV \rightarrow N$ *be a valuation function instantiating logical variables with heap nodes and* $(N, \emptyset, \mu, F) \in \boldsymbol{H}_\emptyset$ *a concrete heap configuration. Then we define* $[\![\cdot]\!] : \text{NExp} \rightarrow N_{nil}$ *for* $x \in LV$, $v \in PV$ *and* $\alpha \in \text{NExp}$ *by:*

$$[\![nil]\!] := nil \qquad [\![v]\!] := v \qquad [\![x]\!] := \beta(x) \qquad [\![*\alpha]\!] := \mu([\![\alpha]\!])$$

Note the semantic difference in comparison to the programming language. In the logic a variable v is interpreted by itself and not by the node it is referencing. This allows the check for identity of program variables without introducing a reference operator. The semantics of PL with respect to concrete heap configurations is quite standard and therefore omitted.

Reasoning about Abstract Computations. When switching to abstract configurations we run into several complications since logical variables can be bound to both concrete and abstract nodes. In the latter case we have to record to *which* concrete node, represented by the abstract node, a variable is bound. This could lead to undefinedness of PL-formulae. The problem mainly occurs in direct comparisons of the form $\alpha = \alpha'$. To solve it we choose the global precision constant M in dependence of the formula $\varphi \in \text{PL}$, assuming from now on that

$$M \geq \sum_{x \in \text{Variables}(\varphi)} \{j + 1 \mid *^j x \text{ occurs in } \varphi\},$$

and introduce the concept of *abstract valuations*.

Given $H \in \boldsymbol{H}_\natural$ and $\varphi \in \text{PL}$, an abstract valuation is of the form $\eta = (\beta, o, \delta)$ where $\beta : PV \to N$ maps logical variables to (abstract) nodes, $o : PV \to \mathbb{M}$ denotes the offset of a variable "inside" an abstract node, and $\delta : PV \to PV \to \mathbb{M}$ is a "distance matrix" for the logical variables (referring to the same abstract node). δ is only defined if both arguments are mapped to the same entity, and o is only different from 1 if the corresponding variable is mapped to an abstract node. The set of all such valuations will be denoted by $\text{Val}_{H,\varphi}$.

Using this concept one can define a function $d_{H,\eta} : \text{NExp} \times \text{NExp} \to \{0, 1, \infty\}$ measuring the "distance" of pointer expressions, where distance here means either 0 if the expressions are mapped onto the same (concrete) node, 1 if the second argument is reachable from the first, or ∞ if neither is the case (see [15] for details).

Definition 5.3. Let $H = (N, A, \mu, F) \in \boldsymbol{H}_\natural$ and $\eta = (\beta, o, \delta) \in \text{Val}_{H,\varphi}$. The satisfaction relation $\models$ for PL-formulae on canonical configurations is then given as follows (omitting the trivial cases):

$$\begin{aligned}
H, \eta &\models f & &\text{iff } f \in F, \text{ where } f \in \text{Flags} \\
H, \eta &\models \alpha_1 = \alpha_2 & &\text{iff } d_{H,\eta}(\alpha_1, \alpha_2) = 0 \\
H, \eta &\models \alpha_1 \leadsto \alpha_2 & &\text{iff } d_{H,\eta}(\alpha_1, \alpha_2) \le 1 \\
H, \eta &\models \exists x : \varphi & &\text{iff } \exists n \in N,\ \textit{off} \in \mathbb{M},\ \textit{dist} : V(\varphi) \to \mathbb{M} \text{ s.t.} \\
& & &\quad H, (\beta_\eta[x/n], o_\eta[x/\textit{off}], \delta_\eta[x/\textit{dist}]) \models \varphi \\
H &\models \varphi & &\text{iff } \exists \eta \in \text{Val}_{H,\varphi} \text{ s.t. } H, \eta \models \varphi \\
[H]_\cong &\models \varphi & &\text{iff } H \models \varphi
\end{aligned}$$

Temporal Pointer Logic. Pointer Logic enables us to express properties of single configurations. However it cannot be used to specify (ongoing) computations, i.e., configuration sequences. To this aim we extend it by temporal operators.

Definition 5.4. *The set of* Temporal Pointer Logic formulae *(TPL-formulae) is given as follows:*

$$\text{TPL} ::= \text{PL} \mid \neg \text{TPL} \mid \text{TPL} \wedge \text{TPL} \mid \boldsymbol{X}\ \text{TPL} \mid \text{TPL}\ \boldsymbol{U}\ \text{TPL}$$

For $\varphi \in \text{TPL}$ we use the the abbreviations $\boldsymbol{F}\varphi := \text{tt}\ \boldsymbol{U}\varphi$ and $\boldsymbol{G}\varphi := \neg \boldsymbol{F}\neg\varphi$.

Note that it is *not* possible to nest PL-quantifiers and temporal operators. To do so it would be necessary to keep track of the object identities between states, which is difficult in the presence of abstract nodes. In addition it would blow up the state space and exclude the use of standard model checking algorithms. Only a few approaches support this idea [11,31]; most other works in the area consider only the *shape* of the heap. Clearly this restriction results in a loss of expressivity, nonetheless we can specify many interesting properties.

Example 5.5. For our server/worker system from Fig. 1 it holds true:

1. **GX** tt (never deadlock, i.e., there is always a successor state)
2. **¬F** err (no pointer errors)
3. **GF** $\exists n : \text{new}_n$ (new objects are created infinitely often)
4. **GF** $\text{spawn}_{\text{worker}}$ (infinitely often worker processes are spawned)

5. $\mathbf{G}(\exists n : \text{new}_n \to \mathbf{F}\ \text{spawn}_{\text{worker}})$
   (for every new object a worker thread is spawned)
6. $\neg\mathbf{G}(\text{spawn}_{\text{worker}} \to \mathbf{F}\ \text{del})$
   (the creation of a worker process does not necessarily result in the deletion of a node, i.e., fairness is not guaranteed)

More general correctness properties are:
7. $\mathbf{F}\ *v = *w$ \hfill (v and w will eventually become aliases)
8. $\mathbf{G}\neg(\exists x : (v \rightsquigarrow x \land w \rightsquigarrow x))$ \hfill (v and w always point to disjoint heap parts)
9. $\mathbf{G}(\forall x : (v \rightsquigarrow x \to (\neg\exists y : (x \rightsquigarrow y \land *y \rightsquigarrow x))))$
   \hfill (v always points to a non-cyclic list)
10. $\mathbf{FG}(\neg\text{leak})$ \hfill (only finitely many memory leaks can occur)
11. $\mathbf{G}(\forall x : (v \rightsquigarrow x \to (\forall y : (y \rightsquigarrow x \to v \rightsquigarrow y))))$ \hfill (v always points to a chain)

As mentioned before TPL specifies computation paths. These are given as sequences of heap configurations according to the Petri net representing the program semantics. By construction, for each marking m there is exactly one $p \in \boldsymbol{H}_\natural/\cong \cup \boldsymbol{H}_\emptyset$ such that $m(p) = 1$.

Definition 5.6. *Let $\mathfrak{P}_\natural = (P, T, src, tgt, \ell, m_0)$ be the abstract (or concrete) semantics of π. For a given run $\rho \in Runs(\mathfrak{P}_\natural)$ the satisfaction relation $\models$ for $\varphi \in$ TPL, assuming w.l.o.g. that the maximal PL-subformulae in φ are closed, is defined as follows (again omitting the trivial cases):*

$\varepsilon \not\models \varphi$
$\rho \models \varphi\ (\in \text{PL})$ iff $\rho \neq \varepsilon\ \land\ \exists p \in P \cap (\boldsymbol{H}_\natural/\cong \cup \boldsymbol{H}_\emptyset) : \rho_0(p) = 1\ \land\ p \models_{\text{PL}} \varphi$
$\rho \models \mathbf{X}\varphi$ iff $\rho[1] \models \varphi$
$\rho \models \varphi \mathbf{U} \psi$ iff $\exists k \leq |\rho| : \rho[k] \models \psi$ and $\forall j < k : \rho[j] \models \varphi$

We write $\mathfrak{P}_\natural \models \varphi$ iff $\rho \models \varphi$ for all $\rho \in Runs(\mathfrak{P}_\natural)$ and $\pi \models \varphi$ iff $\mathfrak{P}^c \otimes \mathfrak{P}_\natural^h \models \varphi$.

Note that finite traces are included in the semantics of TPL. This implies that the equivalence $\neg \mathbf{X}\varphi \leftrightarrow \mathbf{X}\neg\varphi$ does generally *not* hold.

Model Checking Temporal Pointer Logic. The Turing completeness of DLM-programs implies that the model checking problem for TPL-formulae is undecidable. The following theorem shows that it suffices to employ data abstraction to obtain a positive result.

Theorem 5.7. *The data-abstract model checking problem is decidable, i.e., we can decide whether $\mathfrak{P}^c \otimes \mathfrak{P}_\natural^h \models \varphi$.*

Proof. The idea is to evaluate all maximal PL-subformulae on the heap configurations, to label (the transitions of) $\mathfrak{P}_\natural$ by atomic propositions and accordingly eliminate the PL-subformulae in φ to obtain an LTL-formula φ' (see Algorithm 6.4). The next step is to construct two automata $\mathfrak{A}$ and $\mathfrak{B}$ where $\mathfrak{A}$ is a finite automaton recognizing the finite words, and $\mathfrak{B}$ a nondeterministic Büchi-automaton accepting the infinite words satisfying φ'. Then according to [12] the model checking problem is decidable using a formula of the type defined in [32] to formulate the Büchi acceptance condition for $\mathfrak{B}$ and a reduction to the reachability problem for Petri net markings that is decidable in EXPSPACE [17]. □

The result is important but more of theoretical interest due to the high complexity of the problem. Thus we have to apply further simplifications to obtain practically feasible results.

6 Control-Flow Abstraction

The idea of the control-flow abstraction is similar to the data abstraction. Instead of recording for each Petri net place the exact number of tokens we only do this up to a certain resolution. A global constant $C \in \mathbb{N}$ parameterizes the resolution bound. $\mathbb{C} := \{0, ..., C, \star\}$ is used analogously to $\mathbb{M}$. What we obtain is an over-approximation $\mathfrak{P}^c_\natural$ of the concrete control-flow semantics $\mathfrak{P}^c$. The first step is the modification of the Petri net semantics.

Definition 6.1. *An* abstract Petri net *is of the form* $\mathfrak{P} = (P, T, src, tgt, \ell, m_0)$ *with* abstract markings *that are functions of the type* $m : P \to \mathbb{C}$.

Definition 6.2. *Let* $\mathfrak{P} = (P, T, src, tgt, \ell, m_0)$ *be an abstract Petri net,* $m, m' \in Mark(\mathfrak{P})$ *and* $t \in T$. *Then* $\blacktriangleright_t \subseteq Mark(\mathfrak{P}) \times T \times Mark(\mathfrak{P})$ *is given by*[4]:

$m \blacktriangleright_t m' \Leftrightarrow \forall p \in srct : m(p) > 0 \,\wedge\, \forall p \in P:$

$$m'(p) = \begin{cases} m(p) - 1 & \text{if } p \in src(t) \setminus tgt(t) \text{ and } m(p) \neq \star \\ C \text{ or } \star & \text{if } p \in src(t) \setminus tgt(t) \text{ and } m(p) = \star \\ m(p) + 1 & \text{if } p \in tgt(t) \setminus src(t) \\ m(p) & \text{otherwise} \end{cases}$$

The abstract control-flow semantics $\mathfrak{P}^c_\natural$ is defined as the concrete one, but using the abstract transition relation $\blacktriangleright$.

Definition 6.3. *The* abstract semantics *of* π *is the Petri net* $\mathfrak{P}_{\natural\natural} := \mathfrak{P}^c_\natural \otimes \mathfrak{P}^h_\natural$.

If we now want to apply model checking, i.e., verify that a TPL-formula φ is satisfied by $\mathfrak{P}_{\natural\natural}$, we evaluate all maximal PL-subformulae of φ on the heaps in $\mathfrak{P}_{\natural\natural}$, substitute them by atomic propositions, generate the underlying (finite) transition system, label it with atomic propositions according to the evaluation of subformulae, and solve the resulting model checking problem for LTL with finite traces [14].

Algorithm 6.4. *Let* $\mathfrak{P}_{\natural\natural} = (P, T, src, tgt, \ell, m_0)$ *be given and* $\varphi \in$ TPL *the formula to verify. Let* $\Psi := \{\psi \in PL \mid \psi \text{ is a maximal subformula of } \varphi\} = \{\psi_1, ..., \psi_r\}$ *and* $a_1, ..., a_r$ *be atomic propositions.*

1. *Generate a finite transition system* $\mathcal{T} := (\{m \mid m_0 \blacktriangleright^* m\}, m_0, \blacktriangleright, lab)$ *with*

$$lab(m) := \bigcup_{i=1}^{r} \{a_i \mid \exists p \in P \cap \boldsymbol{H}_\natural/_\simeq \,:\, m(p) = 1 \wedge p \models \psi_i\}$$

2. *Solve* $\mathcal{T} \models^?_{LTL} \varphi[\psi_1/a_1, ..., \psi_r/a_r]$ *(admitting finite traces).*

---
[4] Note that $\blacktriangleright_t$ can be nondeterministic for a given transition t.

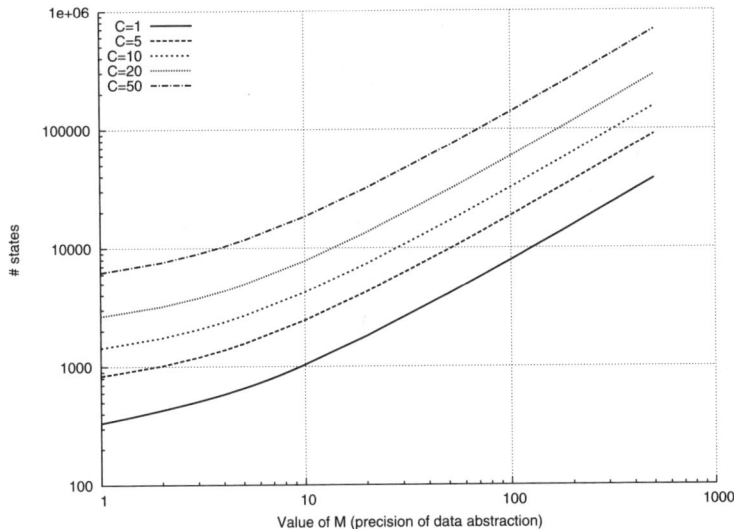

Fig. 5. Size of the state space for the server/worker example

Limitations and Refinement. Due to the over-approximation of the state space, there may exist abstract computations falsifying the property to verify and not corresponding to concrete ones. These *false negatives* can be eliminated through abstraction refinement by increasing the parameters M and C. The size of the state space is a *linear* function wrt. M (and C). This is visualized in Fig. 5 for our server/worker example employing a prototype version of our tool which is currently under development (note the logarithmic scale of both axes). Thanks to the implicit universal quantification over paths in the LTL approach, however, the successful verification of a property in the abstract case implies its correctness in the concrete case, i.e., *false positives* are excluded.

Note that our framework can be easily extended to three truth values, to eliminate false positives. The "don't know" answer would then only be given if the resulting transition system contains both positive *and* negative traces. In the other cases the answer would be an exact "yes" or "no". This would require the additional checking of a CTL formula in the case that the LTL model checker falsifies the property. If the answer is "don't know" a refinement step by increasing M and/or C is necessary.

7 Conclusions and Future Work

We have presented a framework for the verification of concurrent pointer-manipulating programs with dynamic thread creation, unbounded heap size, and destructive updates. Correctness properties are specified using temporal pointer logic (TPL) which is essentially a pointer logic for expressing heap properties enriched with temporal operators. Rather than requiring dedicated algorithms, the TPL model checking problem is reduced to an LTL model checking problem by appropriate abstractions. The trade-off is the restriction to list-like data structures and to static variables as well as the limitation in expressiveness of the logic because object identities are not tracked between configurations.

Currently we are implementing the method to analyze more interesting examples. We are planning to support the user in handling abstract computations which violate a given property, either by deriving concrete counterexamples or by suggesting refinements to eliminate false negatives. Finally we are working on an extension to arbitrary data structures.

Acknowledgments. We would like to thank Ulrich Schrempp for developing the prototype implementation of our analysis framework, which was used for computing the state spaces in the server/worker example.

References

1. Balaban, I., Pnueli, A., Zuck, L.D.: Shape Analysis by Predicate Abstraction. In: Cousot, R. (ed.) VMCAI 2005. LNCS, vol. 3385, pp. 164–180. Springer, Heidelberg (2005)
2. Beyer, D., Henzinger, T.A., Théoduloz, G.: Lazy shape analysis. In: Ball, T., Jones, R.B. (eds.) CAV 2006. LNCS, vol. 4144, pp. 532–546. Springer, Heidelberg (2006)
3. Bouajjani, A., Bozga, M., Habermehl, P., Iosif, R., Moro, P., Vojnar, T.: Programs with lists are counter automata. In: Ball, T., Jones, R.B. (eds.) CAV 2006. LNCS, vol. 4144, pp. 517–531. Springer, Heidelberg (2006)
4. Bouajjani, A., Habermehl, P., Moro, P., Vojnar, T.: Verifying programs with dynamic 1-selector-linked list structures in regular model checking. In: Halbwachs, N., Zuck, L.D. (eds.) TACAS 2005. LNCS, vol. 3440, pp. 13–29. Springer, Heidelberg (2005)
5. Bouajjani, A., Habermehl, P., Rogalewicz, A., Vojnar, T.: Abstract regular tree model checking of complex dynamic data structures. In: Yi, K. (ed.) SAS 2006. LNCS, vol. 4134, pp. 52–70. Springer, Heidelberg (2006)
6. Bozga, M., Iosif, R., Lakhnech, Y.: On logics of aliasing. In: Giacobazzi, R. (ed.) SAS 2004. LNCS, vol. 3148, pp. 344–360. Springer, Heidelberg (2004)
7. Chase, D.R., Wegman, M., Zadeck, F.K.: Analysis of pointers and structures. In: PLDI 1990, pp. 296–310. ACM Press, New York (1990)
8. Dams, D., Namjoshi, K.S.: Shape Analysis through Predicate Abstraction and Model Checking. In: Zuck, L.D., Attie, P.C., Cortesi, A., Mukhopadhyay, S. (eds.) VMCAI 2003. LNCS, vol. 2575, pp. 310–323. Springer, Heidelberg (2002)
9. Das, S., Dill, D.L.: Successive approximation of abstract transition relations. In: LICS 2001, pp. 51–58. IEEE Computer Society Press, Los Alamitos (2001)
10. Das, S., Dill, D.L., Park, S.: Experience with Predicate Abstraction. In: Halbwachs, N., Peled, D.A. (eds.) CAV 1999. LNCS, vol. 1633, pp. 160–171. Springer, Heidelberg (1999)
11. Distefano, D., Katoen, J.-P., Rensink, A.: Safety and liveness in concurrent pointer programs. In: de Boer, F.S., Bonsangue, M.M., Graf, S., de Roever, W.-P. (eds.) FMCO 2005. LNCS, vol. 4111, pp. 280–312. Springer, Heidelberg (2006)
12. Esparza, J.: On the decidability of model checking for several μ-calculi and Petri nets. In: Tison, S. (ed.) CAAP 1994. LNCS, vol. 787, pp. 115–129. Springer, Heidelberg (1994)
13. Gotsman, A., Berdine, J., Cook, B., Sagiv, M.: Thread-modular shape analysis. In: PLDI 2007, pp. 266–277. ACM Press, New York (2007)

14. Havelund, K., Rosu, G.: Testing linear temporal logic formulae on finite execution traces. Technical Report TR 01-08, RIACS (2001)
15. Katoen, J.-P., Noll, T., Rieger, S.: Verifying concurrent list-manipulating programs by LTL model checking. Technical Report 2007-06, RWTH Aachen University, Dept. of Computer Science, Germany (April 2007)
16. Lahiri, S.K., Qadeer, S.: Verifying properties of well-founded linked lists. In: POPL 2006, pp. 115–126. ACM Press, New York (2006)
17. Lambert, J.L.: A structure to decide reachability in Petri nets. Theor. Comput. Sci. 99(1), 79–104 (1992)
18. Lev-Ami, T., Immerman, N., Reps, T.W., Sagiv, S., Srivastava, S., Yorsh, G.: Simulating Reachability Using First-Order Logic with Applications to Verification of Linked Data Structures. In: Nieuwenhuis, R. (ed.) CADE 2005. LNCS (LNAI), vol. 3632, pp. 99–115. Springer, Heidelberg (2005)
19. Manevich, R., Berdine, J., Cook, B., Ramalingam, G., Sagiv, M.: Shape analysis by graph decomposition. In: Grumberg, O., Huth, M. (eds.) TACAS 2007. LNCS, vol. 4424, pp. 3–18. Springer, Heidelberg (2007)
20. Manevich, R., Yahav, E., Ramalingam, G., Sagiv, M.: Predicate abstraction and canonical abstraction for singly-linked lists. In: Cousot, R. (ed.) VMCAI 2005. LNCS, vol. 3385, pp. 181–198. Springer, Heidelberg (2005)
21. Nystrom, E.M., Kim, H.-S., Hwu, W.W.: Bottom-up and top-down context-sensitive summary-based pointer analysis. In: Giacobazzi, R. (ed.) SAS 2004. LNCS, vol. 3148, pp. 165–180. Springer, Heidelberg (2004)
22. O'Hearn, P.W., Yang, H., Reynolds, J.C.: Separation and information hiding. In: POPL 2004, pp. 268–280. ACM Press, New York (2004)
23. Podelski, A., Wies, T.: Boolean Heaps. In: Hankin, C., Siveroni, I. (eds.) SAS 2005. LNCS, vol. 3672, pp. 268–283. Springer, Heidelberg (2005)
24. Reynolds, J.C.: Separation logic: A logic for shared mutable data structures. In: LICS 2002, pp. 55–74. IEEE Computer Society Press, Los Alamitos (2002)
25. Rugina, R., Rinard, M.: Pointer analysis for multithreaded programs. SIGPLAN Not. 34(5), 77–90 (1999)
26. Sagiv, M., Reps, T., Wilhelm, R.: Solving shape-analysis problems in languages with destructive updating. ACM Trans. Program. Lang. Syst. 20(1), 1–50 (1998)
27. Sagiv, M., Reps, T., Wilhelm, R.: Parametric shape analysis via 3-valued logic. ACM Trans. Program. Lang. Syst. 24(3), 217–298 (2002)
28. Salcianu, A., Rinard, M.: Pointer and escape analysis for multithreaded programs. In: PPoPP 2001, pp. 12–23. ACM Press, New York (2001)
29. Vechev, M.T., Yahav, E., Bacon, D.F.: Correctness-preserving derivation of concurrent garbage collection algorithms. In: PLDI 2006, pp. 341–353. ACM Press, New York (2006)
30. Yahav, E.: Verifying safety properties of concurrent Java programs using 3-valued logic. ACM SIGPLAN Notices 36(3), 27–40 (2001)
31. Yahav, E., Reps, T., Sagiv, M., Wilhelm, R.: Verifying Temporal Heap Properties Specified via Evolution Logic. In: Degano, P. (ed.) ESOP 2003 and ETAPS 2003. LNCS, vol. 2618, pp. 204–222. Springer, Heidelberg (2003)
32. Yen, H.-C.: A unified approach for deciding the existence of certain Petri net paths. Inf. Comput. 96(1), 119–137 (1992)
33. Yong, S.H., Horwitz, S.: Pointer-range analysis. In: Giacobazzi, R. (ed.) SAS 2004. LNCS, vol. 3148, pp. 133–148. Springer, Heidelberg (2004)
34. Zhu, J., Calman, S.: Symbolic pointer analysis revisited. In: PLDI 2004, pp. 145–157. ACM Press, New York (2004)

Proofs and Refutations for Probabilistic Refinement

A.K. McIver[1,*], C.C. Morgan[2,*], and C. Gonzalia[1,*]

[1] Dept. Computer Science, Macquarie University, NSW 2109 Australia
[2] School of Comp. Sci. and Eng., Univ. New South Wales, NSW 2052 Australia

Abstract. We consider the issue of finding and presenting counterexamples to a claim "this *spec* is implemented by that *imp*", that is *spec* $\sqsubseteq$ *imp* (refinement), in the context of *probabilistic* systems: using a geometric interpretation of the probabilistic/demonic semantic domain we are able to encode both refinement success and refinement failure as linear satisfaction problems, which can then be analysed automatically by an SMT solver. This allows the automatic discovery of certificates for counterexamples in independently and efficiently checkable form. In many cases the counterexamples can subsequently be converted into "source level" hints for the verifier.

Keywords: Probabilistic systems, counterexamples, quantitative program logic, refinement, constraint solving.

1 Introduction

One of the strengths of standard model checking is its ability to produce counterexamples as concrete evidence that an implementation or model of a system fails to meet its specification. Moreover in some cases the counterexample can aid debugging by pointing to possible causes of the problem [2].

Unfortunately, with *probabilistic* model checking there is not yet an accepted definition for what a counterexample should be, nor is there a tradition for using counterexamples for debugging. In particular, a single computation path or trace is not normally sufficient counterevidence: it is more likely to be a cumulative trend over many traces that leads to suspect behaviour [8], suggesting a probabilistic computation tree as a candidate for a counterexample. A *tree* however cannot easily be presented as a cogent summary of the possible faults, nor does it indicate how to correct them.

The theme of this paper is a novel approach to presenting counterexamples in the context of probabilistic systems, and how it can be used in practice. Our proposal is guided by the following principles which, we believe, are qualities any good counterexample should possess:

P1. A counterexample should produce a *certificate* of failure that is easy to check, independently of the tool that found it; moreover,

---

[*] We acknowledge the support of the Australian Research Council Grant DP0558212.

P2. As far as possible the certificate should relate directly to the program text or system model; and finally,

P3. It should direct the verifier to the possible causes of the problem.

In system verification there is a great variety of behaviours. Whilst identifying the "bad behaviours" amongst the complete set might be hard in the first instance, once observed they should be immediately recognisable as such — in this context that means the counterexample should be checkable with minimum effort. This suggests *P1* and *P2*. Principle *P3* is included as it has the potential to be extremely useful as a debugging tool.

The current proposals [7,8] for counterexamples in probabilistic systems satisfy none of these properties, largely because they are based on probabilistic trace semantics — whilst (sets of) traces do provide evidence, they are neither easily verifiable, nor can they be directly related to the original system model.

Our approach is based on the refinement style of specification exemplified by the refinement calculus [14,1] extended to include probability [15,12]. In this style a specification *spec* is a heavily abstracted system, which is so simple as to be "obviously correct," whereas an implementation *imp* is more detailed, including distributed features or complicated program-code intended to realise some optimisation. Once a set of observable behaviours is agreed on, one writes $spec \sqsubseteq imp$, that *spec is refined by imp*, to mean that all possible behaviours of *imp* are included in those of *spec*.

Our main concern in this paper is when such a hypothesised refinement fails in the probabilistic case. We consider the problems of what constitutes good evidence to refute a refinement, and how can it be used to help the verifier solve the problem, possibly by changing one of *spec* or *imp*. (The former is changed when the counterexample reveals that *spec* is too demanding, and the latter when *imp* contains genuinely incorrect behaviours.)

Our specific contributions in this paper are thus as follows.

1. A description (Sec. 4.3) of how a counterexample to a proposed probabilistic refinement may be encoded as the failure to satisfy a quantitative property: i.e. it is rendered as a term in the quantitative program logic of Morgan and McIver [12];
2. An implemented procedure (Sec. 4) to compute the semantics of a small probabilistic programming language *pGCL*, and an arithmetic solver, which together compute a certificate in the case that refinement fails, showing adherence to Principles *P1* and *P2*;
3. A method (Sec. 4.4) to use the certificate to produce a suspect schedule, in distributed systems for example, thus fulfilling Principle *P3*.

In Sec. 2 we provide a summary of the overall approach, with later sections elaborating the details of the ideas introduced there.

We assume a (finite) state space S; we write $\mathbb{D}X$ for the set of (discrete) distributions over a finite set X, namely the set of 1-summing functions $X \to [0,1]$; given a set K we write $\mathbb{P}K$ for its power set. Given two distributions d, d' and scalar $0 \leq p \leq 1$, we write $d \,{}_p{\oplus}\, d'$ for the distribution $p{\times}d + (1{-}p){\times}d'$. We use an explicit dot for left-associating function application; thus $(f(x))(y)$ becomes $f.x.y$.

2 On Refinement, and Checking for It: An Introduction

Our basic model for operational-style denotations of sequential demonic programs *without probability* is $S \leftrightarrow (S \cup \{\bot\})$ or equivalently $S \to \mathbb{P}S_\bot$, in which (in the latter form) some initial state $s \in S$ is taken by (program denotation) $r \in S \to \mathbb{P}S_\bot$ to any one of the final states $s' \in r.s$. A common convention is that if $\bot \in r.s$ then so also are all $s' \in r.s$ — nontermination (the "improper" final state $\bot$) is catastrophic.

The reason for that last, so-called "fluffing-up" convention (aside from its being generated automatically by the Smyth power-domain over the flat order on $S_\bot$) is that it makes the refinement relation between programs very simple: it is subset, lifted pointwise. Thus we say that $r_1 \sqsubseteq r_2$, i.e. Program r_1 *is refined by* Program r_2, just when for all states s we have $r_1.s \supseteq r_2.s$. The fluffing-up means that the same $\supseteq$-convention that refines by reducing nondeterminism also refines by converting improper $\bot$ (nontermination) into proper behaviour.

Except for nontermination, *result sets* given by $r.s$ are fairly small when the program r is almost deterministic. In that case, from a fixed initial state $s°$ the question of whether $r_1 \sqsubseteq r_2$ can feasibly be established by examining every final state $s' \in r_2.s°$ and checking that also $s' \in r_1.s°$.

Once probability is added, at first things look grim (details in Def. 1 below): there can be non-denumerably many output *distributions* for non-looping programs over a finite, even small, state space: this is because of the "convexity" convention (analogous to fluffing-up) that pure demonic choice $\sqcap$ can be refined by any probabilistic choice ${}_p{\oplus}$ whatever, i.e. for any $0 \leq p \leq 1$. The reason for convexity is to allow, again, refinement via $\supseteq$ in all cases; but its effect is that even the simple program $s := A \sqcap B$ has as result set all distributions $\{\overline{A} \,{}_p{\oplus}\, \overline{B} \mid 0 \leq p \leq 1\}$, where in the comprehension we write $\overline{A}, \overline{B}$ for the point distributions at A, B.[1] Thus if r_2 is being compared for refinement against some r_1, it seems there are uncountably many final distributions to consider.

Luckily the actual situation is not grim at all: those result sets, big though they might be, are convex (and up-) closures of a finite number of distributions, provided S is finite — and even if the program contains loops. (A set D of distributions is convex closed if whenever $d, d' \in D$ then so is $d \,{}_p{\oplus}\, d'$ for any $0 \leq p \leq 1$.) Writing $\lceil \cdot \rceil$ for this closure we are saying that in fact $r.s \in \mathbb{P}\mathbb{D}S_\bot$ is equal to $\lceil D \rceil$ for some finite set of distributions D (depending on r and s). And so by elementary properties of convexity, to check $r_1 \sqsubseteq r_2$ for such programs we need only examine for each $s°$ the (small) sets $D_{1,2}$ of distributions from which $r_{1,2}.s°$ are generated.

This amounts to taking each result distribution $d' \in D_2$ and checking whether that d' is a convex combination of the finitely many distributions in D_1, which

---

[1] Point distributions have probability one at some state and (hence) zero at all others.

–crucially– can be formulated as a linear-constraint problem; and it is not so much worse than in the non-probabilistic case. Even better, however, is that if in fact $d' \notin \lceil D_1 \rceil$, then it is possible to find a certificate for that: because of the *Separating Hyperplane Lemma*, there must be some plane in the Euclidean space[2] containing $D_{1,2}$ with $\lceil D_1 \rceil$ strictly on one side of it and the inconvenient $d' \in \lceil D_2 \rceil$ (non-strictly) on the other. Finding that plane's normal (a tuple of reals that describes the plane's orientation) is *also* a linear-constraint problem, and can be done with the same engine that attempted to show $d' \in \lceil D_1 \rceil$ (but in fact found the opposite).

Thus the overall strategy –and the theme of this paper– is to calculate $D_{1,2}$ for some initial state s° and probabilistic nondeterministic programs given as $r_{1,2} \in S \to \mathbb{PD}S_\bot$, and then for each $d' \in D_2$ to attempt to establish $d' \in \lceil D_1 \rceil$. If that succeeds for all such d''s, declare $r_1 \sqsubseteq r_2$ at s°; but if it fails at some d', then produce a certificate (hyperplane normal) for that failure. (Note that in the automated procedure for finding certificates we only deal with terminating programs.)

As we will see, that certificate can then be used to identify, in a sense "highlight," the key "decision points" through the program r_2 that together caused the refinement failure — and there is our probabilistic counterexample that can be presented to the public and checked –by them independently– using the certificate from the hyperplane.

3 Probabilistic Refinement in Detail

3.1 Definition of Refinement

The transition-style semantics now widely accepted for probabilistic sequential systems models a probabilistic program as a function from initial state to (appropriately structured) sets of distributions over (final) states: each distribution describes the frequency aspects of a *probabilistic choice*, and a *set* of them (if not singleton) represents *demonic nondeterminism*.

Starting with a flat domain $S_\bot \hat{=} S \cup \{\bot\}$, with $\bot \sqsubseteq s$ for all proper states s, we construct $\mathbb{D}S_\bot$, the *discrete distributions over* $S_\bot$ and give it an (flat-induced) order so that for $d, d' \in \mathbb{D}S_\bot$ we have $d \sqsubseteq d'$ just when $d.s \leq d'.s$ for all *proper* s. (Note that $d.\bot > d'.\bot$ might occur to compensate.)

Then a set $D \subseteq \mathbb{D}S_\bot$ is said to be *up-closed* if whenever $d \in D$ and $d \sqsubseteq d'$ then also $d' \in D$; it is *convex* if whenever $d, d' \in D$, so too is $d _p\oplus d'$ for any $0 \leq p \leq 1$; and finally it is *Cauchy closed* if it contains all its limit points with respect to the Euclidean metric. [2] again

Definition 1. *[15,9] The space of (denotations of) probabilistic programs is given by $(\mathbb{C}S, \sqsubseteq)$ where $\mathbb{C}S$ is the set of functions from S to $\mathbb{PD}S_\bot$, restricted to subsets which are* convex, up- *and* Cauchy closed. *The order between programs is induced pointwise (again) so that $r \sqsubseteq r'$ iff $(\forall s \colon S \cdot r.s \supseteq r'.s)$.*

---

[2] See Sec. 3.6.

identity	$[\![\mathsf{skip}]\!].s$	$\hat{=} \ \{\bar{s}\}$
assignment	$[\![x := a]\!].s$	$\hat{=} \ \{\overline{s[x \mapsto a]}\}$
composition	$[\![P; P']\!].s$	$\hat{=} \ \{\sum_{s':S} d.s' \times f'.s' \mid d \in [\![P]\!].s; [\![P']\!] \sqsubseteq f'\}$

where $f' \in S \to \mathbb{D}S_\perp$ and in general $r' \sqsubseteq f'$ means $r'.s \ni f'.s$ for all s.

choice	$[\![\text{if } B \text{ then } P \text{ else } P' \text{ fi}]\!].s$	$\hat{=} \ \text{if } B.s \text{ then } [\![P]\!].s \text{ else } [\![P']\!].s$
probability	$[\![P \ _p\!\oplus P']\!].s$	$\hat{=} \ \{d \ _p\!\oplus d' \mid d \in [\![P]\!].s; d' \in [\![P']\!].s\}$
nondeterminism	$[\![P \sqcap P']\!].s$	$\hat{=} \ \lceil [\![P]\!].s \cup [\![P']\!].s \rceil \ ,$

where in general $\lceil D \rceil$ is the up-, convex- and Cauchy closure of D.

Iteration is defined via a least fixed-point; but we do not use iteration in this paper.

Fig. 1. Relational-style semantics of probabilistic programs [12]

The refinement relation defines when two programs exhibit the same or similar overall behaviour — from Def. 1 we see that a program is more refined by another whenever the extent of nondeterminism is reduced.

We use a small language *pGCL* that generalises Dijkstra's guarded-command language [5] by adding probabilistic choice (and retaining demonic choice); in Fig. 1 we set out how its semantics in the style of Def. 1. Programs without probability behave as usual; programs with probability, but no nondeterminism, abide by classical probability theory; but programs containing both probability *and* nondeterminism can exhibit highly skewed –and confusing– probabilistic behaviour.

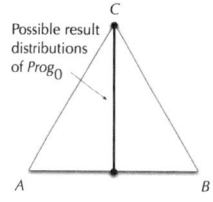

Fig. 2. $Prog_0$'s results (vertical line)

Each point in a triangle defines a discrete distribution over its vertices, here $\{A, B, C\}$, their unique linear combination that gives that point. Since $Prog_0$'s (set of) points is a strict subset of $Prog_1$'s points, we have $Prog_1 \sqsubseteq Prog_0$ and hence also $Prog_0 \not\sqsubseteq Prog_1$.

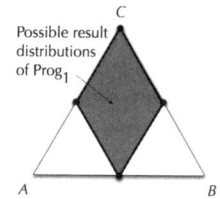

Fig. 3. $Prog_1$'s results (diamond)

Figs. 2 and 3. *Distribution triangles* depict convex result-sets

3.2 Example; and Difficulty with Counterexamples

To illustrate probabilistic refinement, and the difficulties with counterexamples, we consider the two programs below [12, App. A]. Checking $Prog_0$'s text suggests that it establishes $s{=}A$ and $s{=}B$ with equal probabilities; and those probabilities could be as high as 0.5 each (if the outer ⊓ resolves always to the left) or as low as zero (if the ⊓ resolves always to the right). Probabilities in-between (but still equal to each other) result from intermediate behaviours of the ⊓.

Checking $Prog_1$ however suggests more general behaviour. For example, consider the "thought experiment" where we execute $Prog_0$ many times, and keep a record of the results: we expect to see a strong correlation between the number of A's and B's. However with $Prog_1$ we cannot rely on an A, B-correlation, as instead it might correlate B, C while ignoring A altogether.[3]

$$Prog_0 \,\hat{=}\, (s := A \,_{0.5}\!\oplus s := B) \sqcap s := C \qquad (1)$$
$$Prog_1 \,\hat{=}\, (s := A \sqcap s := C) \,_{0.5}\!\oplus (s := B \sqcap s := C) \qquad (2)$$

Figures 2,3 depict the relation between $Prog_0$ and $Prog_1$ according to the semantics at Def. 1, in particular that they seem to be different. But it is not easy to see this experimentally via counterexample: what concrete property can we use to observe the difference? Indeed even if we tabulate, for the two programs, both the maximum and minimum probabilities of all 6 non-trivial result-sets, we get in Fig. 4 the same results *for both programs*.

Allowed final value(s) of s	A	B	C	A, B	B, C	C, A
Maximum possible probability	1/2	1/2	1	1	1	1
Minimum possible probability	0	0	0	0	1/2	1/2

The table illustrates the maximum and minimum probabilities for $Prog_0$ and $Prog_1$ with respect to all non-trivial choices of allowed outcome: the programs are not distinguishable this way. But in a larger context, they are: the composite programs

$$Prog_0;\ \text{if } s{=}C \text{ then } (s := A \,_{0.5}\!\oplus s := B) \text{ fi}$$
and
$$Prog_1;\ \text{if } s{=}C \text{ then } (s := A \,_{0.5}\!\oplus s := B) \text{ fi}$$

are distinguished by the test $s = A$.
This is a failure of compositionality for such (limited) tests [12, App. A.1].

Fig. 4. Maximum and minimum probabilities

The fallback position, that perhaps $Prog_0$ and $Prog_1$ are "observably" equal at this level of abstraction, is not tenable either — for we can define a *context* in which such simple tabulations *do* reveal the difference. Define the program $Prog_2$ to be the conditional if $s{=}C$ then $(s := A \,_{0.5}\!\oplus s := B)$ fi , and compare $Prog_0; Prog_2$ with $Prog_1; Prog_2$. The former establishes $s{=}A$ with probability 1/2; the latter however can produce $s{=}A$ with a probability as low as $1/4$.[3 again]

---

[3] If the $_{0.5}\!\oplus$ goes left, take the ⊓ right — and vice versa.

identity	wp.skip.*expt*	$\hat{=}$	*expt*
assignment	wp.$(x := E)$.*expt*	$\hat{=}$	*expt*$[x := E]$
composition	wp.$(P; P')$.*expt*	$\hat{=}$	wp.P.(wp.P'.*expt*)
choice	wp.(if B then P else P' fi).*expt*.*s*		
		$\hat{=}$	wp.P.*expt*.*s* if $B.s$ else wp.P'.*expt*.*s*
probability	wp.$(P\ _p\oplus\ P')$.*expt*	$\hat{=}$	$p \times$ wp.P.*expt* $+ (1-p) \times$ wp.P'.*expt*
nondeterminism	wp.$(P \sqcap P')$.*expt*	$\hat{=}$	wp.P.*expt* **min** wp.P'.*expt*

The expression *expt* is of non-negative real type over the program variables. As earlier, iteration is given in the usual way via fixed point; but we do not treat iteration here.

Fig. 5. Structural definitions of wp [15,12]

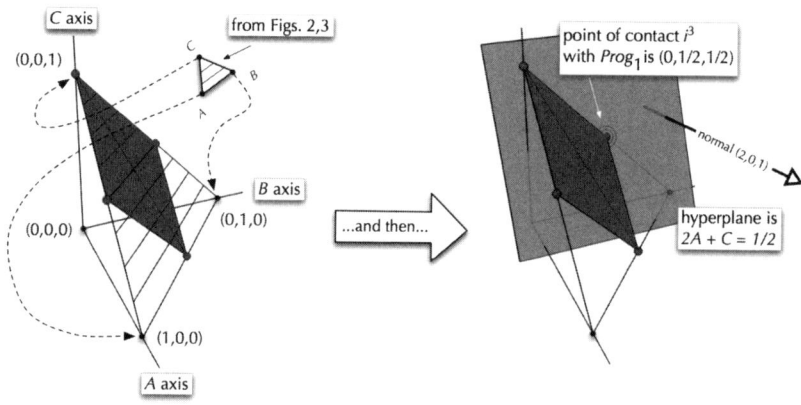

Fig. 6. Position the "distribution triangle" in 3-space, on the base of the non-negative $A+B+C \leq 1$ tetrahedron...

Fig. 7. ... approach from below, with a hyperplane of normal $(2,0,1)$, until a point in some result set is "touched"

The distribution-triangle of Figs. 2,3 becomes the base $A + B + C = 1$ of a tetrahedron in the upwards octant of Euclidean 3-space; a distribution over $\{A, B, C\}$ is now simply a point with the discrete probabilities as its A, B, C co-ordinates.

The random variable defined $(A, B, C) \mapsto (2, 0, 1)$ is represented by an *e*-indexed family of hyperplanes $2A+C = e$ all having the same normal $(2, 0, 1)$. The minimum expected value of that random variable over *any* set of distributions is the least *e* for which the representing hyperplane touches the set. For $Prog_1$'s distributions in particular, that value is $1/2$ (the plane shown in Fig. 7); for $Prog_0$ the *e* would be 1 (touching in fact at all the points in $Prog_0$'s line, that plane not shown).

The fact that the *e*'s for $Prog_0$ and $Prog_1$ are different, for some normal, is what distinguishes the two programs; and, given any normal, the program logic of Fig. 5 can deliver the corresponding *e* directly from the source text of the program.

The "only" problem is to find that distinguishing normal.

Figs. 6 and 7. Distributions in 3-space, and touching hyperplanes

3.3 Expected Values of Random Variables Certify Counterexamples

We are rescued from the difficulties of Fig. 4 by the fact that $Prog_0$ and $Prog_1$ can after all be distinguished statically (rather than via lengthy simulations and statistical tests, as suggested by the above "thought experiment") provided we base our analysis on *random variables* rather than pure probabilities, i.e. *functions* over final states (to reals) rather than simple *sets* of final states.[4]

Rather than ask "What is the minimum guaranteed probability of achieving a given *postcondition* on the final states?" (precisely what was shown above to be non-compositional), we ask "What is the minimum guaranteed expected value of a given *random variable* over the final states?"

In our example above, a distinguishing random variable is e.g. the function $(A, B, C) \mapsto (2, 0, 1)$, giving minimum (in fact guaranteed) expected value 1 for $Prog_0$ but only $1/2$ for $Prog_1$ (from all initial states, for these programs).

3.4 A Logic of Expectation Transformers

The minimum expected values, explained informally in Sec. 3.3, can be found *at the source level* using a quantitative programming logic that generalises Dijkstra's predicate-transformer semantics [5].[5] We call it a logic of *expectation transformers*.

Definition 2. *Random variables (functions of type* $\mathbb{E}S \mathrel{\hat{=}} S \to \mathbb{R}_{\geq 0}$*) are written in the logic as non-negative real-valued expressions over the program variables. They are ordered by pointwise $\geq$. The expectation-transformer denotation of the logic is then $(\mathcal{T}S, \sqsubseteq)$, where $\mathcal{T}S \mathrel{\hat{=}} \mathbb{E}S \to \mathbb{E}S$, and $t \sqsubseteq t'$ iff $(\forall e \colon \mathbb{E}S \cdot t.e \leq t'.e)$.*

With this apparatus we present in Fig. 5 the expectation-transformer logic for $pGCL$; it corresponds to our earlier "set of distribution" semantics of Fig. 1 in the same way as classical predicate transformers correspond to classical relational semantics.

3.5 Equivalence of Relational- and Transformer Semantics

Our two definitions Def. 1 and Def. 2 give complementary views of programs' meaning; crucial for our work here is that those views are equivalent in the following sense:

Theorem 1. *[12,15] Here (and briefly in Sec. 3.6), distinguish the two refinement orders by writing $\sqsubseteq_\mathcal{R}$ for the refinement order given in Def. 1; similarly write $\sqsubseteq_\mathcal{T}$ for the refinement order given in Def. 2. Then for any two pGCL programs P, P' we have $[\![P]\!] \sqsubseteq_\mathcal{R} [\![P']\!]$ iff $\mathsf{wp}.P \sqsubseteq_\mathcal{T} \mathsf{wp}.P'$.*

With Thm. 1 we can use just $\sqsubseteq$ for refinement between $pGCL$ programs, in either semantics, which is why we do not usually distinguish them (thus dropping the subscripts $\mathcal{R}, \mathcal{T}$).

Next we see how a third, geometric view supports this equivalence.

---

[4] This startling innovation is due to Kozen [11]; but he did not treat demonic choice, and so our (non-)compositionality example was not accessible to him.
[5] This is again due to Kozen, again only in the deterministic case [11].

3.6 Distributions and Random Variables in Euclidean Space

Fig. 6 shows how discrete distributions in $\mathbb{D}S_\perp$ can be embedded in $|S|$-dimensional Euclidean space: distribution d becomes a point whose s-coordinate is just $d.s$. (Representing $d.\perp$ is unnecessary, as it is determined by 1-summing.) *Arithmetically* convex sets of distributions become *geometrically* convex sets of points in this space.

Fig. 7 shows how a random variable in $\mathbb{E}S$ can be embedded in the same space: random variable f becomes a (family of) hyperplanes with a collective normal whose s-coordinate is just $f.s$. [6]

The crucial connection is that if the point representing d lies on a plane in the family f then the constant term of that particular plane is the expected value over the distribution d of the random variable that f's normal represents.

Def. 1 -style refinement remains the inclusion of one set of points (imp) wholly within another ($spec$), just as in our earlier Figs. 2,3.

Def. 2 -style refinement is equivalent, but can be formulated in terms of hyperplanes: take any (random-variable-representing-) hyperplane, and position it strictly below the positive octant in the space. (The results sets lie entirely in that octant.) Now move it up –along its normal– until it first touches a point (i.e. distribution) in one of the result sets. The constant term then gives exactly the wp for the program producing that first-touched distribution with respect to the random variable, written as an expectation in the logic of Fig. 5.

Then one program refines another just when for all such planes the less-refined program ($spec$) is always touched before the more-refined one (imp) is — because that means the constant term for $spec$ is always less that that for imp, whence the wp's are similarly ordered as they must be.

The two views justify Thm. 1 informally; we explain it in the contrapositive. If $spec \not\sqsubseteq_\mathcal{R} imp$ then for some initial state $s°$ we have a distribution d' with $d' \in [\![imp]\!].s°$ but $d' \notin [\![spec]\!].s°$. Because $[\![spec]\!].s°$ is convex, by the *Separating Hyperplane Lemma* there must be a plane separating d' from it in the sense that d' is in the plane but $[\![spec]\!].s°$ lies strictly on one side of it.[7] Because our result sets are up-closed, the normal of that plane can be chosen non-negative; and thus if that plane approaches the positive octant from below, it will reach d' in $[\![imp]\!].s°$ strictly before reaching any of $[\![spec]\!].s°$, thus giving $spec \not\sqsubseteq_\mathcal{T} imp$.

The reverse direction is trivial: if $spec \not\sqsubseteq_\mathcal{T} imp$ then some plane reaches $[\![imp]\!].s°$ before it reaches $[\![spec]\!].s°$; hence we cannot have $[\![spec]\!].s° \supseteq [\![imp]\!].s°$; hence $spec \not\sqsubseteq_\mathcal{R} imp$.

---

[6] A hyperplane in N-space is a generalisation of a plane, in 3-space $ax+by+cz = e$. The tuple (a, b, c) is its *normal* and e is its *constant term*.

[7] The *SHP* Lemma states that any point not in a closed and bounded convex set can be *separated* from the set by a plane that has the point on one side and the set strictly on the other.

4 Proofs and Refutations

With the above apparatus we address our main issue: given two $pGCL$ programs $spec, imp$ over some finite state space S, what computational methods can we use either to prove that $spec \sqsubseteq imp$, or to find –and present convincingly– a counterexample? We treat the two outcomes separately.

4.1 Calculating Result Sets

In order to prove refinement, i.e. $spec \sqsubseteq imp$, we must –in effect– investigate every possible outcome (distribution) of the implementation imp (element of its result set) and see whether it is also a possible outcome of the specification $spec$ (is an element of that result set too). Because of the structure of these sets, that they are convex closures of a finite number of "vertex" distribution points,[8] it is enough to check each vertex of the implementation result set against the collection of vertices of the specification result set.

These sets are calculated in the same way (for $spec$ and for imp), simply by "coding up" the relational semantics given in Fig. 1 in a suitable (functional) programming language. The main data-type is *finite set of distributions*, with each distribution being in turn a suitably normalised real-valued function of the finite state space (representable thus as a simple tuple of reals).

We discuss *sequential composition* $S;T$ as an example. Components S and T separately will have been analysed to give structures of type *initial state to set of final distributions*; the composition is implemented by taking the generalised Cartesian product of the T structure –converting it to a set of functions from initial state to final distribution– and then linearly combining the outputs of each of those functions, varying over its initial-state input, using the coefficients given by the probabilities assigned to each state by the S structure in each of its output distributions separately. That gives a set of output distributions for each single output distribution of S; and the union is taken of all of those.

The number of result distributions generated by the program as a whole is determined by the number of syntactic nondeterministic choices and the size of the support of the probabilistic branching, and it is affected by the order in which these occur. For example a D-way demonic branch each of whose components is a P-way probabilistic branch will generate only D distributions (since each P-way branch is a single distribution). However the opposite, i.e. a P-way branch each of whose components is a D-way branch, will generate $|D^P|$ output distributions — because the effect of calculating those distributions for the whole program is simply to convert it to (the representation of) a normal form in which all nondeterministic branching occurs before any probabilistic branching.[9]

---

[8] Sufficient mathematical conditions for this are that either the state space is finite and "raw" nondeterminism $\sqcap$ is finite, with loops allowed. We do not know whether it holds for infinite state spaces with loops, or finite state spaces with general (non-tail) recursion.

[9] For example the program $(x := \pm 1)\,_{1/3}\oplus (x := \pm 2)$ normalises to
$(x := 1\,_{1/3}\oplus 2) \sqcap (x := 1\,_{1/3}\oplus -2) \sqcap (x := -1\,_{1/3}\oplus 2) \sqcap (x := -1\,_{1/3}\oplus -2)$.

Suppose we have M sequentially composed components each one of which is an at most D-way demonic choice between alternatives each of which has at most P non-zero-probability alternatives. The computed results-set is determined by at most $D^{1+P+P^2+\cdots+P^{M-1}}$ vertices. Whilst this makes computing result distributions theoretically infeasible, in practice it is rarely the case that probabilistic and nondeterministic branching interleaves to produce this theoretical worst case.

4.2 Proving Refinement

Now suppose our state-space is of finite size N; then distributions can be represented as as points within Euclidean N-space. The procedure outlined above will thus generate

- for *spec* some set $\boldsymbol{S} \mathrel{\hat=} \boldsymbol{s}^{1..K}$ of N-vectors, and
- for *imp* some (other) set $\boldsymbol{I} \mathrel{\hat=} \boldsymbol{i}^{1..L}$ of N-vectors.

In each case the actual "implied" sets of result distributions are the convex closures $\lceil \boldsymbol{S} \rceil$ and $\lceil \boldsymbol{I} \rceil$ and we are checking that $\lceil \boldsymbol{I} \rceil \subseteq \lceil \boldsymbol{S} \rceil$,

- equivalently that each $\boldsymbol{i}^l \in \lceil \boldsymbol{S} \rceil$,
- equivalently that each $\boldsymbol{i}^l = \boldsymbol{c}^l \cdot \boldsymbol{S}$ for some $\boldsymbol{c}^l$, where $(\cdot)$ is the matrix multiplication of the non-negative 1-summing row-vector $\boldsymbol{c}^l$ of length K and the K-row-by-N-column representation of the set $\boldsymbol{S}$ of distributions,
- equivalently for that l that this constraint set has a solution in scalars $c^l_{1..K}$:
  - $0 \leq c^l_k$ for $1 \leq k \leq K$ and $\sum_{1 \leq k \leq K} c^l_k = 1$;
  - $i^l_n = \sum_{1 \leq k \leq K} c^l_k s^k_n$ for $1 \leq n \leq N$.

That last set of $K+1+N$ (in)equations (for each l) can be dealt with by a suitable satisfaction solver (Sec. 6). If they can be solved, then the refinement holds at that point $\boldsymbol{i}^l$; and if that happens for all $1 \leq l \leq L$ then the refinement holds generally. If not, then we have found an "inconvenient" implementation behaviour $\boldsymbol{i}^l$, and the refinement fails.

We say that *the certificate to support a proposed refinement* is the $K \times L$ matrix $\boldsymbol{c}$ of scalars that gives the appropriate K-wise interpolation of $\boldsymbol{S}$ for each $\boldsymbol{i}^l \in \boldsymbol{I}$. It can be checked as such separately by elementary arithmetic.[10]

In our example, to find the certificate to check the refinement $Prog_1 \sqsubseteq Prog_0$, we need to solve two systems of linear equations, one for each vertex distribution in $Prog_0$'s relational semantics (Fig. 2). For $\boldsymbol{i}^1 \mathrel{\hat=} (1/2, 1/2, 0)$ the system is

- $0 \leq c^1_k$ for $1 \leq k \leq 4$;
- $c^1_1 + c^1_2 + c^1_3 + c^1_4 = 1$;
- $c^1_1(0,0,1) + c^1_2(1/2,0,1/2) + c^1_3(0,1/2,1/2) + c^1_4(1/2,1/2,0) = (1/2,1/2,0)$.

The solution $\boldsymbol{c}^1 = (0,0,0,1)$ thus forms part of the certificate for verifying refinement. The complete certificate would also need the vector $\boldsymbol{c}^2 = (1,0,0,0)$ for $Prog_0$'s other vertex point $(0,0,1)$.

---

[10] These certificates are the essential components of Principles *P1,2* that make our conclusions independent of the correctness of our tools.

4.3 Refuting Refinement

In the case the refinement fails, that is for some $1 \leq l \leq L$ there is no c^l (in the sense of the previous section), we can do better than simply "the solver failed."

We refer to Fig. 7 and its surrounding discussion, and see that if $i^l \notin \lceil S \rceil$ then there must be a hyperplane that separates i^l from $\lceil S \rceil$, i.e. a hyperplane with i^l on one side and all of $\lceil S \rceil$ strictly on the other: in Fig. 7 that is the plane shown, having $i^3 \mathrel{\hat=} (0, 1/2, 1/2)$ non-strictly on its lower side and all of $Prog_0$'s results strictly on the upper side.

Formulated in the expectation logic of Fig. 5, refinement failure $spec \not\sqsubseteq imp$ at some initial state s° requires an expectation $expt$ with the strict inequality wp.$spec.expt.s^\circ$ > wp.$imp.expt.s^\circ$. That $expt$ is given by the normal $(2,0,1)$ of the separating plane in Fig. 7, and wp.$imp.expt.s^\circ$ is its constant term $1/2$ when it touches $Prog_1$ at i^3. To touch $Prog_0$ it would need to move higher, to constant term 1, which is thus the value of wp.$imp.expt.s^\circ$ for that same $expt$ $(A, B, C) \mapsto (2, 0, 1)$.

To find such a hyperplane, we must solve for the N-vector $\boldsymbol{h}$ in the equations

$$- \left(\sum\nolimits_{1 \leq n \leq N} h_n s_n^k\right) > \left(\sum\nolimits_{1 \leq n \leq N} h_n i_n^l\right) \quad \text{for all } 1 \leq k \leq K$$
and the inconvenient l in particular,

thus K inequations in this case.

Note well that if we have obtained i^l from a failure of refinement determined as in Sec. 4.2, then the equations immediately above are guaranteed to have a solution. That solution $\boldsymbol{h}$ together with initial state s° is the *certificate refuting the proposed refinement*.[10] again

In Sec. 4.2 we saw how our example failed for i^3; to find our certificate for that failure we therefore solve

$$h_1/2 + h_2/2 \ > \ h_2/2 + h_3/2 \quad \text{and} \quad h_3 \ > \ h_2/2 + h_3/2 \ ,$$

for which one solution is of course the normal $\boldsymbol{h} \mathrel{\hat=} (2, 0, 1)$ shown in Fig. 7.

We emphasise that simply the failure described in Sec. 4.2 to show some inconvenient d' is not in a convex closure $\lceil S \rceil$ is not above challenge: how do we know the solver itself is not incorrect? The refutation certificate generated for d' by this section –given to us by the hyperplane duality– is independently verifiable, and that is its importance.[11]

4.4 Source-Level Refutation

Finally in this section we consider how to turn the certificate for refuting refinement into a hint presented at the source level.

For our example we imagine a distributed system comprising a number of processors, each executing its local code. A scheduler coordinates the behaviour of the entire system, by determining which of the processors is able to execute

---

[11] Hyperplanes are used similarly in probabilistic process algebras to generate distinguishing contexts [4].

Resulting weakest pre-expectation ↓

$s := A \;_{0.5}\oplus\; s := B$	1
$s := A \;_{0.5}\oplus\; s := C$	1.5
least → $\;\;s := C \;_{0.5}\oplus\; s := B$	0.5
$s := C \;_{0.5}\oplus\; s := C$	1

The pre-expectation is calculated wrt.
$(A, B, C) \mapsto (2, 0, 1)$ in each case.

Fig. 8. The four resolutions of $Prog_1$

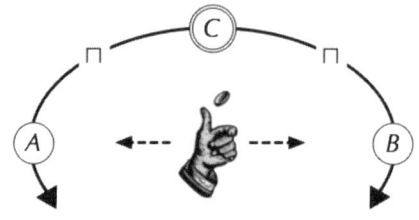

Fig. 9. ⊓-Adversarial scheduling

an (atomic) local execution step; the overall behaviour of the system can be analysed via an interleaving-style semantics [3]. In the most general setting we can represent the scheduler's choice by nondeterminism; in the case that the distributed protocol contains a vulnerability due to the scheduling (i.e. the events can be ordered so as to break the specification) we shall show how the certificate for failure can be used to find automatically the failing schedule.

As an illustration, consider the simple distributed system of Fig. 9 where initially Processor C is scheduled, then a probabilistic choice $_{1/2}\oplus$ is taken whether to continue clockwise or anti-clockwise; the adversarial scheduler can however on the very next step decide whether to remain at C or to move in the direction chosen. One might *specify* with $Prog_0$ that next-in-line Processors A, B should be fairly treated wrt. each other, whether the move occurs or not; but the *implementation* we suggested immediately above first chooses the direction to move via $(s := A) \;_{1/2}\oplus\; (s := B)$, and then demonically either confirms the move (skip), or inhibits it $(s := C)$. The effect is an equivalent but differently written formulation of $Prog_1$ (which we know does *not* refine $Prog_0$):

$$\overbrace{(s := A) \;_{1/2}\oplus\; (s := B)}^{\text{choose schedule}}; \quad \overbrace{\text{skip} \sqcap (s := C)}^{\text{execute schedule, or inhibit}} \qquad (3)$$

Because the witness $expt \;\hat{=}\; (A, B, C) \mapsto (2, 0, 1)$ to $Prog_0 \not\sqsubseteq Prog_1$ is based on *semantics*, it applies to this form (3) of $Prog_1$ too, even though it is now more confusingly presented. (Fig. 8 shows the four resolutions for both $Prog_1$ and (3).) In general, no matter how many statements are composed, the procedure for determining how the nondeterministic choices in the protocol were resolved to violate the refinement can be carried out on each component separately, rear-to-front. This is because the minimised pre-expectation for one component becomes the post-expectation to be minimised for the one immediately before, and so on to the beginning. That greatly reduces the complexity of finding the schedule.[12]

---

[12] This trick is well known in game theory [16].

To see how this works, we take the certificate for failure of $Prog_0 \sqsubseteq Prog_1$, and refer to (3) and Fig. 5 to compute[13]

$$\begin{aligned}
&\ \text{wp.}(\text{skip} \sqcap (s := C)).\langle 2, 0, 1\rangle \\
&= \text{wp.skip.}\langle 2, 0, 1\rangle \ \textbf{min} \ \text{wp.}(s := C).\langle 2, 0, 1\rangle \\
&= \langle 2, 0, 1\rangle \ \textbf{min} \ \langle 1, 1, 1\rangle \\
&= \langle 1, 0, 1\rangle
\end{aligned}$$

Observe how the **min** in the calculation corresponds to the resolution of $\sqcap$ in the code, so that in computing the minimum we also select the bad schedule. In this case, the last-line minimum is achieved from the previous line by taking pointwise choices $(A, B, C) \mapsto \langle right, left, don't\text{-}care\rangle$, which gives the failing schedule for the second statement: at A take $s := C$ (go right); at B take skip (go left); at C take either. Thus the conditional if $s=A$ then $(s := C)$ else skip fi describes concisely and at the source level a schedule that defeats the specification, i.e. if A is suggested by the first statement $(s := A)_{1/2} \oplus (s := B)$ then *inhibit* and stay at C, otherwise *accept* the move to B.

Again we achieve independence from the correctness of our tools,[10] yet again since it is trivial syntactically that our selection *is* a resolution of *imp*; it is also obvious what its single result distribution is *and* that *spec* cannot produce it.

This is a typical failure in such systems: the scheduler "exploits" a probabilistic outcome that the specifier/developer did not realise was a vulnerability.

5 Finding Adversarial Schedules in Distributed Systems

More generally than Sec. 4.4 we fix a set of N processors, each executing "local" code $P_1, \ldots, P_N$ respectively, and overall implementing some protocol. The asynchronous execution of the protocol can be modelled by assuming that each computation step is taken by one of the P_n's, chosen arbitrarily by the adversarial scheduler — in other words is the nondeterministic choice $\sqcap_{1 \leq n \leq N} P_n$, where we have introduced notation for the generalised nondeterministic choice over a finite set; we also write $Prog^K$ for K sequential compositions of the program $Prog$. The analysis of protocols like these normally considers "runs" that define the set of possible execution orders of the P_n's, which execution orders can be made on the basis of the current state. We describe these runs explicitly as follows.

Definition 3. *Given processors's local code $P_1, \ldots, P_N$, an execution schedule is a map $\sigma \in \mathbb{N} \to S \to \{1..N\}$ so that $\sigma.k.s$ defines the number of the processor that would be selected in the k-th step of the protocol if the state at that point were s. We write $\sigma_K \in \{0..K\} \to S \to \{1..N\}$ for the K-bounded execution schedule, namely the schedule σ restricted to the first K steps of the protocol.*

In the following definition we allow P to be subscripted with a function $f \in S \to \{1..N\}$ –rather than a constant– so that P_f from state s behaves as $P_{f.s}$ would; the application of a schedule can then be defined as follows.

---

[13] We abbreviate the expectation using $\langle \cdots \rangle$.

Definition 4. *Let σ_K be an K-bounded execution schedule; the resulting K-bounded execution sequence is then written*

$$(\sqcap_{0 \leq n \leq N} P_n)^{\sigma_K} \;\;\hat{=}\;\; P_{\sigma.0}; \cdots ; P_{\sigma.K}$$

We can now investigate the behaviour of *bounded execution sequences* of the protocol, by considering parameterised specifications. For example, suppose $Spec_K$ denotes a specification of the protocol up to K steps, and our aim is to investigate whether such bounded properties hold of the program.

In such a distributed system, we say that a *certificate to refute a proposed specification* $Spec_K \sqsubseteq (\sqcap_{0 \leq n \leq N} P_n)^K$ is a K-bounded schedule σ_K such that $(\sqcap_{0 \leq n \leq N} P_i)^{\sigma_K}$ is not a refinement of $Spec_K$. The next lemma shows how to compute one.

Lemma 1. *Suppose that $Spec_K \not\sqsubseteq (\sqcap_{1 \leq n \leq N} P_n)^K$, and that $(expt, s^\circ)$ is an (expectation, (initial) state) counterexample pair for the whole failure, as at Sec. 4.3. Define expectations $expt_K \cdots expt_0$ by $expt_K \hat{=} expt$, and $expt_{k-1} \hat{=} \mathsf{wp}.(\sqcap_{1 \leq n \leq N} P_n).expt_k$, for $1 \leq k < K$. Now define the schedule σ_K to give a result $\sigma_K.k \hat{=} f_k$, where each $f_k \in S \to \{1..N\}$ is crafted –as we did at the end of Sec. 4.4– so that $\mathsf{wp}.P_{f_k}.expt_k = \mathsf{wp}.(\sqcap_{1 \leq i \leq n} P_i).expt_k$. Then the resulting σ_K is a counterexample schedule.*

Proof. (Sketch.) As in Sec. 4.4 the hyperplane-generated expectation can "prune" nondeterministic choice from the (purported) implementation so that only the failing behaviour is left: one simply considers all deterministic resolutions and picks the one for which the pre-expectation wrt. the witness is minimised. The formal proof appears elsewhere [13].

We illustrate Lem. 1 with a small example case study elsewhere [13].

Finally we note that once we have the overall certificate $(expt, s^\circ)$, assuming the complexity of computing $\mathsf{wp}.P_n.expt$ is constant for every $expt$ and n, the complexity of breaking it up into a finer-grained failing schedule σ_K is $O(KN)$.

6 Implementing the Search for Certificates

In this section we describe how the search for certificates for failure can be implemented using an SMT solver.

Given two *pGCL* programs *spec* and *imp* we first compute the vertices generating their result distributions, as described in Sec. 4.1; and we formulate the satisfiability problem of Sec. 4.2 to attempt to prove refinement. It is exported to a general SMT solver [6] which, if successful, provides a certificate c of refinement.

If it fails, the dual problem (as Sec. 4.3) is formulated for that failure, with the inconvenient distribution providing the coefficients i_n^l, and then we solve for the hyperplane-normal coefficients h_n. Success there is guaranteed, and the normal $\mathbf{h}$ is the certificate of refutation.

An alternative approach is to attempt first to refute the refinement (Sec. 4.3) for each implementation distribution. If refutation fails for all of them, then we calculate a certificate of refinement (Sec. 4.2).

7 Conclusions and Future Work

We have shown how to generate automatically a witness to the failure of a hypothesised refinement $spec \sqsubseteq imp$. We have not yet specifically automated the subsequent production of a source level certificate generator, although a small change to the wp-generator implemented in the HOL system [10] will be a good place to start.

This work differs significantly from other work using SMT-solvers [7] which is unable to produce an efficiently checkable certificate in the form of an expectation, nor a source-level counterexample.

References

1. Back, R.-J.R., von Wright, J.: Refinement Calculus: A Systematic Introduction. Springer, Heidelberg (1998)
2. Clarke, E., Lu, Y., Grumberg, O., Jha, S., Veith, H.: Counterexample-guided abstraction refinement for symbolic model checking. Journal of the ACM 50(5), 752–794 (2003)
3. Cohen, E.: Separation and reduction. In: Backhouse, R., Oliveira, J.N. (eds.) MPC 2000. LNCS, vol. 1837, pp. 45–59. Springer, Heidelberg (2000)
4. Deng, Y., van Glabeek, R., Morgan, C.C., Zhang, C.: Scalar Outcomes Suffice for Finitary Probabilistic Testing. In: De Nicola, R. (ed.) ESOP 2007. LNCS, vol. 4421, pp. 363–378. Springer, Heidelberg (2007)
5. Dijkstra, E.W.: A Discipline of Programming. Prentice-Hall, Englewood Cliffs (1976)
6. Dutertre, B., de Moura, L.: A Fast Linear-Arithmetic Solver for DPLL(T). In: Ball, T., Jones, R.B. (eds.) CAV 2006. LNCS, vol. 4144, pp. 81–94. Springer, Heidelberg (2006)
7. Gonzalia, C., McIver, A.K.: Automating Refinement Checking in Probabilistic System Design. In: Butler, M., Hinchey, M.G., Larrondo-Petrie, M.M. (eds.) ICFEM 2007. LNCS, vol. 4789, pp. 212–231. Springer, Heidelberg (2007)
8. Han, T., Katoen, J.-P.: Counterexamples in probabilistic model checking. In: Krishnamurthi, S., Odersky, M. (eds.) CC 2007. LNCS, vol. 4420, pp. 72–86. Springer, Heidelberg (2007)
9. He, J., Seidel, K., McIver, A.: Probabilistic models for the guarded command language. Science of Computer Programming 28, 171–192 (1997)
10. Hurd, J., McIver, A.K., Morgan, C.C.: Probabilistic guarded commands mechanised in HOL. In: Cerone, A., de Pierro, A. (eds.) *Proc 4th QAPL*. ENTCS, vol. 112, Elsevier, Amsterdam (2005)
11. Kozen, D.: A probabilistic PDL. Jnl. Comp. Sys. Sci. 30(2), 162–178 (1985)
12. McIver, A.K., Morgan, C.C.: Abstraction, Refinement and Proof for Probabilistic Systems. In: Tech. Mono. Comp. Sci., Springer, New York (2005)
13. McIver, A.K., Morgan, C.C., Gonzalia, C.: Proofs and refutations for probabilistic systems (2007), http://www.ics.mq.edu.au/$\sim$anabel/FM08.pdf
14. Morgan, C.C.: Programming from Specifications, 2nd edn. Prentice-Hall, Englewood Cliffs (1994)
15. Morgan, C.C., McIver, A.K., Seidel, K.: Probabilistic predicate transformers. ACM Trans. Prog. Lang. Sys. 18(3), 325–353 (1996)
16. von Neumann, J., Morgenstern, O.: Theory of Games and Economic Behavior, 2nd edn. Princeton University Press, Princeton (1947)

Assume-Guarantee Verification for Interface Automata

Michael Emmi[1,*], Dimitra Giannakopoulou[2], and Corina S. Păsăreanu[2]

[1] University of California, Los Angeles
mje@cs.ucla.edu
[2] NASA Ames Research Center
{Dimitra.Giannakopoulou,Corina.S.Pasareanu}@email.arc.nasa.gov

Abstract. Interface automata provide a formalism capturing the high level interactions between software components. Checking compatibility, and other safety properties, in an automata-based system suffers from the scalability issues inherent in exhaustive techniques such as model checking. This work develops a theoretical framework and automated algorithms for modular verification of interface automata. We propose sound and complete assume-guarantee rules for interface automata, and learning-based algorithms to automate assumption generation. Our algorithms have been implemented in a practical model-checking tool and have been applied to a realistic NASA case study.

1 Introduction

Modern software systems are comprised of numerous components, and are made larger through the use of software frameworks. Formal analysis of such systems naturally suffers from scalability issues. Modular analysis techniques address this with a "divide and conquer" approach: properties of a system are decomposed into properties of its constituents, each verified separately. Assume-guarantee reasoning [14,21] is a modular formal analysis technique that uses assumptions when checking components in isolation. A simple assume-guarantee rule infers that a system composed of components M_1 and M_2 satisfies safety property P by checking that M_1 under assumption A satisfies P (*Premise 1*) and discharging A on the environment M_2 (*Premise 2*). Finding suitable assumptions can be non-trivial, and has traditionally been performed manually.

Previous work [8] has proposed a framework using learning techniques to automate assumption generation for the aforementioned rule; that work addresses safety property checking for Labeled Transition Systems (LTSs). LTSs interact through synchronization of shared actions, and have been used extensively in the analysis of high-level abstract systems, for example at the architecture level [19]. However, as LTSs do not distinguish between input/output actions that a component can receive/emit, respectively, they are often inadequate for more detailed analyses, testing, or test-case generation [23].

---

[*] This work was completed during an Mission Critical Technologies Inc. internship at NASA Ames.

I/O automata [17] and interface automata [9] are formalisms that differentiate between the input and output actions of a component. The main distinguishing factor between the two formalisms is that I/O automata are required to be *input-enabled*, meaning they must be receptive at every state to each possible input action. For interface automata, some inputs may be illegal in particular states, i.e., the component is not prepared to service these inputs. Two components are said to be *compatible* if in their composition each component is prepared to receive any request that the other may issue.

Compatibility is an important property for the analysis of component-based systems [16]. In the case study we discuss in Section 7, compatibility checking uncovered subtle errors that were undetectable when components were modeled as LTSs. Consequently, parts of the model were unexplored, even though the system is deadlock-free. (Note: these particular errors are undetectable if components are assumed input-enabled, as I/O automata are.)

Checking compatibility and traditional safety properties of interface automata suffers from the inherent scalability issues appearing in model checking techniques. In this work we develop a theoretical framework with automated algorithms for modular verification of systems modeled as interface automata. Specifically, we provide the first sound and complete assume-guarantee rules for checking properties of interface automata. This includes rules for compatibility checking, traditional safety properties, and alternating refinement (the notion of refinement associated with interface automata [9]).

We define a construction that reduces compatibility and alternating refinement to checking error state reachability, by adding to each component transitions to error states. We provide algorithms that automate the application of the assume-guarantee rules by computing assumptions (we provide both a direct and a learning-based construction of the assumptions). Although we reduce compatibility checking to error detection, we cannot simply use the rules and frameworks from our previous work [8]; that work assumed error states to be introduced only by checking the property in *Premise 1* and discharging the assumption in *Premise 2*; in this work error states are also introduced by our reduction. We describe this further in Sections 5 and 6.

For a system where component compatibility has been established we also define an optimized assumption construction when checking traditional safety properties. Our new algorithms have been implemented in the LTSA model checking tool [18] and have been applied to a NASA case study.

2 Background

Labeled Transition Systems. A *labeled transition system* (LTS) A is a tuple $\langle Q, a_0, \alpha A, \delta \rangle$, where Q is a finite set of states, $a_0 \in Q$ is an initial state, αA is a set of observable actions called the *alphabet* of A, and $\delta \subseteq Q \times \alpha A \times Q$ is a transition relation. For readability, we write $a \xrightarrow{\alpha} a'$ when $\langle a, \alpha, a' \rangle \in \delta$, in which case we say that α is *enabled* at a, and that a' is a *destination* of α from a. A state a' is *reachable* from a if there exists $n \in \mathbb{N}$ and sequences $\langle a_i \rangle_{0 \leq i \leq n}$ and

$\langle \alpha_i \rangle_{0 \leq i < n}$ with $a = a_0$ and $a' = a_n$ such that $a_i \xrightarrow{\alpha_i} a_{i+1}$ for $0 \leq i < n$. The LTS A is *deterministic* if δ is a function (i.e., for all $a \in Q$ and $\alpha \in \alpha A$, $a \xrightarrow{\alpha} a'$ for at most one state $a' \in Q$), and is otherwise *non-deterministic*.

We use π to denote a special *error state* without enabled transitions. The *error completion* of A is defined to be the LTS $A^\pi = \langle Q \cup \{\pi\}, a_0, \alpha A, \delta' \rangle$ where δ' agrees with δ, and adds transitions $a \xrightarrow{\alpha} \pi$ for all states a where α is not enabled. We say A is *safe* when π is not reachable from the initial state.

Parallel Composition. The parallel composition operator $\|$ is (up to isomorphism) a commutative and associative operator on LTSs. Given LTSs $A = \langle Q_A, a_0, \alpha A, \delta_A \rangle$ and $B = \langle Q_B, b_0, \alpha B, \delta_B \rangle$, the composition $A \| B$ is an LTS with states $Q_A \times Q_B$,[1] initial state $\langle a_0, b_0 \rangle$, alphabet $\alpha A \cup \alpha B$, and a transition relation defined by the rules (including the symmetric versions):

$$\frac{a \xrightarrow{\alpha} a' \quad a' \neq \pi \quad \alpha \notin \alpha B}{\langle a, b \rangle \xrightarrow{\alpha} \langle a', b \rangle}, \quad \frac{a \xrightarrow{\alpha} a' \quad b \xrightarrow{\alpha} b' \quad a', b' \neq \pi}{\langle a, b \rangle \xrightarrow{\alpha} \langle a', b' \rangle}, \text{ and } \frac{a \xrightarrow{\alpha} \pi}{\langle a, b \rangle \xrightarrow{\alpha} \pi}.$$

Traces. A *trace* t of *length* n on an LTS A is a finite sequence $\langle \alpha_i \rangle_{1 \leq i \leq n}$ of enabled actions on A starting from the initial state: formally, there exist states $a_1, \ldots, a_n \in Q$ such that $a_{i-1} \xrightarrow{\alpha_i} a_i$ for $1 \leq i \leq n$. The set of traces of A is called the *language* of A, denoted $\mathcal{L}(A)$. A trace t may also be viewed as an LTS, called a *trace LTS*, whose language consists of all prefixes of t (including t itself). As the meaning will be clear from the context, we will use t to denote both a trace and a trace LTS. We write $t \downarrow_\Sigma$ for the trace obtained from t by removing every occurrence of an action outside of Σ.

Safety properties. We call a deterministic LTS without the state π a *safety LTS* (any non-deterministic LTS can be made deterministic with the standard algorithm for automata). A safety property P is specified as a *safety LTS* whose language $\mathcal{L}(P)$ defines the set of acceptable behaviors over αP. An LTS M satisfies P, written $M \models P$, if and only if for every trace t of M, $t \downarrow_{\alpha P}$ is a trace of P. Note that $M \models P$ can be checked algorithmically by searching for a trace to π in M composed with the error completion of P.

The L* learning algorithm. Our algorithms for automating assume-guarantee reasoning use the L* algorithm for learning appropriate assumptions. L* was developed by Angluin [3] and later improved by Rivest and Schapire [22]. To synthesize an automaton for a regular language U over alphabet Σ, the algorithm interacts with a "black box", called a *teacher*, who answers questions about U. The teacher answers *membership queries* (given a string s, is $s \in U$?), and *refinement queries* (given an automaton A over Σ, does $\mathcal{L}(A) = U$?). We henceforth refer to the latter query as a *conjecture*, and the former simply as a *query*. If the conjectured automaton A's language is not U, the teacher is obligated to produce a *counterexample trace* in the symmetric difference of $\mathcal{L}(A)$ and U. This algorithm is guaranteed to terminate with a minimal automaton for U which has at most $n + 1$ states, where n is the number of incorrect conjectures.

---
[1] Each state $\langle a, \pi \rangle$ or $\langle \pi, b \rangle$ in the composition is identified with π.

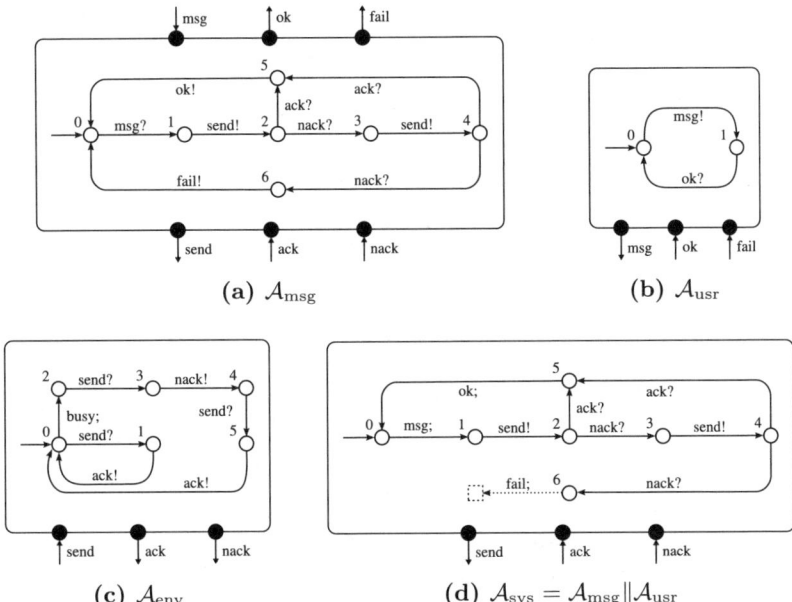

Fig. 1. A messaging system comprised of three components (a, b, and c). The dotted transition to the error state π in (d) originates from the *error completed* automaton $\mathcal{A}^?_{\text{usr}}$ (explained in Sec.3.3), and survives in the composition $\mathcal{A}^?_{\text{msg}} \| \mathcal{A}^?_{\text{usr}}$. We omit other transitions due to error completion for readability.

3 Interface Automata (IA)

Definition 1. *An* interface automaton A *is a tuple* $\langle Q_A, I_A, \alpha A^{\text{I}}, \alpha A^{\text{O}}, \alpha A^{\text{H}}, \delta_A \rangle$ *where* Q_A *is a set of states,* $I_A \in Q_A$ *is the initial state,* αA^{I}, αA^{O}, *and* αA^{H} *are respectively disjoint* input, output, *and* internal *alphabets (we define* $\alpha A = \alpha A^{\text{I}} \cup \alpha A^{\text{O}} \cup \alpha A^{\text{H}}$), *and* $\delta_A \subseteq Q_A \times \alpha A \times Q_A$ *is a transition relation.*

Our running example of composable interface automata is borrowed from [9].

Example 1. The automaton $\mathcal{A}_{\text{msg}}$ (Fig. 1a) transmits messages over a lossy communication channel. The input actions msg, ack, and nack (resp., send, ok, and fail) are depicted by incoming (resp., outgoing) arrows to the enclosing box, and question (resp., exclamation) marks on edge labels. Internal actions (see Fig. 1c) do not appear on the interface boundaries, and suffixed by semicolons on edge labels.

The semantics of interface automata are defined here by reduction to labeled transition systems (LTSs). In particular, given an interface automaton $\langle Q_A, I_A, \alpha A^{\text{I}}, \alpha A^{\text{O}}, \alpha A^{\text{H}}, \delta_A \rangle$, lts($A$) is the LTS $\langle Q_A, I_A, \alpha A, \delta_A \rangle$. We lift the semantics from LTSs by writing $a \xrightarrow{\alpha} a'$ when lts(A) has such a move, we say A is *(non-) deterministic* when lts(A) is, and an action α is *enabled* in a state a when it is in lts(A). The *traces* and the *language* of A are defined similarly.

For the remainder of this section we fix A and B to be interface automata.

Definition 2. *A and B are* composable *when their* signatures *do not conflict, i.e.* $\alpha A^{\mathrm{I}} \cap \alpha B^{\mathrm{I}} = \alpha A^{\mathrm{O}} \cap \alpha B^{\mathrm{O}} = \alpha A^{\mathrm{H}} \cap \alpha B = \alpha A \cap \alpha B^{\mathrm{H}} = \emptyset$.

Example 2. The "user" component of Figure 1b expects that the message-sending component of Figure 1a will never encounter `fail`ure. This implicit assumption is a key feature of IAs; its expressed here by the lack of a `fail?`-labeled edge from state 1 of $\mathcal{A}_{\mathrm{usr}}$.

The communication channel "environment" of Figure 1c either transmits a message on the first attempt, or delays on the first attempt, and transmits on the second. The internal action `busy` is not observed by other components. Both $\mathcal{A}_{\mathrm{usr}}$ and $\mathcal{A}_{\mathrm{env}}$ are composable with the $\mathcal{A}_{\mathrm{msg}}$, albeit on disjoint interfaces.

Note that composable IAs need not have any common actions, but each common action must be an input of one and an output of the other. We identify the set of common actions with $\alpha\mathsf{Shared}(A,B)$.

Definition 3. *When A and B are composable, the* composition *of A and B, written* $A \| B$, *is the interface automaton* $C = \langle Q_C, I_C, \alpha C^{\mathrm{I}}, \alpha C^{\mathrm{O}}, \alpha C^{\mathrm{H}}, \delta_C \rangle$, *where* $\langle Q_C, I_C, \alpha C, \delta_C \rangle = \mathrm{lts}(A) \| \mathrm{lts}(B)$, *and the alphabet is partitioned as*

- $\alpha C^{\mathrm{I}} = \alpha A^{\mathrm{I}} \cup \alpha B^{\mathrm{I}} \setminus \alpha\mathsf{Shared}(A,B)$,
- $\alpha C^{\mathrm{O}} = \alpha A^{\mathrm{O}} \cup \alpha B^{\mathrm{O}} \setminus \alpha\mathsf{Shared}(A,B)$, *and*
- $\alpha C^{\mathrm{H}} = \alpha A^{\mathrm{H}} \cup \alpha B^{\mathrm{H}} \cup \alpha\mathsf{Shared}(A,B)$.

The composition of an IA A and an LTS T is an IA extending A by substituting $\mathrm{lts}(A) \| T$ for $\mathrm{lts}(A)$.

Example 3. Since the constituents of $\mathcal{A}_{\mathrm{sys}}$ (Fig. 1d) synchronize on `fail`, and $\mathcal{A}_{\mathrm{usr}}$ `fail`ure never occurs, there are no transitions from state 6 in the composition. The signature of $\mathcal{A}_{\mathrm{sys}}$ does not mention common actions of $\mathcal{A}_{\mathrm{msg}}$ and $\mathcal{A}_{\mathrm{usr}}$ which have been internalized.

3.1 Compatibility

Although the semantics of a single IA is the same as its underlying LTS, the distinction between input and output actions results in a more stringent behavioral specification between components that cannot be checked for LTSs.

Definition 4. *Given two composable automata A and B, a state $\langle a, b \rangle$ of $A \| B$ is* illegal *if some action $\alpha \in \alpha\mathsf{Shared}(A,B)$ is an enabled output action in a (resp., b), but a disabled input action in b (resp., a).*

Example 4. State 6 of $\mathcal{A}_{\mathrm{sys}}$ (Fig. 1d) is illegal, since `fail` is an enabled output in state 6 of $\mathcal{A}_{\mathrm{msg}}$ and a disabled input in state 1 of $\mathcal{A}_{\mathrm{usr}}$.

Definition 5. *The automaton A is* closed *when* $\alpha A^{\mathrm{I}} = \alpha A^{\mathrm{O}} = \emptyset$, *and is otherwise* open.

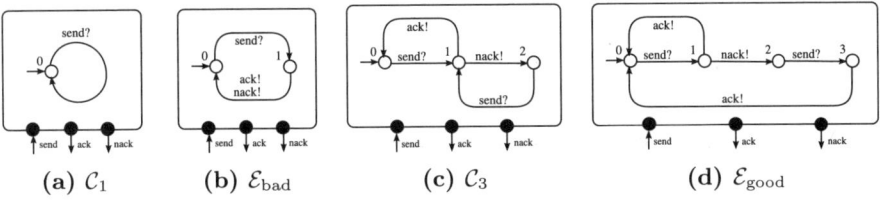

Fig. 2. Four environments for $\mathcal{A}_{\text{sys}}$ (Fig. 1d)

The optimistic notion of compatibility between IAs [9] is associated with the existence of illegal states in their composition. An open automaton with illegal states is not necessarily incompatible with its environments, since illegal states may not be reachable in the composition.

Definition 6. *When $A \| B$ is closed, A and B are said to be* compatible, *written $A \sim B$, if $A \| B$ does not have reachable illegal states.*

3.2 Refinement

For convenience we will write $\alpha \in$ I-Enabled$_A(a)$ (resp., $\alpha \in$ O-Enabled$_A(a)$) when α is an enabled input (resp., output) action in a. The *internal-closure* of a, written H-Closure$_A(a)$, is the set of states reachable from a via internal actions. An *externally observable move*, denoted $a \stackrel{\alpha}{\leadsto} a'$, exists when $a_1 \stackrel{\alpha}{\to} a_2$ for $a_1 \in$ H-Closure$_A(a)$ and $a' \in$ H-Closure$_A(a_2)$, in which case we say a' is an *external destination* from a by α. An action α is an *externally enabled* input (resp., output) in a, written $\alpha \in$ I-ExtEn$_A(a)$ (resp., $\alpha \in$ O-ExtEn$_A(a)$), if α is enabled in all (resp., some) states of H-Closure$_A(a)$.

Definition 7. *A binary relation $\preceq \, \subseteq (Q_A \times Q_B)$ is an* alternating simulation *from A to B if for all $a \in Q_A$ and $b \in Q_B$ such that $a \preceq b$:*

(1) I-ExtEn$_A(a) \supseteq$ I-ExtEn$_B(b)$.
(2) O-ExtEn$_A(a) \subseteq$ O-ExtEn$_B(b)$.
(3) For all actions $\alpha \in$ O-ExtEn$_A(a) \cup$ I-ExtEn$_B(b)$ and states a' such that $a \stackrel{\alpha}{\leadsto} a'$, there exists a state b' such that $b \stackrel{\alpha}{\leadsto} b'$ and $a' \preceq b'$.

We say A refines *B, written $A \preceq B$, if $\alpha A^I \supseteq \alpha B^I$, $\alpha A^O \subseteq \alpha B^O$ and there exists an alternating simulation $\preceq'$ from A to B such that $\langle I_A, I_B \rangle \in \preceq'$.*

Example 5. Figure 2 gives four automata with signatures matching $\mathcal{A}_{\text{env}}$'s (Fig. 1c). One can easily check that $\mathcal{A}_{\text{env}} \preceq \mathcal{E}_{\text{bad}}, \mathcal{E}_{\text{good}}$, but $\mathcal{A}_{\text{env}} \not\preceq \mathcal{C}_1, \mathcal{C}_3$.

The following refinement properties are known [9].

Theorem 1. *The alternating simulation relation over interface automata is reflexive and transitive.*

Theorem 2. *Let A, B, and C be interface automata such that B and C are composable, and $\alpha B^{\mathrm{I}} \cap \alpha C^{\mathrm{O}} \subseteq \alpha A^{\mathrm{I}} \cap \alpha C^{\mathrm{O}}$. If $A \sim C$ and $B \preceq A$, then $B \sim C$ and $B \| C \preceq A \| C$.*

3.3 Checking Compatibility and Refinement

We reduce compatibility and refinement checking to model checking on automata completed with error states.

Definition 8. *The* input *(resp.,* output*) error completion of A, denoted $A^?$ (resp., $A^!$), extends A with the state π and the transition $a \xrightarrow{\alpha} \pi$ whenever α is a disabled input (resp., output) action at a.*

Supposing that A and B are *composable* but incompatible, there must exist a transition to π in $A^? \| B^?$, since either A or B performs an action which the other does not anticipate, causing either $B^?$ or $A^?$, respectively, to move to π. Likewise, if A and B are of the same signature but the behaviors of A are not contained within those of B, then either A performs some output action which B cannot, in which case $B^!$ moves to π, or B performs some input action which A cannot, in which case $A^?$ moves to π.

Theorem 3 (Checking Compatibility). *Let $A \| B$ be a closed automaton. Then $A \sim B$ if and only if π is not reachable in $A^? \| B^?$.*

Theorem 4 (Checking Refinement). *Let A and B be safe interface automata with matching signatures such that B is deterministic. $A \preceq B$ if and only if π is not reachable in $A^? \| B^!$.*

We omit the proofs in the interest of space.

Example 6. $\mathcal{A}_{\mathrm{msg}}$, $\mathcal{A}_{\mathrm{usr}}$, and $\mathcal{E}_{\mathrm{bad}}$ (Figs. 2b, 1a, and 1b) are incompatible since π is reachable in the composition of $\mathcal{A}_{\mathrm{msg}}^?$, $\mathcal{A}_{\mathrm{usr}}^?$, and $\mathcal{E}_{\mathrm{bad}}^?$ by the sequence msg; send; nack; send; nack; fail; (see Fig. 1d). On the other hand, $\mathcal{A}_{\mathrm{env}}$ (Fig. 1c) does not refine $\mathcal{C}_1$ (Fig. 2a) since π is reachable in the composition of $\mathcal{A}_{\mathrm{env}}^?$ and $\mathcal{C}_1^!$ by the sequence send; ack;.

4 Assume-Guarantee Reasoning for Interface Automata

Although in the simple setting of Example 5 the system and environment are relatively small, their composition could, in general, be very complex. We then seek to find a smaller environment model which is descriptive enough to prove the absence of error states in the composition, in the case that there are none.

Figure 3 introduces assume-guarantee rules for reasoning with interface automata. Since composition and compatibility are only defined for composable interface automata, we'll henceforth assume that the automata said to take part in these relations are composable. For the remainder of this section, the symbols M_1, M_2, S, and A range over interface automata, and P denotes a property specified by a safety LTS. Completeness, in the present setting, means that an assumption for use in the premises of rule exists whenever the conclusion holds.

	IA-COMPAT	IA-PROP	IA-ALTREF
Premise 1	$M_1 \sim A$	$M_1 \| A \models P$	$M_1 \sim A \wedge M_1 \| A \preceq S$
Premise 2	$M_2 \preceq A$	$M_2 \models \text{lts}(A)$	$M_2 \preceq A$
Conclusion	$M_1 \sim M_2$	$M_1 \| M_2 \models P$	$M_1 \sim M_2 \wedge M_1 \| M_2 \preceq S$

Fig. 3. Assume-guarantee rules for interface automata. Rule IA-COMPAT gives a modular characterization of compatibility; IA-PROP is the IA instantiation of the classical safety rule [8]; IA-ALTREF modularly establishes alternating refinement with respect to a high-level specification S.

Theorem 5. *IA-COMPAT, IA-PROP, IA-ALTREF are sound and complete.*

Soundness of Rule IA-COMPAT is an immediate consequence of Theorem 2. Soundness of Rule IA-PROP is guaranteed by the soundness of the original rule for transition systems [11, 8]. Soundness of Rule IA-ALTREF is guaranteed by Theorems 1 and 2. Completeness, for any of the rules, follows directly by replacing A with M_2.

Since Rule IA-ALTREF is only meaningful for open systems, and the current work deals with closed systems, its study is deferred for future work.

5 Weakest Assumptions

A central notion in the work on automatic assumption generation for assume-guarantee rules is the construction of a "weakest assumption". For a rule and a given alphabet (the communication alphabet between M_1 and M_2) the weakest assumption A_W is such that, for any assumption A that makes the premises of a rule hold, A necessarily refines A_W, i.e., A_W is as abstract as possible.

Lemma 1. *Given a rule and its associated weakest assumption A_W, the premises of the rule hold for A_W if and only if the conclusion of the rule holds.*

Therefore, to automate assume-guarantee reasoning based on a rule, it is sufficient to build the corresponding A_W and to use it when checking the premises of the rule. We begin with a description of a *direct* construction of the weakest assumptions for various rules. Since this construction involves expensive determinization, we also define in the next section algorithms that learn the traces of A_W *as needed*, using L*. Let us first introduce the following definition.

Definition 9. *The* mirror *of A, written* Mirror(A), *is an automaton identical to A, except for a symmetric alphabet partitioning:* $\alpha \text{Mirror}(A)^I = \alpha A^O$, $\alpha \text{Mirror}(A)^O = \alpha A^I$, *and* $\alpha \text{Mirror}(A)^H = \alpha A^H$.

Rule IA-COMPAT. The weakest assumption A_W of an interface automaton M_1 is an interface automaton with: $\alpha A_W^I = \alpha M_1^O$, $\alpha A_W^O = \alpha M_1^I$, and $\alpha A_W^H = \emptyset$. It is constructed from $M_1^?$ as follows: 1) determinize[2]; 2) remove all transitions to

---

[2] The determinization of our interface automata identifies sets containing π, with π.

π (intuitively, all the inputs that M_1 does not accept lead to error in $M_1^?$, so its environment should not provide these), and 3) mirror the resulting automaton.

The above construction is similar to the property extraction step in the generation of assumptions when checking safety properties of LTSs [11]. However in [11], a completion step adds transitions to an (accepting) sink state. For compatibility, such completion of $M_1^?$ would add outputs ($M_1^?$ is input complete), and would force the environment to accept more inputs than necessary, i.e., the obtained assumption would not be the *weakest*. Also, the extra mirroring step here is needed to obtain a correct representation of the environment.

Rule IA-PROP. As mentioned, Rule IA-PROP is the same as the original rule for LTSs [11,8], so the same notion of a weakest assumption applies. However, in the context of interface automata, the knowledge that $M_1 \sim M_2$ holds may be used for defining a weaker assumption with fewer states than the one in previous work [8]. Let A_W be the weakest assumption for M_2 with respect to M_1 and P, as previously defined [11]. A_W is an interface automaton with: $\alpha A_W^I = \alpha M_1^O \cap \alpha M_2^I$, $\alpha A_W^O = \alpha M_1^I \cap \alpha M_2^O$, and $\alpha A_W^H = \alpha P \cap \alpha M_2^H$. Assume that we already checked $M_1 \sim M_2$ (using e.g. Rule IA-COMPAT) and it holds. We build assumption A_C such that

$$\mathcal{L}(A_C) = \mathcal{L}(A_W) \setminus \{t \mid \exists u \in (\alpha M_1^O)^+ \text{ s.t. } tu \notin \mathcal{L}(A_W)\}.$$

In other words, the assumption does not restrict the behaviors of M_1 by non-acceptance of M_1's outputs (i.e. the assumption is compatible with M_1). A_C is constructed from $M_1 \| P^\pi$ using the same steps of previous work [11], with the following differences. Since $M_1 \sim M_2$ holds, backwards error propagation is performed along *output* transitions *in addition to* internal transitions. Therefore A_C has potentially fewer states than A_W. Moreover, the resulting automaton needs to be mirrored since we are dealing with interface automata.

Lemma 2. *Let $M_1 \sim M_2$, and let A_W and A_C be the assumptions defined above. Then $M_1 \| A_C \models P \land M_2 \models \text{lts}(A_C) \iff M_1 \| M_2 \models P$.*

The above Lemma establishes that A_C, which has at most as many states as A_W, is the weakest assumption. For Rule IA-PROP, we will henceforth use the term weakest assumption (A_W) to refer to A_C.

6 Learning-Based Assume-Guarantee Reasoning

We develop iterative techniques based on L* [3, 22] to check $M_1 \| M_2$ compositionally, by automatically computing the weakest assumptions for Rules IA-COMPAT and IA-PROP. We provide L* with *teachers* using error state reachability analysis to answer membership queries and conjectures. We use L* conjectures as an assumption to check the premises of the rules (using an *oracle* for each premise). When both oracles return OK then the premise is satisfied, and the analysis terminates. Failure of Premise 1 gives L* a counterexample to refine its conjecture, while failure of Premise 2 either corresponds to a real system violation (and the analysis terminates) or gives L* a counterexample for refinement.

The techniques presented here are similar in spirit to existing techniques [8], but must be significantly more complex to address the non-trivial notions of compatibility and alternating refinement (the techniques learn the traces of the new weakest assumptions that we defined in the previous section). Indeed existing algorithms [8] check a strictly weaker property—a consequence of not distinguishing input from output actions.

We make use of the following auxiliary procedures in our L* teachers.

simulate(M,t) returns a set of M-states to which t is a trace, or π with the shortest prefix of t tracing to π, or $\emptyset$ with the shortest prefix of t which is not a trace of M.

analyze(M∥N) returns ERROR(M) (resp., ERROR(N)) when π is reachable in an M-component (resp., N-component) of the composition, and otherwise OK.

Algorithm for compatibility. In our algorithm for obtaining the weakest assumption for Rule IA-COMPAT, we use the procedures in Fig. 4 for answering queries and conjectures. ORACLE 1 uses Theorem 3 to check $M_1 \sim A$, while ORACLE 2 uses Theorem 4 to check $M_2 \preceq A$. If either case fails, the L* teacher emits a counterexample trace witnessing such failure. For the case of ORACLE 2, further analysis determines whether the trace represents an actual incompatibility between M_1 and M_2, or the assumption needs further refinement. If the trace turns out to be an error in M_1, or an error in M_2 which does not block M_1, $M_1 \not\sim M_2$; otherwise the trace is not a feasible incompatibility of the system, so the assumption needs refinement.

procedure QUERY-IA-COMPAT(t)
1: (states,_) := simulate($M_1^?$, t)
2: if $\pi \in$ states then
3:   return NO
4: else if states = $\emptyset$ then
5:   return NO
6: end if
7: return YES

procedure ORACLE1-IA-COMPAT(A)
1: (result,t) := analyze($M_1^?$∥A$^?$)
2: t := t $\downarrow_{\alpha A}$
3: if result = ERROR then
4:   return REFINE(t)
5: else
6:   return OK
7: end if

procedure ORACLE2-IA-COMPAT(A)
1: (result,t) := analyze($M_2^?$∥A$^!$)
2: if result = OK then
3:   return OK
4: end if
5: t := t $\downarrow_{\alpha A}$
6: (states,t') := simulate($M_1^?$, t)
7: if $\pi \in$ states then
8:   return INCOMPATIBLE
9: else if states = $\emptyset$
    or result = ERROR(A) then
10:   return REFINE(t')
11: else if result = ERROR($M_2^?$) then
12:   return INCOMPATIBLE
13: end if

Fig. 4. The L* Teacher for Rule IA-COMPAT

Example 7. Our teacher for Rule IA-COMPAT receives a total of four conjectures when M_1 and M_2 are given by $\mathcal{A}_{\text{sys}}$ and $\mathcal{A}_{\text{env}}$ (Figs. 1d, 1c), respectively. The first and second conjectures are the automata $\mathcal{C}_1$ and $\mathcal{E}_{\text{bad}}$ (Figs. 2a, 2b), respectively, which Example 6 shows violate Premises 2 and 1 of Rule IA-COMPAT. The third conjecture $\mathcal{C}_3$ (Fig. 2c) is also incompatible with $\mathcal{A}_{\text{sys}}$, since the cycle formed between states 1 and 2 allow an arbitrary number of consecutive `nacks`. The final conjecture, $\mathcal{E}_{\text{good}}$ (Fig. 2d) is refined by $\mathcal{A}_{\text{env}}$ and adequate enough to prove compatibility with $\mathcal{A}_{\text{sys}}$.

Algorithm for property safety. Although the LTS safety checking algorithm of [8] can soundly be applied to interface automata, the knowledge about compatibility between automata allows us to develop an optimized algorithm for checking property safety. To do so, we must first consider controllability.

Definition 10. *Let A be an interface automaton, and $t \in \alpha A$ a word. The controllable prefix of t (w.r.t. A), written $\text{ControlPref}_A(t)$ is the longest prefix of t ending in an output or internal action of A.*

Intuitively, the controllable prefix corresponds to the period of time a particular component is dictating a trace. In our optimized safety checking algorithm, we consider incompatibilities arising from any externally controlled sequence appended to the end of the control prefix, not just the particular uncontrollable suffix of the trace. We extend `simulate` to account for this behavior.

`ext_simulate(M,t)` extends `simulate(M,t)` by additionally returning `ERROR` together with the shortest trace to π, when such an error can be reached via a prefix of `t` followed by a sequence of uncontrollable actions.

The key difference between our algorithm (that uses the procedures in Fig. 5 for queries and conjectures) and previous work [8] is that queries here replace the standard automata simulation with `ext_simulate`. The extension accounts for the fact that error states are propagated along output transitions in addition to internal ones in $M_1 \| P^\pi$ (recall, these actions correspond to ones that A cannot control). Moreover, when an assumption must be refined, the teacher returns to L* the controllable prefix of the counterexample that is obtained from reachability analysis (see line 4 in ORACLE 1 and line 5 in ORACLE 2).

Correctness. Granting Lemma 3, we are guaranteed that either L* terminates with the weakest assumption, or that $\mathcal{R}$ does not hold. We omit the proof in the interest of space.

Lemma 3. *Let $\mathcal{R}$ be an assume-guarantee rule in the context of interface automata M_1 and M_2 (and if applicable the safety LTS P), and let A_W be the weakest assumption for $\mathcal{R}$. Then*

(i) QUERY-$\mathcal{R}$(t) *returns* YES *iff* t *is a trace of A_W, and*
(ii) CONJECTURE-$\mathcal{R}$(A) *returns*
   (a) OK *iff the conclusion of $\mathcal{R}$ holds,*
   (b) INCOMPATIBLE *or* PROPERTY_VIOLATION *if the conclusion of $\mathcal{R}$ does not hold, and otherwise*
   (c) *a trace in the symmetric difference of $\mathcal{L}(A)$ and $\mathcal{L}(A_W)$.*

procedure QUERY-IA-PROP(t)
1: (states,_) :=
      ext_simulate($M_1 \| P^\pi$,
      ControlPref$_A$(t))
2: **if** $\pi \in$ states **then**
3:    **return** NO
4: **end if**
5: **return** YES

procedure ORACLE1-IA-PROP(A)
1: (result,t) := analyze($M_1 \| P^\pi \| A$)
2: t := t $\downarrow_{\alpha A}$
3: **if** result = ERROR **then**
4:    **return** REFINE(ControlPref$_A$(t))
5: **else**
6:    **return** OK
7: **end if**

procedure ORACLE2-IA-PROP(A)
1: (result,t) := analyze($M_2 \| A^\pi$)
2: t := t $\downarrow_{\alpha A}$
3: **if** result = ERROR **then**
4:    **if** QUERY-IA-PROP(t) = YES **then**
5:       **return** REFINE(ControlPref$_A$(t))
6:    **else**
7:       **return** PROPERTY VIOLATION
8:    **end if**
9: **else**
10:    **return** OK
11: **end if**

Fig. 5. The L* Teacher for Rule IA-PROP

7 Experience

The ARD Case Study. Autonomous Rendezvous and Docking (ARD) describes a spacecraft's capability of locating and docking with another spacecraft without direct human guidance. In the context of a NASA project, we were given UML statecharts describing an ARD protocol at a high level of abstraction, along with some required properties in natural language, for example: *"good values from at least two sensors are required to proceed to the next mode."*

The model consists of sensors (GPS, StarPlanetTracker, InertialNavigation), used to estimate the current position, velocity, etc. of the spacecraft, and "modes" that constitute a typical ARD system (see Figure 6). The ARD software moves sequentially through the modes, exhibiting different behavior in each. The Orbital-State component takes sensor readings and reports to the mode-related software whether it obtained good readings from enough sensors to calculate a reasonable spacecraft state estimate for ARD. The ARD software enables or disables the orbital state (via enableNavigation and disableNavigation actions, respectively), reads the current estimate (via the read action), and requests for an update of the state estimation (via refresh). The sensors may also fail, as observed through the failed actions.

Study Set-Up. We have extended the LTSA tool [18] to provide support for expressing interface automata and also with algorithms for (1) compatibility and refinement checking and (2) learning-based compositional verification for interface automata for Rules IA-COMPAT and IA-PROP. In an initial study of the ARD system we translated the UML statecharts and their expected properties into LTSs for LTSA; for the current study we refined these LTSs into Interface Automata, resulting in approximately 1000 lines of input code for the LTSA.

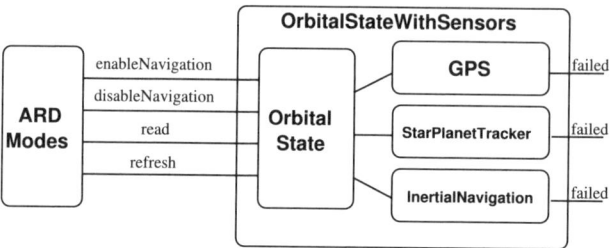

Fig. 6. Architecture of ARD protocol

Model Incompatibilities. Checking compatibility in the ARD system uncovered subtle errors that were undetected in our original study using simple LTS analysis. One incompatibility concerned the OrbitalState sub-system, which is made up of an Estimator and three Counters; the counters record the number of good readings obtained for position, velocity and attitude; estimates are updated through the refresh action. Checking compatibility between the Estimator and the Counters uncovered an error that prevented a significant portion of the system from being exercised.

We illustrate this error with a simplified OrbitalState (see Figures 7 and 8) that estimates position only with a single sensor. When the estimator refreshes, it gets a reading from the sensor. If the reading is sensor_good, the estimator increments the counter. The estimator then gets the counter value get_val; the estimate becomes est_poor when this value is 0, and is otherwise est_good. In intermediate states the estimate is est_updating. Incompatibility between the two components is illustrated by trace: <refresh, sensor_good, increment, get_val, return.1, refresh, sensor_good, increment>, where the estimator tries to increment the counter at its max value. The error occurs because the counter is not reset when it should be (i.e., after each refresh operation). If LTSs were used instead of interface automata, incrementing a counter at its max value would simply not be possible in the composition. Despite this fact, the system would not deadlock, because of the self-loops in the estimator. One could write liveness properties to ensure that certain behaviors are always possible in the system, but it is much simpler and less costly to check for a pre-defined notion of compatibility that does not require specification.

Results and Discussion. After correcting the incompatibilities in the OrbitalState component, we applied our compositional algorithms system-wide level. We divided the ARD model into two components: ARDModes (representing M_1) and OrbitalStateWithSensors (representing M_2); we checked that compatibility and a safety property (the sensor quality property, mentioned earlier) hold. The results in Table 1 compare running LTSA for non-compositional verification with learning-based assume-guarantee reasoning. For each of the runs we report the maximum number of states and transitions explored (separated by the corresponding premise), the analysis time, and the generated assumption's number

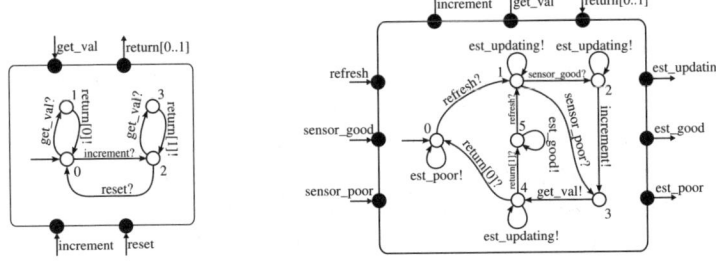

Fig. 7. The ARD counter   **Fig. 8.** The ARD position estimator

Table 1. Analysis results for a NASA ARD model

Check	Non-compositional			Compositional				
	States	Transitions	Time	Rule	States	Transitions	$|A|$	Time
Compatibility	2434K	16612K	37s	IA-COMPAT			35	445s
				Prem. 1	5K	34K		
				Prem. 2	**182K**	**864K**		
Property	2438K	16634K	36s	IA-PROP			74	483s
				Prem. 1	20K	113K		
				Prem. 2	**433K**	**3393K**		

of states. The experiments were run on a 64-bit Sun machine running Windows and a 1GB Java virtual machine.

During compositional verification, the largest state spaces explored were during the second premises for the assume-guarantee rules (highlighted in bold in Table 1). This is approximately one order of magnitude smaller than the state space explored when checking $M_1 \| M_2$ directly. On the other hand, assume-guarantee reasoning took 445s (483s) as compared to 37s (36s) for checking compatibility (resp., safety property) directly. This time penalty is due to the iterative nature of the learning algorithm and to the relatively large number of states in the generated assumption. Previous studies [8,2] on learning for compositional reasoning in other formalisms showed that the approach does not incur such time penalty when smaller assumptions are obtained (i.e., less than 10 states).

The results reported in Table 1 for checking the safety property use the optimized algorithm presented in Section 6. Application of our algorithm from [8] (that views the two components as LTSs and does not take advantage of compatibility) resulted in an assumption of 77 states. The savings in terms of the assumption size (3 states) are not significant in this case. The reason is that the components in our study exhibit behavior where inputs and outputs strictly alternate. More pronounced savings may be obtained in systems where occurrences of chains of output and internal actions may lead to the error state. Finally, we have also experimented with an algorithm that combines Rules IA-COMPAT and IA-PROP: the hybrid algorithm computes an assumption that guarantees both compatibility and property satisfaction. With this algorithm, we obtained an assumption of 94 states (in 3930 seconds). This indicates that checking the two properties separately results in smaller assumptions.

We remark that the largest assumptions built by our frameworks are still much smaller than the components that they represent in the compositional rules (M_1 has over 5K states and M_2 has over 143K states). Therefore, the cost of re-verification, for example, using assume-guarantee reasoning will be much smaller than non-compositional verification.

8 Related Work

Several frameworks have been proposed to support assume-guarantee reasoning [14, 21, 6, 12], but their practical impact has been limited by their need for human input in defining appropriate assumptions. Frameworks using L* to learn assumptions or component interfaces have been developed, for example, in the context of assume-guarantee reasoning of LTSs [11, 8], synthesizing interfaces for Java classes [1], and symbolic model checking using NuSMV [2]. Unlike these approaches, we distinguish input actions from output actions to allow stricter property checking (i.e., ensuring compatibility).

Several optimizations to learning for assume-guarantee reasoning have also been studied. Alternative system decompositions [7, 20] and discovering small interface alphabets [10, 4] may positively affect the performance of learning. Our methods are orthogonal to these, as we consider an extended transition system.

Another approach [13] uses predicate abstraction and refinement to synthesize interfaces for software libraries. This work does not use learning, nor does it reuse the resulting interfaces in assume-guarantee verification. Several approaches have been defined to automatically abstract a component's environment to obtain interfaces [15, 5], however these techniques are not incremental and do not differentiate between inputs and outputs.

9 Conclusion

In this work we have developed a theoretical framework for the automated compositional verification of systems modeled with interface automata. We provide sound and complete assume-guarantee rules, and learning-based algorithms targeting the weakest-possible assumption for each rule. An evaluation of our algorithms on an application of a NASA case study is also presented, based on the implementation of the algorithms in a practical model checking tool.

References

1. Alur, R., Cerny, P., Madhusudan, P., Nam, W.: Synthesis of interface specifications for java classes. In: Proc. 32nd POPL (2005)
2. Alur, R., Madhusudan, P., Nam, W.: Symbolic compositional verification by learning assumptions. In: Proc. 17th CAV (2005)
3. Angluin, D.: Learning regular sets from queries and counterexamples. Inf. Comput. 75(2) (1987)
4. Chaki, S., Strichman, O.: Optimized L* for assume-guarantee reasoning. In: Proc. 13th TACAS (2007)
5. Cheung, S.C., Kramer, J.: Checking safety properties using compositional reachability analysis. TOSEM 8(1) (1999)
6. Clarke, E.M., Long, D.E., McMillan, K.L.: Compositional model checking. In: Proc. 4th LICS (1989)
7. Cobleigh, J.M., Avrunin, G.S., Clarke, L.A.: Breaking up is hard to do: An investigation of decomposition for assume-guarantee reasoning. In: ISSTA (2006)
8. Cobleigh, J.M., Giannakopoulou, D., Păsăreanu, C.S.: Learning assumptions for compositional verification. In: Proc. 9th TACAS (2003)
9. de Alfaro, L., Henzinger, T.A.: Interface automata. In: Proc. 8th ESEC/FSE (2001)
10. Gheorghiu, M., Giannakopoulou, D., Păsăreanu, C.S.: Refining interface alphabets for compositional verification. In: Proc. 13th TACAS (2007)
11. Giannakopoulou, D., Păsăreanu, C.S., Barringer, H.: Assumption generation for software component verification. In: Proc. 17th ASE (2002)
12. Grumberg, O., Long, D.E.: Model checking and modular verification. In: Proc. 2nd CONCUR (1991)
13. Henzinger, T.A., Jhala, R., Majumdar, R.: Permissive interfaces. In: Proc. 10th ESEC/FSE (2005)
14. Jones, C.B.: Specification and design of (parallel) programs. In: Proc. 9th IFIP Congress (1983)
15. Krimm, J.-P., Mounier, L.: Compositional state space generation from Lotos programs. In: Proc. 3rd TACAS (1997)
16. Letier, E., Kramer, J., Magee, J., Uchitel, S.: Monitoring and control in scenario-based requirements analysis. In: Proc. 27th ICSE (2005)
17. Lynch, N., Tuttle, M.: An introduction to input/output automata. Centrum voor Wiskunde en Informatica 2(3) (1989)
18. Magee, J., Kramer, J.: Concurrency: State Models & Java Programs. John Wiley & Sons, Chichester (1999)
19. Magee, J., Kramer, J., Giannakopoulou, D.: Behaviour analysis of software architectures. In: Proc. 1st WICSA (1999)
20. Nam, W., Alur, R.: Learning-based symbolic assume-guarantee reasoning with automatic decomposition. In: Proc. 4th ATVA (2006)
21. Pnueli, A.: In transition from global to modular temporal reasoning about programs. In: Logic and Models of Concurrent Systems (1984)
22. Rivest, R.L., Schapire, R.E.: Inference of finite automata using homing sequences. In: Proc. 21st STOC (1989)
23. Veanes, M., Campbell, C., Schulte, W., Tillmann, N.: Online testing with model programs. In: Proc. 10th ESEC/FSE (2005)

Automated Verification of Dense-Time MTL Specifications Via Discrete-Time Approximation*

Carlo A. Furia[1], Matteo Pradella[2], and Matteo Rossi[1]

[1] Dipartimento di Elettronica e Informazione, Politecnico di Milano, Italy
[2] CNR IEIIT-MI, Milano, Italy
{furia,pradella,rossi}@elet.polimi.it
http://home.dei.polimi.it/lastname/

Abstract. This paper presents a verification technique for dense-time MTL based on discretization. The technique reduces the validity problem of MTL formulas from dense to discrete time, through the notion of *sampling invariance*, introduced in previous work [13]. Since the reduction is from an undecidable problem to a decidable one, the technique is necessarily incomplete, so it fails to provide conclusive answers for some formulas. The paper discusses this shortcoming and hints at how it can be mitigated in practice. The verification technique has been implemented on top of the Zot tool [19] for discrete-time bounded validity checking; the paper also reports on in-the-small experiments with the tool, which show some results that are promising in terms of performance.

Keywords: real-time, metric temporal logic, discretization, dense time, verification techniques, sampling.

1 Introduction

Metric temporal logics such as MTL [18] and TRIO [5] are effective and flexible notations to model and reason about a wide range of systems — real-time, in particular — with varying level of detail. Both MTL and TRIO are parametric with respect to the temporal domain, and permit to describe systems either with a dense or a discrete notion of time [11].

Indeed, when modeling the behavior of real-time systems, the nature of the time domain plays a prominent role, and it must be carefully chosen. From a modeling viewpoint, dense time offers advantages in terms of naturalness and completeness of description, being of the same quality as "physical time", in particular when describing the composition of purely asynchronous processes (which can occur at any instant in time); also, it is usually strictly more expressive than discrete time [2]. Conversely, in practice, discrete-time models are generally more amenable to (automated) verification than dense-time ones. In fact, dense-time formalisms are often undecidable or with highly complex decidability problems

---

* Work partially supported by MIUR under the FIRB ArtDeco project.

[2]; in addition, while verification methods for discrete-time models can often be built upon existing techniques (e.g., for LTL, automata, and untimed formalisms), the native treatment of dense time requires novel, more ingenuous, solutions. In the literature, various techniques have been proposed to mitigate this problem. A significant category of such approaches rely on some notion of *discretization*, which consists in reducing the verification problem from dense to discrete time. Therefore, discretization techniques permit the re-use of existing techniques (and tools), but, for formalisms that are strictly more expressive in their dense-time variant, they are also necessarily *incomplete*, i.e., they fail to give conclusive results on some instances of the verification problem.

In [13], we introduced the notion of *sampling* for temporal logic formulas, an idealization of the physical sampling process. We defined ^R_ZTRIO, a subset of the TRIO metric temporal logic interpreted over *behaviors* (i.e., total functions of time), and we identified a sufficient condition under which ^R_ZTRIO formulas are *sampling invariant* (i.e., such that they can be interpreted consistently over dense-time behaviors and over discrete-time samplings thereof). While the results of [13] were derived for ^R_ZTRIO, it is immediate to translate them for MTL, the reference language in this paper. Hence, in the following we always refer to MTL rather than ^R_ZTRIO, also when citing results from [13].

In the field of formal verification, automata-based techniques have been extensively studied [6]. However, in the last few years, the increased practical efficiency of SAT solvers has rendered SAT-based verification techniques an interesting and viable alternative [3]. These are particularly well-suited in purely logical/descriptive approaches, where both the system to be analyzed and its desired properties (i.e., the entire verification problem) are expressed as temporal logic formulas. In [20], we introduced Zot, a SAT-based verification tool for discrete-time metric temporal logics with past operators (e.g., TRIO and MTL).

In this paper, we build upon the results of [13] and [20] to provide an effective, fully automated technique and tool for the verification of specifications written in dense-time metric temporal logic. Our contribution is twofold. First, the verification technique is introduced and proved sound. The technique relies on *two approximations* (ϕ^+ and ϕ^-) of the formula representing the instance of the verification problem. These approximations represent a mapping of the problem to the discrete-time domain; in other words, they encode information about the samplings of the original dense-time behaviors. Approximations are built parametrically with respect to a chosen length of the sampling period for these samplings. Then, the validity of ϕ^+ over discrete time implies the validity of the original formula over dense time; conversely, the non-validity of ϕ^- over discrete time implies the non-validity of the original formula over dense time. As mentioned above, the technique must be incomplete, i.e., it may happen that the validity check of the approximations yields inconclusive results. This paper discusses how this can be mitigated in practice.

As a second contribution, we demonstrated the practical applicability of the technique by implementing it on top of the Zot validity checker [19], and by performing some experiments. Although limited to a small set of examples, our tests show interesting results; in particular, incompleteness is shown to be not often a practical hurdle (usually because other limitations are more significant, such as the inherent scalability even of discrete-time methods). The tests are thus a first assessment of the feasibility of our discretization techniques.

The paper is organized as follows: Section 1.1 surveys some related works on discretization techniques; Section 2 introduces the MTL subset considered in this paper and recalls the notions of sampling (and sampling invariance) from [13]; Section 3 presents the discretization technique itself; Section 4 briefly describes the implementation and reports on the experiments carried out; finally, Section 5 concludes. For lack of space, we omit some proofs, a few technical details, and several experimental results; we refer the interested reader to [12].

1.1 Related Works

The problem of reducing the dense-time verification problem to the discrete-time one was first explicitly studied in the seminal paper by Henzinger, Manna, and Pnueli [16]. Their discretization techniques are based on the notion of *digitization*; a (semantic) property (i.e., a set of timed state sequences) is digitizable if it is both closed under digitization and closed under inverse digitization. Basically, a property is closed under digitization if all the timed state sequences obtained by digitizing the real-timed state sequences are also integer-timed state sequences of the property; conversely, a property is closed under inverse digitization if all its integer-timed state sequences can be obtained by digitizing some real-timed state sequences of the property. The digitization of a timed state sequence is built by considering all possible roundings, with respect to any threshold $0 \leq \epsilon < 1$, of the timestamps in the timed state sequence. Note that the timestamps are *weakly monotonic*, so that more than one state value can share the same timestamp.

The comparison between the notion of digitization and the notion of sampling invariance — to be recalled in Section 2.2 — shows three main differences (see [10] for details). First, digitization assumes weakly monotonic timed words as semantic models, whereas sampling invariance considers (strongly monotonic) interval-based behaviors; each of these models has its own advantages and disadvantages [17]. Second, it has been shown [10] that the sets of MTL properties that are digitizable and sampling invariant are incomparable, i.e., there are digitizable properties that are not sampling invariant and sampling invariant properties that are not digitizable; this suggests that discretization techniques based on these two notions are likely to have different domains of applicability. Third, whereas sampling invariance is a syntactic property (i.e., it is defined for MTL formulas), digitizability is a semantic notion (i.e., it is defined for sets of timed words); as a consequence it is straightforward to characterize a significant subset of the MTL language whose formulas are sampling invariant, whereas doing the same with respect to digitizability is considerably more complicated [4].

Many subsequent works have applied the notion of digitization of [16], or other notions of discretization, to specific formalisms. In the remainder of this section we briefly report on a few of them, referring to [12] for more examples.

Chakravorty and Pandya [4] apply the notion of digitization to Interval Duration Logic (IDL), a variant of duration calculus where formulas are interpreted over timed state sequences. Overall, they introduce a technique to reduce the validity problem for dense-time IDL formulas to that of discrete-time IDL; this is possible for all IDL formulas that are closed under inverse digitization. However, it is hard to characterize closure under inverse digitization for IDL formulas; to lessen the problem, a new notion of *strong closure under inverse digitization* (SCID) is introduced. It is much simpler to determine if a formula is SCID, and SCID formulas are also closed under inverse digitization. For formulas that are not SCID, they give approximations to stronger and weaker formulas that are SCID. Finally, the validity problem for discrete-time IDL is decidable. Using these techniques, Sharma, Pandya, and Chakravorty [21] experiment with a variety of discrete-time verification tools.

De Alfaro and Manna [7] approach the problem of discretization with reference to the temporal logic TL, a particular flavor of predicative modal logic, and to the timed trace semantics. The authors first introduce the notion of *sample invariance* (not to be confused with our notion of sampling invariance, see Section 2.2): a temporal logic is sample invariant if the formulas of the logic do not distinguish between any two timed traces for which a (sufficiently fine-grained) trace that refines both exists. Then, the notion of *finite variability* is introduced: roughly speaking, a formula ϕ is finitely variable if, for each timed trace, one can find a refinement (called ground trace) such that any subformula of ϕ has a constant truth value within any interval of the refined trace. For finitely variable formulas over ground traces, the satisfaction relation of a formula ϕ in the continuous semantics corresponds to that of $\Omega(\phi)$ in the discrete semantics (where Ω is a suitably defined translation function). The paper states some sufficient syntactic condition for a formula to achieve the finite variability requirement. Based on this, a methodology for continuous-time verification is proposed; it is based on refinement of continuous-time formulas to finitely-variable formulas, which can then be verified in discrete time.

Fainekos and Pappas [9] present a technique for testing specifications written in MITL (an MTL subset) against continuous-time signals by analyzing only discrete samplings of the signals. Their technique shares some underlying motivations and ideas with ours, although the two approaches have complementary scopes: our tool-supported technique provides a partial verification procedure for MTL formulas through discrete-time analysis, whereas [9] discusses practical conditions under which the continuous-time behavior of a dynamical system can be analyzed by means of its discrete-time observations.

2 Preliminaries

2.1 Specification Language: MTL

In this paper, we consider a variant of purely propositional Metric Temporal Logic (MTL, [2]) as the specification language. For brevity, we refer to this variant simply as "MTL".

Let $\mathcal{P}$ be a finite (non-empty) set of atomic propositions, and $\mathcal{I}$ the set of all (possibly unbounded) intervals of the time domain $\mathbb{T}$ with rational endpoints. In this paper $\mathbb{T}$ coincides with either the reals $\mathbb{R}$ (dense time) or the integers $\mathbb{Z}$ (discrete time) — or some subset thereof; we call *bi-infinite* the sets $\mathbb{R}$ and $\mathbb{Z}$, and *mono-infinite* their subsets $\mathbb{R}_{\geq 0}$ and $\mathbb{N} = \mathbb{Z}_{\geq 0}$.

Behaviors are total mappings $b: \mathbb{T} \to 2^{\mathcal{P}}$ that assign to every instant $t \in \mathbb{T}$ the set of propositions $b(t) \subseteq \mathcal{P}$ that are true at t. We denote as $\mathcal{B}_{\mathbb{T}}$ the set of all *behaviors* over $\mathbb{T}$.

MTL Syntax and Semantics

Syntax. The following grammar defines the *syntax* of MTL, where $I \in \mathcal{I}$ and β is a Boolean combination of atomic propositions, i.e., $\beta ::= \mathsf{p} \,|\, \neg \beta \,|\, \beta_1 \wedge \beta_2$ for $\mathsf{p} \in \mathcal{P}$.

$$\phi ::= \beta \,|\, \phi_1 \vee \phi_2 \,|\, \phi_1 \wedge \phi_2 \,|\, \mathsf{U}_I(\beta_1, \beta_2) \,|\, \mathsf{S}_I(\beta_1, \beta_2) \,|\, \mathsf{R}_I(\beta_1, \beta_2) \,|\, \mathsf{T}_I(\beta_1, \beta_2)$$

The basic temporal operator of MTL is the *bounded until* U_I (and its past counterpart *bounded since* S_I), whose subscript I denotes the interval of time over which the operator predicates. However, the results of sampling invariance, recalled in Section 2.2, as well as the discretization techniques introduced in Section 3, are easier to present when referred to MTL formulas that are in a normal form where negations are pushed down to (Boolean combinations of) atomic propositions, and no temporal operators are nested. Therefore, for the sake of simplicity, we introduced directly the MTL syntax for this normal form; hence, we also have the operators *bounded release* R_I and *bounded trigger* T_I — dual of *until* and *since*, respectively — as primitive.

Throughout the paper we omit the explicit treatment of past operators (i.e., S_I and T_I) as it can be trivially derived from that of the corresponding future operators, as shown in [12]. We also assume a number of abbreviations, such as $\bot, \top, \Rightarrow, \Leftrightarrow$, and the following derived operators: $\Diamond_I(\beta) \equiv \mathsf{U}_I(\top, \beta)$, $\overleftarrow{\Diamond}_I(\beta) \equiv \mathsf{S}_I(\top, \beta)$, $\Box_I(\beta) \equiv \mathsf{R}_I(\bot, \beta)$, and $\overleftarrow{\Box}_I(\beta) \equiv \mathsf{T}_I(\bot, \beta)$.

Semantics. MTL *semantics* is defined over behaviors, parametrically with respect to the choice of the time domain $\mathbb{T}$.

$b(t) \models_{\mathbb{T}} \mathsf{p}$	iff	$\mathsf{p} \in b(t)$
$b(t) \models_{\mathbb{T}} \neg \mathsf{p}$	iff	$\mathsf{p} \notin b(t)$
$b(t) \models_{\mathbb{T}} \mathsf{U}_I(\beta_1, \beta_2)$	iff	there exists $d \in I$ such that: $b(t+d) \models_{\mathbb{T}} \beta_2$ and, for all $u \in [0,d]$ it is $b(t+u) \models_{\mathbb{T}} \beta_1$
$b(t) \models_{\mathbb{T}} \mathsf{R}_I(\beta_1, \beta_2)$	iff	for all $d \in I$ it is: $b(t+d) \models_{\mathbb{T}} \beta_2$ or there exists a $u \in [0,d)$ such that $b(t+u) \models_{\mathbb{T}} \beta_1$
$b(t) \models_{\mathbb{T}} \phi_1 \wedge \phi_2$	iff	$b(t) \models_{\mathbb{T}} \phi_1$ and $b(t) \models_{\mathbb{T}} \phi_2$
$b(t) \models_{\mathbb{T}} \phi_1 \vee \phi_2$	iff	$b(t) \models_{\mathbb{T}} \phi_1$ or $b(t) \models_{\mathbb{T}} \phi_2$
$b \models_{\mathbb{T}} \phi$	iff	for all $t \in \mathbb{T}$: $b(t) \models_{\mathbb{T}} \phi$

Whenever for all $b \in \mathcal{B}_{\mathbb{T}} : b \models_{\mathbb{T}} \phi$ we say that ϕ is $\mathbb{T}$-valid and write $\models_{\mathbb{T}} \phi$.

We remark that a global satisfiability semantics is assumed, i.e., the satisfiability of formulas is implicitly evaluated over *all* time instants in the time domain. This permits the direct and natural expression of most common real-time specifications (e.g., time-bounded response) without resorting to nesting of temporal operators. In addition, every generic MTL formulas with nesting temporal operators can be "flattened" to the form we introduced beforehand by introducing auxiliary propositions; in other words flat MTL and full MTL are equi-satisfiable [8,10]. Also notice that our MTL variant uses operators that are *non-strict* in their first argument, i.e., the future and past include the present instant, and the *until* and *since* operators are *matching*, i.e., they require their two arguments to hold together at some instant in I. Other work [14] analyzes the impact of these variants on expressiveness.

MTL$^+$/MTL* Syntax and Semantics. In order to express the discretization relations in Section 3, it is necessary to introduce some variations of the four basic temporal operators *until*, *since*, *release*, and *trigger*, denoted as $\mathsf{U}_I^\uparrow$, $\mathsf{S}_I^\uparrow$, $\mathsf{R}_I^\downarrow$, and $\mathsf{T}_I^\downarrow$, respectively. Notice that they are not part of the language in which dense-time specifications and properties are to be expressed, and they are needed only to illustrate the discretization techniques. We call "MTL$^+$" the *extension* of MTL with these operators, and "MTL*" the variant where we *replace* the operators U_I, S_I, R_I, T_I with $\mathsf{U}_I^\uparrow$, $\mathsf{S}_I^\uparrow$, $\mathsf{R}_I^\downarrow$, and $\mathsf{T}_I^\downarrow$, respectively.

Let us define the semantics of the new variants of *until* and *release*.
$b(t) \models_\mathbb{T} \mathsf{U}_I^\uparrow(\beta_1, \beta_2)$ iff there exists $d \in I$ such that: $b(t+d) \models_\mathbb{T} \beta_2$
 and, for all $u \in [0, d)$ it is $b(t+u) \models_\mathbb{T} \beta_1$
$b(t) \models_\mathbb{T} \mathsf{R}_I^\downarrow(\phi_1, \phi_2)$ iff for all $d \in I$ it is: $b(t+d) \models_\mathbb{T} \phi_2$ or there exists
 a $u \in [0, d]$ such that $b(t+u) \models_\mathbb{T} \phi_1$

Granularity. For an MTL formula ϕ, let $\mathcal{I}_\phi$ be the set of all non-null, finite interval bounds appearing in ϕ. Given a formula ϕ, its *granularity* ρ_ϕ is a pair of values (r_ϕ, R_ϕ) where r_ϕ is the greatest common divisor of the numerators of the elements in $\mathcal{I}_\phi$, and R_ϕ is the least common multiple of the denominators of the elements in $\mathcal{I}_\phi$. For any formula ϕ, we define $\mathcal{D}_\phi$ as the set of positive values δ such that any interval bound in $\mathcal{I}_\phi$ is an integer if divided by δ; it is not difficult to show that $\mathcal{D}_\phi$ can be derived from the granularity ρ_ϕ as the set of all fractions d/D such that: (1) D is a multiple of R_ϕ; and (2) d divides r_ϕ. Also notice that $\mathcal{D}_\phi$ has a maximum (given by r_ϕ/R_ϕ) but no minimum. $\mathcal{D}$ is generalized to sets of formulas Φ in an obvious manner.

2.2 Sampling Invariance

The discretization technique developed in Section 3 is based on the notion of *sampling invariance* [13]. This sub-section recalls the basic definitions and results about sampling invariance that are needed in the remainder; we refer to [13] for details. Note that, although sampling invariance results are presented in terms of bi-infinite time domains, they are valid in the mono-infinite case as well.

The notion of sampling invariance characterizes formulas whose truth value is "consistent" whether they are interpreted over dense-time or discrete-time behaviors. Informally, a formula ϕ is sampling invariant if the discrete-time behaviors that satisfy ϕ coincide with those obtained by "sampling" all the sufficiently slow dense-time behaviors that satisfy another formula ϕ' (where ϕ' is obtained from ϕ by suitably relaxing its interval bounds), and *vice versa* when ϕ is interpreted as a dense-time formula. Below, we recall the precise definition of sampling invariance, after briefly introducing the basic notions that are needed.

Bounded variability. As mentioned above, sampling invariance requires behaviors to be "sufficiently slow", with respect to a chosen period $\delta \in \mathbb{R}_{>0}$. Informally, the truth value of any atomic proposition must change at most once every δ time units; in other words, the change rate is bounded above by $1/\delta$. In fact, this requirement is sometimes called *bounded variability* [22]. The bounded variability requirement can be expressed as an MTL formula χ, which we do not report here for brevity [13]. We denote the set of all dense-time behaviors satisfying χ by $\mathcal{B}_\chi \subset \mathcal{B}_\mathbb{R}$, and we call them χ-regular behaviors. A formula ϕ is called χ-valid if $b \models_\mathbb{R} \phi$ for all $b \in \mathcal{B}_\chi$, and χ-satisfiable if $b \models_\mathbb{R} \phi$ for some $b \in \mathcal{B}_\chi$.

Zeno and Berkeley. A Zeno behavior is one where time progresses only by infinitesimal amounts, and thus it stops, instead of diverging. The name "Zeno" (introduced by Abadi and Lamport [1]) is a reference to the Greek philosopher Zeno of Elea and his paradoxes on time advancement. In this vein, we designate χ-regular behaviors "non-Berkeley" [10], from the Irish philosopher George Berkeley[1] and his investigations arguing against the notion of infinitesimal. So, a behavior is "Berkeley" when it does not obey constraint χ for any value of δ; thus the minimum distance in time between consecutive state changes is infinitesimal. Zeno behaviors are a special case of Berkeley behaviors; more generally, in a Berkeley behavior time can diverge, but with the system becoming arbitrarily "fast". See [10] for more details.

Sampling of a behavior. Let $b \in \mathcal{B}_\mathbb{R}$ be a dense-time behavior. Its *sampling*, with *sampling period* $\delta \in \mathbb{R}_{>0}$, is a discrete-time behavior $b' = \sigma_\delta[b] \in \mathcal{B}_\mathbb{Z}$ that agrees with b at all integer multiples of δ. Formally: $b'(k) = b(k\delta)$ for all $k \in \mathbb{Z}$.[2]

Let us point out a straightforward property of the sampling function $\sigma_\delta[\cdot]$ with respect to the set of behaviors $\mathcal{B}_\chi$.

Lemma 1 (Properties of $\sigma_\delta[\cdot]$). *For any $\delta \in \mathbb{R}_{>0}$, $\sigma_\delta[\cdot]$ is onto and total.*

Adaptation functions. To "switch" from the discrete-time to the dense-time interpretation of a formula ϕ in a way that preserves the truth value of ϕ, one has to "adapt" the interval bounds appearing in ϕ. This adaptation is formalized by two functions $\eta_\delta^\mathbb{R}\{\cdot\}$ and $\eta_\delta^\mathbb{Z}\{\cdot\}$: the former adapts dense-time formulas to be discrete-time ones, while the latter performs the converse.

The exact definition of $\eta_\delta^\mathbb{R}\{\cdot\}$ and $\eta_\delta^\mathbb{Z}\{\cdot\}$, omitted for the lack of space, is given in [13,12]. We note that, if ϕ is an MTL formula, then $\eta_\delta^\mathbb{R}\{\phi\}$ is an MTL* formula and $\eta_\delta^\mathbb{Z}\{\phi\}$ is an MTL formula.

---
[1] See e.g., http://www-groups.dcs.st-and.ac.uk/~history/Biographies/Berkeley.html
[2] The original definition in [13] also introduced a basic offset $z \in \mathbb{R}$, but since it does not play any role in the present discussion we simply take it to be zero.

Sampling invariance. Let us introduce precisely the notion of sampling invariance as a property of MTL formulas.

Theorem 1 (Sampling Invariance [13]). *Any MTL formula ϕ is sampling invariant, that is, for any sampling period δ: (1) (closure under sampling) for all dense-time behavior $b \in \mathcal{B}_\chi$, if $b \models_\mathbb{R} \phi$ then $\sigma_\delta[b] \models_\mathbb{Z} \eta_\delta^\mathbb{R}\{\phi\}$; and (2) (closure under inverse sampling) for all discrete-time behavior $b \in \mathcal{B}_\mathbb{Z}$, if $b \models_\mathbb{Z} \phi$ then $\forall b' \in \mathcal{B}_\chi$ such that $\sigma_\delta[b'] = b$, it is $b' \models_\mathbb{R} \eta_\delta^\mathbb{Z}\{\phi\}$.*

3 Discretization of Dense-Time MTL through Sampling

This section presents a discretization technique to solve the verification problem for MTL specifications.

First of all, given a dense-time MTL formula ϕ and a sampling period $\delta > 0$, we define two functions $\Omega_\delta : \text{MTL} \to \text{MTL}^*$, $O_\delta : \text{MTL} \to \text{MTL}$ that approximate ϕ through the discrete-time formulas $\Omega_\delta(\phi)$ and $O_\delta(\phi)$; basically, these retain some properties of the *samplings* of the dense-time behaviors satisfying ϕ, in a way that allows us to infer the validity of ϕ from the validity of its approximations. For reasons that will become apparent shortly, we name $\Omega_\delta(\phi)$ the *under-approximation* of ϕ, and $O_\delta(\phi)$ the *over-approximation*. They are presented in Sections 3.1 and 3.2, respectively.

In general, the verification problem consists in checking whether a system, described by a *specification* formula ϕ_{sys}, satisfies a given *property* ϕ_{prop}; in other words, whether $b \models_\mathbb{R} \phi_{\text{prop}}$ holds for any behavior b for which $b \models_\mathbb{R} \phi_{\text{sys}}$ holds. Section 3.3 shows how to construct two discrete-time formulas ϕ^+, ϕ^- that are both built upon the over- and under-approximations of ϕ_{sys} and ϕ_{prop}. Then:

– the validity of ϕ^+ over discrete time implies that system ϕ_{sys} satisfies property ϕ_{prop} over dense-time non-Berkeley behaviors;
– the non-validity of ϕ^- over discrete time implies that system ϕ_{sys} does not satisfy property ϕ_{prop} over some non-Berkeley dense-time behavior.

Finally, Section 3.4 shows how the previously introduced approximations can be used in an algorithm to verify a system specified in dense time. The resulting verification technique is however *incomplete*, in that the results from the validity checking of the approximations of a formula can be inconclusive; therefore the algorithm can fail. The incompleteness may be partially mitigated by suitably choosing the sampling period δ, but it cannot be entirely avoided. This is inevitable, since the approximation is a *simplification* of the dense-time verification problem, which cannot be fully captured by discrete-time reasoning only, for a number of well-known reasons [2,15].

3.1 Under-Approximation

The approximation function $\Omega_\delta(\cdot)$ maps dense-time MTL formulas to discrete-time MTL* formulas such that the non-validity of the latter implies the non-validity of the former, over behaviors in $\mathcal{B}_\chi$. More precisely, for MTL formulas such that the chosen sampling period δ is in $\mathcal{D}_\phi$ (see Section 2.1), $\Omega_\delta(\cdot)$ is defined as follows.

$$\begin{aligned}
\Omega_\delta(\beta) &\equiv \beta \\
\Omega_\delta(\phi_1 \wedge \phi_2) &\equiv \Omega_\delta(\phi_1) \wedge \Omega_\delta(\phi_2) \\
\Omega_\delta(\phi_1 \vee \phi_2) &\equiv \Omega_\delta(\phi_1) \vee \Omega_\delta(\phi_2) \\
\Omega_\delta\left(\mathsf{U}_{\langle l,u\rangle}(\phi_1,\phi_2)\right) &\equiv \mathsf{U}^\uparrow_{[l/\delta,u/\delta]}(\Omega_\delta(\phi_1),\Omega_\delta(\phi_2)) \\
\Omega_\delta\left(\mathsf{R}_{\langle l,u\rangle}(\phi_1,\phi_2)\right) &\equiv \mathsf{R}^\downarrow_{\langle l/\delta,u/\delta\rangle}(\Omega_\delta(\phi_1),\Omega_\delta(\phi_2))
\end{aligned}$$

The following lemma, proved in [12], justifies the name *under-approximation*.

Lemma 2 (Under-approximation). *For any MTL formula ϕ, for any $\delta \in \mathcal{D}_\phi$, and for any $b \in \mathcal{B}_\mathbb{Z}$: if $b \not\models_\mathbb{Z} \Omega_\delta(\phi)$ then for all $b' \in \mathcal{B}_\chi$ such that $\sigma_\delta[b'] = b$ it is $b' \not\models_\mathbb{R} \phi$.*

3.2 Over-approximation

The approximation function $O_\delta(\cdot)$ maps dense-time MTL formulas to discrete-time MTL formulas such that the validity of the latter implies the validity of the former, over behaviors in $\mathcal{B}_\chi$. More precisely, for MTL formulas such that the chosen sampling period δ is in $\mathcal{D}_\phi$ (see Section 2.1), $O_\delta(\cdot)$ is defined as follows.

$$\begin{aligned}
O_\delta(\beta) &\equiv \beta \\
O_\delta(\phi_1 \vee \phi_2) &\equiv O_\delta(\phi_1) \vee O_\delta(\phi_2) \\
O_\delta(\phi_1 \wedge \phi_2) &\equiv O_\delta(\phi_1) \wedge O_\delta(\phi_2) \\
O_\delta\left(\mathsf{U}_{\langle l,u\rangle}(\phi_1,\phi_2)\right) &\equiv \mathsf{U}_{[l/\delta+1,u/\delta-1]}(O_\delta(\phi_1),O_\delta(\phi_2)) \\
O_\delta\left(\mathsf{R}_{\langle l,u\rangle}(\phi_1,\phi_2)\right) &\equiv \mathsf{R}_{[l/\delta-1,u/\delta+1]}(O_\delta(\phi_1),O_\delta(\phi_2))
\end{aligned}$$

The following lemma justifies the name *over-approximation*.

Lemma 3 (Over-approximation). *For any MTL formula ϕ, for any $\delta \in \mathcal{D}_\phi$, and for any $b \in \mathcal{B}_\mathbb{Z}$: if $b \models_\mathbb{Z} O_\delta(\phi)$ then for all $b' \in \mathcal{B}_\chi$ such that $\sigma_\delta[b'] = b$ it is $b' \models_\mathbb{R} \phi$.*

Proof (sketch, see also [12]). $O_\delta(\phi)$ is an MTL formula, which is therefore sampling invariant according to Theorem 1, and in particular closed under inverse sampling. Therefore, let $b \in \mathcal{B}_\mathbb{Z}$ such that $b \models_\mathbb{Z} O_\delta(\phi)$. Then the definition of closure under inverse sampling implies that all $b' \in \mathcal{B}_\chi$ such that $b = \sigma_\delta[b']$ satisfy $b' \models_\mathbb{R} \eta_\delta^\mathbb{Z}\{O_\delta(\phi)\}$. According to the definition of $\eta_\delta^\mathbb{Z}\{\cdot\}$ (given in [12, Tab. 3]), one can check that $\eta_\delta^\mathbb{Z}\{O_\delta(\phi)\} \Rightarrow \phi$ is valid. More precisely, $\eta_\delta^\mathbb{Z}\{\cdot\}$ allows one to choose arbitrarily if any interval $\langle l,u\rangle$ of *until* and *since* should be closed or not, so that it is possible to match the original intervals in ϕ. Moreover, $\eta_\delta^\mathbb{Z}\{\cdot\}$ always yields a closed interval in instances of *release* and *trigger*; therefore, it gives either the same subformula as in ϕ, or a *strengthening* of it, when it replaces an open interval with its closure. It is easy to check that this property is lifted to whole formulas. All in all, $b' \models_\mathbb{R} \eta_\delta^\mathbb{Z}\{O_\delta(\phi)\}$ implies $b' \models_\mathbb{R} \phi$.

3.3 System Approximations

Let us now consider a system formally described by an MTL formula $\phi_{\sf sys}$, and a putative property described by another MTL formula $\phi_{\sf prop}$. Verification amounts to proving (or disproving) that all behaviors that satisfy $\phi_{\sf sys}$ also satisfy $\phi_{\sf prop}$.

Let us abbreviate by $\mathrm{Alw}(\phi)$ the nesting MTL formula $\phi \wedge \Box_{(0,+\infty)}(\phi) \wedge \overleftarrow{\Box}_{(0,+\infty)}(\phi)$; $b \models_{\mathbb{T}} \mathrm{Alw}(\phi)$ iff $b \models_{\mathbb{T}} \phi$, for any behavior b, so $\mathrm{Alw}(\phi)$ can be expressed without nesting if ϕ is flat, through the global satisfiability semantics. Then, the verification problem can be reduced to that of determining the validity of the MTL formula $\mathrm{Alw}(\phi_{\sf sys}) \Rightarrow \mathrm{Alw}(\phi_{\sf prop})$. To this end we prove the following.

Proposition 1 (Approximations). *For any MTL formulas ϕ_1, ϕ_2, and for any $\delta \in \mathcal{D}_{\phi_1,\phi_2}$: (1) if $\mathrm{Alw}(\Omega_\delta(\phi_1)) \Rightarrow \mathrm{Alw}(\mathrm{O}_\delta(\phi_2))$ is $\mathbb{Z}$-valid, then $\mathrm{Alw}(\phi_1) \Rightarrow \mathrm{Alw}(\phi_2)$ is χ-valid; and (2) if $\mathrm{Alw}(\mathrm{O}_\delta(\phi_1)) \Rightarrow \mathrm{Alw}(\Omega_\delta(\phi_2))$ is not $\mathbb{Z}$-valid, then $\mathrm{Alw}(\phi_1) \Rightarrow \mathrm{Alw}(\phi_2)$ is not χ-valid.*

Proof. Let $\delta \in \mathcal{D}_{\phi_1,\phi_2}$.

Proof of (1). Assume that $\phi^+ = \mathrm{Alw}(\Omega_\delta(\phi_1)) \Rightarrow \mathrm{Alw}(\mathrm{O}_\delta(\phi_2))$ is $\mathbb{Z}$-valid. That is, for all $b \in \mathcal{B}_\mathbb{Z}$ it is $b \models_\mathbb{Z} \phi^+$; equivalently: either $b \not\models_\mathbb{Z} \Omega_\delta(\phi_1)$ or $b \models_\mathbb{Z} \mathrm{O}_\delta(\phi_2)$. From Lemmas 3 and 2, this implies that for all $b \in \mathcal{B}_\mathbb{Z}$, for all $b' \in \mathcal{B}_\chi$ such that $\sigma_\delta[b'] = b$, it is either $b' \not\models_\mathbb{R} \phi_1$ or $b' \models_\mathbb{R} \phi_2$. Thus, let b' be any dense-time behavior in $\mathcal{B}_\chi$; from Lemma 1, there exists a $b \in \mathcal{B}_\mathbb{Z}$ such that $\sigma_\delta[b'] = b$. We conclude that for all $b' \in \mathcal{B}_\chi$, either $b' \not\models_\mathbb{R} \phi_1$ or $b' \models_\mathbb{R} \phi_2$. All in all, $\mathrm{Alw}(\phi_1) \Rightarrow \mathrm{Alw}(\phi_2)$ is χ-valid.

Proof of (2). We note that the proof of (2) can be obtained from the proof of (1) by duality. Thus, assume that $\phi^- = \mathrm{Alw}(\mathrm{O}_\delta(\phi_1)) \Rightarrow \mathrm{Alw}(\Omega_\delta(\phi_2))$ is not $\mathbb{Z}$-valid. That is, for some $b \in \mathcal{B}_\mathbb{Z}$ it is $b \not\models_\mathbb{Z} \phi^-$; equivalently: $b \models_\mathbb{Z} \mathrm{O}_\delta(\phi_1)$ and $b \not\models_\mathbb{Z} \Omega_\delta(\phi_2)$. From Lemmas 3 and 2, this implies that there exists a $b \in \mathcal{B}_\mathbb{Z}$ such that, for all $b' \in \mathcal{B}_\chi$ such that $\sigma_\delta[b'] = b$, it is $b' \models_\mathbb{R} \phi_1$ and $b' \not\models_\mathbb{R} \phi_2$. Next, Lemma 1 states that, for all $b \in \mathcal{B}_\mathbb{Z}$, there exists some b' such that $b' \in \mathcal{B}_\chi$ and $\sigma_\delta[b'] = b$. We conclude that there exists a $b' \in \mathcal{B}_\chi$ such that $\sigma_\delta[b'] = b$, $b' \models_\mathbb{R} \phi_1$ and $b' \not\models_\mathbb{R} \phi_2$. All in all, $\mathrm{Alw}(\phi_1) \Rightarrow \mathrm{Alw}(\phi_2)$ is not χ-valid. □

3.4 Validity Checking Procedure

Let us finally present the validity checking algorithm based on the approximations described above.

The algorithm takes as input a set of MTL formulas $\phi_{\sf sys}^1, \ldots, \phi_{\sf sys}^m, \phi_{\sf prop}$, where $\phi_{\sf sys}^i$ are the formulas describing the system, and $\phi_{\sf prop}$ is the property to be verified, as well as a suitable value δ. The algorithm checks the validity of $\phi = \bigwedge_{i=1,\ldots,m} \mathrm{Alw}(\phi_{\sf sys}^i) \Rightarrow \mathrm{Alw}(\phi_{\sf prop})$ as follows.

1. For each formula $\gamma \in \phi_{\sf prop} \cup \bigcup_{i=1,\ldots,m} \phi_{\sf sys}^i$, compute the over-approximation $\mathrm{O}_\delta(\gamma)$ and the under-approximation $\Omega_\delta(\gamma)$.
2. Compute:

$$\phi^+ = \bigwedge_{i=1,\ldots,m} \text{Alw}\left(\Omega_\delta\left(\phi_{\text{sys}}^m\right)\right) \Rightarrow \text{Alw}(O_\delta\left(\phi_{\text{prop}}\right));$$
$$\phi^- = \bigwedge_{i=1,\ldots,m} \text{Alw}\left(O_\delta\left(\phi_{\text{sys}}^m\right)\right) \Rightarrow \text{Alw}(\Omega_\delta\left(\phi_{\text{prop}}\right)).$$

3. If ϕ^+ is $\mathbb{Z}$-valid, then ϕ is χ-valid for sampling period δ;
4. otherwise, if ϕ^- is not $\mathbb{Z}$-valid, then ϕ is not χ-valid for sampling period δ;
5. otherwise, fail.

Incompleteness of the Algorithm. The incompleteness of the algorithm in determining the validity of MTL formulas is two-fold. First, the algorithm does not check *all* dense-time behaviors for satisfaction of an MTL formula ϕ, but only those obeying constraint χ for the chosen sampling period δ. Choosing a smaller δ may mitigate this shortcoming, as this amounts to choosing a finer sampling of behaviors or, equivalently, to allowing faster behaviors. However, this may also *not* bring better results. In fact, as δ decreases, not only do the approximation formulas change, but also more behaviors (namely, faster ones) are allowed; thus the effects of shortening the sampling periods are subtle and they may become difficult to predict. We leave a comprehensive study of this phenomenon to future work.

The second source of incompleteness lies in the technique itself, that is based on two different approximations for formula ϕ. Therefore, it is possible that ϕ^+ is non-valid and ϕ^- is valid; in this case, no conclusion about the validity of ϕ can be drawn.

4 Implementation and Experiments

This section describes the implementation of the verification algorithm (Section 4.1), presents two system verification problems (Section 4.2), and reports some of the results obtained in solving them using the tool presented in Section 4.1 (Section 4.3). Several more results can be found in [12].

4.1 Discrete-Time Bounded Validity Checking

The technique introduced in Section 3 reduces the validity-checking problem for MTL formulas over dense time to that over discrete time; the latter is known to be decidable and EXPSPACE-complete [2]. Recently, validity-checking techniques based on the use of propositional satisfiability (SAT) checkers have been developed for discrete-time verification, and they have yielded very encouraging performances in practical tests. Recent variants of these techniques offer the possibility to check completeness.

Zot is an agile and easily extensible bounded satisfiability checker (Zot and the examples described in this section are available for download [19]). The tool supports different logic languages through a multi-layered approach: its core uses PLTL, and a decidable predicative fragment of TRIO (in practice equivalent to $_\mathbb{Z}^\mathbb{R}$TRIO and MTL) is defined on top of it. Zot supports different encodings of temporal logic as SAT problems. Indeed, the user can choose a particular encoding to carry out verification, and the tool loads automatically the corresponding plug-in. At the moment, a few variants of some of the encodings presented in [3] are supported, and the encoding over $\mathbb{Z}$ presented in [20].

In order to assess the practical feasibility of our discretization technique, we verified some examples using Zot. To this end, Zot was extended to accept MTL$^+$ formulas, and to perform the discretization routine on formulas. The experimental results are described in Section 4.3.

4.2 Examples

We modeled two systems: a simple controlled reservoir (similar to the one in [13]), and a coffee machine. They are described only informally here; the exact formalization is given in the Appendix and details are in [12].

The controlled reservoir. The controlled reservoir system consists of a reservoir and a controller. The reservoir can nondeterministically leak and being filled with new liquid by the controller. The level of fluid in the reservoir is described by two predicates: $\ell \geq$ min holds when the level of fluid is above a minimum level, $\ell \geq$ thres holds if the level is above a control threshold, assumed to be higher than the minimum. The system is described by five formulas, shown in the Appendix, stating the behavior of the fluid level under all combinations of filling and leaking, and the control action (filling is triggered as soon as the level goes below the control threshold). The property (1) to be verified requires that, after the system is "initialized" by setting the level above the control threshold, the level stays above the minimum forever in the future:

$$\ell \geq \text{thres} \Rightarrow \Box_{(0,+\infty)}(\ell \geq \text{min}) \qquad (1)$$

The system description is parametric with respect to a single parameter ν. The desired property holds if and only if the sampling period δ equals ν. Otherwise the property does not hold since the sampling period is "too short" with respect to ν: this corresponds to allowing faster behaviors for which the given specification is too weak to assess the desired property (more details can be found in [12]).

The coffee machine. The second example consists in the description of a coffee machine, in operational fashion. We introduce the predicates: prepare_cup, press_button, start_pour, end_pour, get_cup. They represent, respectively, the actions of inserting a new cup in the coffee machine, pressing the button to start the brewing process, beginning and ending of the pouring of coffee, retrieving a cup (presumably filled with coffee) from the machine. We also introduce the predicates: pour, cup_present, coffee_ready, and key_in. They are meant to hold when, respectively, the coffee is pouring into the cup, a cup is inserted in the machine, the coffee has been completely brewed, and a key (to operate the machine, say by recording the coffee credits of the user) is inserted in the machine. Three constants T_1, T_2, T_3 describe the various delays in the operations of the machine; also, a parameter ν is introduced to relate the various delays in a suitable manner (see [12] for details). The behavior of the machine is modeled through ten formulas, shown in the Appendix. From these, two candidate properties of the system should be verified: the first (2) states that the pouring ends only if a key was inserted in the past (between T_3 and $T_1 + T_2 + T_3$ time units ago); the second (3) asserts that a cup is present while the coffee is being poured.

$$\text{end\_pour} \Rightarrow \overleftarrow{\Diamond}_{[T_3, T_1+T_2+T_3]}(\text{key\_in}) \qquad (2)$$

$$\text{pour} \Rightarrow \text{cup\_present} \qquad (3)$$

Some modifications were required in order to obtain a system formalization which avoids some idiosyncrasies of the dense-time description that obstruct the discretization process. They are discussed in [12].

Both candidate properties hold if $\delta = 1$. Otherwise, the properties may not hold, also according to the particular values for the constants T_1, T_2, T_3, which interact in a subtle way. See [12] for more details.

4.3 Experiments

Tables 1–2 report a small sub-set of the results obtained in an array of tests with the discretization techniques and Zot; more of them can be found in [12]. For each test the tables report: the value k of the bound given to Zot (in other words, the size of the explored space); the value of parameter ν in the models; the value of δ, according to which the discretizations are built; the value of other parameters in the models (i.e., T_1, T_2, T_3 in the case of the coffee machine); the outcome of the validity check for the properties to be verified. Each test is done both over mono-infinite domain, and over bi-infinite domain. For each test the tables report, in addition to the outcome ($\top$ means valid, $\bot$ means non-valid, $\sim$ means that the approximation technique has been inconclusive), the net (CPU) time and the total amount of memory taken in the process.

The tests have been performed on a PC equipped with an AMD Athlon64 x2 4600+ processor, 2 Gb of RAM, and Ubuntu GNU/Linux. Zot used GNU CLisp v. 2.39, and MiniSat v. 1.14 as SAT-solving engine.

The reservoir example (in Table 1) is a simple one, and in fact the results are highly predictable and satisfactory. Inconclusive results are never obtained when applying the discretization technique, and the property is confirmed to be valid if and only if $\nu = \delta$. The times and spaces required to obtain the results are always relatively small, and they scale rather well with the increase of the bound. Finally, notice that it usually takes a shorter time to check the validity than to check the non-validity; this is obvious, as the latter requires to submit both ϕ^+ and ϕ^- to the validity checker, while the former checks just ϕ^+.

Table 2 reports some of the results obtained with the coffee machine example. Property (2) is shown to be valid for all the choices of parameters made in the experiments reported in Table 2. The times needed to get this result are rather short, and scale with the length of k. This is reasonable, as the main factors affecting the complexity of the check are the values of the parameters T_1, T_2, T_3, which however stay in a small range in all tests.

Table 1. Checking property (1) of the reservoir example

k	ν	δ	Pr.(1) $\mathbb{T} = \mathbb{N}$ (time / mem)	Pr.(1) $\mathbb{T} = \mathbb{Z}$ (time / mem)
5	10	10	$\top$ (0.2 s / 2.2 Mb)	$\top$ (0.4 s / 2.6 Mb)
5	10	10/3	$\bot$ (0.7 s / 5.8 Mb)	$\bot$ (1.2 s / 9 Mb)
10	10	10	$\top$ (0.6 s / 3.2 Mb)	$\top$ (0.7 s / 4.9 Mb)
10	10	10/3	$\bot$ (1.6 s / 12.1 Mb)	$\bot$ (2 s / 18.1 Mb)
50	10	10	$\top$ (2.8 s / 15.3 Mb)	$\top$ (5.3 s / 23.5 Mb)
50	10	10/3	$\bot$ (8.6 s / 110.8 Mb)	$\bot$ (19.5 s / 149.5 Mb)
100	10	10	$\top$ (9.5 s / 30.4 Mb)	$\top$ (20.2 s / 46.7 Mb)
100	10	10/3	$\bot$ (29.9 s / 361.9 Mb)	$\bot$ (66.1 s / 470.6 Mb)
200	10	10	$\top$ (33.3 s / 60.7 Mb)	$\top$ (72.6 s / 93.1 Mb)
200	10	10/3	$\bot$ (108.6 s / 1240.1 Mb)	$\bot$ (245.1 s / 1588.3 Mb)

Table 2. Checking properties (2) and (3) of the coffee machine example

k	ν	δ	T_1, T_2, T_3	Pr.(2) $\mathbb{N}$ (time / mem)	Pr.(3) $\mathbb{N}$ (time / mem)	Pr.(2) $\mathbb{Z}$ (time / mem)	Pr.(3) $\mathbb{Z}$ (time / mem)
10	1	1	4,4,4	$\top$ (1.8 s / 11.7 Mb)	$\top$ (1.3 s / 9.8 Mb)	$\top$ (3.5 s / 17.9 Mb)	$\top$ (2.6 s / 14.9 Mb)
10	2	1	4,4,4	$\top$ (1.7 s / 11.4 Mb)	$\top$ (1.4 s / 9.5 Mb)	$\top$ (3.4 s / 17.6 Mb)	$\top$ (2.2 s / 14.6 Mb)
10	3	1	10,7,8	$\top$ (3.1 s / 17.4 Mb)	$\sim$ (4.2 s / 35.7 Mb)	$\top$ (7.3 s / 27 Mb)	$\sim$ (8.6 s / 52.5 Mb)
20	1	1	4,4,4	$\top$ (5.1 s / 22.7 Mb)	$\top$ (3.6 s / 18.9 Mb)	$\top$ (11.6 s / 34.7 Mb)	$\top$ (8 s / 28.9 Mb)
20	2	1	4,4,4	$\top$ (4.9 s / 22 Mb)	$\top$ (3.3 s / 18.3 Mb)	$\top$ (10.9 s / 34.1 Mb)	$\top$ (7.6 s / 28.3 Mb)
20	3	1	10,7,8	$\top$ (11.6 s / 33.6 Mb)	$\sim$ (13.8 s / 78.3 Mb)	$\top$ (25.6 s / 52.5 Mb)	$\sim$ (30.4 s / 114.3 Mb)
30	1	1	4,4,4	$\top$ (11 s / 33.6 Mb)	$\top$ (7.7 s / 28.1 Mb)	$\top$ (24 s / 51.6 Mb)	$\top$ (16.7 s / 43 Mb)
30	2	1	4,4,4	$\top$ (10.4 s / 32.7 Mb)	$\top$ (7.1 s / 27.2 Mb)	$\top$ (23.7 s / 51.1 Mb)	$\top$ (16.1 s / 42.2 Mb)
30	3	1	10,7,8	$\top$ (24.2 s / 49.7 Mb)	$\sim$ (28.6 s / 153.3 Mb)	$\top$ (55.5 s / 78.3 Mb)	$\sim$ (65.3 s / 189.2 Mb)
40	1	1	4,4,4	$\top$ (18.4 s / 45 Mb)	$\top$ (12.9 s / 37.3 Mb)	$\top$ (39.6 s / 68.9 Mb)	$\top$ (27.6 s / 57.1 Mb)
40	2	1	4,4,4	$\top$ (17.8 s / 43.8 Mb)	$\top$ (12.3 s / 36.1 Mb)	$\top$ (38.3 s / 67.7 Mb)	$\top$ (26.4 s / 56 Mb)
40	3	1	10,7,8	$\top$ (40.6 s / 66.3 Mb)	$\sim$ (47.8 s / 200 Mb)	$\top$ (89.3 s / 103.8 Mb)	$\sim$ (106.7 s / 284.8 Mb)
50	1	1	4,4,4	$\top$ (27.7 s / 56 Mb)	$\top$ (19.4 s / 46.5 Mb)	$\top$ (60.8 s / 85.8 Mb)	$\top$ (42.1 s / 71.2 Mb)
50	2	1	4,4,4	$\top$ (26.6 s / 54.5 Mb)	$\top$ (18.4 s / 45 Mb)	$\top$ (57.9 s / 84.4 Mb)	$\top$ (39.9 s / 69.8 Mb)
50	3	1	10,7,8	$\top$ (60.8 s / 82.6 Mb)	$\sim$ (71.8 s / 272.1 Mb)	$\top$ (136.2 s / 129.3 Mb)	$\sim$ (160.3 s / 389.1 Mb)

The outcomes of the validity check of the other property (3) are, on the other hand, more varied. As stated when presenting the example, if $\delta = 1$ the second property is valid for the system. While this is confirmed by several of the tests, some cases fall in the incompleteness area of the method, and analyzing the approximations gives inconclusive results. In any case, the time and space required are rather small.

5 Conclusion

We presented a technique to reduce the verification problem for dense-time MTL specifications to the corresponding problem over discrete-time models, based on the notions of *sampling* and *sampling invariance*. In a nutshell, we perform simple syntactic transformations on the MTL formulas to be checked for validity; the resulting formulas retain (partial) information about the discrete-time samplings of the dense-time behaviors described by the the original formulas.

This approach, which considers only a subset of generic MTL formulas, has a two-fold incompleteness: it verifies only "sufficiently slow" dense-time behaviors (although the "speed" of the behaviors can often be modulated), and the analysis of the discretized formulas may yield inconclusive results.

The technique is however simple to implement in practice, and it was used, on top of the Zot bounded validity checker for discrete-time formulas, to carry out some experiments. The results are promising in that they show that the effects of incompleteness can often be mitigated in practice, and the computational effort required to check the discretized formulas is usually acceptably small.

Future work in this line of research will follow three main directions. First, the technique and tool of this paper will be applied to real-life industrial case-studies. Second, our verification technique will be extended to deal with systems described through operational formalisms such as timed automata or Petri nets. Third, methods will be developed to guide the writing of dense-time specifications in a form that is amenable to the application of discretization.

Acknowledgments. We thank Paritosh Pandya for discussions suggesting to apply the notion of sampling to dense-time verification through discretization, Mario Arrigoni Neri for providing a sketch of the coffee machine example, and the anonymous reviewers of several conferences for their remarks.

References

1. Abadi, M., Lamport, L.: An old-fashioned recipe for real-time. ACM TOPLAS 16(5), 1543–1571 (1994)
2. Alur, R., Henzinger, T.A.: Real-time logics: Complexity and expressiveness. Information and Computation 104(1), 35–77 (1993)
3. Biere, A., Heljanko, K., Junttila, T., Latvala, T., Schuppan, V.: Linear encodings of bounded LTL model checking. Logical Methods in Comp. Sci. 2(5:5), 1–64 (2006)
4. Chakravorty, G., Pandya, P.K.: Digiziting interval duration logic. In: Hunt Jr., W.A., Somenzi, F. (eds.) CAV 2003. LNCS, vol. 2725, pp. 167–179. Springer, Heidelberg (2003)
5. Ciapessoni, E., Coen-Porisini, A., Crivelli, E., Mandrioli, D., Mirandola, P., Morzenti, A.: From formal models to formally-based methods: an industrial experience. ACM TOSEM 8(1), 79–113 (1999)
6. Clarke, E.M., Grumberg, O., Peled, D.A.: Model Checking. MIT Press, Cambridge (2000)
7. de Alfaro, L., Manna, Z.: Verification in continuous time by discrete reasoning. In: AMAST 1995. LNCS, vol. 936, pp. 292–306 (1995)
8. D. D'Souza, R. Mohan M., and P. Prabhakar. Eliminating past operators in metric temporal logic. Technical Report IISc-CSA-TR-2006-11 (2006)
9. Fainekos, G.E., Pappas, G.J.: Robust Sampling for MITL Specifications. In: Raskin, J.-F., Thiagarajan, P.S. (eds.) FORMATS 2007. LNCS, vol. 4763, pp. 147–162. Springer, Heidelberg (2007)
10. Furia, C.A.: Scaling up the formal analysis of real-time systems. PhD thesis, DEI, Politecnico di Milano (May 2007)
11. Furia, C.A., Mandrioli, D., Morzenti, A., Rossi, M.: Modeling time in computing: A taxonomy and a comparative survey. Technical Report 2007.22, DEI, Politecnico di Milano (2007)
12. Furia, C.A., Pradella, M., Rossi, M.: Dense-time MTL verification through sampling. Technical Report 2007.37, DEI, Politecnico di Milano (April 2007)
13. Furia, C.A., Rossi, M.: Integrating Discrete- and Continuous-Time Metric Temporal Logics Through Sampling. In: Asarin, E., Bouyer, P. (eds.) FORMATS 2006. LNCS, vol. 4202, pp. 215–229. Springer, Heidelberg (2006)
14. Furia, C.A., Rossi, M.: On the expressiveness of MTL variants over dense time. In: Raskin, J.-F., Thiagarajan, P.S. (eds.) FORMATS 2007. LNCS, vol. 4763, pp. 163–178. Springer, Heidelberg (2007)

15. Henzinger, T.A.: It's about time: Real-time logics reviewed. In: Sangiorgi, D., de Simone, R. (eds.) CONCUR 1998. LNCS, vol. 1466, pp. 439–454. Springer, Heidelberg (1998)
16. Henzinger, T.A., Manna, Z., Pnueli, A.: What good are digital clocks? In: Kuich, W. (ed.) ICALP 1992. LNCS, vol. 623, pp. 545–558. Springer, Heidelberg (1992)
17. Hirshfeld, Y., Rabinovich, A.M.: Logics for real time: Decidability and complexity. Fundamenta Informaticae 62(1), 1–28 (2004)
18. Koymans, R.: Specifying real-time properties with metric temporal logic. Real-Time Systems 2(4), 255–299 (1990)
19. Pradella, M.: Zot (March 2007), http://home.dei.polimi.it/pradella
20. Pradella, M., Morzenti, A., San Pietro, P.: The symmetry of the past and of the future. In: Proc. of ESEC/FSE 2007 (2007)
21. Sharma, B., Pandya, P.K., Chakraborty, S.: Bounded validity checking of interval duration logic. In: Halbwachs, N., Zuck, L.D. (eds.) TACAS 2005. LNCS, vol. 3440, pp. 301–316. Springer, Heidelberg (2005)
22. Wilke, T.: Specifying timed state sequences in powerful decidable logics and timed automata. In: Langmaack, H., de Roever, W.-P., Vytopil, J. (eds.) FTRTFT 1994 and ProCoS 1994. LNCS, vol. 863, pp. 694–715. Springer, Heidelberg (1994)

Appendix: Example Specifications

The reservoir system.

$$\ell \geq \mathsf{min} \wedge \Box_{(0,\nu)}(\mathsf{F}) \Rightarrow \Box_{[\nu,\nu]}(\ell \geq \mathsf{min}) \quad (4)$$

$$\ell \geq \mathsf{thres} \Rightarrow \Box_{[\nu,\nu]}(\ell \geq \mathsf{min}) \quad (5)$$

$$\ell \geq \mathsf{min} \wedge \Box_{(0,\nu)}(\neg \mathsf{F} \wedge \neg \mathsf{L}) \Rightarrow \Box_{[\nu,\nu]}(\ell \geq \mathsf{min}) \quad (6)$$

$$\ell \geq \mathsf{thres} \Rightarrow \ell \geq \mathsf{min} \quad (7)$$

$$\ell < \mathsf{thres} \Rightarrow \mathsf{F} \quad (8)$$

The coffee machine.[3]

$$\mathsf{prepare\_cup} \Rightarrow \overleftarrow{\Diamond}_{(0,T_1)}(\mathsf{press\_button}) \quad (9)$$

$$\mathsf{start\_pour} \Rightarrow \overleftarrow{\Diamond}_{(0,T_2)}(\mathsf{prepare\_cup}) \quad (10)$$

$$\mathsf{end\_pour} \Rightarrow \overleftarrow{\Box}_{[T_3,T_3]}(\mathsf{start\_pour}) \wedge \overleftarrow{\Box}_{[0,T_3)}(\mathsf{pour}) \quad (11)$$

$$\mathsf{press\_button} \Rightarrow \mathsf{key\_in} \quad (12)$$

$$\neg \mathsf{pour} \wedge \bigcirc(\mathsf{pour}) \Leftrightarrow \mathsf{start\_pour} \quad (13)$$

$$\Box_{(0,T_3)}(\mathsf{pour}) \Rightarrow \mathsf{start\_pour} \wedge \Box_{[T_3,T_3]}(\mathsf{end\_pour}) \quad (14)$$

$$\mathsf{start\_pour} \Rightarrow \mathsf{cup\_present} \wedge \neg \mathsf{coffee\_ready} \quad (15)$$

$$\mathsf{cup\_present} \wedge \bigcirc(\neg \mathsf{cup\_present}) \Leftrightarrow \mathsf{get\_cup} \quad (16)$$

$$\mathsf{get\_cup} \Rightarrow \mathsf{coffee\_ready} \quad (17)$$

$$\mathsf{start\_pour} \Rightarrow \Box_{[T_3,T_3]}(\mathsf{end\_pour}) \wedge \Box_{(0,T_3]}(\mathsf{pour}) \quad (18)$$

---

[3] The $\bigcirc(\beta)$ operator is defined as $\mathsf{U}_{(0,+\infty)}(\beta,\top) \vee (\neg \beta \wedge \mathsf{R}_{(0,+\infty)}(\beta,\bot))$.

A Model Checking Language for Concurrent Value-Passing Systems

Radu Mateescu and Damien Thivolle

INRIA Rhône-Alpes / VASY
655, avenue de l'Europe, F-38330 Montbonnot St Martin, France
{Radu.Mateescu,Damien.Thivolle}@inria.fr

Abstract. Modal μ-calculus is an expressive specification formalism for temporal properties of concurrent programs represented as Labeled Transition Systems (LTSs). However, its practical use is hampered by the complexity of the formulas, which makes the specification task difficult and error-prone. In this paper, we propose MCL (*Model Checking Language*), an enhancement of modal μ-calculus with high-level operators aimed at improving expressiveness and conciseness of formulas. The main MCL ingredients are parameterized fixed points, action patterns extracting data values from LTS actions, modalities on transition sequences described using extended regular expressions and programming language constructs, and an infinite looping operator specifying fairness. We also present a method for on-the-fly model checking of MCL formulas on finite LTSs, based on the local resolution of boolean equation systems, which has a linear-time complexity for alternation-free and fairness formulas. MCL is supported by the EVALUATOR 4.0 model checker developed within the CADP verification toolbox.

1 Introduction

Model checking [7] is an automatic, cost-effective method for verifying temporal properties of concurrent finite-state systems. In the action-based framework, where behaviours are represented as Labeled Transition Systems (LTSs), the modal μ-calculus ($L\mu$) [26,38] provides a very expressive way of specifying properties. This fixed point-based logic subsumes virtually all other temporal logics defined in the literature; from this perspective, it can be seen as an "assembly language" for model checking on LTSs, similarly to the λ-calculus in the field of functional programming. The counterbalance of this expressiveness is the inherent complexity of $L\mu$ formulas, even for encoding relatively simple properties, which makes the practical usage of $L\mu$ difficult and error-prone, especially for non-expert users. In practice, higher-level formalisms are needed in order to facilitate the specification task and also to handle in a natural way the data values present in the LTSs generated from value-passing concurrent programs.

Towards this objective, classical temporal logics were extended with mechanisms inspired from regular languages and first-order logic. ETL [44] was the first extension of LTL [34] with regular grammars. BRTL [21] and ECTL* [41] are extensions of CTL [7] and CTL* [12] with Büchi automata. Although they are strictly more powerful than the original ones, these enhanced logics are difficult to employ because of their complicated syntax. In practice, it appears that more concise and readable specifications can be obtained by using regular expressions, as illustrated by the SUGAR [6] extension of CTL and by regular $L\mu_1$ [32], which adds the modalities of test-free PDL [14] to $L\mu_1$, the alternation-free fragment of $L\mu$ [13]. Some extensions of CTL and LTL were further enriched with data and signal handling mechanisms, leading to specialized languages for hardware verification, such as PSL [23] and FORSPEC [3]. As regards $L\mu$, various combinations with first-order logic were proposed, especially in the field of symbolic verification [9,19,36] and of runtime verification [5]. However, no attempt of extending $L\mu$ both with regular expressions and data handling mechanisms was made so far in the framework of model checking for finite-state systems.

The experiences of using regular $L\mu_1$ for specifying temporal properties of industrial systems (ATM switches, asynchronous hardware, etc.) gave us a positive feedback about the gain in readability and conciseness of regular expressions w.r.t. fixed point operators. However, industrial users also formulated two requirements concerning the practical usage and the expressiveness of this logic:

- Temporal properties of value-passing systems must deal with the data values contained in the LTS, in order to avoid tedious updates of the properties for every configuration of the system under analysis (number of processes, values exchanged, etc.). Without parameterization mechanisms, temporal formulas may become prohibitively large because of operator instantiations capturing all relevant data values or expressing repetitions of transition sequences.
- Sometimes it is necessary to characterize precisely the presence of complex cycles (made of regular transition subsequences) in the LTS. In the absence of suitable fairness operators belonging to $L\mu_2$, users can detect complex cycles only by resorting to complicated schemes based on repetitive hiding and bisimulation minimization [4,37].

In this paper, we attempt to fulfill these two requirements by proposing MCL (*Model Checking Language*), an extension of $L\mu$ with various operators aimed at improving the conciseness, readability, and expressiveness of temporal formulas. MCL combines data handling mechanisms (quantified variables and fixed point parameters), extended regular expressions, and constructs inspired from programming languages. All these features contribute to simplify the specification task, by drastically reducing the amount of fixed points and modalities in MCL formulas and allowing specifiers to focus their attention on the description of transition sequences. Fairness properties are expressed in MCL using the infinite looping operator of PDL-Δ [39], which enables a straightforward description of complex unfair sequences.

Besides improving the end-user language, our goal was also to maintain the complexity of verification as low as possible in order to deal with large LTSs. Therefore, as regards fixed point operators, we focused on the alternation-free fragment of MCL, which for dataless formulas coincides with $L\mu_1$ and takes advantage of its linear-time model checking complexity [8]. We reformulate the on-the-fly verification of MCL formulas on LTSs as the local resolution of alternation-free boolean equation systems (BESs), by generalizing the classical procedures used for $L\mu_1$ [1,42]. The infinite looping operator is expressible in $L\mu_2$, the $L\mu$ fragment of alternation depth 2 [13], whose model checking is quadratic; however, we show that this operator can be verified on-the-fly in linear time by proposing an enhanced BES resolution algorithm. This verification method is at the heart of the EVALUATOR 4.0 model checker that we developed within the CADP toolbox [17] using the generic OPEN/CÆSAR environment [15] for on-the-fly exploration of LTSs. As verification engine, the tool employs the generic CÆSAR_SOLVE library [31], which provides several linear-time local resolution algorithms for alternation-free BESs.

The paper is organized as follows. Section 2 defines the MCL language and illustrates its usage through various examples of properties. Section 3 describes the model checking method and the linear-time algorithm for handling the infinite looping operator. Section 4 presents the EVALUATOR 4.0 tool and its application for analyzing the SCSI-2 bus arbitration protocol [2]. Finally, Section 5 summarizes the results and indicates directions for future work.

2 Syntax and Semantics

MCL formulas are interpreted over LTSs of the form $M = \langle S, A, T, s_0 \rangle$, where S is the set of states, A is the set of actions, $T \subseteq S \times A \times S$ is the transition relation, and $s_0 \in S$ is the initial state. A transition $s_1 \xrightarrow{a} s_2 \in T$ indicates that the system can move from state s_1 to state s_2 by performing action a. Actions in A are of the form $c\ v_1...v_n$, where c is a communication channel and $v_1, ..., v_n$ are the values exchanged during a handshake on c. The invisible action $\tau \notin A$ denotes an unobservable behaviour of the system. These LTSs are natural models for value-passing process algebras with early operational semantics, such as full CCS [33] and LOTOS [24].

2.1 Basic MCL: Modal mu-Calculus with Data

A natural way of expressing properties about the values contained in LTS actions is to extend $L\mu$ with data variables, which can be quantified and used as parameters of fixed point operators. Our MCL language follows existing extension proposals [9,19,36] and enhances them by introducing higher-level constructs inspired from programming languages.

Basic MCL (see Fig. 1) consists of data expressions (e), action formulas (α), and state formulas (φ). Expressions are built from data variables $x \in \mathcal{X}$ and functions $f : T_1 \times \cdots \times T_n \to T$. Types bool and nat, equipped with the usual operations, are predefined, and all expressions are assumed to be well-typed. Action formulas are built from action patterns and boolean connectors. Action patterns inspect the structure of actions $c\ v_1...v_n$ by matching values v_i against expressions (clause "$!e_i$") or extracting and storing them in typed variables (clause "$?x_i{:}T_i$") exported to the enclosing formula.

Expressions:	$e ::= x \mid f(e_1, ..., e_n)$
Action formulas:	$\alpha ::= \{c\ !e_1...!e_n\} \mid \{c\ ?x_1{:}T_1...?x_n{:}T_n\}$
	$\mid \neg\alpha \mid \alpha_1 \vee \alpha_2$
State formulas:	$\varphi ::= e \mid \neg\varphi \mid \varphi_1 \vee \varphi_2 \mid \langle\alpha\rangle\ \varphi$
	$\mid$ exists $x_1{:}T_1, ..., x_n{:}T_n.\varphi \mid Y(e_1, ..., e_n)$
	$\mid \mu Y(x_1{:}T_1{:=}e_1, ..., x_n{:}T_n{:=}e_n).\varphi$
	$\mid$ let $x_1{:}T_1{:=}e_1, ..., x_n{:}T_n{:=}e_n$ in
	$\quad\quad \varphi$
	$\quad$ end let
	$\mid$ if φ_1 then φ'_1
	$\quad\quad$ elsif φ_2 then φ'_2 ... else φ'_n
	$\quad$ end if
	$\mid$ case e is
	$\quad\quad p_1 \to \varphi_1 \mid ... \mid p_n \to \varphi_n$
	$\quad$ end case

Expressions:
$$\|x\|\delta = \delta(x)$$
$$\|f(e_1, ..., e_n)\|\delta = f(\|e_1\|\delta, ..., \|e_n\|\delta)$$

Action formulas:
$$[\![\{c\ !e_1...!e_n\}]\!]\delta = \{c\ \|e_1\|\delta... \|e_n\|\delta\}$$
$$[\![\{c\ ?x_1{:}T_1...?x_n{:}T_n\}]\!]\delta = \{c\ v_1...v_n \mid \forall i \in [1,n].v_i \in T_i\}$$
$$[\![\neg\alpha]\!]\delta = A \setminus [\![\alpha]\!]\delta$$
$$[\![\alpha_1 \vee \alpha_2]\!]\delta = [\![\alpha_1]\!]\delta \cup [\![\alpha_2]\!]\delta$$
$$env_{c\ v_1...v_n}(\{c\ ?x_1{:}T_1...?x_n{:}T_n\}) = [v_1/x_1, ..., v_n/x_n] \text{ if } \forall i \in [1,n].v_i \in T_i$$
$$env_a(\alpha) = [\ ] \text{ otherwise}$$

State formulas:
$$[\![e]\!]\rho\delta = \{s \in S \mid \|e\|\delta\}$$
$$[\![\neg\varphi]\!]\rho\delta = S \setminus [\![\varphi]\!]\rho\delta$$
$$[\![\varphi_1 \vee \varphi_2]\!]\rho\delta = [\![\varphi_1]\!]\rho\delta \cup [\![\varphi_2]\!]\rho\delta$$
$$[\![\langle\alpha\rangle\ \varphi]\!]\rho\delta = \{s \in S \mid \exists s \xrightarrow{a} s'.a \in [\![\alpha]\!]\delta \wedge$$
$$s' \in [\![\varphi]\!]\rho(\delta \oslash env_a(\alpha))\}$$
$$[\![\text{exists } x_1{:}T_1, ..., x_n{:}T_n.\varphi]\!]\rho\delta = \{s \in S \mid \exists v_1{:}T_1, ..., v_n{:}T_n.$$
$$s \in [\![\varphi]\!]\rho(\delta \oslash [v_1/x_1, ..., v_n/x_n])\}$$
$$[\![Y(e_1, ..., e_n)]\!]\rho\delta = (\rho(Y))(\|e_1\|\delta, ..., \|e_n\|\delta)$$
$$[\![\mu Y(x_1{:}T_1{:=}e_1, ..., x_n{:}T_n{:=}e_n).\varphi]\!]\rho\delta = (\mu\Phi_{\rho\delta})(\|e_1\|\delta, ..., \|e_n\|\delta)$$
where $\Phi_{\rho\delta} : (T_1 \times \cdots \times T_n \to 2^S) \to (T_1 \times \cdots \times T_n \to 2^S)$,
$$(\Phi_{\rho\delta}(F))(v_1, ..., v_n) = [\![\varphi]\!](\rho \oslash [F/Y])(\delta \oslash [v_1/x_1, ..., v_n/x_n])$$

$$\left[\!\!\left[\begin{array}{l}\text{let } x_1{:}T_1{:=}e_1, ..., \\ x_n{:}T_n{:=}e_n \text{ in } \varphi \text{ end let}\end{array}\right]\!\!\right]\rho\delta = [\![\varphi]\!]\rho(\delta \oslash [\|e_1\|\delta/x_1, ..., \|e_n\|\delta/x_n])$$

$$\left[\!\!\left[\begin{array}{l}\text{if } \varphi_1 \text{ then } \varphi'_1 \text{ elsif } \varphi_2 \text{ then } \varphi'_2 \\ ... \text{ else } \varphi'_n \text{ end if}\end{array}\right]\!\!\right]\rho\delta = \begin{array}{l}\{s \in S \mid \text{if } s \in [\![\varphi_1]\!]\rho\delta \text{ then } s \in [\![\varphi'_1]\!]\rho\delta \\ \quad\text{elsif } s \in [\![\varphi_2]\!]\rho\delta \text{ then } s \in [\![\varphi'_2]\!]\rho\delta \\ \quad ... \text{ else } s \in [\![\varphi'_n]\!]\rho\delta\}\end{array}$$

$$\left[\!\!\left[\begin{array}{l}\text{case } e \text{ is } p_1 \to \varphi_1 \mid \\ ... \mid p_n \to \varphi_n \text{ end case}\end{array}\right]\!\!\right]\rho\delta = \begin{array}{l}\text{if } \|e\|\delta{::}p_1 \text{ then } [\![\varphi_1]\!]\rho(\delta \oslash ext(\|e\|\delta, p_1)) \\ \quad ... \text{ else } [\![\varphi_n]\!]\rho(\delta \oslash ext(\|e\|\delta, p_n))\end{array}$$

Fig. 1. Syntax (upper part) and semantics (lower part) of basic MCL operators

State formulas are built upon parameterized propositional variables $Y \in \mathcal{Y}$ and boolean expressions e by applying boolean connectors, modalities, quantifiers, and parameterized fixed point operators. Each variable Y denotes a function $F : T_1 \times \cdots \times T_n \to 2^S$ belonging to a set $\mathcal{F}$. Derived boolean operators ($\vee$, $\Rightarrow$, and $\Leftrightarrow$) and universal quantification (forall) are defined as usual in terms of $\neg$, $\wedge$, and exists. The necessity modality is the dual of possibility ($[\alpha]\,\varphi = \neg\,\langle\alpha\rangle\,\neg\varphi$) and the maximal fixed point operator is the dual of the minimal one ($\nu Y(...).\varphi = \neg\mu Y(...).\neg\varphi[\neg Y/Y]$, where $[\neg Y/Y]$ denotes the syntactic substitution of Y by $\neg Y$). Quantifiers may contain optional subdomain clauses "$x{:}T$ among $\{e_1\ ...\ e_2\}$" indicating that x takes values between e_1 and e_2. We allow quantification only on finite types equipped with a total order relation; existential and universal quantifiers are merely shorthand notations for (large) disjunctions and conjunctions parameterized by data values.

Fixed point formulas $\sigma Y(...).\varphi$, where $\sigma \in \{\mu, \nu\}$, are assumed to be *syntactically monotonic* [26], i.e., every free occurrence of Y in φ must fall in the scope of an even number of negations. For efficiency of model checking, we consider only *alternation-free* formulas, i.e., without mutual recursion between minimal and maximal fixed point variables, similarly to the $L\mu_1$ fragment [13].

Expressions e and action formulas α are interpreted in the context of a data environment $\delta : \mathcal{X} \to T_1 \cup ... \cup T_n$ assigning values to all free variables occurring in e and α (the environment $\delta \oslash [v/x]$ is identical to δ except for variable x, which is assigned value v). State formulas φ are interpreted also in the context of propositional environments $\rho : \mathcal{Y} \to \mathcal{F}$, which assign functions to all free propositional variables occurring in φ. The parameterized fixed point operators $\sigma Y(x_1{:}T_1{:=}e_1, ..., x_n{:}T_n{:=}e_n).\varphi$ represent both the definition and the call (with the values of $e_1, ..., e_n$ as arguments) of functions $F : T_1 \times \cdots \times T_n \to 2^S$ defined as the corresponding fixed points of monotonic functionals over $T_1 \times \cdots \times T_n \to 2^S$.

To facilitate the handling of data values, we introduce the "let", "if", and "case" operators, inspired from functional programming languages. The branches of "if" and "case" formulas must be exhaustive in order to avoid exceptions and the formulas φ_i used as branch conditions in "if" must not contain free propositional variables in order to preserve syntactic monotonicity. Patterns in "case" formulas are of the form "$x{:}T$" or "$f(p_1, ..., p_n)$", where f is a constructor of the type of e. Variables defined in patterns p_i are visible in the state formulas φ_i of their corresponding branches. The predicate "$v{::}p$" indicates whether value v matches p or not, and $ext(v, p)$ denotes the data environment initializing all variables defined in p with their values extracted from v by pattern-matching.

Action patterns have additional features (not shown in Fig. 1): the two kinds of clauses can be mixed; the wildcard clause "any" matches a value of any type; for dataless actions, brackets can be omitted; and an optional guard "where e" ending the clause list indicates that the action pattern matches an action iff the boolean expression e (which can refer to the variables declared in the clauses "$?x{:}T$" of the action pattern) evaluates to true.

A state satisfies a closed formula φ (notation $s \models \varphi$) iff $s \in [\![\varphi]\!]$. An LTS $M = \langle S, A, T, s_0 \rangle$ satisfies a closed formula φ (notation $M \models \varphi$) iff $s_0 \models \varphi$. Basic

Table 1. Temporal properties formulated using basic MCL operators (upper part) and extended regular operators (lower part). φ_1 and φ_2 involve action patterns, quantifiers, and boolean expressions. φ_3 counts using a parameterized fixed point and φ_4 simulates a simple pushdown automaton for syntactic analysis.

MCL formula	Meaning
φ_1 [true*.{open ?i:nat}.(¬{close !i})*. {open ?j:nat}] (i = j)	Mutual exclusion between processes i and j.
φ_2 [{bcast ?msg:nat}] forall addr:nat. $\mu Y.(\langle$true$\rangle$ true $\wedge$ [¬{recv !msg !addr}] Y)	Inevitable reception of a broadcasted message msg at all its destinations $addr$.
φ_3 νY(c:nat:=0).if c = 3 then $\langle$true*.resp$\rangle$ true else [$req_1 \vee req_2 \vee req_3$] $Y(c+1)$ end if	Potential response after three requests occurring in any order.
φ_4 νX(n:nat:=0).([open_par] $X(n+1) \wedge$ [close_par] $(n > 0 \wedge X(n-1)) \wedge$ [eof] $(n = 0) \wedge$ [¬(open_par $\vee$ close_par $\vee$ eof)] $X(n)$)	No sequence of transitions (tokens) can reach an eof without having well-balanced parentheses.
φ_5 [true*.((¬output)*.input){n+1}] false	Safety of a n-place buffer.
φ_6 [{level ?l:nat}] ((l > max) $\Rightarrow$ [(¬alarm){16}] false $\wedge$ [(¬alarm){0 ... 15}] $\langle$true$\rangle$ true)	Inevitable alarm at most 15 transitions (ticks) after a level reaches a threshold.
φ_7 [true*.{ask ?i:nat}] $\langle$(¬{get !i})*.{get ?j:nat where j $\neq$ i}$\rangle$ @	Starvation of process i in favor of another process j.
φ_8 $\langle$true$^+$.if ¬p_{final} then false end if$\rangle$@	Acceptance condition in a Büchi automaton (p_{final} denotes the repeated states).

MCL allows to express naturally temporal properties involving data values, as illustrated in Table 1. Other data-based properties will be shown in Section 4.

2.2 Extended Regular Operators

Besides the data handling operators of basic MCL, which bring the benefits of parameterization, another kind of useful extension is the ability of specifying transition sequences using regular expressions [6]; in the context of $L\mu$, this can be done naturally by plugging regular expressions inside modalities, similarly to PDL [14]. Although these modalities can be translated into $L\mu_1$ [13], in practice they are much more concise and readable than their fixed point counterparts [32].

The regular formulas (β) we propose in MCL for specifying transition sequences are built from action formulas and various operators stemming from extended regular expressions and programming languages (see Tab. 2). For conciseness, we define the meaning of β formulas by giving their translations to basic MCL when they occur in $\langle\ \rangle$ modalities (dual translations hold for [ ] modalities). The counter-based iteration operators are inspired from the extended regular expressions implemented in string searching tools like the egrep utility available on

Table 2. Syntax and semantics of (a subset of) MCL extended regular operators

Syntax	Meaning	Translation
$\langle \text{nil} \rangle \, \varphi$	Empty seq.	φ
$\langle \beta_1 . \beta_2 \rangle \, \varphi$	Concatenation	$\langle \beta_1 \rangle \, \langle \beta_2 \rangle \, \varphi$
$\langle \beta_1 \| \beta_2 \rangle \, \varphi$	Choice	$\langle \beta_1 \rangle \, \varphi \vee \langle \beta_2 \rangle \, \varphi$
$\langle \beta ? \rangle \, \varphi$	Option	$\varphi \vee \langle \beta \rangle \, \varphi$
$\langle \beta^* \rangle \, \varphi$	Iter. ≥ 0 times	$\mu Y. (\varphi \vee \langle \beta \rangle \, Y)$
$\langle \beta^+ \rangle \varphi$	Iter. ≥ 1 times	$\mu Y. \langle \beta \rangle \, (\varphi \vee Y)$
$\langle \beta\{e\} \rangle \, \varphi$	Iteration e times	$\mu Y (c : \text{nat} := e).$ $\quad$ if $c > 0$ then $\langle \beta \rangle \, Y(c-1)$ $\quad$ else φ end if
$\langle \beta \{e_1 \, ... \, e_2\} \rangle \, \varphi$	Iteration $e_1 \leq e_2$ times	$\mu Y(c_1 : \text{nat} := e_1, c_2 : \text{nat} := e_2 - e_1).$ $\quad$ if $c_1 > 0$ then $\langle \beta \rangle \, Y(c_1 - 1, c_2)$ $\quad$ elsif $c_2 > 0$ then $\qquad \varphi \vee \langle \beta \rangle \, Y(c_1, c_2 - 1)$ $\quad$ else φ end if
$\langle \text{let } x_1 : T_1 := e_1, ..., x_n : T_n := e_n \text{ in }$ β $\text{end let} \rangle \, \varphi$	Variable definition	let $x_1 : T_1 := e_1, ..., x_n : T_n := e_n$ in $\quad \langle \beta \rangle \, \varphi$ end let
$\langle \text{if } \varphi_1 \text{ then } \beta_1$ $\text{elsif } \varphi_2 \text{ then } \beta_2 \, ... \, \text{else } \beta_n$ $\text{end if} \rangle \, \varphi$	Conditional	if φ_1 then $\langle \beta_1 \rangle \, \varphi$ elsif φ_2 then $\langle \beta_2 \rangle \, \varphi$...else $\langle \beta_n \rangle \, \varphi$ end if
$\langle \text{case } e \text{ is}$ $p_1 \rightarrow \beta_1 \mid ... \mid p_n \rightarrow \beta_n$ $\text{end case} \rangle \, \varphi$	Selection	case e is $p_1 \rightarrow \langle \beta_1 \rangle \, \varphi \mid ... \mid p_n \rightarrow \langle \beta_n \rangle \, \varphi$ end case
$\langle \text{while } \varphi_1 \text{ do } \beta \text{ end while} \rangle \, \varphi_2$	Initial test loop	$\mu Y. \text{if } \varphi_1 \text{ then } \langle \beta \rangle \, Y \text{ else } \varphi_2 \text{ end if}$

UNIX systems. These operators turn out to be as useful for specifying transition sequences as their egrep counterparts are for describing character strings (see, e.g., formulas φ_5 and φ_6 in Tab. 1). However, when one must handle the data values contained in actions and characterize the intermediate states occurring on a sequence, more sophisticated operators become necessary.

The "if" operator generalizes the testing operator "?φ" of PDL [14], which allows to specify a formula φ about an intermediate state of a sequence denoted by a regular formula. The "?φ" operator is formulated in MCL as if $\neg \varphi$ then false end if. The "let" and "case" operators are the sequence counterparts of the corresponding state operators. Note that exhaustiveness of branches in the "if" and "case" regular formulas is not mandatory: if none of the branch conditions is satisfied, the formula denotes the empty sequence, exactly as in sequential programming languages. The "while" iteration operator specifies repetitions of subsequences driven by their source states. Originally, the "if" and "while" operators were introduced in *well-structured* PDL [20], a syntactic extension of PDL intended to enforce a disciplined use of the testing operator.

The regular modalities defined in Table 2 can deal only with finite transition sequences and thus can specify only simple fairness properties, such as the fair reachability [35] of an action a, described as $[(\neg a)^*] \langle(\neg a)^*.a\rangle$ true. To specify more complex fairness properties, we use the infinite looping operator $\Delta\beta$ of PDL-Δ [39], noted $\langle\beta\rangle$ @ in MCL, which states the existence of an infinite (unfair) sequence made by concatenating subsequences satisfying β (see formula φ_7 in Tab. 1). This operator is equivalent to the $\nu Y.\langle\beta\rangle Y$ formula [13]; by expanding β using the rules in Table 2, the resulting formula belongs to $L\mu_2$ or $L\mu_1$, depending whether β contains iteration operators or not. The $\langle\beta\rangle$ @ operator captures the Büchi acceptance condition (see formula φ_8 in Tab. 1), unexpressible in $L\mu_1$.

Expressiveness: The dataless fragment of MCL (i.e., with no occurrences of data variables) contains the operators of $L\mu_1$, the regular modalities of PDL (embedded in $L\mu_1$ [13]), and the infinite looping operator, which belongs to $L\mu_2$ [13]. This fragment strictly includes PDL-Δ, which in turn subsumes LTL (see formula φ_8 in Tab. 1) and CTL* [43]. Data variables do not, strictly speaking, increase expressiveness: since we work on finite LTSs, all possible instances of data variables or fixed point parameters related to the LTS could be expanded statically. This is however uncompatible with the on-the-fly model checking approach, which does not assume an *a priori* knowledge of the entire LTS.

3 Model Checking Method

We are interested in the on-the-fly model checking of an alternation-free MCL formula φ on an LTS $M = \langle S, A, T, s_0\rangle$, which consists in determining whether s_0 satisfies φ or not by exploring T in a forward manner starting at s_0. We proceed by generalizing the method used for model checking $L\mu_1$ formulas [1,8] and their extensions with PDL regular modalities [32]: the verification problem is reformulated as the local resolution of a boolean equation system (BES) [28], which is performed using specialized algorithms such as those in [31].

3.1 Translation into Parameterized BESs

The reformulation of the verification problem roughly consists of four steps, illustrated in the table below. The MCL formula φ serving as example states that every number p inserted into an empty 5-place buffer will be potentially delivered after 4 internal transitions denoting the moves of p between contiguous buffer cells. The first three steps transform φ syntactically, and the fourth one involves semantic information coming from the LTS.

1. The normalization step inserts new propositional variables at appropriate places in order to capture all occurrences of "hidden" fixed points underlying regular modalities with iterations (e.g., νY_1) and to ensure that every data variable occuring free in a subformula must be a parameter of the propositional variable dominating the subformula (e.g., $\mu Z_1(q:\mathsf{nat}{:=}p)$).

2. The translation to parameterized PDL with recursion (PDLR) [32] brings the formula to an equivalent equational form. Here we focus on alternation-free PDLR systems, without cyclic dependencies between equation blocks. Every fixed point subformula induces an equation, which (due to normalization) is self-contained w.r.t. its data parameters.

3. The translation to parameterized HML with recursion (HMLR) [27] simplifies the modalities by expanding the regular formulas according to their semantics given in Table 2. Duplication of subformulas is avoided by introducing new equations, in such a way that the size of the HMLR system remains linear w.r.t. the initial MCL formula.

4. The final step makes a kind of product between the HMLR system and the LTS, producing a parameterized BES (PBES) [29] in which a boolean variable $Y_s(v_1, ..., v_n)$ is true iff state s satisfies $Y(v_1, ..., v_n)$. The evaluation of the boolean formulas in the right-hand sides allows to traverse the LTS transitions in a forward way, suitable for on-the-fly verification.

MCL formula	$[\text{true}^*.\{put\ ?p\text{:nat}\}]\ \langle \tau\{4\}.\{get\ !p\}\rangle\ \text{true}$
Normalized formula	$\nu Y_1.\ [\text{true}^*.\{put\ ?p\text{:nat}\}]\ \mu Z_1(q\text{:nat}{:=}p).\ \langle \tau\{4\}.\{get\ !q\}\rangle\ \text{true}$
PDLR system	$\left\{ Y_1 \stackrel{\nu}{=} [\text{true}^*.\{put\ ?p\text{:nat}\}]\ Z_1(p) \right\}$ $\left\{ Z_1(q\text{:nat}) \stackrel{\mu}{=} \langle \tau\{4\}.\{get\ !q\}\rangle\ \text{true} \right\}$
HMLR system	$\left\{ Y_1 \stackrel{\nu}{=} [\text{true}^*]\ [\{put\ ?p\text{:nat}\}]\ Z_1(p) \right\}$ $\left\{ Z_1(q\text{:nat}) \stackrel{\mu}{=} \langle \tau\{4\}\rangle\ \langle\{get\ !q\}\rangle\ \text{true} \right\}$ $\left\{ Y_1 \stackrel{\nu}{=} [\{put\ ?p\text{:nat}\}]\ Z_1(p) \wedge [\text{true}]\ Y_1 \right\}$ $\left\{ \begin{array}{l} Z_1(q\text{:nat}) \stackrel{\mu}{=} Z_2(q, 4) \\ Z_2(q, c\text{:nat}) \stackrel{\mu}{=} \text{if } c > 0 \text{ then } \langle \tau \rangle\ Z_2(q, c-1) \\ \qquad \text{else } \langle\{get\ !q\}\rangle\ \text{true end if} \end{array} \right\}$
PBES	$\left\{ Y_{1\,s} \stackrel{\nu}{=} \bigwedge_{s \stackrel{put\ m}{\rightarrow} s'} Z_{1\,s'}(m) \wedge \bigwedge_{s \rightarrow s'} Y_{1\,s'} \right\}_{s \in S}$ $\left\{ \begin{array}{l} Z_{1\,s}(q\text{:nat}) \stackrel{\mu}{=} Z_{2\,s}(q, 4) \\ Z_{2\,s}(q, c\text{:nat}) \stackrel{\mu}{=} \text{if } c > 0 \text{ then } \bigvee_{s \stackrel{\tau}{\rightarrow} s'} Z_{2\,s'}(q, c-1) \\ \qquad \text{else } \bigvee_{s \stackrel{get\ q}{\rightarrow} s'} \text{true end if} \end{array} \right\}_{s \in S}$

The evaluation of an MCL formula on the initial state s_0 of an LTS is reduced to the resolution of a variable instance $Y_{s_0}(v_1, ..., v_n)$ defined by the first equation block of the corresponding PBES. This is carried out by expanding the PBES incrementally, starting at $Y_{s_0}(v_1, ..., v_n)$ and evaluating the formula in the right-hand side of its equation, which in turn will generate new variable instances, and so on. If the number of generated instances is finite, the expanded PBES portion is converted into a plain BES by associating a boolean variable $Y_{s,v_1,...,v_n}$ to each variable instance $Y_s(v_1, ..., v_n)$, based on the isomorphism of the lattices $(T_1 \times \cdots \times T_n \to \text{bool})^{|S|}$ and $\text{bool}^{|T_1|\cdots|T_n|\cdot|S|}$. Then, the value of $Y_{s_0,v_1,...,v_n}$ is obtained by locally solving the resulting BES using the linear-time algorithms of [31]. The incremental expansion of the PBES to a plain BES and the local resolution are performed simultaneously, since both of them rely upon a forward exploration of the dependencies between (instances of) boolean variables.

3.2 Handling of the Infinite Looping Operator

When β contains iterations, the $\langle \beta \rangle$ @ operator corresponds to a $L\mu_2$ formula; although we cannot directly use alternation-free BES resolution, we can still devise a linear-time algorithm for evaluating it on an LTS. The PDLR system equivalent to $\langle \beta \rangle$ @ contains two mutually recursive equation blocks $\{Y \stackrel{\nu}{=} Z\}$ and $\{Z \stackrel{\mu}{=} \langle \beta \rangle Y\}$. The BES obtained by applying the translation given in Section 3.1 has the form $\{Y_s \stackrel{\nu}{=} Z_s\}$, $\{Z_s \stackrel{\mu}{=} \vee_{s \xrightarrow{\beta} s'} Y_{s'}\}$. The shorthand notation $\vee_{s \xrightarrow{\beta} s'}$ means the existence of a sequence relating s and s' and satisfying β; in general, this is further expanded into several disjunctive equations, e.g., the block $\{Z_s \stackrel{\mu}{=} \vee_{s \xrightarrow{(a^*.b)^*.c} s'} Y_{s'}\}$ becomes $\{Z_s \stackrel{\mu}{=} \vee_{s \xrightarrow{c} s'} Y_{s'} \vee W_s, W_s \stackrel{\mu}{=} \vee_{s \xrightarrow{b} s'} Z_{s'} \vee \vee_{s \xrightarrow{a} s'} W_{s'}\}$. To solve such a BES, we abusively merge its two blocks into a single disjunctive μ-block $B = \{Y_s \stackrel{\mu}{=} Z_s, Z_s \stackrel{\mu}{=} \vee_{s \xrightarrow{\beta} s'} Y_{s'}\}$ and take care to preserve the original semantics during local resolution. A state s satisfies $\langle \beta \rangle$ @ iff it has an outgoing infinite sequence made of subsequences satisfying β. If there is no such sequence going out of s, then the formula is false, which is also the value of Y_s obtained by solving B. Otherwise, the infinite sequence ends with a cycle (because the LTS is finite) going through some variable $Y_{s'}$; to force Y_s to true, it is sufficient to detect the cycle and set $Y_{s'}$ to true, which will propagate back to Y_s.

The local resolution algorithm A4 [31] solves a disjunctive BES by performing a depth-first search (DFS) of the associated *boolean graph* [1], which encodes the dependencies between boolean variables. The DFS starts at the vertex (variable) of interest x and, when it encounters a true constant, it propagates it back to x via the disjunctive variables present on the DFS stack, which become true as well. Furthermore, all visited variables that may reach the true constant must also be set to true, in order to avoid multiple traversals of the boolean graph during subsequent invocations of A4 (this happens when the subformula from which the block was generated is nested within other temporal operators) and to keep a linear-time complexity for the overall resolution. Since these variables belong to the partially explored strongly connected components (SCCs) covering the DFS stack, A4 also performs SCC detection using Tarjan's algorithm [40].

Algorithm A4$_{cyc}$ (see Fig. 2) extends A4 with the ability to detect cycles going through certain marked variables (such as $Y_{s'}$ above), indicated by a predicate *marked*. When such a cycle is detected, the marked variable becomes true, and its value will propagate back to x via disjunctive variables, exactly like an ordinary true constant. A simple way to detect these cycles is to check, every time a SCC is identified, whether it contains such a variable or not. A more efficient solution is to do the check only when traversing a cycle-closing edge (lines 20–23), i.e., a "back" or a "cross" edge in the DFS terminology [40]. To avoid searching the DFS stack for marked variables, we use an additional $stack_2$, which contains all marked variables present on the DFS stack and evolves synchronously with it. Then, it is sufficient to check that the target variable of a cycle-closing edge has a "lowlink" number [40] smaller than the DFS number of the variable on top of $stack_2$. Thus, cycles containing marked variables are always detected before the exploration of the last encountered SCC is completed.

```
 1. var $A : 2^V$ ; $k$ : nat ; $stack : V^*$ ; $stack_2 : V^*$ ;
 2. $A := \emptyset$ ; $k := 0$ ; $stack := nil$ ;
 3. function $\text{A4}_{cyc}$ $(x : V, (V, E, L), marked : V \to$ bool$)$ : bool is
 4.    var $v, stable : V \to$ bool ; $n, p, low : V \to$ nat ;
 5.       $y, z : V$ ; $val$ : bool ;
 6.    if $|E(x)| = 0$ then
 7.       if $L(x) = \vee$ then $v(x) :=$ false else $v(x) :=$ true end if ;
 8.       $stable(x) :=$ true
 9.    else
10.       $v(x) :=$ false;
11.       $stable(x) :=$ false
12.    end if ;
13.    $p(x) := 0$ ; $n(x) := k$ ; $k := k + 1$ ; $low(x) := n(x)$ ;
14.    $A := A \cup \{x\}$ ; $stack := push(x, stack)$ ;
15.    if $marked(x)$ then $stack_2 := push(stack_2)$ end if ;
16.    while $p(x) < |E(x)|$ do
17.       $y := (E(x))_{p(x)}$ ;
18.       if $y \in A$ then
19.          $val := v(y)$ ;
20.          if $\neg stable(y) \wedge n(y) < n(x)$ then
21.             $low(x) := min(low(x), n(y))$ ;
22.             if $low(x) \leq n(top(stack_2))$ then $val :=$ true end if
23.          end if
24.       else
25.          $val := \text{A4}_{cyc}$ $(y, (V, E, L))$
26.          $low(x) := min(low(x), low(y))$
27.       end if ;
28.       if $val$ then
29.          $v(x) :=$ true ; $stable(x) :=$ true ;
30.          $p(x) := |E(x)|$
31.       else
32.          $p(x) := p(x) + 1$
33.       end if
34.    end while ;
35.    if $v(x) \vee low(x) = n(x)$ then
36.       repeat
37.          $z := top(stack)$ ; $v(z) := v(x)$ ;
38.          $stable(z) :=$ true ; $stack := pop(stack)$
39.       until $z = x$
40.    end if ;
41.    if $x = top(stack_2)$ then $stack_2 := pop(stack_2)$ end if ;
42.    return $v(x)$
43. end
```

Fig. 2. Local resolution of a disjunctive μ-block with marked cycle detection

Complexity of model checking: Algorithm A4$_{cyc}$ runs in $O(|V|+|E|)$ time and $O(|V|)$ memory, where V is the set of boolean graph vertices (boolean variables) and E is the set of dependencies between them (boolean operators). Since A4 can handle PDL [31], it provides together with A4$_{cyc}$ a linear-time on-the-fly model checking procedure for PDL-Δ, improving over the classical quadratic procedure obtained by translating PDL-Δ to $L\mu_2$ [13]. Given that $\langle \beta \rangle$ @ captures the Büchi acceptance condition, A4$_{cyc}$ could also serve as verification back-end for LTL; the SCC detection (which is not needed for LTL model checking [22]) is necessary for ensuring a linear-time complexity when $\langle \beta \rangle$ @ occurs nested within branching-time operators and is therefore evaluated multiple times.

Dataless formulas of MCL are evaluated with a time and space complexity $O(|\varphi| \cdot (|S| + |T|))$ using BES resolution [31]. The operators of CTL and PDL-Δ, which cover the quasi-totality of practical needs, are evaluated with a space complexity $O(|\varphi| \cdot |S|)$ using A4 and A4$_{cyc}$. Data variables of infinite types may lead to divergence of model checking, because the number of boolean variable instances produced by expansion from PBESs to BESs can be unbounded. Therefore, parameterized fixed points should be used with the same care as recursive functions in programming languages (note however that cycles $Y_s(v_1, ..., v_n) \to \cdots \to Y_s(v_1, ..., v_n)$ do not harm, since BES resolution algorithms can handle cyclic dependencies between variables). The evaluation of all extended regular operators given in Table 2 is guaranteed to converge, because their expansion to BESs always creates a finite number of variable instances, bounded by the values of iteration counters and/or the number of LTS states.

4 Implementation and Use

The model checkers Evaluator 3.x and 4.0: A verification method similar to that given in Section 3, but restricted to dataless formulas, is at the core of the EVALUATOR 3.x model checker [31,32] of CADP [17], which evaluates formulas of regular $L\mu_1$ on LTSs on-the-fly. The tool is based on the generic LTS exploration API defined by OPEN/CÆSAR [15] and therefore is language-independent. The implicit BES produced by reformulating the verification problem is solved on-the-fly using the local resolution algorithms of the generic CÆSAR_SOLVE library [31]. These algorithms rely upon various exploration strategies of boolean graphs: plain DFS, optimized DFS for the memory-efficient resolution of disjunctive/conjunctive or acyclic BESs, breadth-first search (BFS), etc. The tool is also able to generate examples and counterexamples (LTS portions explaining the verification result) using the BES approach proposed in [30]. To facilitate the specification task, derived temporal operators can be defined as macros parameterized by subformulas and grouped into reusable libraries, several of which are currently available (defining CTL [7], Action-based CTL [10], and the property patterns proposed in [11]). EVALUATOR 3.x served to validate more than 30 industrial case-studies over the last 7 years[1], and is currently used by BULL, STMicroelectronics, and CEA/LETI for checking asynchronous hardware [37].

---
[1] See http://www.inrialpes.fr/vasy/cadp/case-studies

The verification method described in Section 3 is at the core of the new version EVALUATOR 4.0 (38 000 lines of code) that we developed within CADP. The new tool[2] brings two major enhancements w.r.t. its previous versions 3.x:

- The MCL language presented in Section 2 (which is a conservative extension of regular $L\mu_1$, the input language of versions 3.x) is now accepted as input, thus allowing to express temporal properties involving data. The presence of data parameters significantly reduces the size of temporal specifications, by avoiding tedious repetitions of formulas caused by instantiations of parameters with values contained in the LTS actions.
- The infinite looping operator $\langle ... \rangle @$ is now fully implemented (versions 3.x only accepted iteration-free regular formulas inside the $\langle ... \rangle @$ operator) using the linear time algorithm $A4_{cyc}$, thus allowing to verify elaborated fairness properties on-the-fly. The presence of $\langle ... \rangle @$ makes MCL more expressive than both $L\mu_1$ and LTL, enabling to specify the existence of complex unfair cycles in LTSs, which was previously verifiable using CADP only by means of bisimulation checking [4,37].

Besides the operators defined in Section 2, EVALUATOR 4.0 also accepts weak modalities as in observational $L\mu$ [38]. The new tool is fully upward compatible with the versions 3.x: it accepts existing specifications written in regular $L\mu_1$, uses the same on-the-fly verification engine CÆSAR_SOLVE, offers the same diagnostic features, and keeps the same macro-definition mechanism, allowing the existing libraries of derived operators to be directly reused in MCL specifications.

Model checking of data-based fairness properties using Evaluator 4.0: We illustrate below the use of EVALUATOR 4.0 for verifying the behaviour of the SCSI-2 bus arbitration protocol [2], based on the LOTOS specification given in [16], available in the demo_31 of CADP. The SCSI-2 protocol handles the access of devices (disks and controllers) to a bus. Devices are assigned unique numbers (priorities) in the range $[0, n-1]$. We consider a configuration containing one controller with number n_c and $n-1$ disks. The controller communicates with disk i by sending commands "*cmd i*"; after a disk receives a command, it processes it and responds to the controller with a "*rec i*" action (*reconnect* in the SCSI-2 terminology). To perform an emission or a reception, each device must get access to the bus; when several devices are requesting the bus, the device with the highest number obtains it. This priority-based arbitration raises a question about fairness: are the low priority disks always able to dialog with the controller?

It turns out that this is not the case, as it was determined experimentally by engineers at BULL [16]. The unfair behaviours of the SCSI-2 protocol are precisely captured by the following MCL formula, expressing the existence of infinite execution sequences on which disks with numbers $i < n_c$ are continuously preempted from accessing the bus by disks with higher priority:

[true*.{ *cmd* ?*i*:nat where $i < n_c$ }]
   forall *j*:nat among $\{i+1 \ ... \ n-1\}$.
      $(j \neq n_c) \Rightarrow \langle (\neg\{rec \ !i\})^*.\{cmd \ !j\}.(\neg\{rec \ !i\})^*.\{rec \ !j\} \rangle @$

---

[2] See http://www.inrialpes.fr/vasy/cadp/man/evaluator.html

This property was impossible to express and verify precisely using the earlier versions EVALUATOR 3.x, which did not support the infinite looping operator. Using version 4.0, we checked that the above formula holds for several values of n and n_c (see the table below). The experiments were carried out on a 731 MHz, 1 GByte Pentium III machine. For each experiment, we give the size of the LTS, its generation time in seconds (for comparison with on-the-fly verification time), the size of the underlying BES, and the local resolution time. The BES contains a ν-block and a μ-block encoding the necessity modality and the infinite looping subformula, respectively. We also indicate how many times A4$_{cyc}$ was invoked for solving variables of the inner μ-block; each invocation denotes the evaluation of the $\langle ... \rangle$ @ subformula on a state reached after an appropriate "$cmd\ i$" action. The peak of memory usage was 182 MBytes (for $n = 5$ and $n_c = 4$). For each value of n, we observe a linear growth of the BES size and resolution time w.r.t. the value of n_c, which directly influences the effort of evaluating the formula.

cfg.		LTS		gen.	BES		res.	calls to
n	n_c	states	trans.	time	vars.	opns.	time	A4$_{cyc}$
3	0	2 060	4 630	0.73	2 061	4 631	1.30	0
	1	2 060	4 628	0.74	4 148	7 479	1.40	255
	2	2 060	4 628	0.74	4 698	8 284	1.39	255
4	0	56 169	154 752	1.71	56 170	154 753	3.52	0
	1	56 169	154 749	1.71	113 571	233 840	5.05	8 670
	2	56 169	154 749	1.71	148 444	282 024	5.87	13 005
	3	56 169	154 749	1.71	154 709	292 308	5.88	13 005
5	0	1 384 022	4 499 242	29.94	1 384 023	4 499 243	75.86	0
	1	1 384 022	4 499 238	29.78	2 710 057	6 341 224	125.74	221 085
	2	1 384 022	4 499 238	30.06	3 655 692	7 657 871	162.08	368 475
	3	1 384 022	4 499 238	30.00	4 219 664	8 446 999	182.81	442 170
	4	1 384 022	4 499 238	30.05	4 304 560	8 598 936	184.63	442 170

We successfully checked several other MCL properties on the SCSI-2 protocol, among which a safety property expressing that the difference between the number of commands received and reconnections sent by a disk i varies from 0 to 8 (the size of the buffers associated to disks):

$$\nu Y(c:\text{nat}:=0).([\ \{cmd\ !i\}\ ]\,((c < 8) \land Y(c+1)) \land$$
$$[\ \{rec\ !i\}\ ]\,((c > 0) \land Y(c-1)) \land [\ \neg(\{cmd\ !i\} \lor \{rec\ !i\})\ ]\,Y(c))$$

This property is also expressible in plain $L\mu$, but requires 9 nested maximal fixed point operators (one for each value of the counter c) and 27 box modalities.

5 Conclusion and Future Work

The specification of temporal properties in $L\mu$ is a difficult task that requires a significant training and experience. By proposing MCL, a user-friendly extension of $L\mu$, we attempted to facilitate this task for branching-time, action-based properties interpreted on LTSs; our effort goes in the same direction as existing enhancements of state-based temporal logics [3,5,6,23]. Our model checking method, based on reformulating the problem as a BES resolution, provides a natural evaluation engine for parameterized fixed points on finite LTSs; infinite-state systems could be handled using symbolic resolution of PBESs [18]. The restriction to the alternation-free MCL fragment, motivated by efficiency, is compensated by the ability of the infinite looping operator to handle fairness properties. The local BES resolution algorithm A4$_{cyc}$ that we proposed for evaluating this operator yields a linear-time on-the-fly model checking procedure for PDL-Δ, despite its embedding in $L\mu_2$ [13].

We plan to continue our work along several directions. Firstly, a tighter coupling is needed between EVALUATOR 4.0 and the data types and functions of the program under verification: this can be done by appropriately extending the LTS exploration API defined by OPEN/CÆSAR with data manipulation features. Secondly, MCL can be enhanced with the operators of other logics, such as (action-based) LTL, which can be translated using the infinite looping operator. Finally, a distributed version of EVALUATOR 4.0 can be obtained by coupling it with distributed BES resolution algorithms [25].

References

1. Andersen, H.R.: Model Checking and Boolean Graphs. TCS 126(1), 3–30 (1994)
2. ANSI. Small Computer System Interface-2. Standard X3.131-1994
3. Armoni, R., Fix, L., Flaisher, A., et al.: The ForSpec Temporal Logic: A New Temporal Property-Specification Language. In: Katoen, J.-P., Stevens, P. (eds.) ETAPS 2002 and TACAS 2002. LNCS, vol. 2280, pp. 211–296. Springer, Heidelberg (2002)
4. Arts, T., Benac Earle, C., Derrick, J.: Development of a Verified Erlang Program for Resource Locking. STTT 5(2-2), 205–220 (2004)
5. Barringer, H., Goldberg, A., Havelund, K., Sen, K.: Rule-Based Runtime Verification. In: Steffen, B., Levi, G. (eds.) VMCAI 2004. LNCS, vol. 2937, pp. 44–57. Springer, Heidelberg (2004)
6. Beer, I., Ben-David, S., Eisner, C., Fisman, D., Gringauze, A., Rodeh, Y.: The Temporal Logic Sugar. In: Berry, G., Comon, H., Finkel, A. (eds.) CAV 2001. LNCS, vol. 2102, pp. 363–367. Springer, Heidelberg (2001)
7. Clarke, E., Grumberg, O., Peled, D.: Model Checking. MIT Press, Cambridge (2000)
8. Cleaveland, R., Steffen, B.: A Linear-Time Model-Checking Algorithm for the Alternation-Free Modal Mu-Calculus. FMSD 2(2), 121–147 (1993)
9. Dam, M.: Model Checking Mobile Processes (Full version). Research Report RR 94:1, Swedish Institute of Computer Science, Kista, Sweden (1994)
10. De Nicola, R., Vaandrager, F.W.: Action versus State Based Logics for Transition Systems. In: LITP 1990. Lncs, vol. 469, pp. 407–419 (1990)
11. Dwyer, M.B., Avrunin, G.S., Corbett, J.C.: Patterns in Property Specifications for Finite-State Verification. In: ICSE 1999, pp. 411–420 (1999)
12. Emerson, E.A., Halpern, J.Y.: Sometimes and Not Never Revisited: On Branching versus Linear Time Temporal Logic. J. ACM 33(1), 151–178 (1986)
13. Emerson, E.A., Lei, C.-L.: Efficient Model Checking in Fragments of the Propositional Mu-Calculus. In: LICS 1986, pp. 267–278 (1986)

14. Fischer, M.J., Ladner, R.E.: Propositional Dynamic Logic of Regular Programs. JCSS 18(2), 194–211 (1979)
15. Garavel, H.: OPEN/CAESAR: An Open Software Architecture for Verification, Simulation, and Testing. In: Steffen, B. (ed.) ETAPS 1998 and TACAS 1998. LNCS, vol. 1384, pp. 68–84. Springer, Heidelberg (1998)
16. Garavel, H., Hermanns, H.: On Combining Functional Verification and Performance Evaluation Using CADP. In: Eriksson, L.-H., Lindsay, P.A. (eds.) FME 2002. LNCS, vol. 2391, pp. 410–429. Springer, Heidelberg (2002)
17. Garavel, H., Lang, F., Mateescu, R., Serwe, W.: CADP 2006: A Toolbox for the Construction and Analysis of Distributed Processes. In: Damm, W., Hermanns, H. (eds.) CAV 2007. LNCS, vol. 4590, pp. 158–163. Springer, Heidelberg (2007)
18. Groote, J.F., Willemse, T.A.C.: Parameterised Boolean Equation Systems. TCS 343, 332–369 (2005)
19. Groote, J.F., Mateescu, R.: Verification of Temporal Properties of Processes in a Setting with Data. In: Haeberer, A.M. (ed.) AMAST 1998. LNCS, vol. 1548, pp. 74–90. Springer, Heidelberg (1998)
20. Halpern, J.Y., Reif, J.H.: The Propositional Dynamic Logic of Deterministic, Well-structured Programs. TCS 27(1–2), 127–165 (1983)
21. Hamaguchi, K., Hiraishi, H., Yajima, S.: Branching Time Regular Temporal Logic for Model Checking with Linear Time Complexity. In: CAV 1990. Lncs, vol. 531 (1990)
22. Holzmann, G.: The SPIN Model Checker. Addison-Wesley, Reading (2003)
23. IEEE. PSL: Property Specification Language. Std. P1850, IEEE (2004)
24. ISO/IEC. LOTOS — A Formal Description Technique Based on the Temporal Ordering of Observational Behaviour. Int. Std. 8807, ISO — OSI, Genève (1989)
25. Joubert, C., Mateescu, R.: Distributed On-the-Fly Model Checking and Test Case Generation. In: Valmari, A. (ed.) SPIN 2006. LNCS, vol. 3925, pp. 126–145. Springer, Heidelberg (2006)
26. Kozen, D.: Results on the Propositional μ-calculus. TCS 27, 333–354 (1983)
27. Larsen, K.G.: Proof Systems for Hennessy-Milner logic with Recursion. In: Dauchet, M., Nivat, M. (eds.) CAAP 1988. LNCS, vol. 299, pp. 215–230. Springer, Heidelberg (1988)
28. Mader, A.: Verification of Modal Properties Using Boolean Equation Systems. In: VERSAL 8, Bertz Verlag, Berlin (1997)
29. Mateescu, R.: Local Model-Checking of an Alternation-Free Value-Based Modal Mu-Calculus. In: VMCAI 1998. University Ca'Foscari of Venice (1998)
30. Mateescu, R.: Efficient Diagnostic Generation for Boolean Equation Systems. In: Schwartzbach, M.I., Graf, S. (eds.) ETAPS 2000 and TACAS 2000. LNCS, vol. 1785, pp. 251–265. Springer, Heidelberg (2000)
31. Mateescu, R.: CÆSAR_SOLVE: A Generic Library for On-the-Fly Resolution of Alternation-Free Boolean Equation Systems. STTT 8(1), 37–56 (2006)
32. Mateescu, R., Sighireanu, M.: Efficient On-the-Fly Model-Checking for Regular Alternation-Free Mu-Calculus. SCP 46(3), 255–281 (2003)
33. Milner, R.: Communication and Concurrency. Prentice-Hall, Englewood Cliffs (1989)
34. Pnueli, A.: A Temporal Logic of Concurrent Programs. TCS 13, 45–60 (1981)
35. Queille, J.-P., Sifakis, J.: Fairness and Related Properties in Transition Systems — A Temporal Logic to Deal with Fairness. Acta Informatica 19, 195–220 (1983)
36. Rathke, J., Hennessy, M.: Local Model Checking for a Value-Based Modal μ-calculus. Report 5/96, Univ. of Sussex (1996)

37. Salaün, G., Serwe, W., Thonnart, Y., Vivet, P.: Formal Verification of CHP Specifications with CADP — Illustration on an Asynchronous Network-on-Chip. In: ASYNC 2007, pp. 73–82. IEEE, Los Alamitos (2007)
38. Stirling, C.: Modal and Temporal Properties of Processes. Springer, Heidelberg (2001)
39. Streett, R.: Propositional Dynamic Logic of Looping and Converse. Information and Control 54, 121–141 (1982)
40. Tarjan, R.E.: Depth First Search and Linear Graph Algorithms. SIAM J. of Computing 1(2), 146–160 (1972)
41. Thomas, W.: Linear Time, Branching Time and Partial Order in Logics and Models for Concurrency. Lncs, vol. 354
42. Vergauwen, B., Lewi, J.: A Linear Algorithm for Solving Fixed-Point Equations on Transition Systems. In: Raoult, J.-C. (ed.) CAAP 1992. LNCS, vol. 581, pp. 322–341. Springer, Heidelberg (1992)
43. Wolper, P.: A Translation from Full Branching Time Temporal Logic to One Letter Propositional Dynamic Logic with Looping. Unpublished manuscript (1982)
44. Wolper, P.: Temporal Logic Can Be More Expressive. Information and Control 56(1/2), 72–99 (1983)

Verification of Mondex Electronic Purses with KIV: From a Security Protocol to Verified Code

Holger Grandy, Markus Bischof, Kurt Stenzel,
Gerhard Schellhorn, and Wolfgang Reif

{grandy,stenzel,schellhorn,reif}@informatik.uni-augsburg.de

Abstract. We present a verified JavaCard implementation for the Mondex Verification Challenge. This completes a series of verification efforts that we made to verify the Mondex case study starting at abstract transaction specifications, continuing with an introduction of a security protocol and now finally the refinement of this protocol to running source code. We show that current verification techniques and tool support are not only suitable to verify the original case study as stated in the Grand Challenge but also can cope with extensions of it resulting in verified and running code. The Mondex verification presented in this paper is the first one that carries security properties proven on an abstract level to an implementation level using refinement.

1 Introduction

The Mondex [22] case study is a significant contribution to the Verified Software Repository [4] [37] which has its origin in the Grand Challenge in Software Verification [18]. Mondex is an electronic purse application for smart cards. It was originally implemented by Mastercard and became famous for being one of the first applications to be verified according to the highest criteria of ITSEC [8]. The challenge is the machine assisted verification of Mondex smart cards security properties. It was first done by paper and pencil proofs by Stepney, Cooper and Woodcock [34]. A lot of groups recently showed that their verification tools and methods can cope with the case study (e.g. [25] [2] [17] [38] [20]). Some small errors were found in the original case study. Our group also solved the challenge in [30] and [29] using Abstract State Machines (ASM) [6] and ASM Refinement [5] [26] [27] with the interactive theorem prover KIV [1]. Furthermore, we extended the case study by introducing a suitable cryptographic security protocol in [15], while the original specifications do not deal with explicit cryptography, but only assume messages to be unforgeable. We also introduced an UML-based modelling framework for security protocols in general and used it to model Mondex in [24].

In this paper we adopt our refinement method for security protocol implementations (already presented in [12]), to the verification of a Mondex implementation. The code we are verifying is running on Java smart cards [35]. Besides the original Mondex challenge, this paper addresses especially the problems of

Data Abstraction and of Complex Heap Data Structures as stated in a current verification challenge [21].

We prove that our implementation preserves the Mondex security properties. First, security is proved for the abstract levels. Then, the refinement theory carries the properties over to the concrete level. All proofs and the implementation are available on the Web [19]. Fig. 1 shows an overview of our specification and verification layers for Mondex. The levels 1 and 2 are the A and C levels of the original case study, using ASMs as the specification language. The third layer introduces cryptography and was not present in the original specification. Level 4 is the JavaCard implementation level. The refinement from level 3 to 4 is the main content of this paper.

Sect. 2 will introduce Mondex, Sect. 3 describes the source code. Sect. 4 in-

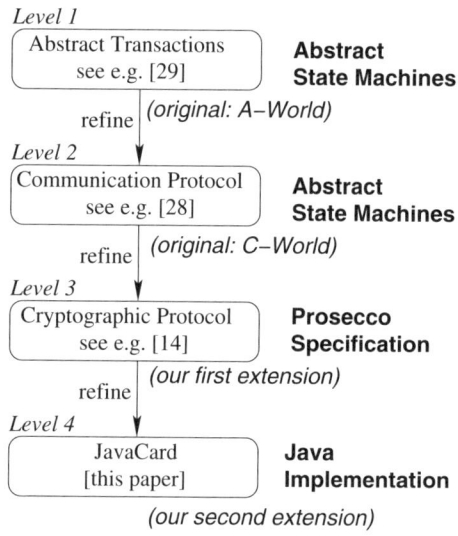

Fig. 1. Our Mondex layers

troduces Java in KIV and the refinement framework, Sect. 5 explains the proof strategy. Sect. 6 compares the approach to related work.

2 Mondex in a Nutshell

Mondex smart cards are electronic purses, that store an amount of money. They can be used to pay by transferring money from one purse (called the FROM Purse) to another one (the TO Purse). Those transactions are assumed to be possibly faulty. While the most abstract level in the case study only uses non-deterministic choice between successful money transfer or loss of money (both possible in one atomic step), the first refinement introduces a protocol using five different messages, together forming a transaction. All messages can be lost during transmission, thereby leading to an error on any of the cards in any state. Level 2 also uses an ether of messages which are currently in transit. Receiving a message is basically taking an arbitrary one out of the ether. Thereby replay attacks are modeled by adding the possibility of taking the same message out more than once. Besides that, there is no explicit attacker analyzing messages or generating new ones. Also there is no cryptography on this level: all messages are assumed to be unforgeable. Any error during one protocol run (like receiving a replayed message) leads to logging of the current transaction. The first refinement shows that the log entries correctly represent the lost money on level 1. This was shown e.g. in [30].

The original verification of Mondex ends at our level 2. Level 3 now introduces cryptography for this protocol using the PROSECCO specification approach [14] [13], which is also based on Abstract State Machines. We chose this approach because PROSECCO already provides lots of specification libraries for security protocols and is well integrated into the KIV system. PROSECCO contains an explicit Dolev-Yao attacker [9] who is analyzing and building messages. The ether of level 2 is now modelled using explicit input queues. Also additional participants (like the terminal or the card holder) are introduced to get closer to reality. We proved that this protocol is a correct refinement of level 2 [29]. A symmetric secret key shared between all the authentic purses is used to encrypt most messages and thereby ensures that the attacker cannot generate forged critical messages. Some details on level 2 and level 3 were already given in [15]. Our Java implementation of Mondex on level 4 is a correct refinement of the abstract ASM specification on level 3.

The protocol of level 3 and 4 is shown in Fig. 2. After the purses' data was queried, the two messages STARTTO and STARTFROM set up the transaction by sending one purse the data of the other. Every purse has a name and a sequence number. The latter is used to avoid replay attacks. The first messages establish a transaction context called PayDetails, consisting of both purse names, both sequence numbers and the money in transfer. The messages REQ(uest), VAL(ue), and ACK(knowledge) are used to transfer money. All messages contain the PayDetails of the current transaction. The

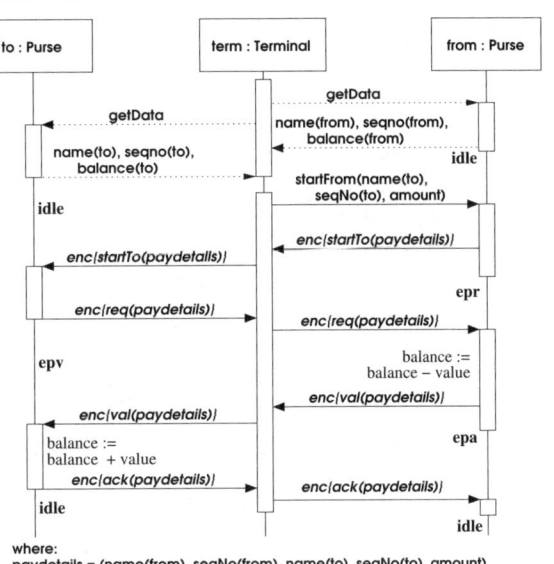

Fig. 2. The Mondex Protocol

FROM purse withdraws money from its balance after receiving a correct REQ and before sending VAL, whereas the TO Purse deposits the same amount after receiving VAL and before sending ACK. Sending STARTTO as a response to STARTFROM is a slight modification of the original protocol of [34], because we found a possible attack in [29]. Another modification is the addition of an explicit getData message to query the sequence number, the name and the current balance of a purse, which is necessary in a realistic environment. Furthermore the messages STARTTO, REQ, VAL and ACK are secured by symmetrically encrypting them with a shared secret key (also shown by *italic* font and prefix enc in Fig. 2). STARTFROM and getData messages are not encrypted. Those protocol modifications and extensions do not incur any problems with the security properties since we proved that this is a correct refinement of level 2 [29].

3 An Implementation of Mondex

3.1 Data Types and Communication

One of the main problems for a correct refinement from an abstract specification is the correct mapping of data types from specification to implementation. Level 3 uses a algebraic data type called Document with various subtypes for modelling messages. For Mondex, we will need the following ones: A Document is either ⊥ (an empty document), an IntDoc representing an arbitrary large integer, or the result of cryptographic encryption of a document doc using the cryptographic key key (i.e. EncDoc(key, doc)). Arbitrary protocol data (like the purse's name or sequence number) is modeled using the IntDoc type. Messages in communication protocols are composed of those basic data types. To model composition the Document type also contains the Doclist constructor, which contains a list of documents (Documentlist). The Documentlist type itself can either be the empty list [] or a composition of a Document and another Documentlist. This gives a mutual recursive algebraic specification of a free data type Document:

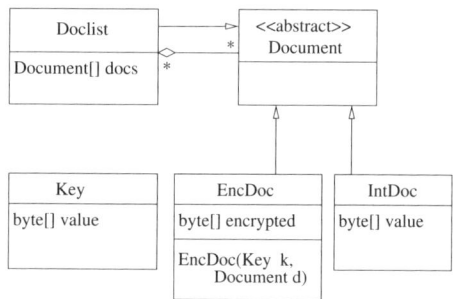

Fig. 3. Mondex Document classes

Document = ⊥ |
        IntDoc(value : int) |
        EncDoc(key : Key, doc : Document) |
        Doclist(docs : Documentlist)
Key = mkKey(value : int)
Documentlist =   [ ] | . + .(first : Document, rest : Documentlist)

The implementation uses a Java class type `Document` to implement this abstract type, resulting in the classes of Fig. 3. We use `byte[]` as the representation of the integer values in the abstract type. Those classes and the mapping from the abstract to the concrete world was described in more detail in [11].

We implement a communication interface, which contains `send` and `receive` methods for the Document type. This is the `SimpleComm` interface:

```
1  public interface SimpleComm {
2      public Document receive();
3      public void send(Document d);}
```

An embedding of this `SimpleComm` interface into JavaCard will be introduced in Sect. 3.3

3.2 Purse Functionality

Using the communication interface, the Purse functionality benefits from the high-level Java class type Document instead of low-level byte sequences. The resulting implementation works as follows[1]:

```
1   public class Purse{
2     SimpleComm comm; Document payDetails, name;
3     short exLogCounter; Document[] exLog;
4     ...
5     public void step() {
6       Document outdoc = null;
7       if(exLogCounter < exLog.length){
8         Document indoc = comm.receive();
9         ... //decrypt and check indoc
10        switch(getInsByte(indoc)) {
11          case START_FROM: outdoc = startFrom(indoc); break;
12          ... // same for other steps
13          case ACK:                      ack(indoc);     break;
14          default:                       abort();        break;}
15        if(outdoc!=null) comm.send(outdoc);}}}
```

The Purse class uses the SimpleComm.receive() method to receive the next input (line 8). Since in a smart card implementation the exception log must have a bounded length (it is unbounded in the original case study, the refinement to bounded lengths is done from level 2 to 3), it is first checked, whether the log is already full (line 7). The exception log is implemented using a field Document[] exLog of class Purse. We use an additional field exLogCounter, which stores the index of the next free exception log entry. A full log can be checked by comparing this field to the maximum log length constant. If the log is full, no further step is performed (the restriction to fixed length exception logs itself is already introduced on the abstract level 3). If space is available, the input document structure is decrypted (if necessary, line 9) and its structure is checked. Level 3 already introduced a document format for all the Mondex messages of Fig. 2. For example, the ACK message is:

$$\left. \begin{array}{l} \text{EncDoc(} \\ \quad \text{mkKey(THESECRETKEY),} \quad \} \text{ Crypto Key} \\ \quad \text{Doclist(} \\ \quad\quad \text{IntDoc(ACK)} \quad \} \text{ Type Flag} \\ \quad\quad + \text{Doclist(} \quad \text{IntDoc(name}_{\text{from}}) + \text{IntDoc(seqno}_{\text{from}}) \\ \quad\quad\quad + \text{IntDoc(name}_{\text{to}}) + \text{IntDoc(seqno}_{\text{to}}) \quad \} \text{ Pay Details} \\ \quad\quad\quad + \text{IntDoc(amount))))} \end{array} \right\} \text{Encrypted Message}$$

The other messages (except STARTFROM, which is slightly shorter) have the same structure. This structure maps directly to Java Documents.

---

[1] For the sake of readability we slightly pretty printed the programs for this paper. The original verified programs can be found on the web [19].

After checking the input structure, the `getInsByte` method (line 9 above) returns the type of the input message and the correct protocol step method (e.g. ack(...), line 13) is chosen. The `ack()` method now has to check whether the PayDetails are correct and that it is no replayed message from an older protocol run. Since the PayDetails are also implemented using the `Document` type (using a field `Document payDetails` in class `Purse`), we can do this by calling a generic equals Method on Document (line 3 below):

```
1  private void ack(Document indoc) {
2    indoc = getPaydetails(indoc);
3    if(!payDetails.equals(indoc)){ abort(); return; }
4    state = STATE_IDLE;}
```

The `abort()` method now only has to check whether the current state is critical (line 2 below). Money can only be lost if the TO Purse is in state EPV or the FROM Purse is in state EPA (see Fig. 2). If we are in a critical state, the current PayDetails have to be copied to the exception log exLog (using the method copyLogPDs, line 3):

```
1  private void abort() {
2    if(state==STATE_EPA || state == STATE_EPV) {
3      exLog[exLogCounter] = copyLogPDs();
4      exLogCounter++;}
5    state = STATE_IDLE;}
```

ack() is relatively short. In contrast, the `startFrom()` method has to perform more checks, since it has to set up the PayDetails correctly:

```
1  private Document startFrom(Document indoc) {
2    Document othername = checkName(indoc);
3    short value = checkBalance(indoc);
4    short otherSeqNo = checkSeqNo(indoc);
5    if(   32767 == sequenceNo || otherSeqNo == -1
6       || value == -1 || othername == null) {
7      abort(); return null;}
8    if(state != STATE_IDLE) abort();
9    if(exLogCounter < exLog.length) {
10     setPaydetails(name, sequenceNo, othername,
11                   otherSeqNo, value);
12     sequenceNo++; state = STATE_EPR;
13     return generateOutmsg(START_TO);}
14   else return null;}
```

First it has to check, whether the transmitted name of the TO Purse is authentic and different from the FROM purse name (in this implementation all names with a length of 8 bytes are authentic[2]). This is checked in the method

---

[2] Authenticity of names is a concept introduced in the abstract levels of Mondex, used to distinguish real Mondex cards from faked ones. The original case study does not state which names are authentic. Note that a check of authenticity of names using e.g. cryptographic signatures does not add any security to the Mondex application. All security of Mondex is based on the encryption and the sequence numbers.

checkName (line 2). Also the amount of money to be deposited must be positive and smaller than the current balance (checkBalance, line 3) and the transmitted sequence number of the other purse must be reasonable (checkSeqNo, line 4). Since the sequence number is a short value, we only allow a further protocol run, if the maximum sequence number (32767) is not yet reached. This restriction was already made on the abstract PROSECCO level 3. The three check methods return an error value (null or -1), if anything is wrong. In those cases, we simply abort and stop (line 7). If we receive a STARTFROM message when we are in not in the IDLE state, we abort and continue afterwards (line 8). This is an extension of the original case study where STARTFROM is only accepted in IDLE. The approach of the original case study would have the negative effect that every new transaction started directly after a previously interrupted transaction would fail, too. This is not what a user expects in reality. If all parameter checks are successful, we store the PayDetails, increment the sequence number and generate a STARTTO return message (lines 10 to 13).

3.3 Embedding in Javacard

The implementation of Mondex runs on Java smart cards. Those cards communicate with APDUs (Application Protocol Data Units), which are essentially byte arrays. To use Java Document classes on Java smart cards we provide a transformation layer that encodes and decodes instances of the Document classes to byte sequences and sends them over the APDU interface. This can be combined with certain checks on the structure of incoming and outgoing messages. An attacker generating for example non well-formed APDU messages has no chance of attacking the protocol, if all those invalid inputs are filtered out in a transformation layer before even starting with the real protocol functionality. We have implemented and proved correct such a transformation layer in [11] for normal network communication and adopted it here to the use on Java smart cards.

The Purse class uses the SimpleComm interface to communicate. The embedding of SimpleComm in the JavaCard world is is done schematically as described in the following code:

```
1   public class PurseAppletWrapper
2     extends javacard.framework.Applet implements SimpleComm{
3       Document input; Purse protocolimpl;
4       public void process(APDU apdu){
5         ...
6         input = decode(apdu.getBuffer());
7         protocolimpl.step();}
8       public Document receive(){ return input; }
9       public void send(Document d){
10        byte[] outbytes = encode(d);
11        ... //copy outbytes to apdu buffer and send them }
12      //for an implementation of encode and decode see [11]
13      private byte[] encode(Document d){...}
14      private Document decode(byte[] b){...}}
```

In JavaCard, every execution of a protocol step on the card is started by a call of the `Applet.process(APDU apdu)` method (line 4). Therefore the byte array input, which is wrapped in the parameter `apdu` of this method, is decoded into a Java `Document` pointer structure (line 6). Then a `step()` Method on the `Purse` implementation class is called (line 7). This method uses `receive()`, which returns the decoded input `Document`. It will also eventually call `send(Document)`, which encodes the output and sends it over the APDU interface (line 10-11).

Additionally, the encoding scheme can be used to deal with cryptography (not shown above), which is inherently necessary for Mondex: If we want to encrypt a `Document` object with a certain key, we can simply encode it to an array of bytes using the encoding scheme and then use the standard Java cryptographic architecture to encrypt this array using the given key's value. This is also the reason why our `EncDoc` class contains an array of bytes as the encrypted value. The only assumption we have to make here is the standard assumption about perfect cryptography used in almost all approaches to security protocol verification: cryptography can only be broken when knowing the right key.

All together, the `Purse` class implementation consists of over 600 lines of code, not counting the various `Document` classes and the encoding/decoding implementation. All classes verified for this case study have around 1800 lines, which is quite a large number for *interactive* source code verification.

4 Refinement Method

We described our refinement framework for Java protocol implementations using another case study in [12]. The method is based on the Java calculus in KIV [32] [33]. For the Mondex verification, ASM Refinement theory [5] is used in a variant which is preserving invariants over the refinement [27] [3]. Every method call of the `step` method in the implementation corresponds to exactly one step of the abstract specification. Our refinement approach consists of the following steps (described in more detail in [12]):

1. **Specify the Implementation Level (Level 4, Fig. 1):** First specify the implementation level as a copy of the abstract PROSECCO level. Then replace the part of the abstract specification dealing with the Mondex purse steps with a call of the Java `Purse.step()` method. Further replace the abstract initialization with a constructor call for `Purse`. This is possible within KIV, since both ASM Verification and Java Verification are based on the same logical background framework, Dynamic Logic (DL) [16] and algebraic specifications. ASMs are modeled using the programs of DL , Java Verification is done by extending the program operators of DL by introducing an explicit memory model for the heap, as described later. So we can add

---

[3] In [12], standard Data Refinement theory is used. ASM Refinement is used in all the other levels of our Mondex refinements, and ASM Refinement was shown to be a generalization of Data Refinement [28]. So, technically this does not make any difference, because all our proof obligations are standard 1:1 refinement properties.

the heaps of the Java purses as an additional state function to the ASM. Then we execute the Java implementation using those heaps to define the concrete agents' behaviour.
2. **Data Transformation for Inputs:** Insert a data transformation function from abstract input Documents to Java objects before the actual call of the Java implementation Purse.step().
3. **Data Transformation for Outputs:** Insert a data transformation function from Java objects to abstract output Documents after the actual call of the Java implementation Purse.step().
4. **Simulation Relation:** Find a simulation relation R, that maps the abstract PROSECCO state to the concrete Java state using data transformation functions that are similar to input/output transformation. Additionally, find suitable invariants for the abstract and concrete levels.
5. **Prove Initialization:** Prove that the Java constructor call of Purse leads to a Java state, where a corresponding initial abstract state can be found in which the simulation relation holds.
6. **Prove Correctness:** Prove that if the simulation relation holds and if we execute a sequence of data input transformation to Java, call of Purse.step() and data output transformation back to Documents, we then find a step of the abstract ASM purse specification which results in a state where the simulation relation holds again.

We will describe these steps in more detail now. The state of the PROSECCO ASM is given by different state functions, which map an agent to some data, where agent is a free data type specifying the protocol participants:
Agent = purse(int : name) | terminal | user(int : name) | attacker
For the Mondex purses, the level 3 ASM specification uses the state functions:

inputs : agent $\to$ documentlist	input messages of each agent
seqNo : agent $\to$ int	current sequence numbers
balance : agent $\to$ int	current balances
payDetails : agent $\to$ Document	current transaction details
exLog : agent $\to$ Documentlist	current exception logs

To define the ASM rules for the agents on level 3, we use macro definitions MACRO#(input; output) with input parameters input and input/output parameters output. For an agent representing a purse, the rule is:

```
1    PURSE#(agent, ... ;inputs, exLog, balance, ...)
2      if inputs(agent)  ≠  []  ∧  # exLog(agent) < MAXLENGTH
3      then let indoc = inputs(agent).first in
4        inputs(agent) := rest(inputs(agent));
5          //check the input and decrypt
6          ...
7          if is_startfrom(indoc) then STARTFROM#(...)
8          else if ... then ...
9          if is_ack(indoc) then ACK#(...)
10         else if insbyte = 0 then ABORT#(...);
11     SEND#(outdoc, ...; inputs)
```

The abstract specification first selects the next available input from the inputs state function (if one is available and the log is not yet full, line 2 and 3). Then the inputs state function is updated accordingly (line 4), and the received Document is cut off (rest(...)). After checking the input message, a case distinction over the type of the message is performed, and the matching ASM Macro for that protocol step is executed (just as in the implementation).

Now we have to define the concrete specification layer for the refinement. The purse ASM rule is now substituted with a Java implementation. Since no other agent protocol definitions are modified, and since those other definitions still use the Documents to communicate, we keep the inputs state function on the concrete level. We introduce data transformation functions from and to the Java world before and after our protocol step. This will be done by Macros TOSTORE and FROMSTORE. TOSTORE takes an input document from inputs and transforms it into the Java world, FROMSTORE does the inverse. For this, we have to take a look at how the state of Java programs is modeled in KIV [32] [33]. Since KIV is a very elaborated system for the verification using Dynamic Logic and algebraic specifications, we have a huge library of algebraically specified data types. The state of Java programs is modeled explicitly using an algebraic data type in KIV, too. This is the store data type. A store defines a mapping from a tuple of a reference (a pointer to an object or array) and a field (a field of a class or an array index) to a Java value. A Java value can be a primitive value like an int or short, or a reference representing a pointer to another object. This allows representation of arbitrary pointer structures. We write st[r.f] for the access to field f of reference r in store st.

Now back to refinement, we store the states of the Java purses using another state function cstore : agent $\rightarrow$ store. The functions seqNo, balance, ... of the abstract level are not present on the refined level, since their values are contained in the corresponding fields of the Purse inside the store. Formally, we have the state functions:

inputs : agent $\rightarrow$ documentlist   current input messages of each agent
cstore : agent $\rightarrow$ store   current Java heaps

Java programs are now integrated into the logic by extending the Box and Diamond operators of Dynamic Logic (shown here only for Diamond):

$\langle st; \alpha \rangle\ \phi$ states that Java program α terminates if executed in the context of store st and afterwards formula ϕ holds

With those operators, KIV provides a sequent calculus for the complete sequential part of Java [10]. We do not perform any transformation on the Java code we verify, the running original source code is verified. With those modified DL operators, the concrete purse step is defined as:

```
1   JAVAPURSE(agent, ... ;inputs, cstore, ...)
2       TOSTORE( agent , inputs ; cstore );
3       st₀ := cstore ( agent );
4       choose st with ⟨st₀; Purse.instance.step();⟩ (st₀ = st) in
5           cstore ( agent ) := st ;
6           FROMSTORE( agent , st ; outdoc );
7           SEND( outdoc , ... ; inputs )
```

The current Purse object is stored in a static field Purse.instance which is set by the constructor as a Singleton. First the input from inputs(agent) is transformed into cstore using TOSTORE (line 2), then step() is called (line 4) on a Purse object in the context of the heap of that agent (which is st_0 = cstore(agent), line 3). As described later, step() then calls SimpleComm.receive() to get the input and calls SimpleComm.send() to produce some output, which we transform afterwards from the store into variable outdoc using FROMSTORE (line 6). Finally, the SEND macro is used (as on the abstract level) to update the inputs function for the receiver of the document (line 7).

The next step is to define, how concrete Java states and abstract ASM states relate to each other. This is done in the simulation relation R. It defines that the Java state is the same as the corresponding abstract state. For example, for the exception log in the JavaCard program, this means that the array of exception log entries exLog from index 0 to index exLogCounter is (transformed to the abstract world) equal to the abstract exLog state function. For Document classes, a generic transformation function java2doc : reference $\times$ store $\rightarrow$ Document is defined for this purpose. It takes a store and a reference pointing to some Document Java object and constructs the corresponding abstract Document. Using a simple recursion, this is lifted to lists of references java2doc : referencelist $\times$ store $\rightarrow$ Documentlist. Additionally, we use a function getarray : reference$\times$ startindex$\times$ length$\times$ store $\rightarrow$ referencelist to extract the references contained in an array in the store. Using such functions, the property for the exception log is:

exLogCorrect(cstore, exLog) $\leftrightarrow$ ($\forall$ agent. is_purse(agent) $\rightarrow$
    java2doc(getarray(cstore(agent)[Purse.instance.exLog], 0,
                      cstore(agent)[Purse.instance.exLogCounter], cstore(agent)),
        cstore(agent)) = exLog(agent))

Similar definitions are needed for all the different state functions. Besides such value definitions, a lot of invariants, both for the concrete and the abstract level are needed: a good example for the abstract level is the property that the exLog is always shorter or equally long as the MAXLENGTH. Additionally, all exception log entries have the correct format of PayDetails. Another example is that all purses always share the same secret key, and that the attacker never knows it.

On the concrete level, one needs the property that the exLogCounter is always smaller than the exLog.length. Here again all exception log entries have to be well-formed. This is a lot harder to formulate than on the abstract level since we are now talking about pointer structures. For example, one has to deal with properties like sharing among the pointers or cyclic structures. Those structures must be ruled out.

The whole invariant for the concrete level is way too long to be presented here. It can be viewed on the web [19]. It consists of 87 properties, all of them again divided into lots of different formulas. For example, the pure value mapping between abstract and concrete world requires 8 properties, the invariant on the abstract level 21 and the invariant on the Java level requires 58 different properties.

Using such a simulation relation now directly translates the security properties of the abstract world to the implementation. It follows directly from refinement theory that for the concrete balances and for the concrete exception log entries the same properties hold as on the abstract level. This is because the simulation relation simply states that their values are equal (modulo transformation from Java pointer structures to abstract data types). Thereby, all security properties (which are all invariants on the state) of the abstract world hold for the implementation as well.

5 Proof Strategy and Experiences

The proof strategy for the case study is symbolic execution of the Java program, extended by the use of lemmata for every method that is called on the way. The main proof obligation for correct refinement of the Purse step is (abbreviating the abstract state to astate and the concrete state to cstate): In every abstract state astate, in which the simulation relation R holds with some concrete state cstate, we have to show that if we do a step of the concrete JAVAPURSE , then a step of abstract PURSE exists, after which the simulation relation holds again with the new abstract and concrete states. In Dynamic Logic, this is:

$\quad$ R(astate, cstate)
$\to \langle\!|$JAVAPURSE(cstate)$|\rangle$ $\langle$PURSE(astate)$\rangle$ R(astate, cstate)

We now can use symbolic execution for JAVAPURSE, leading to a formula that contains a sequence of TOSTORE, `Purse.step` and FROMSTORE. Using further symbolic execution on the `step` method at some point will lead to the switch case distinction of the implementation deciding which protocol method to call. Each protocol step is now treated by formulating a lemma, which discards the Java method call for the protocol functionality and the corresponding abstract specification ASM rule. Those lemmata have to state that the Java method, when given the same input, behaves the same as the corresponding abstract ASM macro. E.g. for STARTFROM we have schematically:

$\quad$ R(astate, cstate)
$\quad \wedge\ ...$ // some more preconditions about structure of inputs and state
$\quad \wedge\ $st $=$ cstore(agent) $\wedge$ java2doc(in, st) $=$ indoc
$\to\ \langle$st/Document out $=$ `Purse.instance.startfrom(in);`$\rangle$
$\quad\quad\quad \langle$STARTFROM#(agent, indoc; outdoc, astate)$\rangle$
$\quad\quad\quad\quad\quad$ (java2doc(out, st) $=$ outdoc $\wedge$ R(astate, setStore(agent, cstate, st))

where setStore(agent, cstate, st) updates cstate by setting the new Java store st for the given agent.

Using such lemmata the method calls in the Java program are discarded one after another together with the corresponding abstract specification. Finally the simulation relation holds on the resulting states. The same strategy is then applied to prove those lemmata themselves, meaning that for STARTFROM more lemmata about `checkName` or `setPaydetails` are formulated and proven the same way until we reach methods not containing other method calls. This is quite similar to the approach used in Design by Contract [23], but making it more specific by linking Java methods to abstract ASM program definitions as shown above.

The verification described was done using the KIV system for the protocol steps STARTFROM and ACK. Although these are only 2 of 6 different protocol steps, the verification nevertheless covered almost 85% of the total lines of code of the Purse class. This is because the other protocol steps are nearly symmetric to those two (STARTTO is nearly the same as STARTFROM, REQ and VAL are equal to ACK). So, we can state that the verification done gives a representative insight on the case study. One of the hardest parts was getting the invariant right. This is not really a matter of difficulty, more a matter of complexity, because the state of the Java program and of the abstract specification is not trivial. The most important part of the proofs was the formulation of suitable lemmata, which can divide the complexity of the overall case study into smaller parts. Especially sometimes a method called early in the program ensured properties needed late in the program, but this was not predictable in the first iteration of the proofs. All together, the Java KIV project for Mondex, consisting of the abstract specification, its invariants, the concrete specification and finally the refinement proof, took around 4200 lines of specification and 600 lines of Java code for Purse, around 1800 in total. Over 1700 theorems where formulated, which took 85000 proof steps (with an automation degree of around 70%). This is not counting any libraries, like the transformation functions for abstract Documents to Java and vice versa and basic libraries for PROSECCO, refinement theory or simple data types. Nevertheless, the Mondex case study heavily accounted to the growth of those libraries too. The time needed for verifying the case study is hard to measure, but it certainly was more than half a year of verification for one person. Most of the pure verification work was done in a master's thesis.

6 Related Work

A lot of work has already been done for Mondex on more abstract specification levels as mentioned in the introduction. Since all of them are not focusing on source code verification we omit a detailed explanation of those approaches in this paper.

The most important work that is closely related to what we are presenting in this paper is the verification by Tonin and Schmitt presented in [31] and in more detail in a technical report [36]. They also claim to verify an implementation of the Mondex case study for smart cards in JavaCard. Furthermore, they state to have verified the security properties of the original Mondex case study on the code level. Their approach uses JML[7] annotations for every method and class and generates proof obligations from those annotations to be discarded using the KeY Verification System [3]. There is no abstract specification and no refinement theory. However, their implementation does not really implement the case study in the sense that one could use the code on a real smart card and it would be secure. That is because they do not use cryptography in their implementation and therefore have very strong assumptions about the environment the cards are used in. Without using cryptography, a malicious attacker can easily generate a faked smart card and use it for payment, thereby generating money. They also assume that a terminal exists which generates all the messages for the protocol instead of generating the messages by the cards themselves. But the latter, combined with the need for cryptography in a *real* implementation, is postulated in the original case study. The corresponding original technical monograph [34] clearly states on p. 1 that "All security measures have to be implemented on the card" and "Once released into the field, each purse is on its own: it has to ensure the security of all its transactions without recourse to a central controller.". In the work of Schmitt and Tonin, every card only answers "OK" or "Error" to every input. Such a smart card can easily be faked. Also their formalization of the security properties of Mondex does not capture the original work in all their aspects. The property "All value accounted" (which states that no money is really lost but correctly logged in the exception logs on the cards) is formulated without using the exception logs in the formalization. They argue that this is because JML lacks the abilily to formulate causality between different operations, and argue that their formalization still captures the essence of the security property. But actually, their implementation contains a bug in the handling of the exception logs. All previous exception log entries are changed by side effect when adding a new exception log entry because there is a problem with pointer sharing. So the security property "All value accounted", which states that the exception logs really captures exactly the lost money due to failed transactions *cannot* hold in their implementation. They did not find that bug, because their proof obligations do not state anything about the contents of the log entries. Summarizing, in our opinion their work can be viewed as an additional specification of the Mondex case study using the Java programming language as a kind of specification language, rather than an actual implementation of it, which is usable and secure in the real world. Our aim in this work, however, was to achieve the latter.

7 Conclusion

We presented a verification of the Mondex case study starting at abstract specifications and ending at the proof of correctness and security of an implementation in Java. The result is based on several techniques ranging from refinement theories, implementation techniques, encoding and decoding of messages in the implementation, modelling and specification of security protocols on an abstract level. It is, to our best knowledge, the largest and most comprehensive approach to the Mondex case study. We succeded showing that current elaborated verification tools like KIV can cope with the challenge of verifying such applications.

References

1. Balser, M., Reif, W., Schellhorn, G., Stenzel, K.: KIV 3.0 for Provably Correct Systems. In: Hutter, D., Traverso, P. (eds.) FM-Trends 1998. LNCS, vol. 1641, Springer, Heidelberg (1999)
2. Banach, R., Jeske, C., Poppleton, M., Stepney, S.: Retrenching the purse: The balance enquiry quandary, and generalised and (1,1) forward refinements. Fundamenta Informaticae 77 (2006)

3. Beckert, B., Hähnle, R., Schmitt, P.H. (eds.): Verification of Object-Oriented Software. LNCS (LNAI), vol. 4334. Springer, Heidelberg (2007)
4. Bicarregui, J., Hoare, C.A.R., Woodcock, J.C.P.: The verified software repository: a step towards the verifying compiler. Formal Aspects Computing 18(2), 143–151 (2006)
5. Börger, E.: The ASM Refinement Method. Formal Aspects of Computing 15(1–2), 237–257 (2003)
6. Börger, E., Stärk, R.F.: Abstract State Machines—A Method for High-Level System Design and Analysis. Springer, Heidelberg (2003)
7. Burdy, L., Cheon, Y., Cok, D., Ernst, M., Kiniry, J., Leavens, G.T., Rustan, K., Leino, M., Poll, E.: An overview of JML tools and applications. International Journal on Software Tools for Technology Transfer 7(3) (2005)
8. UK ITSEC Certification Body. UK ITSEC SCHEME CERTIFICATION REPORT No. P129 MONDEX Purse. Technical report, UK IT Security Evaluation and Certification Scheme (1999)
9. Dolev, D., Yao, A.C.: On the security of public key protocols. In: Proc. 22th IEEE Symposium on Foundations of Computer Science, pp. 350–357. IEEE, Los Alamitos (1981)
10. Gosling, J., Joy, B., Steele, G.: The Java Language Specification. Addison-Wesley, Reading (1996)
11. Grandy, H., Bertossi, R., Stenzel, K., Reif, W.: ASN1-light: A Verified Message Encoding for Security Protocols. In: Software Engineering and Formal Methods, SEFM, IEEE Press, Los Alamitos (2007)
12. Grandy, H., Stenzel, K., Reif, W.: A Refinement Method for Java Programs. In: Bonsangue, M.M., Johnsen, E.B. (eds.) FMOODS 2007. LNCS, vol. 4468, pp. 221–235. Springer, Heidelberg (2007)
13. Haneberg, D.: Sicherheit von Smart Card – Anwendungen. PhD thesis, University of Augsburg, Augsburg, Germany (in German) (2006)
14. Haneberg, D., Grandy, H., Reif, W., Schellhorn, G.: Verifying Smart Card Applications: An ASM Approach. In: Davies, J., Gibbons, J. (eds.) IFM 2007. LNCS, vol. 4591, pp. 313–332. Springer, Heidelberg (2007)
15. Haneberg, D., Schellhorn, G., Grandy, H., Reif, W.: Verification of Mondex Electronic Purses with KIV: From Transactions to a Security Protocol. Formal Aspects of Computing 20(1) (January 2008)
16. Harel, D., Kozen, D., Tiuryn, J.: Dynamic Logic. MIT Press, Cambridge (2000)
17. Haxthausen, A.E., George, C., Schütz, M.: Specification and Proof of the Mondex Electronic Purse. In: 1st Asian Working Conference on Verified Software, AWCVS 2006, UNU-IIST Reports 348, Macau (2006)
18. Hoare, S.T.: The Ideal of Verified Software. In: Ball, T., Jones, R.B. (eds.) CAV 2006. LNCS, vol. 4144, pp. 5–16. Springer, Heidelberg (2006)
19. Web presentation of the Mondex case study in KIV. URL, http://www.informatik.uni-augsburg.de/swt/projects/mondex.html
20. Kong, W., Ogata, K., Futatsugi, K.: Algebraic Approaches to Formal Analysis of the Mondex Electronic Purse System. In: Davies, J., Gibbons, J. (eds.) IFM 2007. LNCS, vol. 4591, pp. 393–412. Springer, Heidelberg (2007)
21. Leavens, G.T., Leino, K.R.M., Müller, P.: Specification and verification challenges for sequential object-oriented programs. Formal Aspects of Computing 19(2) (June 2007)
22. MasterCard International Inc., http://www.mondex.com
23. Meyer, B.: Applying "design by contract". IEEE Computer 25(10), 40–51 (1992)

24. Moebius, N., Haneberg, D., Schellhorn, G., Reif, W.: A Modeling Framework for the Development of Provably Secure E-Commerce Applications. In: International Conference on Software Engineering Advances 2007, IEEE Press, Los Alamitos (2007)
25. Ramananadro, T., Jackson, D.: Mondex, an electronic purse: specification and refinement checks with the alloy model-finding method (2006), http://www.eleves.ens.fr/home/ramanana/work/mondex/
26. Schellhorn, G.: Verification of ASM Refinements Using Generalized Forward Simulation. Journal of Universal Computer Science (J.UCS) 7(11) (2001)
27. Schellhorn, G.: ASM Refinement Preserving Invariants. In: Proceedings of the 14th International ASM Workshop, ASM 2007, Grimstad, Norway (2007)
28. Schellhorn, G.: ASM Refinement and Generalizations of Forward Simulation in Data Refinement: A Comparison. Journal of Theoretical Computer Science 336(2-3), 403–435 (2005)
29. Schellhorn, G., Grandy, H., Haneberg, D., Moebius, N., Reif, W.: A Systematic Verification Approach for Mondex Electronic Purses using ASMs. In: Dagstuhl seminar on Rigorous Methods for Software Construction and Analysis, LNCS. Springer, to appear (older version available as Techn. Report 2006-27 at [19] (2008)
30. Schellhorn, G., Grandy, H., Haneberg, D., Reif, W.: The Mondex Challenge: Machine Checked Proofs for an Electronic Purse. In: Misra, J., Nipkow, T., Sekerinski, E. (eds.) FM 2006. LNCS, vol. 4085, pp. 16–31. Springer, Heidelberg (2006)
31. Schmitt, P.H., Tonin, I.: Verifying the Mondex case study. In: Software Engineering and Formal Methods, SEFM, IEEE Press, Los Alamitos (2007)
32. Stenzel, K.: A Formally Verified Calculus for Full Java Card. In: Rattray, C., Maharaj, S., Shankland, C. (eds.) AMAST 2004. LNCS, vol. 3116, pp. 491–505. Springer, Heidelberg (2004)
33. Stenzel, K.: Verification of Java Card Programs. PhD thesis, Universität Augsburg, Fakultät für Angewandte Informatik (2005)
34. Stepney, S., Cooper, D., Woodcock, J.: AN ELECTRONIC PURSE Specification, Refinement, and Proof. Technical monograph PRG-126, Oxford University Computing Laboratory (July 2000)
35. Sun Microsystems Inc. Java Card 2.2 Specification (2002), http://java.sun.com/products/javacard/
36. Tonin, I.: Verifying the mondex case study. The KeY approach. Techischer Bericht 2007-4, Fakultät für Informatik, Universität Karlsruhe (2007)
37. Woodcock, J.: First steps in the verified software grand challenge. IEEE Computer 39(10), 57–64 (2006)
38. Woodcock, J., Freitas, L.: Z/Eves and the Mondex Electronic Purse. In: Barkaoui, K., Cavalcanti, A., Cerone, A. (eds.) ICTAC 2006. LNCS, vol. 4281, pp. 15–34. Springer, Heidelberg (2006)

Incremental Development of a Distributed Real-Time Model of a Cardiac Pacing System Using VDM

Hugo Daniel Macedo[1], Peter Gorm Larsen[2], and John Fitzgerald[3]

[1] Minho University, Portugal
[2] Engineering College of Aarhus, Denmark
[3] School of Computing Science, Newcastle University, UK
hmacedo@di.uminho.pt, pgl@iha.dk, John.Fitzgerald@ncl.ac.uk

Abstract. The construction of formal models of real-time distributed systems is a considerable practical challenge. We propose and illustrate a pragmatic incremental approach in which detail is progressively added to abstract system-level specifications of functional and timing properties via intermediate models that express system architecture, concurrency and timing behaviour. The approach is illustrated by developing a new formal model of the cardiac pacemaker system proposed as a "grand challenge" problem in 2007. The models are expressed using the Vienna Development Method (VDM) and are validated primarily by scenario-based tests, including the analysis of timed traces. We argue that the insight gained using this staged modelling approach will be valuable in the subsequent development of implementations, and in detecting potential bottlenecks within suggested implementation architectures.

1 Introduction

Formal models have a valuable role to play in validating requirements and designs for real-time distributed systems in early development stages. Rapid feedback from the analysis of such models has the potential to reduce the risk of expensive re-working as a consequence of the late-stage detection of defects. However, models that incorporate the description of functionality alongside timing behaviour and distribution across shared computing resources are themselves potentially complex. Moving too rapidly to such a complex model can increase modelling and design costs in the long run. In order to gain full value from formal modelling and analysis, a systematic approach to constructing and validating models is required.

Our current work is focussed on the development and industrial application of formal modelling techniques that satisfy the requirements discussed above. We have developed and applied technology based on the Vienna Development Method (VDM) [1,2,3] and its tool support (VDMTools [4]). Recent work has developed modelling abstractions and test-based analysis tools that support the object-oriented description of distributed real-time systems [5,6]. Our experience applying formal modelling techniques in a variety of industry sectors suggests that an approach to modelling such distributed real-time systems should permit the staged and controlled construction of a formal model, with opportunities for validation at each stage. We have proposed such a staged approach as part of the methodological guidelines accompanying the VDMTools [7].

This paper reports a study in which we have assessed the feasibility of applying an incremental approach to model construction by developing a model for an artificial cardiac pacemaker [8]. The pacemaker specification is that it includes system-level requirements affecting hardware as well as software. We demonstrate how such cross-disciplinary requirements can be introduced gradually into a model in a phased fashion, along with validation of functional and timing requirements.

The Pacemaker specification has been offered by the Software Quality Research Laboratory at McMaster University as a pilot problem in the Grand Challenge in Verified Software [9] and this paper is believed to represent the first attempt at its treatment. However, the present study does not aim to provide comprehensive coverage of the Pacemaker challenge. The intention is to use the problem to pilot the incremental method in an industrially relevant context, using the available tools, as a precursor to tackling more substantial challenges, including the full Pacemaker and other real-time systems.

We introduce the Pacemaker system in Section 2. Section 3 briefly introduces the VDM technology used, our phased approach to model construction and the tool support. The progressive development of the Pacemaker model is described, illustrated by extracts from the series of VDM models developed (Section 4). The test-based approach to validation is discussed in Section 5, including how timing conditions can be checked using this technology. Finally Sections 6 and 7 discuss related work and draw conclusions from the study.

2 The Pacemaker System and Environment

In this study, the pacemaker is treated as an embedded system operating in an environment containing the heart. We first review the elements of the environment that interact with the pacemaker (Section 2.1) and then consider the elements of the pacemaker system itself (Section 2.2).

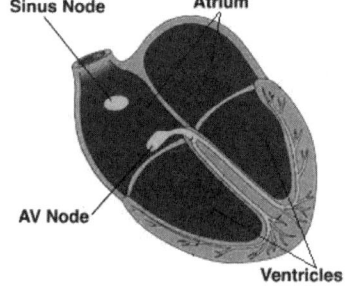

Fig. 1. The natural pacemaker

2.1 Environment: The Heart

The human heart serves as a pump for the circulatory system. It is a muscular shell around four chambers (called atria and ventricles) which contract and relax periodically under the control of natural electrical stimuli. A natural pacemaker orchestrates the functioning of the pump, discharging electrical pulses at specific points (see Fig. 1). In normal functioning, a discharge made at the sinus node subsequently reaches the atrioventricular (AV) node which amplifies it, stimulating the ventricles. If the natural pacemaker is malfunctioning, a physical condition termed Bradycardia may arise in which the heart rate falls below the level expected for the patient. To normalise the heart rate, an artificial pacemaker may be implanted to aid or replace the natural pacemaker. Physicians measure the heart's performance using, among other parameters, the bpm (beats per minute) rate of the heart. We use the term *pulse* and *pulses per minute* in reference to pacemaker activity, whereas *beat* and *beats per minute* refer to heart activity.

2.2 System: Artificial Pacemaker

An artificial pacemaker (referred to subsequently as a *pacemaker* [10]) is a system composed of:

Leads: One or more wires, normally two, that both sense and discharge electric pulses.
Device: The implanted batteries and controller.
Device Controller-Monitor (DCM): An external unit that interacts with the device using a wireless connection (not modelled in this paper.)
Accelerometer: A unit inside the device measuring body motion in order to allow modulated pacing.

A typical configuration consists of one lead attached to the right atrium and another to the right ventricle. The pacemaker has several operating modes that address different malfunctions of the natural pacemaker. The specification document [8] identifies 18 operating modes controlling 26 variables and each of the variables can be configured within a value range. Most of the variables are time-related parameters, defining such properties as the interval between a pace in the atrium and the ventricle or the number of pulses per minute the device should deliver to a given chamber.

The operating modes of the device are classified using a code consisting of three or four characters. For the examples in this paper, the code elements are: chamber(s) paced ("O" for none, "A" for atrium, "V" for ventricle, "D" for both), chamber(s) sensed (same codes), response to sensing ("O" for none in this paper) and a final optional "R" to indicate the presence of rate modulation in response to the physical activity of the patient as measured by the accelerometer. "X" is a wildcard used to denote any letter (i.e. "O", "A", "V" or "D"). Thus "DOO" is an operating mode in which both chambers are paced but no chambers are sensed, and "XXXR" denotes all modes with rate modulation.

3 VDM Modelling Technology for Distributed Real-Time Systems

In our modelling work, we have used VDM [1]. Three dialects of the VDM modelling language are in use, each supporting different forms of system specification.

VDM-SL [2] provides facilities for the functional specification of sequential systems with basic support for modular structuring. VDM++ [3] extends VDM-SL with features for object-oriented modelling and concurrency. VICE (VDM++ In Constrained Environments) further extends VDM++ with features for describing real-time computations [11] and distributed systems [5]. Each dialect has formally defined syntax, static and dynamic semantics which extend those of the ISO Standard VDM-SL language [12]. For a detailed introduction to VDM++, the reader is referred to the texts and the VDM Portal [13]. In the remainder of this section, we focus on the features of VDM++ and VICE that have a major role in the modelling of distributed real-time systems.

3.1 Basic VDM Notations

A model in VDM-SL, is composed of type definitions built from simple abstract types such as *bool* or *nat*, and type constructors such as sequences and records. Types may be restricted by predicate invariants. Persistent state variables may be defined. Operations that may modify the state can be defined implicitly, using pre- and postcondition expressions, or explicitly, using imperative statements. Functions are similar to operations except they may not refer to state variables, and are side-effect free.

An object-oriented model in VDM++ is composed of class specifications which may use single or multiple inheritance. The internals of each class definition are similar to those of a regular VDM-SL model. each object's persistent state consists of typed *instance variables*. Operations in VDM++ are re-entrant and their invocation is defined with synchronous (rendezvous) semantics. Operation execution may be constrained by specifying a permission predicate [14], a Boolean expression over *history counters* that acts as a guard for the operation, for example to express mutual exclusion. History counters are maintained per object to count the number of requests (#req), activations (#act) and completions (#fin) per operation.

VDM++ classes may be active or passive. Active classes represent entities that have their own thread of control; passive classes are always manipulated from the thread of control of another active class. A thread is a sequence of statements that is executed to completion, at which point the thread dies. The thread is created whenever the object is created but the thread needs to be started explicitly using a *start* operator. For reactive systems it is possible to specify threads that do not terminate.

Extensions to VDM++ (VICE) support the description and analysis of real-time embedded and distributed systems [5,15]. These include primitives for modelling deployment to a distributed hardware architecture and support for asynchronous communication. Two predefined classes, *BUS* and *CPU*, are available to the specifier to construct the distributed architecture in the model. User-defined classes can be instantiated and deployed on specific *CPU*s. The communication topology between the computation resources in the model can be described using the *BUS* class.

The semantics of VDM++ is extended with a notion of time such that any thread that is running on a computation resource or any message that is in transit on a communication resource can cause time to elapse. Models that contain only one computation resource are compatible to models in plain VDM++.

Operations may be specified as asynchronous in VICE, allowing the caller to resume its own thread of control after the call is initiated. A new thread is created, scheduled and started to execute the body of the asynchronous operation. Statements (*duration* and *cycles*) may be used in operation bodies to specify time delays that are, respectively independent of or dependent upon processor capacity. The time delay incurred by the message transfer over the *BUS* can be made dependent on the size of the message being transferred.

3.2 An Incremental Approach to Model Construction

Faced with the challenge of developing VDM++ models of distributed real-time systems, we have proposed a staged approach [7] which reflects the capabilities of each of the VDM modelling languages.

The analysis of informally expressed requirements leads to a first abstract model giving system-level specification of behaviour. The basic VDM-SL language is well suited to this level of description. Based on the abstract model, we introduce a static architecture, creating a sequential (i.e. non-concurrent) model with structure expressed using the features of VDM++. This model would then be extended to become a concurrent VDM++ design model. The concurrent design model itself is then extended with real-time information using the VICE extensions, and additionally distribution over processors can be described also using the VICE extensions. At this stage it may prove necessary to revisit the concurrent design model, since design decisions made at that stage may prove to be infeasible when real-time information is added to the model (for instance, the model may not be able to meet its deadlines).

The ability to validate the intermediate models developed in this process makes it possible to identify requirements and design defects at an early stage. The initial abstract model need not be directly executable, but subsequent models are likely to be so, making it possible to conduct extensive tests in order to validate design decisions. The VDMTools are intended to provide extensive support for scenario-based testing as a form of validation.

We do not claim that the models introduced at each stage in our approach are formal refinements of their predecessors, although this may sometimes be the case. Our intended output is a comprehensive model of the target system that can serve as a basis for subsequent development, possibly using refinement. We are therefore introducing detail in a staged manner, where the executions at each level might, informally, be seen as providing a finer level of granularity than its predecessor.

3.3 VDM Tool Support

VDM is supported by an industry-strength tool set, VDMTools, owned and developed by CSK Systems [16]. VDM and VDMTools have been used successfully in several large-scale industrial projects, e.g. [17,4]. The tools offer syntax, type and integrity checking capabilities, code generators, a pretty printer and an application programmer interface. The main support for model validation is by

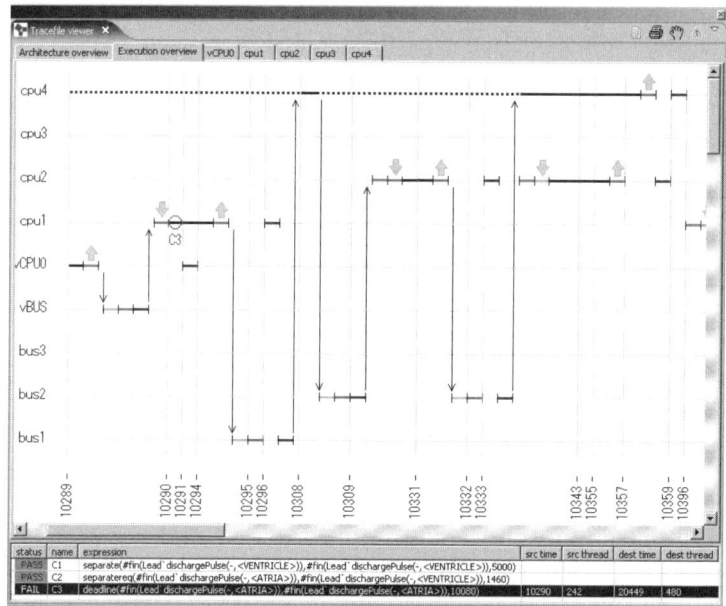

Fig. 2. Showtrace tool demonstrating validation conjecture violation

means of an interpreter allowing the execution of models written in the large executable subset of the language.

Scenarios defined by the user are essentially test cases consisting of scripts invoking the model's functionality. The interpreter executes the script over the model and returns observable results as well as an *execution trace* containing, for each event, a time stamp and an indication of the part of the model in which it appeared. A separate tool (an Eclipse plug-in) called *showtrace* has been developed for reading execution traces, displaying them graphically so that the user can readily inspect behaviour after the execution of a scenario, and thereby gain insight into the ordering and timing of exchange of messages, activation of threads and invocation of operations.

The existing tools have been further extended to allow explicit logical statements of expected system-level timing properties (termed *timing conjectures*) which can be checked against execution traces [6]. Fig. 2 shows the *showtrace* output resulting from the analysis of three validation conjectures (C1-C3) from the pacemaker study (see Section 5). The main window shows a fragment of the execution trace, with time on the horizontal axis. Processing on each architectural unit is shown by horizontal lines (colours are used to denote thread start-up, kill and scheduling). Thin arrows indicate message passing and fat arrows indicate thread swapping. The conjectures are shown at the bottom of the window. Circular marks on the traces show conjecture violations, e.g. the circle showing a counterexample to the timing conjecture C3, where an event occurrence breaches an expected temporal separation.

4 The Pacemaker Models

We describe the incremental development of a model of the Pacemaker challenge problem conducted in order to evaluate the incremental development approach outlined above using an industrially relevant application. At this stage, we have not attempted a comprehensive attack on the Pacemaker problem. In this context, the overall purpose of the modelling work on the Pacemaker has been to clarify and validate the system's informally stated requirements as defined at [8], from where additional tutorial material on cardiac timing cycles and pacing modes is also available. A full-scale attempt on the pacemaker challenge would also rely on extensive domain background from texts [10] and domain experts.

Following our staged approach, in order to manage the complexity of the model itself, the construction was done in four steps, each involving the construction of a new model at a lower level of abstraction from its predecessor. We will term them *Abstract, Sequential, Concurrent* and *Distributed Real-Time* (DR-T) respectively.

Of the 19 modes of the pacemaker, eight have been modelled so far, covering 18 of the 26 controlling variables. The initial *Abstract* model consists of several modules totalling 652 lines of VDM-SL. The three subsequent object-oriented models are larger but of almost equal size: the *Sequential* model is 872 lines of VDM++ and the *Concurrent* model is 879 lines whereas the *DR-T* model is 811 lines of VDM++. So the *Abstract* model is a bit smaller and simpler than the *Sequential* model. Although the sizes of the sequential, concurrent and DR-T models are similar, they get progressively more complex as they include concurrency and the distribution.

Note that we do not claim that this is a *formal* refinement process. The initial *Abstract* model is informally refined by a *Sequential* model by adding structuring information. Neither of these models the concurrency of the environment and the system; instead they simulate fixed time steps controlled from the environment. In the *Concurrent* model both the environment and the relevant parts of the system are organised with concurrent threads that are synchronized by permission predicates. In each of these three models, time is present explicitly as an abstraction whereas in the final *Distributed Real-Time* model time is implicit, allowing us to express more realistic timing behaviour while validating this model.

4.1 Abstract Model

The first model is expressed in VDM-SL, the simplest of the VDM modelling languages, lacking the object-orientation and concurrency features of VDM++. It is organised in modules, each of which corresponds to an operating mode of the pacemaker and defines a single function PacemakerM (where M is the mode), derived from the requirements. The key type and function definitions have the following form:

```
SenseTimeline = set of (Sense * Time);
ReactionTimeline = set of (Reaction * Time);
functions
PacemakerM (inp : SenseTimeline) r : ReactionTimeline
post ...
```

where `Sense` and `Reaction` are enumerated types representing the presence or absence of a pulse. Each `PacemakerM` function is expressed in VDM-SL in an implicit style by means of a postcondition characterising the events trace that should result from correct functioning of the pacemaker over an input sense trace. The implicit style is used because it is not intended that the function should be directly executed; it serves primarily as a means of clarifying requirements.

The abstract models support the formalisation of our understanding of the system requirements. For example, during construction of the abstract models it became apparent that the requirements in [8] for some modes place constraints on ventricular pace events even when the ventricle is not being paced. Domain experts later reported this is an error in the natural language specification. We also identified areas of incompleteness, for example the requirements as modelled in `PacemakerDOO` [18] do not take account of certain unstated requirements on intervals between atrium pulses.

The post-conditions of the `PacemakerM` functions have the potential to serve as test oracles on the models developed in subsequent phases, provided suitable abstraction functions are implemented. The post-condition formulations were also valuable and we were also able to use them to help design the validation conjectures that were applied to the analysis of the final (distributed real-time) model. For example, the following post-condition from `PacemakerDOO` gives rise to the validation conjecture C2 used on test traces and shown in Section 5.2:

```
forall mk_(<ATRIA>,ta) in set r &
   (exists mk_(<VENTRICLE>,tv) in set r & tv = ta + FixedAV);
```

4.2 Sequential and Concurrent Models

The sequential design model describes both the data that is to be computed, and how it is to be structured into static classes, without commitment to a specific dynamic architecture. The Pacemaker model is structured around a class `Pacemaker` coexisting with an `Environment` class in a given `World`. Figure 3 shows the classes that are common to all the VDM++ models and their associations. The diagram is derived automatically from the VDM++ models using the VDMTools link to IBM Rational Rose. In the generated class diagram, we do not show associations arising from the use of public static methods. However, the public static instance variables in the `Pacemaker` class are shown as directed associations (labelled '+$') sign from `Pacemaker` to the relevant target class.

The main feature of the static architecture is its division into the environment and the pacemaker system. The `Environment` class controls the production of stimuli delivered via `Leads`. The `Pacemaker` class represents the technical system. The `HeartController` class monitors incoming stimuli and generates pulses. The `RateController` class is used for rate adaptation control in "XXXR" operating modes, and will not be further discussed in this paper (for full details see [18,19]) and the `Accelerometer` class is coping with the motion data.

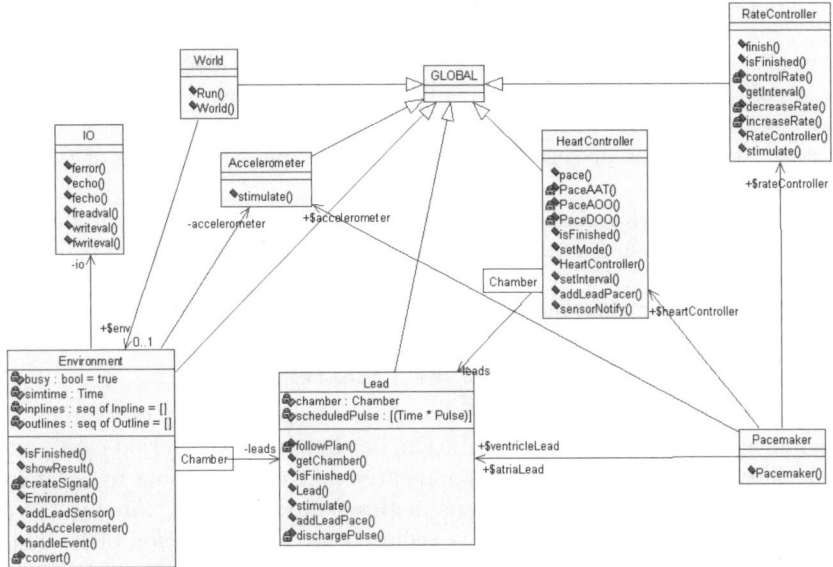

Fig. 3. A UML class diagram describing the common static structure

The initial sequential model is then used to analyse the system behaviour without taking concurrency issues into account. In the sequential step, the environment affects the flow-of-control by passing signals to the pacemaker system. The environment also provides the simulated time increments using an additional Timer class (not shown in Figure 3). This model is executable and so may be validated with respect to informal requirements by running tests through the VDM++ interpreter.

In the sequential model the environment class contains an explicit Run operation which operates a form of command loop, stepping through the input timeline of sensed events, delivering signals to the system (through the operation createSignal). Having created the signals, it calls a Step operation in rateController and later in heartController, the two parts of the system model that will become concurrent in subsequent models. In addition the global time variable is stepped forward.

In the third phase of model development concurrency is introduced. The static structure is maintained with the exception of a more elaborate modelling of time enabling synchronisation of time in concurrent threads [18]. The environment model is freed of the responsibility to control the system model but still controls the time. The concurrent model has the same structure as the sequential one, but the lock-step stepping mechanism is substituted by threading and synchronisation. With the introduction of concurrency the need for synchronisation arises and this is achieved through the use of VDM++ permission predicates. We claim that the main benefit of this model is to study and find possible concurrency issues, for instance, we have found some race conditions caused by errors introduced in our specification that were corrected at this level.

4.3 Distributed Real-Time Model

The final step in model construction is the introduction of distribution over CPUs in a topology determined by the configuration of a bus. Time "annotations" allow time to be built in and managed by the VDM++ interpreter so again the static structure is preserved except that the explicit modelling of time now disappears.

The deadlines and periods in the requirements [8] are stated in milliseconds and in certain cases in fractions of milliseconds. We therefore use 0.1 ms as the unit of time below.

The `Environment` class now only delivers signals to the system as a periodic thread:

```
thread periodic (1000,10,900,0) (createSignal);
```

The operation `createSignal` will be invoked approximately every 1000 time units and a jitter of up to 10 time units can be allowed for the periodic invocation of this thread. The third parameter indicates that there is going to be at least 900 time units between two wake-ups of this periodic thread. Finally, the last parameter indicates that no offset is required for the invocation of it. This is a feature that is most valuable if a number of threads are started at the same time, and there is a desire to carry them out in a special order.

The `createSignal` operation looks at the remaining input events in the input lines (`inplines`) which each have a time associated with them. If this time has been reached for one or more of the events the relevant leads and accelerometer must be notified. It is defined as:

```
createSignal : () ==> ()
createSignal () ==
  (if len inplines > 0
   then (dcl curtime : Time := time,
             done : bool := false;
         while not done do
           let mk_(sensed,chamber,accinfo,stime)= hd inplines
             in if stime <= curtime
                then
                (leads(chamber).stimulate(sensed);
                 accelerometer.stimulate(accinfo);
                 inplines := inplines(2,...,len(inplines));
                 done := len inplines = 0
                )
                else done := true
        );
   if len inplines = 0 then busy := false;
  );
```

Expressing Time Requirements. Time "annotations" are used to record the durations allocated to particular actions. For example, consider the requirement that "The Atrial pulse width must be 0.4 milliseconds." [8], appendix. This is a requirement on the operation that describes the discharge of a pulse. The `duration` statement of VDM++ is used to specify the width (40 in the 0.1 ms units).

```
private async
dischargePulse : Pulse * Chamber ==> ()
dischargePulse (p,c) ==
   if(c = <ATRIUM>)
     duration(40) World'env.handleEvent(p,c,time);
```

Notice also the use of `async` so that the caller of this operation will not block waiting for it to terminate.

Modelling the System Distribution. The system class defines the distribution architecture. Instance variables are defined as follows (all declared public static) to define the physical objects present in the system architecture:

```
atriumLead      : Lead          := new Lead(<ATRIUM>);
ventricleLead   : Lead          := new Lead(<VENTRICLE>);
accelerometer   : Accelerometer := new Accelerometer();
rateController  : RateController := new RateController();
heartController : HeartController := new HeartController();
```

The architectural components in the model are, for the purposes of illustration, four CPUs. Each CPU definition in the model indicates the scheduling policies (Fixed Priority (FP) and First-Come-First-Served (FCFS) respectively) and processor capacity (number of cycles per unit time). For the CPUs that will just run a single thread we used a FCFS scheduling algorithm. For the case of CPU4 that contains both the `rateController` and `heartController` threads we opted for a fixed priority policy, assuming that the stimulation of the patient heart is more important than adjusting the rate of the stimulation.

```
cpu1 : CPU := new CPU(<FCFS>,3E2);
cpu2 : CPU := new CPU(<FCFS>,3E2);
cpu3 : CPU := new CPU(<FCFS>,3E2);
cpu4 : CPU := new CPU(<FP>   ,3E2);
```

In order to define the communication topology, we create three bus objects linking the specified CPUs with a certain bandwidth (1E6) and the chosen network control protocol, in this case FCFS.

```
bus1 : BUS := new BUS(<FCFS>,1E6,{cpu1,cpu4});
bus2 : BUS := new BUS(<FCFS>,1E6,{cpu2,cpu4});
bus3 : BUS := new BUS(<FCFS>,1E6,{cpu3,cpu4});
```

The final element in this system class is the constructor operation that deploys the functionality across the resources. Here the leads are deployed on two processors (representing the physical wires and lead controllers) and the accelerometer is deployed using the same approach. The remaining devices are deployed on `cpu4`:

```
public Pacemaker: () ==> Pacemaker
Pacemaker () ==
  (cpu1.deploy(atriumLead);
   cpu2.deploy(ventricleLead);
   cpu3.deploy(accelerometer);
   cpu4.deploy(rateController);
   cpu4.deploy(heartController);
   cpu4.setPriority(HeartController'pace,3);
   cpu4.setPriority(RateController'adjustRate,1);
  );
```

Implicitly there is always a virtual CPU and BUS where elements run that are not explicitly deployed to a CPU. Also the communication between objects in different CPUs with no explicit bus connecting them will occur using the virtual bus.

Whenever a Lead is stimulated it simply delegates this stimulus on to the statically declared heartController as a notification:

```
public
stimulate : Sense ==> ()
stimulate (s) ==
  Pacemaker'heartController.sensorNotify(s,chamber);
```

When the heartController is notified it adds the new signal that has been sensed to a mapping of sensed entries and that is then taken into account subsequently by a periodic thread determining whether a pace is necessary depending upon the mode of operation of the pacemaker.

```
public
sensorNotify : Sense * Chamber ==> ()
sensorNotify (s,c) ==
  sensed := sensed ++ {c |-> s};
```

5 Validation

5.1 Validation of Abstract, Sequential, Concurrent and DR-T Models

A systematic testing approach [3] was used to validate the models derived during the staged development process. "Validation" in this context refers to the activity of gaining confidence that the formal models developed are consistent with the requirements expressed in the requirements document [8]. A comprehensive model of the full Pacemaker specification would additionally entail domain experts in both the setting of validation conjectures and the detailed review of the model; for the initial study reported here, we had only limited access to domain expertise.

Test scenarios were defined to model interesting situations such as the absence of input pulses. These were run over the several models while collecting the test coverage data for each model. Tests developed for the abstract model can be used, adapted, as regression tests in the later model development phases.

To validate the sequential model we used the re-shaped scenarios, augmenting them with new tests derived from the process of constructing and debugging of the model and its algorithmic subtleties. The validation process involves loading the chamber senses into the Environment which will deliver them at the correct time to the respective lead. During the simulation reactions (pulses delivered by the leads) were collected by the environment and then displayed. All of the test scenarios were reused in the validation of the *Concurrent* model and the *DR-T* model using the same paradigm.

5.2 Timing Conjectures and Their Validation

The capabilities of VDMTools have been extended to support automated checking of timing-related conjectures on traces derived from runs of test scenarios over VDM++ models [6]. A simple language of standard conjecture forms has been defined and the semantics have been embedded directly into the tool set. The result of checking conjectures on a trace is displayed using the trace display format, with conjecture violation points identified as shown in Figure 2. These timing conjectures are not part of the requirements; they are assertions that the developers expect to hold over the traces derived from scenario executions. The timing conjectures analysed so far in this pilot study are naive; a fuller set would be derived from interactions with domain experts in a full-scale modelling and verification study.

The forms of timing conjecture used in the pacemaker study are: *separations*, *required separations* and *deadlines* [6]. Separation conjectures describe a minimum separation between occurrences of specified events, should the events occur. A *Separation* conjecture is a 5-tuple $separate(e_1, c, e_2, d, m)$ where e_1 and e_2 are the names of events, c is a state predicate, d is the minimum acceptable delay between an occurrence of e_1 and the next following occurrence of e_2 provided that c evaluates to true at the occurrence time of e_1. If c evaluates to false when e_1 occurs, the validation conjecture holds independently of the occurrence time of e_2. The Boolean flag m, when set to true, indicates a requirement that the occurrence numbers of e_1 and e_2 should be equal. This allows the designer to record conjectures that describe some coordination between events. The *Required separation* conjecture is similar to the separation conjecture but additionally requires that e_2 does indeed occur. The *Deadline* conjecture places a maximum delay on the occurrence of e_2. Again, the m option may be used to link the occurrence numbers of the events. A validation conjecture $deadline(e_1, c, e_2, d, m)$; if c holds, d is the maximum tolerable delay between e_2 and e_2.

Validation conjectures can be proposed for the test scenarios on the Distributed Real-Time model. For example, a conjecture might be stated that the minimum delay between a ventricular pace event and the next ventricular pace shall be 500 ms. After converting it to the modelled time unit i.e. 0.1 ms, this is expressed as the following conjecture C1:

```
separate(#fin(Lead'dischargePulse(-,<VENTRICLE>), true,
         #fin(Lead'dischargePulse(-,<VENTRICLE>), 5000, false)
```

A requirement that, after an atrial event there must be a ventricular pace after 150 ms (± 4 ms), leads to the following conjecture which includes a requirement that the second event occurs, C2:

```
separatereq(#fin(Lead'dischargePulse(-,<ATRIUM>), true,
            #fin(Lead'dischargePulse(-,<VENTRICLE>), 1460, true)
```

A requirement on the maximum delay between pulses being, say, 100 ±8 ms would be expressed as a deadline conjecture as follows, C3:

```
deadline(#fin(Lead'dischargePulse(-,<ATRIUM>), true,
         #fin(Lead'dischargePulse(-,<ATRIUM>), 1080, false)
```

The three validation conjectures above have been applied to test runs of the validation scenarios. In several cases this identified violations in the model and in this way the model could be improved as such bottlenecks were discovered [20,21].

6 Related Work

Efforts are being made to support the incremental development of formal models, but has not so far been extended to model-oriented specifications of real-time systems with explicit deployment. Work in SCTL/MUST [22] addresses the iterative production of early-stage models of real-time systems. As in our approach, validation by testing is supported and the model production process feeds back into requirements scenarios. The Credo project [23] focuses on modelling and analysis of evolutionary structures for distributed services and also includes formal models similar to those described here but without so far considering deployment issues. Our incremental approach also has similarities with refinement-oriented approaches, such as those in event-based B work [24] but here the focus is more on the formal aspects of the refinement, not explicitly addressing time or deployment.

Related work by Suhaib et al. [25] proposes a methodology derived from that of eXtreme Programming, in which "user stories" are expressed as LTL formulae representing properties which are model-checked. On each iteration, new user stories are addressed. The ordering of properties is significant for the practical tractability of the analysis on each iteration. In the context of research on real-time UML [26], a combination of UML and SDL [27] with a rigorous semantic foundation. However, in this work the ability to carry out the validation is more limited when deployment is considered. Burmester et al. [28] describe support for an iterative development process for real-time system models in extended UML by means of compositional model checking, and Uchitel et al. [29] address the incremental development of message sequence charts, again model-checking the models developed in each iteration.

Regarding our particular pacemaker example, we believe that the McMaster pilot problem example has not previously been attacked. It is always a challenge to be first with a new case study and the work presented here should only be seen as the first step in attacking the pacemaker challenge. From the cardiac pacing domain, the work that comes closest to ours is that of Liu and others addressing safety analysis of a pacemaker product line using state-based modelling [30]. They have a very similar split between the environment and system; the main difference is that they use Rhapsody's executable state models for simulations in contrast to our model-oriented specification supporting deployment. The focus there is on safety analysis while ours is on the incremental development of models.

7 Concluding Remarks and Further Work

Our objective in the work reported here was to assess the feasibility of using an incremental approach in the production of a useful model of an industrially relevant real-time distributed system. The pacemaker case study suggests that such an approach can yield a viable model that can be subjected to validation against system-level properties at an early stage in the development process. The study encourages us to apply the approach to a wider range of examples. The study revealed that the regression test suite built from the validation activities on the intermediate models was valuable in validating the later, more complex models.

It is important to stress that we have not attempted a comprehensive attack on the full Pacemaker specification [8]. Our validation activity in particular, has been preliminary. We would like as a next stage to seek domain expert involvement in the definition of validation conjectures.

The scheduling models in the current VICE formalism limit the range of exploration supported. An important future task is extending this range and increasing the configurability of the model set. In the pacemaker example, we would like to explore a wider range of scheduling assumptions.

Our approach has been pragmatic, driven by the aim of providing a fully formal modelling approach with a low barrier to industrial adoption. As a consequence we have emphasised validation by animation rather than verification by proof. The state of the art in VDM tool support reflects this. Facilities such as the application programmer interfaces and dynamic link libraries in VDMTools allow for co-simulation [31,32] in which models of the environment (e.g. a Matlab model of electrical activity in the heart) can be linked to VDM++ models of discrete event controllers. We plan to do this for the Pacemaker application in order to explore the fault tolerance characteristics of alternative candidate architectures.

Looking forward to proof-based verification, modern implementations of proof support for VDM [33] currently handle a subset of the modelling language but require further work to adapt them to the needs of distributed real-time models in VDM++. Once the tool support is enhanced, enabling analysis of proof obligations for the Pacemaker model, this will be carried out.

We have not yet dealt with the relationship between the incremental addition of detail and formal refinement. In particular, we would like to be able to drive useful proof obligations out of the "refinement" steps. An examination of this issue must address the treatment of atomicity in the abstract and sequential models (for example in handling the maintenance of invariants). To encourage adoption, we feel it is essential that we automate a larger part of the validation process.

Acknowledgments. We are grateful to Brian Larson of Boston Scientific and to anonymous FM'08 referees for comments and suggestions on this paper. José

Nuno Oliveira, Shin Sahara, Marcel Verhoef, Sander Vermolen and Zoe Andrews contributed to the development of the formalism, tool and method extensions. Fitzgerald's work is supported by the EU Framework 7 Deploy project and the UK EPSRC platform project on Trustworthy Ambient Systems.

References

1. Jones, C.B.: Systematic Software Development Using VDM, 2nd edn. Prentice-Hall International, Englewood Cliffs (1990), ISBN 0-13-880733-7
2. Fitzgerald, J., Larsen, P.G.: Modelling Systems – Practical Tools and Techniques in Software Development. Cambridge University Press, The Edinburgh Building (1998), ISBN 0-521-62348-0
3. Fitzgerald, J., Larsen, P.G., Mukherjee, P., Plat, N., Verhoef, M.: Validated Designs for Object–oriented Systems. Springer, New York (2005)
4. Fitzgerald, J.S., Larsen, P.G.: Triumphs and Challenges for the Industrial Application of Model-Oriented Formal Methods. In: Margaria, T., Philippou, A., Steffen, B., eds.: Proc. 2nd Intl. Symp. on Leveraging Applications of Formal Methods, Verification and Validation (ISoLA 2007) Also Technical Report CS-TR-999, School of Computing Science, Newcastle University (2007)
5. Verhoef, M., Larsen, P.G., Hooman, J.: Modeling and Validating Distributed Embedded Real-Time Systems with VDM++. In: Misra, J., Nipkow, T., Sekerinski, E. (eds.) FM 2006. LNCS, vol. 4085, pp. 147–162. Springer, Heidelberg (2006)
6. Fitzgerald, J.S., Larsen, P.G., Tjell, S., Verhoef, M.: Validation Support for Real-Time Embedded Systems in VDM++. In: Cukic, B., Dong, J. (eds.) Proc. HASE 2007: 10th IEEE High Assurance Systems Engineering Symposium, November 2007, pp. 331–340. IEEE, Los Alamitos (2007)
7. C.S.K.: Development Guidelines for Real Time Systems using VDMTools. Technical report, CSK Systems (2008)
8. Boston Scientific: Pacemaker system specification. Technical report, Boston Scientific (January 2007),
   http://www.cas.mcmaster.ca/sqrl/_SQRLDocuments/PACEMAKER.pdf
9. Woodcock, J.: First Steps in the Verified Software Grand Challenge. Computer 39(10), 57–64 (2006)
10. Ellenbogen, K.A., Wood, M.A.: Cardiac Pacing and ICDs, 4th edn. Blackwell, Malden (2005)
11. Mukherjee, P., Bousquet, F., Delabre, J., Paynter, S., Larsen, P.G.: Exploring Timing Properties Using VDM++ on an Industrial Application. In: Bicarregui, J., Fitzgerald, J. (eds.) Proceedings of the Second VDM Workshop (September 2000),
    www.vdmportal.org
12. Larsen, P.G., Hansen, B.S., et al.: Information technology – Programming languages, their environments and system software interfaces – Vienna Development Method – Specification Language – Part 1: Base language (December 1996)
13. Overture Group: The VDM Portal (2007), http://www.vdmportal.org
14. Lano, K.: Logic specification of reactive and real-time systems. Journal of Logic and Computation 8(5), 679–711 (1998)
15. Verhoef, M., Larsen, P.G.: Interpreting Distributed System Architectures Using VDM++ – A Case Study. In: Sauser, B., Muller, G. (eds.) 5th Annual Conference on Systems Engineering Research (March 2007),
    http://www.stevens.edu/engineering/cser/

16. CSK: VDMTools homepage (2007), http://www.vdmtools.jp/en/
17. Kurita, T., Oota, T., Nakatsugawa, Y.: Formal specification of an embedded IC for cellular phones. In: Proceedings of Software Symposium 2005. Software Engineers Associates of Japan, June 2005, pp. 73–80 (in Japanese)
18. Macedo, H.: Validating and Understanding Boston Scientific Pacemaker Requirements. Master's thesis, Minho University, Portugal (October 2007)
19. Macedo, H.: VDM models of the Pacemaker Challenge (2007), http://www.vdmportal.org/twiki/bin/view/Main/PacemakerCaseStudy
20. Sørensen, R.A., Nygaard, J.M.: Evaluating Distributed Architectures using VDM++ Real-Time Modelling with a Proof of Concept Implementation. Master's thesis, Enginering College of Aarhus (December 2007)
21. Verhoef, M.: Modeling and Validation Distributed Embedded Real-Time Systems. PhD thesis, Radboud University Nijmegen (2008)
22. Vilas, A.F., Arias, J.J.P., Redondo, R.P.D., Martinez, A.B.B.: Formalizing Incremental Design in Real-time Area: SCTL/MUS-T. In: Proceedings of the 26 th Annual International Computer Software and Applications Conference (COMPSAC 2002), IEEE, Los Alamitos (2002)
23. de Boer, F.: CREDO: Modeling and analysis of evolutionary structures for distributed services (2007), http://www.cwi.nl/projects/credo/
24. Lecomte, T.: Event B Reference Manual. Technical report, MATISSE/ClearSy (2001)
25. Suhaib, S.M., Mathaikutty, D.A., Shukla, S.K., Berner, D.: XFM: An Incremental Methodology for Developing Formal Models. ACM Transactions on Design Automation of Electronic Systems 10(4), 589–609 (2005)
26. Douglas, B.P.: Real Time UML – Advances in the UML for real-time systems, 3rd edn. Addison-Wesley, Reading (2004)
27. de Jong, G.: A UML-Based Design Methodology for Real-Time and Embedded Systems. In: Proceedings of the 2002 Design, Automation and Test in Europe Conference and Exhibition (DATE 2002), IEEE, Los Alamitos (2002)
28. Burmester, S., Giese, H., Hirsch, M., Schilling, D.: Incremental Design and Formal Verification with UML/RT in the FUJABA Real-Time Tool Suite. In: Proceedings of the International Workshop on Specification and vaildation of UML models for Real Time and embedded Systems, SVERTS 2004, UM (2004)
29. Uchitel, S., Kramer, J., Magee, J.: Incremental Elaboration of Scenario-Based Specifications and Behavior Models Using Implied Scenarios. ACM Transactions on Software Engineering and Methodology 13(1), 37–85 (2004)
30. Jing Liu, J.D., Lutz, R.: Safety analysis of software product lines using state-based modeling. Journal of Systems and Software 80(11), 1879–(1892)
31. Verhoef, M., Visser, P., Hooman, J., Broenink, J.: Co-simulation of Distributed Embedded Real-Time Control Systems. In: Davies, J., Gibbons, J. (eds.) IFM 2007. LNCS, vol. 4591, pp. 639–658. Springer, Heidelberg (2007)
32. Andrews, Z.H., Fitzgerald, J.S., Verhoef, M.: Resilience Modelling through Discrete Event and Continuous Time Co-Simulation. In: Proc. 37th Annual IFIP/IEEE Intl. Conf. on Dependable Systems and Networks (Supp. Volume), June 2007, pp. 350–351. IEEE Computer Society Press, Los Alamitos (2007)
33. Vermolen, S.: Automatically Discharging VDM Proof Obligations using HOL. Master's thesis, Radboud University Nijmegen, Computer Science Department (August 2007)

Industrial Use of Formal Methods for a High-Level Security Evaluation

Boutheina Chetali and Quang-Huy Nguyen

Gemalto, Security Labs
6 rue de la Verrerie, 92197 Meudon Cedex, France
{boutheina.chetali,quang-huy.nguyen}@gemalto.com

Abstract. This paper presents an effective use of formal methods for the development and for the security certification of smart card software. The approach is based on the Common Criteria's methodology that requires the use of formal methods to prove that a product implements the claimed security level. This work led to the world-first certification of a commercial Java Card^{TM} product involving all formal assurances needed to reach the highest security level. For this certification, formal methods have been used for the design and the implementation of the security functions of the Java Card system embedded in the product. We describe the refinement scheme used to meet the Common Criteria's requirements on formal models and proofs. In particular, we show how to build the proof that the implementation ensures the security objectives claimed in the security specification. We also provide some lessons learned from this important application of formal methods to the smart cards industry.

1 Introduction

Common Criteria (ISO 15408) becomes nowadays a well-established standard to evaluate the security of IT products. This standard, that defines seven levels of security from EAL1 to EAL7[1], requires the use of formal methods for the high-level evaluations (5 to 7). From a practical point of view, the main goal is to protect the assets of the product against risks and threats. The assurance scale is used to evaluate the effectiveness of the security mechanisms ensuring this protection. The high levels of the Common Criteria (CC) allow the user to protect high value assets against significant risks using security engineering techniques and a rigorous development environment. Those security engineering techniques include formal methods for the design and the development of the product.

In a security-sensitive industry as smart cards manufacturing, the level of CC certificate becomes an important differential factor: for the clients, a high-level Common Criteria certificate is a measurable assurance on the security of the product.

In the industry, the EAL4 level that is the common security level required for smart cards, provides assurance that the claimed security functions are present in the code. It is an indication of where the functions are located. But the correctness of that code, *w.r.t.* the security policies, is simply checked by the evaluator.

---
[1] EAL stands for Evaluation Assurance Level.

The code is only tested with the requirement that the test is structured. The requirements of the EAL7 level give, not only the assurance that the security functions are implemented, but also that these functions are correct w.r.t. the security policies defined in the security target of the product.

In order to obtain a high-level certificate (EAL5-7), the CC requires to follow the software engineering waterfall model and to use formal methods to build the different descriptions of the product, starting from its security specification down to its implementation. The correspondence between the different refinement levels are proved using the underlying tool.

In this paper, we present an industrial project that led to the world-first certification of a smart card product using formal models and proofs in all refinement levels. This work produces an augmented EAL4 certificate[2] in which the Java Card system meets all the formal requirements of the EAL7 level. We describe the technical approach developed to fulfill the EAL7 requirements and show the added value in terms of security. Using the Java Card firewall security function as an example, the key elements are detailed, showing how the security objectives defined in the security specification are represented, proved in the different formal descriptions and then, are ensured by the implementation of the product.

In this project, all formal models and proofs have been developed using Coq [1], a proof assistant based on higher-order type theories. This choice was firstly motivated by the safeness of Coq that is based on well-studied mathematical foundations and is defensively implemented: only a tiny kernel needs to be trusted and all Coq proofs are rechecked by this kernel. Secondly, the expressive power of the logics underlying Coq allowed us to deal efficiently with the (universally) quantified security properties.

The rest of this paper is organized as follows. Section 2 recalls the product development cycle required by the CC methodology and in particular the refinement scheme that is followed along this paper. Section 3 presents the security target and one of the security objectives implemented by our Java Card system, *i.e.*, the firewall, that will be used to illustrate the present approach. Section 4 describes the different formal representations of the product. Section 5 presents the correctness proof of the stepwise refinement and Section 6 explains how this refinement ensures that the implementation fulfills the security objectives. We discuss the related work and give some concluding remarks in Section 7.

2 CC Waterfall Model

The Common Criteria define several classes of activities (development, test, configuration management, vulnerability analysis, operation, maintenance, etc) and a set of requirements for each class. The developer has to fulfill the requirements in order to demonstrate to the evaluator that the product meets its claimed security level. Amongst these classes, the **ADV** class deals with the product development, and describes the (security of the) product at different levels of detail starting

---
[2] Certificate Ref. DCCSI-2007/19 delivered by the French Certification Body (DCSSI) on September 2007 (see also http://www.gemalto.com/php/pr_view.php?id=239).

from the informal security specification, *i.e.*, the security target (ST), down to the implementation (ADV_IMP). The levels of description are the *security functional specification* (ADV_FSP), the *high level design* (ADV_HLD) of the product in terms of sub-systems and the *low-level design* (ADV_LLD) in terms of modules. The main goal of this class is to gain confidence that the security functions are correctly implemented in the source code of the product. The EAL7 level requires that the three descriptions of the security design of the product, *i.e.*, FSP, HLD, LLD and the security policy, are formal models. Hence correspondences between adjacent models are formal proofs. In practice, the application of these requirements is challenging because their fulfillment depends on the used formal method (the language and the underlying tool). Several questions may be raised here:

- How safe is a theorem prover ?
- Should we trust the automatic proofs done by a model checker or a deductive proof with a theorem prover ?
- How to interpret the concept of refinement between two formal models ?

In addition to the development of practical models and proofs, there are also other challenges to deal with:

1. how to ensure the correspondence between the Security Target, an informal document and the two adjacent ones that are formal
2. how to ensure the correspondence between the most detailed level, that is formal, and the implementation of the product

Figure 1 resumes our refinement scheme for the EAL7 requirements which deals with these challenges in an effective way. This scheme not only fulfills the CC requirements but also allows to certify the security policy on the product using formal techniques. In the following, we will describe how this scheme is applied to the evaluation of our Java Card system.

3 Security Target

The security target is the security specification of the product. It is the main document of a CC evaluation used as a reference of the *claimed security*. The main goal of this document is to describe the efforts done by the developer to protect the assets of the product. The security target is then the result of the risk analysis and describes all the elements to be evaluated, in particular (see Figure 1):

- a set of **security objectives**, that counters the identified threats to the security of the assets
- a set of **security functional requirements**[3], that defines the security behavior of the product, and necessary to *meet* the security objectives
- a set of **security functions**, that claim to *implement* the functional requirements

---

[3] The functional requirements (SFR) are selected from a dictionary provided by the CC.

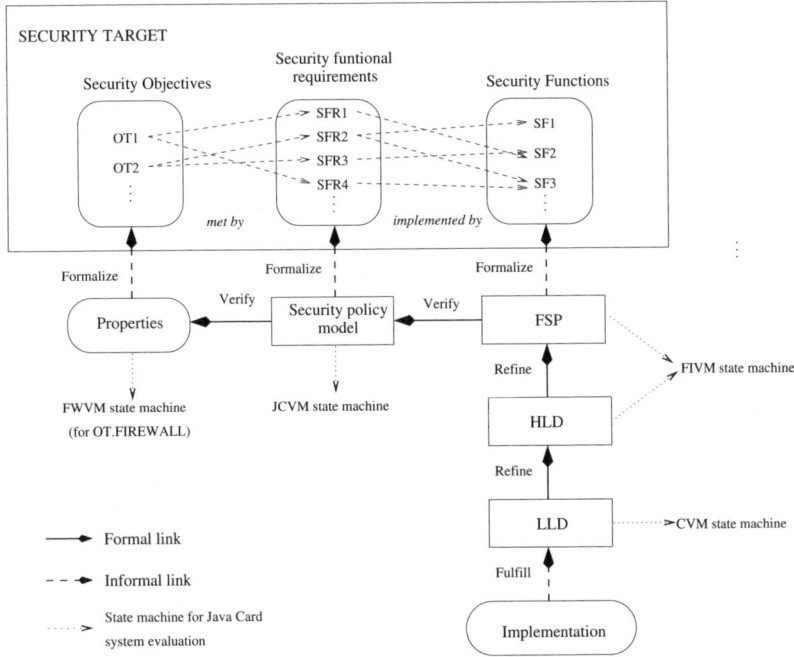

Fig. 1. A practical EAL7 refinement scheme

The assurance that the product meets its security objectives, *i.e.*, that the **security objectives** are achieved by the **security functions**, is derived from two conditions:

a) confidence in the *correctness* of the implementation of the security functions, *i.e.*, the assessment whether they are correctly implemented; and
b) confidence in the *effectiveness* of the security functions, *i.e.*, the assessment whether they actually satisfy the stated security objectives.

The refinement scheme presented in Figure 1 substitutes *formal proof* for *confidence* to fulfill the EAL7 requirements.

3.1 Java Card Firewall as a Security Objective

Figure 2 overviews the software architecture of a Java-embedded smart card. The scope of the EAL7 evaluation is the Java Card system that consists of the virtual machine[4], the API written in Java and the native API.

The virtual machine plays a central role: it securely interprets the bytecodes and makes calls to the API if necessary. The virtual machine is usually implemented

---

[4] Here, the virtual machine also includes the Java Card Runtime Environment that is sometimes described separately.

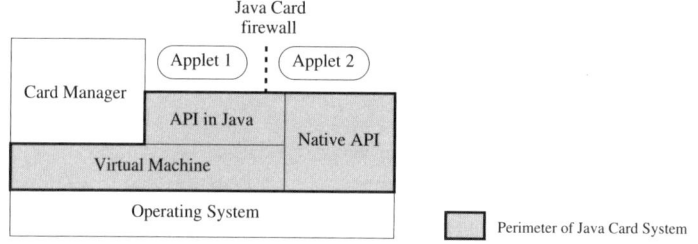

Fig. 2. Java Card system inside the card architecture

in a low-level programming language such as C for performance reasons. The functional behavior of the virtual machine is defined by Sun in [2] and [3].

Java Card API [4] provides the applets with commonly used functions such as the operations on array data-type, access to the card resource, remote method invocation, etc. Many API methods are written in Java but some of them are implemented in a native language (C) in order to speed up the low-level operations. An API method may also be a mixture of Java code and native API calls. Java Card API is part of the Java Card system and obviously participates in its security functions. However, in this paper, we only concentrate on the virtual machine due to space limitations. The refinement scheme of the API is not very different from that of the virtual machine, but requires some adaptation and is described in [5] for native API and in [6] for Java API.

The security target contains the objectives required for the Java Card system (see [7] for the complete list of objectives). Amongst them, several objectives have been formalized[5]. The most complex and demanding objective is the following:

OT.FIREWALL : the Java Card *platform shall ensure the isolation between the applet executions.*

This objective prevents the objects owned by one applet from being used by another applet without explicit sharing. The isolation between the applets covers two security properties: *confidentiality* and *integrity*. The confidentiality ensures that during its execution, an applet cannot read the information stored in the other applets. The integrity ensures that during its execution, an applet cannot modify the information stored in the other applets.

3.2 Security Policy Model of Java Card Firewall

The second component of the security target is a set of security functional requirements describing the security behavior of the product. Examples of functional requirements are :

1. The security functions (of the product) shall require each user to identify itself before authorizing any other actions on behalf of that user.

---

[5] Not all objectives can be formalized. For example, some of the security objectives provide assurance against physical attacks. These objectives are not formalizable in the current state of the art.

2. The security functions (of the product) shall explicitly authorize access of subjects to objects based on the following rules: R_1, R_2, etc.

The product security policy (TSP) is then the set of rules that regulate how assets are managed, protected and distributed, expressed by the security functional requirements. Those policies could be explicitly stated by the functional requirements, *e.g.*, the second one above, or are implicit *e.g.*, the first one. They are all the security policies enforced by the product, e.g. the audit policy, the management policy, the encryption policy, etc. But only a subset of those policies can be formalized, because modeling certain policies is currently beyond the state of the art. Generally, access control and information flow control policies are required to be formalized.

From EAL5 to EAL7, the CC requires a formal security policy model and a demonstration that the formal security policy *implements* the informal security policies described in the security target. The set of CC requirements to be met by the models and the associated proofs are called the ADV_SPM.

For our Java Card system, the formal security policy model (TSPM) is made of two abstract state machines, called JCVM (Java Card Virtual Machine), and FWVM (Firewall Virtual Machine).

The JCVM state machine is the complete defensive formalization of the virtual machine. The JCVM *states* represent the card states that are composed of the installed applets, the runtime data of the virtual machine (*i.e.*, the frame stack and the heap), the static data, the transaction log, etc. A JCVM *transition* corresponds to the execution a Java Card bytecode that transforms a card state into another card state.

The FWVM state machine formalizes all the access control and information flow control rules defining the firewall control of Sun (see Chapter 6 of [3]). FWVM is an abstraction of JCVM that only defines the transitions and the card components that are related to the reference data-type. Indeed, the firewall control authorizes an access according to the *reference* of its target. In other words, the other data-types are not concerned by this control and are not considered in FWVM. Similarly, the bytecodes that do not require an access through the firewall are not included in FWVM.

The demonstration, that the TSPM implements the informal security policies of the security target, may be done in the two following steps[6]:

1. provide a correspondence between the rules and characteristics of the functional requirements and the mathematical objects (sets, predicates, functions, etc) which are the formal counterpart in the security policy model.
2. as the objectives are met by the functional requirements, and the security policy model formalizes the functional requirements, the objectives are then *properties*[7] that the model must verify.

---

[6] Details on the interpretation of the CC requirements for formal models and proofs can be found in the document [8] issued by the German Certification Body (BSI).

[7] Generally, due to the fact that the objective is too abstract, there is no direct translation between an objective and a property, but mainly an objective represents a set of properties.

In a previous work [9], it has been proved that the firewall control rules are sufficient to ensure the *confidentiality* aspect of OT.FIREWALL providing that the embedded applets have been bytecode verified and there is not shared element between them. In other words, the FWVM provides a formalization of the confidentiality aspect of OT.FIREWALL and is the property that the JCVM must verify.

The *integrity* aspect is formalized as a theorem on JCVM stating that if the two applets do not share any element, then the execution of an applet does not modify the memory zone owned by the other applet. More formally, let A_1 and A_2 be two applets belonging two different security contexts. If they do not share any element (for example, through a *shareable interface*), then for all JCVM transitions on A_1, the heap spaces belonging to A_2 before and after the transition are identical.

3.3 Java Card Firewall as a Security Function

The last component of the security target is a high-level definition of the **security functions** claimed to *implement* the **security functional requirements**(see Figure 1). In the case of the firewall, a function named *SF.Firewall* describes the rules of the access control and information flow control during the execution of the bytecodes that may give access to an object in the card memory. This description is informal. The security target includes a *rationale*, made of a table and explanatory text showing the coverage of the security requirements by the security functions, i.e. that each SFR is implemented by at least one security function.

4 Formal Refinement of the Product

We presented the security target, that is the security specification describing the expected security behavior (security functional requirements and security functions) of the product. The following sections will describe the design of the security functions of the product, using the refinement process described in Figure 1. The description starts with the security functional specification.

4.1 Functional Specification

The functional specification (FSP for short) is a high-level description of the user-visible interface and the behavior of the product security functions.

The functional specification of the Java Card virtual machine is formalized by an abstract state machine, called the FIVM (Formal Internal Virtual Machine), that is a refinement of the JCVM. This refinement is based on the fact that the applets to be interpreted by the FIVM are linked and are already checked by a bytecode-verifier. The difference between FIVM and JCVM resides essentially on the two following features:

1. The FIVM interprets linked applets whose data structures are optimized to speed up the execution. The linking process transforms the indirect references into the absolute addresses in the card memory, and initializes the static data structures. In other words, FIVM references are absolute while a JCVM reference consists of a segment and an offset.
2. FIVM is not as defensive as JCVM. When interpreting a bytecode, JCVM performs static checks on the arguments to detect typing errors. Because FIVM operates on applets that have been bytecode verified, these static checks are not necessary. In other words, FIVM concentrates on the execution of the applets and only handles the runtime errors (exceptions or internal errors).

As for the JCVM, the FIVM transitions are the executions of the bytecodes and the FIVM states are the card states. FIVM is an abstract state machine because its states are opaque: the state components (*i.e.,* the installed applets, the heap, the frame stack, the static data, etc) are not fully refined but are abstract data-types. Thus, the access operations to these components are also abstract: only their signatures are given in the FSP. This refinement keeps the FSP independent of any implementation of the product. Indeed, the concrete data structures are only instantiated in the implementation.

In the FSP, the execution of a bytecode is formalized by a pre-condition and a post-condition. The pre-condition specifies the conditions on the card state before the execution while the post-condition specifies the effects of the execution.

Functional Specification of the Security Functions. The correspondence between the security target and the security functional specification must be provided in order to give assurance that all the security functions are covered. The coverage is a mapping between the security functions, as identified in the security target, and the formal functional specification. The mapping shall demonstrate that the FSP is a complete and consistent representation of the security functions. In our case, the security target is an informal document and the FSP is a formal model, the mapping consists in pointing the mathematical objects that are used in the FSP model to specify a given security function.

The firewall security function is formalized as a set of firewall control rules in the pre-conditions of the bytecodes that provide access to card resource. If a rule is not satisfied, then the execution is switched to the error case where a security exception is thrown. The list of bytecodes and the informal specification of the rules are described in Chapter 6 of [3].

4.2 High Level Design

The High Level Design (HLD for short) describes the product in terms on subsystems participating to the enforcement of the security. The functional specification of the security functions, must be refined in a high level design. This refinement will indicate in which sub-system each security function is implemented.

In our approach, the HLD model describes the computational behavior of the virtual machine, refining the specification of the security functions in terms of *algorithms*. It is close to the FSP model because it is formalized using the same FIVM state machine. The difference between these two description levels relies on the modeling style. On one hand, the FSP describes a security function using logical predicates to relate its pre-condition (on the input state) and its post-condition (on the output state). On the other hand, the HLD specifies the security function by a (total) function that computes the output from the input. For example, the HLD model of a bytecode defines an executable algorithm that handles all possible cases of the execution (nominal, errors and exceptions). The FSP of this bytecode lists the possible couples of input state and output state. In other words, the HLD gives an algorithmic description of the security function and is more close to a real implementation than the FSP, which is abstract because not every relation is realizable.

Because the HLD also uses the FIVM whose states are abstract, this model is still independent of the implementation. Indeed, the components of the virtual machine are not concretely defined. These components will be defined in the low-level design model that is **implementation-dependent**.

Sometimes, there exist different algorithms to implement an execution specified in the FSP[8]. In that case, the HLD becomes implementation-dependent because it must choose a concrete algorithm. This is the case of the Java Card API methods whose the HLD contains all necessary details and the LLD is not needed anymore [6].

4.3 Low Level Design

The Low-level Design (LLD for short) describes the product in terms of modules that participate in the enforcement of the security. The modules are the refinement of the HLD sub-systems. The LLD is built using a new state machine[9] that is called CVM (Concrete Virtual Machine). Contrary to the FIVM, the CVM is fully defined by concrete data structures and takes into account the optimizations done by the implementation. For example, the frame stack is defined such as the different frames share part of their structure in order to reduce the RAM consumption. Because the data structures and the optimizations are implementation-dependent, the LLD is actually a refinement of the HLD by following the implementation of the product.

5 Correctness

We have described the formal models that correspond to the stepwise refinement (Figure 1) of the product development. We will describe how the correctness of the refinement steps is formalized and proved upon the different state machines.

---

[8] An execution is a set of traces of the abstract machine.
[9] Even if the LLD is only required to be semi-formal in EAL7.

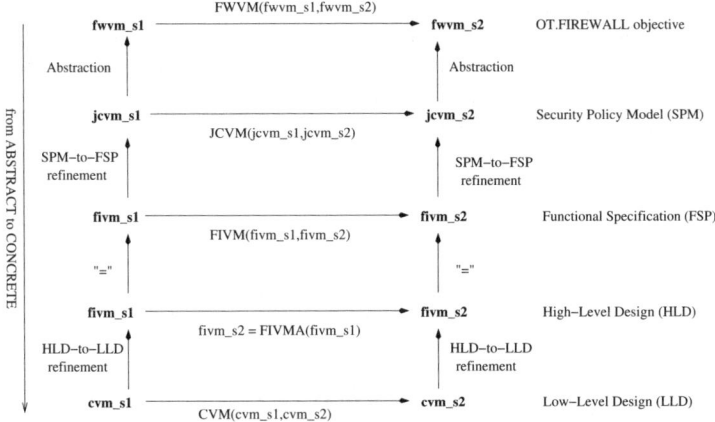

Fig. 3. Theorems of correctness

5.1 Theorems of Correctness

The correctness of each refinement step between two representations is stated as a commutative property between the two corresponding state machines as described in Figure 3. A commutative theorem states that for each transition (*i.e.*, for each bytecode execution) in the refined representation, there exists a corresponding transition in the abstract representation.

Theorem 1 (Correctness of refinement). *A transition between two states s_1 and s_2 on the state machine $\mathcal{M}$ is denoted by $\mathcal{M}(s_1, s_2)$. Let $\mathcal{R}$ be a refinement relation between the states of $\mathcal{M}_1$ and $\mathcal{M}_2$. Assume that the two initial states of a transition are related by $\mathcal{R}$. The refinement from $\mathcal{M}_1$ to $\mathcal{M}_2$ is said to be correct if the two final states are also related by $\mathcal{R}$:*

$$\mathcal{R}(s_1, v_1) \wedge \mathcal{M}_1(s_1, s_2) \Rightarrow \exists v_2. \mathcal{M}_2(v_1, v_2) \wedge R(s_2, v_2)$$

This generic theorem has been used to define:

- the commutation between FWVM and JCVM which implies that the firewall rules are satisfied by JCVM. By combining with the result of a previous work [9], we conclude that the confidentiality aspect of OT.FIREWALL is verified by the TSP model. The integrity aspect of OT.FIREWALL is formalized and proved on JCVM as a separate theorem.
- the correspondence between the TSP model and the FSP *i.e.*, the commutation between JCVM and FIVM which implies that the security functions specified in FSP fulfills the objectives ensured by JCVM and hence, OT.FIREWALL.
- the HLD-LLD correspondence *i.e.*, the commutation between FIVM and CVM which implies that the security functions are correctly refined from the HLD to the LLD.

The refinement from the FSP to the HLD is a specific step because both these models are built on the same FIVM state machine. The refinement between the HLD and the FSP is correct if the algorithms defined in the HLD fulfill their specifications defined in the FSP. In Hoare logic, a function f fulfills its precondition Pre_f and postcondition $Post_f$ if:

$$\forall xy : y = f(x) \Rightarrow Pre_f(x) \Rightarrow Post_f(y)$$

where x, y respectively represent the input and the output of f.

In our case, this amounts to proving:

$$\forall fivm\_s1 \, fivm\_s2 : fivm\_s2 = FIVMA(fivm\_s1) \Rightarrow FIVM(fivm\_1, fivm\_s2)$$

where $FIVMA$ denotes the HLD function and $FIVM$ denotes the FSP predicate relating the two FIVM states.

To resume, the proof of the commutative theorems in Figure 3 demonstrates that the security objective OT.FIREWALL is verified by all formal representations of the product.

5.2 Proof Scheme and Experiences

The proof of the correctness theorems described above is done for each transition of the state machines (*i.e.*, for each bytecode execution). The general structure of a bytecode execution can be seen as a tree whose leaves are the access operations to the card state (*i.e.*, to the machine states in the formal models). These operations consist in reading or modifying a state component (heap, frame stack, static data, etc). The internal nodes of the execution tree are the constructs used to express the execution flow, *e.g.*, assigning, branching (if... then... else), looping. The general proof scheme for the commutation of two state machines on a bytecode execution is described as follows:

1. Decompose the bytecode execution into more simple operations in both two machine states until the access operations are reached.
2. Prove the correctness for each decomposition step: because the definitions of the bytecode in both models follow the same structure, this proof is feasible.
3. Apply the appropriate refinement hypotheses to get the correctness for the access operations: the refinement hypotheses define the relation between the two state machines *i.e.*, the mapping between their components.

This proof scheme is closely related to the structure of the bytecode execution. For example, if the byte code execution is a recursive function, then for proving the correctness of the decomposition steps over it, a proof by induction is needed. Furthermore, because the execution needs to cover all possible error cases, the proof must be done on all of its execution paths.

In many cases, this leads to a huge and unreadable proof script. Actually, one of the difficulties we encountered in this work is the maintenance of the proof scripts. Indeed, a modification in the model usually requires a significant adaptation of the proof script. For example, a modification on an internal node of the execution tree implies the modification of all the proof branches passing through this node: new quantified variables are introduced and the tactic calls are changed. In order to ease the proof readability and maintenance, the following methodology has been used:

- respect several "coding rules" while writing proof scripts: (1) adding comments for each branching point; (2) properly naming the quantified variables instead of using the generated names by Coq (these generated names are numbered and make proof maintenance costly); (3) using one-step Coq tactics and not automatic ones that make proof debugging costly because their effects are too complex to be traced.
- define new tactics to replace the repetitive proof scripts: the proof of our theorems does not require complex proof search. It is usually up to the user to provide the right arguments to the tactics according to the proof context. This does not favor the use of the automatic decision procedures. In contrast, many parts of the proof scripts are repetitive and can be factorized by the user-defined tactics.

In total, more than 1600 theorems have been proved using the standard Coq tactics and some 150 user-defined tactics. This work has shown that the proof mode of the interactive provers still needs to be improved to reduced the maintenance cost. Actually, in the "proof-as-programming" paradigm proposed by theorem provers based on type theories, a theorem is seen as a specification. Proving the theorem corresponds to writing a program that fulfills this specification. For software engineering, numerous tools have been developed to help the developers to debug, maintain and improve their programs. The equivalent tools in proof engineering are still missing or are very specific to an application domain (*e.g.,* model-checking based tools).

6 Ensuring Security Objectives by the Implementation

The main goal of the CC evaluation process is that the developer of the product demonstrate to the evaluator that the most detailed, or least abstract, product representation is an accurate, consistent, and complete instantiation of the security functions of the security target. This is accomplished by showing the correspondence between adjacent representations at a certain level of rigor. In our approach, the refinement process described in the previous sections formally proves that the security functions, and then the security objectives are verified by the low level model of the product. But how about the last description that is the implementation of the product in C language ?

In the idea case, one may automatically generate the implementation of the product from the (formal) LLD using a formal tool. Hence the implementation will ensure the security objectives *by construction*. This approach has been tested for part of the Java Card (such as the bytecode-verifier) in some previous work (see for example [10]). However, the prohibitive size and the poor performance of the generated code prevent it from being embedded into a smart card. Beside the cost, the size of the embedded code is crucial for the viability of services offered by the card. Hence, the footprint of the Java Card system needs to be minimized to save the space for application data such as the biometric images or phone-book. In terms of performance, the generated code needs to be optimized. However, a generic optimization by the code generator is usually difficult while a particular optimization (by hand) may jeopardize the benefits of the formal verification. Last but not least, a CC evaluation is generally required when the product is already developed, *i.e.,* on an existing implementation. All these constraints make that solution not satisfactory for the moment.

Another direction is to formalize the semantics of C and then, to prove the correspondence between the LLD model and the C code (see for example [11]). In the current state of the art, this approach is not sufficiently developed to deal with an industrial C implementation.

From a CC point of view, because the LLD model is formal while the implementation is informal, the refinement between them is only required to be semi-formal by the EAL7 level. In other words, the correspondence between the elements in the LLD model and in the code must only be showed in a structured and complete manner. In this work, this correspondence is showed by a hypertext document using a precise and complete code-to-spec review. For any data structure and function, the LLD model and C implementation are linked, and the semantics of C source code is informally checked.

In particular, for the OT.FIREWALL security objective, we check that the SF.Firewall rules formalized in the LLD are effectively implemented in the C code of the bytecodes that require the firewall to access to card resource.

7 Concluding Remarks

In this paper, we present the use of formal methods techniques for the security design and development of a smart card product. This methodology has been evaluated and led to a CC certificate. The approach consists of the specification of the security objectives that the product has to meet and their stepwise refinement into security functions to be implemented in the code. All the refinements steps, from the security target down to the implementation, have been described and the chain provides a formal proof that the security functions are correctly implemented.

In our knowledge, this project is the biggest development that has been done in Coq with more than 117 000 lines of code. This code includes the different state machines and the proof of 1 640 theorems. Most of these theorems require an interactive proof. This work allowed us to detect and fix several bugs in the implementation, in particular in the Java Card API. Some of them have been described in [5,6].

The main difficulties we encountered in this work are the first and last step of correspondence of the development chain. The first one is a correspondence between an informal description and two formal models, *i.e.*, between the security target, and the formal functional security specification or the formal security policy model. The second correspondence is between the formal model of the low-level design and the C description of the implementation.

The first correspondence is the classic problem of the conformity of a formal model *w.r.t.* the informal specification. The specification in our case is the security specification (Security Target) of the product. The formal models are the security policy model and the formal functional specification of the security functions. The main achievement of this work is the correspondence between the security policy model and the security **objectives** and functional requirements of the security target. We applied the interpretation proposed in [8] using the objectives as security **properties** to be proved on the formal model describing the functional **behavior** of the policy. It is important to note that the CC is a security standard that provides a set of requirements for the developer and for the evaluator and provides a Common Evaluation Methodology (CEM). But at the start of this work there were no guidelines nor methodology for the EAL5-7 levels, e.g. no recommendation for the verification tool to use. Therefore the use of formal methods for the complete chain of the design was a challenge. Consequently, the successful evaluation of our security policy model and its correspondence with the security target is a major forward step for the state of the art.

The second difficulty is the final refinement step, between the formal low-level design of the product and the C implementation. This correspondence has been done with a code-to-spec review providing a mapping between Coq objects and C objects. Obviously, this correspondence requires a structured C implementation with a minimum of complexity. Future work on this direction may focus on the compilers. In fact, even if the C code could be generated automatically by a *trusted* formal verification tool, the code will then be compiled by an untrusted tool. The next goal will be then to certify the compiler (formally proving its correctness) to complete the chain. Several research projects are following this direction (see for example [12] and [13]).

Applying formal methods to the security of smart cards in general, and of Java Card in particular, has been studied by numerous researchers in the last ten years ([14] and [15] provide a survey of their work). However, most of them concentrate on building formal analysis tools or on formalizing part of the Java Card system. A high-level CC evaluation requires a more important efforts to build and to prove several models of the complete system.

That may explain why very few high-level evaluations of smart card software have been conducted, and all of them are at the EAL5 level (see for example, http://www.ssi.gouv.fr/site_documents/certificats/cible2007_16en.pdf for such an evaluation). At that level only the security policy model is required to be formal. The other descriptions, functional specification, high level design and low level design are semi-formal (generally UML models). The result is that at the EAL5 level, the security functions are semi-formally designed and tested. From the CC view, this level is applicable when the user requires *"a high level of independently assured security in a planned development and require a rigorous development approach without incurring unreasonable costs attributable to specialist security engineering techniques"* [16]. Therefore, this level could be sufficient with the time-to-market constraint in the smart card industry but the **open**[10] and **multi-applications**[11] constraints justify the additional costs of using *"specialist security engineering techniques"* such as formal methods. But for customers from fast-moving industries like mobile telecommunications and retail banking, the applications to be hosted in smart cards are becoming more sophisticated and more sensitive. For example, one of the most promising market is the *mobile banking* where the user uses his mobile phone for payment (transport, goods, etc). This business model requires applications from different sectors, here finance and telecommunication, to collaborate on the same card to provide the requested services. In this context, the card (application) security is crucial as several embedded applications are combined in a complex architecture. The use of formal techniques is then advocated to minimize the risk to the integrity and the confidentiality of the data handled by the card.

Our approach has proposed a new kind of evaluation where the complete product is certified according to the state of the art, but where the main security properties have been ensured using formal methods. The resulting certificate, an EAL4 augmented by formal assurances, is a major breakthrough in the CC certifications and in smart card security. The (EAL7) formal assurances provided for this product mean that the integrity and the confidentiality of the application data in a multi-application card have been mathematically proved. The formal assurances from the EAL7 certification level add an extra dimension to the Java Card system implementation. They provide a protection against significant security risks normally reserved for high-value assets.

References

1. The Coq Development Team. The Coq Proof Assistant., http://coq.inria.fr/
2. Sun Microsystems. Java Card 2.2 Virtual Machine Specification (2002), http://www.javasoft.com/products/javacard
3. Sun Microsystems. Java Card 2.2 Runtime Environment Specification (2002), http://www.javasoft.com/products/javacard
4. Sun Microsystems. Java Card 2.2 Application Programming Interface (2002), http://www.javasoft.com/products/javacard
5. Nguyen, Q.-H., Chetali, B.: Certifying Native Java Card API by Formal Refinement. In: Domingo-Ferrer, J., Posegga, J., Schreckling, D. (eds.) CARDIS 2006. LNCS, vol. 3928, pp. 313–328. Springer, Heidelberg (2006)
6. Andronick, J., Nguyen, Q.-H.: Certifying an Embedded Remote Method Invocation Protocol. In: Proc. of the 23th ACM Symposium on Applied Computing (SAC 2008), pp. 352–359. ACM Press, New York (2008)

---

[10] The card is *open* if it allows to download applications in post-issuance.
[11] A multi-applications card is a card with more that one user application, i.e. a credit-debit application embedded with a e-purse on the same card.

7. Sun Microsystems. Java Card System Protection Profile Collection - Version 1.1 (2003), http://java.sun.com/products/javacard/pp.html
8. Bundesam für Sicherheit der Informationstechnik (BSI). Evualuation methodology for CC assurance classes for EAL5+, June, Version 1.00. Ref. AIS34 (2004)
9. Andronick, J., Chetali, B., Ly, O.: Using Coq to Verify Java Card Applet Isolation Properties. In: Basin, D., Wolff, B. (eds.) TPHOLs 2003. LNCS, vol. 2758, pp. 335–351. Springer, Heidelberg (2003)
10. Bert, D., Boulmé, S., Potet, M.-L., Requet, A., Voisin, L.: Adaptable Translator of B Specifications to Embedded C Programs. In: Araki, K., Gnesi, S., Mandrioli, D. (eds.) FME 2003. LNCS, vol. 2805, pp. 94–113. Springer, Heidelberg (2003)
11. Andronick, J., Chetali, B., Paulin-Mohring, C.: Formal Verification of Security Properties of Smart Card Embedded Source Code. In: Fitzgerald, J.S., Hayes, I.J., Tarlecki, A. (eds.) FM 2005. LNCS, vol. 3582, pp. 302–317. Springer, Heidelberg (2005)
12. Leroy, X.: Formal certification of a compiler back-end or: programming a compiler with a proof assistant. In: Procs. of POPL 2006, pp. 42–54. ACM Press, New York (2006)
13. Blazy, S., Dargaye, Z., Leroy, X.: Formal verification of a c compiler front-end. In: Misra, J., Nipkow, T., Sekerinski, E. (eds.) FM 2006. LNCS, vol. 4085, pp. 460–475. Springer, Heidelberg (2006)
14. Barthe, G., Dufay, G.: Formal Methods for Smartcard Security. In: Aldini, A., Gorrieri, R., Martinelli, F. (eds.) FOSAD 2005. LNCS, vol. 3655, pp. 133–177. Springer, Heidelberg (2005)
15. Hartel, P.H., Moreau, L.: Formalising the Safety of Java, the Java Virtual Machine and Java Card. ACM Computing Surveys 33(4), 517–558 (2001)
16. Common Criteria, http://www.commoncriteria.org/

Secret Ninja Formal Methods

Joseph R. Kiniry[1] and Daniel M. Zimmerman[2]

[1] School of Computer Science and Informatics, University College Dublin,
Belfield, Dublin 4, Ireland
kiniry@acm.org
[2] Institute of Technology, University of Washington, Tacoma,
Tacoma, Washington 98402, USA
dmz@acm.org

Abstract. The use of formal methods can significantly improve software quality. However, many instructors and students consider formal methods to be too difficult, impractical, and esoteric for use in undergraduate classes. This paper describes a method, used successfully at several universities, that combines ninja stealth with the latest advances in formal methods tools and technologies to integrate applied formal methods into software engineering courses.

1 Enter the Ninja

Software development tools and techniques based on formal methods hold great promise for improving software quality. Unfortunately, many undergraduate computer science and software engineering curricula include no formal methods instruction beyond the introduction of basic concepts such as the assertion and the loop invariant. Moreover, even when formal methods concepts are introduced, they tend not to be used outside of toy examples. Many students and instructors, it seems, believe that the very words "formal methods" imply writing equations on paper for hours on end with no computers in sight. Those who have never used modern formal tools and techniques generally consider formal methods to be irrelevant to "real" computer programming.

Our goal is not only for our students to *use* formal methods in their software design and implementation process, but also for them to *enjoy* doing so. To accomplish this lofty goal, we employ *shinobi-iri*[1] (stealth and entering methods)—we sneak up on our blissfully unaware students, slip a dose of formal methods into their coursework and development environments, then with a thunderclap disappear in a puff of smoke.

We teach our students to design software systems using a (formal) notation that appears to be merely structured English, and to implement them using sophisticated tool support that is almost entirely hidden behind simple instructor-provided scripts and IDE plugins. Details about the automated theorem proving,

---

[1] The terminology of the ninja may be inscrutable to the uninitiated; the curious reader may more intensively exercise his *chōhō* (espionage skill) at http://en.wikipedia.org/wiki/Ninjutsu.

static code analysis, runtime assertion generation, and other processes underlying the system are not revealed to the students until after they have implemented software projects. By the time our initiates realize they are using "formal methods" in developing their software, they have experienced firsthand what formal methods can do for them, and are likely to continue to follow in their masters' silent footsteps.

Over the past 10 years we have used this approach to varying degrees, with considerable success, in classes taught at the California Institute of Technology, Radboud University Nijmegen, University College Dublin, and the University of Washington, Tacoma. And, while we are aware of the formal methods teaching literature [1], we and the colleagues with whom we have corresponded about teaching know of no other academics that combine the tools and techniques described herein to practice formal methods ninjutsu in their classrooms.

2 The Ninja Arts

A formal methods ninja has many subtle and effective techniques at his command. We use only a few of these in our classrooms. In this section, we briefly introduce the formal methods concepts we use and then discuss the tools we employ in the software development process. For more details on any of these formal methods or tools, please see the cited sources.

2.1 Formal Methods

Assertions. The assertion [2] is a core concept we use and emphasize in software design and development. Our notion and use of assertions are much broader than just formal assertions in program code; we also classify informal documentation of conceptual constraints and compiler pragmas [3], both of which are encoded as semantic properties in BON and JML (see below), and logging messages as forms of assertions.

Design by Contract. Design by Contract (DBC) [4] is a design technique for object-oriented software that uses assertions to document and enforce restrictions on data and specify class and method behavior. Contracts are used throughout the *entire process* of creating a software system, from analysis and design to implementation and maintenance.

BON. The Business Object Notation (BON) [5] is an analysis and design method for object-oriented software originally developed for use with the Eiffel programming language. We use an extended version of BON (EBON) that folds user-defined domain-specific languages into BON. We use BON instead of UML because BON is simple and has a clear semantics.

JML. The Java Modeling Language (JML) [6] is a specification language for Java programs. It is used both to write class and method contracts in a DBC style and to specify properties beyond simple partial correctness of method specifications and class invariants. We use JML both because its Java-like syntax is easy for students to learn and because it has excellent tool support.

Underlying Semantics. Underlying the concepts in our realization of DBC, BON, and JML is a rich set of semantics embodied in several logics and tools. A detailed discussion of these semantics is beyond the scope of this paper; however, we will highlight how some of them are naturally expressed to the students in Section 3.

2.2 Tools and Technologies

The main "hook" that we use to get students interested in and excited about trying new development techniques is *tool support*. In fact, we consider the existence of rich, high quality, automated tools *mandatory* for any kind of real adoption of applied formal methods. Moreover, such tools must be integrated into development environments with which students are already familiar.

The tools that we use include some that we have helped develop and some from other teams with which we have little interaction. The former is motivated not by selfishness, but by the principle that we should "eat our own *mochi*."[2] We believe that one cannot propose and provide a tool to the software developers of the world unless one *at least* uses the tool himself, preferably in the tool's own development.

Common JML Tools. The *Common JML* tool suite [6] contains several tools, nearly all of which we use in teaching. The tool suite includes a JML typechecker (`jml`), a JML compiler (`jmlc`) that compiles JML specifications into runtime checks, a runtime assertion checking environment (`jmlrac`), an augmented version of Javadoc (`jmldoc`) that generates browsable documentation containing specifications, and a unit test generating framework (`jmlunit`, discussed below).

Although these tools are quite easy to use, as `jmlc` behaves very much like `javac`, `jmldoc` very much like `javadoc`, etc., our young apprentices need not learn their details as we provide pre-defined build configurations (using GNU Make, Ant, and Eclipse) for them to use.

For example, a freshman programmer need only type `make build` in a shell to generate a full runtime assertion checking build of his project. The same applies to the GNU Make targets `test`, `docs`, etc. Similar targets exist in the predefined Ant build scripts and Eclipse build configurations. Using these predefined build targets, students catch errors in their programs early and often, in reliable and repeatable ways.

In addition, students get to see their hard work on writing documentation and specifications published in an attractive format for all the world, or at least

---

[2] Others "eat their own dog food". We prefer *mochi*, a delicious Japanese treat made of glutinous rice pounded into paste and molded into shape.

their fellow students, to see. In fact, publishing documentation in this fashion sometimes initiates intra-class rivalries where different teams try to "out-doc" each other, delving into the use of more sophisticated code and documentation presentation mechanisms such as MathML in Javadoc, fancy hyperlinked source processors like Doxygen, etc.

JUnit with JML. Using the Common JML tool `jmlunit`, one can generate arbitrary numbers of different unit tests for an annotated API. Contracts are used as test oracles and data values are identified manually by the developer.

In some of our courses, when appropriate, we generate tests for the students to use and simply provide a build system with a `test` target. The students do not know how these (thousands of) tests are generated, nor do they really care... at first. All they care about is that, by running the automated tests occasionally, they know what piece of code is responsible for a given test failure (as they are taught that precondition failures are the fault of the caller and postcondition failures are the fault of the implementer), and can more easily find and fix bugs.

This style of automated project evaluation is the first example of how we align assessment and project process, development methodology, and code quality in our teaching. Through the use of such stealthy alignment, students are inclined to take "suggestions" like full documentation coverage seriously, as not doing so impacts their grades.

ESC/Java2. The problem with relying solely upon runtime checking and unit testing, even in the presence of tens of thousands of tests, is that one can neither test for the absence of errors nor test a subsystem that is not yet completely implemented. We believe that students need feedback on the quality and correctness of their system's architecture and specified behavior *before* the implementation is complete. To achieve this, the true formal methods ninja reaches into his *shinobi shokozu*[3] for static checkers.

ESC/Java2 is an extended static checker for Java [7]. It *statically* analyzes JML-annotated Java modules (classes and interfaces)—it does not run the code, but instead checks the code and its annotations at compile time. Its capabilities are twofold: (1) it identifies common programming errors like null pointer dereferences, class cast exceptions, out-of-bounds array indexing, etc.; (2) it performs lightweight full-functional verification, ensuring that program code conforms to (sometimes quite rich) specifications written in JML. That is, ESC/Java2 modularly and statically checks that each method body fulfills its contract.

We note a few points about our use of ESC/Java2. First, students run the tool unknowingly, via a build system, exactly as they run the JML compiler and other tools. Second, students are encouraged to run this tool early and often, as static checking is modular and does not depend upon having a running system. Finally, students do not know what kind of (very complex) analysis is being rapidly and efficiently performed in the background; they know only that error

---

[3] The traditional garb of the ninja, which we wear when giving all our ninja-related conference talks.

messages that look exactly like those produced by `javac` or `gcc` are displayed on their screens or, if they are using Eclipse, that problem markers and red squiggles dynamically appear in their editors.

The fact that ESC/Java2 is carrying out weakest precondition and strongest postcondition reasoning on a Hoare logic using several different automated theorem provers sails over the students' heads like a errant *shuriken* (throwing star). This *hensōjutsu* (disguise and impersonation technique) is highly effective, and only when a student wonders aloud or asks in class how this build rule performs its magic do we begin to reveal the true nature of the connections between this tool and the seemingly highly abstract "nonsense" the student may have witnessed in theory courses.

It is essential that we carefully approach this dialogue. Subtlety is critical, as pushing this formal material, or its connection to the tools being used, too hard can cause the students to crack. It is better to let the advanced students ask the questions, investigate the material on their own, and espouse the ideas, methods, and tools to their less enthusiastic fellow students. Finding the fulcra in the classroom is critical to developing the students' *juhakkei* (ninja skills).

Moodle. We use a *Moodle*-based Virtual Learning Environment (VLE) in our teaching[4]. We use our Moodle servers for typical course-related purposes: posting lecture slides; hosting web and email forums for discussing course organization and concepts; providing a course calendar for scheduling lectures, special tutorials, and instructor/teaching assistant/student group collaborative hack sessions; posting, collecting, and grading homework assignments; and referencing supplementary materials like book lists and tutorials. However, we also integrate our VLE with our collaborative development environment (see below) and our development methodology.

In particular, we use two Moodle components in an integrated fashion. First, we use the Moodle's wiki module to document and evolve the class project's co-analysis and co-design (see the discussion in Section 3 for more information). Second, we use the Moodle's support for automatic implicit dictionary entry hyperlinking to document and cross-reference all concepts identified during the analysis phase of our software development method. The result of these two approaches is that, at any point in time, a student or instructor can: (a) browse the current project architecture, or any previous version thereof, in the wiki; (b) make updates and proposals directly in the wiki; and (c) jump to a single consistent set of concept definitions, as written during concept analysis.

GForge. All project development is managed via a web-based Collaborative Development Environment (CDE). We have used a GForge server for the past several years[5]. CDEs like the GForge provide a variety of services including web forums, email lists, version control repository management and browsing, user

---

[4] Our Moodles are all available via the KindSoftware research group website.
[5] The UCD GForge server that contains hundreds of student projects is http://sort.ucd.ie/.

polls, a ticket tracker (for features, bugs, patches, etc.), release and download services, etc.

Students are taught not only how to wield a CDE and its critical dependent services (especially version control and ticket tracking), but also how to integrate these practices with their groups' work. In particular, we have an extensive code standard [8] with domain-specific code annotations that students use to communicate about, and through, their system artifacts.

For example, in addition to Javadoc annotations (which are used extensively), we provide special pragmas written in a familiar Javadoc-like syntax. These special pragmas include everything from informal markup (such as copyright, version information, and bug and feature tracking cross-references) to formal annotations about concurrency semantics and time and space complexity.

The students feel like they are just writing normal Javadoc-like documentation. This is our ninja 気 (*qi*, a kind of "life force" or "spiritual energy") flowing through the students, mesmerizing them into believing they are doing something quite simple. In fact, these annotations have formal semantics that are statically checked by the tools we supply.

In summary, by integrating our VLE, our CDE, and project analysis, design, development, deployment, and maintenance, we more deeply engage the students and accurately measure (and potentially reward) their participation, as our VLE and CDE both stealthily track user actions in great detail.

Eclipse and its Plugins. Students are encouraged to use rich editors and development environments. In fact, they receive lectures on, and homework about, the classic yin and yang of `emacs` and `vi`. But many students, in the end, use Eclipse. Thus, we provide a rich set of pre-configured Emacs features and Eclipse plugins and align assessment with the regular use of these tools. In particular, we use plugins for evaluting code standard conformance (CheckStyle), code complexity analysis (NCSS and, in future classes, Metrics), and source and bytecode-level design and implementation analysis to find common programming errors (PMD and FindBugs).

Each of these plugins provides interactive feedback to students, who are easily dazzled by such *kayakujutsu* (pyrotechnics and explosives), while subtly and stealthily training them to use better design and programming practices. Little do they know that our plugins are "tuned" with an eye toward developing *formally verifiable* software. That is, the rigorous practices that our students follow, and the results against which they are assessed, are those necessary to develop robust, reliable, dependable software of very high quality.

Other Common Software Engineering Tools. A number of other concepts, tools, and practices are introduced, with complementary homework assignments, in our courses. As mentioned earlier, build systems like GNU Make and Apache Ant are used. Version control systems like RCS, CVS, and Subversion are critical, and thus introduced early in the semester so that all homeworks can be stored, and sometimes submitted, via commits. Also, unit testing frameworks like JUnit are used.

The aforementioned assessments encourage students to learn about each of these tools. Additionally, as previously stated, student inertia is overcome by precise *bōryaku* (military strategy) in the form of pre-written build system specifications, initial extensive (but not complete) unit tests, and pre-configured version control repositories. This encourages our students to follow the *Way of the Formal Methods Ninja*.

Reflecting on Our Technology Choices. While some of these choices in concepts, tools, technologies, and languages are predictable, many are also surprising. Why not use UML instead of EBON? Why not use Eiffel instead of Java?

Most applied formal methods ninjas have extensive experience with these alternative choices, and these weapons are indeed found in our *dōjō*. However, while we would love to use, for example, Eiffel in instruction, all ninjas have limitations imposed by the local *daimyō* (i.e., the head of the department). Moreover, some choices, at least in the domain of rigorous software development, are simply poor ones, and we avoid them.

3 Ninjutsu in the Classroom

Every ninja knows that his choice of weapon must be appropriate for the situation at hand; a bad choice can mean the difference between victory and defeat. The software development process we teach our students illuminates the right situations and wrong situations in which to use each tool and technique previously described. In this process, no executable code is written until *after* the important engineering work has taken place.

Our process is derived from the BON process [5], but has been modified over the years with an aim toward developing verifiable software, and is conducted as *co-analysis* and *co-design*—rather than lecturing at our students, we run interactive analysis and design sessions with active student involvement. Students propose and argue over terminology (Section 3.1), debate the best informal interface (Section 3.2) and type specification (Section 3.4) for each concept, and argue over appropriate formal specifications (Section 3.5). The remainder of this section describes our six-fold path of software development and gives an example of a single software concept as it travels the path. This concept is necessarily limited in complexity so that we can, within this manuscript, depict multiple steps of its journey; for further, more complex application examples, our course websites and example projects are available online.

3.1 Concept Analysis

The first step in the process, *concept analysis*, involves identifying and naming the important concepts (also sometimes called *entities*, *properties*, or, most often, *classifiers*) in the desired software system and collecting them into *clusters*, sets of related classifiers. We explicitly do *not* use the word "class" at this stage, because we want the students to think about basic concepts rather than about software artifacts such as classes, interfaces, and objects. In fact, students are forbidden from using words like "class", "variable", "array", and "loop".

We ask the students to analyze things from the real world, such as desks and automobiles. In a recent class (the video of which is available on the course website), the students analyzed a desk and identified several important associated concepts: a leg, a top, a drawer, a knob (for the drawer), screws, etc.

A more complicated system than a desk (such as a cellular automaton simulator or a Tetris-like game, both examples that we have used in our classes) requires more concepts. At this stage of the process, the goal is to devise a set of classifiers that is *as small as possible* while capturing all the important concepts of the desired system.

3.2 Queries, Commands and Constraints

Once the students have devised a set of concepts for their system, the next step is to identify the queries, commands, and constraints associated with each concept. A *query* is a question that an concept must answer, such as "How tall are you in feet?"; a *command* is a directive that a concept must obey, such as "Open your drawer!"; and a *constraint* is a restriction on query responses or command contexts, such as "A desk must be made of at least one material." or "An open drawer cannot be opened." Composite query/commands (and query/queries) such as "Lock your drawer and tell me whether it was already locked!" are not allowed.

Students identify the queries, commands, and constraints for each concept as simple sentences using a restricted English vocabulary. This vocabulary includes the following: the concept names identified during concept analysis; numbers; comparison terms ("at least", "at most", etc.); articles; and some common nouns and verbs. Each query must end with a question mark, each command with an exclamation point, and each constraint with a period. When reading queries and commands aloud in class, this punctuation is overemphasized to drive the point home. This reinforces the fact that composite queries and commands are forbidden, because such mixed constructs cannot be written as simple English questions or exclamations.

By the end of this co-analysis step, the students and the instructor (recall that much of this process is performed initially *with* the instructor, thus *co*-analysis) have identified queries, commands, and constraints for every concept. Similar to the concept analysis, the goal is to have as few of these as possible while capturing the important characteristics of the concepts. Figure 1 shows a set of queries, commands, and constraints for a simple desk with a single drawer. This is by no means the only possible such set of queries, commands, and constraints; for instance, the length, width, and height are (roughly) what we consider "useful" sizes for a desk.

Queries

How tall are you in feet? / How wide are you in feet? / How deep are you in feet? / What materials are you made of? / Is your drawer open? / Is your drawer locked?

Commands

Open your drawer! / Close your drawer! / Lock your drawer! / Unlock your drawer!

Constraints

A desk must be between 2 and 8 feet tall. / A desk must be between 2 and 20 feet wide. / A desk must be between 2 and 8 feet deep. / A desk must be made of at least one material. / An open drawer cannot be opened. / A closed drawer cannot be closed. / A locked drawer cannot be opened.

Fig. 1. Queries, commands, and constraints associated with a simple desk

3.3 Java Module Skeletons

After identifying the queries, commands, and constraints, it is finally time for the students to start using a programming language, which at our current universities, for good or ill, is Java. However, students do not write any executable code at this stage. Instead, the concepts identified during analysis are refined into Java modules (classes, abstract classes, and interfaces, as appropriate) and primitive types, and clusters are refined into Java packages. Only a subset of the concepts identified in the first stage are refined into Java modules—there is rarely a one-to-one correspondence between concepts and module skeletons by the end of this step.

The queries, commands, and constraints associated with each concept are (literally) cut-and-pasted into the appropriate module as specially-formatted comments. Every module created in this step also has a Javadoc comment, which is likewise cut-and-pasted from its concept's definition.

Our simple desk concept is refined into a Java class *SimpleDesk*, and we assume the existence of a Java module for *Material*. We do not need new Java modules for the dimensions, which are represented by existing primitive types (e.g., `float`, `double`). Figure 2 shows the Java class skeleton for *SimpleDesk*.

3.4 Method Signatures

Having created the Java modules, the students move on to writing method signatures for each concept. Each query or command has exactly one method signature associated with it. Method signatures associated with queries must have non-`void` return types, and method signatures associated with commands must have `void` return types. The parameter types and return types of the methods

```
package formalmethods.ninja.furniture;

/**
 * A representation of a desk with a single drawer.
 *
 * @author Daniel M. Zimmerman
 * @author Joseph R. Kiniry
 * @version 9 November 2007
 */

public class SimplifiedDesk
{
  // @bon query

  // @query How tall are you in feet?
  // @query How wide are you in feet?
  // @query How deep are you in feet?
  // @query What materials are you made of?
  // @query Is your drawer open?
  // @query Is your drawer locked?

  // @bon command

  // @command Open your drawer!
  // @command Close your drawer!
  // @command Lock your drawer!
  // @command Unlock your drawer!

  // @bon constraint

  // @constraint A desk must be between 2 and 8 feet tall.
  // @constraint A desk must be between 2 and 20 feet wide.
  // @constraint A desk must be between 2 and 8 feet deep.
  // @constraint A desk must be made of at least one material.
  // @constraint An open drawer cannot be opened.
  // @constraint A closed drawer cannot be closed.
  // @constraint A locked drawer cannot be opened.
}
```

Fig. 2. Java class skeleton for a simple desk

are chosen from among the previously-created Java module skeletons and the core Java libraries and primitive types.

Every method has a Javadoc comment, which is written entirely using cut-and-paste. The `@return` tag of a query is exactly the original English query ("What materials are you made of?"), and the method description of a command is exactly the original English command. Method parameters, if any, are named starting with articles (`the_width`, `a_material`) or indexed with numbers (`material_1`, `material_2`). All these guidelines are automatically checked against our code standard using the aforementioned static style checker.

At this stage, each method body consists of exactly the following: (1) the JML assertion `//@ assert false`; (2) the Java assertion `assert false`; and (3) for methods with return types, the Java statement `return null` (or a return of an appropriate default value of a primitive type, such as 0 for integral types). This default body enables the classes to compile before the methods are implemented, and also allows our tools to properly analyze the methods, as this initial implementation both signals that the method has not been implemented (differentiating it from a legal empty implementation) and is the "bottom" implementation with respect to refinement. Of course, our initiates do not know or understand these theoretical subtleties; they merely know that this is a very practical way to generate method stubs.

Figure 3 shows the *SimpleDesk* class with method signatures; for space reasons, we omit some of the methods.

3.5 JML Specifications

The method signatures from the previous step are the translation of the queries and commands into Java. The next step is the addition of JML specifications in the form of basic preconditions and postconditions on methods, and the translation of the BON constraints into JML invariants. Also, every query is labeled with the JML annotation "`pure`", which indicates that the method does not change any system state.

For example, the constraint "A desk must have at least one leg." (on a more complex desk class than the one in our example) might be translated into both a class invariant (`0 < numberOfLegs()`) and a precondition on the method `removeLeg` (`1 < numberOfLegs()`). These specifications are written collaboratively (remember, this is *co*-design); young students are only expected to be able to read them, while older, more advanced students are expected to be able to write them as well.

Figure 4 shows the *SimpleDesk* class from Figure 3 after JML specifications have been added.

3.6 Method Bodies and Fields

The final step, which takes place only after all method signatures and JML specifications are completed, is when the students, working individually or in teams, finally get to write executable code. They take this step without our direct involvement.

At this point, programming is something of a fill-in-the-blanks exercise. All the students need to do is write code in each method to fulfill the specification, concretize fields to represent essential data, and (optionally) write a `main()` method somewhere to actually run the system. They are encouraged to implement methods in a bottom-up fashion, focusing on "leaf" methods and simple queries first and complex methods later.

Recall that students have thousands of pre-generated test cases as well as tools like ESC/Java2 at their disposal. They are encouraged to regularly run these tests and tools as they write their code. In the vast majority of cases, the code that students write at this stage "just works" on the first try; this is a very different result from the code written in most introductory software engineering classes, and gives students a concrete sense of accomplishment.

```java
package formalmethods.ninja.furniture;

import java.util.Collection;

/**
 * A representation of a desk with a single drawer.
 *
 * @author Daniel M. Zimmerman
 * @author Joseph R. Kiniry
 * @version 9 November 2007
 */
public class SimpleDesk {
  // @bon query

  /** @return How tall are you in feet? */
  public float height() {
    //@ assert false;
    assert false;
    return 0.0f;
  }

  // width() and depth() are symmetric with height()

  /** @return What materials are you made of? */
  public Collection<Material> materials() {
    //@ assert false;
    assert false;
    return null;
  }

  /** @return Is your drawer open? */
  public boolean isDrawerOpen() {
    //@ assert false;
    assert false;
    return false;
  }

  // isDrawerLocked() is symmetric with isDrawerOpen()

  // @bon command

  /** Open your drawer! */
  public void openDrawer() {
    //@ assert false;
    assert false;
  }

  // closeDrawer(), lockDrawer(), and unlockDrawer() are symmetric with openDrawer()

  // @bon constraint

  // @constraint A desk must be between 2 and 8 feet tall.
  // @constraint A desk must be between 2 and 20 feet wide.
  // @constraint A desk must be between 2 and 8 feet deep.
  // @constraint A desk must be made of at least one material.
  // @constraint An open drawer cannot be opened.
  // @constraint A closed drawer cannot be closed.
  // @constraint A locked drawer cannot be opened.
}
```

Fig. 3. Java class skeleton with method signatures for a simple desk

```java
package formalmethods.ninja.furniture;

import java.util.Collection;

/**
 * A representation of a desk with a single drawer.
 *
 * @author Daniel M. Zimmerman
 * @author Joseph R. Kiniry
 * @version 9 November 2007
 */
public class SimpleDesk {
  // @bon query

  /** @return How tall are you in feet? */
  public /*@ pure */ float height() {
    //@ assert false;
    assert false;
    return 0.0f;
  }

  // width() and depth() are symmetric with height()

  /** @return What materials are you made of? */
  //@ ensures \result.size() >= 1;
  public /*@ pure */ Collection<Material> materials() {
    //@ assert false;
    assert false;
    return null;
  }

  /** @return Is your drawer open? */
  public /*@ pure */ boolean isDrawerOpen() {
    //@ assert false;
    assert false;
    return false;
  }

  // isDrawerLocked() is symmetric with isDrawerOpen()

  // @bon command

  /** Open your drawer! */
  //@ requires !isDrawerOpen();
  //@ requires !isDrawerLocked();
  //@ ensures isDrawerOpen();
  public void openDrawer() {
    //@ assert false;
    assert false;
  }

  // closeDrawer(), lockDrawer(), and unlockDrawer() are symmetric with openDrawer()

  // @bon constraint
  // @constraint A desk must be between 2 feet and 8 feet tall.
  //@ public invariant 2.0 <= height() && height() <= 8.0;
  // (width and depth constraints and invariants are symmetric with height)
  // (other constraints have no corresponding invariants)
}
```

Fig. 4. Java class skeleton with JML specifications for a simple desk

4 Notes from the Dōjō

We now reflect upon some of our choices, successes and failures, and student reactions in our classrooms. To date, we have received primarily informal student feedback through in-class and online anonymous questionnaires, the results of which are public and available via the aforementioned website. The qualitative evidence from this feedback suggests that the training we provide in our formal methods *dōjō* is both well-received and successful. However, we recognize that more quantitative evidence is necessary to refine our training techniques, and are currently undertaking a study to gather data about student adoption of formal methods.

Student reactions to several of our choices have been excellent. As previously mentioned, Java is used in other courses at all the universities where we have used this approach, and the students are comfortable with it. JML feels just like Java with a handful of extra keywords, the tool support for JML with Java 1.4 is very good, and students generally enjoy using our enriched Eclipse and the Moodle online course management system. Also, students seem to enjoy our process and adopt it well, and many use it in subsequent software engineering and design courses.

On the other hand, our tool arsenal is currently lacking in two main respects. First, EBON tool support is poor. We provide a minimal shell script for extracting BON specifications from annotated Java code and use both EiffelStudio and BlueJ for carrying out the initial design stages of our approach. However, these tools are not a perfect fit, as EiffelStudio does not support Java and BlueJ does not support BON. Work is underway on new tools to directly support EBON, and we will quickly adopt these tools once they become available. In fact, the first version of our new BON specification checker, BONC, was released recently and is now being used in our software engineering courses.

Second, because JML does not currently support Java 1.5 language features such as generics, enhanced `for` loops, and autoboxing, the contexts in which we can use the JML tools are more limited than we would like. Students that have already been exposed to these language features are (understandably) reluctant to do without them in order to use the tools. Projects such as JML4 [9] that aim to update JML for use with current Java virtual machines will alleviate this problem in the near future.

In addition to these tool-related shortcomings, we have received significant negative feedback about the user interface of the GForge. We have therefore decided to replace the GForge with a Trac server for the current academic year. Trac's excellent interface and integration of a wiki, a tracker, and version control allow us to eliminate the haphazard use of various suboptimally-realized subsystems in the Moodle (e.g., its wiki) and the GForge.

We have customized our Trac server significantly, using over a dozen plugins to enrich its capabilities for our teaching practices. One of these plugins supports Mylyn, an Eclipse feature for task management that we will use in some classes this year. With Mylyn, students are able to interact with the Trac server directly from within Eclipse. Mylyn also provides support for context-aware, task-focused software development—a style we have taught previously, but have been unable to enforce.

5 Conclusion

We hope that you, the reader, have not been offended by our ninja metaphors and are, perhaps, intrigued by our unique integration of applied formal methods into undergraduate instruction. We welcome your inquiries, and have made large amounts of quality pedagogical materials available including slides, projects, videos, tutorials, papers, etc. Perhaps you, too, might enter our *dōjō* and adopt the *Way of the Formal Methods Ninja*.

References

1. Dean, C.N., Hinchey, M.G. (eds.): Teaching and Learning Formal Methods. Academic Press, London (1996)
2. Hoare, S.T.: Towards the Verifying Compiler. In: Aichernig, B.K., Maibaum, T.S.E. (eds.) Formal Methods at the Crossroads. From Panacea to Foundational Support. LNCS, vol. 2757, pp. 151–160. Springer, Heidelberg (2003)
3. Grogono, P.: Comments, assertions, and pragmas. ACM SIGPLAN Notices 24(3) (1989)
4. Jézéquel, J., Meyer, B.: Design by contract: The lessons of Ariane, January 1997, pp. 129–130. IEEE Computer Society Press, Los Alamitos (1997)
5. Waldén, K., Nerson, J.M.: Seamless Object-Oriented Software Architecture - Analysis and Design of Reliable Systems. Prentice-Hall, Inc., Englewood Cliffs (1995)
6. Burdy, L., Cheon, Y., Cok, D., Ernst, M., Kiniry, J., Leavens, G.T., Leino, K., Poll, E.: An overview of JML tools and applications. In: International Journal on Software Tools for Technology Transfer (February 2005)
7. Kiniry, J.R., Cok, D.R.: ESC/Java2: Uniting ESC/Java and JML. In: Barthe, G., Burdy, L., Huisman, M., Lanet, J.-L., Muntean, T. (eds.) CASSIS 2004. LNCS, vol. 3362, pp. 108–128. Springer, Heidelberg (2005)
8. Kiniry, J.R.: The KindSoftware coding standard. Technical report, KindSoftware Research Group, UCD (2005), `http://secure.ucd.ie/`
9. Chalin, P., James, P.R., Karabotsos, G.: An integrated verification environment for JML: Architecture and early results. In: Sixth International Workshop on Specification and Verification of Component-Based Systems (SAVCBS), Cavtat, Croatia, September 2007, pp. 47–53 (2007)

Specification and Checking of Software Contracts for Conditional Information Flow*

Torben Amtoft[1], John Hatcliff[1], Edwin Rodríguez[1], Robby[1], Jonathan Hoag[1], and David Greve[2]

[1] Kansas State University Manhattan, KS 66506, USA
{tamtoft,hatcliff,edwin,robby,jch5588}@cis.ksu.edu
[2] Rockwell Collins Cedar Rapids, IA, USA
dagreve@rockwellcollins.com

Abstract. Information assurance applications providing *Multi-Level Secure* (MLS) solutions must often implement information flow policies that are *conditional* in the sense that data is allowed to flow between system components only when the system satisfies certain state predicates. However, existing specification and verification environments, such as SPARK, used to develop such applications, are capable of capturing only unconditional information flows. Motivated by the need to better formally specify and certify MLS applications in industrial contexts, we present an enhancement of the SPARK system that enables specification, inference, and compositional checking of conditional information flow contracts. We report on the use of this framework for a collection of SPARK examples.

1 Introduction

National and international infrastructures as well as commercial services are increasingly relying on complex distributed systems that share information with *Multiple Levels of Security* (MLS). These systems often seek to coalesce information with mixed security levels into information streams that are targeted to particular clients. For example, in a national emergency response system, some data will be privileged (*e.g.*, information regarding availability of military assets, and deployment orders for those assets) and some data will be public (*e.g.*, weather and mapping information).

The *Multiple Independent Levels of Security* (MILS) architecture [25] proposes to make development, accreditation, and deployment of MLS-capable systems more practical, achievable, and affordable by providing a certified infrastructure *foundation for systems that require assured information sharing*. In the MILS architecture, systems are developed on top of: (a) a "separation kernel", a concept introduced by Rushby [21]

---

* This work was supported in part by the US National Science Foundation (NSF) awards 0454348, 0429141, and CAREER award 0644288, the US Air Force Office of Scientific Research (AFOSR), and Rockwell Collins. The authors gratefully acknowledge insightful comments from Matt Benke at the US Department of Defense, and the assistance of Rod Chapman and Trevor Jennings of Praxis High Integrity Systems in obtaining SPARK examples and running the SPARK tools.

which guarantees isolation and controlled communication between application components deployed in different virtual "partitions" supported by the kernel, and (b) MLS middleware services such as "high assurance guards" that allow information to flow between various partitions, and between trusted and untrusted segments of a network, only when certain *conditions* are satisfied.

Researchers at the Rockwell Collins Advanced Technology Center are industry leaders in certifying MILS components according to standards such as the Common Criteria (EAL 6/7) that mandate the use of formal methods. For example, Rockwell Collins engineers carried out the certification of the hardware-based separation kernel in Rockwell Collins' AAMP7 processor (this was the first such certification of a MILS separation kernel and it formed the initial draft of the Common Criteria Protection Profile for Separation Kernels). Product groups at Rockwell Collins are building several different information assurance products on top of the AAMP7 that leverage the underlying MILS architecture. These products are often programmed using the SPARK subset of Ada [7]. A motivating factor for the use of SPARK is that it includes annotations (formal contracts for procedure interfaces) for specifying and checking information flow [9]. These annotations often play a key role in the certification of such products. The SPARK language and associated tool-set is the only commercial product that we know of which can support checking of code-level information flow contracts, and SPARK provides a number of well-designed and effective capabilities for specifying and verifying properties of highly critical implementations.

Even with SPARK, however, developers are sometimes unable to provide complete, machine-checkable arguments for the correctness of information assurance products. This is due to certain limitations in the SPARK information flow framework, in particular: SPARK information flow annotations are unconditional (e.g., they capture such statements as "executing procedure P may cause information to flow from input variable X to output variable Y"), but MLS security policies are often conditional (e.g., "data from input variable X is only allowed to flow to output variable Y when state variables G_1 and G_2 satisfy certain conditions"). Thus, SPARK currently can neither capture nor support verification of certain critical aspects of MLS security policies (treating such conditional flows as unconditional flows in SPARK is an over-approximation that leads to many false alarms).

In previous work, Amtoft and Banerjee have developed Hoare logics that enable compositional reasoning about information flow [2,1]. Inspired by challenge problems from Rockwell Collins, these logics were extended to support conditional information flow [4]. While the logic as presented in [4] exposed some foundational issues, it only supported intraprocedural analysis, it required developers to specify information flow loop invariants, the verification algorithm was not yet fully implemented (and thus no experience was reported), and the core logic was not mapped to a practical method contract language capable of supporting compositional reasoning in industrial settings.

In this paper, we address these limitations by describing how the logic can provide a foundation for a practical information flow contract language capable of supporting compositional reasoning about conditional information flows. The specific contributions of our work are as follows:

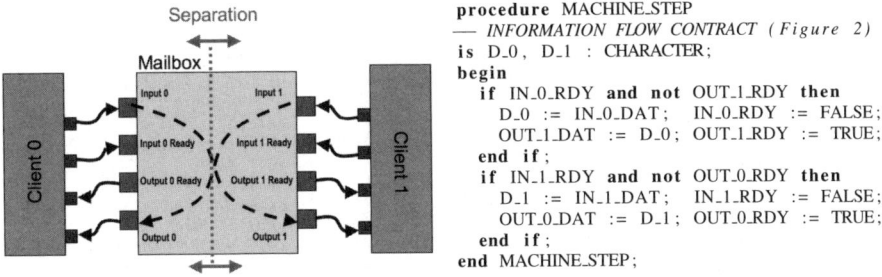

Fig. 1. Simple MLS Guard - mailbox mediates communication between partitions

- we propose an extension to SPARK's information flow contract language that supports conditional information flow, and we describe how the logic of [4] can be used to provide a semantics for the resulting framework,
- we extend the algorithm of [4] to support procedure calls and thus modularity,
- we present a strategy for automatically inferring conditional information flow invariants for while loops, thus significantly reducing developers' annotation burden,
- we provide an implementation that can automatically generate conditional information flow contracts from unannotated source code, and
- we report on experiments applying the implementation to a collection of examples.

Recent efforts for certifying MILS separation kernels [13,14] applied ACL2 [16] or PVS [19] theorem provers to formal models; extensive inspections were then required by certification authorities to establish the correspondence between model and source code. Because our approach is directly integrated with code, it complements these earlier efforts by: (a) removing the "trust gaps" associated with inspecting behavioral models (built manually), and (b) allowing many verification obligations to be discharged earlier in the life cycle by developers while leaving only the most complicated obligations to certification teams. Moreover, our logic-based approach provides a foundation for producing independently auditable and machine-checkable *evidence* of correctness and MILS policy compliance as recommended [15] by the National Research Council's Committee on Certifiably Dependable Software Systems.

2 Example

Figure 1 illustrates the conceptual information flows in a fragment of a simplistic MLS component. Rockwell Collins engineers constructed this example to illustrate, to NSA and industry representatives, the specification and verification challenges facing the developers of MLS software. The "Mailbox" component in the center of the diagram mediates communication between two client processes – each running on its own partition in the separation kernel. *Client 0* writes data to communicate in the memory segment *Input 0* that is shared between *Client 0* and the mailbox, then it sets the *Input 0 Ready* flag. The mailbox process polls its ready flags; when it finds that, *e.g.*, *Input 0 Ready* is set and *Output 1 Ready* is cleared (indicating that *Client 1* has already consumed data

```
--#  global  in out  IN_0_RDY,  IN_1_RDY,
--#                  OUT_0_RDY, OUT_1_RDY,
--#                  OUT_0_DAT, OUT_1_DAT;
--#          in      IN_0_DAT,  IN_1_DAT;
--#  derives
--#    OUT_0_DAT from IN_1_DAT, OUT_0_DAT,
--#                   OUT_0_RDY, IN_1_RDY &
--#    OUT_1_DAT from IN_0_DAT, OUT_1_DAT,
--#                   IN_0_RDY, OUT_1_RDY &
--#    IN_0_RDY  from IN_0_RDY, OUT_1_RDY &
--#    IN_1_RDY  from IN_1_RDY, OUT_0_RDY &
--#    OUT_0_RDY from OUT_0_RDY, IN_1_RDY &
--#    OUT_1_RDY from OUT_1_RDY, IN_0_RDY;
                       (a)
```

```
--# derives
--#    OUT_0_DAT from
--#      IN_1_DAT when
--#        (IN_1_RDY and not OUT_0_RDY),
--#      OUT_0_DAT when
--#        (not IN_1_RDY or OUT_0_RDY),
--#      OUT_0_RDY, IN_1_RDY &
--#    OUT_1_DAT from
--#      IN_0_DAT when
--#        (IN_0_RDY and not OUT_1_RDY),
--#      OUT_1_DAT when
--#        (not IN_0_RDY or OUT_1_RDY),
--#      OUT_1_RDY, IN_0_RDY
                       (b)
```

Fig. 2. (a) SPARK information flow contract for Mailbox example. (b) Fragment of same example with proposed conditional information flow extensions (Section 4).

deposited in the *Output 1* slot in a previous communication), then it copies the data from *Input 0* to *Output 1* and clears *Input 0 Ready* and sets *Output 1 Ready*. The communication from *Client 1* to *Client 0* follows a symmetric set of steps. The actions to be taken in each execution frame are encoded in SPARK by the MACHINE_STEP procedure of Fig. 1.

Figure 2(a) shows SPARK annotations for the MACHINE_STEP procedure, whose information flow properties are captured by derives annotations. It requires that each parameter and each global variable referenced by the procedure be classified as in (read only), out (written, and initial values [values at call point] are unread), or in out (written, and initial values read). For a procedure P, variables annotated as in or in out are called *input variables* and denoted IN_P; variables annotated as out or in out are *output variables* and denoted as OUT_P. Each output variable x_o must have a derives annotation indicating the input variables whose initial values are used to directly or indirectly calculate the final value of x_o. One can also think of each derives clause as expressing a dependence relation (or program slice) between an output variable and the input variables that it transitively depends on (via both data and control dependence). For example, the second derives clause specifies that on each MACHINE_STEP execution the output value of OUT_1_DAT is possibly determined by the input values of several variables: from IN_0_DAT when the Mailbox forwards data supplied by *Client 0*, from OUT_1_DAT when the conditions on the ready flags are not satisfied (OUT_1_DAT's output value then is its input value), and from OUT_1_RDY and IN_0_RDY because these variables *control* whether or not data flows from *Client 0* on a particular machine step (*i.e.*, they *guard* the flow).

While upper levels of the MILS architecture require reasoning about lattices of security levels (*e.g.*, *unclassified*, *secret*, *top secret*), the policies of infrastructure components such as separation kernels and guard applications usually focus on data separation policies (reasoning about flows between components of program state), and we restrict ourselves to such reasoning in this paper.

No other commercial language framework provides automatically checkable information flow specifications, so the use of the information flow checking framework in SPARK is a significant step forward. As illustrated above, SPARK derives clauses can be used to specify flows of information from input variables to output variables, but they do not have enough expressive power to state that information only flows under specific conditions. For example, in the Mailbox code, information from IN_0_DAT only flows to OUT_1_DAT when the flag IN_0_RDY is set and the flag OUT_1_READY is cleared. Unfortunately, the SPARK derives cannot distinguish the flag variables as guards nor phrase the conditions under which the guards allow information to pass or be blocked. This means that guarding logic, which is central to many MLS applications including those developed at Rockwell Collins, *is completely absent from the checkable specifications* in SPARK. In general, the lack of ability to express *conditional* information flow not only inhibits automatic verification of guarding logic specifications, but also results in imprecision which cascades and builds throughout the specifications in the application.

3 Foundations of SPARK Conditional Information Flow

The SPARK subset of Ada is designed for programming and verifying high assurance applications such as avionics applications certified to DO-178B Level A. It deliberately omits constructs that are difficult to reason about such as dynamically created data, pointers, and exceptions. Below, we present the syntax of a simple imperative language with assertions that one can consider to be an idealized version of SPARK.

Assertions
$\phi ::= B \mid \phi \wedge \phi$
$\quad \mid \phi \vee \phi \mid \neg \phi$

Expressions
$A ::= x \mid c \mid A \text{ op } A$
$B ::= A \text{ bop } A$

Commands
$S ::= \text{skip} \mid x := A \mid \text{assert}(\phi)$
$\quad \mid S\,;S \mid \text{if } B \text{ then } S \text{ else } S$
$\quad \mid \text{call } p \mid \text{while } B \text{ do } S$

Features of SPARK that we do not consider here include the package and inheritance structure, records, and arrays. From these, only arrays present conceptual challenges. Our current implementation treats arrays as atomic entities, just as SPARK does. The extended version of this paper [5] describes how our logical approach can reason about individual elements of arrays (giving more precision than SPARK), a feature which is currently being included in our implementation. We consider both arithmetic (A) and boolean (B) expressions where we use $x, y, \ldots$ to range over variables, c to range over integer constants, p to range over named (parameterless) procedures, op to range over arithmetic operators in $\{+, \times, \text{mod}, \ldots\}$, and bop to range over comparison operators in $\{=, <, \ldots\}$. Using parameterless procedures simplifies our exposition; our implementation supports procedures with parameters (there are no conceptual challenges in this extended functionality). For an expression E (arithmetic or boolean), we write $\text{fv}(E)$ for the variables occurring free in E, and $E[A/x]$ for the result of substituting in E all occurrences of x by A.

The semantics of an arithmetic expression $[\![A]\!]$ is a function from stores into values, where a value ($v \in Val$) is an integer n and where a *store* $s \in Store$ maps variables to values; we write $dom(s)$ for the domain of s and write $[s|x \mapsto v]$ for the store that is like s except that it maps x into v. Similarly, $[\![B]\!]_s$ denotes a boolean. A command transforms the store into another store; hence its semantics is given in relational style, in the form $s[\![S]\!]s'$. For some S and s, there may not exist any s' such that $s[\![S]\!]s'$;

this can happen if a **while** loop does not terminate, or an **assert** fails. The details of the semantics are standard and thus omitted; implicitly we assume a global procedure environment P that for each p returns a relation between input and output stores.

Assertions ϕ are also called 1-assertions since they represent predicates on a single program state; we write $s \models \phi$ to denote that ϕ holds in s following the standard semantics. We write $\phi \vartriangleright_1 \phi'$ if whenever $s \models \phi$ also $s \models \phi'$. As usual we define $\phi_1 \to \phi_2$ as $\neg \phi_1 \vee \phi_2$; we also define *true* as $0 = 0$, and *false* as $0 = 1$.

Reasoning about information flow in terms of non-interference: MILS seeks to prevent security breaches that can occur via unauthorized/unintended information flow from one partition to another; thus previous certification efforts for MILS components have among the core requirements included the classical property of *non-interference* [12] which (in this setting) states: for every pair of runs of a program, if the runs agree on the initial values of one partition's data (but may disagree on the data of other partitions) then the runs also agree on the final values of that partition's data.

Capturing non-interference and secure information flow in a compositional logic: The logic developed in [2] was designed to verify specifications of the following form: *given two runs of P that initially agree on variables $x_1 \ldots x_n$, the runs agree on variables $y_1 \ldots y_m$ at the end of the runs*. This includes non-interference as a special case (let $x_1 \ldots x_n$, and $y_1 \ldots y_m$, be the variables of one partition). We may express such a specification, which makes the "end-to-end" (input to output) aspect of verifying confidentiality explicit, in Hoare-logic style as $\{x_1 \bowtie, \ldots, x_n \bowtie\} \, P \, \{y_1 \bowtie, \ldots, y_m \bowtie\}$, where the *agreement assertion* $x \bowtie$ is satisfied by a *pair* of states, s_1 and s_2, if $s_1(x) = s_2(x)$. With P the example program from Sect. 2, we would have, e.g.,

$$\{\text{IN\_1\_DAT}\bowtie, \text{OUT\_0\_DAT}\bowtie, \text{IN\_1\_RDY}\bowtie, \text{OUT\_0\_RDY}\bowtie\} \, P \, \{\text{OUT\_0\_DAT}\bowtie\}.$$

To capture conditional information flow, recent work [4] by Banerjee and Amtoft introduced *conditional* agreement assertions, also called *2-assertions*. They are of the form $\phi \Rightarrow E \bowtie$ which is satisfied by a pair of stores if either at least one of them does not satisfy ϕ, or they agree on the value of E:

$$s \,\&\, s_1 \models \phi \Rightarrow E\bowtie \text{ iff whenever } s \models \phi \text{ and } s_1 \models \phi \text{ then } [\![E]\!]_s = [\![E]\!]_{s_1}.$$

We use $\theta \in \mathbf{2Assert}$ to range over 2-assertions. For $\theta = (\phi \Rightarrow E\bowtie)$, we call ϕ the antecedent of θ and write $\phi = ant(\theta)$, and we call E the consequent of θ and write $E = con(\theta)$. We often write $E\bowtie$ for $true \Rightarrow E\bowtie$. We use $\Theta \in \mathcal{P}(\mathbf{2Assert})$ to range over sets of 2-assertions (where we often write θ for the singleton set $\{\theta\}$), with conjunction implicit. Thus, $s\&s_1 \models \Theta$ iff $\forall \theta \in \Theta : s\&s_1 \models \theta$.

Fig. 3(a) illustrates a simple derivation using conditional information flow assertions that answers the question: what is the source of information flowing into variable OUT_0_DAT? The natural way to read the derivation is from the bottom up (since our algorithm works "backwards"). Thus, for OUT_0_DAT$\bowtie$ to hold after execution of P, we must have D_1$\bowtie$ before line 3 (since data flows from D_1 to OUT_0_DAT), IN_1_DAT$\bowtie$ before line 2 (since data flows from IN_1_DAT to D_1), and before line 1 IN_1_RDY$\bowtie$ and OUT_0_RDY$\bowtie$ (since they *control* which branch of the condition is taken), along with conditional assertions. The pre-condition shows that the value of OUT_0_DAT

```
   {IN_1_RDY ∧ ¬OUT_0_RDY ⇒ IN_1_DATĸ,
    ¬IN_1_RDY ∨ OUT_0_RDY ⇒ OUT_0_DATĸ,
    IN_1_RDYĸ, OUT_0_RDYĸ}
1. if IN_1_RDY and not OUT_0_RDY then
   {IN_1_DATĸ}
2.   D_1 := IN_1_DAT; IN_1_RDY := false;
   {D_1ĸ}
3. OUT_0_DAT := D_1; OUT_0_RDY := true;
   {OUT_0_DATĸ}
4. fi
   {OUT_0_DATĸ}
              (a)
```

Summary information for p with $\text{OUT}_p = \{x\}$

derives x from y,
   z when $y > 0$,
   w when $y \leq 0$

Procedure call

$\{z > 7 \Rightarrow v\kappa, z > 5 \Rightarrow u\kappa, z > 5 \Rightarrow y\kappa,$
$z > 5 \wedge y > 0 \Rightarrow z\kappa, z > 5 \wedge y \leq 0 \Rightarrow w\kappa\}$
call p
$\{x > 5 \wedge z > 7 \Rightarrow v\kappa,$
$x > 7 \wedge z > 5 \Rightarrow (x+u)\kappa\}$
              (b)

Fig. 3. (a) A derivation for the mailbox example, illustrating the handling of conditionals. (b) An example illustrating the handling of procedure calls (Section 5).

depends *unconditionally* on IN_1_RDY and OUT_0_RDY, and *conditionally* on IN_1_DAT and OUT_0_DAT, just as we would expect.

Relations between agreement assertions: We define $\Theta \triangleright_2 \Theta'$ to hold iff for all s, s_1: whenever $s \& s_1 \models \Theta$ then also $s \& s_1 \models \Theta'$. In development terms, when $\Theta \triangleright_2 \Theta'$ holds we can think of Θ as a *refinement* of of Θ', and Θ' an *abstraction* of Θ. For example, $\{x\kappa, y\kappa\}$ refines $x\kappa$ by adding an (unconditional) agreement assertion, and $z < 10 \Rightarrow x\kappa$ refines $z < 7 \Rightarrow x\kappa$ by weakening the antecedent of a 2-assertion.

We define a function *decomp* that converts arbitrary 2-assertions into assertions with only variables as consequents: $decomp(\Theta) = \{\phi \Rightarrow x\kappa \mid \phi \Rightarrow E\kappa \in \Theta, x \in \text{fv}(E)\}$. For example, $decomp(\phi \Rightarrow (x+y)\kappa) = \{\phi \Rightarrow x\kappa, \phi \Rightarrow y\kappa\}$.

Fact 1. *For all Θ, $decomp(\Theta)$ is a refinement of Θ.*

The converse does not hold, with a counterexample being $s \& s_1 \models (x + y)\kappa$ but not $s \& s_1 \models x\kappa$ or $s \& s_1 \models y\kappa$, as when $s(x) = s_1(y) = 3, s(y) = s_1(x) = 7$.

4 Conditional Information Flow Contracts

4.1 Foundations of Flow Contracts

The syntax of a SPARK derives annotation for a procedure P (as illustrated in Figure 2(a)) can be represented formally as a relation $\mathcal{D}_P$ between OUT_P and $\mathcal{P}(\text{IN}_P)$. A particular clause $\text{derives}(x, \bar{y}) \in \mathcal{D}_P$ declares that the final value of output variable x depends on the input values of variables $\bar{y} = y_1, \ldots, y_k$. The correctness of such a clause as a contract for P can be expressed in terms of the logic of the preceding section, as requiring the triple $\{\bar{y}\kappa\}\ S\ \{x\kappa\}$ where S is the body of procedure P and where $\bar{y}\kappa$ is a shorthand for $\{y_1\kappa, \ldots, y_k\kappa\}$.

Because $\mathcal{D}_P$ contains multiple clauses (one for each output variable of P), it captures multiple "channels" of information flow through P. Therefore, we cannot simply describe the semantics of a multi-clause derives contract $\{\text{derives}(x, \bar{y}), \text{derives}(z, \bar{w})\}$ as $\{(\bar{y}\bar{w})\kappa\}\ S\ \{x\kappa, z\kappa\}$ because this would confuse the dependencies associated with x and z, i.e., it would allow z to depend on $\bar{y}$. Accordingly, the full semantics of SPARK derives contracts is supported by what we term a *multi-channel version* of the logic which is extended to include *indexed agreement assertions* $x \bowtie_c$ indexed by a channel identifier c – which one can associate with a particular output variable. In the multi-channel logic, the confused triple above can now be correctly stated as $\{\bar{y}\bowtie_x, \bar{w}\bowtie_z\}\ S\ \{x\bowtie_x, z\bowtie_z\}$. (Alternatively, we could have *two* single-channel triples: $\{\bar{y}\bowtie\}\ S\ \{x\bowtie\}$ and $\{\bar{w}\bowtie\}\ S\ \{z\bowtie\}$.) The algorithm to be given in Sect. 5 extends to the multi-channel version of the logic in a straightforward manner, and our implementation supports the multi-channel version of the logic. For simplicity, we present the semantics of contracts using the single-channel version of the logic.

We now give a more convenient notation for triples of the form $\{\Theta\}\ P\ \{\Theta'\}$. A flow judgement κ is of the form $\Theta \leadsto \Theta'$, with Θ the precondition and with Θ' the postcondition. We say that $\Theta \leadsto \Theta'$ is valid for command S, written $S \models \Theta \leadsto \Theta'$, if whenever $s_1 \& s_2 \models \Theta$ and $s_1 [\![S]\!] s_1'$ and $s_2 [\![S]\!] s_2'$ then also $s_1' \& s_2' \models \Theta'$ (if the 2-assertions in the precondition hold for input states s_1 and s_2, the postcondition must also hold for associated output states s_1' and s_2').

4.2 Language Design for Conditional SPARK Contracts

The logic of the preceding section is potentially much more powerful than what we actually want to expose to developers – instead, we view it as a "core calculus" in which information flow reasoning is expressed. To determine how much of the power of the logic we wish to expose to developers in enhanced SPARK conditional information flow contracts, our design goals are: (1) writing the contracts should be as simple as possible, (2) the contracts should be able to capture common idioms of MILS information guarding, (3) the contract checking framework should be compositional so as to support MILS goals, and (4) there should be a natural progression (e.g., via formal refinements) from unconditional derives statements to conditional statements.

Simplifying assertions: The agreement assertions from the logic of Sect. 3 have the form $\phi \Rightarrow E\bowtie$. Here E is an arbitrary expression (not necessarily a variable), whereas SPARK derives statements are phrased in terms of IN/OUT variables only. We believe that including arbitrary expressions in SPARK conditional derives statements would add significant complexity for developers, and our experimental studies have shown that little increase in precision would be gained by such an approach. Instead, we retain the use of expression-based assertions $\phi \Rightarrow E\bowtie$ only during intermediate (automated) steps of the analysis. Appealing to Fact 1, we have a canonical way of strengthening, at procedure boundaries, $\phi \Rightarrow E\bowtie$ to $\phi \Rightarrow w_1\bowtie, \ldots, \phi \Rightarrow w_k\bowtie$ where $\mathrm{fv}(E) = \{w_1, \ldots, w_k\}$. A second simplification relates to the fact that the core logic allows both pre- and post-conditions to be conditional (e.g., $\{\phi_1 \Rightarrow E_1\bowtie\}\ P\ \{\phi_2 \Rightarrow E_2\bowtie\}$ where ϕ_1 and ϕ_2 may differ). Based on discussions with developers at Rockwell Collins and initial experiments, we believe that this would expose too much power/complexity to developers leading to unwieldy contracts and confusion about the underlying semantics. Accordingly, we are currently pursuing an approach in which only preconditions can be conditional. Combining these two simplifications, SPARK derives clauses are extended to allow conditions on input variables as follows:

```
derives x from    y₁ when φ₁,   ...,   yₖ when φₖ
```

$\{\Theta\}\ (R) \Longleftarrow \mathbf{skip}\ \{\Theta'\}$ iff $R = \{(\theta, u, \theta) \mid \theta \in \Theta'\}$ and $\Theta = \Theta'$

$\{\Theta\}\ (R) \Longleftarrow \mathbf{assert}(\phi_0)\ \{\Theta'\}$ iff $R = \{((\phi \wedge \phi_0) \Rightarrow E\kappa, u, \phi \Rightarrow E\kappa) \mid \phi \Rightarrow E\kappa \in \Theta'\}$ and $\Theta = dom(R)$

$\{\Theta\}\ (R) \Longleftarrow x := A\ \{\Theta'\}$ iff $R = \{(\phi[A/x] \Rightarrow E[A/x]\kappa, \gamma, \phi \Rightarrow E\kappa) \mid \phi \Rightarrow E\kappa \in \Theta'\}$,
where $\gamma = m$ iff $x \in fv(E)$, and $\Theta = dom(R)$

$\{\Theta\}\ (R) \Longleftarrow S_1\ ;S_2\ \{\Theta'\}$ iff $\{\Theta''\}\ (R_2) \Longleftarrow S_2\ \{\Theta'\}$ and $\{\Theta\}\ (R_1) \Longleftarrow S_1\ \{\Theta''\}$
and $R = \{(\theta, \gamma, \theta') \mid \exists \theta'', \gamma_1, \gamma_2 : (\theta, \gamma_1, \theta'') \in R_1, (\theta'', \gamma_2, \theta') \in R_2\}$, where $\gamma = m$ iff $\gamma_1 = m$ or $\gamma_2 = m$

$\{\Theta\}\ (R) \Longleftarrow \mathbf{if}\ B\ \mathbf{then}\ S_1\ \mathbf{else}\ S_2\ \{\Theta'\}$
iff $\{\Theta_1\}\ (R_1) \Longleftarrow S_1\ \{\Theta'\}$, $\{\Theta_2\}\ (R_2) \Longleftarrow S_2\ \{\Theta'\}$, $R = R'_1 \cup R'_2 \cup R'_0 \cup R_0$, and $\Theta = dom(R)$,
where $R'_1 = \{((\phi_1 \wedge B) \Rightarrow E_1\kappa, m, \theta') \mid \theta' \in \Theta'_m, (\phi_1 \Rightarrow E_1\kappa, \_, \theta') \in R_1\}$
and $R'_2 = \{((\phi_2 \wedge \neg B) \Rightarrow E_2\kappa, m, \theta') \mid \theta' \in \Theta'_m, (\phi_2 \Rightarrow E_2\kappa, \_, \theta') \in R_2\}$
and $R'_0 = \{(((\phi_1 \wedge B) \vee (\phi_2 \wedge \neg B)) \Rightarrow B\kappa, m, \theta') \mid \theta' \in \Theta'_m, (\phi_1 \Rightarrow E_1\kappa, \_, \theta') \in R_1, (\phi_2 \Rightarrow E_2\kappa, \_, \theta') \in R_2\}$
and $R_0 = \{(((\phi_1 \wedge B) \vee (\phi_2 \wedge \neg B)) \Rightarrow E\kappa, u, \theta') \mid \theta' \in \Theta'_u, (\phi_1 \Rightarrow E\kappa, u, \theta') \in R_1, (\phi_2 \Rightarrow E\kappa, u, \theta') \in R_2\}$
and $\Theta'_m = \{\theta' \in \Theta' \mid \exists(\_, m, \theta') \in R_1 \cup R_2\}$ and $\Theta'_u = \Theta' \setminus \Theta'_m$

$\{\Theta\}\ (R) \Longleftarrow \mathbf{call}\ p\ \{\Theta'\}$
iff $R = R_u \cup R_0 \cup R_m$ and $\Theta = dom(R)$,
where $R_u = \{(rm^+_{\text{OUT}_P}(\phi) \Rightarrow E\kappa, u, \phi \Rightarrow E\kappa) \mid (\phi \Rightarrow E\kappa) \in \Theta' \wedge fv(E) \cap \text{OUT}_P = \emptyset\}$
and $R_0 = \{(rm^+_{\text{OUT}_P}(\phi) \Rightarrow x\kappa, m, \phi \Rightarrow E\kappa) \mid (\phi \Rightarrow E\kappa) \in \Theta' \wedge fv(E) \cap \text{OUT}_P \neq \emptyset \wedge x \in fv(E) \wedge x \notin \text{OUT}_P\}$
and $R_m = \{(rm^+_{\text{OUT}_P}(\phi) \wedge \phi^y_x \Rightarrow y\kappa, m, \phi \Rightarrow E\kappa)$
$\mid (\phi \Rightarrow E\kappa) \in \Theta' \wedge x \in fv(E) \cap \text{OUT}_P \wedge \phi^y_x \Rightarrow y\kappa$ among preconditions for $x\kappa$ in p's summary $\}$

$\{\Theta\}\ (R) \Longleftarrow \mathbf{while}\ B\ \mathbf{do}\ S_0\ \{\Theta'\}$
iff $R = R_u \cup R_m$ and $\Theta = dom(R)$, where for each x (in X) we inductively in i define $\phi^i_x, \Theta^i, R^i, \psi^i_x$ by
$\phi^0_x = \bigvee\{\phi \mid \exists E : (\phi \Rightarrow E\kappa) \in \Theta' \wedge x \in fv(E)\}$, $\Theta^i = \{\phi^i_x \Rightarrow x\kappa \mid x \in X\}$, $\{\_\}\ (R^i) \Longleftarrow S_0\ \{\Theta^i\}$
$\psi^i_x = \bigvee\{\phi \mid \exists(\phi \Rightarrow E\kappa, \_, \_) \in R^i,\ x \in fv(E)\ \text{or}\ x \in fv(B),\ \exists(\theta, m, \theta') \in R^i,\ \phi \in \{ant(\theta), ant(\theta')\}\}$
$\phi^{i+1}_x = \mathbf{if}\ \psi^i_x \triangleright_1 \phi^i_x\ \mathbf{then}\ \phi^i_x\ \mathbf{else}\ \phi^i_x \vee \psi^i_x$,
and j is the least i such that $\Theta^i = \Theta^{i+1}$, and $R_m = \{(\theta, m, \theta') \mid \theta' \in \Theta'_m \wedge \theta \in \Theta^j \cup \{true \Rightarrow 0\kappa\}\}$
and $R_u = \{(\phi \Rightarrow E\kappa, u, \theta') \mid \theta' \in \Theta'_u, E = con(\theta'), (fv(E) = \emptyset, \phi = true) \vee (fv(E) \neq \emptyset, \phi = \bigvee_{x \in fv(E)}(\phi^j_x))\}$,
and $\Theta'_m = \{\theta' \in \Theta' \mid \exists x \in fv(con(\theta')) : \exists(\_, m, \_ \Rightarrow x\kappa) \in R^j\}$ and $\Theta'_u = \Theta' \setminus \Theta'_m$

Fig. 4. The Precondition Generator

Here $\phi_1 \ldots \phi_k$ are boolean expressions on the pre-state of the associated procedure P. Thus, the above specification can be read as "The value of variable x at the conclusion of executing P (for *any* final state s') is derived from those y_j where ϕ_j holds in the pre-state s from which s' is computed." Figure 2(b) shows how this can be used to specify conditional flows for procedure MACHINE_STEP in Fig. 1.

Design methodology separating guard logic from flow logic: The lack of conditional assertions in post-conditions has the potential to introduce imprecision. Yet, we believe the above approach to conditional expressions can be effective for the following reason: we have observed that information assurance application design tends to factor out the *guarding logic* (i.e., the pieces of state and associated state changes that determine *when* information can flow) from the code which propagates information. This follows a common pattern in embedded systems in which the control logic is often factored out from data computation logic.

Contract abstraction and refinement: For a practical design and development methodology, it is important to consider notions of contract abstraction (generalization) and refinement – ideally, conditional contracts should be a refinement of unconditional contracts. For example, we believe it will be easier to introduce conditional contracts into workflows if developers can: (1) make a rough cut at specifying information flows without conditions, and (2) systematically refine to produce conditional contracts, perhaps assisted by expert verification engineers. Conversely, if developers decide not to pursue a verification approach based on our conditional contracts, we want them to be able to safely abstract all conditional contracts back to unconditional SPARK contracts.

We now establish the desired notion of contract refinement (in terms of the general underlying calculus instead of its limited exposure in SPARK), by defining a relation between flow judgements: $\kappa_1 \vartriangleright_\kappa \kappa_2$, pronounced "$\kappa_1$ refines κ_2", to hold iff for all commands S, whenever $S \models \kappa_1$ then also $S \models \kappa_2$. To gain the proper intuition about contract refinement, it is important to note that the refinement relation is contra-variant in the pre-condition and co-variant in the post-condition: given $\kappa_1 \equiv \Theta_1 \leadsto \Theta_1'$ and $\kappa_2 \equiv \Theta_2 \leadsto \Theta_2'$, if $\Theta_2 \vartriangleright_2 \Theta_1$ and $\Theta_1' \vartriangleright_2 \Theta_2'$ then $\kappa_1 \vartriangleright_\kappa \kappa_2$. For example, $x \bowtie \leadsto y \bowtie \vartriangleright_\kappa x \bowtie, y \bowtie \leadsto y \bowtie$ holds because $x \bowtie, y \bowtie \vartriangleright_2 x \bowtie$ (Section 3). Intuitively, this captures the fact that a contract can always be *abstracted* to a weaker one by stating that the output variables may depend on additional input variables. This illustrates that our contracts capture "may" dependence modalities: output y *may* depend on both inputs x and y, but a refinement $x \bowtie \leadsto y \bowtie$ shows that output y need not depend on input y (the contract before refinement is an *over-approximation* of dependence information). Also, we have $(z<7 \Rightarrow x \bowtie \leadsto y \bowtie) \vartriangleright_\kappa (x \bowtie \leadsto y \bowtie)$ which realizes our design goals of achieving: (a) a formal refinement by adding conditions to a contract, and (b) a formal (safe) abstraction by removing conditions.

5 A Precondition Generation Algorithm

We define in Fig. 4 an algorithm Pre for inferring preconditions from postconditions. We write $\{\Theta\}\ (R) \Longleftarrow S\ \{\Theta'\}$ when, given command S and postcondition Θ', Pre returns a precondition Θ for S that is designed so as to be sufficient to establish Θ', and a relation R that associates each 2-assertion $\theta \in \Theta'$ with the 2-assertions in Θ needed to establish θ. R captures dependences between variables before and after the execution of S, and it also supports reasoning about multiple channels of information flow as discussed in Sect. 4.1, e.g., if $\{y_1y_2 \bowtie_x, y_1y_3 \bowtie_z\}\ S\ \{x \bowtie_x, z \bowtie_z\}$ then R will relate y_1 to x and to z, y_2 to x, and y_3 to z. More precisely, we have $R \subseteq \Theta \times \{m, u\} \times \Theta'$ where tags m,u are mnemonics for "modified" and "unmodified"; if $(\theta, u, \theta') \in R$ then additionally it holds that S modifies no "relevant" variable, where a "relevant" variable is one occurring in the consequent of θ'. We use γ to range over $\{m, u\}$, and write $dom(R) = \{\theta \mid \exists (\theta, \_, \_) \in R\}$ and $ran(R) = \{\theta' \mid \exists (\_, \_, \theta') \in R\}$.

Correctness results: If $\{\Theta\}\ (\_) \Longleftarrow S\ \{\Theta'\}$ then Θ is indeed a precondition (but not necessarily the *weakest* such) that is strong enough to establish Θ', as stated by:

Theorem 2 (Correctness). *Assume* $\{\Theta\}\ (\_) \Longleftarrow S\ \{\Theta'\}$. *Then* $S \models \Theta \leadsto \Theta'$. *That is, if* $s\&s_1 \models \Theta$, *and* s', s_1' *are such that* $s\ [\![S]\!]\ s'$ *and* $s_1\ [\![S]\!]\ s_1'$, *then* $s'\&s_1' \models \Theta'$.

Note that Theorem 2 is termination-*in*sensitive; this is not surprising given our choice of a relational semantics (but see [3] for a logic-based approach that is termination-sensitive). Also note that correctness is phrased directly wrt. the underlying semantics, unlike [2,1] which first establish the semantic soundness of a logic and next provide a sound implementation of that logic. Theorem 2 is proved [5] much as the corresponding

Specification and Checking of Software Contracts   239

result [4] (that handled a language with heap manipulation but without procedure calls and without automatic computation of loop invariants), by establishing some auxiliary properties (e.g., the R component) that have largely determined the design of Pre.

Intraprocedural analysis: We now explain the various clauses of Pre in Fig. 4, where the clause for **skip** is trivial. For an assignment $x := A$, each 2-assertion $\phi \Rightarrow E\ltimes$ in Θ' produces exactly one 2-assertion in Θ, given by substituting A for x (as in standard Hoare logic) in ϕ as well as in E; the connection is tagged m when x occurs in E. For example, if S is $x := w$ then R might contain the triplets $(q > 4 \Rightarrow w\ltimes, m, q > 4 \Rightarrow x\ltimes)$ and $(w > 3 \Rightarrow z\ltimes, u, x > 3 \Rightarrow z\ltimes)$. The rule for $S_1 ; S_2$ works backwards, first computing S_2's precondition which is then used to compute S_1's; the tags express that a consequent is modified iff it has been modified in either S_1 or S_2. The rule for **assert** allows us to weaken 2-assertions, by strengthening their antecedents; this is sound since execution will abort from stores not satisfying the new antecedents.

To illustrate and motivate the rule for conditionals, we shall use Fig. 3(a) where, given postcondition OUT_0_DAT$\ltimes$, the **then** branch generates (as the domain of R_1) precondition IN_1_DAT$\ltimes$ which by R'_1 contributes the first conditional assertion of the overall precondition. The **skip** command in the implicit **else** branch generates (as the domain of R_2) precondition OUT_0_DAT$\ltimes$ which by R'_2 contributes the second conditional assertion of the overall precondition. We must also capture that two runs, in order to agree on OUT_0_DAT after the conditional, must agree on the value of the test B; this is done by R'_0 which generates the precondition $(\mathit{true} \wedge B) \vee (\mathit{true} \wedge \neg B) \Rightarrow B\ltimes$; optimizations (not shown) in our algorithm simplify this to $B\ltimes$ and then use Fact. 1 to split out the variables in the conjuncts of B into the two unconditional assertions of the overall precondition. Finally, assume the postcondition contained an assertion $\phi \Rightarrow E\ltimes$ where E is not modified by either branch: if also ϕ is not modified then $\phi \Rightarrow E\ltimes$ belongs to both R_1 and R_2, and hence by R_0 also to the overall precondition; if ϕ is modified by one or both branches, R_0 generates a more complex antecedent for $E\ltimes$.

Interprocedural analysis: Recall from Sect. 4.2 that for a procedure summary, we allow only variables as consequents, and allow conditional assertions only in the preconditions. At a call site **call** p, antecedents in the call's postcondition will carry over to the precondition, *provided* that they do not involve variables in OUT$_P$. Otherwise, since our summaries express variable dependencies but not functional relationships, we cannot state an exact formula for modifying antecedents (unlike what is the case for assignments). Instead, we must conservatively strengthen the preconditions, by weakening their antecedents; this is done by an operator rm^+ such that if $\phi' = rm_X^+(\phi)$ (where $X =$ OUT$_p$) then ϕ logically implies ϕ' where ϕ' does not contain any variables from X. A trivial definition of rm^+ is to let it always return true (which drops all conditions associated with X), but we can often get something more precise; for instance, we can choose $rm_{\{x\}}^+(x > 7 \wedge z > 5) = (z > 5)$.

Equipped with rm^+, we can now define the analysis of procedure call, as done in Fig. 4 and illustrated in Fig. 3(b). In Fig. 4, R_u deals with assertions (such as $x > 5 \wedge z > 7 \Rightarrow v\ltimes$ in the example) whose consequent has not been modified by the procedure call (its "frame conditions" determined by the OUT declaration). For an assertion whose consequent E has been modified (such as $x > 7 \wedge z > 5 \Rightarrow (x+u)\ltimes$),

Table 1. Experiment Data (excerpts)

Package.Procedure Name	LoC	C	L	P	O	SF	Flows 1	Flows 2	Cond. Flows 1	Cond. Flows 2	Gens. 1	Gens. 2	Time (seconds) 1	Time (seconds) 2
Autopilot.AP.Altitude.Pitch.Rate.History_Average	10	0	1	0	1	2	5	3	0	0	0	0	0.047	0.063
Autopilot.AP.Altitude.Pitch.Rate.Calc_Pitchrate	13	2	0	2	2	7	17	8	0	0	15	15	0.000	0.015
Autopilot.AP.Altitude.Pitch.Target_Rate	17	4	0	1	1	3	53	4	42	0	142	46	0.015	0.015
Autopilot.AP.Heading.Roll.Target_ROR	15	3	0	1	1	2	4	3	0	0	26	26	0.000	0.000
Autopilot.AP.Heading.Roll.Target_Rate	11	2	0	1	1	3	9	4	0	0	14	14	0.000	0.000
Autopilot.AP.Control	19	1	0	13	8	46	58	54	0	0	63	51	0.016	0.032
Autopilot.Scale.Scale_Movement	22	4	0	2	1	4	47	10	46	9	0	0	0.016	0.000
Minepump.Logbuffer.ProtectedWrite	8	1	0	0	5	9	9	9	4	4	0	0	0.031	0.047
Mailbox.MACHINE_STEP	17	2	0	0	6	16	18	18	12	12	0	0	0.047	0.062
Mailbox.Main	6	0	1	1	6	16	54	22	0	0	2	2	0.031	0.016
BoilerWater-Monitor.FaultIntegrator.Test	11	3	0	0	4	11	46	22	42	18	0	0	0.047	0.047
BoilerWater-Monitor.FaultIntegrator.Main	11	0	1	6	2	2	14	4	0	0	0	0	0.016	0.016
Lift-Controller.Poll	22	2	1	3	2	9	77	12	43	0	0	0	0.031	0.031
Lift-Controller.Traverse	18	0	1	11	3	10	210	13	66	0	0	0	0.281	0.063
Missile_Guidance.Clock_Read	12	2	0	0	3	5	13	11	10	8	0	0	0.047	0.047
Missile_Guidance.Extrapolate_Speed	13	2	0	2	2	7	14	10	6	4	36	16	0.000	0.000
Missile_Guidance.Code_To_State	12	3	0	0	1	7	15	9	14	8	0	0	0.000	0.000
Missile_Guidance.Transition	20	4	0	2	1	9	3527	63	3524	62	4	4	0.156	0.125
Missile_Guidance.Drag_cfg.Calc_Drag	21	4	0	1	1	3	37	3	34	0	0	0	0.000	0.000
Missile_Guidance.Nav.Handle_Airspeed	18	4	0	4	3	13	117	28	110	25	18	18	0.000	0.000
Missile_Guidance.Nav.Estimate_Height	21	5	0	2	2	11	60	18	57	16	4	4	0.000	0.000

we must ensure that the variables of E agree after the procedure call (when the antecedent holds). For those not in OUT_p (such as u), this is done by R_0 (which expresses some "semi frame conditions"); for those in OUT_p (such as x), this is done by R_m which utilizes the procedure summary (contract) of the called procedure.

Synthesizing loop invariants: For while loops (the only iterative construct), the idea is to consider assertions of the form $\phi_x \Rightarrow x \bowtie$ and then repeatedly analyze the loop body so as to iteratively weaken the antecedents until a fixed point is reached. Illustratively:

```
while i < 7 do
   if odd(i)
   then r := r + v; v := v + h
   else v := x;
   i := i + 1
{r⋈}
```

Iteration	0	1	2	3	
	false	false	false	false	$\Rightarrow h \bowtie$
	false	true	true	true	$\Rightarrow i \bowtie$
	true	true	true	true	$\Rightarrow r \bowtie$
	false	odd(i)	odd(i)	odd(i)	$\Rightarrow v \bowtie$
	false	false	¬odd(i)	true	$\Rightarrow x \bowtie$

Here we are given $r \bowtie$ as postcondition; hence the initial value of r's antecedent is *true* whereas all other antecedents are initialized to *false*. The first iteration updates v's antecedent to odd(i) (we use odd(i) as a shorthand for $i \bmod 2 = 1$), since v is used to compute r when i is odd, and also updates i's antecedent to *true*, since (the parity of) i is used to decide whether r is updated or not. The second iteration updates x's antecedent to ¬odd(i), since in order for two runs to agree on v when i is odd, they must have agreed on x in the previous iteration when i was even. The third iteration updates x's antecedent to *true*, since in order for two runs to agree on x when i is even, then must agree on x always (as x doesn't change). We have now reached a fixed point. It is noteworthy that even though the postcondition mentions $r \bowtie$, and r is updated using v which in turn is updated using h, the generated precondition does not mention h, since the parity of i was exploited. This shows [4] that even if we should only aim at producing contracts where all assertions are unconditional, precision may still be improved if the analysis engine makes internal use of *conditional* assertions.

In the general case, however, fixed point iteration may not terminate. To ensure termination, we need a "widening operator" $\triangledown$ on 1-assertions, with the following properties: *(a)* for all ϕ and ψ, ψ logically implies $\psi \triangledown \phi$, and also ϕ logically implies $\psi \triangledown \phi$; *(b)* if for all i we have that ϕ^{i+1} is of the form $\phi^i \triangledown \psi$, then the chain $\{\phi^i \mid i \geq 0\}$ eventually stabilizes. A trivial widening operator is the one that always returns *true*, in effect converting conditional agreement assertions into unconditional. A less trivial option will utilize a number of assertions, say $\psi_1 \ldots \psi_k$, and allow $\psi \triangledown \phi = \psi_j$ if ψ_j is logically implied by ψ as well as by ϕ; such assertions may be given by the user if he has a hint that a suitable invariant may have one of $\psi_1 \ldots \psi_k$ as antecedent.

6 Evaluation

The algorithm of Section 5 provides a foundation for automatically *inferring* contracts from implementations, but can also be used for *checking* `derives` contracts supplied by a developer: the verification condition will be that the contract pre-condition implies the inferred pre-condition. In principle, this approach may reject a sound contract since the inference algorithm does not always generate the weakest pre-condition.

There is much merit in a methodology that encourages writing of the contract *before* writing/checking the implementation. However, one of our strategies for injecting our techniques into industrial development groups is to pitch the tools as being able to discover more precise conditional specifications to supplement conventional SPARK `derives` contracts already in the code; thus we focus the experimental studies of this section on the more challenging problem of automatically inferring *conditional* contracts starting from code with no existing `derives` annotations.

For each procedure P with $\text{OUT}_P = \{w_1, \ldots, w_k\}$, the algorithm analyzes the body wrt. a post-condition $w_1 \bowtie_1, \ldots, w_k \bowtie_k$. Since SPARK disallows recursion, we simply move in a bottom-up fashion through the call-graph – guaranteeing that a contract exists for each called procedure. When deployed in actual development, one would probably allow developers to tweak the generated contracts (e.g., by removing unnecessary conditions for establishing end-to-end policies) before proceeding with contract inference for methods in the next level of the call hierarchy. However, in our experiments, we used autogenerated contracts for called methods without modification. All experiments were run under JDK 1.6 on a 2.2 GHz Intel Core2 Duo.

Code bases: Embedded security devices are the initial target domain for our work, and the security-critical sections to be certified from these code bases are often relatively small, *e.g.*, roughly 1000 LOC for one Rockwell Collins high assurance product and 3000 LOC for a device recently certified by Naval Research Labs researchers [14]. For our evaluation, we consider a collection of five small to moderate size applications from the SPARK distribution, in addition to an expanded version of the mailbox example of Section 2. Of these, the *Autopilot* and *Missile Control* applications are the most realistic. There are well over 250 procedures in the code bases, but due to space constraints, in Table 1 we list metrics for only the most complex procedures from each application (see [27] for the source code of all the examples). Columns **LOC**, **C**, **L**, and **P** report the number of non-comment lines of code, conditional expressions, loops, and procedure calls in each method. Our tool can run in two modes. The first mode (identified as version **1** in Table 1) implements the rules of Figure 4 directly, with just one small optimization: a collection of boolean simplifications are introduced, e.g., simplifying assertions of the form $true \wedge \phi \Rightarrow E \bowtie$ to $\phi \Rightarrow E \bowtie$. The second mode (version **2** in Table 1) enables a collection of simplifications aimed at compacting and eliminating redundant flows from the generated set of assertions. One simplification performed is elimination of assertions with *false* in the antecedent (these are trivially true), and elimination of duplicate assertions. Also, it eliminates simple entailed assertions, such as $\phi \Rightarrow E \bowtie$ when $true \Rightarrow E \bowtie$ also appears in the assertion set.

Typical refinement power of the algorithm: Column **O** gives the number of OUT variables of a procedure (this is equal to the number of `derives` clauses in the original SPARK contract), and Column **SF** gives the number of *flows* (total number of IN/OUT pairs) appearing in the original contract. Column **Flows** gives the number of flows generated by different versions of our algorithm. This number increases over **SF** as SPARK flows are refined into conditional flows (often creating two or more conditioned flows for a particular IN/OUT variable pair). The data shows that the compacting optimizations often substantially reduce the number of flows; the practical impact of this is to substantially increase the readability/tractability of the contracts. Column **Cond. Flows** indicates the number of flows from **Flows** that are conditional. We expect to see the refining power of our approach in procedures with conditionals (column **C**) primarily, but we also see increases in precision that is due to conditional contracts of called procedures (column **P**). In a few cases we see a blow-up in the number of conditional flows. The worse case is `MissileGuidance.Transition`, which contains a case statement with each branch containing nested conditionals and procedure calls with conditional contracts – leading to an exponential explosion in path conditions. Only a few variables in these conditions lie in what we consider to be the "control logic" of the system. The tractability of this example would improve significantly with the methodology suggested earlier in which developers declare explicitly the guarding variables (such as `IN_1_RDY` of Fig. 1), thus allowing the algorithm to omit tracking of conditional flows not associated with declared guard variables. A manual inspection of each inferred contract showed that the algorithm usually produces conditions that an expert would expect.

Efficiency of inference algorithm: As can be see in the **Time** columns, the algorithm is quite fast for all the examples, usually taking a little longer in version **2** (all optimizations on). However, for some examples, version **2** is actually faster; these are the cases of procedures with calls to other procedures. Due to the optimizations, the callees now have simpler contracts, simplifying the processing of the caller procedures.

Sources of loss of precision: We would like to determine situations where our treatment of loops or procedure calls leads to abstraction steps that discard conditional information. While this is difficult to determine for loops (one would have to compare to the most precise loop invariant – which would need to be written by hand), Column **Gens.** indicates the number of conditions dropped across processing of procedure calls. The data shows, and our experience confirms, that the loss of precision is not drastic (in some cases, one wants conditions to be discarded), but more experience is needed to determine the practical impact on verification of end-to-end properties.

7 Related Work

The theoretical framework for the SPARK information flow framework is provided by Bergeretti and Carré [9] who presents a compositional method for inferring and checking dependences among variables. That approach is flow-sensitive, whereas most security type systems [26,6] are flow-*in*sensitive as they rely on assigning a security level ("high" or "low") to each variable. Chapman and Hilton [10] describe how SPARK information flow contracts could be extended with lattices of security levels and how the SPARK Examiner could be enhanced to check conformance of flows to particular security levels. Those ideas could be applied directly to provide security levels of flows in our framework. Rossebo *et al.*[20] show how the existing SPARK framework can be applied to verify various *unconditional* properties of a MILS Message Router. Apart from Spark Ada, there exists several tools for analyzing information flow properties, notably Jif (Java + information flow) which is based on [17]), and Flow Caml [22].

The seminal work on agreement assertions is [2], whose logic is flow-sensitive, and comes with an algorithm for computing (weakest) preconditions, but the approach does not integrate with programmer assertions. To address that, and to analyze heap-manipulating languages, the logic of [1] employs *three* kinds of primitive assertions: agreement, programmer, and region (for a simple alias analysis). But, since those can be combined only through conjunction, programmer assertions are not smoothly integrated, and it is not possible to capture *conditional* information flows. That was what motivated Amtoft & Banerjee [4] to introduce conditional agreement assertions, for a heap-manipulating language. This paper integrates that approach into the SPARK setting (whose lack of heap objects allows us to omit the "object flow invariants" of [4]) for practical industrial development, adds interprocedural contract-based compositional checking, adds an algorithm for computing loop invariants (rather than assuming the user provides them), and provides an implementation as well as reports on experiments.

A recently popular approach to information flow analysis is *self-composition*, first proposed by Barthe et al. [8] and later extended by, e.g., Terauchi and Aiken [24] and (for heap-manipulating programs) Naumann [18]. Self-composition works as follows: for a given program S, a copy S' is created with all variables renamed (primed); with the observable variables say x, y, then non-interference holds provided the sequential composition $S; S'$ when given precondition $x = x' \wedge y = y'$ also ensures postcondition $x = x' \wedge y = y'$. This is a property that can be checked using existing static verifiers.

Darvas et al. [11] use the KeY tool for interactive verification of non-interference; information flow is modeled by a dynamic logic formula, rather than by assertions.

When it comes to *conditional* information flow, the most noteworthy existing tool is the slicer by Snelting et al [23] which generates *path conditions* in program dependence graphs for reasoning about end-to-end flows between specified program points/variables. In contrast, we provide a contract-based approach for *compositional* reasoning about conditions on flows with an underlying logic representation that can provide external evidence for conformance to conditional flow properties. We have recently received the implementation of the approach in [23], and we are currently investigating the deeper technical connections between the two approaches.

Finally, we have already noted how our work has been inspired by and aims to complement previous ground-breaking efforts in certification of MILS infrastructure [13,14]. While the direct theorem-proving approach followed in these efforts enables proofs of very strong properties beyond what our framework can currently handle, our aim is to dramatically reduce the labor required, and the potential for error, by integrating automated techniques directly on code, models, and developer workflows to allow many information flow verification obligations to be discharged earlier in the life cycle.

8 Conclusion

We have presented what we believe to be an effective and developer-friendly framework for specification and automatic checking of conditional information flow properties, which are central to verification and certification of information applications hoping to provide MLS solutions. The directions that we are pursuing are inspired directly by challenge problems presented to us by industry teams using SPARK to develop MLS components. The initial prototyping and evaluation of our framework has produced promising results, and we are pressing ahead with evaluating our techniques against actual product codebases developed at Rockwell Colins. A crucial concern in this effort will be to develop design and implementation methodologies for (a) exposing and checking conditional information flows, (b) specifying and checking security levels of data along conditional flows, and (c) investigating a more precise treatment of arrays as presented in the extended version of this paper [5].

References

1. Amtoft, T., Bandhakavi, S., Banerjee, A.: A logic for information flow in object-oriented programs. In: 33rd Principles of Programming Languages (POPL), pp. 91–102 (2006)
2. Amtoft, T., Banerjee, A.: Information Flow Analysis in Logical Form. In: Giacobazzi, R. (ed.) SAS 2004. LNCS, vol. 3148, pp. 100–115. Springer, Heidelberg (2004)
3. Amtoft, T., Banerjee, A.: A logic for information flow analysis with an application to forward slicing of simple imperative programs. Science of Comp. Prog. 64(1), 3–28 (2007)
4. Amtoft, T., Banerjee, A.: Verification condition generation for conditional information flow. In: 5th ACM Workshop on Formal Methods in Security Engineering (FMSE), pp. 2–11 (2007); A long version, with proofs, appears as technical report KSU CIS TR 2007-2
5. Amtoft, T., Hatcliff, J., Rodriguez, E., Robby, Hoag, J., Greve, D.: Specification and checking of software contracts for conditional information flow (extended version). Technical Report SAnToS-TR2007-5, KSU CIS (2007), http://www.sireum.org
6. Banerjee, A., Naumann, D.A.: Stack-based access control and secure information flow. Journal of Functional Programming 2(15), 131–177 (2005)
7. Barnes, J.: High Integrity Software – the SPARK Approach to Safety and Security. Addison-Wesley, Reading (2003)
8. Barthe, G., D'Argenio, P., Rezk, T.: Secure information flow by self-composition. In: Foccardi, R. (ed.) CSFW 2004, pp. 100–114. IEEE Press, Los Alamitos (2004)
9. Bergeretti, J.-F., Carré, B.A.: Information-flow and data-flow analysis of while-programs. ACM TOPLAS 7(1), 37–61 (1985)

10. Chapman, R., Hilton, A.: Enforcing security and safety models with an information flow analysis tool. In: SIGAda 2004, Atlanta, Georgia, November 2004, pp. 39–46. ACM, New York (2004)
11. Darvas, A., Hähnle, R., Sands, D.: A theorem proving approach to analysis of secure information flow. In: Hutter, D., Ullmann, M. (eds.) SPC 2005. LNCS, vol. 3450, pp. 193–209. Springer, Heidelberg (2005)
12. Goguen, J.A., Meseguer, J.: Security policies and security models. In: IEEE Symposium on Security and Privacy, pp. 11–20 (1982)
13. Greve, D., Wilding, M., Vanfleet, W.M.: A separation kernel formal security policy. In: 4th International Workshop on the ACL2 Prover and its Applications (ACL2-2003) (2003)
14. Heitmeyer, C.L., Archer, M., Leonard, E.I., McLean, J.: Formal specification and verification of data separation in a separation kernel for an embedded system. In: 13th ACM Conference on Computer and Communications Security (CCS 2006), pp. 346–355 (2006)
15. Jackson, D., Thomas, M., Millett, L.I. (eds.): Software for Dependable Systems: Sufficient Evidence? National Academies Press, Washington (2007); Committee on Certifiably Dependable Software Systems, National Research Council
16. Kaufmann, M., Manolios, P., Moore, J.S.: Computer-Aided Reasoning: An Approach. Kluwer Academic Publishers, Dordrecht (2000)
17. Myers, A.C.: JFlow: Practical mostly-static information flow control. In: POPL 1999, San Antonio, Texas, pp. 228–241. ACM Press, New York (1999)
18. Naumann, J.D.A.: From Coupling Relations to Mated Invariants for Checking Information Flow. In: Gollmann, D., Meier, J., Sabelfeld, A. (eds.) ESORICS 2006. LNCS, vol. 4189, pp. 279–296. Springer, Heidelberg (2006)
19. Owre, S., Rushby, J.M., Shankar, N.: PVS: A prototype verification system. In: Kapur, D. (ed.) CADE 1992. LNCS, vol. 607, Springer, Heidelberg (1992)
20. Rossebo, B., Oman, P., Alves-Foss, J., Blue, R., Jaszkowiak, P.: Using SPARK-Ada to model and verify a MILS message router. In: Proceedings of the International Symposium on Secure Software Engineering (2006)
21. Rushby, J.: The design and verification of secure systems. In: 8th ACM Symposium on Operating Systems Principles, vol. 15(5), pp. 12–21 (1981)
22. Simonet, V.: Flow Caml in a nutshell. In: Hutton, G. (ed.) First APPSEM-II workshop, March 2003, pp. 152–165 (2003)
23. Snelting, G., Robschink, T., Krinke, J.: Efficient path conditions in dependence graphs for software safety analysis. ACM TOSEM 15(4), 410–457 (2006)
24. Terauchi, T., Aiken, A.: Secure information flow as a safety problem. In: Hankin, C., Siveroni, I. (eds.) SAS 2005. LNCS, vol. 3672, pp. 352–367. Springer, Heidelberg (2005)
25. Vanfleet, M., Luke, J., Beckwith, R.W., Taylor, C., Calloni, B., Uchenick, G.: MILS: Architecture for high-assurance embedded computing. CrossTalk: The Journal of Defense Software Engineering (August 2005)
26. Volpano, D., Smith, G., Irvine, C.: A sound type system for secure flow analysis. Journal of Computer Security 4(3), 167–188 (1996)
27. Sireum website, http://www.sireum.org

JML Runtime Assertion Checking: Improved Error Reporting and Efficiency Using Strong Validity

Patrice Chalin and Frédéric Rioux

Dependable Software Research Group,
Dept. of Computer Science and Software Engineering, Concordia University
chalin@encs.concordia.ca, fred@dsrg.org

Abstract. The Java Modeling Language (JML) recently switched to an assertion semantics based on "strong validity" in which an assertion is taken to be valid precisely when it is defined and true. Elsewhere we have shared our positive experiences with the realization and use of this new semantics in the context of ESC/Java2. In this paper, we describe the challenges faced by and the redesign required for the implementation of the new semantics in the JML Runtime Assertion Checker (RAC) compiler. Not only is the new semantics effective at helping developers identify formerly undetected errors in specifications, we also demonstrate how the realization of the new semantics is more efficient—resulting in more compact instrumented code that runs slightly faster. More importantly, under the new semantics, the JML RAC can now compile sizeable JML annotated Java programs (like ESC/Java2) which it was unable to compile before.

1 Introduction

The assertion semantics of the Java Modeling Language (JML) [13, 17], a behavioral interface specification language for Java, was formerly founded on a classical definition of validity. Elsewhere we have demonstrated that

- this semantics was not faithfully implemented [4] by either of the two main JML tools [1] (namely, `jmlc`, the JML Runtime Assertion Checker (RAC) Compiler and ESC/Java2) and that in any case,
- a comprehensive survey of programmers, mainly from industry, indicated that this is not the semantics that they want [3].

Hence, a new assertion semantics for JML based on "strong validity" was recently proposed [2, 4] and adopted [20, §2.7]. Under such a semantics, an assertion is taken as valid when its evaluation does not result in partial functions being applied to values outside their domain and, the assertion evaluates to true. In terms of runtime assertion checking (RAC), this means that an assertion is considered valid if and only if its evaluation (terminates and) results in true without raising an exception.

We have begun the realization of the new assertion semantics in ESC/Java2 [4]. In this paper, we explain how the JML RAC has been adapted to conform to the new semantics and some of the challenges that we faced. We also demonstrate how the

```
public class Person {
  /*@ spec_public */ private String name;   // a spec_public field
  /*@ spec_public */ private int age;        // can be used in public specs
  //@ public invariant age >= 0;
  //@ requires age >= 0;
  public Person(String n, int age) { this.name = n; this.age = age; }

  //@ ensures age == \old(age) + 1;
  public void birthday() { age++; }
}
```

Fig. 1. Person class annotated with JML

realization of the new semantics helped us find new bugs in JML specifications and that it is more efficient, resulting in smaller instrumented bytecode that runs slightly faster. More importantly, under the new semantics, the JML RAC can now compile sizeable JML annotated Java programs (like ESC/Java2) which it was unable to compile before.

This paper first compares both the old classical and new assertion semantics before giving more details on the JML RAC and its design. Then, we present an overview of how we had to modify the JML RAC to support the new assertion semantics and how we assessed the validity of our work.

2 JML Assertion Semantics

Among other things, the Java Modeling Language brings Design by Contract to Java [6, 18]. Hence, in particular, classes can be annotated with invariants and methods adorned with contracts expressed using preconditions and postconditions inside Java comments starting with a leading "@"—see Fig. 1. Invariants, pre- and post-conditions are expressed using *assertions*, which in the case of JML, consist of (the side-effect free subset of) Java boolean expressions enhanced with some extra operators and constructs—such as logical implication (==>) and quantifiers (\forall, \exists) [20].

2.1 Classical Assertion Semantics

The old classical JML semantics assumed that assertions, even if their syntax is very close to that of Java, are to be interpreted as formulas of a classical logic. Under such an interpretation, computational issues that can introduce undefinedness such as short-circuiting of logical operators, exceptions, runtime errors, and informal assertions are not explicitly modeled [7, p.29]. Instead, partial functions are modeled as *underspecified total functions* [19]. Hence, partial functions applied to values outside their domains are assigned a fixed, though unspecified value.

2.2 RAC Approximation of the Old Semantics through Game-playing

Conformant with this view of assertions, the JML RAC-compiled bytecode will always consider an assertion as satisfied or violated; it will never be declared as invalid. Since the evaluation of Java expressions can naturally lead to exceptions, the RAC still has to deal with undefinedness. In its attempt to emulate classical two-valued logic from Java's three-valued operational semantics, the RAC resorts to a game-playing strategy as we explain next.

Table 1. Game played by the JML RAC to approximate classical logic

	Value assigned to ...		Value of top-level assertion
	(*informal*)	x/0 == y	
!(* informal *) && x/0 == y i.e. !*angelic* && *demonic*	False	False	False
! (* informal *) && !(x/0 == y) i.e. !*angelic* && !*demonic*	False	True	False
(* informal *) || !(x/0 == y) i.e. *angelic* || !*demonic*	True	True	True

In the JML RAC, undefinedness comes in two flavors: *demonic* and *angelic* [7, pp.30-31]. Demonic undefinedness arises from various runtime errors or exceptions that are generated when an assertion expression is evaluated. Angelic undefinedness comes from the attempt to evaluate something that is not executable (e.g., an informal predicate or some categories of quantified expression). The JML RAC adopts a game-playing strategy in its attempt to deal with the two kinds of undefinedness. That is, generally, the smallest Boolean subexpression containing an undefined term will be treated as either true or false depending on the evaluation context. For demonic undefinedness the JML RAC tries to choose a truth value for the undefined subexpression that will make the top-level assertion false; whereas for angelic undefinedness the RAC will try to make the top-level assertion true [7]. When both angelic and demonic undefinedness occurs in the same expression, they each try to influence the top-level assertion in the best way they can to meet their respective goals. Table 1 illustrates the game being played.

Classical logic does not feature conditional Boolean operators such as conditional conjunction (&&). Under the old JML semantics, Java's conditional operators were mapped into their classical non-conditional counterparts. This implied that the JML assertion E1 && E2 is equivalent to E2 && E1 [19]. In order to preserve that behavior, the JML RAC evaluated both of its operands when the evaluation of the first operand is exceptional [7, p.27]. Such a scheme can be confusing for developers since it leads to the evaluation of syntactically correct Java expressions differently if done in a Java or JML context as illustrated in Table 2. For both expressions, JML will interpret a logical or between something (possibly) undefined and something true; hence always yielding true in such a case. Java on the other hand will throw an exception upon a null pointer dereference.

2.3 New Semantics Based on Strong Validity

The original JML RAC semantics guessed a truth value for an invalid assertion; using the new semantics, an assertion can be satisfied (evaluated true), violated (false) or

Table 2. Semantic differences between Java and JML

	true || x.length > 0	x.length > 0 || true
Java	Always true	if x is not null: true. Otherwise: NullPointerException.
JML	Always true	Always true

invalid (when evaluation does not complete successfully) [4]. Violated and invalid assertions are reported as distinct kinds of error.

Handling Undefinedness. In our implementation of the new semantics, all logical operators behave in the same way in both Java and JML. For instance, a conditional disjunction or conjunction whose left-hand subexpression is exceptional would cause the resulting expression to be exceptional no matter what the right-hand subexpression refers to. When an exception or runtime error occurs while evaluating part of an assertion, that exception causes the entire assertion to be invalid and the user to be notified. In other words, as soon as demonic undefinedness occurs, the evaluation of the assertion is halted, and the assertion is reported as invalid.

The concept of angelic undefinedness cannot be as easily factored out. As was mentioned earlier, such undefinedness was associated with non-executable subexpressions and was treated in a way that ensured the top-level expression would be "*as true as possible*". We do not want assertion expression evaluation to have the overhead of game playing. In the new semantics, if an assertion is non-executable (in its entirety or in part) then the entire assertion is tagged as non-executable. While most non-executable assertions can be detected at compile-time, the rest can only be discovered at runtime. While it is possible to warn the user that some of the assertions may be non-executable, it is not always possible to precisely say if it will *always* be non-executable [7, 23].

Whether a non-executable assertion should play a role in the overall truth value of a specification depends on what the developer wants. In some cases (e.g. during preliminary development, when there is a higher occurrence of incomplete specifications), one might be willing to ignore them by treating the assertion in which they occur as equivalent to true. However, in other situations, to gain extra confidence and ensure that the specifications are entirely verified, one may prefer to have non-executable assertions be reported and make the specification verification fail since they cannot be enforced or verified. Non-executable assertions can either be simplified to true or false, depending on the setting of a JML RAC compilation flag. Trying to factor out non-executable expressions from an assertion while trying to infer a truth value to the expression would mimic the game played by the previous semantics. We believe non-executable assertions should be avoided as they provided very little in the context of automated program verification.

3 JML Runtime Assertion Checker (RAC), Old Semantics

The JML RAC is part of the Common JML tools suite—formerly known as the ISU JML tool suite. It uses a "compilation-based approach" for translating JML specifications into runtime checking bytecode [7]. Unlike static checkers, which verify program properties at compile-time, the JML RAC enables dynamic checking by generating bytecode that verifies that specifications are satisfied during program execution. When an assertion fails, the JML RAC-compiled code generates a runtime error. The remainder of this section describes the design and operation of the RAC under the old semantics. (As will be seen in the next section, the design changes required to implement the new semantics have been quite localized.)

The JML RAC is built on top of the MultiJava (MJ) compiler and uses the JML Checker[1] for type checking JML specifications and as the front-end for building an Abstract Syntax Tree (AST). JML specification clauses are translated

```
public int x, y;
//@ requires b && x < y;
public void m(boolean b) {...}
```

Fig. 2. A simple method precondition

into *assertion methods*. For each Java method, three RAC assertion methods are generated: one for precondition checking and two for postcondition checking (i.e., for normal and exceptional termination). The JML-specified Java methods are instrumented using a wrapper approach. The instrumentation process takes the original body of a method and extracts it into a private method with a uniquely defined name. The original signature of the method is used for the newly created wrapper method hence replacing it. The wrapper implements the specification checking logic by calling the original body and assertion methods when required. Not only are the preconditions and postconditions associated with the method called, but some class-related assertion methods are also called (e.g., for invariant and constraint checking [18]). The control flow of the wrapper approach to method instrumentation is presented in [7, §4.1].

3.1 Code Instrumentation

Every Java class compiled with the JML RAC contains not only its normal content (as would be generated by, e.g., `javac`), but also an embedding of its specification and how to verify it at runtime. Instrumentation code is generated on a per classifier, per method, per field, and per assertion basis [9]. Most generated instrumentation code gives rise to an overhead that is linear and foreseeable, though for assertion expressions interpreted under the old semantics it used to be polynomial (at least quadratic!) as we shall soon illustrate.

3.1.1 General Assertion Evaluation

Under the old semantics, JML RAC-generated code that evaluates an assertion expression tended to be rather verbose because expression evaluation had to emulate classical two-valued logic while playing an optimization game with angelic and demonic undefinedness. Hence, for example, the JML RAC made extensive use of new variables: as a rule of thumb, *every* subexpression had an associated new internal variable used to hold its value. Moreover, each step in the evaluation was done separately and had again its own new internal variable, and sometimes its own try block. For example, a simple precondition such as the one given in Fig. 2 was translated into 59 lines of instrumentation code and used 7 new internal variables—see Fig. 3. Upon reading the code, one may notice the right-hand side of the && operator is evaluated if the left-hand side is exceptional; as mentioned earlier, this different from the Java semantics for that operator.

3.1.2 RAC Generated Code Exceeded JVM and Class File Format Limits

The JML RAC's attempt to implement an assertion semantics based on classical two-valued logic caused the instrumented code to be *much* larger than the source. We note

---

[1] MultiJava: http://multijava.sourceforge.net/; Java Modeling Language (JML): http://www.jmlspecs.org/.

```
 1|  try {
 2|    // eval of &&
 3|    boolean rac$v0 = true;
 4|    boolean rac$v1 = false, rac$v2 = false;
 5|    // arg 1 of &&
 6|    try {
 7|      rac$v0 = b;
 8|    }
 9|    catch (JMLNonExecutableException jml$e0) {
10|      rac$v2 = true;
11|    }
12|    catch (java.lang.Exception jml$e0) {
13|      rac$v1 = true;
14|    }
15|    if (rac$v0) {
16|      // arg 2 of &&
17|      try {
18|        boolean rac$v3 = false, rac$v4 = false;
19|        int rac$v5 = 0;
20|        int rac$v6 = 0;
21|        try {
22|          rac$v5 = this.x;
23|        }
24|        catch (JMLNonExecutableException jml$e0) {
25|          rac$v4 = true;
26|        }
27|        catch (java.lang.Exception jml$e0) {
28|          rac$v3 = true;
29|        }
30|        if (!rac$v3) {
31|          try {
32|            rac$v6 = this.y;
33|          }
34|          catch (JMLNonExecutableException jml$e0) {
35|            rac$v4 = true;
36|          }
37|          catch (java.lang.Exception jml$e0) {
38|            rac$v3 = true;
39|          }
40|        }
41|        if (rac$v3) { rac$v0 = false; }
42|        else if (rac$v4) { rac$v0 = true; }
43|        else try {
44|          rac$v0 = rac$v5<rac$v6;
45|        }
46|        catch (JMLNonExecutableException jml$e0) {
47|          rac$v0 = true;
48|        }
49|        catch (java.lang.Exception jml$e0) {
50|          rac$v0 = false;
51|        }
52|      }
53|      catch (JMLNonExecutableException jml$e0) {
54|        rac$v2 = true;
55|      }
56|      catch (java.lang.Exception jml$e0) {
57|        rac$v1 = true;
58|      }
59|    }
60| }
```

Fig. 3. Instrumentation code evaluating "requires b && x < y" (old RAC semantics)

here that in some cases, the generated code was so large that a Java compiler would be unable to process it. For example, in the ESC/Java2 project, there are a few classes that could not be compiled using the JML RAC. One of these classes (`javafe.ast.-TypeDeclElem`) has an automatically generated postcondition composed of a conjunction of 118 implications. Unfortunately, the instrumented code generated for verifying the postcondition consisted of 15,816 lines of Java which no compiler can successfully compile. This is because the assertion method which checks the postcondition had a top-level catch block that was too far away from its try block (due to limitations of the JVM instruction set and the Java class file format, the two blocks must compile into byte code that is no more than 65535 bytes apart [21, §4.10]). Of course, methods with such postconditions are rather rare, but the fact is that the evaluation of expressions following the original semantics JML RAC does not scale and cannot cope with heavily specified code. Users should obtain benefits from writing richer specifications rather than be penalized.

4 JML RAC Redesign in Support of Strong Validity

4.1 Expression Evaluation

Representing Assertions as a Single Java Expression. Most of the time, an assertion's body can be evaluated exactly as written (i.e., without having to declare new variables for each subexpression). The possible outcomes of such an evaluation are true, false, or an error/exception. Hence, if we choose not to model partial functions by underspecified total functions, the evaluation of expressions becomes quite straightforward, helping us overcome some of the practical limitations mentioned earlier.

Expression Evaluation under the Old Semantics. Expression-evaluation code was generated by RAC expression translators implemented as AST visitors [12]. Given an expression to be translated, an expression translator would walk the expression AST and build a compound "node" that contained the instrumentation code to evaluate the expression at runtime. Such a node could either be wrapped with a try-catch block or not. A high-level translator used such nodes whenever it needed for that expression to be evaluated while generating the wrapper assertion methods [7].

The translation process was achieved by visiting every subexpression of a given top-level expression and generating nodes to evaluate the subexpressions. As was mentioned earlier, a new variable was usually defined to hold the value of a subexpression. Each of the subexpression nodes was stored on a stack. When all of the expressions had been visited, the stack of nodes was used to generate an all encompassing node that, most often, was wrapped in a try-catch block before being returned to the sender. We briefly note that proper handling of quantified expressions is quite involved (e.g. requiring specialize heuristic-based static analysis in order to decide how, if possible, to evaluate them). Hence we will only describe the handling of quantified expressions in Section 0 for the new semantics.

New Approach to Expression Evaluation. The implementation of the new semantics requires alternate expression translators. For this reason, we created a new general expression translator usable almost as a simple drop-in replacement for the old (top-level) translators. Under the new semantics, there is no need to evaluate subexpressions separately through the use of newly declared variables. Precedence of operators is embedded in the AST and hence, an appropriate use of parentheses while visiting the tree avoids the need for variables. Since, in the new semantics, a clause is either entirely executable or not at all, a new runtime exception was created to short-circuit evaluation code generation in the event that one of the subexpressions is found to be non-executable at compile-time. At runtime, the expression is evaluated in a top-level try-block that catches two things: (i) `JMLNonExecutableException`s (Fig. 4), and (ii) all other errors and exceptions. `JMLNonExecutableException`s cause an entire assertion to immediately simplify to true (as was mentioned in Section 0, a command line option allows developers to change this default to false). Any other exception or error thrown while evaluating an expression is caught and wrapped in a `JMLEvaluationError` before being re-thrown.

4.2 Handling Quantified Expressions

Quantified expressions, unlike other simpler expressions, cannot have their evaluation code mechanically derived. They have to be analyzed beforehand. In order to properly analyze quantified expressions and derive the best way to verify them at runtime, the JML RAC provides a special package and translator that, like the other high-level translators, uses the (base) expression translator to evaluate expressions. In order to reuse the existing quantifier evaluation package while implementing our new direct expression evaluation approach, we decided to wrap the output of the quantifier translator into an inner class that is used in the evaluation of the assertion instead of the quantified expression as described in [23].

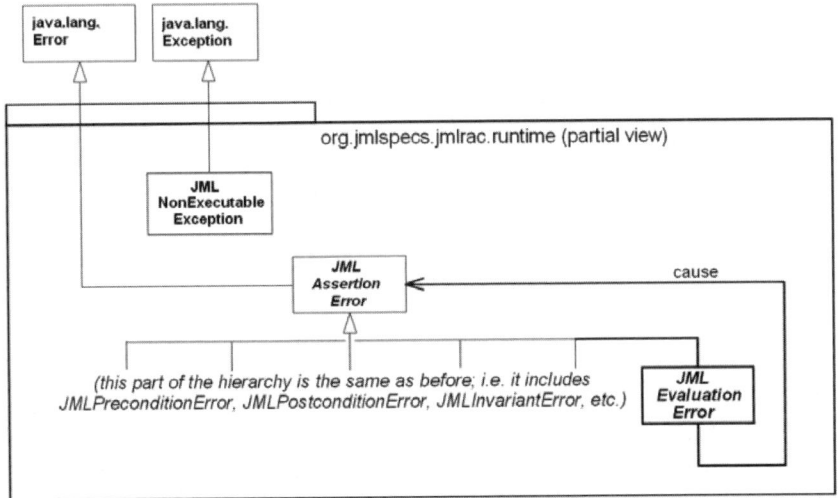

Fig. 4. Modified error hierarchy of the JML RAC runtime package

```
public static ArrayList myList = new ArrayList();

//@ requires (x > y) || (x < 0) ||
//@   (\forall Object obj;
//@          myList.contains(obj); obj instanceof Integer);
public void m(int x, int y) {...}
```

Fig. 5. Sample assertion containing a quantified subexpression

Consider the specification fragment of Fig. 5. Under the new semantics, RAC code for the method's precondition is as shown in Fig. 6. Note that the try block starts with the definition of the inner class rac$v4 whose eval() method performs the evaluation of the quantified subexpression. The statement following the inner class definition instantiates the class. Finally, the last statement of the try block, marked (*), is the one that can be clearly seen to correspond to the requires clause expression of Fig. 5.

5 Validation: Assessment and Statistics

Basic Validation: Regression Testing. The Common JML tool suite is supported by an extensive collection of automated tests. These tests, numbering in the thousands, help developers ensure the integrity of the tool suite following any modification. The test suite for the JML RAC consists of approximately 500 test files, each containing several test cases. Out of those, more than 375 are grouped under the racrun package, whose purpose is to test the runtime behavior of RAC-compiled code—this is in contrast to, e.g., testing the behavior of the JML RAC. In particular, the racrun package is meant to test all JML statements and expressions individually and in various combinations. The test coverage of the racrun package is considered sufficiently complete. For the purpose of testing the new assertion semantics we adapted the racrun

```
try {
    class rac$v4 {
        public boolean eval() {
            boolean rac$v0 = false;
            java.util.Collection rac$v1 = new java.util.HashSet();
            java.util.Collection rac$v3 = MyClass.myList;
            rac$v1.addAll(rac$v3);
            java.util.Iterator rac$v2 = rac$v1.iterator();
            rac$v0 = true;
            while (rac$v0 && rac$v2.hasNext()) {
                java.lang.Object obj = (java.lang.Object) rac$v2.next();
                rac$v0 = (!(MyClass.myList.contains(obj))
                    || obj instanceof java.lang.Integer);
            }
            return rac$v0;
        }
    }
    rac$v4 rac$v0Evaluator = new rac$v4();
    rac$pre4 = (((x > y) || (x < 0)) || rac$v0Evaluator.eval()); // (*)
} catch (JMLNonExecutableException rac$v5$nonExec) {
    rac$pre4 = true;
} catch (Throwable rac$v6$cause) {
    JMLChecker.exit();
    throw new JMLRacExpressionEvaluationError("Invalid Expression in
        \"FM08.java\", line 36, character 10", rac$v6$cause);
}
```

Fig. 6. RAC Code for precondition evaluation of method m()

package to support the expected output of the new semantics and ensured that all unit tests passed successfully.

Testing Code Generation Robustness. Aside from `racrun` tests, we also successfully compiled all the JML *model classes*, which are heavily annotated classes that specify abstract data types such as sequences, sets and bags. The model classes extensively use of the features of JML. Such a test suite helped us discover some design flaws that surfaced in rare circumstances. Most of them were for situations where operator precedence is not preserved during the translation from JML to Java.

While the `racrun` package gave us confidence in the behavior of the generated code, ensuring that the model classes could yield properly formed instrumented source code when compiled using the new assertion semantics demonstrated the robustness of the code generation for the new semantics.

Assessing Improved Capabilities. One of the goals of the JML community is to use its own tools. As was mentioned earlier, prior attempts to compile ESC/Java2 [11] with the JML RAC demonstrated that for a few source files, it would generate instrumentation code that had such large try blocks that it was impossible to represent them

```
1|try {
2|    rac$pre0 = (b && (this.x < this.y));
3|} catch (JMLNonExecutableException rac$v0$nonExec) {
4|    rac$pre0 = true;
5|} catch (Throwable rac$v1$cause) {
6|    JMLChecker.exit();
7|    throw new JMLRacExpressionEvaluationError("Invalid Expression in \"...\", line 5, ...", rac$v1$cause);
8|}
```

Fig. 7. Evaluation of precondition in the modified RAC

Table 3. ESC/Java2 source code statistics for `escjava` and `javafe` packages

Source code size (measured in MB)	Old Semantics	New Sem.	Δ	New/Old
`Escjava` Instrumented source code	33.6	26.5	7.1	≈ 78.9%
`Escjava` Instrumented bytecode	12.2	9.8	2.4	≈ 80.3%
`Javafe` Instrumented source code	35.5 30.5*	21.7 21.6*	13.8 8.9*	≈ 61.1% ≈ 70.8%*
`Javafe` Instrumented bytecode	10.7	8.0	2.7	≈ 74.8%

* Adjusted measurement in which we removed the code size for two files that could not be compiled under the old semantics due to the excessive size of try blocks in the instrumentation code.

in bytecode. We verified that with the new semantics, such a problem did not happen as all files were amenable to RAC compilation. Moreover, for the files that compiled using both semantics, we gathered statistics to measure the overall reduction in code size.

Measurements and Code Size Statistics. Throughout our assessment of the new semantics, we gathered some measurements that demonstrated an improvement in both size and performance of JML RAC-instrumented code. In order to understand the source of such an improvement, one should consider that the new semantics generates much less code to evaluate expressions than the previous semantics did, in part due to its more coarse approach, but mostly because it no longer plays the angelic vs. demonic undefinedness game for invalid expressions. Moreover, that code always takes advantage of short-circuited logical operators and does not try to assign a truth value to exceptional expressions. For instance, the instrumentation code of Fig. 3 (59 LOC) is reduced to only 8 lines of code under the new semantics—Fig. 7.

We observed that the `racrun` test package executes on average 8% faster than the version using the original semantics (average of 96.0s vs. 88.3s in five independent runs). Such an evaluation includes the parsing, checking, code generation, compilation, run and validation against expected output files of over 375 tests files. While using the new semantics on ESC/Java2 source, both the generated instrumented source code and bytecode showed a significant size reduction, as illustrated in Table 3. E.g., for the ESC/Java2 `escjava` package (301 classes), the instrumented source code using the new semantics was only 78.9% the size of the one instrumented with the original semantics (for this metric, we had the JML compiler emit the Java source corresponding to the instrumented runtime checking code that it would otherwise create a `.class` file for). For the instrumented bytecode, the new/original semantics ratio was of 80.5%. The compiler front end of ESC/Java2 (`javafe` package, 216 classes) displayed similar improvements in size. Two classes in the `javafe` package could not be compiled under the old semantics due to the excessive size of try blocks. If we factor out those two abnormally large (and uncompilable) instrumented source files, the new/original size ratio goes from 61.1% to 70.8%.

6 Effectiveness at Finding Bugs

Using the new RAC semantics, approximately 45 previously undetected errors have been found in JML specifications of the sample and model files (307 files, 77KLOC) included with the JML distribution. It should be noted that most of these sample and model files have been in use since 2002; some are from published specifications that

```
public /*@pure*/ class NaturalNumber implements TotallyOrderedCompareTo,... {
    /*@ spec_public */ private final BigInteger value;

    //@ public normal_behavior
    //@   ensures \result == value.compareTo(n.value);
    public int compareTo(NaturalNumber n) {
        return value.compareTo(n.value);
    }

    //@ also public normal_behavior
    //@   requires o instanceof NaturalNumber ...
    //@   ensures \result == ...;
    public int compareTo(Object o) throws ClassCastException {
        return value.compareTo(((NaturalNumber)o).value);
    }

    /*@ public normal_behavior
      @   requires !isZero() && exponent.equals(ZERO);
      @   ensures \result.equals(ONE);
      @ also
      @   forall NaturalNumber v;
      @   requires !(exponent.equals(ZERO)) &&
      @     exponent.compareTo(BigInteger.valueOf(Integer.MAX_VALUE)) <= 0; // (*)
      @ ... */
    public NaturalNumber pow(NaturalNumber exponent) { ... }
...
```

Fig. 8. Excerpt from the JML model class **NaturalNumber**

have appeared in peer-reviewed books or articles and hence have been carefully been reviewed by both human readers and/or analyzed by other JML tools. Of the errors found, slightly more than half are the specification equivalent of common programming errors (such as null dereferences[2] and array index out of bound errors) as well as some common object-oriented programming pitfalls.

As an example of the latter, consider the excerpt of the NaturalNumber model class, slightly simplified due to space constraints, given in Fig. 8. (Note that all declarations of reference types, with the exception of local variables, are non-null by default in JML unless annotated with /*@nullable*/ [5].) Under the new semantics, unit testing reports a ClassCastException during the precondition evaluation of the second spec-case at (*). Given this information one can easily see that the developer forgot to include a compareTo(BigInteger) method, and hence the call to compareTo at (*) resolves to compareTo(Object), resulting in a meaningless method contract due to the undefinedness of the precondition.

Most of the remaining errors had to do with recursive specification constructs. A simple example of such an error is illustrated by the excerpt from the specification for java.lang.Boolean given in Fig. 9. Notice how the model field theBoolean is represented by the expression "booleanValue()" and yet, the contract of booleanValue() defines it to be equal to the model field theBoolean. Hence each is defined in terms of the other. (Note that a JML *model field* is a specification-only field used to represent an abstraction of part of an object's or a class' state, for non-static and static fields respectively. The binding between the model field's value and the concrete state is given in the form of a represents clause.)

---

[2] A potential null-dereference is shown in Fig. 10—see the underlined occurrence of nextNode.

```
public final /*@ pure @*/ class Boolean ... {
    //@ public model boolean theBoolean;
    //@ represents theBoolean <- booleanValue();

    /*@ public normal_behavior
      @    assignable \nothing;
      @    ensures \result == theBoolean;
      @*/
    public boolean booleanValue();
    ...
}
```

Fig. 9. Excerpt from the JML API specification for **java.lang.Boolean**

```
//@ model import org.jmlspecs.models.JMLObjectSequence;

public class OneWayNode {   // Singly Linked Node
    /*@spec_public*/ protected /*@nullable*/ Object entry;
    /*@spec_public*/ protected /*@nullable*/ OneWayNode nextNode;

    //@ public model JMLObjectSequence entries;
    //@ public model JMLObjectSequence allButFirst; ...
    //@ protected represents entries <- allButFirst.insertFront(entry);
    //@ protected represents allButFirst <- (nextNode == null)
    //@      ? new JMLObjectSequence() : nextNode.entries;
    ...
}

public class TwoWayNode extends OneWayNode { // Doubly Linked Node
    /*@spec_public*/ protected /*@nullable*/ TwoWayNode prevNode;

    //@ public model JMLObjectSequence prevEntries; ...
    //@ protected represents prevEntries <- (prevNode == null)
    //@      ? new JMLObjectSequence()
    //@      : prevNode.prevEntries.insertBack(prevNode.entry);

    /*@ public normal_behavior
      @   assignable prevEntries;
      @   ensures prevEntries.equals(\old(prevEntries).insertBack(newEntry))
      @        && \not_modified(nextNode.entries);
      @*/
    public void insertBefore(/*@nullable*/ Object newEntry) {...}
}
```

Fig. 10. Classes from the **org.jmlspecs.samples.list.node** package

An example that is more involved is treated next. Consider the code excerpt from two classes in org.jmlspecs.samples.list.node package (Fig. 10): OneWayNode, used to build singly-linked lists and TwoWayNode used to build doubly-linked lists[3]. A OneWayNode contains an entry and a possibly-null reference to a next node (nextNode). TwoWayNodes extend OneWayNodes by adding a possibly-null reference to a previous node (prevNode). Two model fields are defined for a OneWayNode: entries which is the sequence of Object entries contained in the linked list rooted at this node; allButFirst, as the name implies, is the sequence of Object entries contained in the linked list rooted at this.nextNode, provided it is not null. Similarly, TwoWayNode defines the model field prevEntries to be the sequence of entries contained in the linked list rooted at this node but by following the prevNode field.

---

[3] Note that in the JML distribution, the specifications for these two classes are each spread over three files since use was made of JML's specification refinement feature. Since this feature is somewhat involved, a simplified—though equivalent—version of the classes and their specifications is given here.

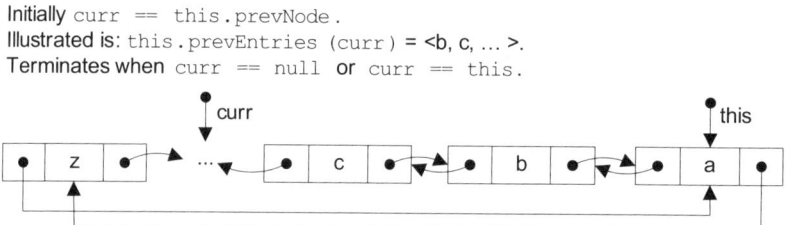

Fig. 11. Evaluation of **TwoWayNode.prevEntries** (terminates even for circular lists)

Running the test suite for this package using RAC instrumented versions of these classes reports a null-dereference error on nextNode.entries in the postcondition of TwoWayNode.insertBefore(). More interestingly is the fact that under the new semantics, a stack overflow error is reported. While at first we believed that the error might have been caused by a bug in our implementation of the new assertion semantics, inspection of the error reports allowed us to identify bugs in the specifications. Notice that the definitions of the representations of OneWayNode.entries, OneWayNode.allButFirst and TwoWayNode.prevEntries are all subject to looping forever if the nodes are part of a cyclic list. The main point here is that under the old semantics, the stack overflow caused by the use of any one of these three model fields would have been caught and translated into some truth value that would make true the overall assertion in which they occurred as subexpressions! A corrected specification for prevEntries is given in Fig. 12—the corrections for the other two model fields are

```
public class TwoWayNode extends OneWayNode
{
  protected /*@nullable*/ TwoWayNode prevNode;
  /*@ public model JMLObjectSequence prevEntries; ...
    @ protected represents prevEntries <- prevEntries();
    @
    @ public model pure JMLObjectSequence prevEntries() {
    @    // To detect cycles we use a helper function.
    @    return prevEntries(prevNode);
    @ }
    @
    @ public model pure
    @    JMLObjectSequence prevEntries(nullable TwoWayNode curr) {
    @    return (curr == null
    @             // the following disjunct prevents infinite recursion
    @             || curr == this)
    @           ? new JMLObjectSequence()
    @           : prevEntries(curr.getPrevNode()).insertBack(curr.getEntry());
    @ }*/

    ...

    /*@ public normal_behavior
      @    assignable prevEntries;
      @    ensures prevEntries.equals(\old(prevEntries).insertBack(newEntry))
      @         && (nextNode != null ==> \not_modified(nextNode.entries));
      @*/
    public void insertBefore(/*@nullable*/ Object newEntry) {
       ...
    }
}
```

Fig. 12. TwoWayNode **specification now correctly handling lists with cycles**

similar. Note how prevEntries is represented by the prevEntries() model method which returns the sequence of entries in the nodes reachable from this by following prevNode links until either null is reached or we have cycled by to this—see the illustration of **Fig.** 11. With this change, all tests pass under the new semantics.

7 Related Work

The use of program assertions as an aid in verifying the correctness of programs was first explored by Alan Turing in the late 40s. Over the decades, this idea was further refined by Computer Science founding fathers such as Goldstine, von Neumann, McCarthy, Floyd, Hoare and others [15, 16]. An early milestone in this vein was Hoare's 1969 Axiomatic Basis for Computer Programming where the pre- and postconditions of Hoare triples were expressed by means of assertions [14]. Early on, assertions were also introduced as a distinct construct in mainstream programming languages, and eventually, Hoare triples found their way into the programmer's tool box in the form of a method known as Design by Contract (DbC) [22]. A comprehensive report on the history of runtime assertion checking can be found in Clarke and Rosenblum's IMPACT report [10].

To our knowledge, all programming languages (or programming language extensions) supporting the use of plain inline assertions or DbC at runtime also support an assertion semantics like the one recently adopted for JML. The main reason is that it results in the simplest and most efficient runtime checking code. It remains a challenge to find a proper balance between minimalist instrumentation code with less useful error reporting in cases where assertions fail due to undefinedness vs. more accurate error reporting (which requires extra try-catch blocks to catch exceptions and wrap them up in another more meaningful exception before re-throwing it).

Another related challenge is to preserve soundness of the new assertion semantics in the context of static checkers like ESC/Java2. In [3, 4], we show how this can be achieved by making use of definedness predicates. Use of definedness predicates allows us to keep on using provers for classical logic (even though the new assertion semantics is essentially that of a three-valued logic). We note that the increase in processing time required for definedness checking in ESC/Java2 is currently less than 2% [4]. This is fairly small compared to the increase in static error detection offered by the adoption of strong validity (especially for API specifications for which little more than type checking was provided before).

A few other tools that make direct or indirect use of jmlc will be able to upgrade to the new semantics merely by making use of the new version of the compiler. This is the case for JmlUnit, a tool that can help developers create JUnit tests using JML specifications as oracles [8], and the SpEx-JML model checker [26]. Being build on the Bogor framework [24], SpEx-JML makes use of jmlc's core translation module to render runtime checking code for JML constructs. By making use of the new version of jmlc, SpEx-JML will in effect be implementing a form of model checking based on three-valued logic (in the spirit of [25]).

8 Conclusion

The work reported here was conducted as part of an ongoing effort to bring strong validity into all of the main JML verification tools. Using ESC/Java2, we have demonstrated the effectiveness of the new semantics by showing how it uncovered about 50 errors in the (143) API specifications of the java.* package [4, §6.1]. In applying the JML RAC (also with the new semantics), we have uncovered a comparable number of bugs in the JML model classes and specification samples which are a part of the JML distribution.

As future work we plan to finalize a few unresolved issues. For example, under the former RAC semantics, the value of \old expressions[4] that occur in method postconditions are evaluated before preconditions. This often leads to runtime errors under the new semantics since the evaluation of the \old expressions is meant to be guarded by the preconditions. That is, the pre-state evaluation of the \old expressions should be done if and only if the corresponding preconditions evaluate to true. We also need to better address the issue of short circuiting the evaluation of an assertion when one of its subexpressions raises an exception because it is non-executable. Currently we simplify the entire assertion to true; ideally we would want to simplify the smallest top-level conjunct that contains the non-executable subexpression.

References

[1] Burdy, L., Cheon, Y., Cok, D.R., Ernst, M.D., Kiniry, J.R., Leavens, G.T., Leino, K.R.M., Poll, E.: An Overview of JML Tools and Applications. International Journal on Soft-ware Tools for Technology Transfer (STTT) 7(3), 212–232 (2005)

[2] Chalin, P.: Reassessing JML's Logical Foundation. In: Proceedings of the 7th Workshop on Formal Techniques for Java-like Programs (FTfJP 2005), Glasgow, Scotland (July 2005)

[3] Chalin, P.: Are the Logical Foundations of Verifying Compiler Prototypes Matching User Ex-pectations? Formal Aspects of Computing 19(2), 139–158 (2007)

[4] Chalin, P.: A Sound Assertion Semantics for the Dependable Systems Evolution Verifying Compiler. In: Proceedings of the Int'l Conf. on Soft. Eng. (ICSE), pp. 23–33 (2007)

[5] Chalin, P., James, P.R.: Non-null References by Default in Java: Alleviating the Nullity Annotation Burden. In: Proceedings of the ECOOP, pp. 227–247 (2007)

[6] Chalin, P., Kiniry, J., Leavens, G.T., Poll, E.: Beyond Assertions: Advanced Specification and Verification with JML and ESC/Java2. In: de Boer, F.S., Bonsangue, M.M., Graf, S., de Roever, W.-P. (eds.) FMCO 2005. LNCS, vol. 4111, pp. 342–363. Springer, Heidelberg (2006)

[7] Cheon, Y.: A Runtime Assertion Checker for the Java Modeling Language., Iowa State Uni-versity, Ph.D. Thesis, also TR #03-09 (April 2003)

[8] Cheon, Y., Leavens, G.T.: A Simple and Practical Approach to Unit Testing: The JML and JUnit Way. In: Proceedings of the ECOOP, pp. 231–255. Springer, Heidelberg (2002)

[9] Cheon, Y., Leavens, G.T.: A Contextual Interpretation Of Undefinedness For Runtime Assertion Checking. In: Proc. Int'l Symp. on Automated Analysis-driven Debugging (2005)

---

[4] The occurrence of \old(e) in a post condition refers to the pre-state value of e.

[10] Clarke, L.A., Rosenblum, D.S.: A Historical Perspective on Runtime Assertion Checking in Software Development. ACM SIGSOFT SEN 31(3), 25–37 (2006)
[11] Cok, D.R., Kiniry, J.R.: ESC/Java2: Uniting ESC/Java and JML. In: Barthe, G., Burdy, L., Huisman, M., Lanet, J.-L., Muntean, T. (eds.) CASSIS 2004. LNCS, vol. 3362, pp. 108–128. Springer, Heidelberg (2005)
[12] Gamma, E., Helm, R., Johnson, R., Vlissides, J.: Design Patterns: Elements of Reusable Ob-ject-Oriented Software. Addison-Wesley, Reading (1995)
[13] Gary, T.L., Albert, L.B., Clyde, R.: Preliminary Design of JML: A Behavioral Interface Specification Language for Java. SIGSOFT Softw. Eng. Notes 31(3), 1–38 (2006)
[14] Hoare, C.A.R.: An axiomatic basis for computer programming. Commun. ACM 12(10), 576–580 (1969)
[15] Hoare, C.A.R.: Assertions: A Personal Perspective. IEEE Annals of the History of Computing 25(2), 14–25 (2003)
[16] Jones, C.B.: The early search for tractable ways of reasoning about programs. IEEE Annals of the History of Computing 25(2), 26–49 (2003)
[17] Leavens, G.T., Baker, A.L., Ruby, C.: JML: A Notation for Detailed Design. In: Haim Kilov, B.R., Simmonds, I. (eds.) Behavioral Specifications of Businesses and Systems, pp. 175–188. Kluwer, Dordrecht (1999)
[18] Leavens, G.T., Cheon, Y.: Design by Contract with JML (2006), http://www.jmlspecs.org
[19] Leavens, G.T., Cheon, Y., Clifton, C., Ruby, C., Cok, D.R.: How the design of JML accommodates both runtime assertion checking and formal verification. Science of Computer Programming 55(1-3), 185–208 (2005)
[20] Leavens, G.T., Poll, E., Clifton, C., Cheon, Y., Ruby, C., Cok, D., Müller, P., Kiniry, J., Chalin, P.: JML Reference Manual (2007), http://www.jmlspecs.org
[21] Lindholm, T., Yellin, F.: The Java Virtual Machine Specification. Prentice-Hall, Englewood Cliffs (1999)
[22] Meyer, B.: Applying Design by Contract. Computer 25(10), 40–51 (1992)
[23] Rioux, F.: Effective and Efficient Design by Contract for Java. M.Comp.Sc. thesis, Concordia University, Montréal, Québec (2006)
[24] Robby, E., Rodríguez, M.B., Dwyer, M.B., Hatcliff, J.: Checking JML specifications using an extensible software model checking framework. International Journal on Software Tools for Technology Transfer (STTT) 8(3), 280–299 (2006)
[25] Sagiv, M., Reps, T., Wilhelm, R.: Parametric shape analysis via 3-valued logic. ACM ToPLaS 24(3), 217–298 (2002)
[26] SAnToS, SpEx Website (2003), http://spex.projects.cis.ksu.edu

Provably Correct Runtime Monitoring*
(Extended Abstract)

Irem Aktug[1], Mads Dam[2], and Dilian Gurov[1]

[1] Royal Institute of Technology (KTH), Sweden
[2] Access Linneaus Center, Royal Institute of Technology (KTH), Sweden

Abstract. Runtime monitoring is an established technique for enforcing a wide range of program safety and security properties. We present a formalization of monitoring and monitor inlining, for the Java Virtual Machine. Monitors are security automata given in a special-purpose monitor specification language, ConSpec. The automata operate on finite or infinite strings of calls to a fixed API, allowing local dependencies on parameter values and heap content. We use a two-level class file annotation scheme to characterize two key properties: (i) that the program is correct with respect to the monitor as a constraint on allowed program behavior, and (ii) that the program has an instance of the given monitor embedded into it, which yields state changes at prescribed points according to the monitor's transition function. As our main application of these results we describe a concrete inliner, and use the annotation scheme to characterize its correctness. For this inliner, correctness of the level II annotations can be decided efficiently by a weakest precondition annotation checker, thus allowing on-device checking of inlining correctness in a proof-carrying code setting.

1 Introduction

Program monitoring is a firmly established and efficient approach for enforcing a wide range of program security and safety properties [6,10,5,9]. Several approaches to program monitoring have been proposed in the literature. In "explicit" monitoring, target program actions are intercepted and tested by some external monitoring agent [10]. A variant, examined by Schneider and Erlingsson [6], is monitor inlining, under which target programs are rewritten to include the desired monitor functionality, thus making programs essentially self-monitoring. This eliminates the need for a runtime enforcement infrastructure which may be costly on small devices. Also, it opens the possibility for third party developers to use inlining as a way of providing runtime guarantees to device users or their proxies. This, however, requires that users are able to trust that inlining has been performed correctly. In this work we propose a formalization of monitoring and monitor inlining as a first step towards addressing this concern.

---

* This work was partially funded by the S3MS project, IST-STREP-27004. The second author was partially supported by the Swedish Research Council grant 2003-6108.

We focus on monitors as security automata that operate on calls to some fixed API from a target program given as an abstract Java Virtual Machine (JVM) class file. Automaton transitions are allowed to depend locally on argument values, heap at time of call and (normal or exceptional) return, and return value. Our main contributions are characterizations, in terms of JVM class files annotated by formulas in a suitable Floyd-like program logic, of the following two conditions on a program:

1. That the program is policy-adherent.
2. The existence of a concrete representation of the monitor state inside the target program itself, as an inlined monitor which is compositional, in the sense that manipulations of the monitor state do not cross method call boundaries.

The annotations serve as an important intermediate step towards a decidable annotation validity problem, once the inliner is suitably instantiated. Compositionality allows validity to be checked per method. This is uncontroversial, and satisfied by all inliners we know of.

By these results, the verification of a concrete inliner reduces to proof of validity of the corresponding annotations. We use this to prove correctness for an inlining scheme which is introduced in the paper. We also sketch how, for a program inlined by such an inliner, the annotations can be completed to produce a fully annotated program for which validity can be efficiently decided. Such a fully annotated program can then be used by a bytecode weakest precondition checker in a proof-carrying code setting to certify monitor compliance to a third party such as a mobile device.

Related Work A closely related result is the recent work on type-based monitor certification by Hamlen et al [8]. That work focuses on per-object monitoring rather than the "per-session" model considered here. Also, their results are restricted to one particular inliner, whereas we give a characterization of a whole class of compositional inliners.

Our results can be seen as providing theoretical underpinnings for the earlier work by Schneider and Erlingsson [6]. The PoET/PSLang framework developed by Erlingsson represents monitors as Java snippets connected by an automaton superstructure. The code snippets are inserted into target programs at suitable points to implement the inlined monitor functionality. This approach, however, makes many monitor-related problems such as policy adherence and correctness undecidable. To overcome this, we base our results on a restricted monitor specification language, ConSpec [3], developed in the context of the EU project S3MS.

Organization In section 2 we present the JVM model used in this paper. Sections 3 and 4 introduce the automaton model in concrete and symbolic forms, the ConSpec language, and relations between the three. In section 5 we give an account of monitoring by interleaved co-execution of a target program with a monitor, and establish the equivalence of policy adherence and co-execution. In section 6, the two annotation levels are presented, and the main characterization theorems are proved. In section 7 an inliner and its correctness are presented. We also sketch how to produce, for this inliner, fully annotated programs with a decidable validity problem. Finally, in section 8 we conclude and discuss future work. Due to space limitations, many technical details, all proofs and further examples are delegated to a technical report [1].

2 Program Model

We briefly present the components of JVM used in this paper.

Types Fix sets of class names $c \in \mathbb{C}$, method names $m \in \mathbb{M}$, and field names $f \in \mathbb{F}$. A type $\tau \in \mathit{Type}$ is either a primitive type, not further specified, or an object type, determined by a class name c. An object type determines a set of fields and methods defined through its class declaration. Class declarations induce a class hierarchy, and $c_1 <: c_2$ if c_1 is a subclass of c_2. If c is the smallest superclass (under $<:$) of c' that contains an explicit definition of $c.m$ then c defines $c'.m$. Single inheritance ensures that definitions are unique, if they exist.

Values and Methods Values of object type are (typed) locations $\ell \in \mathit{Loc}$, mapped to objects by a heap $h \in \mathbb{H}$, a partial assignment of objects to locations. Objects determine typed fields and methods, using standard dot notation, and $type(\ell, h)$ is the type of ℓ in h, if defined. A method definition is an environment Γ (usually elided) taking a method reference $M = c.m$ to a definition (P, H) consisting of a method body (instruction sequence) P, and an exception handler array H. Method overloading is not considered. The notation $M[L] = I$ indicates that $\Gamma(M) = (P, H)$ and $P(L)$ is defined and equal to the instruction I. The exception handler array H is a partial map from integer indices to exception handlers. An exception handler (b, e, t, c) catches exceptions of type c and its subtypes raised by instructions in the range $[b, e)$ and transfers control to address t, if it is the topmost handler that covers the instruction for this exception type.

Machine Configurations, Transitions and Type Safety A *configuration* of the JVM is a pair $C = (R, h)$, where R is a stack of activation records of the form either (M, pc, s, lv) for some method reference M, program counter pc, operand stack s, and local variables lv, or, for exceptional states, of the form $(\ell)_e$, where ℓ is the location of an exceptional object. $\mathit{Unhandled}(C)$ holds if C has an exceptional frame on top of the frame stack, and the current method does not have a handler for the exception. We assume a standard *transition relation* $\longrightarrow_{\mathrm{JVM}}$ on JVM configurations (cf. [7]). An *execution* E of a program (class file) T is then a (possibly infinite) sequence of JVM configurations $C_1 C_2 \ldots$ where C_1 is an initial configuration consisting of a single, normal activation record with an empty stack, no local variables, M as a reference to the main method of P, $pc = 1$, Γ set up according to T, and for each $i \geq 1$, $C_i \longrightarrow_{\mathrm{JVM}} C_{i+1}$. We restrict attention to configurations that are *type safe*, in the sense that heap contents match the types of corresponding locations, and that arguments and return/exceptional values for primitive operations as well as method invocations match their prescribed types. The Java bytecode verifier serves, among other things, to ensure that type safety is preserved under machine transitions.

API Method Calls The only non-standard aspect of $\longrightarrow_{\mathrm{JVM}}$ is the treatment of API methods. We assume a fixed API for which we have access only to the signature, but not the implementation, of its methods. We therefore treat API method calls as atomic instructions with a non-deterministic semantics. Our approach hinges on our ability to recognize such method calls. This property is destroyed by the *reflect* API, which is left out of consideration. Among the method invocation instructions, we discuss here only `invokevirtual`; the remaining invoke instructions are treated similarly.

3 Security Policies and Automata

Let T be a program for which we identify a set of *security relevant actions* A. Each execution of T determines a corresponding set $\Pi(\mathrm{T}) \subseteq A^* \cup A^\omega$ of finite or infinite traces of actions in A. A *security policy* is a predicate on such traces, and T *satisfies* a policy $\mathcal{P}$ if $\mathcal{P}(\Pi(\mathrm{T}))$.

The notion of security automata was introduced by Schneider [11]. We view a *security automaton* over alphabet A as an automaton $\mathcal{A} = (Q, \delta, q_0)$ where Q is a countable set of states, $q_0 \in Q$ is the initial state, and $\delta : Q \times A \rightharpoonup Q$ is a (partial) transition function. All $q \in Q$ are viewed as accepting. A security automaton $\mathcal{A}$ induces a security policy $\mathcal{P}_\mathcal{A} \subseteq 2^{A^* \cup A^\omega}$ through its language $L_\mathcal{A}$ by $\mathcal{P}_\mathcal{A}(X) \Leftrightarrow X \subseteq L_\mathcal{A}$.

In this study, we focus on security automata which are induced by policies in the ConSpec language (see section 4) and therefore are named *ConSpec automata*. The security relevant actions are method calls, represented by the class name and the method name of the method, along with a sequence of values that represent the actual arguments. We partition the set of security relevant actions into *pre-actions* $A^\flat \subseteq \mathbb{C} \times \mathbb{M} \times Val^* \times \mathbb{H}$ and *post-actions* $A^\sharp \subseteq RVal \times \mathbb{C} \times \mathbb{M} \times Val^* \times \mathbb{H} \times \mathbb{H}$, corresponding to method invocations and returns. Both types of actions may refer to the heap prior to method invocation, while the latter may also refer to the heap upon termination and to a return value from $RVal = Val \cup \{exc\}$ where exc is used to mark exceptional return from a method call[1]. The partitioning on security relevant actions induces a corresponding partitioning on the transition function δ of ConSpec automata into a function $\delta^\flat$ on pre-actions, and a function $\delta^\sharp$ on post-actions.

4 ConSpec: A Monitor Specification Language

A monitor specification in ConSpec determines a collection of security relevant actions (sra's), a security state, and for each security relevant action, a transition rule, using a guarded command-like syntax. In addition, in [3] a scope declaration is introduced which is ignored in this paper. As an example, consider the following specification:

---

[1] We disregard the exceptional value since we do not, as yet, put constraints on these in ConSpec policies.

```
SECURITY STATE bool accessed   = false; bool permission = false;

BEFORE File.Open(string path, string mode, string access)
PERFORM mode.equals("CreateNew")                          -> { skip; }
        mode.equals("Open") && access.equals("OpenRead")  -> { accessed = true; }

AFTER bool answer = GUI.AskConnect()
PERFORM answer   -> { permission = true; }
        !answer  -> { permission = false; }

BEFORE Connection.Open(string type, string address)
PERFORM !accessed || permission -> { permission = false; }
```

The sra's are self-explanatory. The security state is a pair of boolean variables accessed and permission, which record whether an existing file has been accessed and if a permission has been obtained. The example policy contains three *clauses* that state the conditions for and effect of the security relevant actions. The sra of a clause is identified by the signature of the method mentioned in the clause. The *modifiers* BEFORE and AFTER (or EXCEPTIONAL) indicate whether it is the call of, or the normal (or exceptional) return from, the method that is security relevant. For each sra, there can exist at most one event clause per modifier in the policy. In order to determine if the policy allows an sra, the guards of the corresponding clause are evaluated *top to bottom* using the current value of the security state variables and the values of the relevant program variables. If none of the conditions hold for the current sra, it is violating and no more sra's are allowed by the policy.

Fix a set *Svar* of security state variables and a set *Var* of program variables. The security state variables of ConSpec are restricted to strings, integers and booleans. Expressions *Exp* and boolean expressions *BoolExp* over $Svar \cup Var$ can access object fields and use standard arithmetic and boolean operations. Strings can be compared for equality or prefix.

The formal semantics of ConSpec policies is defined in terms of *symbolic security automata*, which in turn induce ConSpec automata.

Definition 1 (Symbolic Security Automaton). *A symbolic security automaton is a tuple* $\mathcal{A}_s = (q_s, A_s, \delta_s, Init_s)$, *where:*

(i) $q_s = Svar$ *is the initial and only state;*
(ii) $Init_s : q_s \to Val$ *is an initialization function;*
(iii) $A_s = A_s^\flat \cup A_s^\sharp$ *is a countable set of symbolic actions, where:*
$A_s^\flat \subseteq \mathbb{C} \times \mathbb{M} \times (Type \times Var)^*$ *and* $A_s^\sharp \subseteq \{(Type \times Var) \cup \{exc\}\} \times \mathbb{C} \times \mathbb{M} \times (Type \times Var)^*$ *are the symbolic pre- and post-actions, respectively;*
(iv) $\delta_s = \delta_s^\flat \cup \delta_s^\sharp$ *is a symbolic transition relation, where:*
$\delta_s^\flat \subseteq A_s^\flat \times BoolExp \times (q_s \to Exp)$ *and* $\delta_s^\sharp \subseteq A_s^\sharp \times BoolExp \times (q_s \to Exp)$ *are the symbolic pre- and post-transitions, respectively.*

ConSpec policies and symbolic automata are two very similar representations. The security state variables of a ConSpec policy determines the state of the symbolic automaton. Each sra clause gives rise to one symbolic action, and each guarded command of the clause gives rise to a symbolic transition consisting of the sra itself, the guard of the guarded command in conjunction with negations

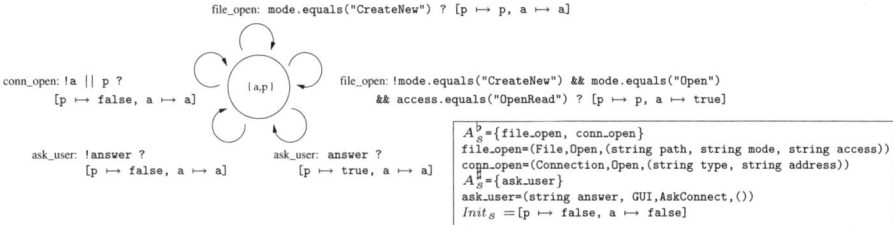

Fig. 1. Symbolic Automaton for the Example Policy

of the guards that lie above it in the clause, and the effect of the guarded command. The updates to security state variables, which are presented as a sequence of assignments in ConSpec, are captured in the automaton as functions that return one ConSpec expression per symbolic state variable, determining the value of that variable after the update. In fig. 1 we illustrate the construction on the earlier example, using "a" for accessed and "p" for permission.

Symbolic automata are converted to ConSpec automata without too much effort. The details are given in [1]. Here it suffices to note that states in the induced ConSpec automaton are members of the lifted function space $(q_s \to Val)_\perp$. The bottom element, in particular, is used only as the target of post-transitions that are disallowed (has an unsatisfied boolean guard) in the symbolic automaton; it has no outgoing transitions.

5 Monitoring with ConSpec Automata

In this section we formalize the enforcement language of a ConSpec automaton as a set of finite strings of security relevant actions. Each target transition can give rise to zero, one, or two security relevant actions, namely, in the latter case, a pre-action followed by a post-action. Accordingly, we define the security relevant pre-action, $act^b(C)$, of the configuration C, and the corresponding post-action, $act^\sharp(C_1, C_2)$, as in the table below. If none of the conditions of the table hold, the corresponding action is ϵ.

$act^b(C)$	Condition
(c, m, s, h_b)	$C = ((M, pc, s \cdot [d] \cdot s', lv) \cdot R, h^b)$ $M[pc] = $ invokevirtual $c'.m$ c defines $type(d, h^b).m$ $type(h^b, d) <: c'$ $(c, m, s, h^b) \in A^b$
$act^\sharp(C_1, C_2)$	Condition
$(v, c, m, s, h^b, h^\sharp)$	$C_1 = ((M, pc, s \cdot d \cdot s', lv) \cdot R, h^b)$ $M[pc] = $ invokevirtual $c'.m$ $C_2 = ((M, pc+1, v \cdot s', lv) \cdot R, h^b)$ c defines $type(h^b, d).m$ $type(h^b, d) <: c'$ $(v, c, m, s, h^b, h^\sharp) \in A^\sharp$
$(exc, c, m, s, h^b, h^\sharp)$	$C_1 = ((M, pc, s \cdot d \cdot s', lv) \cdot R, h^b)$ $M[pc] = $ invokevirtual $c'.m$ $C_2 = ((b)_e \cdot (M, pc, s \cdot d \cdot s', lv) \cdot R, h^b)$ c defines $type(h^b, d).m$ $type(h^b, d) <: c'$ $(exc, c, m, s, h^b, h^\sharp) \in A^\sharp$

We obtain the *security relevant trace*, $srt_A(w)$, of an execution w by lifting the operations $act^\flat$ and $act^\sharp$ co-inductively to executions in the following way:

$$srt_A(\epsilon) = \epsilon \qquad srt_A(C) = act^\flat(C)$$
$$srt_A(C_1 C_2 \cdot w) = act^\flat(C_1) \cdot act^\sharp(C_1, C_2) \cdot srt_A(C_2 \cdot w)$$

Then a target program T *adheres* to a policy $\mathcal{P}$, if the security trace of each execution of T is in the enforcement language of the corresponding automaton $\mathcal{A}_\mathcal{P}$, i.e. $\forall E \in \Pi(T).\ srt_A(E) \in L_{\mathcal{A}_\mathcal{P}}$.

Program-Monitor co-execution. A basic application of a ConSpec automaton is to execute it alongside a target program to monitor for policy compliance. We can view such an execution as an interleaving $w = (C_0, q_0)(C_1, q_1) \cdots$ such that C_0 and q_0 is the initial configuration and state of T and $\mathcal{A}$, respectively, and such that for each consecutive pair $(C_i, q_i)(C_{i+1}, q_{i+1})$, either the target (only) progresses: $C_i \longrightarrow_{JVM} C_{i+1}$ and $q_{i+1} = q_i$ or the automata (only) progresses: $C_{i+1} = C_i$ and $\exists a \in A.\ \delta(q_i, a) = q_{i+1}$. In the former case we write $(C_i, q_i) \longrightarrow_{JVM} (C_{i+1}, q_{i+1})$, and in the latter case we write $(C_i, q_i) \longrightarrow_{AUT} (C_{i+1}, q_{i+1})$. We can w.l.o.g. assume that at most one of these cases apply, for instance by tagging each interleaving step.

The first projection function $w \downarrow 1$ on interleavings $w = (C_1, q_1)(C_2, q_2) \cdots$ extracts the underlying execution sequence $C'_1 C'_2 \cdots$ such that $C'_1 = C_1$, and $C'_2 = C_1$ if $(C_1, q_1) \longrightarrow_{AUT} (C_2, q_2)$ and $C'_2 = C_2$ otherwise, and so on. To extract the automaton states and the security relevant actions, we use the (co-inductive) function *extract*:

$$extract((C_1, q_1)(C_2, q_2)w) = q_1 q_2\, extract((C_2, q_2)w)$$

if $(C_1, q_1) \longrightarrow_{AUT} (C_2, q_2)$,

$$extract((C_1, q_1)(C_2, q_2)w) = act^\flat(C_1) act^\sharp(C_1, C_2) extract((C_2, q_2)w),$$

if $(C_1, q_1) \longrightarrow_{JVM} (C_2, q_2)$, $extract(C, q) = act^\flat(C)$, and $extract(\epsilon) = \epsilon$. Note that $extract(w)$ may well be finite even if w is infinite.

Definition 2 (Co-Execution). *Let $E^\flat = \{qq'a^\flat \mid q, q' \in Q, a^\flat \in A^\flat, \delta^\flat(q, a^\flat) = q'\}$, $E^\sharp = \{a^\sharp qq' \mid q, q' \in Q, a^\sharp \in A^\sharp, \delta^\sharp(q, a^\sharp) = q'\}$. An interleaving w is a co-execution if $extract(w) \in (E^\flat \cup E^\sharp)^* \cup (E^\flat \cup E^\sharp)^\omega$.*

In other words, an interleaving is a co-execution, if the sequence of extracted automaton states corresponds to an automaton run for the security relevant trace of the underlying execution.

Theorem 1 (Correctness of Monitoring by Co-execution). *The program T adheres to policy $\mathcal{P}$ if, and only if, for each execution $C_1 C_2 \cdots$ of T there is a co-execution w for the automaton $\mathcal{A}_\mathcal{P}$ such that $w \downarrow 1 = C_1 C_2 \cdots$.*

6 Specification of Monitoring

We specify monitor inlining correctness using annotations in a Floyd-style logic for bytecode. The idea behind our annotation scheme is the following. In a first annotation, referred to as the *policy* (or, level I) *annotation*, we define a monitor for the given policy by means of "ghost" variables, updated before or after every security relevant action according to the symbolic automaton induced by the given security policy. In a second annotation, referred to as *synchronisation check annotation* (or level II), we add assertions that check at all relevant program points that the actual inlined monitor (represented by global program variables) agrees with the specified one (represented by ghost variables).

6.1 Language of Ghost Annotations

Assertions Methods are augmented with annotations that determine assertions on the extended state (current configuration and current ghost variable assignment), and actions on ghost variables. Let g range over ghost variables, $i \in \omega$, and let Op (Bop) range over a standard, not further specified, collection of unary and binary operations (comparison operations) on strings and integers. Assertions a, and expressions e used in assertions, have the following shape:

$$e ::= \bot \mid v \mid g \mid e.f \mid s[i] \mid Op\ e \mid e\ Op\ e$$
$$a ::= e\ Bop\ e \mid e : c \mid \neg a \mid a \wedge a \mid a \vee a$$

Here, $s[i]$ is the value at the i'th position of the current operation stack, if defined, and $\bot$ otherwise, and $e : c$ is a class membership test.

Ghost Variable Assignments Ghost variables are assigned using a single, guarded multi-assignment of the form

$$\vec{gs} := a_1 \to \vec{e_1} \mid \cdots \mid a_m \to \vec{e_m} \tag{1}$$

such that the arities (and types) of $\vec{gs}$ and the $\vec{e_i}$ match. The idea is that the first assignment $\vec{gs} := \vec{e_i}$ is assigned such that the guard a_i is true in the current extended state. If no guard is true, the ghost state is assigned the constant $\bot$-vector. This happens, in particular, when $m \leq 0$ in (1) above, which we write as $\vec{gs} := ()$.

Method Annotations. A target program is annotated by an extended environment, Γ^*, which maps method references M to tuples $(P, H, A, Requires, Ensures, Exsures)$ such that *Requires*, *Ensures* and *Exsures* are assertions, and such that A is an assignment to each program point $n \in Dom(P)$ of a sequence, ψ, of atomic annotations, either an assertion or a ghost variable assignment.

Annotation Semantics In the absence of ghost variable assignments the notion of annotation validity is the expected one, i.e. that the assertions annotating any given program point (or the point of exceptional return) are all guaranteed to be valid. To extend this account to ghost variables, we use a rewrite semantics, shown on table 1. In the table, extended configurations are triples of the form (ψ, C, σ) such that ψ is the sequence of annotations remaining to be evaluated

Table 1. Operational Semantics of Annotations

$$(1) \quad \frac{Assert(a, C, \sigma)}{\Gamma^* \vdash (a\psi, C, \sigma) \to (\psi, C, \sigma)}$$

$$(2) \quad \frac{\| a_1 \| (C, \sigma) = \text{TRUE}, \quad m > 0}{\Gamma^* \vdash ((\vec{gs} := a_1 \to \vec{e_1} | \cdots | a_m \to \vec{e_m})\psi, C, \sigma) \to (\psi, C, \sigma[\| \vec{e_1} \| (C, \sigma)/\vec{gs}])}$$

$$(3) \quad \frac{\| a_1 \| (C, \sigma) \neq \text{TRUE}, \quad m > 0}{\Gamma^* \vdash ((\vec{gs} := a_1 \to \vec{e_1} | \cdots | a_m \to \vec{e_m})\psi, C, \sigma) \to ((\vec{gs} := a_2 \to \vec{e_2} | \cdots | a_m \to \vec{e_m})\psi, C, \sigma)}$$

$$(4) \quad \frac{}{\Gamma^* \vdash ((\vec{gs} := ())\psi, C, \sigma) \to (\psi, C, \sigma[\vec{\bot}/\vec{gs}])}$$

$$(5) \quad \frac{C \longrightarrow_{\text{JVM}} C' \quad Unexc(C')}{\Gamma^* \vdash (\epsilon, C, \sigma) \to (A(\Gamma^*(M(C')))(pc(C')), C', \sigma)}$$

$$(6) \quad \frac{C \longrightarrow_{\text{JVM}} C', \quad Unhandled(C')}{\Gamma^* \vdash (\epsilon, C, \sigma) \to (Exsures(\Gamma^*(M(C))), C', \sigma)} \quad (7) \quad \frac{C \longrightarrow_{\text{JVM}} C' \quad Handled(C')}{\Gamma^* \vdash (\epsilon, C, \sigma) \to (\epsilon, C', \sigma)}$$

for the current program point in C. We use abbreviations M, pc, A, *Requires*, *Ensures*, and *Exsures* for the first to sixth projections, respectively. *Unexc* holds of a configuration that does not have an exceptional frame on the top of the stack, and $Unexc(C) \Leftrightarrow \neg(Handled(C) \vee Unhandled(C))$. The side condition $Assert(a, C, \sigma)$ always returns true, but as a sideeffect causes the arguments to be "asserted", e.g. to appear on some output channel. For rule (6), note that unhandled exceptions causes the assertions in the *Exsures* clause to be asserted.

Definition 3 (Validity). *A program annotated according to the rules set up above is* valid *for the annotated environment Γ^*, if all predicates asserted as a result of a Γ^*-derivation $(\psi_0, C_0, \sigma_0) \longrightarrow_{\text{JVM}} \cdots \longrightarrow_{\text{JVM}} (\psi_n, C_n, \sigma_n) \longrightarrow_{\text{JVM}} \cdots$ are valid, where ψ_0 is $Requires(\Gamma^*(\langle \text{main} \rangle)) \cdot A_{\langle \text{main} \rangle}[1]$, C_0 is an initial configuration, and $\sigma_0 = \bot$.*

6.2 Policy Annotations (Level I)

The *policy annotations* define a monitor for the given policy by means of a ghost state. The ghost state is initialized in the precondition of the $\langle \text{main} \rangle$ method and updated at relevant points by annotating all the methods defined by the classes of the target program. We call each such method an *application method*. We assume that $\langle \text{main} \rangle$ is not called by any application method (including itself) and that all exceptions that may be raised by a security relevant instruction (i.e. an instruction that may lead to a security relevant action) are covered by a handler. We also assume that the exception handling is structured such that the only way an instruction in an exception handler gets executed is if an exception has been raised and caught by the handler that the instruction belongs to. Finally, we assume w.l.o.g. that there are no jumps to instructions below method invocations.

Updating the Specified Security State. The updates to the specified security state are done according to the transitions of the symbolic automaton. If the automaton does not have a transition for a security relevant method call, the call is violating and the corresponding annotation sets the value of the specified state to undefined. Such a program should terminate without executing the next security relevant action in order to adhere to the policy. This is specified by asserting, as a precondition to each security relevant method invocation and at updates to the ghost state, that the ghost state is not undefined. If a security relevant instruction may cause a pre-action (an unexceptional post-action) of the automaton, then a ghost assignment annotation is inserted as a precondition (as a postcondition) to this instruction. Finally, if the instruction can cause an exceptional post-action, the update is inserted as a precondition to the first instruction of each exception handler that covers the instruction.

Preliminary Definitions In the definitions below, fix a program T and a policy $\mathcal{P}$. Let $\mathcal{A}_s = (q_s, A_s, \delta_s, Init_s)$ be the symbolic automaton induced by $\mathcal{P}$. We define the set $A_s^e \subseteq A_s^\sharp$ of exceptional symbolic post-actions as those which have the value exc as their first component. Given a symbolic action set A'_s, the function $RS((c,m), A'_s)$ returns those subclasses c' of c for which the method $(c'.m)$ is defined by a class c'' such that A'_s has an action with the reference $(c''.m)$. The variables of $\vec{gs}$ are named identical to the security state variables of the automaton. The ghost variable g_{pc} records labels of security relevant instructions. and ghost variables g stack values. For an expression mapping $E : q_s \to Exp$, let $\vec{e_E}$ denote the corresponding expression tuple, and for a boolean ConSpec expression $b \in BoolExp$, let a_b denote the corresponding assertion.

Level I Annotation We define the annotations for every method M, through three arrays of annotations: a pre-annotation array $A_M^\flat[i]$, a post-annotation array $A_M^\sharp[i][j]$, and an exceptional annotation array $A_M^e[i][k]$, where i ranges over the instructions of method M. The second index $j \in \{0,1\}, k \in \{0,1,2\}$ indicates whether the annotation will be placed as a precondition of the instruction ($j, k = 0$), as a precondition to the next instruction ($j, k = 1$), or as a precondition to all the exception handlers of the instruction ($k = 2$). The predicate *Handler* holds for a label L and a method M if $(L_1, L_2, L, c) \in H_M$ for some labels L_1, L_2, and class name c. In addition, we define $Exc(L, M)$ as the sequence of all annotations $A_M^e[L'][2]$ where L' is a security relevant instruction and there exists an exception handler $(L_1, L_2, L, c) \in H_M$ such that $L_1 \leq L' < L_2$, and as ϵ if such an L' does not exist.

Given these annotations, the *level I annotation* of program T is given for each application method M as a precondition $Requires_M^I$ and an array A_M^I of annotation sequences defined as follows (where $L > 0$):

$$Requires_M^I = \begin{cases} (\vec{gs} := \vec{e_{Init_s}}) \cdot (g_{pc} := 0) & \text{if } M = \langle \texttt{main} \rangle \\ (g_{pc} := 0) & \text{otherwise.} \end{cases}$$

$A_M^I[1] = A_M^\flat[1] \cdot A_M^\sharp[1][0] \cdot A_M^e[1][0]$

$A_M^I[L] = \begin{cases} Exc(L, M) \cdot A_M^\flat[L] \cdot A_M^\sharp[L][0] \cdot A_M^e[L][0] & \text{if} Handler(L, M) \\ A_M^\sharp[L-1][1] \cdot A_M^e[L-1][1] \cdot A_M^\flat[L] \cdot A_M^\sharp[L][0] \cdot A_M^e[L][0] & \text{otherwise} \end{cases}$

The annotation $Requires_M$ resets the value of g_{pc} and, if $M = \langle \texttt{main} \rangle$, also initializes the ghost state using function $Init_s$ of the automaton.

After Annotations For every method M, the elements of the post-annotation array $A_M^\sharp[L]$ are defined for each label L as follows:

(i) If the instruction at label L is not an `invokevirtual` instruction or is of the form $M[L] = $ `invokevirtual` $c.m$ where $RS((c,m), A_s^\sharp \setminus A_s^e) = \emptyset$, we define the pre- and postconditions to be empty: $A_M^\sharp[L][0] = A_M^\sharp[L][1] = \epsilon$

(ii) Otherwise, if the instruction at label L is of the form $M[L] = $ `invokevirtual` $c.m$ with $c.m : (\gamma \to \tau)$ and $|\gamma| = n$ and $RS((c,m), A_s^\sharp \setminus A_s^e) = \{c_1', \ldots, c_p'\}$, then the precondition of the instruction saves the arguments and the object in ghost variables:

$$A_M^\sharp[L][0] = ((g_0, \ldots, g_{n-1}, g_{\text{this}}) := (\text{s}[0], \ldots, \text{s}[n])) \cdot \textit{Defined}^\sharp$$

The assertion $\textit{Defined}^\sharp$ checks if the ghost variables are defined:

$$\textit{Defined}^\sharp = ((g_{\text{this}} : c_1' \vee \ldots \vee g_{\text{this}} : c_p') \Rightarrow (\overrightarrow{gs} \neq \overrightarrow{\bot}))$$

while the postcondition of the instruction uses these saved values to compute the new security state:

$$A_M^\sharp[L][1] = (\overrightarrow{gs} := \alpha_1 \mid \cdots \mid \alpha_m \mid \alpha)$$

where the α_k are the guarded expressions $(\overrightarrow{gs} \neq \overrightarrow{\bot}) \wedge g_{\text{this}} : c_i' \wedge a_b \rho_i \to \overrightarrow{e_E} \rho_i$ where class c'' defines (c_i', m) and there exists $a_s^\sharp = (\tau\, x, c'', m, (\tau_0\, x_0, \ldots, \tau_{n-1}\, x_{n-1}))$, $a_s^\sharp \in A_s^\sharp \setminus A_s^e$ such that $(a_s^\sharp, b, E) \in \delta_s^\sharp$. The substitution ρ_i is defined as $[\text{s}[0]/x, g_0/x_0, \ldots, g_{n-1}/x_{n-1}, g_{this}/\text{this}]$. Finally, $\alpha = \neg(g_{\text{this}} : c_1' \vee \ldots \vee g_{\text{this}} : c_p') \to \overrightarrow{gs}$.

The annotation arrays $A_M^\flat$ and A_M^e are defined similarly (see [1] for details).

Each execution of a program that is valid w.r.t. level I annotations for policy $\mathcal{P}$ is a co-execution of the program and the automaton for $\mathcal{P}$, where the automaton states are given by the ghost state; hence the program adheres to $\mathcal{P}$.

Theorem 2 (Correctness of Level I Annotations). *Program T annotated with level I annotations for policy $\mathcal{P}$ is valid, if and only if T adheres to $\mathcal{P}$.*

6.3 Synchronisation Check Annotations (Level II)

An inlined program can be expected to contain an explicit representation of the security state, an *embedded state*, which is updated in synchrony with the execution of security relevant actions. The level II annotations aim to capture this idea in a generic form that is independent of the design choices a specific inliner may make. To this end, we make two assumptions on the inliner. We require that the embedded state is in agreement with the ghost state immediately prior to execution of a security relevant action. This condition would be violated by, for example, an optimized inliner which determines in advance that a fixed sequence of security relevant actions is permissible and reflects this to the embedded state through only a single update. The second assumption we make in this section is that updates to the embedded state are made *locally*, that is by the method that executes the security relevant method call. The specified and the embedded states are synchronized then at all call points.

For simplicity we assume that the embedded state is determined as a fixed vector $\vec{ms}$ of global static variables of the target program, of types corresponding pointwise to the type of ghost state vector $\vec{gs}$. The *synchronisation assertion* is the equality $\vec{gs} = \vec{ms}$, and the *level II annotations* are formed by appending the synchronization assertion to the level I annotations of each application method M at the following points: (i) each annotation $A(\Gamma^*(M))(i)$ such that $P(\Gamma^*(M))(i)$ is an invoke or a return instruction, and (ii) the annotation $Exsures(\Gamma^*(M))$.

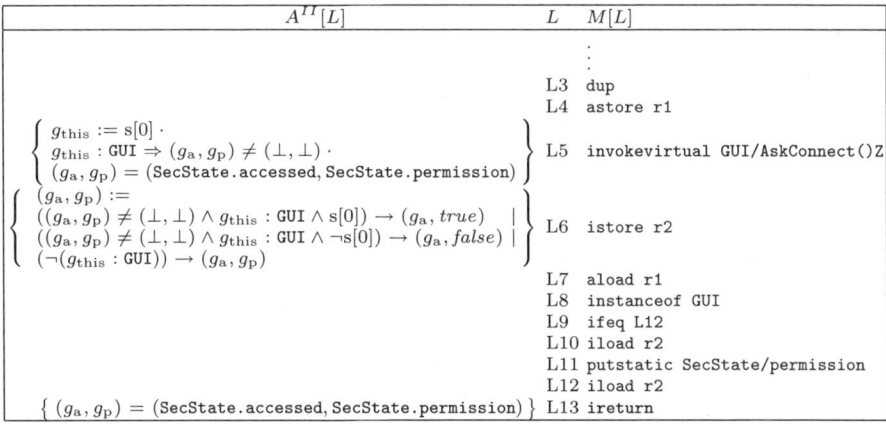

Fig. 2. An application method with level II annotations for the example policy

Level II Annotation Example. An application method annotated with level II annotations for the example policy of section 4 is shown in fig. 2. The ghost state is represented by the ghost variables g_a and g_p, i.e. $\vec{gs} = (g_a, g_p)$. The embedded state consists of the static fields accessed and permission of the SecState class. It is assumed that the class GUI does not have any subclasses. The annotated method is valid since the embedded state is updated as is described by the policy, after a call to the method GUI.AskConnect. The annotations are enclosed by braces and placed on the left of the instruction label they are associated with.

Level II Characterization. We now explain in what sense the level II annotations characterize the two conditions assumed in this section (the synchronous update assumption, and the method-local update assumption).

Consider a program T with a level II annotated environment Γ^*. Consider an execution $E = C_0 C_1 \cdots$ from an initial configuration C_0 of T. The index i is a *sampling point* if one of the following three conditions holds:

(i) the top frame of C_i has the shape $(M, pc, s, f) \cdot R; h$, and $M[pc]$ is either an invokevirtual instruction, or a return instruction;
(ii) the configuration C_{i-1} has the shape $(M, pc, s, f) \cdot R; h$ where $M[pc]$ is an invokevirtual instruction, and C_i, the shape $(N, 1, \epsilon, f')(M, pc, s, f) \cdot R; h$;
(iii) alternatively, $Unhandled(C_i)$.

We can then construct a sequence $w(E, \vec{ms}) = (C_0, q_0)(C_1, q_1) \cdots$ such that: q_0 is the initial automaton state, for all sampling points $i > 0$, $q_i = C_i(\vec{ms})$, where $C_i(\vec{ms})$ denotes the value of $\vec{ms}$ in configuration C_i, and for any two consecutive sampling points i and i', for all $j : i \leq j < i'$, $q_j = q_i$.

The role of the sequence $w(E, \vec{ms})$ is similar to that of interleavings in section 5. However, the sequence $q_0 q_1 \cdots$ may not necessarily correspond to an automaton run: the intermediate automaton state is not sampled when a post-action is followed by a pre-action without an intermediate method boundary crossing, as there is no well-defined point where this might be done. The construction also needs to account for the method-local nature of embedded state updates. For this reason, we define the operation $extract_{II}$, taking sequences w to strings over the alphabet $Q \cup A \cup \{\mathtt{I}\}$ where $\mathtt{I}$ is a distinguished symbol, by the following conditions:

- $extract_{II}((C_1, q_1)(C_2, q_2)w) = q_1\, act^\flat(C_1)\, act^\sharp(C_1, C_2) q_2\, extract_{II}((C_2, q_2)w)$, if C_1 is an API method call.
- $extract_{II}((C_1, q_1)(C_2, q_2)w) = q_1 \mathtt{I} q_2\, extract_{II}((C_2, q_2)w)$, if C_1 is an application method call and $Unexc(C_2)$, i.e. C_2 is a method entry point.
- $extract_{II}((C, q)w) = q\mathtt{I}q\, extract_{II}(w)$, if C is a return point from an application method, either normal or exceptional.
- $extract_{II}((C_1, q_1)(C_2, q_2)w) = extract_{II}((C_2, q_2)w)$, otherwise.
- $extract_{II}((C, q)) = q\, act^\flat(C)$ if C is a method call and ϵ otherwise.

Definition 4 (Method-local Co-execution). *Let*

$\Sigma_0 = \{\mathtt{I}, q, a^\flat, a^\sharp \mid q \in Q, a^\flat \in A^\flat, a^\sharp \in A^\sharp\}$,
$\Sigma_1 = \{\mathtt{I}\} \cup Q \cup E^\flat \cup E^\sharp \cup \{a^\sharp qq'a^\flat \mid \exists q''. \delta^\flat(q, a^\flat) = q'', \delta^\sharp(q'', a^\sharp) = q'\}$,
$\Sigma_2 = \{qq'q'', qq'q, \mathtt{I}qq'a^\sharp, \mathtt{I}qq'\mathtt{I}, \mathtt{I}qq'q', qa^\sharp q',$
$\quad\quad qa^\flat a^\sharp q', a^\flat qq'q', a^\flat qq'\mathtt{I}, a^\flat qq'a^\sharp, q\mathtt{I}q', qa^\flat q' \mid q \neq q' \neq q''\}$

A sequence w is a method-local co-execution, if

$$extract_{II}(w) \in (\Sigma_1^* \cup \Sigma_1^\omega) \setminus (\Sigma_0^* \cdot \Sigma_2 \cdot (\Sigma_0^* \cup \Sigma_0^\omega))$$

We can then extend theorem 2 to the situation where a target program T has a monitor for the given policy inlined into it.

Theorem 3 (Level II Characterization). *The level II annotation of T with embedded state $\vec{ms}$ is valid if, and only if, for each execution E of T, the sequence $w(E, \vec{ms})$ is a method-local co-execution.*

7 Correctness of Inlining

As an application of the annotation scheme described in the previous section, we characterize the correctness of a class of inliners in the flavor of PoET/PSLang [6]. We first describe the operation of a simple inliner that embeds, in target programs, a method-local monitor for a ConSpec policy.

Description of Inlining The inliner adds a class definition to the program. The static variables of this class serve as the embedded state. Since this class is not in the original namespace, the embedded state is safe from interference by the target. For each clause in the policy, a piece of bytecode is created, which evaluates, in turn, the guards of guarded commands and either updates the security state according to the update block associated with the first condition that holds or quits the program if none of them hold.

The rewriting process consists of identifying method invocation instructions that lead to security relevant actions (security relevant instructions), and for each such instruction, inserting code produced by policy compilation in an appropriate manner. The inliner inserts, immediately before the security relevant instruction, code that records the object the method is called for, and the arguments (and possibly parts of the heap) in local variables. Then, code for the relevant BEFORE clauses of the policy (if any) is inserted. Next, the object and the method arguments are restored on the stack. If there are AFTER clauses in the policy for the instruction, first the return value (if any) is recorded in a local variable, the code compiled from the AFTER clauses is inlined, followed by code to restore the return value on the stack. Finally, if there are EXCEPTIONAL clauses for the instruction, an exception handler is created that covers only the method invocation instruction and catches all types of exceptions. It is placed highest amongst the handlers for this label in the handler list, so that whenever the instruction throws an exception, this handler will be executed. The code of this exception handler consists of code created for the related EXCEPTIONAL clauses and ends by rethrowing the caught exception. All (original) exception handlers of the program that cover the security relevant instruction are redirected to cover this last throw instruction instead.

Due to virtual method call resolution, execution of an invocation instruction can give rise to different security relevant actions. The inliner inserts code to resolve, at runtime, the signature of the method that is called, using the type of the object that the method is invoked on, and information on which methods have been overridden. A check to compare this signature against the signature of the event mentioned in the clause is prepended to code compiled for the clause.

Correctness of Inlining Inliners as described above are expected to satisfy the following property. Let $\mathcal{P}$ be a policy, T a program and $M[L]$ be a post-security relevant instruction $M[L]$ of the inlined program T'. Let $M[L] =$ invokevirtual $(c.m)$ for some c and m, $\alpha_1, \ldots, \alpha_m$ be the guarded expressions $g_{\text{this}} : c'_i \wedge a_b \rho_i \rightarrow \overrightarrow{e_E}\rho_i$, $1 \leq i \leq m$, and α be $\neg(g_{\text{this}} : c'_1 \vee \ldots \vee g_{\text{this}} : c'_p) \rightarrow \overrightarrow{gs}$, induced, by the policy, for $M[L]$ as described in section 6.2. Furthermore, let r_{this} be the local variable used by the inliner to record the reference of the object $M[L]$ operates on. Then the weakest pre-condition of the block of code inlined immediately after the instruction $M[L]$ in T' w.r.t. the synchronisation assertion $\overrightarrow{gs} = \overrightarrow{ms}$ is the logical assertion

$$\bigwedge_{1 \leq i \leq m} r_{\text{this}} : c'_i \wedge a_b \rho'_i \rightarrow \overrightarrow{gs} = \overrightarrow{e_E}\rho'_i$$
$$\wedge \neg(r_{\text{this}} : c'_1 \vee \ldots \vee r_{\text{this}} : c'_p) \rightarrow \overrightarrow{gs} = \overrightarrow{ms}$$

The blocks inlined above and at the exception handlers of security relevant instructions can be specified similarly.

We claim that it is possible to devise an inliner in accordance with the description above. Let I be such an inliner, and let I(T,$\mathcal{P}$) denote the program T inlined by I for the policy $\mathcal{P}$. Our implementation of such an inliner is found at [2].

The following result shows that programs inlined for a policy contain a monitor as characterized by theorem 3, and that level II annotations can be efficiently completed to a "fully" annotated program for which annotation validity, and hence policy adherence, is decidable. In the result, *local validity* refers to logical validity of the verification conditions resulting from a fully annotated program (see [4] for details).

Theorem 4. *Let $\mathcal{P}$ be a ConSpec policy and T a program.*

(i) The inlined program I(T,$\mathcal{P}$) is valid with respect to the level II annotation for this policy.

(ii) For I(T,$\mathcal{P}$), the level II annotation can be efficiently extended to an annotation so that: (a) the extended annotation is locally valid (in terms of the pre- and postconditions of the individual instructions) if and only if the level II annotation is valid (in terms of definition 3), and (b) local validity is decidable.

An extended (or level III) annotation as referred to above can be obtained by: (a) annotating all non-inlined instructions with the synchronisation assertion $\vec{gs} = \vec{ms}$, (b) extending the annotation to inlined instructions by means of a syntactic weakest precondition function $wp(M[L])$ (as defined in [4]), and (c) collapsing every annotation to an equivalent single assertion (see [1] for details).

As a corollary of theorem 2 and the above result, every program inlined with the described inliner adheres to the policy it was inlined for.

Corollary 1 (Correctness of Inlining). *Let $\mathcal{P}$ be a ConSpec policy and T be a program. The inlined program I(T,$\mathcal{P}$) adheres to the policy.*

Another corollary of theorem 4 is that the inlined program I(T,$\mathcal{P}$) yields only method-local co-executions. This is so since programs that validate level III annotations validate also level II annotations and thus theorem 3 applies to inlined programs.

As a consequence, a level III annotation as described above can be used for on-device checking of inlining correctness in a proof-carrying code setting.

8 Conclusion

This extended abstract presents a specification language for security policies in terms of security automata, and a two-level class file annotation scheme in a Floyd-style program logic for Java bytecode, characterizing two key properties: (i) that a program adheres to a given policy, and (ii) that the program has an embedded method-compositional monitor for this policy. The annotation scheme thus characterizes a whole class of monitor inliners. As an application, we describe a concrete inliner and prove its correctness. For this inliner, validity of the annotations can be decided efficiently using a weakest precondition annotation checker, thus allowing the annotation scheme to be used in a proof-carrying code setting for certifying monitor compliance. This idea is currently being developed within the European S3MS project.

Future effort will focus on generalizing the level II annotations by formulating suitable state abstraction functions to extend the present approach to programs that are not inlined but still self-monitoring. Another interesting challenge is to extend the annotation framework to programs with threading.

Acknowledgements. Thanks are due to Andreas Lundblad for discussions on many issues relating to this paper, and to Johan Linde for his work on the inliner tool.

References

1. Aktug, I., Dam, M., Gurov, D.: Provably correct runtime monitoring. Technical Report TRITA-CSC-TCS 2008:1, CSC KTH (2007), http://www.csc.kth.se/~irem/S3MS/TechRep07.pdf
2. Aktug, I., Linde, J.: An inliner tool for mobile platforms, http://www.csc.kth.se/~irem/S3MS/Inliner/
3. Aktug, I., Naliuka, K.: ConSpec – a formal language for policy specification. In: Piessens, F., Massacci, F. (eds.) Proc. of The First Int. Workshop on Run Time Enforcement for Mobile and Distributed Systems (REM 2007). Electronic Notes in Theoretical Computer Science, vol. 197-1, pp. 45–58 (2007)
4. Bannwart, F.Y., Müller, P.: A logic for bytecode. In: Proc. of BYTECODE 2005. ENTCS, vol. 141-1, pp. 255–273 (2005)
5. Bauer, L., Ligatti, J., Walker, D.: Composing security policies with Polymer. In: Proc. of the ACM SIGPLAN Conf. on Prog. Lang. Design and Implementation, pp. 305–314 (2005)
6. Erlingsson, Ú., Schneider, F.B.: IRM enforcement of Java stack inspection. In: IEEE Symp. on Security and Privacy, p. 246. IEEE Computer Society Press, Los Alamitos (2000)
7. Freund, S.N., Mitchell, J.C.: A type system for object initialization in the Java bytecode language. ACM Trans. Program. Lang. Syst. 21(6), 1196–1250 (1999)
8. Hamlen, K.W., Morrisett, G., Schneider, F.B.: Certified in-lined reference monitoring on .NET. In: Proc. of the ACM SIGPLAN Workshop on Programming Languages and Analysis for Security (PLAS 2006), June 2006, pp. 7–16 (2006)
9. Hamlen, K.W., Morrisett, G., Schneider, F.B.: Computability classes for enforcement mechanisms. ACM Trans. Program. Lang. Syst. 28(1), 175–205 (2006)
10. Havelund, K., Rosu, G.: Synthesizing monitors for safety properties. In: Katoen, J.-P., Stevens, P. (eds.) ETAPS 2002 and TACAS 2002. LNCS, vol. 2280, pp. 342–356. Springer, Heidelberg (2002)
11. Schneider, F.B.: Enforceable security policies. ACM Trans. Infinite Systems Security 3(1), 30–50 (2000)

A Schedulerless Semantics of TLM Models Written in SystemC Via Translation into LOTOS

Olivier Ponsini and Wendelin Serwe

INRIA, 655, avenue de l'Europe, 38334 Saint-Ismier Cedex, France
{olivier.ponsini,wendelin.serwe}@inria.fr

Abstract. TLM (Transaction-Level Modeling) was introduced to cope with the increasing complexity of Systems-on-Chip designs by raising the modeling level. Currently, TLM is primarily used for system-level functional testing and simulation using the SystemC C++ API widely accepted in industry. Nevertheless, TLM requires a careful handling of asynchronous concurrency. In this paper, we give a semantics to TLM models written in SystemC via a translation into the process algebra LOTOS, enabling the verification of the models with the CADP toolbox dedicated to asynchronous systems. Contrary to other works on formal verification of TLM models written in SystemC, our approach targets fully asynchronous TLM without the restrictions imposed by the SystemC simulation semantics. We argue that this approach leads to more dependable models.

1 Introduction

Systems-on-Chip combine several hardware components with embedded software in a single integrated circuit. TLM (Transaction-Level Modeling) was introduced to cope with the increasing complexity and time-to-market pressure of Systems-on-Chip by using reference descriptions closer to system-level. Compared to traditional RTL (Register Transfer Level) based design flows, TLM reduces both the development time of virtual test platforms and the simulation time, allowing to run the embedded software earlier and to perform functional testing of the system.

TLM is still a rather informal concept. In this paper, we use the definition given in [4]. TLM models describe both system architecture and behavior. The hardware part of a system is not required to be completely detailed, but only to be sufficient to develop and run the embedded software. A TLM model is a set of interconnected modules, whose behavior is represented by asynchronous concurrent processes communicating only through transactions and events. Dealing with asynchronous concurrency is known to be difficult due to the many possible interleavings of concurrent tasks. TLM models are no exception: explicitly and completely defining the synchronizations between processes is the key to ensure model correctness; unfortunately, this is also very error prone, so that formal validation techniques are required.

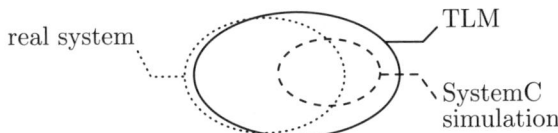

Fig. 1. Observable system behaviors

In general, TLM models are written in system-level design languages, among which the SystemC standard [16] has become the most popular. SystemC is a C++ library providing (1) types, methods, and macros to describe systems, including hardware, at various abstraction levels and (2) a simulation kernel, in particular a scheduler, to simulate the execution of the modeled systems. Simulation greatly helps functional validation, yet it is well-known that testing cannot prove the absence of errors, since exhaustiveness is impossible (at reasonable cost). This holds all the more for asynchronous concurrent systems, where the process interleaving space must be covered in addition to the data space. On the other hand, formal methods and tools dedicated to concurrent systems have a proper handling of asynchronous concurrency and can guarantee a property for all possible executions of a system.

Moreover, and to the contrary of the nondeterministic and asynchronous nature of TLM, the scheduler of the SystemC simulation kernel is nonpreemptive, has synchronous features, and imposes that for the same input the order of process execution does not vary from run to run. These properties of the scheduler are useful for testing and debugging, since they allow to reproduce a simulation run. However, they do not suit verification needs since they restrict the set of executions. Thus, as will be shown in Sect. 3.3, one may miss executions leading to erroneous states of the system.

Figure 1 compares the possible observable behaviors of different models and the real system. A TLM model is an abstraction of the real system, thus its behavior does not always exactly coincide with the behavior of the real system; further differences might be introduced during synthesis, since the step from TLM to hardware is not formally defined. A model based on the SystemC scheduler can only exhibit a subset of the TLM model behaviors. We advocate that verification over the increased number of behaviors of TLM leads to more dependable models and thus to more dependable embedded software. Therefore, we aim at a formal semantics of TLM models written in SystemC independent from the SystemC scheduler and its simulation semantics.

The contribution of this paper is a formal semantics of TLM defined via a translation from a TLM-subset of SystemC into the standard process algebra LOTOS [8], so as to enable the use of CADP (Construction and Analysis of Distributed Processes) [3], a rich formal verification toolbox that allows on the fly, compositional model-checking and equivalence checking of asynchronous systems. The translation has the following features:

- It regards SystemC as a description language for TLM and does not superimpose the SystemC simulation semantics to TLM semantics. This allows

to exhibit behaviors that might occur if the embedded software were run on hardware, but that would not be revealed by simulation with SystemC.
- It is parameterized to control asynchronous behaviors according to verification needs; in particular, the SystemC scheduler semantics can be reproduced if required.
- It preserves the architectural hierarchy (encapsulation of modules) of the SystemC description, since TLM models are not flattened to an unstructured set of processes. This facilitates compositional verification as well as going back and forth from the formal model to the SystemC code.

The rest of the paper is organized as follows. Related work is presented in Sect. 2. Section 3 surveys TLM and SystemC and discusses the limitations of the SystemC simulation semantics. The translation itself and a brief introduction to LOTOS are given in Sect. 4. Some experimental results are discussed in Sect. 5. Section 6 concludes.

2 Related Work

Both TLM and SystemC lack an authoritative semantics to which formal approaches could refer. As for TLM, there is no standard definition: [17] is a proposal seeking better interoperability between TLM models but it is still incomplete. The works addressing the issue of giving a formal semantics for TLM and/or SystemC differ mainly as regards the formal methods used and level of abstraction, *e.g.* cycle-accurate RTL, algorithmic level, or the so-called transaction levels, themselves divided into TLM PV (Programmer's view) untimed models and TLM PVT (PV + Timing) timed models. Focussing on a particular level allows to optimize the formal model, but may require to choose a subset of SystemC constructs. For instance, SystemC signals are important to RTL but not to TLM. The chosen level may also determine the target formalism: for instance, synchronous models seem adequate for RTL, whereas asynchronous models seem appropriate for TLM.

We distinguish four main lines of work targeting either low-level SystemC, full SystemC, TLM with SystemC, or TLM alone.

SystemC was initially designed as a language for modeling circuits, providing low-level hardware constructs such as hardware signals. A first line of work targets this low-level SystemC. For instance, [5] addresses temporal property checking for SystemC RTL level descriptions. [14] proposes an operational semantics for low-level SystemC, which uses distributed Abstract State Machines but limits asynchrony to two modules: the SystemC scheduler and the set of all SystemC processes, i.e. there is no asynchrony between the SystemC processes. [18, 6] define a denotational semantics for a restricted subset of SystemC. In this paper, we are interested in modeling of systems above this low-level SystemC.

A second line of work targets full SystemC, *i.e.* low-level SystemC as well as higher levels of abstraction. Various formalisms have been used to give a semantics to full SystemC, *e.g.* labeled Kripke structures [10], synchronous languages [19], Petri nets [9] or process algebra [12]. Contrary to our proposal, these approaches do not take advantage of the higher abstraction levels, in particular they are tied to the synchronous features of low-level SystemC. Moreover, most of these works flatten the hierarchical description allowed by SystemC.

A third line of work is interested in dedicated methods for TLM descriptions written in SystemC. In [13], a verification tool chain for TLM is developed upon synchronous communicating automata, with interfaces to synchronous languages and their model checkers. Recently, [20] proposed an encoding of a TLM-subset of SystemC in PROMELA, allowing a connection with verification tools based on asynchronous formalisms. However, these works have in common with the previous ones to integrate the SystemC scheduler as part of the formalized model, either explicitly [9, 13] or implicitly [10, 12, 19, 20]. Whereas the problem of covering more schedules is an active research direction (see [7] for instance), these works do not depart from the SystemC simulation semantics and its restrictions on the possible schedules, *e.g.* nonpreemption. Our work belongs to this third line, since we give a formal semantics to a TLM-subset of SystemC: we translate the PV level of TLM into the process algebra LOTOS. More importantly, we aim at verification of TLM, and distinguish between SystemC as a description language and SystemC as a simulation tool, *i.e.* we give a formal semantics to TLM models written in SystemC, not to TLM models as simulated by SystemC. Thus, in contrast to other works, our formal semantics of TLM does not integrate the SystemC scheduler and the simulation semantics it implies.

The fourth line consists in relatively few works interested in formalizing TLM models not written in SystemC. For instance, [21] presents the modeling of an on-chip bus protocol in LOTOS at TLM level. Seeking more generality, [15] gives first a formal definition of what a transaction should be (according to criteria applying to transactions in databases) and then derives guidelines how to implement complying transactions in SystemC, considering the SystemC scheduler specificities. Our approach is just the opposite: we start from a SystemC implementation of a TLM model and translate it into a formal language.

3 TLM Subset of SystemC

Although TLM is in principle not tied to a particular language, the SystemC standard [16] has gained wide acceptance for describing TLM models. In this section, we first outline the SystemC subset relevant to TLM PV. Then, we describe the SystemC scheduler and its limitations as regards verification.

3.1 TLM Principles

Basically, a TLM model is a set of components whose behavior and communication aspects are clearly separated. The behavior of a component is captured by a set of concurrent processes. Communication between modules is captured by transactions, which can transfer data and/or trigger events.

TLM models range over several abstraction subclasses whose boundaries depend mainly on timing accuracy and data granularity. In this work, we focus on

PV models as this level is intended for embedded software development and functional verification. PV models are untimed and the data granularity should fit the intended application rather than the hardware micro-architecture (*e.g.* a frame for a video processing unit, rather than the actual bus packets or hardware signals).

The PV model of computation is summed up by four points [4, p. 34]:

1. concurrent execution of independent processes,
2. respect for causal dependencies between processes using system synchronization,
3. bit-true behavior, and
4. bit-true communication.

Points (1) and (2) define an asynchronous model of computation where process interleavings are only controlled by explicit synchronizations between processes; points (3) and (4) ensure that functional verification is possible.

3.2 SystemC Description Language

The SystemC C++ library defines classes and convenience macros to describe system architectures. The components of a system are *modules* (`SC_MODULE`) whose behavior is specified by a set of processes. For simulation efficiency and synthesis concerns, SystemC distinguishes several kinds of processes, but we focus, without loss of generality, on *threads* (`SC_THREAD`). To our knowledge, TLM models have a static number of processes; thus, we do not handle process spawning.

Modules contain *ports* (`sc_port`) through which they communicate with other modules. Ports are connected either to other ports or *channels*.

Channels are used to encapsulate communication protocols, they are either primitive or hierarchical. Primitive channels, *e.g.* `sc_signal`, are only used in modeling levels lower than PV. Hierarchical channels are not very different from other modules.[1] Hence, we will not make the distinction in the sequel.

A *transaction* is a call of a method in another module (through a port). The calling process executes the code encapsulated in the other module. The two involved modules exchange data through method parameters and return value. Methods used for transactions are declared in *interfaces* (`sc_interface`) inherited by the module implementing the transaction.

Processes can also synchronize via *events* (`sc_event`). A process can suspend its execution waiting for a specific event e (`wait(e)`). When e is notified (`e.notify()`), all suspended processes waiting for e resume their execution; if there is no waiting process, the notification is lost.

Finally, SystemC has also constructs related to timing and to synchrony — *e.g.* delayed wait and notification, update-request mechanism of primitive channels — implemented in its simulation kernel by the so-called *delta-cycles*. These

---

[1] The difference between hierarchical channels and ordinary modules is that the former also inherit from interfaces specifying the implemented transactions.

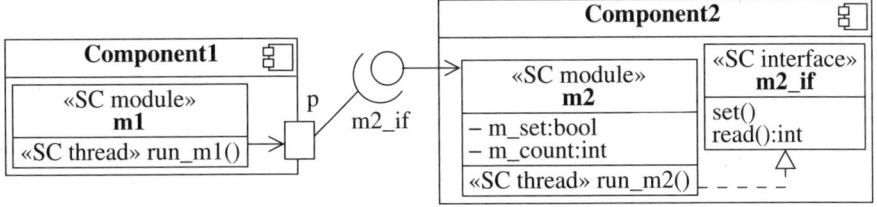

Fig. 2. UML diagram of the set-counter example

features are inherited from earlier versions, before the language was extended to support TLM, and they are not relevant to our discussion of the PV level.

For illustration, we use the set-counter example depicted in Fig. 2. Its SystemC code is:

```
SC_MODULE(M1) {
  sc_port<m2_if> p;
  SC_CTOR(M1) { SC_THREAD(run_m1); }
  void run_m1() { p->set(); cout << p->read(); }
};
class m2_if: virtual public sc_interface {
  virtual void set() = 0;
  virtual int  read() = 0;
};
SC_MODULE(M2): public m2_if {
  SC_CTOR(M2): m_set(false), m_count(0) {
    SC_THREAD(run_m2);
  }
  void run_m2() {
    while(true) { wait(e); m_count++; m_set=false; }
  }
  void set() { m_set=true; e.notify(); }
  int read() { return m_count; }
private:
  sc_event e; bool m_set; int m_count;
};
int sc_main (int argc, char *argv[]) {
  M1 m1("module1");  M2 m2("module2");
  m1.p.bind(m2); sc_start(-1); return 0;
}
```

Module m2 allows module m1 to set a flag (m_set) and to read how many times it was set. The program entry point sc_main instantiates the two modules and binds port p of m1 to module m2. Thus, in the thread run_m1, method calls p->set() and p->read() are transactions, in which run_m1 executes the methods set and read defined in m2. These two methods are declared in interface m2_if inherited by module m2. Transaction set sets data member m_set to true and notifies event e. Transaction read returns the value of counter m_count.

The behavior of m2 is described by run_m2: it waits for the notification of e, increments m_count and resets m_set.

3.3 SystemC Scheduler

In order to simulate the concurrent execution of several processes on a single processor, the SystemC simulation kernel uses a scheduler to select the process gaining control of the processor. In this section, we discuss two limitations, as regards verification, of the SystemC scheduler: immutable order of process execution and nonpreemption.

Immutable Order of Process Execution. Except for explicit synchronizations, TLM does not impose any order of execution of processes: they run concurrently with an asynchronous semantics. Synchronizations between processes define a partial order on process interleavings, allowing several different schedules. Although the choice of a schedule by the SystemC scheduler is implementation dependent, the SystemC standard [16] requires that all the simulation runs with the same input will choose the same schedule. This helps debugging since it allows to easily reproduce an erroneous behavior of the system. The downside is that other schedules may lead to different erroneous behaviors that will never show up with SystemC simulation.

In the set-counter, asynchronous concurrency means that the wait(e) statement of process run_m2 can occur either before or after process run_m1 has performed the transaction p->set(), *i.e.* either before or after event e is notified. This leads to two different system behaviors.

If the notification of e occurs *before* the wait, then the event is lost and run_m2 will deadlock since it will eventually wait for an event that will not be notified anymore. If the notification of e occurs *after* the wait, then run_m2 will resume its execution and eventually proceed.

These two behaviors are intended in TLM. However, the SystemC scheduler imposing an order of process execution no matter the number of simulation runs, only one out of the two behaviors will be simulated. Hence, simulation may miss the deadlock.

This deadlock can be prevented by replacing the statement wait(e) by while(!m_set) wait(e). With this modification, a correct synchronization between the wait of run_m2 and the notification of event e by run_m1 is ensured.

Non-preemption. The SystemC scheduler is not preemptive, *i.e.* a process runs without interruption until it explicitly gives control back with a wait statement. This is known as collaborative multithreading and is generally found easier to program with than preemptive multithreading, *e.g.* it simplifies access control to shared variables. However, this major difference with the concurrent model of computation of TLM may hide interleavings intended in the model and the final system.

For instance, when run_m1 gains control, it performs the two transactions, set and read, in a row. Although run_m2 is resumed by transaction set, with the simulation semantics of SystemC, this second process has no chance to execute before run_m1 explicitly gives control back, *i.e.* on termination in this case. Therefore, the value of m_count read by run_m1 during the transaction read is never updated by run_m2.

However, in real asynchronous concurrency as in TLM, once process run_m2 is resumed, the update of m_count could occur before or after run_m1 performs its transaction read. Therefore, the value of m_count read by run_m1 can either be the updated one or not. These two behaviors are intended in the TLM model, but only the second one is permitted by the SystemC scheduler. Hence, this synchronization problem between successive transactions is missed by simulation, and by formal semantics based on the SystemC simulation semantics.

4 Translation of the TLM-Subset of SystemC into LOTOS

In this section, we briefly present LOTOS and outline the translation of TLM descriptions written in SystemC into LOTOS. In the following, $\overline{L}$ denotes a list $L_1, \ldots, L_n$ of, depending on context, gates, variables, type-variable couples or values. We use the set-counter without deadlock as a running example.

4.1 LOTOS

The standard process algebra LOTOS (Language Of Temporal Ordering Specification) [8] allows to describe asynchronous concurrent processes communicating and synchronizing by *rendez-vous* on *gates*. LOTOS specifications are composed of a data part and a behavior part. For a complete description of LOTOS, we refer the reader to existing tutorials, such as [1]; in the following we briefly introduce the notions occurring in the examples of this paper.

Data values and operations are described by algebraic specifications in the style of ACTONE [2]. Types define a collection of *sorts*, *operations* on sorts and *equations* describing the meaning of operations. The verification toolbox CADP also allows to use external C data types. In the examples of this paper, we suppose that we are given an implementation of Booleans and natural numbers.

Behaviors are expressed by *terms* combining processes with algebraic operators. Figure 3 gives a grammar of behaviors; lower case identifiers stand for terminals and upper case identifiers for non terminals (P is a process name, G a gate name, X a variable name, S a sort name, and F a function name).

The semantics of LOTOS is formally defined by labeled transition systems. Here, we only sketch the meaning. A *rendez-vous* "G $\overline{O}$; B" on a gate G allows to communicate several values $\overline{O}$, called *offers*, either for emission (!) or reception (?); then behavior B is executed. Hidden gates $\overline{G}$ of B in "hide $\overline{G}$ in B" are unobservable, and unavailable for synchronization with other behaviors. "B_1 [] B_2" implements a nondeterministic choice between behaviors B_1 and B_2. "B_1 |[$\overline{G}$]| B_2" is the parallel composition of B_1 and B_2 synchronizing on the gates $\overline{G}$; pure *interleaving* "B_1 ||| B_2" is the special case where $\overline{G}$ is empty.

$$\begin{aligned}
B ::= &\ G\ O_1 \ldots O_n\ ;\ B & rendez\text{-}vous \\
      &|\ \texttt{hide}\ G_1, \ldots, G_n\ \texttt{in}\ B & hiding \\
      &|\ B_1\ \texttt{[]}\ B_2 & choice \\
      &|\ B_1\ \texttt{|||}\ B_2 & interleaving \\
      &|\ B_1\ |[G_1, \ldots, G_n]|\ B_2 & parallel \\
      &|\ B_1 >> \texttt{accept}\ X_1 : S_1, \ldots, X_n : S_n\ \texttt{in}\ B_2 & sequence \\
      &|\ \texttt{exit}(V_1, \ldots, V_n) & termination \\
      &|\ [V] -> B & guard \\
      &|\ \texttt{let}\ X : S = V\ \texttt{in}\ B & variable\ definition \\
      &|\ P[G_1, \ldots, G_m](V_1, \ldots, V_n) & process\ call \\
O ::= &\ !V\ |\ ?X : S & offer \\
V ::= &\ X\ |\ F(X_1, \ldots, X_n) & value
\end{aligned}$$

Fig. 3. Grammar of LOTOS behaviors

Synchronization on gates with offers only occurs if the offers are compatible (same number and types, same values for matching emissions). In the sequence "$B_1 >> \texttt{accept}\ \overline{X\!:\!S}\ \texttt{in}\ B_2$", on successful termination, behavior B_1 uses the operator "$\texttt{exit}(\overline{V})$" to pass results $\overline{V}$ of types $\overline{S}$ to B_2 through variables $\overline{X}$ (of types $\overline{S}$). A behavior B can be *guarded* by a Boolean expression V: "$[V] -> B$". A "$\texttt{let}\ X\!:\!S\!=\!V\ \texttt{in}\ B$" construct allows to define a variable X of sort S that can be used in B and is initialized to value V. Finally, a behavior B can be encapsulated in a recursive process P as follows: "$\texttt{process}\ P\ [\overline{G}](\overline{X\!:\!S}):\ E := B\ \texttt{endproc}$" where E is either $\texttt{noexit}$ or $\texttt{exit}(\overline{S})$.

4.2 Overview of the Translation

Our translation into LOTOS maps SystemC threads, transactions, shared variables, and modules into the single concept of LOTOS process. SystemC types are translated into LOTOS types. Two additional LOTOS processes are required. The *event manager* process is an implementation of the event communication mechanism used in TLM. The *lock manager* process is not the translation of a TLM concept. It is added to the LOTOS model so as to adjust the degree of asynchrony to verification needs.

Several LOTOS implementations may exist for a given concept (*e.g.* event communication). Due to lack of space, we will only briefly mention these alternatives. Translation of shared variables and locks are based on standard techniques from process algebra (e.g. [11]). In the following, we will write thread for a LOTOS process corresponding to the translation of a SystemC thread.

4.3 Variables of Modules

A variable v of a module can be shared, *i.e.* accessed by several threads or transactions of the module. If this is not the case, the variable is added as a parameter of the thread using it. Otherwise, it is necessary to introduce a dedicated process $\texttt{shared}_v$ that offers rendez-vous to read and write v. In LOTOS, this supplementary process avoids synchronizations between processes accessing the same shared variables.

If the type of v is Bool, $shared_v$ can be defined as:

```
process shared_v [read_v, write_v] (v : Bool) : noexit :=
   read_v !v; shared_v [read_v, write_v] (v) []
   write_v ?new_v : Bool; shared_v [read_v, write_v] (new_v)
endproc
```

A single process comprising all read/write rendez-vous suffices to handle all shared variables of a module.

Moreover, if a shared variable of a module m is accessed by threads of m and by threads of other modules, then it is necessary to duplicate the gates accessing this variable in order to avoid n-ary rendez-vous between the threads of m and the other threads. This is the case in the set-counter example with the shared variables of module m2: m_set (resp., m_count) is accessed for reading (resp., writing) by both run_m2 and transaction set (resp., read). Consequently, we introduce the two supplementary gates w_m_set_ext and r_m_count_ext that will be used by the transactions. The LOTOS code for the shared variables of module m2 is:

```
process shared_var [w_m_set, r_m_set, w_m_count, r_m_count,
                    w_m_set_ext, r_m_count_ext]
                   (m_set : Bool, m_count : Nat) : noexit :=
   w_m_set ?v : Bool;
   shared_var [w_m_set, r_m_set, w_m_count, r_m_count, w_m_set_ext,
               r_m_count_ext] (v, m_count)
 []
   r_m_set !m_set;
   shared_var [w_m_set, r_m_set, w_m_count, r_m_count, w_m_set_ext,
               r_m_count_ext] (m_set, m_count)
 []
   w_m_count ?v : Nat;
   shared_var [w_m_set, r_m_set, w_m_count, r_m_count, w_m_set_ext,
               r_m_count_ext] (m_set, v)
 []
   r_m_count !m_count;
   shared_var [w_m_set, r_m_set, w_m_count, r_m_count, w_m_set_ext,
               r_m_count_ext] (m_set, m_count)
 []
   w_m_set_ext ?v : Bool;
   shared_var [w_m_set, r_m_set, w_m_count, r_m_count, w_m_set_ext,
               r_m_count_ext] (v, m_count)
 []
   r_m_count_ext !m_count;
   shared_var [w_m_set, r_m_set, w_m_count, r_m_count, w_m_set_ext,
               r_m_count_ext] (m_set, m_count)
endproc
```

4.4 Locks

For various reasons (*e.g.* debugging, efficiency, knowledge of the system), it may be desirable to control the level of asynchrony in (parts of) the LOTOS model. This is possible using different *locking* strategies: locks ensure mutually exclusive execution of selected code parts. For instance, one lock per module acquired by each transaction of the module prevents simultaneous transactions in the same target module, whereas a single global lock acquired by each thread reproduces the nonpreemptive semantics of the SystemC scheduler. Several lock granularities for different parts of the system can be used to fine tune the desired behaviors of a model.

One or several lock manager processes can propose rendez-vous to acquire or release locks on gates lock and free. These gates may take an offer identifying a desired lock if a centralized lock manager is used for several locks.

To illustrate the use of locks with the set-counter, we implement a locking policy that prevents transactions and the thread of m2 from executing simultaneously. Thus, a thread or a transaction starts by acquiring the lock of m2, which is then freed only on suspension or termination. The corresponding lock manager process is:

```
process lock_manager[lock,free](m2_locked : Bool) : noexit :=
   [not(m2_locked)] -> lock !m2; lock_manager[lock,free](true)
   []
   free !m2; lock_manager[lock,free](false)
endproc
```

4.5 Event Communication

For an event e, an event manager process is used to record which processes are waiting for e and to resume them all nondeterministically on notification of event e. A wait(e) is translated into a sequence suspend !id_p !e; resume !id_p where id_p is the identifier of the waiting process. A e.notify() translates into a rendez-vous notify !e; if a process p is waiting for e, the event manager offers a rendez-vous resume !id_p to resume p.

For each process p possibly waiting for an event e (this can be known statically), we use one Boolean parameter of the event manager to record whether p is waiting for e or not. An event manager for an event e with two possible waiting processes $p1$ and $p2$ can then be defined as:

```
process event_manager[notify,resume,suspend]
                    (id_p1_e, id_p2_e:Bool): noexit :=
   suspend !id_p1 !e;
   event_manager[notify,resume,suspend](true,id_p2_e)
   []
   suspend !id_p2 !e;
   event_manager[notify,resume,suspend](id_p1_e,true)
   []
```

```
(notify !e;
(
    ([id_p1_e]->resume !id_p1; exit [] [not(id_p1_e)]->exit)
   |||
    ([id_p2_e]->resume !id_p2; exit [] [not(id_p2_e)]->exit)
) >> event_manager [notify,resume,suspend](false,false) )
endproc
```

For each process, an additional Boolean parameter can suffice to encode whether the process is waiting for a conjunction or disjunction of events. Finally, a single process may manage all event/process combinations, or several processes can be used to manage events local to groups of modules.

In the set-counter, there is only one event and run_m2 is the only thread waiting for it, so the event manager is simpler than the more generic one above:

```
process event_manager [n, r, s](b_run_m2 : Bool) : noexit :=
  s; event_manager[n, r, s](true)
  []
  [not (b_run_m2)] -> n; event_manager[n, r, s](b_run_m2)
  []
  [b_run_m2] -> n; r; event_manager[n, r, s](false)
endproc
```

4.6 Threads and Transactions

A SystemC thread T is translated into a LOTOS process whose behavior is the translation of the body of T. C++ constructs occurring in threads are translated as follows: an assignment to a local variable becomes a let construct, a conditional branching becomes a choice between behaviors guarded by mutually exclusive conditions ([cond]->if_part [] [not(cond)]->else_part), a loop becomes a recursive process, and a method call becomes either a process call or a call to a C function if the method only processes data without synchronizing. In this latter case, CADP calls the C function to compute a value if needed.

A transaction is also translated into a process P. Unlike threads, transactions may have input (request) and output (response). Inputs become parameters of P while outputs become results returned by P via the exit operator. Calling a transaction through a port is calling the corresponding process – which one is statically known.

In the set-counter example, there are two transactions, set and read. Their translation is:

```
process set[lock,free,notify,w_m_set_ext] : exit :=
  lock !m2;
  w_m_set_ext !true; notify;
  free !m2; exit
endproc

process read[lock,free,r_m_count_ext] : exit(Nat) :=
  lock !m2;
```

```
  r_m_count_ext ?n:Nat;
  free !m2; exit(n)
endproc
```

Then, the translation of thread `run_m1` calling the transactions is:

```
process run_m1[lock,free,notify,cout,w_m_set_ext,
               r_m_count_ext] : noexit :=
  set[lock,free,notify,w_m_set_ext]
    >> read[lock,free,r_m_count_ext]
      >> accept n:Nat in cout !n; stop
endproc
```

Finally, the translation of thread `run_m2` is:

```
process run_m2[lock,free,resume,suspend,r_m_set,w_m_set,
               r_m_count,w_m_count] : noexit :=
  lock !m2; run2[lock,free,resume,suspend,r_m_set,w_m_set,
                 r_m_count,w_m_count]
where
  process run2[lock,free,resume,suspend,r_m_set,w_m_set,
               r_m_count,w_m_count] : noexit :=
    r_m_set ?v:Bool;
    (
      [not(v)]-> suspend; free !m2; resume; lock !m2;
        run2[lock,free,resume,suspend,r_m_set,w_m_set,
             r_m_count,w_m_count]
    []
      [v]-> r_m_count ?n:Nat; w_m_count !n+1; w_m_set !false;
        run2[lock,free,resume,suspend,r_m_set,w_m_set,
             r_m_count,w_m_count]
    )
  endproc
endproc
```

4.7 Modules and Complete System

A SystemC module is translated into a parallel composition of the process handling its state variables with the translation of its threads.

As an example, the following is a translation of a module M with two threads P_1 and P_2, which use the gates $\overline{A_{\text{int}}} = \overline{A_{\text{int}_1}} \cup \overline{A_{\text{int}_2}}$ to access variables of M and the gates $\overline{A_{\text{ext}}} = \overline{A_{\text{ext}_1}} \cup \overline{A_{\text{ext}_2}}$ to access variables of other modules. Contrary to SystemC, transactions are not encapsulated in the owner module[2]. Consequently, the scoping rules of LOTOS require M to expose its variables via gates (here $\overline{A_t}$) to make them accessible to threads of other modules (through transactions of M).

---

[2] This solution has been investigated and leads either to complex handling of contexts, or to duplication of code; it is not exposed here.

```
process M[notify,resume,suspend,At,Aint,Aext] : noexit :=
   shared_var [Aint,At](var)
 |[Aint]|
   (P1[notify,resume,suspend,Aint1,Aext1]
   |||
    P2[notify,resume,suspend,Aint2,Aext2])
endproc
```

The module m2 of the set-counter is translated into:

```
process m2[lock,free,notify,resume,suspend,
           w_m_set_ext,r_m_count_ext] : noexit :=
   hide r_m_set,w_m_set,r_m_count,w_m_count in
   (
     shared_var[w_m_set,r_m_set,w_m_count,r_m_count,
                w_m_set_ext,r_m_count_ext] (false,0)
    |[w_m_set,r_m_set,w_m_count,r_m_count]|
     run_m2[lock,free,resume,suspend,r_m_set,w_m_set,
            r_m_count,w_m_count]
   )
endproc
```

Module m1 contains only one thread, thus m1 is translated into a call to run_m1.

The entire system is the parallel composition of all modules with the event and lock managers. Modules are synchronized with each other on the gates to access their variables (the union of the $\overline{A_{ext}}$ and $\overline{A_t}$ gates).

Finally, the translation of the entire set-counter system is:

```
(
  ( run_m1[lock,free,notify,cout,w_m_set_ext,r_m_count_ext]
   |[w_m_set_ext,r_m_count_ext]|
    m2[lock,free,notify,resume,suspend,
       w_m_set_ext,r_m_count_ext]            )
 |[notify,resume,suspend]|
   event_manager[notify,resume,suspend](false)
)
|[lock,free]| lock_manager[lock,free](false)
```

5 Experimental Results

We developed the LOTOS model of the set-counter without deadlock using two locking policies: without (a global lock has to be acquired by each thread and released on suspension or termination) and with thread preemption (no lock at all). The former reproduces the behaviors of the TLM model observable with the SystemC simulation kernel. The latter allows transaction interleavings, as required by TLM semantics. We also wrote a μ-calculus formula expressing what values of the counter may be read by initiator module m1 (cf. Sect. 3.3).

For both versions, we used CADP [3] to generate the corresponding automata and check the property (as expected, it holds only with preemption). We also

Table 1. Results for the set-counter example

i=initiator t=target		1i 1t	2i 1t	1i 2t	2i 2t	3i 2t
w/ preemption	generation time (s)	1.1	1	1.4	1.8	28.4
	number of states	77	1,201	1,109	48,149	1,940,977
	formula checking (s)	0.1	0.3	0.1	0.7	35.8
w/o preemption	generation time (s)	1	1	1.4	1.5	1.5
	number of states	35	141	149	770	3,334
	formula checking (s)	< 0.1	< 0.1	< 0.1	< 0.1	1.1
checking w/o $\subsetneq$ w/ (s)		1.4	1.7	2.7	32.6	450.4

verified that, modulo branching equivalence, the model without preemption was included in the model with preemption, but not vice versa.

Table 1 shows the results for different configurations of initiator (m1) and target (m2) modules. When several targets are available, each initiator performs set and read transactions with each target in sequence. Experiments were done on a Sun UltraSparc IIIi 1.6 GHz with 2 GB memory running Solaris 10 (time is in seconds and "generation" refers to the automata construction from LOTOS).

As a consequence of showing more behaviors, preemptive models (lines "w/") produce automata with a greater number of states than nonpreemptive models (lines "w/o"). However, first experiments show that minimization with respect to branching bisimulation reduces automata of preemptive models by factors up to 10^3. Therefore, compositional approaches might be very effective.

6 Conclusion

TLM models are nondeterministic and asynchronous, as may be the underlying hardware. Hence, they are difficult to apprehend and formal methods can help their understanding and verification. Since there is no formal semantics of TLM, most verification approaches refer to the simulation semantics of SystemC and its nonpreemptive scheduler. Such approaches cannot exhibit all behaviors of a TLM model, possibly leaving errors undetected, as we have shown in this paper.

We presented a translation from a TLM-subset of SystemC into LOTOS using a schedulerless semantics; our translation can be easily tuned to support the nonpreemptive semantics as a particular case. Although the interleaving semantics abstraction of concurrency, in which our approach is rooted, may not always correspond to physical true concurrency, it is widely accepted and proved efficient in many application domains. Experimenting our translation on several TLM models with CADP, we showed that our semantics is a strict superset of a nonpreemptive one and that the additional behaviors may reveal errors.

Automating a translation of TLM into LOTOS is a difficult task, since the former is informal whereas the latter has a precise formal semantics. The formalization of TLM is a necessary first step, to which the translation rules of this paper contribute.

References

[1] Bolognesi, T., Brinksma, E.: Introduction to the ISO Specification Language Lotos. Computer Networks and ISDN Systems 14(1), 25–59 (1988)
[2] Ehrig, H., Mahr, B.: Fundamentals of Algebraic Specification 1: Equations and Initial Semantics. EATCS Monographs on Theoretical Computer Science, vol. 6 (1985)
[3] Garavel, H., Lang, F., Mateescu, R., Serwe, W.: CADP 2006: A Toolbox for the Construction and Analysis of Distributed Processes. In: Damm, W., Hermanns, H. (eds.) CAV 2007. LNCS, vol. 4590, pp. 158–163. Springer, Heidelberg (2007)
[4] Ghenassia, F. (ed.): Transaction-Level Modeling with SystemC: TLM Concepts and Applications for Embedded Systems. Springer, Heidelberg (2005)
[5] Große, D., Drechsler, R.: CheckSyC: An Efficient Property Checker for RTL SystemC Designs. ISCAS 4, 4167–4170 (2005)
[6] Habibi, A., Tahar, S.: Design and Verification of SystemC Transaction-Level Models. IEEE Transactions on VLSI Systems 14(1), 57–68 (2006)
[7] Helmstetter, C., Maraninchi, F., Maillet-Contoz, L., Moy, M.: Automatic Generation of Schedulings for Improving the Test Coverage of Systems-on-a-Chip. In: FMCAD, 171–178 (2006)
[8] ISO/IEC. Lotos – A Formal Description Technique Based on the Temporal Ordering of Observational Behaviour. International Standard 8807, ISO, Genève (1989)
[9] Karlsson, D., Eles, P., Peng, Z.: Formal Verification of SystemC Designs Using a Petri-net Based Representation. In: DATE, pp. 1228–1233 (2006)
[10] Kroening, D., Sharygina, N.: Formal Verification of SystemC by Automatic Hardware/Software Partitioning. In: MEMOCODE, pp. 101–110 (2005)
[11] Magee, J., Kramer, J.: Concurrency: State Models and Java Programs, 2nd edn., April 2006. Wiley, Chichester (2006)
[12] Man, K.L.: SystemC^{FL}: A Formalism for Hardware/Software Codesign. European Conference on Circuit Theory and Design 1, 193–196 (2005)
[13] Moy, M., Maraninchi, F., Maillet-Contoz, L.: LusSy: A Toolbox for the Analysis of Systems-on-a-Chip at the Transactional Level. In: ACSD, June 2005, pp. 26–35 (2005)
[14] Müller, W., Ruf, J., Hoffmann, D., Gerlach, J., Kropf, T., Rosenstiel, W.: The Simulation Semantics of SystemC. In: DATE, March 2001, pp. 64–70 (2001)
[15] Niemann, B., Haubelt, C.: Towards a Unified Execution Model for Transactions in TLM. In: MEMOCODE, pp. 103–112 (2007)
[16] Open SystemC Initiative. IEEE Standard SystemC Language Reference Manual. IEEE Computer Society. IEEE Std 1666-2005 (2006)
[17] Rose, A., Swan, S., Pierce, J., Fernandez, J.-M.: Transaction Level Modeling in SystemC. In: Open SystemC Initiative (2005), http://www.systemc.org
[18] Salem, A.: Formal Semantics of Synchronous SystemC. In: DATE, pp. 376–381 (2003)
[19] Talpin, J.-P., Guernic, P.L., Shukla, S.K., Gupta, R.: A Compositional Behavioral Modeling Framework for Embedded System Design and Conformance Checking. International Journal of Parallel Programming 33(6), 613–643 (2005)
[20] Traulsen, C., Cornet, J., Moy, M., Maraninchi, F.: A SystemC/TLM Semantics in Promela and Its Possible Applications. In: Bošnački, D., Edelkamp, S. (eds.) SPIN 2007. LNCS, vol. 4595, pp. 204–222. Springer, Heidelberg (2007)
[21] Wodey, P., Camarroque, G., Baray, F., Hersemeule, R., Cousin, J.-P.: LOTOS Code Generation for Model Checking of STBus Based SoC: The STBus Interconnect. In: MEMOCODE, June 2003, pp. 204–213 (2003)

A Rigorous Approach to Networking: TCP, from Implementation to Protocol to Service

Tom Ridge[1], Michael Norrish[2], and Peter Sewell[1]

[1] University of Cambridge
[2] NICTA

Abstract. Despite more then 30 years of research on protocol specification, the major protocols deployed in the Internet, such as TCP, are described only in informal prose RFCs and executable code. In part this is because the scale and complexity of these protocols makes them challenging targets for formalization.

In this paper we show how these difficulties can be addressed. We develop a high-level specification for TCP and the Sockets API, expressed in the HOL proof assistant, describing the byte-stream service that TCP provides to users. This complements our previous low-level specification of the protocol internals, and makes it possible for the first time to state what it means for TCP to be correct: that the protocol implements the service. We define a precise abstraction function between the models and validate it by testing, using verified testing infrastructure within HOL. This is a pragmatic alternative to full proof, providing reasonable confidence at a relatively low entry cost.

Together with our previous validation of the low-level model, this shows how one can rigorously tie together concrete implementations, low-level protocol models, and specifications of the services they claim to provide, dealing with the complexity of real-world protocols throughout.

1 Introduction

Real-world network protocols are usually described in informal prose RFCs, which inevitably have unintentional ambiguities and omissions, and which do not support conformance testing, verification of implementations, or verification of applications that use these protocols. Moreover, there are many subtly different realisations, including the TCP implementations in BSD, Linux, WinXP, and so on. The Internet protocols have been extremely successful, but the cost is high: there is considerable legacy complexity that implementors and users have to deal with, and there is no clear point of reference. To address this, we have developed techniques to put practical protocol design on a rigorous footing, to make it possible to specify protocols and services with mathematical precision, and to do verified conformance testing directly against those specifications. In this paper we demonstrate our approach by developing and validating a high-level specification of the service provided by TCP: the dominant data transport protocol (underlying email and the web), which provides reliable duplex byte streams, with congestion control, above the unreliable IP layer.

Our specification deals with the full complexity of the service provided by TCP (except for performance properties). It includes the Sockets API (`connect`, `listen`, etc.), hosts, threads, network interfaces, the interaction with ICMP and UDP, abandoned connections, transient and persistent connection problems, unexpected socket closure, socket self-connection and so on. The specification comprises roughly 30 000 lines of (commented) higher-order logic, and mechanized tool support has been essential for work on this scale. It is written using the HOL system [11]. The bulk of the definition is an operational semantics, using idioms for timed transition relations, record-structured state, pattern matching and so on.

We relate this service-level specification to our previous protocol description by defining, again in HOL, an abstraction function from the (rather complex) low-level protocol states, with sets of TCP segments on the wire, flow and congestion control data, etc., to the (simpler) service-level states, comprising byte streams and some status information. This makes explicit how the protocol implements the service.

The main novelty of the approach we take here is the *validation* of this abstraction function. Ideally, one would *prove* that the abstraction relationship holds in all reachable states. Given the scale and complexity of the specifications, however, it is unclear whether that would be pragmatically feasible, especially with the limited resources of an academic team. Accordingly, we show how one can validate the relationship by verified testing. We take traces of the protocol-level specification (themselves validated against the behaviour of the BSD TCP implementation), and verify (automatically, and in HOL) that there are corresponding traces of the service-level specification, with the abstraction function holding at each point. Our previous protocol-level validation, using a special-purpose symbolic evaluator, produced symbolic traces of the protocol-level specification. We now *ground* these traces, using a purpose-built constraint solver to instantiate variables to satisfy any outstanding constraints, and use a new symbolic evaluator to apply the abstraction function and check that the resulting trace lies in the service-level specification. By doing this all within HOL, we have high confidence in the validation process itself.

Obviously, such testing cannot provide complete guarantees, but our experience with the kind of errors it detects suggests that it is still highly discriminating (partly due to the fact that it examines the internal states of the specifications at every step along a trace) and one can develop useful levels of confidence relatively quickly.

In the following sections, we first recall our previous protocol model (Sect. 2), before describing the new service-level specification (Sect. 3) and abstraction function (Sect. 4), giving small excerpts from each. We then discuss the validation infrastructure, and the results of validation (Sect. 5). Finally, we discuss related work and conclude.

2   Background: Our Previous Low-Level Protocol Model

Our previous low-level specification [5,6] characterises TCP, UDP and ICMP at the protocol level, including hosts, threads, the Sockets API, network interfaces and segments on the wire. As well as the core functionality of segment retransmission and flow control, TCP must handle details of connection setup and tear-down, window scaling, congestion control, timeouts, optional TCP features negotiated at connection setup, interaction with ICMP messages, and so on. The model covers all these. It is parameterized by the OS, allowing OS-dependent behaviour to be specified cleanly; it is also non-deterministic, so as not to constrain implementations unnecessarily.

This level of detail results in a model of roughly 30 000 lines of (commented) higher-order logic (similar in size to the implementations, but structured rather differently). As further evidence of its accuracy and completeness, it has been successfully used as the basis for a Haskell implementation of a network stack [13].

The main part of the protocol model (the pale shaded region below) is the *host labelled transition system*, or *host LTS*, describing the possible interactions of a host OS: between program threads and host via calls and returns of the Sockets API, and between host and network via message sends and receives. The protocol model uses the host LTS, and a model of the TCP, UDP and ICMP segments on the wire, to describe a network of communicating hosts.

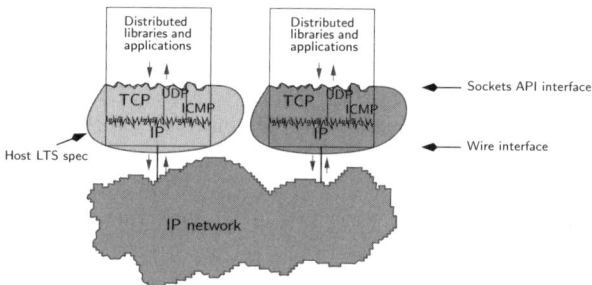

The host labelled transition relation, $h \xrightarrow{lbl} h'$, is defined by some 148 rules for the socket calls (5–10 for each interesting call) and some 46 rules for message send/receive and for internal behaviour. An example of one of the simplest rules is given in Fig. 1. The rule describes a host with a blocked thread attempting to send data to a socket. The thread becomes unblocked and transfers the data to the socket's send queue. The send call then returns to the user.

The transition $h \, (\!\!|...|\!\!) \xrightarrow{\tau} h \, (\!\!|...|\!\!)$ appears at the top, where the thread pointed to by *tid* and the socket pointed to by *sid* are unpacked from the original and final hosts, along with the send queue *sndq* for the socket. Host fields that are modified in the transition are highlighted. The initial host has thread *tid* in state SEND2, blocking attempting to send *str* to *sndq*. After the transition, *tid* is in state RET(OK...), about to return to the user with str'', the data that has not been sent, here constrained to be the empty string.

The bulk of the rule is the condition (a predicate) guarding the transition, specifying when the rule applies and what relationship holds between the input and output states. The condition is simply a conjunction of clauses, with no temporal ordering. The rule only applies if the state of the socket, *st*, is either ESTABLISHED or CLOSE_WAIT. Then, provided send_queue_space is large *send_3* **tcp: slow nonurgent succeed** Successfully return from blocked state having sen t data

$h \; (\!|ts := ts \oplus (tid \mapsto \boxed{(\text{SEND2}(sid, *, str, opts))_d});$
  $socks := socks \oplus \quad [(sid, \text{SOCK}(\uparrow fid, sf, \uparrow i_1, \uparrow p_1, \uparrow i_2, \uparrow p_2, *, \mathbf{F}, cantrcvmore,$
    $\text{TCP\_Sock}(st, cb, *, \boxed{sndq}, \boxed{sndurp}, rcvq, rcvurp, iobc)))]\!|\rangle$

$\xrightarrow{\tau}$

$h \; (\!|ts := ts \oplus (tid \mapsto \boxed{(\text{RET}(\text{OK}(\mathbf{implode} \; str'')))}_{\text{sched\_timer}});$
  $socks := socks \oplus \quad [(sid, \text{SOCK}(\uparrow fid, sf, \uparrow i_1, \uparrow p_1, \uparrow i_2, \uparrow p_2, *, \mathbf{F}, cantrcvmore,$
    $\text{TCP\_Sock}(st, cb, *, \boxed{sndq + + str'}, \boxed{sndurp'}, rcvq, rcvurp, iobc)))]\!|\rangle$

$st \in \{\text{ESTABLISHED}; \text{CLOSE\_WAIT}\} \land$
$space \in \text{send\_queue\_space}(sf.n(\text{SO\_SNDBUF}))$
  $(\mathbf{length} \; sndq)(\text{MSG\_OOB} \in opts)$
  $h.\text{arch} \; cb.t\_maxseg \; i_2 \land$
$space \geq \mathbf{length} \; str \land$
$str' = str \land str'' = [] \land$
$sndurp' = \mathbf{if} \; \text{MSG\_OOB} \in opts \; \mathbf{then} \; \uparrow(\mathbf{length}(sndq + + str') - 1) \; \mathbf{else} \; sndurp$

HOL syntax For optional data items, $*$ denotes absence (or a zero IP or port) and $\uparrow x$ denotes presence of value x. Concrete lists are written $[1, 2, 3]$ and appending two lists is written using an infix $++$. Records are written within angled brackets $(\!|...|\!)$. Record fields can be accessed by dot notation or by pattern-matching. Record fields may be overridden: $cb' = cb \; (\!|irs := seq|\!)$ states that the record cb' is the same as the record cb, except that field $cb'.irs$ has the value seq. The expression $f \oplus [(x, y)]$ or $f \oplus (x \mapsto y)$ denotes the finite map f updated to map x to y.

Fig. 1. Protocol-level model, example rule

enough, str is appended to the $sndq$ in the final host. Lastly, the urgent pointer $sndurp'$ is set appropriately.

Although the bulk of the model deals with the relatively simple Sockets API, with many rules like that of Fig. 1, the real complexity arises from internal actions that are largely invisible to the Sockets user, such as retransmission and congestion control. For example, the rule *deliver_in_3* (not shown) that handles normal message receipt comprises over 1 000 lines of higher-order logic.

The model has been validated against several thousand real-world network traces, designed to test corner cases and unexpected situations. Of these, 92% are valid according to the model, and we believe that for many purposes the model is sufficiently accurate — certainly enough to be used as a reference, in conjunction with the standard texts.

3 The New Service-Level Specification

The service-level specification, illustrated below, describes the behaviour of a network of hosts communicating over TCP, as observed at the Socket APIs of the connections involved. It does not deal with TCP segments on the wire (though it necessarily does include ICMP and UDP messages).

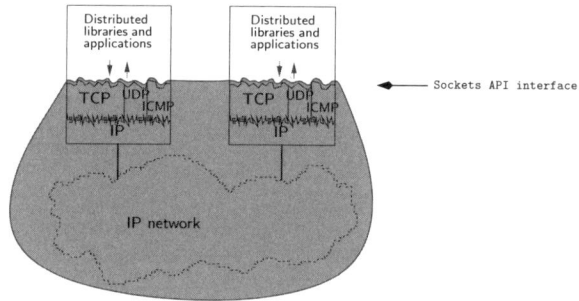

In principle one could derive a service-level specification directly from the protocol model, taking the set of traces it defines and erasing the TCP wire segment transitions. However, that would not give a *usable* specification: one in which key properties of TCP, that users depend on, are clearly visible. Hence, we built the service-level specification by hand, defining a more abstract notion of host state, an abstract notion of stream object, and a new network transition relation, but aiming to give the same Sockets-API-observable behaviour.

The abstract host states are substantially simpler than those of the protocol-level model. For example, the protocol-level TCP control block contains 44 fields, including retransmit and keep-alive timers; window sizes, sequence position and scaling information; timestamping and round trip times. Almost none of these are relevant to the service-level observable behaviour, and so are not needed in the service-level TCP control block. Along with this, the transition rules that define the protocol dynamics, such as *deliver_in_3*, become much simpler. The rules that deal with the Sockets API must be adapted to the new host state, but they remain largely as before. The overall size of the specification is therefore not much changed, at around 30 000 lines (including comments).

A naive approach to writing the individual rules would be to existentially quantify those parts of the host state that are missing at the service level (and then to logically simplify as much as possible). However, this would lead to a highly non-deterministic and ultimately less useful specification. Instead, we relied on a number of invariants of the low-level model, arguing informally that, given those, the two behaviours match. We rely on the later validation to detect any errors in these informal arguments.

In the rest of this section we aim to give a flavour of the service-level specification, referring the interested reader to the complete specification online [23].

The heart of the specification is a model of a bidirectional TCP connection as a pair of unidirectional byte streams between Sockets endpoints:

- **unidirectional stream :**
tcpStream =⦇ i : ip; (* source IP *)
p : port; (* source port *)
$flgs$: streamFlags;
$data$: byte list;
$destroyed$: bool⦈

The data in the stream is a byte list. Further fields record the source IP address and port of the stream, control information in the form of flags, and a boolean indicating whether the stream has been destroyed at the source (say, by deleting the associated socket). Some of these fields are shared with the low-level specification, but others are purely abstract entities. Note that although a stream may be destroyed at the source, previously sent messages may still be on the wire, and might later be accepted by the receiver, so we cannot simply remove the stream when it is destroyed. Similarly, if the source receives a message for a deleted socket, a RST will typically be generated, which must be recorded in the stream flags of the destroyed stream. These flags record whether the stream is opening (SYN,$SYNACK$), closing normally (FIN) or abnormally (RST).

– **stream control information :**
streamFlags =⟨| SYN : bool; (* SYN, no ACK *)
　　　　　　$SYNACK$: bool; (* SYN with ACK *)
　　　　　　FIN : bool;
　　　　　　RST : bool|⟩

This control information is carefully abstracted from the protocol level, to capture just enough structure to express the user-visible behaviour. Note that the SYN and $SYNACK$ flags may be set simultaneously, indicating the presence of both kinds of message on the wire. The receiver typically lowers the stream SYN flag on receipt of a SYN: even though messages with a SYN may still be on the wire, subsequent SYNs will be detected by the receiver as invalid duplicates of the original. A bidirectional stream is then just an unordered pair (represented as a set) of unidirectional streams.

The basic operations on a byte stream are to read and write data. The following defines a write from Sockets endpoint (i_1, p_1) to endpoint (i_2, p_2).

– **write flags and data to a stream :**
write$(i_1, p_1, i_2, p_2)(flgs, data)s\ s' =$ (
　$\exists in_-\ out\ in'\ out'$.
　sync_streams$(i_1, p_1, i_2, p_2)s(in_-, out) \wedge$
　sync_streams$(i_1, p_1, i_2, p_2)s'(in', out') \wedge$
　$in' = in_- \wedge$
　$out'.flgs =$
　⟨| $SYN := (out.flgs.SYN \vee flgs.SYN)$;
　　$SYNACK := (out.flgs.SYNACK \vee flgs.SYNACK)$;
　　$FIN := (out.flgs.FIN \vee flgs.FIN)$;
　　$RST := (out.flgs.RST \vee flgs.RST)$|⟩ $\wedge$
　$out'.data = (out.data + + data))$

Stream s' is the result of writing $flgs$ and $data$ to stream s. Stream s consists of a unidirectional input stream in_- and output stream out, extracted from the bidirectional stream using the auxiliary sync_streams function. Similarly s', the state of the stream after the write, consists of in' and out'. Since we are writing *send_3* **tcp: slow nonurgent succeed** Successfully return from blocked state having sent data

$$(h \langle\!| ts := ts \oplus (tid \mapsto \boxed{(\text{SEND2}(sid, *, str, opts))_d});$$
$$socks := socks \oplus [(sid, \text{SOCK}(\uparrow fid, sf, \uparrow i_1, \uparrow p_1, \uparrow i_2, \uparrow p_2, *, \mathbf{F}, cantrcvmore,$$
$$\text{TCP\_Sock}(st, cb, *)))]|\!\rangle,$$
$$S_0 \oplus [(streamid\_of\_quad(i_1, p_1, i_2, p_2), \boxed{s})], M)$$
$$\xrightarrow{\tau}$$
$$(h \langle\!| ts := ts \oplus (tid \mapsto \boxed{(\text{RET}(\text{OK}(\text{implode } str'')))_{sched\_timer}});$$
$$socks := socks \oplus [(sid, \text{SOCK}(\uparrow fid, sf, \uparrow i_1, \uparrow p_1, \uparrow i_2, \uparrow p_2, *, \mathbf{F}, cantrcvmore,$$
$$\text{TCP\_Sock}(st, cb, *)))]|\!\rangle,$$
$$S_0 \oplus [(streamid\_of\_quad(i_1, p_1, i_2, p_2), \boxed{s'})], M)$$

$st \in \{\text{ESTABLISHED}; \text{CLOSE\_WAIT}\} \wedge$
$space \in \text{UNIV} \wedge$
$space \geq \textbf{length } str \wedge$
$str' = str \wedge str'' = [\,] \wedge$
$flgs = flgs \langle\!| SYN := \mathbf{F}; SYNACK := \mathbf{F}; FIN := \mathbf{F}; RST := \mathbf{F} |\!\rangle \wedge$
$write(i_1, p_1, i_2, p_2)(flgs, str')s\ s'$

Fig. 2. Service-level specification, example rule

to the output stream, the input stream remains unchanged, $in' = in_-$. The flags on the output stream are modified to reflect $flgs$. For example, SYN is set in $out'.flgs$ iff $flgs$ contains a SYN or $out.flgs$ already has SYN set. Finally, $out'.data$ is updated by appending $data$ to $out.data$.

Fig. 2 gives the service-level analogue of the previous protocol-level rule. The transition occurs between triples $(h \langle\!|...|\!\rangle, S_0 \oplus [...], M)$, each consisting of a host, a finite map from stream identifiers to streams, and a set of UDP and ICMP messages. The latter do not play an active part in this rule, and can be safely ignored. Host state is unpacked from the host as before. Note that protocol-level constructs such as $rcvurp$ and $iobc$ are absent from the service-level host state. As well as the host transition, there is a transition of the related stream s to s'. The stream is unpacked from the finite map via its unique identifier $streamid\_of\_quad(i_1, p_1, i_2, p_2)$, derived from its quad.

As before, the conditions for this rule require that the state of the socket st must be ESTABLISHED or CLOSE_WAIT. Stream s' is the result of writing string str' and flags $flgs$ to s. Since $flgs$ are all false, the write does not cause any control flags to be set in s', although they may already be set in s of course.

This rule, and the preceding definitions, demonstrate the conceptual simplicity and stream-like nature of the service level. Other interesting properties of TCP are clearly captured by the service-level specification. For example, individual writes do not insert record boundaries in the byte stream, and in general, a read returns only part of the data, uncorrelated with any particular write. The model also makes clear that the unidirectional streams are to a large extent independent. For example, closing one direction does not automatically cause the other to close.

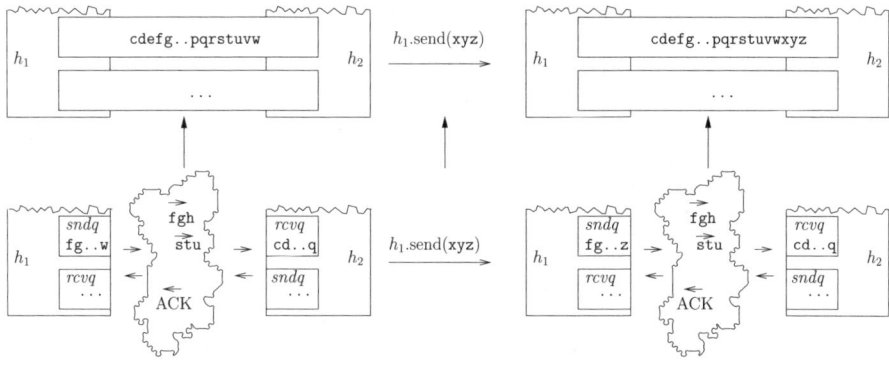

Fig. 3. Abstraction function, illustrated (data part only)

4 The Abstraction Function

While the service specification details *what* service an implementation of TCP provides to the Sockets interface, the abstraction function details *how*. The abstraction function maps protocol-level states and transitions to service-level states and transitions. A protocol-level network consists of a set of hosts, each with their own TCP stacks, and segments on the wire. The abstraction function takes this data and calculates abstract byte streams between Sockets API endpoints, together with the abstract connection status information.

The latter is the more intricate part, but we can give only a simple example here: the *destroyed* flag is set iff either there is no socket on the protocol-level host matching the quad for the TCP connection or the state of the TCP socket is CLOSED.

The former is illustrated in Fig. 3. For example, consider the simple case where communication has already been established, and the source is sending a message to the destination that includes the string "abc...xyz", of which bytes up to "w" have been moved to the source *sndq*. Moreover, the destination has acknowledged all bytes up to "f", so that the *sndq* contains "fgh...uvw", and *snd_una* points to "f". The destination *rcvq* contains "cde...opq", waiting for the user to read from the socket, and *rcv_nxt* points just after "q".

	↓ *snd_una* ↓ *rcv_nxt*
message	...abcdefghijklmnopqrstuvwxyz...
source *sndq*	fghijklmnopqrstuvw
destination *rcvq*	cdefghijklmnopq
DROP($rcv\_nxt - snd\_una$)$sndq$	rstuvw
stream	cdefghijklmnopqrstuvw

The data that remains in the stream waiting for the destination endpoint to read, is the byte stream "cdefghijklmnopqrstuvw". This is simply the destination *rcvq* with part of the source *sndq* appended: to avoid duplicating the shared part of the byte sequence, ($rcv\_nxt - snd\_una$) bytes are dropped from *sndq* before appending it to *rcvq*.

- **unidirectional abstraction function :**
abs_hosts_one_sided$(i_1, p_1, i_2, p_2)(h, msgs, i) = ($
  (* messages that we are interested in, including oq and iq *)
  let $(hoq, iiq) =$
    case $(h.oq, i.iq)$ **of** $((msgs)_{\_1}, (msgs')_{\_2}) \to (msgs, msgs')$ **in**
  let $msgs = $ **list_to_set** $hoq \cup msgs \cup ($**list_to_set** $iiq)$ **in**
  (* only consider TCP messages ... *)
  let $msgs = \{msg \mid TCP\ msg \in msgs\}$ **in**
  (* ...that match the quad *)
  let $msgs = msgs \cap $
    $\{msg \mid msg = msg \langle\!| is_1 := \uparrow i_1; ps_1 := \uparrow p_1; is_2 := \uparrow i_2; ps_2 := \uparrow p_2 |\!\rangle\}$ **in**

  (* pick out the send and receive sockets *)
  let $smatch\ i_1\ p_1\ i_2\ p_2\ s = $
    $((s.is_1, s.ps_1, s.is_2, s.ps_2) = (\uparrow i_1, \uparrow p_1, \uparrow i_2, \uparrow p_2))$ **in**
  let $snd\_sock = Punique\_range(smatch\ i_1\ p_1\ i_2\ p_2)h.socks$ **in**
  let $rcv\_sock = Punique\_range(smatch\ i_2\ p_2\ i_1\ p_1)i.socks$ **in**
  let $tcpsock_of\ sock = $ **case** $sock.pr$ **of**
    $TCP1\_hostTypes\ \$TCP\_PROTO\ tcpsock \to tcpsock$
    $\|\ \_3 \to ERROR$"abs_hosts_one_sided:tcpsock_of"
  in
  (* the core of the abstraction function is to compute $data$ *)
  let $(data :$ **byte list**$) =$ **case** (snd_sock, rcv_sock) **of**
    $(\uparrow(\_8, hsock), \uparrow(\_9, isock)) \to ($
      let $htcpsock = tcpsock\_of\ hsock$ **in**
      let $itcpsock = tcpsock\_of\ isock$ **in**
      let $(snd\_una, sndq) = (htcpsock.cb.snd\_una, htcpsock.sndq)$ **in**
      let $(rcv\_nxt, rcvq) = (itcpsock.cb.rcv\_nxt, itcpsock.rcvq)$ **in**
      let $rcv\_nxt = tcp\_seq\_flip\_sense\ rcv\_nxt$ **in**
      let $sndq' = DROP(($**num**$(rcv\_nxt - snd\_una)))sndq$ **in**
      $rcvq ++ sndq')$

    $\|\ (\uparrow(\_8, hsock), *) \to ($
      let $htcpsock = tcpsock\_of\ hsock$ **in**
      $htcpsock.sndq)$

    $\|\ (*, \uparrow(\_9, isock)) \to ($
      let $itcpsock = tcpsock\_of\ isock$ **in**
      let $(rcv\_nxt : tcpLocal\ seq32, rcvq :$ **byte list**$) = $
        $(tcp\_seq\_flip\_sense(itcpsock.cb.rcv\_nxt), itcpsock.rcvq)$ **in**
      $rcvq ++(stream\_reass\ rcv\_nxt\ msgs))$

    $\|\ (*, *) \to ERROR$"abs_hosts_one_sided:data"
  in
  $\langle\!|\ i := i_1;$
  $p := p_1;$
  $flgs := $
    $\langle\!|\ SYN := (\exists msg.msg \in msgs \wedge msg = msg\ \langle\!|\ SYN := \mathbf{T}; ACK := \mathbf{F} |\!\rangle);$
    $SYNACK := (\exists msg.msg \in msgs \wedge msg = msg\ \langle\!|\ SYN := \mathbf{T}; ACK := \mathbf{T} |\!\rangle);$
    $FIN := (\exists msg.msg \in msgs \wedge msg = msg\ \langle\!|\ FIN := \mathbf{T} |\!\rangle);$
    $RST := (\exists msg.msg \in msgs \wedge msg = msg\ \langle\!|\ RST := \mathbf{T} |\!\rangle)$
    $|\!\rangle;$
  $data := data;$
  $destroyed := ($**case** snd_sock **of**
    $\uparrow(sid, hsock) \to ((tcpsock_of\ hsock).st = $ CLOSED$)$
    $\|\ * \to \mathbf{T})$
  $|\!\rangle)$

Fig. 4. Abstraction function, excerpt

An excerpt from the HOL definition appears in Fig. 4. It takes a quad (i_1, p_1, i_2, p_2) identifying the TCP connection, a source host h, a set of messages $msgs$ on the wire, and a destination host i, and produces a unidirectional stream. It follows exactly the previous analysis: $(rcv\_nxt - snd\_una)$ bytes are dropped from $sndq$ to give $sndq'$, which is then appended to $rcvq$ to give the data in the stream.

Note that, in keeping with the fact that TCP is designed so that hosts can retransmit any data that is lost on the wire, this abstraction does not depend on the data in transit — at least for normal connections in which neither endpoint has crashed.

For a given TCP connection, the full abstraction function uses the unidirectional function twice to form a bidirectional stream constituting the service-level state. As well as mapping the states, the abstraction function maps the transition labels. Labels corresponding to visible actions at the Sockets interface, such as a `connect` call, map to themselves. Labels corresponding to internal protocol actions, such as the host network interface sending and receiving datagrams from the wire, are invisible at the service level, and so are mapped to τ, indicating no observable transition. Thus, for each protocol-level transition, the abstraction function gives a service-level transition with the same behaviour at the Sockets interface. Mapping the abstraction function over a protocol-level trace gives a service-level trace with identical Sockets behaviour. Every valid protocol-level trace should map to a valid service-level trace.

5 Experimental Validation

How can we ensure that TCP implementations (written in C), our previous protocol-level model (in HOL), and our new service-level specification (also in HOL) are consistent? Arguing that a small specification corresponds to a simple real-world system can already be extremely challenging. Here, we are faced with very large specifications and a very complex real-world system. Ideally one would verify the relationship between the protocol and service specifications by proving that their behaviours correspond, making use of the abstraction function. One would also prove that the Sockets behaviour of the endpoint implementations (formalized using a C semantics) conformed to the protocol model.

Proving the relationships between the levels in this way would be a very challenging task indeed. One of the main barriers is the scale of TCP implementations, including legacy behavioural intricacies of TCP and Sockets, which were not designed with verification in mind.

Hence, we adopt the pragmatic approach of validating the specifications to provide reasonable confidence in their accuracy. Note that for TCP the implementations are the de facto standard. In producing specifications after the fact, we aim to validate the specifications against the implementation behaviour. Our techniques could equally well be used in the other direction for new protocol designs. Our service-level validation builds on our earlier protocol-level work [5,6], so we begin by recalling that.

Protocol-level validation. We instrumented a test network and wrote tests to drive hosts on the network, generating real-world traces. We then ensured that the protocol specification admitted those traces by running a special-purpose symbolic model checker in HOL, correcting the specification, and iterating, when we discovered errors. Because it is based directly on the formal specification, and deals with all the internal state of hosts, the checker is extremely rigorous, producing a machine checked proof of admissibility for each successfully validated trace. Obviously no testing-based method can be complete, but this found many issues in early drafts of the specification, and also identified a number of anomalies in TCP implementations.

Service-level validation. For the service-level validation of this paper, we began with a similar instrumented test network, but collected double-ended traces, capturing the behaviour of two interacting hosts, rather than just one endpoint. We then used our previous symbolic evaluation tool to discover symbolic traces of the protocol-level model that corresponded to the real-world traces. That is a complex and computationally intensive process, involving backtracking depth-first search and constraint simplification, essentially to discover internal host state and internal transitions that are not explicit in the trace.

We then *ground* these symbolic traces, finding instantiations of their variables that satisfy any remaining constraints, to produce a ground protocol-level trace in which all information is explicit. Given such a ground trace, we can map the abstraction function over it to produce a candidate ground service-level trace.

It is then necessary to check validity of this trace, which is done with a service-level test oracle. As at the protocol level, we wrote a new special-purpose service-level checker in HOL which performs symbolic evaluation of the specification with respect to ground service-level traces. Crucially, this checking process is much simpler than that at the protocol level because all host values, and all transitions, are already known. All that remains is to check each ground service-level transition against the specification.

The most significant difference between the old and new checkers is that the former had to perform a depth-first search to even determine which rule of the protocol model was appropriate. Because that work has already been done, and because the two specifications have been constructed so that their individual rules correspond, the service-level checker does not need to do this search. Instead, it can simply check the service-level version of the rule that was checked at the protocol level, dealing with each transition in isolation. In particular, this means that the service-level checker need not attempt to infer the existence of unobservable τ-transitions.

Another significant difference between the two checkers is that the service-level checker can aggressively search for instantiations of existentially quantified variables that arise when a rule's hypothesis has to be discharged. At the protocol level, such variables may appear quite unconstrained at first appearance, but then become progressively more constrained as further steps of the trace are processed.

For example, a simplified rule for the `socket` call might appear as

$$\frac{fd \notin \mathsf{usedfds}(h_0)}{h_0 \langle\!| socks := socks |\!\rangle \xrightarrow{tid \cdot \mathsf{socket}()} h_0 \langle\!| socks := socks \oplus (sid, fd) |\!\rangle}$$

stating that when a socket call is made, the host h_0's socks map is updated to associate the new socket (identified by *sid*) with file-descriptor *fd*, subject only to the constraint that the new descriptor not already be in use. (This underspecification is correct on Windows; on Unix, the file-descriptor is typically the next available natural number.)

In the protocol-level checker, the *fd* variable must be left uninstantiated until its value can be deduced from subsequent steps in the trace. In the service-level checker, both the initial host and the final host are available because they are the product of the abstraction function applied to the previously generated, and ground, protocol trace. In a situation such as this, the variable from the hypothesis is present in the conclusion, and can be immediately instantiated.

In other rules of the service-level specification, there can be a great many variables that occur only in the hypothesis. These are existentially quantified, and the checker must determine if there is an instantiation for them that makes the hypothesis true. The most effective way of performing this check is to simplify, apply decision procedures for arithmetic, and to then repeatedly case-split on boolean variables, and the guards of if-then-else expressions to search for possible instantiations.

The above process is clearly somewhat involved, and itself would ordinarily be prone to error. To protect against this we built all the checking infrastructure within HOL. So, when checking a trace, we are actually building machine-checked proofs that its transitions are admitted by the inductive definition of the transition relation in the specification.

Results. Our earlier protocol-level validation involved several thousand traces designed to exercise the behaviour of single endpoints, covering both the Sockets API and the wire behaviour. To produce a reasonably accurate specification, we iterated the checking and specification-fixing process many times.

For the service-level specification, we have not attempted the same level of validation, simply due to resource constraints. Instead, we have focused on developing the method, doing enough validation to demonstrate its feasibility. Producing a specification in which one should have high confidence might require another man-year or so of testing — perfectly feasible, and a tiny amount of effort in terms of industrial protocol stack development, but unlikely to lead to new research insights. That said, most of the Sockets API behaviour does not relate to the protocol dynamics and is common between the two specifications, so is already moderately well tested. In all, 30 end-to-end tests were generated, covering a variety of connection setup and tear-down cases and end-to-end communication, but not including packet loss, reordering, duplication, and severe delay. After correcting errors, all these traces were found to validate successfully.

To illustrate how discriminating our testing process is, we mention two errors we discovered during validation. At the protocol-level, a TCP message moving from a host output queue to the wire corresponds to an unobservable τ event at the service level. Naively we assumed the host state would be unchanged, since the output queue at the service-level carries only ICMP and UDP messages.

However, this is not correct, since the transmission of a TCP message alters the timer associated with the output queue, increasing its value. The update to the timer permits the host to delay sending the ICMP and UDP messages. Without this side-effect, the service-level specification effectively required ICMP and UDP messages to be sent earlier than they would otherwise have been. To correct this error, the service specification had to allow the timer to be updated if at the protocol-level there was potentially a TCP message on the queue that might be transferred to the wire. Another error arose in the definition of the abstraction function. The analysis of the merging of the send and receive queues on source and destination hosts, described in Sect. 4, was initially incorrect, leading to streams with duplicated, or missing, runs of data. Fortunately this error was easy to detect by examining the ground service-level trace, where the duplicated data was immediately apparent.

Our validation processes check that certain traces are included in the protocol-level or service-level specification. As we have seen, this can be a very discriminating test, but it does not touch on the possibility that the specifications admit too many traces. That cannot be determined by reference to the de facto standard implementations, as a reasonable specification here must be looser than any one implementation. Instead, one must consider whether the specifications are strong enough to be useful, for proving properties of applications that use the Sockets API, or (as in [13]) as a basis for new implementations.

6 Related Work

This work builds on our previous TCP protocol model [5,6], and we refer the reader there for detailed discussion of related work. We noted that "to the best of our knowledge, however, no previous work approaches a specification dealing with the full scale and complexity of a real-world TCP". This also applies to the service-level specification. As before, this is unsurprising: we have depended on automated reasoning tools and on raw compute resources that were simply unavailable in the 1980s or early 1990s. Our goals have also been different, and in some sense more modest, than the correctness theorems of traditional formal verification: we have not attempted to *prove* that an implementation of TCP satisfies the protocol model, or that the protocol satisfies the service-level specification.

There is a vast literature devoted to verification techniques for protocols, with both proof-based and model checking approaches, e.g. in conferences such as CAV, CONCUR, FM, FORTE, ICNP, SPIN, and TACAS. The most detailed rigorous specification of a TCP-like protocol we are aware of is that of Smith [22], an I/O automata specification and implementation, with a proof that one satisfies the other, used as a basis for work on T/TCP. The protocol is still substantially idealised, however. Later work by Smith and Ramakrishnan uses a similar model to verify properties of a model of SACK [21]. A variety of work addresses radically idealised variants of TCP [8,9,19,10,3,15,16]. Finally, Postel's PhD thesis used early Petri net protocol models descriptively [18].

Implementations of TCP in high-level languages have been written by Biagioni in Standard ML [2], by Castelluccia *et al.* in Esterel [7], and by Kohler *et al.* in Prolac [12]. As for any implementation, allowable non-determinism means they cannot be used as oracles for conformance testing.

For concurrent and distributed systems, there are many abstraction-refinement techniques, such as abstraction relations (which include our abstraction function) and simulation relations, see [14] for an overview. As an example of these techniques, Alur and Wang address the PPP and DHCP protocols [1]. For each they check refinements between models that are manually extracted from the RFC specification and from an implementation. Although these techniques are widely used in verification, to the best of our knowledge, they have never been applied previously to real-world protocols on the scale of TCP.

7 Conclusion

Summary. We presented a formal, mechanized, service-level specification of TCP, tackling the full detail of the real-world protocol. The specification is appropriate for formal and informal reasoning about applications built above the Sockets layer, and about the service that TCP and TCP-like protocols provide to the Sockets layer. The service-level specification stands as a precise statement of end-to-end correctness for TCP. We also presented a formal abstraction function from our previous protocol-level model of TCP to the service-level specification, thereby explaining how stream-like behaviour arises from the protocol level. We used novel validation tools, coupled with the results of previous work, to validate both the service specification and the abstraction function. The specification, abstraction function, and testing infrastructure were developed entirely in HOL.

On the practice of protocol design. This paper is the latest in a line of work developing rigorous techniques for real-world protocol modelling and specification [20,24,17,5,6,4]. In most of this work to date we have focused on post-hoc specification of existing infrastructure (TCP, UDP, ICMP, and the Sockets API) rather than new protocol design, though the latter is our main goal. This is for two reasons. Firstly, the existing infrastructure is ubiquitous, and likely to remain so for the foreseeable future: these wire protocols and the Sockets API are stable articulation points around which other software shifts. It is therefore well worth characterising exactly what they are, for the benefit of both users and implementers. Secondly, and more importantly, they are excellent test cases. There has been a great deal of theoretical work on idealised protocols, but, to develop rigorous techniques that can usefully be applied, they must be tested with realistic protocols. If we can deal with TCP and Sockets, with all their accumulated legacy of corner cases and behavioural quirks, then our techniques should certainly be applicable to new protocols. We believe that that is now demonstrated, and it is confirmed by our experience with design-time formalisation and conformance testing for an experimental MAC protocol for an optically switched network [4].

In recent years there has been considerable interest in 'clean slate' networking design, and in initiatives such as FIND and GENI. Protocols developed in such work should, we argue, be developed as trios of running implementation, rigorous specification, and verified conformance tester between the two. Modest attention paid to this at design time would greatly ease the task — for example, specifying appropriate debug trace information, and carefully identifying the deterministic parts of a protocol specification, would remove the need for backtracking search during validation. Declarative specification of the intended protocol behaviour, free from the imperative control-flow imposed by typical implementation languages, enables one to see unnecessary behavioural complexities clearly. Verified conformance testing makes it possible to keep implementations and specifications in sync as they are developed. Together, they should lead to cleaner, better-understood and more robust protocols, and hence to less costly and more robust infrastructure.

More specifically to TCP, we see two main directions for future work. One is simply to scale up our validation process, covering a wide variety of common protocol stacks, increasing confidence still further by testing against more traces, identifying and testing additional invariants of connection states, and so forth, and producing a packaged conformance tester for TCP implementations. This would be useful, and on an industrial scale would be a relatively small project (compared, perhaps, to the QA effort involved in developing a new protocol stack), but doing this for an existing protocol may be inappropriate for a small research group. The weight of legacy complexity here is very large, so non-trivial resources (perhaps several man-years) would be needed to cope with the detail, but the basic scientific questions, of *how* to do this, have now been solved. Doing this for *new* protocols, on the other hand, seems clearly worthwhile, even with very limited resources.

The second, more research-oriented, question, is to consider not just validation of end-to-end functional correctness (as we have done here), but properties such as end-to-end performance. Ultimately one could envisage proving network-wide properties, such as network stability, thereby connecting highly abstract properties of these protocols to the low-level details of their implementations.

Acknowledgements. We gratefully acknowledge the use of the Condor facility in the Computer Laboratory, work of Adam Biltcliffe on testing infrastructure, and support from a Royal Society University Research Fellowship (Sewell) and EPSRC grants EPC510712 and GRT11715. NICTA is funded by the Australian Government's Backing Australia's Ability initiative, in part through the Australian Research Council.

References

1. Alur, R., Wang, B.-Y.: Verifying Network Protocol Implementations by Symbolic Refinement Checking. In: Berry, G., Comon, H., Finkel, A. (eds.) CAV 2001. LNCS, vol. 2102, pp. 169–181. Springer, Heidelberg (2001)

2. Biagioni, E.: A structured TCP in Standard ML. In: Proc. SIGCOMM (1994)
3. Billington, J., Han, B.: On defining the service provided by TCP. In: Proc. ACSC: 26th Australasian Computer Science Conference, Adelaide (2003)
4. Biltcliffe, A., Dales, M., Jansen, S., Ridge, T., Sewell, P.: Rigorous protocol design in practice: An optical packet-switch MAC in HOL. In: Proc. ICNP (November 2006)
5. Bishop, S., Fairbairn, M., Norrish, M., Sewell, P., Smith, M., Wansbrough, K.: Rigorous specification and conformance testing techniques for network protocols, as applied to TCP, UDP, and Sockets. In: Proc. SIGCOMM 2005 (August 2005)
6. Bishop, S., Fairbairn, M., Norrish, M., Sewell, P., Smith, M., Wansbrough, K.: Engineering with logic: HOL specification and symbolic-evaluation testing for TCP implementations. In: Proc. POPL (2006)
7. Castelluccia, C., Dabbous, W., O'Malley, S.: Generating efficient protocol code from an abstract specification. IEEE/ACM Trans. Netw. 5(4), 514–524 (1997)
8. Chkliaev, D., Hooman, J., de Vink, E.: Verification and Improvement of the Sliding Window Protocol. In: Garavel, H., Hatcliff, J. (eds.) ETAPS 2003 and TACAS 2003. LNCS, vol. 2619, pp. 113–127. Springer, Heidelberg (2003)
9. Fersman, E., Jonsson, B.: Abstraction of communication channels in Promela: A case study. In: Havelund, K., Penix, J., Visser, W. (eds.) SPIN 2000. LNCS, vol. 1885, pp. 187–204. Springer, Heidelberg (2000)
10. Hofmann, R., Lemmen, F.: Specification-driven monitoring of TCP/IP. In: Proc. 8th Euromicro Workshop on Parallel and Distributed Processing (January 2000)
11. The HOL 4 system, Kananaskis-3 release, http://hol.sourceforge.net
12. Kohler, E., Kaashoek, M.F., Montgomery, D.R.: A readable TCP in the Prolac protocol language. In: Proc. SIGGCOMM 1999, August 1999, pp. 3–13 (1999)
13. Li, P., Zdancewic, S.: Combining events and threads for scalable network services. In: Proc. PLDI, pp. 189–199 (2007)
14. Lynch, N., Vaangdrager, F.: Forward and backward simulations – Part I: Untimed systems. Information and Computation 121(2), 214–233 (1995)
15. Murphy, S.L., Shankar, A.U.: A verified connection management protocol for the transport layer. In: Proc. SIGCOMM, pp. 110–125 (1987)
16. Murphy, S.L., Shankar, A.U.: Service specification and protocol construction for the transport layer. In: Proc. SIGCOMM, pp. 88–97 (1988)
17. Norrish, M., Sewell, P., Wansbrough, K.: Rigour is good for you, and feasible: reflections on formal treatments of C and UDP sockets. In: Proceedings of the 10th ACM SIGOPS European Workshop, September 2002, pp. 49–53 (2002)
18. Postel, J.: A Graph Model Analysis of Computer Communications Protocols. University of California, Computer Science Department, PhD Thesis (1974)
19. Schieferdecker, I.: Abruptly-terminated connections in TCP. In: Proc. Int. Workshop on Applied Formal Methods In System Design (1996)
20. Serjantov, A., Sewell, P., Wansbrough, K.: The UDP calculus: Rigorous semantics for real networking. In: Proc. TACS 2001 (October 2001)
21. Smith, M.A., Ramakrishnan, K.K.: Formal specification and verification of safety and performance of TCP selective acknowledgment. IEEE/ACM Trans. Netw. 10(2), 193–207 (2002)
22. Smith, M.A.S.: Formal verification of communication protocols. In: Proc. FORTE IX/PSTV XVI (1996)
23. The Netsem Project. Web page, http://www.cl.cam.ac.uk/users/pes20/Netsem/
24. Wansbrough, K., Norrish, M., Sewell, P., Serjantov, A.: Timing UDP: Mechanized Semantics for Sockets, Threads, and Failures. In: Le Métayer, D. (ed.) ESOP 2002 and ETAPS 2002. LNCS, vol. 2305, pp. 278–294. Springer, Heidelberg (2002)

Constraint Prioritization for Efficient Analysis of Declarative Models

Engin Uzuncaova and Sarfraz Khurshid

The University of Texas at Austin
Austin, TX 78712
{uzuncaov,khurshid}@ece.utexas.edu

Abstract. The declarative modeling language Alloy and its automatic analyzer provide an effective tool-set for building designs of systems and checking their properties. The Alloy Analyzer performs bounded exhaustive analysis using off-the-shelf SAT solvers. The analyzer's performance hinges on the complexity of the models and so far, its feasibility has been shown only within limited bounds. We present a novel optimization technique that defines program slicing for declarative models and enables efficient analyses exploiting partial solutions. We present an algorithm that computes transient slices for Alloy models by partitioning them into a base and a derived slice. A satisfying solution to the base slice is systematically extended to generate a solution for the entire model, while unsatisfiability of the base implies unsatisfiability of the entire model.

By generating slices, our approach enables constraint prioritization, where the base slice assumes higher priority than the derived slice. Compared to the complete model, base and derived slices represent smaller and, ideally, simpler sub-problems, which, in turn, enables efficient analyses for the underlying SAT solvers. Our approach analyzes the structure of a given model and constructs a set of candidate slicing criteria. Our prototype tool, Kato, performs a small-scope analysis for each criterion to determine whether declarative slicing optimization provides any performance gain and, if so, to select a criterion that is likely to provide an optimal performance enhancement. The experimental results show that, with declarative slicing, it is possible to achieve significant improvements compared to the Alloy Analyzer.

1 Introduction

Testing and verification become more challenging as software systems grow in complexity. Automated techniques are even more critical today to achieve a certain level of confidence in software quality. Alloy [5] is a declarative modeling language that can be used for building designs of systems. Together with its fully automatic analyzer [6], Alloy provides an effective tool-set for checking system properties.

Alloy is a first-order relational logic with transitive closure, which allows expressing rich structural properties using succinct and intuitive path expressions. The Alloy Analyzer translates Alloy models into Boolean formulas using a *scope*—bound on the universe of discourse—provided by the user, and uses off-the-shelf Boolean satisfiability (SAT) solvers to generate a satisfying instance for and determine the consistency and feasibility of the Boolean formulas. Since Alloy's analysis is valid with respect to a given bound, the analyzer's failure to generate a satisfying instance does not amount to a proof of non-existence of satisfying instances. It is therefore natural for Alloy users to (iteratively) check the formulas using a bound as large as is feasible within the amount of time they have.

The Alloy Analyzer already incorporates a variety of optimizations to improve the solving time by generating optimized Boolean formulas such as symmetry-breaking and type-based reduction of variables [10]. In past work [7], we presented a suite of optimizations inspired by traditional compiler optimizations, such as common subexpression elimination and loop unrolling, to perform source-to-source translations on Alloy models to enable the SAT solvers to perform more efficiently. However, the main limitation with the analyzer is that it generates one (typically large) SAT problem, which can choke the underlying solver.

In this paper, we present a new class of optimizations, *declarative slicing*, which are inspired by program slicing for imperative languages [14] but are applicable to analyzable declarative languages, in general, and Alloy, in particular. We present a novel algorithm for slicing declarative models. Given an Alloy model, our prototype tool, Kato, uses a *slicing criterion* to partition the model into a *base* and a *derived slice*. A base slice consists of a subset of the model constraints that constrains only the relations specified by the slicing criterion. A satisfying instance for the base is systematically extended into a satisfying instance for the entire model using the derived slice, while unsatisfiability of the base implies unsatisfiability of the entire model.

We use the partial solution support in the KodKod relational engine [11] for extending a satisfying instance of a base slice to a satisfying instance for the original model. We first generate a partial instance solving the base slice, and then we conjoin that instance with the constraints defined on the derived slice and re-execute the analyzer. Since slices typically consist of only a strict subset of the original model, the slices translate to smaller Boolean formulas with fewer variables. Even though this method executes SAT twice, each time it executes on, ideally, a simpler Boolean formula than the one that represents the whole model, which enables more efficient analysis for the underlying SAT solvers.

Slicing enables *constraint prioritization* [15] since a base slice assumes a higher priority than the derived slice. However, the potential performance improvement of using declarative slicing depends on how a given model is partitioned into slices. Kato performs a static analysis of the model to identify a set of *candidate slicing criteria*, where each criterion defines a valid base slice for the model. The candidate set is formed using the *free variables* that appear in each constraint. To select a slicing criterion that would provide a *likely* optimal performance gain, we perform a heuristic evaluation. The evaluation performs declarative slicing for each slicing criterion for a small scope and considers the overall solving time as the basis for selection.

While slicing in the context of Alloy is not a new idea because, for example, the Alloy Analyzer only translates the formulas that are relevant to the command being analyzed (akin to dead code elimination), we present a fundamentally different approach to slicing. Our slicing algorithm introduces a *transient* notion of slicing for Alloy models. Even though we partition the given model into a base and a derived slice, the partitioning is to optimize the underlying analysis, and the final result pertains to the complete model. Our technique thus, applies even when the entire model is *necessary* to compute the result of the analysis. This contrasts even with traditional program slicing for imperative languages, where only the computed slice is of interest and the rest of the code is considered irrelevant and hence ignored [14].

We have evaluated the potential speedup in solving time that Kato can provide using a suite of benchmark examples that model structurally complex data. The results evince the existence of opportunities for significant performance gains. This paper builds on our FSE 2006 poster presentation [12] and ICSE 2007 tool demonstration [13] and makes the following contributions:

- We introduce the notion of transient program slicing for declarative specifications;
- We present an algorithm that computes transient slices for Alloy models by partitioning them into base and derived components;
- We present an algorithm for solving declarative models using slices; and,
- We present experimental results that show significant opportunities for optimizing analyses of Alloy models using slicing.

2 Example: Binary Search Tree

This section illustrates our optimization technique using a binary search tree example. We describe the example using Alloy notations [5]. Section 4 presents a more detailed discussion of our approach.

2.1 Alloy Model: Binary Search Tree

Consider a binary search tree [2], which is acyclic, satisfies the search constraints, has parent pointers and caches the number of nodes in the tree. The Alloy model for this data structure is shown in Figure 1.

The keyword sig is a declaration and introduces a set of (indivisible) atoms; the signatures BinaryTree and Node respectively declare a binary tree atom and a set of node atoms. The *fields* of a signature declare *relations*. The field root introduces a relation of type (BinaryTree x Node) and left, right and parent relations of type (Node x Node). lone indicates that these relations are partial functions. The field key declares a partial relation of type (Node x Int) and specifies that the tree stores integer values at each node, where Int is a built-in Alloy type that represents the domain of integers. size relation has a type (Tree x Int) and caches the number of nodes in the tree.

The Acyclic *predicate* constrains the structure to be acyclic. The predicate is a universally quantified (all) formula which represents an implicit conjunction of three sub-formulas. The expression t.root.*(left+right) defines all the nodes reachable from the root node following zero or more traversals along the left and right children. The operator '*' denotes reflexive-transitive closure. The first sub-formula uses the quantifier lone to say that all nodes are either left or right child of another node or none. The second sub-formula says that a node's itself is not reachable by following its left and right children. The operator '+' denotes set union and '~' denotes transpose of a relation.The expression n.^(left+right) represents the set of

```
sig BinaryTree { root : lone Node }

sig Node {
  left, right, parent : lone Node,
  key : Int }

pred Acyclic(t:Tree) {
  all n: t.root.*(left+right) {
    lone n.~(left+right)
    n !in n.^(left+right)
    no n.left & n.right }}

pred Search(t:Tree) {
  all n: t.root.*(left+right) {
    all n': n.left.*(left+right) | int n'.key < int n.key
    all n': n.right.*(left+right) | int n.key < int n'.key }}

pred Parent(t:Tree) {
  all n, n': t.root.*(left+right) | n in n'.(left+right) ⇔ n' = n.parent
  no t.root.parent }

pred Size(t:Tree) {
  int t.size = #(t.root.*(left+right)) }

pred Generate[t:Tree] {
  Acyclic[t] && Search[t] && Parent[t] && Size[t]}

run Generate exactly 1 Tree, exactly 8 Node
```

Fig. 1. Alloy model for binary search tree. The model captures `acyclicity`, `search`, `size` and `parent` constraints.

all nodes reachable from n following one or more traversals along the `left` and `right` fields. The operator '^' denotes transitive closure. The third sub-formula says that left and right children are distinct using the set intersection operator '&'.

The `Search` predicate defines the ordering over the integer values stored at each node using a nested quantification. The keyword `int` represents the actual integer value denoted by the expression it precedes, for instance, 'n.key'. The operator '<' is used for integer comparison.

The `Parent` predicate defines the parent pointer for each node and that `root` node has no parent. The operator '⇔' represents bi-implication.

The `Size` predicate constrains the `size` field to represent the number of nodes in the tree. The '#' operator denotes the set cardinality.

To instruct the analyzer, we formulate the `Generate` predicate specifying the constraints and write a `run` command stating that we want to generate a binary search tree with exactly 8 nodes.

Performance of the Alloy Analyzer: Invoked on the `Generate` predicate, the analyzer takes 4.05 seconds on average to generate a binary search tree with exactly 8 nodes. An instance satisfying all the model constraints is illustrated in Figure 7(b). As the scope increases the solving time increases significantly; for example, the analyzer takes 128.78 seconds for scope 12 and 538.54 seconds for scope 16 on average. Due to the increasing size of the generated Boolean problem, the Alloy Analyzer (the underlying SAT solver) fails to generate a binary search tree instance beyond scope 16 within a reasonable time (1 hour).

Declarative Slicing: We next illustrate how using declarative slicing can improve the solving time. We compare our approach against the *conventional* use of the analyzer, where models are solved in a single execution of the underlying SAT solver. Given the same Alloy model for binary search tree, Kato identifies a set of candidate slicing criteria and selects a likely optimal one by evaluating each criterion for a small scope. For the binary search tree example, Kato identifies the following set of relations as the slicing criterion:

$$c = \{\text{root, left, right, parent}\}$$

The base and the derived slices are generated based on the given criterion. With declarative slicing, we solve the base slice first and then conjoin that instance with the constraints defined on the derived slice and re-execute the analyzer with this new SAT problem. Our approach improves the solving time significantly, where it takes 0.77 second on average to generate a binary search tree with exactly 8 nodes. An illustration of declarative slicing is shown in Figure 7. This amounts to a performance gain of 5.24 times. As opposed to the behavior observed with the conventional approach, the analysis time does not increase drastically as the scope increases. It takes 1.81 seconds for scope 12 and 2.90 seconds for scope 16. In addition, we were able to generate a binary search tree with 32 nodes in 23.84 seconds on average using the same slicing criterion, which is far beyond the largest scope, 16, we were able to reach with the conventional approach.

3 Background: Alloy and Program Slicing

3.1 Alloy

Alloy [5] is a first-order declarative language based on sets and relations. The Alloy Analyzer [6] is a tool for automatically analyzing models written in Alloy. The analyzer translates Alloy models into boolean formulas and uses off-the-shelf SAT technology to solve the formulas. The analyzer consists of the following: a front-end that parses Alloy models into an intermediate representation (IR), a set of optimizations on this IR, and a back-end that translates IR into boolean formulas.

Each Alloy model consists of data (i.e., sets and relations), formulas that constrain data, and commands that represent invocations of the analyzer. The formulas can be structured using predicates (i.e., parameterized formulas that can be invoked elsewhere), which the analyzer inlines. Additionally, each analysis specifies a *scope* (i.e., a bound on the size of basic sets within which to check the formulas). The analyzer translates a conjunction of all formulas relevant to the command being executed into a boolean formula—the boolean formula has a solution iff there are some sets and relations that satisfy all the constraints represented by the relevant Alloy formulas (thus providing a satisfying instance). Alloy is a relational language; every expression in Alloy denotes a relation (or a set in the case of a relation of arity one). Even the scalars are represented as singleton sets. More details of the Alloy language are available elsewhere [5].

3.2 Constraint Partitioning and Prioritization

Yuan et. al. introduces *constraint prioritization* to address some of the challenges in constraint-based verification of electronic designs [15]. Instead of solving a set of constraints as a whole, some constraints may assume higher priority than others. In such a case, the variables constrained by the lower-priority constraints can be decided using the valuations to the higher-priority constraints. For example, in our binary search tree example, one can generate a binary tree based on the constraints pertaining to the tree properties and then assign integer values to the nodes in this tree to satisfy the search constraints. However, they also note that the necessary information for how to partition the constraints is usually only known by the user. They propose that the user can either provide priorities or specify the constrained variables for each constraint.

Given a set of constraints, *constraint prioritization* enables identifying independent subsets of those constraints that can be analyzed independently and/or incrementally. Yuan et.al. [15] presents a framework for constrained functional verification, where prioritization is used as a technique to minimize representation of constraints and complexity of constraint solving as well. Constraint prioritization provides for enhanced expressiveness of constraints, but simplification of complicated constraint system into manageable blocks which make constraint solving more efficient.

Yuan et al. also uses *constraint partitioning* to partition constraints by identifying disjoint input variable support within the constraint, which enables solving each partition separately. While this approach is based on the assumption that disjoint sets of variables exist in a constraint, our approach follows a partitioning approach based on the semantic information observed in Alloy models. In either way, the main benefit of partitioning is reduction in problem size and, therefore, more efficient SAT solving.

4 Our Approach

4.1 Alloy Language Structure

An Alloy model consists of first-order logic formulas over free variables (relations). Figure 2 shows the language syntax for a subset of Alloy along with how free variables are computed for each formula type. An Alloy instance represents a valuation to all the declared relations such that the formulas evaluate to true; in other words, all the model constraints are satisfied. Mathematically, an instance i is a function from a set of relations R to a power set of tuples 2^T where each tuple consists of indivisible atoms, i.e., i: R -> 2^T. Thus, for each Alloy relation, an instance gives the set of tuples that valuate the relation.

Language Syntax	Free Variables

$model ::= relDecl^*\ formula$

$formula\ `f ::=$
    $formula\ binOp\ formula$ $f_v(f.left)\ \cup\ f_v(f.right)$
    $mult\ expr$ $f_v(f.expr)$
    not $formula$ $f_v(f.formula)$
    $expr\ [\textbf{not}]compOp\ expr$ $f_v(f.left)\ \cup\ f_v(f.right)$
    $quantifier\ varDecl^+\ formula$ $f_v(f.formula)\ -\ f_v(f.varDecl)$

$expr\ e ::=$
    $expr\ binExprOp\ expr$ $f_v(e.left)\ \cup\ f_v(e.right)$
    $unaryOp\ expr$ $f_v(e.expr)$
    rel $e.identifier$
    var $\emptyset$

$relDecl\ r ::= rel : arity$ $\cup\ f_v(r.rel)$
$varDecl\ v ::= var : expr$ $f_v(v.expr)\ -\ f_v(v.var)$
$rel ::=$ identifier
$var ::=$ identifier
$arity ::= 1\ |\ 2\ |\ ...$

$binOp ::=$ **and** $|$ **or** $|$ **implies** $|$ **iff**
$mult ::=$ **one** $|$ **lone** $|$ **some** $|$ **no**
$compOp ::=$ **in** $|$ **=**
$quantifier ::=$ **all** $|$ **some**
$binExprOp ::=$ **+** $|$ **&** $|$ **−** $|$ **.** $|$ **→** $|$ **++**
$unaryOp ::=$ **~** $|$ **^** $|$ *****

Fig. 2. On the left column, a subset of the Alloy language syntax is shown. For each language construct, right column shows how corresponding set of free variables are computed.

To solve a formula, the Alloy Analyzer uses a scope that bounds the universe of discourse. The Kodkod back-end of the Alloy Analyzer allows specifying a scope using two bounds: a *lower* bound and an *upper* bound on the set of tuples that any valuation of a relation may take. Any instance must satisfy the following property: for every relation, each tuple in the lower bound must be present in the instance and no tuple that is not in the upper bound may be present in the instance. Hence, a lower bound represents a partial solution for a given model. Kodkod's support for partial solution is one of the key advantages for efficient analysis. Mathematically, a bound b is a pair of two functions: a lower bound l and an upper bound u, each of type R -> 2^T. An instance can equivalently be viewed as a bound b = [l, u], where l = u.

Thus, an Alloy model can be seen as a triple $\langle d,\ s,\ b \rangle$, where d represents the data elements, i.e., declared relations, s represents the formula that constrains the data elements (i.e., constraints), and b represents the bound on the universe discourse. We assume (without loss of generality) that s is a conjunction of several sub-formulas, i.e., $s = \bigwedge s_i$.

4.2 Declarative Slicing

Declarative slicing is an optimization technique that exploits partial solutions for efficient analysis of declarative specifications. It is inspired by program slicing for imperative languages [14], and is applicable to analyzable declarative languages, in general,

```
1    all n: t.root.*(left+right) | lone n.~(left+right)              //{root, left, right}
2    all n: t.root.*(left+right) | n !in n.^(left+right)              //{root, left, right}
3    all n: t.root.*(left+right) | no n.left & n.right                //{root, left, right}
4    all n: t.root.*(left+right) {                                    //{root, left, right, key}
         all n': n.left.*(left+right) | int n'.key < int n.key }
5    all n: t.root.*(left+right) {                                    //{root, left, right, key}
         all n': n.right.*(left+right) | int n.key < int n'.key }
6    all n, n': t.root.*(left+right) |                                //{root, left, right, parent}
         n in n'.(left+right) ⇔ n' = n.parent
7    no t.root.parent                                                 //{root, parent}
8    int t.size = #(t.root.*(left+right))                             //{root, left, right, size}
```

Fig. 3. $Free\ variables$ for each sub-formula is shown next to it in parenthesis. This form is equivalent to the original model.

and Alloy, in particular. Our technique introduces an alternative way to analyze Alloy models and provides significant performance enhancement compared to the conventional use of the Alloy Analyzer.

With declarative slicing, an Alloy model is partitioned into a *base* and a *derived* slice, where each slice is a disjoint subset of the model constraints. A base slice is defined by a *slicing criterion*, c, which is a set of relations to be constrained by the constraints in the base slice. Given a model and a slicing criterion, our algorithm (Figure 4) generates the base and the derived slices. The base slice is analyzed first and then the constraints in the derived slice are used to extend a satisfying instance for the base into a satisfying instance for the entire model (Figure 5).

Considering all the relations declared in a given Alloy model, there can be many different slicing criteria, hence many different base slices. We refer to the set of all possible criteria for a model as the set of candidate slicing criteria. Note that a model itself can also be considered as a slice with a slicing criterion consisting all the declared relations. Recall that slicing optimization aims at improving the performance of the Alloy analyzer by generating smaller and, ideally, simpler sub-problems from the complete model: The performance gain that can be achieved varies based on the partitioning defined by a particular slicing criterion. From the set of all candidate criteria, we select a criterion that would provide a *likely* optimal improvement in solving time using a heuristic evaluation (Section 4.3). Next, we describe the notion of *slice*, the algorithm for constraint partitioning and how we solve Alloy models using slices.

Definition 1. Let R be the set of all relations. Let R_b and R_d partition R. Let f_b be the formulas in f that only involve relations in R_b. Let I be the set of all instances of f. Let I_b be the set of all valuations to relations in R_b and I_d be the set of all valuations to relations in R_d. R_b defines a *base slice* if and only if:

$$\forall i_b \in I_b \mid f_b(i_b) \Rightarrow \exists i_d \in I_d \mid f(i_b + \!\!+ i_d)$$

Essentially, a base instance represents a partial solution for the complete model and the key idea behind declarative slicing is to extend this solution to a complete solution using the derived slice. However, it is also possible for a particular partial instance to a base slice, there is no way to extend it to a complete instance using the given scope. Such cases can be handled by using an enumerating SAT solver, such as mchaff [8]. Enumerating partial instances continues until there is one that can be extended, which we refer to as *filtering*. Indeed, if no such partial solution is found it means that the complete model is unsatisfiable for the given scope. Therefore, it is imperative to identify a base slice properly (if there exists any) to prevent inefficient applications of declarative slicing.

Constraint Partitioning. To generate slices, we use a *constraint partitioning* algorithm as described in Figure 4. The algorithm traverses the abstract syntax tree (AST) of a given model and evaluates each formula based on the provided slicing criterion. For this, a preprocessing is performed on the AST before the algorithm starts. First, the composite constraints (e.g., nested quantified formulas) are broken into sub-formulas by a mechanical transformation. This form represents the model as a conjunction of sub-formulas. Figure 3 shows this form for the binary search tree model (Section 2).

Next, the algorithm computes the free variables for each sub-formula. Figure 2 shows how free variables are computed for a subset of the Alloy language constructs. Free variables for a formula states which variables (relations in Alloy models) are constrained by that formula. Free variables for the sub-formulas of the binary search tree model are also shown in Figure 3.

After the initial preprocessing, each sub-formula is evaluated based on the given slicing criterion: If a formula contains a free variable that is not part of the slicing criterion it is deleted from the model; hence, it is not included the base slice and added to the derived slice. As a result, the algorithm generates two disjoint subsets from the model's sub-formulas, where the conjunction of the base slice s_b and the derived slice s_d is equivalent to the original model, $s: s \Leftrightarrow s_b \wedge s_d$. Figure 6 show an example for how base and derived slices are formed.

Approach for Slicing-based Constraint Solving. We provide an algorithm (Figure 5), which enables a fully automatic solver for declarative slicing. The algorithm takes as

```
⟨Formula, Formula⟩ Slicer(Model s, Set⟨Relation⟩ c){
    Formula base = s.formulas();
    Formula drv = true;
    Set⟨Relation⟩ R = s.relations();
    for(Formula f: s.formulas()){
        if (f_v(f) ⊄   c){
            base = base.remove(f);
            drv = drv.and(f);
        }
    }
    return ⟨base, drv⟩;
}
```

Fig. 4. Algorithm for slicing an Alloy model

```
Instance SlicingSolver (Model s, Set⟨Relation⟩ c){
    Slice s_b, s_d = Slicer(s, c);
    Bound bound = s_b.bound().update(null);
    Iterator⟨Instance⟩ itr = Alloy.solveAll(s_b, bound);

    Instance I, I_b = itr.getNext();

    while(I_b.outcome == SAT){
        bound = s_d.bound().update(I_b);
        I = solve(s_d, bound);
        if(I.outcome() == SAT)
            break;
        else
            I_b = itr.getNext();
    }
    return I;
}
```

Fig. 5. Algorithm for analyzing an Alloy model using base and derived slices

c = {root, left, right}

s_b = all n: t.root.*(left+right) | lone n.~(left+right)
      all n: t.root.*(left+right) | n !in n.^(left+right)
      all n: t.root.*(left+right) | no n.left & n.right

s_d: all n: t.root.*(left+right) {all n': n.left.*(left+right) | int n'.key < int n.key }
    all n: t.root.*(left+right) { all n': n.right.*(left+right) | int n.key < int n'.key }
    all n, n': t.root.*(left+right) | n in n'.(left+right) ⇔ n' = n.parent
    no t.root.parent
    int t.size = #(t.root.*(left+right))

Fig. 6. For the given slicing criterion, the base and the derived slices represent a disjoint subset of the sub-formulas shown in Figure 3

input an Alloy model, s, and a slicing criterion for the base slice, c, and generates a satisfying instance for the model by analyzing the base and the derived slices and combining their solutions. Successive calls are made to the analyzer to generate a complete instance satisfying all the model constraints. We first generate an instance for the base, and then extend the instance with respect to the derived slice. In case a base instance cannot be extended to a complete solution, we continue enumerating the base instances until either a satisfying instance is found or all the base instances are exhausted. The later case implies the unsatisfiability of the entire model.

The algorithm extends a base instance into an instance for the complete model by conjoining the base instance with the derived slice. This is achieved by tightening the bound for the derived slice, which forces the lower and upper bounds to be equal to the

valuations in the base instance for the base relations (s_d.bound().update(I_b)).
This guarantees the satisfaction of base constraints in the final solution. In addition, the
final solution includes valuations for the relations constrained by the derived slice and
satisfies the derived constraints on all relations.

Illustration. Consider the base and the derived slices in Figure 6. Invoking the Alloy
Analyzer on the base slice results in the following valuation, I_b, for scope 3, which is
graphically illustrated in Figure 7(a):

```
BinaryTree = { BT0 }      Node = { N0, N1, N2 }
root = { <BT0, N0> }      left = { <N0, N1> }
right = { <N0, N2> }
```

We run the analyzer on the derived slice and set the lower and upper bounds for the free
variables that are solved for base (i.e., BinaryTree, Node, root, left and right) to
the values in the instance I_b. The analyzer generates a satisfying solution for the entire
model, I, by combining the valuations in I_b with the new relations Int, size, key and
parent:

```
Int = { 0, 1, 2 }         key = { <N0, 1> <N1, 0>, <N2, 2> }
size = { <BT0, 3> }       parent = { <N1, N0>, <N2, N0> }
```

Figure 7 (b) graphically illustrates this tree, which is indeed a binary *search* tree.

4.3 Selecting a *Likely* Optimal Criterion

Previous section described the declarative slicing optimization in detail. It is important
to note that the efficiency of the optimization heavily depends on the selected slicing
criterion. We introduce a heuristic evaluation approach as an enabling technique for
the declarative slicing optimization. Using sub-formulas and free variables generated
during initial preprocessing (Figure 3), we identify a set of *candidate* slicing criteria.
Each criterion in this set represents a valid partitioning. We evaluate each candidate for a
small scope to; (1) determine whether the optimization is likely to produce a significant
performance gain, and (2) if so, select a likely optimal criterion.

Intuitively, slicing criteria could be selected from the power set of declared relations
for a given model. However, such an approach would cause a substantial amount of
analysis overhead to find an optimal criterion; for example, the binary search tree model

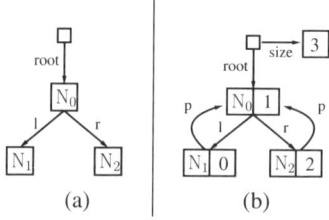

Fig. 7. Base and complete solution. (a) An acyclic binary tree. (b) An acyclic binary search tree
with size field and parent pointers. The small unlabeled square represents the BinaryTree
atom BT0; nodes N_0, N_1, N_2 are Node atoms. Edges represent valuations of binary relations.

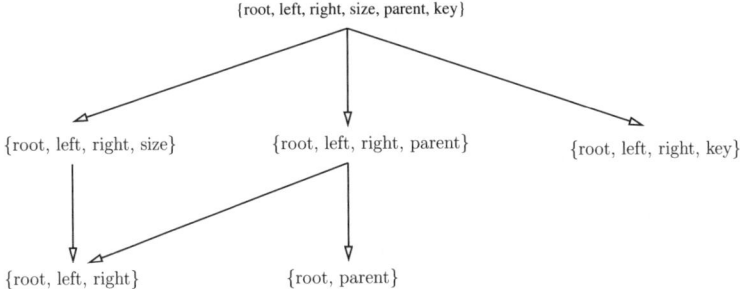

Fig. 8. Partially ordered set of free variables for the binary search tree model

we used earlier declares 6 relations, which results in 64 distinct set of relations that could be use as slicing criteria.

Slicing (constraint partitioning), ρ can be thought of as a function from a slicing criterion, c, to a base slice, s_b,: $\rho : c \rightarrow s_b$. Given a random criterion, it may map to an empty slice, i.e., there is no constraint in the model that constrains only the relations in that criterion. For example, using {root,left} as the slicing criterion for the binary search tree example would map to an empty slice: $\rho(\{\text{root,left}\}) \rightarrow \emptyset$. This indicates that a slicing criterion, c, is valid candidate if and only if there is at least one sub-formula s_i that the set of its free variables is a subset of c: $f_v(s_i) \subseteq c$.

Using this as the basis of our approach, we use free variables of the sub-formulas to prune the candidate set, where each distinct set of free variables is a candidate slicing criterion. Using the binary search tree example again, we identify that there are only 5 different slicing criteria that would map to a base slice (numbers next to each criterion indicate the sub-formulas from Figure 3 to be included in the base slice):

$\rho(\{\text{root, left, right}\})$ $\rightarrow s_b = 1 \land 2 \land 3$
$\rho(\{\text{root, left, right, key}\})$ $\rightarrow s_b = 1 \land 2 \land 3 \land 4 \land 5$
$\rho(\{\text{root, left, right, parent}\}) \rightarrow s_b = 1 \land 2 \land 3 \land 6$
$\rho(\{\text{root, left, right, size}\})$ $\rightarrow s_b = 1 \land 2 \land 3 \land 8$
$\rho(\{\text{root, parent}\})$ $\rightarrow s_b = 7$

The set of candidate slicing criteria can also be shown as a partially ordered set using subset inclusion as in Figure 8. The partially ordered set of free variables reflects a hierarchy of criteria, as in this case, including only 5 criteria. The topmost criterion includes all the declared relations in the binary search tree model, which defines a base slice as the complete model. Following the downward arrows, each criterion defines a smaller base slice, where the criteria at the bottom defines the smallest possible base slices that can be generated for the model. This approach helps us work with a small candidate set; however, we still have to try each criterion to select an optimal one.

Heuristic Evaluation. Once the candidate set is generated, we perform a *small-scope analysis* on each slicing criterion. The analysis executes the declarative slicing optimization with each candidate criterion and evaluates the results with respect to performance. The assumption is that the performance observed during small-scope analysis indicates the performance for larger scopes as well. As a result of the evaluation, we expect to find a criterion that is likely to provide an optimal performance gain. In case there is none, declarative slicing is not effective for the given model due to the fact that we cannot find an appropriate partitioning.

For each candidate criterion, we collect and evaluate overall analysis time and relative complexity of the Boolean formulas generated by the Alloy Analyzer. If an optimal base slice exists, we expect to be able to observe it through these variables. Note that, we compare the performance against the conventional use of the Alloy analyzer. Next, we describe each variable and why they are important to measure performance of the analyzer.

Overall Analysis Time: *Overall analysis time T* consists of both the time required to translate an Alloy model into a Boolean formula and the time spent during SAT solving. Generally, translation takes much less time than SAT solving. A proper slicing criterion would be likely to yield a *significantly* better overall analysis time for declarative slicing, T_{ds}, compared to the conventional use, T_{conv}: $\lambda_T = T_{conv} \div T_{ds} > 1$.

Complexity of the Boolean Formula: *Complexity C* of a Boolean formula (generated by the analyzer) can be expressed with respect to the number of variables and clauses used in that formula: $\langle V, C \rangle$. With our slicing optimization, we generate two smaller sub-problems representing the same Boolean formula; i.e., base,$\langle V_b, C_b \rangle$, and derived, $\langle V_d, C_d \rangle$. While the total number of primary variables is equal to the original formula, $V = V_b + V_d$, the total number of clauses used for the base and the derived slices decreases: $C_b + C_d < C$. This is because each slice contains a subset of the model constraints defined on a subset of the relations. We expect a proper partitioning to yield a ratio greater than 1 for complexity: $\lambda_C = C_{conv} \div (C_b + C_d) > 1$.

5 Experiments

The sections first presents experimental results, and then presents a discussion of our technique and some future work.

5.1 Results

We present evaluation for three Alloy models: binary search tree, doubly-linked list, and red-black tree [2]. We run the experiments with our prototype tool, Kato, implemented as an extension to the KodKod relational engine and use MiniSat SAT solver [3]. The experiments were run on a Windows XP machine with 1.8 GHz processor using Java 2 SDK 1.5.

Table 9 summarizes the results we obtained from small scope analysis for each subject. Binary search tree and doubly linked list models are solved for scope 8 and red-black tree for scope 7 due to the model's complexity. While doubly linked list is a cyclic data structure, the tree subjects are acyclic. Red-black tree can be seen as a more constrained version of binary search tree, where nodes have color attributes. We generated 10 different instances for each criterion. The overall analysis times, T_{conv} and T_{ds}, represents the average time to generate one instance. Detailed times for base and derived slices are not tabulated due to space considerations. The number of clauses for

slicing criteria	solving time			clauses		
	T_{conv}	T_{ds}	λ_T	C_{conv}	$\langle C_b, C_d \rangle$	λ_C
Binary Search Tree (scope=8)						
$\{root, left, right\}$	4.12	0.82	5.01	23496	$\langle 8319, 10826 \rangle$	1.23
$\{root, left, right, size\}$	4.12	0.81	5.06	23496	$\langle 9543, 9636 \rangle$	1.23
$\{root, left, right, parent\}$	4.12	0.79	5.29	23496	$\langle 9324, 10388 \rangle$	1.19
$\{root, left, right, key\}$	4.12	7.24	0.57	23496	$\langle 21251, 1365 \rangle$	1.04
Doubly Linked List (scope=8)						
$\{header, next\}$	2.34	0.12	19.50	19177	$\langle 7076, 4003 \rangle$	1.73
$\{header, next, size\}$	2.34	0.12	19.50	19177	$\langle 7636, 3600 \rangle$	1.71
$\{header, next, prev\}$	2.34	0.09	26.00	19177	$\langle 8058, 3731 \rangle$	1.63
$\{header, next, key\}$	2.34	3.89	0.60	19177	$\langle 18125, 676 \rangle$	1.02
Red-Black Tree (scope=7)						
$\{root, left, right, color\}$	4.61	0.42	10.89	14379	$\langle 7621, 3743 \rangle$	1.27
$\{root, left, right, color, size\}$	4.61	0.48	9.65	14379	$\langle 8140, 3366 \rangle$	1.25
$\{root, left, right, color, size, parent\}$	4.61	0.61	7.52	14379	$\langle 8834, 3110 \rangle$	1.20

Fig. 9. The results obtained from small-scope analysis for subject models. For space considerations, criteria causing filtering are not included in the table. One important observation is the consistency between the λ_T and λ_C values.

each Boolean formula generated by the Alloy analyzer is also shown in the table. The analyzer finds satisfying solutions for all three subject models.

The speed-up in solving time, λ_T, and the reduction in the formula size, λ_C, are used for selecting a likely optimal slicing criterion as highlighted for each subject. Overall analysis times indicate significant performance gains for some of the slicing criteria, while some others provide either a smaller or negative gain. While we use the speed-up as the basis for evaluation, the performance gain and complexity reduction variables are consistent with each other for all cases, which we consider as an interesting point for further exploration. Our assumption is that the criterion with the highest positive gain represents a likely optimal base slice. Indeed, when we run declarative slicing optimization with the identified criteria on the binary tree and the linked list models, we achieve substantial performance improvements for larger scopes. This is mainly because as the scope increases SAT problems face a state explosion problem, where slicing addresses this issue by generating smaller sub-problems. While the conventional approach fails to generate instances for binary search tree beyond scope 16, Kato is able to test scope 32 only within 24 seconds on average. Similarly, Kato can generate doubly linked list instances with 32 nodes in 20.59 seconds on average using the slicing criterion identified by our approach.

While we were also able to achieve speed-ups for the red-black tree, the largest scope we were able to reach with declarative slicing was 14. For the same model, the conventional approach failed to generate instances for scope 8. In its simplest terms, this is because the red-black tree is a more complex data structure; therefore, the analysis cannot scale. In the declarative slicing case, note that every criteria (except the ones causing filtering) contains the `color` field, which causes most of the complex constraints to be included in each corresponding base slice. While declarative slicing helps the analyzer to scale, for this reason, it is not as significant as the other subject models.

In addition to the tabulated criteria, there some others that cause filtering, i.e., not all base instances can be extended for that particular base slice (not included due to space considerations). Main reason for this is that the generated base slice is underconstrained and satisfying instances for those slices are often invalid with respect to the complete model. These are identified during analysis and discarded from the candidate set, which is crucial for pruning the candidate set even further. For all subject models, the results indicate that declarative slicing optimization enables efficient analysis and our approach identifies a likely optimal slicing criterion.

5.2 Discussion

Our approach for slicing declarative models opens a new avenue for developing a range of novel optimizations for analyzing Alloy models. To illustrate, consider the `Search` constraints for binary search tree (Section 2). There is no reason why we must use a SAT solver or a Java program for that matter to computes the values of keys. We could instead use a dedicated solver, such as the Omega library [9] or CVC-lite [1], for integer constraints. Thus, Kato enables the use of a variety of solvers (and optimizations as well) in conjunction, and we plan to explore this further.

Currently, Kato makes successive invocations to the analyzer and the underlying SAT solver to identify a proper base slice. As the experiment results suggest, there is a direct correlation between the overall analysis time and the size of the Boolean formula generated by the analyzer. We strongly believe that more efficient techniques can be developed by introducing a tighter integration between the semantic and structural properties of declarative models and the internal decision procedures of SAT solvers. We are planning to explore ways to use such properties to directly influence the decision procedures, such as branching heuristics and learning procedures [16], within SAT solvers.

It is worth pointing that the problem of generating boolean formulas that optimize analysis of underlying SAT solvers is particularly challenging because the performance of SAT solvers cannot be described in any simple terms. There are two guiding heuristics in the field: reducing the number of variables tends to reduce the solving time (presumably because it reduces the search space that the SAT solver must explore) and increasing the number of constraints also tends to reduce the solving time (again because it reduces the search space). These are just heuristics and do not hold always [4]. In the context of Alloy the problem is even more interesting because of the semantic information associated with models and the optimizations done internally. We plan to systematically explore these issues.

6 Conclusion

We have presented declarative slicing, a novel optimization that defines program slicing for declarative models and enables efficient analyses exploiting partial solutions. As opposed to the conventional use of the analyzer, where models are solved in a single execution of the underlying SAT solver, our approach identifies two sub-problems for a model and solves each problem separately and combines their solution. This not only enables the Alloy Analyzer to scale to larger scopes, but it is also complementary to the other optimizations addressing the scalability problem. Since the slices generated by the incremental analysis are valid SAT problems, our optimization can be used in conjunction with other optimizations to further improve the performance. The experimental results show that it is possible to achieve a significant improvement in the solving time for Alloy models. We believe analyses based on program slicing hold a lot of promise for efficiently checking declarative specifications.

References

1. Barrett, C., Berezin, S.: CVC Lite: A new implementation of the cooperating validity checker. In: Proc. of the 16th Int'l Conference on Computer Aided Verification(CAV) (July 2004)
2. Cormen, T.H., Leiserson, C.E., Rivest, R.L.: Introduction to Algorithms. The MIT Press, Cambridge (1990)
3. Een, N., Sorensson, N.: An extensible sat-solver. In: Proc. of the 6th Int'l Conference on Theory and Applications of Satisfiability Testing (2003)
4. Ganai, M.K., Zhang, L., Ashar, P., Gupta, A., Malik, S.: Combining strengths of circuit-based and CNF-based algorithms for a high-performance SAT solver. In: Proc. of the 39th Conference on Design Automation (DAC), June 2002, pp. 747–750 (2002)
5. Jackson, D.: Software Abstractions: Logic, Language and Analysis. The MIT Press, Cambridge (2006)
6. Jackson, D., Schechter, I., Shlyakhter, I.: ALCOA: The Alloy constraint analyzer. In: Proc. of the 22nd Int'l Conference on Software Engineering (ICSE), Limerick, Ireland (June 2000)
7. Marinov, D., Khurshid, S., Bugrara, S., Zhang, L., Rinard, M.: Optimizations for Compiling Declarative Models into Boolean Formulas. In: Bacchus, F., Walsh, T. (eds.) SAT 2005. LNCS, vol. 3569, pp. 187–202. Springer, Heidelberg (2005)
8. Moskewicz, M.W., Madigan, C.F., Zhao, Y., Zhang, L., Malik, S.: Chaff: Engineering an efficient SAT solver. In: Proc. of the 38th Conference on Design Automation (DAC) (2001)
9. Pugh, W.: The Omega test: A fast and practical integer programming algorithm for dependence analysis. Communications of the ACM 31(8) (August 1992)
10. Shlyakhter, I.: Declarative Symbolic Pure Logic Model Checking. PhD thesis, MIT (February 2005)
11. Torlak, E., Jackson, D.: Kodkod: A relational model finder. In: Proc. of the 13th Int'l Conference on Tools and Algorithms for Construction and Analysis of Systems (TACAS) (2007)
12. Uzuncaova, E., Khurshid, S.: Program slicing for declarative models. In: Proc. of the 14th ACM SIGSOFT Symposium on the Foundations of Software Engineering (FSE), Portland, OR (November 2006) (poster paper)
13. Uzuncaova, E., Khurshid, S.: Kato: A program slicing tool for declarative specifications. In: Proc. of the 29th Int'l Conference on Software Engineering (ICSE) (May 2007) (Research Demo)
14. Weiser, M.: Program slicing. In: Proc. of the 5th Int'l Conference on Software Engineering (ICSE), March 1981, pp. 439–449. IEEE Computer Society Press, Los Alamitos (1981)
15. Yuan, J., Pixley, C., Aziz, A.: Constraint-Based Verification. Springer, Heidelberg (2006)
16. Zhang, L., Malik, S.: The quest for efficient boolean satisfiability solvers. In: Proc. of the 8th Conference on Automated Deduction (CADE) (July 2002)

Finding Minimal Unsatisfiable Cores of Declarative Specifications

Emina Torlak, Felix Sheng-Ho Chang, and Daniel Jackson

MIT Computer Science and Artificial Intelligence Laboratory
{emina,fschang,dnj}@mit.edu

Abstract. Declarative specifications exhibit a variety of problems, such as inadvertently overconstrained axioms and underconstrained conjectures, that are hard to diagnose with model checking and theorem proving alone. *Recycling core extraction* is a new coverage analysis that pinpoints an irreducible unsatisfiable core of a declarative specification. It is based on resolution refutation proofs generated by *resolution engines*, such as SAT solvers and resolution theorem provers. The extraction algorithm is described, and proved correct, for a generalized specification language with a *regular* translation to the input logic of a resolution engine. It has been implemented for the Alloy language and evaluated on a variety of specifications, with promising results.

1 Introduction

As Dijkstra famously noted, testing can only show the presence of errors and not their absence. Establishing the absence of errors has been a major motivation for more complete analyses, such as model checking and theorem proving. Yet, despite the advantages such analyses often bring in bug-detecting ability, it is not always clear what level of confidence is warranted when no bugs are reported.

The main reason for doubting the result of a successful analysis is simply that the theorem being checked might not be the right one, and might fail to capture the notion of correctness that will actually be required in the context of use. When the artifact being checked is a model (rather than the actual implementation of a system), there is an additional concern that the model may not be faithful to the system it purports to represent.

It may seem that this problem is not amenable to a technical solution. In fact, however, the most common faults in a model or theorem that undermine the credibility of an analysis can be exposed by a kind of 'coverage analysis' that highlights those portions of the model and theorem that were used to establish that the theorem held for the model. Portions that are not highlighted, contrary to the expectations of the user, are evidence that the analysis was inadequate.

This idea has been explored as "vacuity detection" [1, 2] in the context of model checking, although the very definition of the problem is somewhat intricate. In the context of checking declarative specifications (as written in languages such as Alloy, Z, VDM, B, OCL, and so on), the notion of coverage has a particularly simple formulation. A constraint, whether occurring in the model being checked or in the theorem being asserted, is covered (and subsequently highlighted) if it was used in the proof that the theorem follows from the model.

This approach has been implemented as a feature of the Alloy Analyzer [3,4], but until recently has not been particularly useful since the highlighting has been too conservative, often including constraints that were not in fact used. This paper presents a new algorithm, RCE, that has been incorporated into the tool, and which gives superior results. RCE is proven to give results that are sound (meaning that constraints that are not highlighted are definitely irrelevant) and minimal (meaning that removing the highlighting on a constraint would make the result unsound). Its performance is compared to three simpler algorithms: OCE, the one previously implemented in the Alloy Analyzer, which runs faster than RCE but is not minimal, and typically highlights 2 to 3 times as many constraints; and NCE and SCE, which are sound and minimal, but run much more slowly than RCE.

As illustrated in the next section, coverage analysis mitigates a variety of problems that can arise in practice: inadvertently overconstraining the model (so that behaviours that should be included are de facto excluded); using a theorem that is not strong enough (so that bad behaviours are accepted); and setting the analysis bounds too small, so that the analyzer does not examine a sufficiently large space of possibilities. This last problem is a liability only of checkers (such as the Alloy Analyzer) that artificially bound the space, and is not suffered by theorem provers. Nevertheless, provers do suffer from the other two problems, and the algorithm presented here will therefore work for them too.

The underlying mechanism used is *unsat core extraction*, a facility of some SAT solvers. The core of an unsatisfiable formula (presented in CNF as a set of boolean clauses) is a subset of the formula that is also unsatisfiable. Every unsatisfiable formula is its own core, but a smaller core is more useful. SAT solvers do not generally provide minimal cores, which would require too much computation to produce.

Exploiting an unsat core facility is not straightforward, however, since the core returned by the SAT solver must be translated back into the high-level specification language before being shown to the user. Efficient compilations into SAT employ a variety of elaborations and transformations that result in a complex relationship between the original specification formula and the boolean formula passed to the solver. Consequently, a small core at the boolean level may be translated back to a large core at the specification level.

The new algorithm has two key ideas. The first idea is that, rather than attempting to minimize the core at the boolean level, to map the core back and apply reductions (by testing the removal of candidate constraints) at the specification level. The second idea is to identify, using the proof returned by the solver, and the mapping between levels, those boolean clauses that were generated during a proof of unsatisfiability, and which will still hold when a specification-level constraint is removed. By adding these clauses to the formula presented to the SAT solver, the algorithm allows the solver to reuse the results of inferences that were previously made. It is well known that careful exploitation of learned clauses is essential for improving SAT solver performance in general, so it is not surprising that it plays an important role in this application also.

Although the scheme was developed for analyzing coverage of Alloy specifications that are translated to boolean formulas, it has more general applicability. The paper therefore defines the context rather abstractly. The source language can take any form so long as its translation to the target language satisfies some basic properties that the paper defines. The target language can be any clausal language, and any prover is suitable if it can return a proof as a resolution graph.

2 A Small Example

As a motivating example, consider the problem of formalizing a key ingredient in our core extraction algorithm—a proof of unsatisfiability expressed as a resolution graph. To make the problem more concrete, our challenge is to specify what it means to refute a set of propositional clauses via resolution. A more generic definition that also applies to first order clauses is given in §3.2.

Figure 1 shows an Alloy [5] solution to this problem.[1] The keyword "sig" introduces a set of atoms, called a signature. A field within a signature defines a relation of some arity whose leftmost column is the signature itself. For example, neg is a function from literals to their negations, and assign is a ternary relation that maps each Instance to a partial function from Literals to Booleans. The keyword "extends" specifies a containment relationship between sets. So, True and False are subsets of Boolean. The constraints that immediately follow a signature declaration hold for all atoms of that signature. For example, the constraint on line 18 means that the edges of every Refutation are free of cycles.

A Refutation has three components: sources, resolvents, and edges. The sources relation maps a Refutation to the nonempty set of clauses that it refutes. These clauses cannot include the conflict clause. The resolvents relation defines the set of clauses that are derivable from the sources via resolution, defined by the resolve predicate. The resolvents of a valid refutation must include the conflict clause. The edges relation describes the resolution relationships among the sources and resolvents of a refutation. Every resolvent is a target of some edge, and the source of that edge is a clause used in resolution derivation of the target. The remaining definitions are straightforward.

2.1 Sample Analyses

We validate an Alloy model against an assertion that we believe to be true by instructing the Alloy Analyzer [6] to check that the conjunction of the model and the negation of the assertion is unsatisfiable. The check is performed with respect to a finite *scope*, which bounds the number of atoms that the Analyzer may assign to each signature in the model. If the assertion is invalid in the given

---

[1] A simpler example motivating the use of unsatisfiable cores, with a slower-paced introduction to Alloy, can be found in the paper by Shlyakhter et al. [3].

scope, the Analyzer produces a *counterexample*—an assignment of values to sets and relations that satisfies the model but violates the assertion. The absence of a counterexample, however, does not necessarily constitute a proof of validity. Rather, it indicates one of the following:

1. the assertion is valid but the model is too strong,
2. the assertion and the model are both valid,
3. the assertion is too weak, or
4. the scope is too small.

Each of these cases leads to an identifiable pattern of minimal cores, discussed below.

Case 1: The Model is Too Strong. The first case is probably the most common. It happens when a part of the model itself is overconstrained, admitting either no solutions or just the uninteresting ones. As a result, many assertions follow trivially from the model.

```
1   abstract sig Boolean {}                    // The set of booleans is partitioned into
2   one sig True, False extends Boolean {}     // singleton sets True and False.

3   sig Literal { neg: Literal }               // Each literal has an associated negation.
4   fact { neg = ~neg ∧ (no iden ∩ neg) }      // Negation is symmetric and irreflexive.

5   sig Clause { lits: set Literal }           // Each clause contains a set of literals.
6   one sig Conflict extends Clause {} { no lits }  // One empty clause is denoted Conflict.
7   fact { ∀ c: Clause \ Conflict | some c.lits }   // Every clause other than Conflict is nonempty.
8   fact { ∀ c: Clause | no c.lits ∩ c.lits.neg }   // No clause has both a literal and its negation.

9   pred resolve [c1, c2, r: Clause] {         // Resolving clauses c1 and c2 yields r if
10     ∃ x: c1.lits ∩ c2.lits.neg |            // c1 contains some literal x, c2 contains !x,
11     r.lits = (c1.lits ∪ c2.lits) \ (x ∪ x.neg)  // and r is a union of c1 and c2 minus x and !x.
12  }

13  sig Refutation {                           // Each refutation consists of
14     sources: some Clause \ Conflict,        // a set of nonempty clauses called 'sources,'
15     resolvents: set Clause,                 // a set of clauses called 'resolvents,' and
16     edges: (sources ∪ resolvents)→resolvents // a set of edges from clauses to resolvents,
17  }{                                         // such that
18     no ^edges ∩ iden                        // 1) The edge relation is acyclic;
19     ∀ r: resolvents | some edges.r          // 2) Every resolvent has some incoming edges;
20     Conflict ⊆ resolvents                   // 3) The empty clause is a resolvent;
21     ∀ n1, n2: sources ∪ resolvents |        // 4) For every source or resolvent n1 and n2
22     ∀ r: resolvents |                       //    for every resolvent r
23     ((n1 ∪ n2)→r ⊆ edges                    //    there are two edges ⟨n1, r⟩ and ⟨n2, r⟩
24     ⇔ resolve[n1, n2, r])                   //    if and only if n1 and n2 resolve to r.
25  }

26  sig Instance {
27     clauses: some Clause,                   // Each instance has a nonempty set of clauses,
28     assign: Literal→lone Boolean            // and each literal is assigned at most one value.
29  }{
30     ∀ lit: clauses.lits |                   // Each mentioned literal is assigned a value,
31     assign[lit] = Boolean \ assign[lit.neg] // and its negation has the opposite value.
32     ∀ c: clauses | True ⊆ assign[c.lits]    // Each clause has at least one true literal.
33  }
```

Fig. 1. A buggy formalization of resolution refutation

The example in Fig. 1 contains a bona fide error that one of the authors made in the first version of the model. It was revealed by checking that a set of clauses cannot have both an instance and a refutation:

check { ∀ i: Instance | ∄ ref: Refutation | ref.sources = i.clauses } **for** 3

The Analyzer confirms that the assertion has no counterexamples in a scope of 3, and highlights these constraints as a minimal cause of unsatisfiability:

```
 5  sig Clause { lits: set Literal }
 8  fact { ∀ c: Clause | no c.lits ∩ c.lits.neg }
13  sig Refutation {
16    edges: (sources ∪ resolvents)→resolvents
17  }{
19    ∀ r: resolvents | some edges.r
20    Conflict ⊆ resolvents
21    ∀ n1, n2: sources ∪ resolvents |
22    ∀ r: resolvents |
23      ((n1 ∪ n2)→r ⊆ edges
24      ⇔ resolve[n1, n2, r])
25  }
    check { ∀ i: Instance | ∄ ref: Refutation | ref.sources = i.clauses } for 3
```

Increasing the analysis scope to 4, 5, and 6 yields the same result: the definition of Instance is not needed to prove the assertion. What's wrong?

Examining the highlighted lines more closely reveals that the definition of refutation edges is too strong. It forces each Refutation to have at least one resolvent (line 20) and to therefore include at least one edge (line 19). But, the constraints on lines 21-24 and line 8 prevent any edge from existing. To see why, let $\langle c_1, c_2 \rangle$ be an edge between some clauses c_1 and c_2. The formula on lines 21-24 simplifies to $(c_1 \cup c_1) \rightarrow c_2 \subseteq$ edges $\Leftrightarrow$ resolve$[c_1, c_1, c_2]$ when c_2 is substituted for r and c_1 for n1 and n2. By our hypothesis, $\langle c_1, c_2 \rangle \subseteq$ edges, so resolve$[c_1, c_1, c_2]$ must be true. The definition of resolution (Fig. 1, lines 10-11), however, says that c_1 must contain both a literal and its negation, which contradicts the constraint on line 8. A revised definition of edges is given below:

```
21  edges = {                              // For every source or resolvent n, for every
22    n: sources ∪ resolvents, r: resolvents |   // resolvent r, ⟨n, r⟩ is an edge if there is
23    one edges.r \ n ∧                    // a unique clause m!=n such that ⟨m, r⟩
24    resolve[n, edges.r \ n, r]  }        // is an edge, and n and m resolve to r.
```

Case 2: The Model and Assertion are Both Valid. A valid model and a valid assertion produce cores that highlight both the assertion and all the definitions to which it pertains. When we revise the definition of edges and check the previous assertion against the revised model, the Analyzer, once again, finds no counterexample within a scope of 3. But, the derived core now includes the entire definition of Clause, Refutation, and Instance. Moreover, it remains the same with increasing scope, suggesting that the model and the assertion are both valid.

Case 3: The Assertion is Too Weak. A valid assertion that exercises only a small portion of a model is called *weak*. By themselves, weak assertions are not harmful, but they can be misleading. If the modeler believes a weak assertion covers all or most of the model, he can miss real errors in the parts of the model that are not exercised. For example, the following assertion is supposed to validate the Instance definition. It states that, if an instance satisfies a set of clauses, then it must also satisfy all subsets of those clauses:

check { ∀ i: Instance, cs: set i.clauses | cs ⊆ lits.(i.assign.True) } for 3

The Analyzer finds no counterexample, but produces the following minimal core that, once again, does not include more constraints as the scope is increased:

```
26  sig Instance {
29  }{
32    ∀ c: clauses | True ⊆ assign[c.lits]
33  }
    check { ∀ i: Instance, cs: set i.clauses | cs ⊆ lits.(i.assign.True) } for 3
```

The problem here is that the assertion covers only the highlighted part of the Instance definition, when the intention was to cover the definition in its entirety. That is, the assertion was intended to fail if any part of the Instance definition was wrong. But, if we had, for example, accidentally omitted the "lone" keyword from the declaration of assign (Fig. 1, line 28), which ensures that each literal gets at most one value, checking this assertion would not produce a counterexample.

Case 4: The Scope is Too Small. The last case is the easiest to diagnose: if the scope is too small, the minimal core usually increases when the analysis is repeated in a larger scope. In the case of a valid assertion, the core will stop increasing after a while. For an invalid one, the core will often continue to grow with scope until the scope becomes large enough to reveal a counterexample. The following assertion, which states that the edges of a resolution graph never point to source clauses, illustrates this scenario:

check { ∀ ref: Refutation | no (ref.edges).(ref.sources) } for 2

In the search scope of 2, no counterexample exists and the unsatisfiable core includes only the assertion and the definition of resolution edges:

```
13  sig Refutation {
17  }{
21    edges = {
22      n: sources ∪ resolvents, r: resolvents |
23      one edges.r \ n ∧
24      resolve[n, edges.r \ n, r] }
25  }
    check { ∀ ref: Refutation | no (ref.edges).(ref.sources) } for 2
```

As we increase the scope, however, the core expands to include more and more of the model—Refutation, Clause, and Literal definitions—until a counterexample is found in a scope of 5. The assertion is invalid because the sources of a refutation graph can be redundant; i.e. they can include a clause that is derivable from other source clauses via resolution.

3 Finding Minimal Cores

The *Simple* and *Recycling Core Extractor* (SCE and RCE) are new algorithms for finding minimal unsatisfiable cores of declarative specifications. They were developed in the context of the Alloy language and SAT-based analysis, but are independent of either. Both SCE and RCE are applicable to any specification language that can be translated to the input language of some resolution engine as described in §3.1-3.3. Unlike the alternatives (§3.4), they guarantee minimality (§3.6) at a reasonable cost (§4).

3.1 Specifications and Cores

A *declarative specification* is a conjunction of constraints on variables $v_i \in V$ that range over a universe U of values. A *model* or an *instance* of a *satisfiable* specification is a binding of $v_i \in V$ to elements of U that makes the specification true. An *unsatisfiable* specification has no models, but it has one or more *unsatisfiable cores*—subsets of the specification's constraints which are themselves unsatisfiable. Such a core is *minimal* if removing any one of its constraints causes the remainder of the core to become satisfiable.

We assume that a declarative specification $S = s_1 \wedge \ldots \wedge s_k$ is encoded in a language $\mathcal{L}$ as a directed, acyclic Abstract Syntax Graph (ASG) with k roots. The remaining constraints on the structure of ASGs capture the usual syntactic rules for declarative languages. In particular, the leaves of the ASG are variables $v_i \in V$ and constants in U, and each internal node n computes a predetermined function $f : U^{|n|} \to U$ of its children, $c_1, \ldots, c_{|n|}$.

The meaning of an ASG node n with respect to a binding $b : V \mapsto U$ is computed by applying the function f to the values of n's children: $[\![n]\!]b = f([\![c_1]\!]b, \ldots, [\![c_{|n|}]\!]b)$. The root nodes compute Boolean functions whose conjunction is the value of S as a whole. Hence, S is satisfiable if there is a binding for the variables $v_i \in V$ that induces the value *true* in the roots of its ASG. In the remainder of the paper, we will take S to mean "the ASG of S."

3.2 Resolution Engine

Invalidity of a specification can be proved by converting it to a clausal logic and then applying a suitable *resolution engine* to the generated clauses. At its simplest, a resolution engine is a procedure that applies resolution to a set of clauses in conjunctive normal form until it detects a conflict or determines satisfiability. Because resolution is refutation complete [7], a resolution engine is guaranteed to terminate on an unsatisfiable clause set with a proof of its unsatisfiability. This proof takes the form of a *resolution refutation* (Fig. 2), defined as follows:

Definition 1 (Resolution refutation). *Let C and R be sets of clauses such that C is unsatisfiable and $R \setminus C$ contains the empty (conflict) clause, denoted by $c_\emptyset$. Let E be a set of edges from $C \cup R$ to R. A directed acyclic graph $G = (C, R, E)$ is a resolution refutation of C iff*

1. the sources of G are in C;
2. each $r \in R$ is the result of resolving some clauses $s_0, s_1, \ldots, s_k \in C \cup R$, represented by $\langle s_0, r \rangle, \ldots, \langle s_k, r \rangle \in E$ (which are the only edges in E); and,
3. $c_\emptyset$ is a sink of G.

The sources of a resolution refutation $G = (C, R, E)$ that are connected to $c_\emptyset$ form an unsatisfiable core of C. The core of C with respect to (C, R, E) is denoted by $\{c \in C \mid c_\emptyset \in E^*(c)\}$, where E^* is the reflexive transitive closure of E and $E^*(c)$ is the relational image of c under E^*.

The behavior of a resolution engine on an arbitrary clause set depends on the decidability of its input language. For example, a SAT solver [8,9,10] will eventually produce a model or a refutation for every set of propositional clauses, while a theorem prover [11,12,13] will run forever on some sets of first order clauses. We abstract away from the particulars of the concrete engines' behavior with a partial function $\mathcal{E} : \mathbb{P}(C) \to G$ that maps each unsatisfiable clause set to a resolution refutation. The remaining sets in the domain of $\mathcal{E}$ are taken to resolution graphs that do not include $c_\emptyset$ (indicating satisfiability).

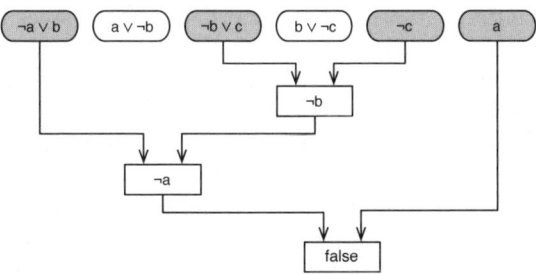

Fig. 2. Resolution refutation of $(a = b) \wedge (b = c) \wedge \neg(a \Rightarrow c)$. Core clauses are shaded in gray. The false square designates the conflict clause.

3.3 Translation

There are many ways to translate an ASG to a set of clauses in conjunctive normal form (e.g. [14,15,16]). The details of such a translation are unimportant for its use with our core extraction algorithms, as long as it is *regular* in the following sense:

Definition 2 (Regular Translation). *A procedure $\mathcal{T} : \mathcal{L} \to \mathbb{P}(C)$ is a regular translation from the specification language $\mathcal{L}$ to the clausal logic $\mathbb{P}(C)$ iff*

1. *a specification $S \in \mathcal{L}$ is unsatisfiable iff $\mathcal{T}(S)$ is unsatisfiable;*
2. *the translation of a specification $S \in \mathcal{L}$ is the union of the translations of its constraints: $\mathcal{T}(S) = \mathcal{T}_S(roots(S)) = \cup_{s \in roots(S)} \mathcal{T}_S(s)$, where $\mathcal{T}_S(s)$ is the translation of the constraint s in the context of the specification S; and,*
3. *the translation of the constraints $\sigma = roots(S) \cap roots(S')$ is context independent up to a renaming: $\mathcal{T}_S(\sigma) = r(\mathcal{T}_{S'}(\sigma))$ for some bijection r over the symbols (i.e. variable, constant, function, and predicate names) used in $\mathcal{T}(S) \cup \mathcal{T}(S')$, lifted to clauses and sets of clauses in the obvious way.*

Informally, a regular translation takes a specification to an equisatisfiable set of clauses, in a context independent way. For example, suppose that we have two specifications $S = \exists x.p(x)$ and $S' = (\forall x.q(x)) \wedge (\exists x.p(x))$ whose free variables range over a universe of two atoms, $\{a_0, a_1\}$. A regular translation $\mathcal{T}$ of these specifications to propositional logic might generate the clauses $\mathcal{T}(S) = (v_0 \vee v_1)$ and $\mathcal{T}(S') = v_0 \wedge v_1 \wedge (v_2 \vee v_3)$. In the context of S, the value of the predicate p on atoms a_0 and a_1 is represented by boolean variables v_0 and v_1, respectively. In the context of S', p is represented by v_2 and v_3. As a result, the translation of the constraint $\exists x.p(x)$ is not context-free. But, it is context independent, because $\mathcal{T}_S(\exists x.p(x))$ and $\mathcal{T}_{S'}(\exists x.p(x))$ are equivalent up to the renaming of v_0 to v_2 and v_1 to v_3.

3.4 Basic Core Extraction Algorithms

The *Naive Core Extractor* (NCE) is the most basic algorithm for extracting minimal cores of declarative specifications (Fig. 3a). It starts with an initial core K that contains all roots of the unsatisfiable specification S (line 1). The initial core is then pruned, one constraint at a time, by discarding all constraints u for which a regular translation of $K \setminus \{u\}$ is unsatisfiable (lines 3-8). This pruning step is sound since the regularity of the translation guarantees that $\mathcal{T}(K \setminus \{u\})$ and $K \setminus \{u\}$ are equisatisfiable. In the end, K contains a minimal core of S.

Because it calls the computationally expensive resolution procedure once for each constraint, NCE tends to be unacceptably slow for large specifications with small, hard cores. Shlyakhter et al. [3] addressed this problem with the *One-Step Core Extractor* (OCE) algorithm which sacrifices minimality for scalability. OCE (Fig. 3b) simply returns all roots of S whose translations include clauses connected to the conflict clause $c_\emptyset$ in a refutation of $\mathcal{T}(S)$. The set of constraints computed in this way is an unsatisfiable core of S (§3.6, Thm. 1), but it is usually not minimal.

3.5 Simple and Recycling Core Extraction

The *Simple Core Extractor* (SCE) combines the core-pruning loop of NCE with the core-extraction technique of OCE (Fig. 3c). In particular, SCE is NCE with the following modifications: initialize K with a core of S instead of S (line 14), and reduce K to a core of $K \setminus \{u\}$ instead of $K \setminus \{u\}$ itself in the iterative step (line 21). Correctness and minimality of SCE's output are discussed in §3.6.

Although it avoids unnecessary calls to the resolution engine, SCE is still wasteful. By applying $\mathcal{E}$ solely to $\mathcal{T}_S(K \setminus \{u\})$ on line 19, it discards all the clauses that $\mathcal{E}$ has learned about $\mathcal{T}_S(K \setminus \{u\})$ in previous iterations (while refuting $\mathcal{T}_S(K)$). When these clauses are recycled, SCE turns into the *Recycling Core Extractor* algorithm (RCE).

The pseudocode for RCE is shown in Fig. 3d. As before, line 24 initializes K to the unsatisfiable core of S extracted from $\mathcal{E}(\mathcal{T}(S))$. Lines 29-30 construct $\mathcal{T}(K \setminus \{u\})$ (from the already computed translations of the roots of S) and collect the clauses, called *resolvents*, that $\mathcal{E}$ had already learned about $\mathcal{T}(K \setminus \{u\})$. These are simply all resolvents reachable from $\mathcal{T}(K \setminus \{u\})$ but not from the other clauses previously fed to $\mathcal{E}$. If they include the conflict clause $c_\emptyset$, u is discarded (line 32)

NCE(S: $\mathcal{L}$, $\mathcal{T}$: $\mathcal{L} \to \mathbb{P}(C)$, $\mathcal{E}$: $\mathbb{P}(C) \to G$)
1 $K \leftarrow roots(S)$
2 $M \leftarrow \{\}$
3 **while** $K \not\subseteq M$ **do**
4    $u \leftarrow pick(K \setminus M)$
5    $M \leftarrow M \cup \{u\}$
6    $(C, R, E) \leftarrow \mathcal{E}(\mathcal{T}(K \setminus \{u\}))$
7   **if** $c_\emptyset \in R$ **then**
8      $K \leftarrow K \setminus \{u\}$
9 **return** K

(a) Naive Core Extractor

OCE(S: $\mathcal{L}$, $\mathcal{T}$: $\mathcal{L} \to \mathbb{P}(C)$, $\mathcal{E}$: $\mathbb{P}(C) \to G$)
10 $(C, R, E) \leftarrow \mathcal{E}(\mathcal{T}(S))$
11 $K \leftarrow \{s \in roots(S) \mid c_\emptyset \in E^*(\mathcal{T}_S(s))\}$
12 **return** K

(b) One-Step Core Extractor

SCE(S: $\mathcal{L}$, $\mathcal{T}$: $\mathcal{L} \to \mathbb{P}(C)$, $\mathcal{E}$: $\mathbb{P}(C) \to G$)
13 $(C, R, E) \leftarrow \mathcal{E}(\mathcal{T}(S))$
14 $K \leftarrow \{s \in roots(S) \mid c_\emptyset \in E^*(\mathcal{T}_S(s))\}$
15 $M \leftarrow \{\}$
16 **while** $K \not\subseteq M$ **do**
17    $u \leftarrow pick(K \setminus M)$
18    $M \leftarrow M \cup \{u\}$
19    $(C, R, E) \leftarrow \mathcal{E}(\mathcal{T}_S(K \setminus \{u\}))$
20   **if** $c_\emptyset \in R$ **then**
21      $K \leftarrow \{s \in K \setminus \{u\} \mid c_\emptyset \in E^*(\mathcal{T}_S(s))\}$
22 **return** K

(c) Simple Core Extractor

RCE(S: $\mathcal{L}$, $\mathcal{T}$: $\mathcal{L} \to \mathbb{P}(C)$, $\mathcal{E}$: $\mathbb{P}(C) \to G$)
23 $(C, R, E) \leftarrow \mathcal{E}(\mathcal{T}(S))$
24 $K \leftarrow \{s \in roots(S) \mid c_\emptyset \in E^*(\mathcal{T}_S(s))\}$
25 $M \leftarrow \{\}$
26 **while** $K \not\subseteq M$ **do**
27    $u \leftarrow pick(K \setminus M)$
28    $M \leftarrow M \cup \{u\}$
29    $C' \leftarrow \mathcal{T}_S(K \setminus \{u\})$
30    $R' \leftarrow R \setminus E^*(C \setminus C')$
31   **if** $c_\emptyset \in R'$ **then**
32      $K \leftarrow K \setminus \{u\}$
33   **else**
34      $(C'', R'', E'') \leftarrow \mathcal{E}(C' \cup R')$
35   **if** $c_\emptyset \in R''$ **then**
36        $(C, R, E) \leftarrow (C', R' \cup R'', E'' \cup (E \triangleright R'))$
37        $K \leftarrow \{s : K \setminus \{u\} \mid c_\emptyset \in E^*(\mathcal{T}_S(s))\}$
38 **return** K

(d) Recycling Core Extractor

Fig. 3. Core extraction algorithms. S is an unsatisfiable specification, $\mathcal{T}$ is a regular translation, and $\mathcal{E}$ is a resolution engine. Star (*) means reflexive transitive closure, $r(X)$ is the relational image of X under r, and $\triangleright$ is range restriction.

because there must be some other constraint in $K \setminus \{u\}$ whose translation contributes the same or a larger set of clauses to the core of C as u. Otherwise, line 34 applies $\mathcal{E}$ to $\mathcal{T}(K \setminus \{u\})$ and its resolvents. If the result is a refutation, the invalidity of K can be proved without u. Before we can extract the u-free core from (C'', R'', E''), however, we have to fix it: (C''', R''', E''') is not a valid refutation of S because its sources include the resolvents for $\mathcal{T}(K \setminus \{u\})$. So, lines 36-37 fix the proof and set K to the corresponding core, which excludes at least u.

3.6 Correctness and Minimality of SCE and RCE

Both SCE and RCE rely on OCE's core extraction technique to reduce the number of calls to the resolution engine. Establishing the correctness of OCE's output is therefore the first step to proving the correctness of SCE and RCE:

Theorem 1. *Let $G = (C, R, E)$ be a resolution refutation for $C = \mathcal{T}(S)$, a regular translation of the unsatisfiable specification S. Then, $K = \{s \in roots(S) \mid c_\emptyset \in E^*(\mathcal{T}_S(s))\}$ is an unsatisfiable core of S.*

Proof. Let S' be a specification whose roots are K, i.e. $roots(S') = K$. Because $\mathcal{T}$ is regular, $\mathcal{T}(S') = \mathcal{T}_{S'}(roots(S')) = \mathcal{T}_{S'}(K) = r(\mathcal{T}_S(K))$ for some renaming r. Let $C_K = \mathcal{T}_S(K)$, $R_K = E^*(C_K)$ and $E_K = E \triangleright R_K$, where $\triangleright$ is range restriction. By Def. 1 and the construction of K, the graph $G_K = (C_K, R_K, E_K)$ is a resolution refutation of $\mathcal{T}_S(K)$, and, letting $r(G_K)$ denote G_K with r applied to all of its vertices, $r(G_K)$ is a resolution refutation of $r(\mathcal{T}_S(K)) = \mathcal{T}(S')$. Hence, by regularity of $\mathcal{T}$, S' is unsatisfiable and, by the semantics of ASGs, so is K. □

We can now show that RCE produces a minimal unsatisfiable core of the input specification S, if the input engine terminates on each invocation. Since RCE reduces to SCE when R' is set to the empty set on line 30, the following is also a proof of SCE's correctness and minimality:

Theorem 2. *If it terminates, RCE(S, $\mathcal{T}$, $\mathcal{E}$) returns a minimal unsatisfiable core of S, where S is an unsatisfiable specification, $\mathcal{T}$ is a regular translation, and $\mathcal{E}$ a resolution engine.*

Proof. Let K be the output of RCE(S, $\mathcal{T}$, $\mathcal{E}$). We first show that K is unsatisfiable and then that it is minimal. By Thm. 1, the constraints assigned to K by line 24 form an unsatisfiable core of S. The only other lines that assign K are lines 32 and 37. Suppose that the condition on line 31 is true. Then, by Def. 1 and construction of C' and R', $(C', R', E \triangleright R')$ is a resolution refutation for $C' = \mathcal{T}_S(K \setminus \{u\})$ which, by regularity of $\mathcal{T}$, is equivalent (up to a renaming) to $\mathcal{T}(K \setminus \{u\})$. Hence, $K \setminus \{u\}$ is unsatisfiable, so line 32 will never remove a relevant constraint from K. For line 37 to execute, the condition on line 35 must hold. If it does, line 36 executes first, establishing (C, R, E) as a resolution refutation for $C = C' \equiv_r \mathcal{T}(K \setminus \{u\})$ (Defs. 1, 2). This and Thm. 1 ensure that the constraints assigned to K in line 37 form an unsatisfiable core of $K \setminus \{u\}$.

Now, suppose that K is not minimal. Then, there is a constraint $s \in K$ such that $K \setminus \{s\}$ is unsatisfiable. Lines 26 and 28 ensure that s is picked at least once on line 27. Because $K \setminus \{s\}$ is invalid, either the condition on line 31 or that on line 35 holds, causing s to be removed from K—a contradiction. □

4 Experimental Results

We have implemented both SCE and RCE for the Alloy language, with MiniSat [8] as the resolution engine and Kodkod [14] as the (regular) translation procedure from Alloy to propositional clauses. These implementations were evaluated against the basic algorithms (NCE and OCE) on two sets of problems: fifteen TPTP [17] benchmarks and six problems from the Alloy4 distribution [6]. The chosen problems come from a variety of fields (software engineering, medicine, geometry, etc.), include 4 to 59 constraints, and exhibit a wide range

	problem	size	scope	variables	clauses	transl (sec)	solve (sec)	initial core	min core	OCE (sec)	NCE (sec)	SCE (sec)	RCE (sec)	tRCE (sec)
Alloy	Trees	4	7	407396	349384	10	98	4	4	1	7	7	7	7
	RingElection	10	8	59447	187381	1	49	9	9	2	59	7	8	9
	Lists.empties	12	60	2547216	7150594	74	12	7	6	9	196	89	86	86
	Lists.reflexive	12	14	34914	91393	1	23	10	5	3	134	120	158	96
	Lists.symmetric	12	8	7274	17836	0	27	12	7	3	150	115	93	85
	Hotel	59	5	22407	55793	0	0	53	29	0	27	14	11	11
TPTP	ALG212	6	7	1072203	1027000	7	63	6	5	1	103	104	107	98
	COM008	14	9	6154	9845	0	1	14	10	0	190	193	235	166
	NUM374	14	3	6874	18938	0	0	14	6	0	3	3	3	3
	TOP020	14	10	2554114	4262733	21	113	2	2	6	826	10	10	10
	SET943	18	5	5333	12541	0	0	14	4	0	19	18	15	13
	SET948	20	14	339132	863889	5	36	10	6	1	754	247	359	254
	SET967	20	4	14641	45112	0	0	10	2	0	454	181	142	142
	GEO091	26	10	106329	203303	9	108	24	7	3	1129	652	105	105
	GEO092	26	8	48500	91285	3	7	24	7	0	120	99	70	51
	GEO158	26	8	46648	88234	3	38	25	7	2	175	107	45	45
	GEO115	27	9	109002	188782	6	85	25	7	2	675	278	63	86
	LAT258	27	7	205621	336912	2	11	26	20	0	95	87	70	70
	GEO159	28	8	87214	195200	10	57	24	7	1	223	83	50	50
	MED007	41	35	130777	265702	2	67	24	7	1	>3600	>3600	176	91
	MED009	41	35	130777	265703	2	71	26	7	1	>3600	>3600	85	76

Fig. 4. Experimental results. The notation ">3600" means that an algorithm was unable to produce a core for the specified problem in the given scope within one hour. Gray shading highlights the best running time among NCE, SCE, RCE, and trained RCE (tRCE).

of behaviors. In particular, eleven are theorems (i.e. unsatisfiable conjunctions of axioms and negated conjectures); four are assumed to be (counter)satisfiable but have no known finite models; two are unsatisfiable in some universes and satisfiable in others; and four have neither an assumed status nor any known finite models.

Each problem p was tested for satisfiability in scopes of increasing sizes until a failing scope $s_{\text{fail}}(p)$ was reached in which either a model was found or all three minimality-guaranteeing algorithms failed to produce a result for that scope within 5 minutes (300 seconds). Then, because our implementation of RCE is parameterized by a "resolution distance" d that controls which resolvents are reused in each iteration[2], RCE was automatically trained using a scope of $0.75 * (s_{\text{fail}}(p) - 1)$ to estimate the best d for the problem p. Once the experimental parameters were determined, the algorithms were tested on each problem using a scope of $s_{\text{fail}}(p) - 1$. All experiments were performed on a 2×3 GHz Dual-Core Intel Xeon with 2 GB of RAM, with a cut-off time of one hour (3600 seconds).

The results are shown in Fig. 4. The first three columns show the name of the problem, the number of constraints it contains, and the scope in which it was tested. The next two columns contain the number of propositional variables and clauses produced by the translator. The "transl (sec)" and "solve (sec)" columns show the time, in seconds, taken by the translator to generate the problem and the SAT solver to produce the initial refutation. The "initial core" and "min

---

[2] A relevant resolvent $r \in R'$ (Fig. 3d, line 30) is recycled if all paths from r to a source in C' (Fig. 3d, line 29) contain at most d edges.

	problem	N-score	NCE/RCE	NCE/tRCE	average speed-up
easy	NUM374	-0.34	1.04	0.95	
	SET943	0.12	1.29	1.44	RCE: 1.48x
	SET967	0.53	3.20	3.20	tRCE: 1.56x
	Trees	0.59	1.08	1.08	
	COM008	0.60	0.81	1.14	
medium	Hotel	1.08	2.54	2.54	
	RingElection	1.73	7.13	6.31	
	ALG212	1.82	0.96	1.05	
	Lists.empties	1.87	2.28	2.29	
	LAT258	1.89	1.36	1.36	RCE: 2.45x
	Lists.symmetric	2.13	1.61	1.77	tRCE: 2.59x
	GEO092	2.14	1.73	2.35	
	Lists.reflexive	2.21	0.85	1.40	
	SET948	2.70	2.10	2.97	
	GEO158	2.86	3.90	3.89	
hard	GEO159	3.08	4.49	4.48	
	TOP020	3.13	85.26	85.76	
	GEO115	3.23	10.74	7.82	RCE: 29.04x
	GEO091	3.32	10.78	10.77	tRCE: 32.65x
	MED007	3.36	20.51	39.54	
	MED009	3.38	42.47	47.53	

(a) RCE and tRCE versus NCE

	problem	S-score	SCE/RCE	SCE/tRCE	average speed-up
easy	NUM374	-0.34	1.05	0.96	
	SET943	-0.03	1.21	1.36	
	SET967	0.18	1.28	1.28	RCE: 1.08x
	TOP020	0.35	0.99	1.00	tRCE: 1.11x
	Trees	0.59	1.08	1.08	
	COM008	0.60	0.82	1.16	
	RingElection	0.65	0.87	0.77	
	Hotel	0.99	1.31	1.31	
medium	Lists.empties	1.12	1.04	1.04	
	ALG212	1.82	0.97	1.06	
	LAT258	1.82	1.24	1.24	
	Lists.reflexive	2.06	0.76	1.25	RCE: 1.27x
	GEO092	2.09	1.43	1.94	tRCE: 1.43x
	Lists.symmetric	2.13	1.24	1.36	
	SET948	2.16	0.69	0.97	
	GEO158	2.83	2.39	2.39	
	GEO159	2.99	1.67	1.66	
hard	MED007	3.06	20.51	39.54	
	MED009	3.13	42.47	47.53	RCE: 18.41x
	GEO115	3.18	4.42	3.22	tRCE: 24.13x
	GEO091	3.27	6.23	6.22	

(b) RCE and tRCE versus SCE

Fig. 5. Comparison of minimal core extractors based on problem difficulty

core" columns present the number of constraints in the initial core found by OCE and the minimal core found by the minimality-guaranteeing algorithms. The remaining columns show core extraction time, in seconds, for each algorithm.

On average, RCE outperforms NCE and SCE by a factor of 10 and 4, respectively; its trained variant (tRCE) is roughly 11 times faster than NCE and 6 times faster than NCE. These overall averages, however, do not take into account the wide variance in difficulty among the tested problems. A more useful comparison of the minimality-guaranteeing algorithms is given in Fig. 5, where we classify the problems according to their difficulty for NCE (Fig. 5a) and SCE (Fig. 5b), and then report how well the RCE variants perform on the problems deemed as "easy", "moderately hard" or "hard" for the competing algorithms.

To assess the difficulty of a given problem for NCE, we compute its *N-score*, and rate it as easy if the score is less than 1, hard if the score is 3 or more, and moderately hard otherwise. The N-score for a specification S is $\log_{10}((s - m) * t + m * t * .01)$, where s is the size of the specification, m is the size of its minimal core, and t is the time, in seconds, taken by the SAT solver to determine that S is unsatisfiable. Note that the N-score for a problem measures how much work NCE has to do to eliminate irrelevant constraints from the specification, which is approximated by predicting that NCE will take $(s - m) * t$ seconds to prune away the $(s - m)$ irrelevant constraints. (The formula assumes that it takes only 1 percent of the initial time to throw out a relevant constraint because of the ability of modern SAT solvers to find satisfying assignments very quickly.) The difficulty of a problem for SCE is computed in a similar way; the S-score of a given problem is $\log_{10}((s' - m) * t + m * t * .01)$, where s' is the size of the initial (one-step) core.

Unsurprisingly, OCE outperforms both SCE and RCE in terms of execution time. However, it generates cores that are on average 2.4 times larger than the corresponding minimal cores. For 20 out of 21 (95%) of the tested problems, the OCE core included at least 50% of the original constraints. In contrast, only 7 out of 21 (33%) minimal cores included at least half of the original constraints.

5 Related Work

The problem of finding unsatisfiable cores of sets of constraints has been studied in the context of linear programming [18], propositional satisfiability [19, 20, 21, 22, 23, 24, 25], and finite model finding [3]. Chinneck and Dravnieks' [18] deletion filtering algorithm for linear constraints is similar to NCE: given an infeasible linear program LP, the algorithm tests each functional constraint for membership in an Irreducible Infeasible Subset (i.e. minimal unsatisfiable core) by removing it from LP and applying a linear programming solver to the result. If the reduced LP is infeasible, the constraint is permanently removed, otherwise it is kept. The remaining algorithms in [18] are specific to linear programs, and there is no obvious way to adapt them to other domains.

Most of the work on extracting small unsatisfiable cores comes from the SAT community. Several practical algorithms [20, 24, 25] have been proposed for finding small, but not necessarily minimal, cores of propositional formulas. Zhang and Malik's algorithm [25], for example, works by extracting a core from a refutation, feeding it back to the solver, and repeating this process until the size of the extracted core no longer decreases. A few proposed algorithms provide strong optimality guarantees—such as returning the smallest minimal core [22, 23] or all minimal cores [21, 26, 27, 28] of a boolean formula—at the cost of scaling to problems that are orders of magnitude smaller than those handled by the approximation algorithms. The Complete Resolution Refutation (CRR) algorithm by Dershowitz et al. [19] strikes an attractive balance between scalability and optimality: it finds a single minimal core but scales to large real-world formulas. CRR was one of the inspirations for our work and is, in fact, an instantiation of RCE for propositional logic, with a SAT solver as a resolution engine and the identity function as the translation procedure.

The work by Shlyakhter et al. [3] is most closely related to ours. It proposes the One-Step Core Extractor (OCE) for declarative specifications in a language reducible to propositional logic. As discussed in previous sections, OCE is faster than RCE but produces cores that are two to three times larger than the corresponding minimal cores.

6 Conclusions

We have presented *recycling core extraction*, a new method for finding minimal unsatisfiable cores of declarative specification, and compared it to two simpler algorithms, NCE and SCE. On hard problems, the base recycling extraction algorithm (RCE), which reuses all available learned clauses, is about 29x faster than NCE and 18x faster than SCE. But even greater speed-ups can be achieved with a simple variant of RCE that is trained to recycle a fixed subset of the available resolvents in each iteration.

RCE has so far been used as a coverage analysis for hand-crafted formal models within the interactive modeling environment of the Alloy Analyzer. It seems likely, however, that RCE will be applicable in other settings, particularly those involving large, automatically generated specifications, enabling its use for coverage analysis in code checking [29,30,31] and declarative configuration [32].

References

1. Chockler, H., Kupferman, O., Vardi, M.Y.: Coverage metrics for temporal logic model checking. LCNS 2031, 528 (2001)
2. Kupferman, O., Vardi, M.Y.: Vacuity detection in temporal model checking. In: Conference on Correct Hardware Design and Verification Methods, pp. 82–96 (1999)
3. Shlyakhter, I., Seater, R., Jackson, D., Sridharan, M., Taghdiri, M.: Debugging overconstrained declarative models using unsatisfiable cores. In: ASE 2003 (2003)
4. Shlyakhter, I.: Declarative Symbolic Pure Logic Model Checking. PhD thesis, Massachusetts Institute of Technology, Cambridge, MA (2005)
5. Jackson, D.: Software Abstractions: logic, language, and analysis. MIT Press, Cambridge (2006)
6. Chang, F.: Alloy analyzer 4.0 (2007), http://alloy.mit.edu/alloy4/
7. Robinson, J.A.: A machine-oriented logic based on the resolution principle. J. ACM 12(1), 23–41 (1965)
8. Eén, N., Sörensson, N.: An Extensible SAT-solver. In: Giunchiglia, E., Tacchella, A. (eds.) SAT 2003. LNCS, vol. 2919, pp. 502–518. Springer, Heidelberg (2004)
9. Goldberg, E., Novikov, Y.: BerkMin: A fast and robust SAT solver. In: DATE 2002, pp. 142–149 (2002)
10. Mahajan, Y.S., Fu, Z., Malik, S.: zchaff2004: An efficient SAT solver. In: SAT (Selected Papers), pp. 360–375 (2004)
11. Kalman, J.A.: Automated Reasoning with Otter. Rinton Press (2001)
12. Riazanov, A.: Implementing an Efficient Theorem Prover. PhD Thesis, The University of Manchester, Manchester (2003)
13. Weidenbach, C.: Combining superposition, sorts and splitting. In: Handbook of automated reasoning, pp. 1965–2013 (2001)
14. Torlak, E., Jackson, D.: Kodkod: A Relational Model Finder. In: Grumberg, O., Huth, M. (eds.) TACAS 2007. LNCS, vol. 4424, pp. 632–647. Springer, Heidelberg (2007)
15. Claessen, K., Sörensson, N.: New techniques that improve MACE-style finite model finding. In: CADE-19 Workshop on Model Computation, Miami, FL (2003)
16. Baumgartner, P., Fuchs, A., de Nivelle, H., Tinelli, C.: Computing finite models by reduction to function-free clause logic. In: Journal of Applied Logic (2007)
17. Sutcliffe, G., Suttner, C.: The TPTP Problem Library: CNF Release v1.2.1. Journal of Automated Reasoning 21(2), 177–203 (1998)
18. Chinneck, J.W., Dravnieks, E.W.: Locating minimal infeasible constraint sets in linear programs. ORSA Journal of Computing 3(2), 157–158 (1991)

19. Dershowitz, N., Hanna, Z., Nadel, A.: A Scalable Algorithm for Minimal Unsatisfiable Core Extraction. In: Biere, A., Gomes, C.P. (eds.) SAT 2006. LNCS, vol. 4121, pp. 36–41. Springer, Heidelberg (2006)
20. Goldberg, E., Novikov, Y.: Verification of proofs of unsatisfiability for CNF formulas. In: DATE 2003 (2003)
21. Liffiton, M.H., Sakallah, K.A.: On Finding All Minimally Unsatisfiable Subformulas. In: Bacchus, F., Walsh, T. (eds.) SAT 2005. LNCS, vol. 3569, pp. 173–186. Springer, Heidelberg (2005)
22. Lynce, I.: On computing minimum unsatisfiable cores. In: SAT 2004 (2004)
23. Mneimneh, M., Lynce, I., Andraus, Z.: A Branch-and-Bound Algorithm for Extracting Smallest Minimal Unsatisfiable Formulas. In: Bacchus, F., Walsh, T. (eds.) SAT 2005. LNCS, vol. 3569, pp. 467–474. Springer, Heidelberg (2005)
24. Oh, Y., Mneimneh, M., Andraus, Z., Sakallah, K., Markov, I.: Amuse: A minimally-unsatisfiable subformula extractor. In: DAC, ACM/IEEE, pp. 518–523 (2004)
25. Zhang, L., Malik, S.: Extracting small unsatisfiable cores from unsatisfiable boolean formula. In: SAT 2003 (2003)
26. Grégoire, E., Mazure, B., Piette, C.: Extracting MUSes. In: ECAI 2006, Trento, Italy, pp. 387–391 (2006)
27. Grégoire, E., Mazure, B., Piette, C.: Local-search extraction of MUSes. Constraints Journal 12(3), 324–344 (2007)
28. Grégoire, E., Mazure, B., Piette, C.: Boosting a complete technique to find MSS and MUS thanks to a local search oracle. In: IJCAI 2007, Hyderabad, India, vol. 2, pp. 2300–2305 (2007)
29. Dennis, G., Chang, F., Jackson, D.: Modular verification of code. In: ISSTA 2006, Portland, Maine (2006)
30. Dolby, J., Vaziri, M., Tip, F.: Finding bugs efficiently with a sat solver. In: ESEC-FSE 2007, pp. 195–204. ACM, New York (2007)
31. Taghdiri, M.: Automating Modular Program Verification by Refining Specifications. PhD thesis, Massachusetts Institute of Technology (2007)
32. Yeung, V.: Declarative configuration applied to course scheduling. Master's thesis, Massachusetts Institute of Technology, Cambridge (2006)

Precise Interval Analysis vs. Parity Games

Thomas Gawlitza and Helmut Seidl

TU München, Institut für Informatik, I2
85748 München, Germany
{gawlitza,seidl}@in.tum.de

Abstract. In [8], a practical algorithm for precise interval analysis is provided for which, however, no non-trivial upper complexity bound is known. Here, we present a lower bound by showing that precise interval analysis is at least as hard as computing the sets of winning positions in parity games. Our lower-bound proof relies on an encoding of parity games into systems of particular integer equations. Moreover, we present a simplification of the algorithm for integer systems from [8]. For the given encoding of parity games, the new algorithm provides another algorithm for parity games which is almost as efficient as the discrete strategy improvement algorithm by Vöge and Jurdziński [17].

1 Introduction

Interval analysis as introduced by Cousot and Cousot [3,4] tries to determine at compile-time for each variable x and program point v in a program an as tight interval as possible which is guaranteed to contain all values of x when reaching program point v. This problem is of fundamental importance for program optimizations such as safe removal of array bound checks as well as the certification of absence of arithmetic overflows. The problem with interval analysis, though, is that the lattice of all intervals has infinite ascending chains implying that acceleration techniques are needed to enforce fixpoint iteration to terminate. One such acceleration technique is the widening and narrowing approach of Cousot and Cousot [3,4] which, however, results in algorithms which may fail to return the least solution of the given system of equations extracted from the program.

Recently, the problem of interval analysis has attracted new attention. In [15] Su and Wagner identified a class of polynomial solvable range constraints for interval analysis which can be solved *precisely*. This class admits full addition. Multiplication and intersection are restricted in such a way that at least one of the arguments must be a constant interval. Leroux and Sutre [13] extend this result by providing an acceleration-based algorithm for solving interval constraints with *full* multiplication and restricted intersection in cubic time *precisely*. In [2], Gaubert et al. suggest strategy iteration as an alternative method for computing solutions of interval equations with full intersections. Their method still fails to return the least solution in some cases. Computing the *least* solution to the interval equations introduced for interval analysis will be called *precise* interval analysis in the sequel. In [8], we reduce precise interval analysis to solving systems of integer equations for which we propose another variant of strategy iteration which is guaranteed to return the least solution. The practical efficiency of any algorithm based on strategy iteration depends on the number of strategies encountered during the iteration. Although we never have observed more than a linear number of strategies, no non-trivial upper bound to this number is known. Thus, one might think of other methods to obtain not only a practical, but also provably polynomial algorithm for precise interval analysis. Here we show that, if such an algorithm exists, it also solves a long standing open problem, namely, to compute the winning regions of a parity game in polynomial time.

This lower-bound proof uses a reduction similar to the reductions of parity games to mean payoff games and discounted payoff games [10,14]. A different class of interval constraints is considered in [1] where Bordeaux et al. prove that computing the least fixpoint is **NP**-hard. This strong lower bound, however, relies on the explicit use of a square-root operator and thus cannot easily be carried over to our class where only linear operations on intervals are allowed.

Our encoding of parity games does not only give a lower-bound argument for precise interval analysis, but also allows to use methods for integer systems to solve parity games. As our second contribution, we therefore present a new version of the algorithm from [8] for integer systems which is significantly simpler. Similar to the algorithm in [8], the new algorithm is based on strategy iteration. The original algorithm, however, relies on an instrumentation of the underlying lattice to guide strategy improvement. This extra overhead is now avoided. Via our encoding, the new method for integer systems also provides a very simple algorithm for parity games. Compared to the discrete strategy improvement algorithm of Vöge [17,16], the valuations to determine the next strategy needed by our algorithm are just mappings from positions to integers.

The paper is organized as follows. In section 2, we introduce basic notions and the concepts of parity games and systems of integer equations. In section 3, we show how one can reduce the computation of the winning regions and the winning strategies for a parity game to the computation of the least solution of systems of particular integer equations. In section 4, we show how computing least solutions of these integer equations can be reduced to precise interval analysis — thus completing the lower-bound proof for interval analysis. In section 5, we present the novel strategy iteration algorithm for solving systems of integer equations. Moreover, we organize the strategy iteration in such a way that, for simple integer equations, i.e., for equations with addition of constants only, the number of maxima with constants no longer affects the asymptotic complexity. Since the systems obtained from our reduction from parity games are simple, the reduction together with the new algorithm for integer equations provides another strategy iteration algorithm for parity games. Each improvement step of this algorithm requires at most quadratically many operations on integers of length $\mathcal{O}(d \cdot \log n)$ where n is the number of positions and d is the maximal rank of the parity game.

2 Notation and Basic Concepts

As usual, $\mathbb{N}$ and $\mathbb{Z}$ denote the set of natural numbers excluding 0 and the set of integers, respectively. We write $\mathbb{N}_0$ for $\mathbb{N} \cup \{0\}$. Given a relation $R \subseteq A \times B$ and a subset $A' \subseteq A$ we write $A'R$ for the set $\{b \in B \mid \exists a \in A' : (a,b) \in R\}$. Our complexity results will be stated w.r.t. a uniform cost measure where we count memory accesses and arithmetic operations for $\mathcal{O}(1)$.

Parity Games. A *parity game* is a tuple $G = (V_\vee, V_\wedge, E, r)$. $V_\vee$ and $V_\wedge$ are disjoint finite sets of *positions* owned by the $\vee$-player and the $\wedge$-player, respectively. We will always write V for the set $V_\vee \cup V_\wedge$. The set $E \subseteq V^2$ is a finite set of possible *moves* with $\{v\}E \neq \emptyset$ for every position $v \in V$, i.e., there is no sink. Finally, $r : V \to \mathbb{N}_0$ is the *rank function* which assigns a *rank* $r(v)$ to every position v.

A *play* over G is an infinite word $w = v_1 v_2 \cdots$ with $(v_i, v_{i+1}) \in E$ for $i \in \mathbb{N}$. Let $m(w) := \max\{r(v) \mid v \in V \text{ occurs infinitely often in } w\}$. The play w is won by the $\vee$-player (resp. $\wedge$-player) iff $m(w)$ is odd (resp. even). A position $v \in V$ is called $\vee$-*winning* (resp. $\wedge$-*winning*) iff the $\vee$-player (resp. $\wedge$-player) can enforce that every play starting at v is won by the $\vee$-player (resp. $\wedge$-player). The set of all $\vee$-winning (resp. $\wedge$-winning) positions is called the $\vee$-*winning region* (resp. $\wedge$-*winning region*).

A mapping $\sigma_\vee : V_\vee \to V$ with $\sigma_\vee(v) \in \{v\}E$ for every $v \in V_\vee$ is called a *positional* $\vee$-*strategy*. Dually, a mapping $\sigma_\wedge : V_\wedge \to V$ with $\sigma_\wedge(v) \in \{v\}E$ for every $v \in V_\wedge$ is called a *positional* $\wedge$-*strategy*. A play w is *consistent* with the positional $\vee$-strategy $\sigma_\vee$ iff $\sigma_\vee(v_\vee) = v$ for every finite prefix $w'v_\vee v$ of w with $v_\vee \in V_\vee$. Dually, a play w is *consistent* with the positional $\wedge$-strategy $\sigma_\wedge$ iff $\sigma_\wedge(v_\wedge) = v$ for every finite prefix $w'v_\wedge v$ of w with $v_\wedge \in V_\wedge$. It is well-known that positional strategies are sufficient (memoryless determinacy) [6]. This means: there exists a positional $\vee$-strategy $\sigma_\vee$ such that every play w which starts at a $\vee$-winning position and which is consistent with $\sigma_\vee$ is won by the $\vee$-player. Such a positional $\vee$-strategy is called *winning*. Dually, there exists a positional $\wedge$-strategy $\sigma_\wedge$ (called *winning*) such that every play w which starts at a $\wedge$-winning position and which is consistent with $\sigma_\wedge$ is won by the $\wedge$-player.

Given a positional $\vee$-strategy $\sigma_\vee$ (resp. $\wedge$-strategy $\sigma_\wedge$) we write $G(\sigma_\vee)$ (resp. $G(\sigma_\wedge)$) for the parity game $(V_\vee, V_\wedge, (E \cap V_\wedge \times V) \cup \sigma_\vee, r)$ (resp. $(V_\vee, V_\wedge, (E \cap V_\vee \times V) \cup \sigma_\wedge, r)$) [1]. Thus, the parity game $G(\sigma_\vee)$ (resp. $G(\sigma_\wedge)$) is obtained from G by removing all moves which cannot be used in any play which is consistent with $\sigma_\vee$ (resp. $\sigma_\wedge$). A $\vee$-strategy $\sigma_\vee$ (resp. $\wedge$-strategy $\sigma_\wedge$) is winning iff every play w in $G(\sigma_\vee)$ (resp. $G(\sigma_\wedge)$) which starts from a $\vee$-winning position (resp. $\wedge$-winning position) is won by the $\vee$-player (resp. $\wedge$-player).

Systems of Integer Equations. We briefly introduce systems of integer equations (cf. [8]). Let $\overline{\mathbb{Z}}$ denote the complete lattice $\mathbb{Z} \cup \{-\infty, \infty\}$ equipped with the natural ordering. We extend the operations addition $+ : \overline{\mathbb{Z}} \times \overline{\mathbb{Z}} \to \overline{\mathbb{Z}}$ and multiplication $\cdot : \overline{\mathbb{Z}} \times \overline{\mathbb{Z}} \to \overline{\mathbb{Z}}$ to the operands $-\infty$ and ∞:

$$x + (-\infty) = -\infty \quad \text{for all } x \in \overline{\mathbb{Z}}$$
$$0 \cdot x = 0 \quad \text{for all } x > -\infty$$
$$x \cdot \infty = \infty \quad \text{for all } x > 0$$
$$x \cdot \infty = -\infty \quad \text{for all } x < 0$$
$$x + \infty = \infty \quad \text{for all } x > -\infty$$
$$x \cdot (-\infty) = -\infty \quad \text{for all } x > 0$$
$$x \cdot (-\infty) = \infty \quad \text{for all } x < 0$$

A system $\mathcal{E}$ of integer equations is a sequence of equations $\mathbf{x}_i = e_i$ for $i = 1, \ldots, n$, where the variables $\mathbf{x}_i$ on the left-hand sides are pairwise distinct and the right-hand sides e_i are expressions e built up from constants and variables by means of addition, multiplication with constants as well as minimum ("$\wedge$") and maximum ("$\vee$"):

$$e ::= a \mid \mathbf{x} \mid e_1 + e_2 \mid b \cdot e_1 \mid e_1 \wedge e_2 \mid e_1 \vee e_2$$

---

[1] Here a mapping $f : A \to B$ is considered as the relation $\{(a, f(a)) \mid a \in A\}$.

where e_1, e_2 are expressions, $\mathbf{x}$ is a variable, $a, b \in \overline{\mathbb{Z}}$, $b \geq 1$. We assume that $b\cdot$ has the highest operator precedence followed by $+$, $\wedge$ and $\vee$ which has the lowest operator precedence. We write $|\mathcal{E}|$ for the number of subexpressions occurring in right-hand sides of $\mathcal{E}$. Thus, $|\mathcal{E}|$ is independent of the sizes of numbers occurring in $\mathcal{E}$. We denote the set of variables of $\mathcal{E}$ by $\mathbf{X}_\mathcal{E}$. We drop the subscript whenever $\mathcal{E}$ is clear from the context. The system $\mathcal{E}$ is called *disjunctive*, if it does not contain $\wedge$-expressions, and it is called *conjunctive*, if it does not contain $\vee$-expressions. A system without $\vee$- and $\wedge$-expressions is called *basic*. If $\mathcal{E}$ denotes the system $\mathbf{x}_i = e_i$, $i = 1, \ldots, n$, then, for $a, b \in \overline{\mathbb{Z}}$ with $a \leq b$, $\mathcal{E}|_{[a,b]}$ denotes the system $\mathbf{x}_i = (e_i \wedge b) \vee a$, $i = 1, \ldots, n$.

Under a variable assignment μ, i.e., a function which maps variables from $\mathbf{X}$ to values from $\overline{\mathbb{Z}}$, an expression e evaluates to a value $[\![e]\!]\mu \in \overline{\mathbb{Z}}$:

$$[\![a]\!]\mu = a \qquad [\![\mathbf{x}]\!]\mu = \mu(\mathbf{x}) \qquad [\![e_1 + e_2]\!]\mu = [\![e_1]\!]\mu + [\![e_2]\!]\mu$$
$$[\![b \cdot e]\!]\mu = b \cdot [\![e]\!]\mu \qquad [\![e_1 \vee e_2]\!]\mu = [\![e_1]\!]\mu \vee [\![e_2]\!]\mu \qquad [\![e_1 \wedge e_2]\!]\mu = [\![e_1]\!]\mu \wedge [\![e_2]\!]\mu$$

where e, e_1, e_2 are expressions, $\mathbf{x}$ is a variable, $a, b \in \overline{\mathbb{Z}}$, $b \geq 1$. Together with the point-wise ordering the set of variable assignments $\mathbf{X} \to \overline{\mathbb{Z}}$ forms a complete lattice. A *solution* of $\mathcal{E}$ is a variable assignment μ which satisfies all equations of a system $\mathcal{E}$, i.e. $\mu(\mathbf{x}_i) = [\![e_i]\!]\mu$ for all i. A variable assignment μ with $\mu(\mathbf{x}_i) \leq [\![e_i]\!]\mu$ (resp. $\mu(\mathbf{x}_i) \geq [\![e_i]\!]\mu$) is called a pre-solution (resp. post-solution) of $\mathcal{E}$. Since every right-hand side e_i induces a monotonic function $[\![e_i]\!]$, Knaster-Tarski's fixpoint Theorem implies that every system $\mathcal{E}$ of integer equations has a least solution μ^*, i.e., $\mu^* \leq \mu$ for every solution μ of $\mathcal{E}$. The least solution μ^* is the greatest lower bound of all post-solutions. We refer to computing the least solution of a system $\mathcal{E}$ as solving the system $\mathcal{E}$.

We will also define strategies for systems of integer equations. Let $M(\mathcal{E})$ denote the set of all $\vee$-expressions occurring in $\mathcal{E}$. Moreover, let $M_c(\mathcal{E}) \subseteq M(\mathcal{E})$ denote the set of $\vee$-expression $e \vee e'$ occurring in $\mathcal{E}$ where at least one of the arguments e, e' is constant, i.e. it does not contain any variable. Let $M_{nc}(\mathcal{E}) := M(\mathcal{E}) \setminus M_c(\mathcal{E})$. A $\vee$-*strategy* π for $\mathcal{E}$ is a function mapping every expression $e_1 \vee e_2$ in $M(\mathcal{E})$ to one of the subexpressions e_1, e_2. For an expression e we write $e\pi$ for the expression obtained from e by recursively replacing every $\vee$-expression with the respective subexpression selected by the $\vee$-strategy π, i.e.:

$$a\pi = a \qquad \mathbf{x}\pi = \mathbf{x} \qquad (e_1 + e_2)\pi = e_1\pi + e_2\pi$$
$$(b \cdot e)\pi = b \cdot e\pi \qquad (e_1 \vee e_2)\pi = (\pi(e_1 \vee e_2))\pi \qquad (e_1 \wedge e_2)\pi = e_1\pi \wedge e_2\pi$$

where e, e_1, e_2 are expressions, $\mathbf{x}$ is a variable, $a, b \in \overline{\mathbb{Z}}$, $b \geq 1$. Assuming that $\mathcal{E}$ is the system $\mathbf{x}_i = e_i$, $i = 1, \ldots, n$, we write $\mathcal{E}(\pi)$ for the system $\mathbf{x}_i = e_i\pi$, $i = 1, \ldots, n$. The definitions for $\wedge$-strategies are dual.

Systems of *simple* integer equations are of a particular interest. We call an expression e *simple* iff it is of the following form:

$$e ::= c \mid \mathbf{x} \mid e + a \mid e_1 \vee e_2 \mid e_1 \wedge e_2$$

where e, e_1, e_2 are simple expressions, $\mathbf{x}$ is a variable, $a \in \mathbb{Z}$, $c \in \overline{\mathbb{Z}}$. I.e., at least one argument of every $+$-expression is a constant. An integer equation $\mathbf{x} = e$ is called *simple* iff e is simple.

We define the relation $\to$ between expressions of $\mathcal{E}$ by $e \to e'$ iff e' is an immediate subexpression of e or e is a variable and e' is the right-hand side of e, i.e., $e = e'$ is an equation of $\mathcal{E}$. A sequence $p = e_1, \ldots, e_k$ of expressions occurring in $\mathcal{E}$ is called a *path* in $\mathcal{E}$ iff $e_i \to e_{i+1}$ for $i = 1, \ldots, k-1$. The path is called *simple* iff no expression occurs twice in it. The path $e_1, \ldots, e_k$ is called a *cycle* iff $e_k \to e_1$. The weight $w(p)$ of a path $p = e_1, \ldots, e_k$ is the sum $\sum_{i=1}^{k} w(e_i)$ where $w(e)$ equals a if $e \equiv e' + a$ for some expression e' and $a \in \mathbb{Z}$, and $w(e)$ equals 0 otherwise. We call a system $\mathcal{E}$ of simple integer equations *non-zero* iff $w(c) \neq 0$ for every simple cycle c in $\mathcal{E}$.

Example 1. Consider the following systems of simple integer equations:

$$\mathcal{E}_1 = \mathbf{x}_1 = \mathbf{x}_2 + 2, \mathbf{x}_2 = \mathbf{x}_1 + (-1) \quad \mathcal{E}_2 = \mathbf{x}_1 = \mathbf{x}_2 + 2 \vee \mathbf{x}_2 + 1, \mathbf{x}_2 = \mathbf{x}_1 + (-1)$$

The system $\mathcal{E}_1$ is non-zero, because the only simple cycle in $\mathcal{E}_1$ (up to cyclic permutations) is $\mathbf{x}_1, \mathbf{x}_2 + 2, \mathbf{x}_2, \mathbf{x}_1 + (-1)$ which has weight 1. The system $\mathcal{E}_2$ is not non-zero, because the simple cycle $\mathbf{x}_1, \mathbf{x}_2 + 1, \mathbf{x}_2, \mathbf{x}_1 + (-1)$ has weight 0. □

A variable assignment μ with $-\infty < \mu(\mathbf{x}) < \infty$, $\mathbf{x} \in \mathbf{X}$ is called *finite*. We have:

Lemma 1. *Every non-zero system $\mathcal{E}$ of simple equations has at most one finite solution.*

Proof. Note that, if we rewrite an expression in $\mathcal{E}$ using distributivity, then the resulting system is still non-zero. Let $\mathbf{X}_\mathcal{E}^{rhs}$ denote the set of variables occurring in right-hand sides of $\mathcal{E}$. We proceed by induction on $|\mathbf{X}_\mathcal{E}^{rhs}|$. If $|\mathbf{X}_\mathcal{E}^{rhs}| = 0$, then the statement is fulfilled, since there is exactly one solution.

Let $|\mathbf{X}_\mathcal{E}^{rhs}| > 0$ and $\mathbf{x} \in \mathbf{X}_\mathcal{E}^{rhs}$. Consider the equation $\mathbf{x} = e$. We consider the case where e contains the variable $\mathbf{x}$. Because of distributivity, we can w.l.o.g. assume that $\mathbf{x} = e$ is of the form $\mathbf{x} = ((\mathbf{x} + c) \wedge e_1) \vee e_2$. where e_1 and e_2 are such that no $\vee$ occurs within a $\wedge$-expression and no $\wedge$-expression occurs within a +-expression. We say that such an expression is in disjunctive normal form. Since $\mathcal{E}$ is non-zero, we know that $c \neq 0$. We only consider the case that $c > 0$. The other case is similar. First of all, observe that, for every finite variable assignment μ, the following holds:

$$\mu(\mathbf{x}) = [\![((\mathbf{x} + c) \wedge e_1) \vee e_2]\!]\mu \quad \text{implies} \quad \mu(\mathbf{x}) = [\![e_1 \vee e_2]\!]\mu. \tag{1}$$

Let μ_1 and μ_2 be finite solutions of $\mathcal{E}$. Let $\mathcal{E}'$ denote the system of simple equations obtained from $\mathcal{E}$ by replacing the equation $\mathbf{x} = e$ with the equation $\mathbf{x} = e_1 \vee e_2$. The system $\mathcal{E}'$ is non-zero. (1) implies that μ_1 and μ_2 are finite solutions of $\mathcal{E}'$. Since we can repeat this step, we can w.l.o.g. assume that the variable $\mathbf{x}$ does not occur within $e_1 \vee e_2$. We now replace every occurrence of $\mathbf{x}$ in right-hand sides of $\mathcal{E}'$ by $e_1 \vee e_2$ and obtain a system $\mathcal{E}''$. This system is again non-zero and μ_1 and μ_2 are finite solutions of $\mathcal{E}''$. Thus, since $|\mathbf{X}_{\mathcal{E}''}^{rhs}| = |\mathbf{X}_\mathcal{E}^{rhs}| - 1$, the induction hypotheses implies $\mu_1 = \mu_2$. □

3 From Parity Games to Systems of Integer Equations

In this section we reduce computing winning regions and winning strategies for parity games to solving systems of integer equations. Thus, the latter computational problem is as least as hard as solving parity games. It is an intriguing open problem to determine the precise complexity of parity games. What is known is that this problem is in **UP** ∩ **co–UP** [10]. A first subexponential algorithm has been presented in [11]. Whether or not, however, parity games can be solved in polynomial time, is still unknown.

Let us fix a parity game $G = (V_\vee, V_\wedge, E, r)$. Let $n := |V|$ be the number of positions, $d := \max r(V) = \max \{r(v) \mid v \in V\}$ the maximal rank and $m := n^{d+1}$. In order to compute the winning regions, we consider the system $\mathcal{E}_G$ of integer equations which we define subsequently. From the least solution μ^* of $\mathcal{E}_G|_{[-m,m]}$ we will deduce the winning regions as well as winning strategies for both players. For every position $v \in V$ we introduce a fresh variable $\mathbf{x}_v$, i.e., $\mathbf{X}_{\mathcal{E}_G} := \{\mathbf{x}_v \mid v \in V\}$. Let

$$\delta_r = -(-n)^r.$$

Observe that δ_r is less than 0 whenever r is even and greater than 0 whenever r is odd. Moreover, δ_r is chosen such that $(n-1)|\delta_{r'}| < |\delta_r|$ whenever $r' < r$. This important property ensures that, for $k \leq n$, the sum $\delta_{r_1} + \cdots + \delta_{r_k}$ is greater than 0 iff the most relevant rank within $\{r_1, \ldots, r_k\}$ is odd. We construct $\mathcal{E}_G$ as follows. For every position $v \in V_\vee$ we add the equation

$$\mathbf{x}_v = (\mathbf{x}_{v_1} \vee \cdots \vee \mathbf{x}_{v_k}) + \delta_{r(v)}$$

where $\{v\}E = \{v_1, \ldots, v_k\}$. For every position $v \in V_\wedge$ we add the equation

$$\mathbf{x}_v = (\mathbf{x}_{v_1} \wedge \cdots \wedge \mathbf{x}_{v_k}) + \delta_{r(v)}$$

where $\{v\}E = \{v_1, \ldots, v_k\}$. We illustrate this reduction by an example.

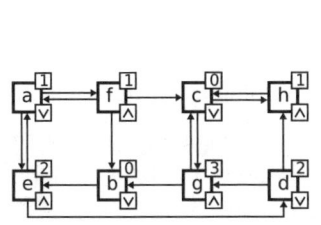
(a) The parity game G of example 2

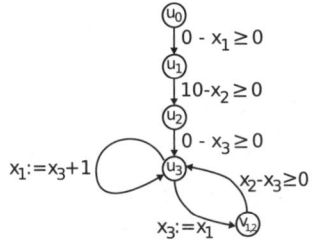
(b) Affine program P_C of example 5

Fig. 1.

Example 2. Consider the parity game $G = (V_\vee, V_\wedge, E, r)$ (from [16]) where

- $V_\vee = \{a, b, c, d\}$ and $V_\wedge = \{e, f, g, h\}$
- $E = \{(a, f), (a, e), (b, e), (c, g), (c, h), (d, g), (d, h), (e, a), (e, d), (f, a),$
  $(f, b), (f, c), (g, b), (g, c), (h, c)\}$
- $r(b) = r(c) = 0, r(a) = r(f) = r(h) = 1, r(d) = r(e) = 2, r(g) = 3$

which is illustrated in figure 1 (a). The system $\mathcal{E}_G|_{[-m,m]}$ is given as

$$\begin{array}{ll}
\mathbf{x}_a = (\mathbf{x}_e \vee \mathbf{x}_f) + 8 \wedge m \vee -m & \mathbf{x}_b = \mathbf{x}_e + (-1) \wedge m \vee -m \\
\mathbf{x}_c = (\mathbf{x}_g \vee \mathbf{x}_h) + (-1) \wedge m \vee -m & \mathbf{x}_d = (\mathbf{x}_g \vee \mathbf{x}_h) + (-64) \wedge m \vee -m \\
\mathbf{x}_e = (\mathbf{x}_a \wedge \mathbf{x}_d) + (-64) \wedge m \vee -m & \mathbf{x}_f = (\mathbf{x}_a \wedge \mathbf{x}_b \wedge \mathbf{x}_c) + 8 \wedge m \vee -m \\
\mathbf{x}_g = (\mathbf{x}_b \wedge \mathbf{x}_c) + 512 \wedge m \vee -m & \mathbf{x}_h = \mathbf{x}_c + 8 \wedge m \vee -m
\end{array}$$

where $m = 4096$. □

We summarize statements about $\mathcal{E}_G$ and $\mathcal{E}_G|_{[-m,m]}$ in the following Lemma:

Lemma 2. *1. $|\mathbf{X}_{\mathcal{E}_G}| = |\mathbf{X}_{\mathcal{E}_G|_{[-m,m]}}| = n$;*
2. $|M(\mathcal{E}_G)| = |E \cap V_\vee \times V| - |V_\vee|$ and $|M(\mathcal{E}_G|_{[-m,m]})| = |E \cap V_\vee \times V| - |V_\vee| + n$;
3. The size of occurring numbers is bounded by $(d+1) \log_2 n$;
4. The systems $\mathcal{E}_G$ and $\mathcal{E}_G|_{[-m,m]}$ of simple equations are non-zero.

Proof. We only prove the fourth statement. Since there exists a one-to-one mapping f from the set of simple cycles in $\mathcal{E}_G|_{[-m,m]}$ onto the set of simple cycles in $\mathcal{E}_G$ with $w(c) = w(f(c))$ for every simple cycle c in $\mathcal{E}_G|_{[-m,m]}$, we only have to show that $\mathcal{E}_G$ is non-zero. W.l.o.g., let

$$c = \mathbf{x}_1, e_1 + \delta_{r(v_1)}, \ldots, \mathbf{x}_2, e_2 + \delta_{r(v_2)}, \ldots, \mathbf{x}_k, e_k + \delta_{r(v_k)}$$

be a simple cycle in $\mathcal{E}_G$ where $\mathbf{x}_1, \ldots, \mathbf{x}_k$ are the only expressions in the sequence c which are variables. Thus $k \leq n$. Let $J := \{j \in \{1,\ldots,k\} \mid |\delta_{r(v_j)}| = \max_{i=1,\ldots,k} |\delta_{r(v_i)}|\}$. Let r denote the only rank in the set $r(\{v_j \mid j \in J\})$. Note that $k - |J| \leq n - 1$ and $|\delta_r| > (n-1)|\delta_{r-1}|$. We get:

$$|w(c)| = |\sum_{i=1}^k \delta_{r(v_i)}| = |\sum_{i \in J} \delta_{r(v_i)} + \sum_{i \in \{1,\ldots,k\} \setminus J} \delta_{r(v_i)}|$$
$$= ||J|\delta_r + \sum_{i \in \{1,\ldots,k\} \setminus J} \delta_{r(v_i)}| \geq |\delta_r| - \sum_{i \in \{1,\ldots,k\} \setminus J} |\delta_{r(v_i)}|$$
$$\geq |\delta_r| - (k - |J|)|\delta_{r-1}| \geq |\delta_r| - (n-1)|\delta_{r-1}| > 0$$

It follows $w(c) \neq 0$. □

Thus, by Lemma 1 and 2, $\mathcal{E}_G|_{[-m,m]}$ has exactly one solution which is finite.

Example 3. The unique solution μ^* of $\mathcal{E}_G|_{[-4096,4096]}$ in example 2 is given by
$\mu^*(\mathbf{x}_a) = -4080, \mu^*(\mathbf{x}_b) = -4096, \mu^*(\mathbf{x}_c) = 4095, \mu^*(\mathbf{x}_d) = 4032,$
$\mu^*(\mathbf{x}_e) = -4096, \mu^*(\mathbf{x}_f) = -4088, \mu^*(\mathbf{x}_g) = -3584, \mu^*(\mathbf{x}_h) = 4096.$ □

The next Lemma states that we can reassemble the unique solution of $\mathcal{E}_G|_{[-m,m]}$ by a $\vee$-strategy for $\mathcal{E}_G$. This is similar to the memoryless determinacy of parity games.

Lemma 3. *Let μ^* denote the unique finite solution of $\mathcal{E}_G|_{[-m,m]}$. There exists a $\vee$-strategy (resp. $\wedge$-strategy) π for $\mathcal{E}_G$ such that μ^* is the unique solution of $\mathcal{E}_G(\pi)|_{[-m,m]}$. Moreover, π can be computed from μ^* in time $\mathcal{O}(|\mathcal{E}_G|)$.*

Proof. We only prove the $\vee$-strategy case. Let π be the $\vee$-strategy defined by

$$\pi(e_1 \vee e_2) = \begin{cases} e_1 & \text{if } [\![e_1]\!]\mu^* \geq [\![e_2]\!]\mu^* \\ e_2 & \text{if } [\![e_1]\!]\mu^* < [\![e_2]\!]\mu^* \end{cases}$$

for every expression $e_1 \vee e_2$ occurring in $\mathcal{E}_G$. The system $\mathcal{E}_G(\pi)|_{[-m,m]}$ is non-zero and μ^* is a solution of $\mathcal{E}_G(\pi)|_{[-m,m]}$. Thus, Lemma 1 implies that μ^* is the only solution of $\mathcal{E}_G(\pi)|_{[-m,m]}$. The complexity statement follows from the fact that the $\vee$-strategy π can be computed by evaluating each right-hand side once. □

Before going further we consider the special case that no player has a choice.

Lemma 4. *Let $G = (V_\vee, V_\wedge, E, r)$ be a parity game where only one move is possible for every position, i.e., $|\{v\}E| = 1$ for every $v \in V_\vee \cup V_\wedge$. Let μ^* be the unique finite solution of $\mathcal{E}_G|_{[-m,m]}$. Then $\mu^*(\mathbf{x}_v) > 0$ iff v is a $\vee$-winning position.*

Proof. Since the winning regions partition the set of positions, we only have to show that $\mu^*(\mathbf{x}_v) > 0$ for every $\vee$-winning position v. Let v be a $\vee$-winning position. Let

$$w = v'_1 \cdots v'_{k'} \cdot (v_1 \cdots v_k)^\omega$$

denote the only game which can be played on G starting at v. We can assume that $v'_1, \ldots, v'_{k'}, v_1, \ldots, v_k$ are pair-wise distinct. Then $k + k' \leq n$ and $k \geq 1$. Since w is won by the $\vee$-player, the highest rank h which occurs in $r(v_1), \ldots, r(v_k)$ is odd. Thus $\delta_h > 0$. Let j be the smallest $j \in \{1, \ldots, k\}$ with $r(v_j) = h$. The system $\mathcal{E}_G|_{[-m,m]}$ contains the equations

$$\mathbf{x}_{v_i} = \mathbf{x}_{v_{(i+1) \bmod k}} + \delta_{r(v_i)} \wedge m \vee -m, \quad i = 1, \ldots, k.$$

Thus, since $\sum_{i=1}^{k} \delta_{r(v_i)} \geq \delta_h - (k-1)|\delta_{h-1}| > 0$, it follows that $\mu^*(\mathbf{x}_{v_j}) = m$. Since $\sum_{i=1}^{k'} \delta_{r(v'_i)} + \sum_{i=1}^{j-1} \delta_{r(v_i)} \leq (n-1)|\delta_d| = (n-1)n^d < n^{d+1} = m$, we get $\mu^*(\mathbf{x}_{v'_1}) > 0$. □

We establish a one-to-one correspondence between positional strategies for G and strategies for $\mathcal{E}_G$. For a positional $\vee$-strategy $\sigma_\vee$ (resp. $\wedge$-strategy $\sigma_\wedge$) for G, we write $\pi(\sigma_\vee)$ (resp. $\pi(\sigma_\wedge)$) for the $\vee$-strategy (resp. $\wedge$-strategy) for $\mathcal{E}_G$ which corresponds to $\sigma_\vee$ (resp. $\sigma_\wedge$). More precisely, the $\vee$-strategy $\pi(\sigma_\vee)$ is defined by

$$\pi(\sigma_\vee)(\mathbf{x}_{v_1} \vee \cdots \vee \mathbf{x}_{v_k}) = \mathbf{x}_{v_j} \quad \text{for } \{v\}E = \{v_1, \ldots, v_k\} \text{ and } \sigma_\vee(v) = v_j.$$

The $\wedge$-strategy $\pi(\sigma_\wedge)$ is defined analogously. Since the mapping π is one-to-one, the inverse π^{-1} exists which maps strategies for $\mathcal{E}_G$ to positional strategies for G. By construction, $\mathcal{E}_{G(\sigma)} = \mathcal{E}_G(\pi(\sigma))$ and thus $\mathcal{E}_{G(\sigma)}|_{[-m,m]} = \mathcal{E}_G(\pi(\sigma))|_{[-m,m]}$ for every $\vee$-strategy (resp. $\wedge$-strategy) σ for G.

Let μ^* denote the unique solution of $\mathcal{E}_G|_{[-m,m]}$. By Lemma 3 we can compute a $\vee$-strategy $\pi_\vee$ for $\mathcal{E}_G$ such that μ^* is the unique solution of $\mathcal{E}_G(\pi_\vee)|_{[-m,m]}$. The next Lemma in particular states that $\pi^{-1}(\pi_\vee)$ is a $\vee$-winning strategy for G.

Lemma 5. *Let $G = (V_\vee, V_\wedge, E, r)$ be a parity game. Let μ^* be the unique solution of $\mathcal{E}_G|_{[-m,m]}$. Then $\mu^*(\mathbf{x}_v) > 0$ (resp. $\mu^*(\mathbf{x}_v) \leq 0$) iff v is a $\vee$-winning (resp. $\wedge$-winning) position. Moreover, winning strategies for both players can be computed from μ^* in time $\mathcal{O}(|E|)$. More precisely, if $\pi_\vee$ (resp. $\pi_\wedge$) is a $\vee$-strategy (resp. $\wedge$-strategy) for $\mathcal{E}_G$ such that μ^* is the unique solution of $\mathcal{E}_G(\pi_\vee)|_{[-m,m]}$ (resp. $\mathcal{E}_G(\pi_\wedge)|_{[-m,m]}$), then $\pi^{-1}(\pi_\vee)$ (resp. $\pi^{-1}(\pi_\wedge)$) is $\vee$-winning (resp. $\wedge$-winning).*

Proof. We only show the statement for the ∨-player. The statement for the ∧-player can be shown dually. Let W denote the ∨-winning region in G. Let $\Sigma_\vee$ (resp. $\Sigma_\wedge$) denote the set of ∨-strategies (resp. ∧-strategies) for G. Given some $\sigma_\vee \in \Sigma_\vee$ and some $\sigma_\wedge \in \Sigma_\wedge$, we write $W_{\sigma_\vee}$ (resp. $W_{\sigma_\vee \sigma_\wedge}$) for the ∨-winning region in $G(\sigma_\vee)$ (resp. $G(\sigma_\vee)(\sigma_\wedge)$). Let $\Pi_\vee$ (resp. $\Pi_\wedge$) denote the set of ∨-strategies (resp. ∧-strategies) for $\mathcal{E}_G$. Given some $\pi_\vee \in \Pi_\vee$ and some $\pi_\wedge \in \Pi_\wedge$, we write $\mu_{\pi_\vee}$ (resp. $\mu_{\pi_\vee \pi_\wedge}$) for the unique solution of $\mathcal{E}_G(\pi_\vee)|_{[-m,m]}$ (resp. $\mathcal{E}_G(\pi_\vee)(\pi_\wedge)|_{[-m,m]}$). Lemma 4 implies

$$W_{\sigma_\vee \sigma_\wedge} = \{v \in V \mid \mu_{\pi(\sigma_\vee)\pi(\sigma_\wedge)}(\mathbf{x}_v) > 0\} \text{ for all } \sigma_\vee \in \Sigma_\vee \text{ and all } \sigma_\wedge \in \Sigma_\wedge. \quad (2)$$

Let us fix some $\sigma_\vee \in \Sigma_\vee$. Lemma 3 implies that there exists some $\pi_\wedge \in \Pi_\wedge$ such that $\mu_{\pi(\sigma_\vee)\pi_\wedge} = \mu_{\pi(\sigma_\vee)}$. Let $\sigma'_\wedge \in \Sigma_\wedge$. We have $\mu_{\pi(\sigma_\vee)\pi(\sigma'_\wedge)} \geq \mu_{\pi(\sigma_\vee)} = \mu_{\pi(\sigma_\vee)\pi_\wedge}$. Thus (2) implies $W_{\sigma_\vee \sigma'_\wedge} \supseteq W_{\sigma_\vee \pi^{-1}(\pi_\wedge)}$. Since $\sigma'_\wedge$ was chosen arbitrarily, we have $W_{\sigma_\vee} = W_{\sigma_\vee \pi^{-1}(\pi_\wedge)}$. Since $\sigma_\vee$ was also chosen arbitrarily, (2) implies

$$W_{\sigma_\vee} = \{v \in V \mid \mu_{\pi(\sigma_\vee)}(\mathbf{x}_v) > 0\} \text{ for all } \sigma_\vee \in \Sigma_\vee. \quad (3)$$

Lemma 3 implies that there exists some $\pi_\vee \in \Pi_\vee$ such that $\mu_{\pi_\vee} = \mu^*$. Let $\sigma'_\vee \in \Sigma_\vee$. We have $\mu_{\pi(\sigma'_\vee)} \leq \mu^* = \mu_{\pi_\vee}$. Thus (3) implies $W_{\sigma'_\vee} \subseteq W_{\pi^{-1}(\pi_\vee)}$. Since $\sigma'_\vee$ was chosen arbitrarily, we have $W = W_{\pi^{-1}(\pi_\vee)}$ which means that $\pi^{-1}(\pi_\vee)$ is a ∨-winning strategy in G. Using (3) we get $W = \{v \in V \mid \mu^*(\mathbf{x}_v) > 0\}$. The complexity statement is obvious. □

Example 4. Consider again example 2 and example 3. Positions c, d and h are ∨-winning positions, since $\mu^*(\mathbf{x}_c), \mu^*(\mathbf{x}_d), \mu^*(\mathbf{x}_h) > 0$. Conversely, a, b, e, f, g are ∧-winning positions, since $\mu^*(\mathbf{x}_a), \mu^*(\mathbf{x}_b), \mu^*(\mathbf{x}_e), \mu^*(\mathbf{x}_f), \mu^*(\mathbf{x}_g) < 0$. A ∨-strategy $\pi_\vee$ for $\mathcal{E}_G$ such that μ^* is the unique solution of $\mathcal{E}_G(\pi_\vee)|_{[-m,m]}$ is given by

$$\pi_\vee(\mathbf{x}_e \vee \mathbf{x}_f) = \mathbf{x}_f \qquad \pi_\vee(\mathbf{x}_g \vee \mathbf{x}_h) = \mathbf{x}_h.$$

Thus $\sigma := \pi^{-1}(\pi_\vee)$, given by $\sigma(a) = f, \sigma(c) = h, \sigma(d) = h$ is ∨-winning. □

Thus we get the main result for this section as a corollary of Lemma 5.

Theorem 1. *The problem of computing winning regions for parity games is* **P**-*time reducible to solving systems of integer equations.* □

4 From Systems of Integer Equations to Interval Analysis

We now reduce solving systems of integer equations to precise interval analysis for affine programs (cf. e.g. [12]). Let $\mathcal{I}$ denote the set of closed intervals in $\mathbb{Z}$, i.e.,

$$\mathcal{I} = \{\emptyset\} \cup \{[a,b] \subseteq \mathbb{Z} \mid a,b \in \overline{\mathbb{Z}} \text{ and } \infty > a \leq b > -\infty\}.$$

Let $\mathcal{B} := \{I_1 \times \cdots \times I_n \mid I_i \in \mathcal{I}, i = 1, \ldots, n\} \subseteq 2^{\mathbb{Z}^n}$. $(\mathcal{B}, \subseteq)$ is a complete lattice. Elements from $\mathcal{B}$ are called boxes. We define $\alpha : 2^{\mathbb{Z}^n} \to \mathcal{B}$ by

$$\alpha(X) = \bigcap_{B \in \mathcal{B}, B \supseteq X} B \in \mathcal{B}, \qquad X \subseteq \mathbb{Z}^n.$$

The box $\alpha(X)$ is the smallest box which is a super-set of X.

Subsequently we discuss affine programs. Let us fix a set $\mathbf{X}_P = \{\mathbf{x}_1, \ldots, \mathbf{x}_n\}$ of program variables. Then a *state* in the concrete semantics which assigns values to the variables is conveniently modeled by a vector $x = (x_1, \ldots, x_n) \in \mathbb{Z}^n$; x_i is the value assigned to variable $\mathbf{x}_i$. Note that we distinguish variables and their values by using a different font. In this paper, we only consider statements of the following forms:

(1) $\quad \mathbf{x}_j := a + \sum_{i=1}^n a_i \cdot \mathbf{x}_i \qquad$ (2) $\quad a + \sum_{i=1}^n a_i \cdot \mathbf{x}_i \geq 0$

where $a, a_1, \ldots, a_n \in \mathbb{Z}$. We use an abstract fixpoint semantics which associates a box $B = I_1 \times \cdots \times I_n \in \mathcal{B}$ to each program point. Each statement $s \in \mathsf{Stmt}$ induces a transformation $[\![s]\!] : \mathcal{B} \to \mathcal{B}$, given by

$[\![\mathbf{x}_j := a + \sum_{i=1}^n a_i \cdot \mathbf{x}_i]\!] B = \alpha(\{(x_1, \ldots, x_{j-1}, a + \sum_{i=1}^n a_i \cdot x_i, x_{j+1}, \ldots, x_n)$
$\qquad\qquad\qquad\qquad\qquad | \; (x_1, \ldots, x_n) \in B\})$

$[\![a + \sum_{i=1}^n a_i \cdot \mathbf{x}_i \geq 0]\!] B = \alpha(\{(x_1, \ldots, x_n) \in B \mid a + \sum_{i=1}^n a_i \cdot x_i \geq 0\})$

where $B \in \mathcal{B}$. We emphasize that $[\![s]\!]$ is the best abstract transformer w.r.t. the natural concrete semantics (cf. [5]). The branching of an *affine program* is non-deterministic. Formally, an *affine program* is given by a *control flow graph* $P = (N, T, \mathsf{st})$ that consists of a set N of *program points*, a set $T \subseteq N \times \mathsf{Stmt} \times N$ of *(control flow) edges* and a special *start point* $\mathsf{st} \in N$. Then, the abstract fixpoint semantics V of P is characterized as the least solution of the following system of constraints:

(1) $\quad \mathbf{V}[\mathsf{st}] \supseteq \mathbb{Z}^n \qquad$ (2) $\quad \mathbf{V}[v] \supseteq [\![s]\!](\mathbf{V}[u]) \quad$ for each $(u, s, v) \in T$

where the variables $\mathbf{V}[v]$, $v \in N$ take values in $\mathcal{B}$. We denote the components of the abstract fixpoint semantics V by $V[v]$ for $v \in N$. We emphasize that we focus on *precise* interval analysis which means that it is not sufficient to compute a small solution of the above constraint system. We in fact want to compute the least solution.

Assume that $\mathcal{E}$ denotes a system of integer equations. In place of $\mathcal{E}$ we consider a system $\mathcal{C}$ of integer constraints where each constraint is of one of the following forms

(1) $\quad \mathbf{x} \geq c \qquad$ (2) $\quad \mathbf{x} \geq a + \sum_{i=1}^k a_i \cdot \mathbf{x}_i \qquad$ (3) $\quad \mathbf{x} \geq \mathbf{x}_1 \wedge \mathbf{x}_2$

where $c \in \overline{\mathbb{Z}} \setminus \{-\infty\}, a, a_1, \ldots, a_k > 0$, $\mathbf{x}, \mathbf{x}_1, \mathbf{x}_2$ are variables. This can be done w.o.l.g. since, for every system $\mathcal{E}$ of integer equations, we can compute a system $\mathcal{C}$ of integer constraints of the above form whose least solution gives us the least solution of $\mathcal{E}$ in linear time. Furthermore, we assume w.l.o.g. that, for every variable $\mathbf{x}$, there exists exactly one constraint of the form (1). This can be done w.o.l.g., since we can identify the set of variables $\mathbf{x}$ with $\mu^*(\mathbf{x}) = -\infty$ in time $\mathcal{O}(n \cdot |\mathcal{E}|)$. We can remove these variables and obtain a system whose least solution maps every variable to a value strictly greater than $-\infty$. Additionally, we can compute a lower bound $c_\mathbf{x} \in \mathbb{Z}$ for each variable $\mathbf{x}$, i.e. $\mu^*(\mathbf{x}) \geq c_\mathbf{x}$, in time $\mathcal{O}(n \cdot |\mathcal{E}|)$ by performing n lock-step fixpoint computation steps.

We construct the affine program $P_\mathcal{C} = (N, T, \mathsf{st})$ as follows. Let $\{\mathbf{x}_1, \ldots, \mathbf{x}_n\}$ denote the set of variables used in $\mathcal{C}$. We choose

$$N := \{\mathsf{st}, u_1, \ldots, u_n\} \cup \{v_{k_1, k_2} \mid \mathbf{x}_j \geq \mathbf{x}_{k_1} \wedge \mathbf{x}_{k_2} \text{ is a constraint of } \mathcal{C}\}$$

as the set of program points and identify st with u_0. We construct the set T of control-flow edges as follows. For every constraint $\mathbf{x}_j \geq c$ of $\mathcal{C}$ we add the control-flow edge

$$(u_{j-1}, c - \mathbf{x}_j \geq 0, u_j).$$

For every constraint $\mathbf{x}_j \geq a + \sum_i a_i \cdot \mathbf{x}_{k_i}$ of $\mathcal{C}$ we add the control-flow edge

$$(u_n, \mathbf{x}_j := a + \sum_i a_i \cdot \mathbf{x}_{k_i}, u_n).$$

For every constraint $\mathbf{x}_j \geq \mathbf{x}_{k_1} \wedge \mathbf{x}_{k_2}$ of $\mathcal{C}$ we add the control-flow edges

$$(u_n, \mathbf{x}_j := \mathbf{x}_{k_1}, v_{k_1,k_2}) \quad \text{and} \quad (v_{k_1,k_2}, \mathbf{x}_{k_2} - \mathbf{x}_j \geq 0, u_n).$$

Then we can obtain the least solution of $\mathcal{C}$ from the abstract fixpoint semantics V of P:

Lemma 6. *Let μ^* denote the least solution of $\mathcal{C}$ and $(I_1, \ldots, I_n) := V[u_n]$. Then, for every $i = 1, \ldots, n$, $\mu^*(\mathbf{x}_i)$ equals the upper bound of the interval I_i.* □

Example 5. Consider the following system $\mathcal{E}$ of integer constraints:

$$\mathbf{x}_1 = 0 \vee \mathbf{x}_3 + 1 \qquad \mathbf{x}_2 = 10 \qquad \mathbf{x}_3 = \mathbf{x}_1 \wedge \mathbf{x}_2$$

By performing 3 rounds of lock-step fixpoint iteration we get that the value of the variable $\mathbf{x}_3$ is as least 0. Thus, in place of $\mathcal{E}$, we consider the following system $\mathcal{C}$ of integer constraints. $\mathcal{E}$ and $\mathcal{C}$ have the same least solution.

$$\mathbf{x}_1 \geq 0 \qquad \mathbf{x}_1 \geq \mathbf{x}_3 + 1 \qquad \mathbf{x}_2 \geq 10 \qquad \mathbf{x}_3 \geq 0 \qquad \mathbf{x}_3 \geq \mathbf{x}_1 \wedge \mathbf{x}_2$$

The least solution μ^* of $\mathcal{E}$ is given by $\mu^*(\mathbf{x}_1) = 11, \mu^*(\mathbf{x}_2) = 10, \mu^*(\mathbf{x}_3) = 10$. Figure 1 (b) shows the corresponding affine program $P_\mathcal{C}$. Let V denote the abstract fixpoint semantics of $P_\mathcal{C}$. Then $V[u_3] = [-\infty, 11] \times [-\infty, 10] \times [-\infty, 10]$. □

Combining Theorem 1 and Lemma 6 we get our lower bound result:

Theorem 2. *The problem of computing winning regions of parity games is $\mathbf{P}$-time reducible to precise interval analysis for affine programs.* □

5 Solving Integer Equations

In this section we present a simplified method for computing least solutions of systems of integer equations. As the algorithm in [8], our new algorithm essentially iterates over suitable $\vee$-strategies where, for each attained strategy, we determine the *greatest* solution of the corresponding conjunctive system. Our key contribution is to show that this idea also works, if instrumentation of the underlying lattice as in [8] is abandoned.

Assume that μ^* denotes the least solution of the system $\mathcal{E}$ of integer equations. A $\vee$-*strategy improvement operator* $P_\vee$ is a function which maps a pair (π, μ) to an *improved* $\vee$-strategy $\pi' := P_\vee(\pi, \mu)$, where π is a $\vee$-strategy for $\mathcal{E}$ and $\mu \leq \mu^*$ is a pre-solution of $\mathcal{E}$ and the following holds:

$$\pi' \neq \pi \text{ whenever } \mu < \mu^* \text{ and } \pi'(e_1 \vee e_2) \in \begin{cases} \{e_1, \pi(e_1 \vee e_2))\} & \text{if } [\![e_1]\!]\mu > [\![e_2]\!]\mu \\ \{e_2, \pi(e_1 \vee e_2))\} & \text{if } [\![e_1]\!]\mu < [\![e_2]\!]\mu \\ \{\pi(e_1 \vee e_2)\} & \text{if } [\![e_1]\!]\mu = [\![e_2]\!]\mu \end{cases}$$

If not further specified $P_\vee$ means any $\vee$-strategy improvement operator. We define the $\vee$-strategy improvement operator $P_\vee^{eager}$ by

$$P_\vee^{eager}(\pi,\mu)(e_1 \vee e_2) = \begin{cases} e_1 & \text{if } [\![e_1]\!]\mu > [\![e_2]\!]\mu \\ e_2 & \text{if } [\![e_1]\!]\mu < [\![e_2]\!]\mu \\ \pi(e_1 \vee e_2) & \text{if } [\![e_1]\!]\mu = [\![e_2]\!]\mu \end{cases}$$

where π is a $\vee$-strategy for $\mathcal{E}$ and $\mu \leq \mu^*$ is a pre-solution of $\mathcal{E}$. This is basically the $\vee$-strategy improvement operator used in [9].

Assume that $\mathcal{E}$ is a system of *basic* integer equations. We define the set $\mathcal{D}(\mathcal{E})$ of *derived constraints* as the smallest set of constraints of the form $\mathbf{x} \leq e$ such that (1) $\mathbf{x} \leq e \in \mathcal{D}(\mathcal{E})$ whenever $\mathbf{x} = e$ is an equation of $\mathcal{E}$; and (2) $\mathbf{x} \leq e'' \in \mathcal{D}(\mathcal{E})$ whenever $\mathbf{x} \leq e$, $\mathbf{x}' \leq e' \in \mathcal{D}(\mathcal{E})$ and e'' is obtained from e by replacing $\mathbf{x}'$ with e'. For a system $\mathcal{E}$ of conjunctive equations we define the set $\mathcal{D}(\mathcal{E})$ of derived constraints by $\mathcal{D}(\mathcal{E}) := \bigcup_\pi$ is a $\wedge$-strategy for $\mathcal{E}$ $\mathcal{D}(\mathcal{E}(\pi))$. Let $\mathcal{E}$ be a system of conjunctive equations. For every $\mathbf{x} \leq e \in \mathcal{D}(\mathcal{E})$ and every pre-solution μ of $\mathcal{E}$ we have $[\![\mathbf{x}]\!]\mu \leq [\![e]\!]\mu$. A pre-solution μ of $\mathcal{E}$ is called *($\mathcal{E}$-)feasible* iff (1) $e = -\infty$ whenever $\mathbf{x} = e$ is an equation of $\mathcal{E}$ with $[\![e]\!]\rho = -\infty$; and (2) $[\![\mathbf{x}]\!]\mu = [\![e]\!]\mu$ implies $[\![\mathbf{x}]\!]\mu = \infty$ for all derived constraints $\mathbf{x} \leq e \in \mathcal{D}(\mathcal{E})$ where $\mathbf{x}$ occurs in e.

Example 6 (feasibility). There exists no feasible pre-solution of the system $\mathbf{x}_1 = \mathbf{x}_1 \wedge 10$. Every variable assignment which maps $\mathbf{x}_1$ to values between 1 and 10 is a feasible pre-solution of the system $\mathbf{x}_1 = 2 \cdot \mathbf{x}_1 \wedge 10$. □

Lemma 7. *1. Let $\mathcal{E}$ be a conjunctive system of integer equations and μ be a feasible pre-solution of $\mathcal{E}$. Every pre-solution $\mu' \geq \mu$ of $\mathcal{E}$ is feasible.*
2. Let $\mathcal{E}$ be a system of integer equations, π a $\vee$-strategy for $\mathcal{E}$, μ a feasible pre-solution of $\mathcal{E}(\pi)$ and $\pi' := P_\vee(\pi,\mu)$. Then μ is a feasible pre-solution of $\mathcal{E}(\pi')$. □

Let $\mathcal{E}$ be the system $\mathbf{x}_1 = e_1, \ldots, \mathbf{x}_n = e_n$ and μ^* the least solution of $\mathcal{E}$. Our strategy improvement algorithm is given as algorithm 1. It starts with a $\vee$-strategy $\overline{\pi}$ for $\mathcal{E}$ and *feasible* pre-solution $\overline{\mu} \leq \mu^*$ of $\mathcal{E}(\pi)$.

Algorithm 1. Computing Least Solutions of Systems of Integer Equations

---
$\pi \leftarrow \overline{\pi}$; $\mu \leftarrow \overline{\mu}$;
while (μ is not a solution of $\mathcal{E}$) {
 $\quad \pi \leftarrow P_\vee^{eager}(\pi,\mu)$; $\quad \mu \leftarrow$ least solution of $\mathcal{E}(\pi)$ that is greater than or equal to μ;
}
return μ;

By induction one can show that algorithm 1 returns the least solution μ^* of $\mathcal{E}$ whenever it terminates (cf. [8]). In order to obtain an upper bound to the number of iterations, we first show that every system of conjunctive equations has at most one feasible solution.

Lemma 8. *Assume that the greatest solution μ^* of the system $\mathcal{E}$ of conjunctive equations is feasible. Then μ^* is the only feasible solution of $\mathcal{E}$.*

Proof. Assume that $\mathcal{E}$ denotes the system $\mathbf{x}_i = e_i$, $i = 1, \ldots, n$. We first prove the statement for a system $\mathcal{E}$ of *basic* equations. Let $\overline{\mathbf{X}}(\mathcal{E})$ denote the set of variables occurring in right-hand sides of $\mathcal{E}$. Let μ be a feasible solution of $\mathcal{E}$. We show by induction on $|\overline{\mathbf{X}}(\mathcal{E})|$ that $\mu = \mu^*$. This is obviously fulfilled, if $|\overline{\mathbf{X}}(\mathcal{E})| = 0$. Thus, consider an equation $\mathbf{x}_i = e_i$ of $\mathcal{E}$ where $\mathbf{x}_i$ occurs in a right-hand side e_j of $\mathcal{E}$.

Assume that e_i does not contain $\mathbf{x}_i$. We obtain a system $\mathcal{E}'$ from $\mathcal{E}$ by replacing all occurrences of $\mathbf{x}_i$ in right-hand sides with e_i. Since $\mathcal{D}(\mathcal{E}') \subseteq \mathcal{D}(\mathcal{E})$, μ, μ^* are feasible solutions of $\mathcal{E}'$. Since $|\overline{\mathbf{X}}(\mathcal{E}')| = |\overline{\mathbf{X}}(\mathcal{E})| - 1$, the induction hypothesis implies $\mu = \mu^*$.

Assume now that e_i contains $\mathbf{x}_i$. Since $\mathbf{x}_i \leq e_i \in \mathcal{D}(\mathcal{E})$ and μ, μ^* are feasible solutions we get $[\![\mathbf{x}_i]\!]\mu = [\![\mathbf{x}_i]\!]\mu^* = \infty$. Thus μ, μ^* are solutions of the system $\mathcal{E}'$ obtained from $\mathcal{E}$ by replacing the equation $\mathbf{x}_i = e_i$ with $\mathbf{x}_i = \infty$ and then replacing all occurrences of the variable $\mathbf{x}_i$ in right-hand sides with ∞. Since $\mathcal{D}(\mathcal{E}') \subseteq \mathcal{D}(\mathcal{E})$, μ, μ^* are feasible solutions of $\mathcal{E}'$. Since $|\overline{\mathbf{X}}(\mathcal{E}')| = |\overline{\mathbf{X}}(\mathcal{E})| - 1$, the induction hypothesis implies $\mu = \mu^*$. Thus the statement holds for systems of basic equations.

Now assume that $\mathcal{E}$ is a system of *conjunctive* equations. In order to derive a contradiction, assume that $\mu < \mu^*$ is a feasible solution of $\mathcal{E}$. Then μ is a feasible solution of $\mathcal{E}(\pi)$ for some $\wedge$-strategy π. Thus μ is the greatest solution of $\mathcal{E}(\pi)$. The greatest solution of $\mathcal{E}(\pi)$ is greater than or equal to μ^*. Thus, $\mu \geq \mu^*$ — contradiction. □

Consider algorithm 1. Let π_j be the $\vee$-strategy π after the execution of the first statement in the j-th iteration. Let μ_j be the variable assignment μ at this point and μ'_j the variable assignment μ after the j-th iteration. The sequence (μ'_j) is strictly increasing until the least solution is reached. Lemma 7 implies that, for every j, μ_j and μ'_j is a feasible presolution of $\mathcal{E}(\pi_j)$. Thus, Lemma 8 implies that μ'_j is the greatest solution of $\mathcal{E}(\pi_j)$. This has two important consequences. The first consequence is that, since $\mathcal{E}(\pi_j)$ is a system of *conjunctive* equations, the greatest solution μ'_j can be computed in time $\mathcal{O}(|\mathbf{X}_\mathcal{E}| \cdot |\mathcal{E}|)$ using Bellman-Ford's algorithm (cf. [7]). The second consequence is that every strategy π_j is considered at most once. Otherwise, there exist $j' > j$ such that $\pi_{j'} = \pi_j$ implying that $\mu'_{j'} = \mu'_j$ which is a contradiction to the fact that (μ'_j) is strictly increasing. Thus, the number of iterations is bounded by the number of $\vee$-strategies.

In order to give a precise characterization of the run-time, let $\Pi(m)$ denote the maximal number of updates of strategies necessary for a system with m $\vee$-subexpressions. Thereby we assume that $\overline{\pi}$ and $\overline{\mu}$ are given. $\Pi(m)$ is trivially bounded by 2^m.

Until now we have assumed that we have a $\vee$-strategy $\overline{\pi}$ and a feasible pre-solution $\overline{\mu} \leq \mu^*$ of $\mathcal{E}(\overline{\pi})$ at hand. In order to lift this restriction, we consider $\mathcal{E}^{\vee -\infty}$ in place of $\mathcal{E}$ which we define to be the system $\mathbf{x}_1 = e_1 \vee -\infty, \ldots, \mathbf{x}_n = e_n \vee -\infty$. Then we can choose $\overline{\pi}$ to be the $\vee$-strategy which maps every top-level $\vee$-expression $e_i \vee -\infty$ of $\mathcal{E}^{\vee -\infty}$ to $-\infty$. Accordingly, we choose $\overline{\mu}$ to be the variable assignment which maps every variable to $-\infty$. Then $\overline{\mu} \leq \mu^*$ is a feasible solution of $\mathcal{E}^{\vee -\infty}(\overline{\pi})$.

We now show that the number of updates of strategies necessary for computing the least solution of $\mathcal{E}^{\vee -\infty}$ is $n + \Pi(m)$ although $|M(\mathcal{E}^{\vee -\infty})| = m + n$. We have:

Lemma 9. $\mu'_n(\mathbf{x}_i) = -\infty$ iff $\mu^*(\mathbf{x}_i) = -\infty$ for $i = 1, \ldots, n$. □

Let $i \in \{1, \ldots, n\}$. Lemma 9 implies $\mu^*(\mathbf{x}_i) \geq \mu'_j(\mathbf{x}_i) = -\infty$ for all $j \geq n$ iff $\mu'_n(\mathbf{x}_i) = -\infty$ Since μ'_j is a feasible solution of $\mathcal{E}(\pi_j)$, we get $\pi_j(e_i \vee -\infty) = \pi_n(e_i \vee -\infty)$ for all $j \geq n$. Thus, after n iterations we can consider the following iterations as iterations for the system obtained by replacing every right-hand side $e_i \vee -\infty$ with $\pi_n(e_i \vee -\infty)$. This system has m $\vee$-expressions. Thus, the number of iterations is bounded by $n + \Pi(m)$. Summarizing, we have:

Theorem 3. *The least solution of a system $\mathcal{E}$ of integer equations can be computed in time $\mathcal{O}(|\mathbf{X}_\mathcal{E}| \cdot |\mathcal{E}| \cdot \Pi(|M(\mathcal{E})|))$.* □

In contrast to the algorithm presented in [8], our new algorithm no longer relies on an instrumentation of the underlying lattice. For systems of *simple* integer equations we can improve on the number of iteration, if we use a different improvement operator.

Assume now that $\mathcal{E}$ is a system of *simple* integer equations. We now also consider partial $\vee$-strategies π, i.e., the domain $dom(\pi)$ of a partial $\vee$-strategy π is a subset of $M(\mathcal{E})$. Then we set

$$(e \vee e')\pi = \begin{cases} (\pi(e \vee e'))\pi & \text{if } e \vee e' \in dom(\pi) \\ e\pi \vee e'\pi & \text{if } e \vee e' \notin dom(\pi). \end{cases}$$

Let $M \subseteq M(\mathcal{E})$. We define the $\vee$-strategy improvement operator $P_\vee^M$ by

$$P_\vee^M(\pi, \mu) = \begin{cases} P_\vee^{eager}(\pi, \mu)|_M \cup \pi|_{M(\mathcal{E}) \setminus M} & \text{if } P_\vee^{eager}(\pi, \mu)|_M \neq \pi|_M \\ P_\vee^{eager}(\pi, \mu) & \text{if } P_\vee^{eager}(\pi, \mu)|_M = \pi|_M. \end{cases}$$

Intuitively, $P_\vee^M$ first tries to improve at $\vee$-expressions from M. Only if such an improvement is not possible, $\vee$-expressions from $M(\mathcal{E}) \setminus M$ are considered.

Assume that $\mathcal{E}$ is a system of *conjunctive simple* equations. All derived constraints in $\mathcal{D}(\mathcal{E})$ can be rewritten to the form $\mathbf{x} \leq \mathbf{y} + a$ or $\mathbf{x} \leq c$ where $\mathbf{x}, \mathbf{y}$ are variables, $a \in \mathbb{Z}$ and $c \in \overline{\mathbb{Z}}$. We call $\mathcal{E}$ *feasible* iff $a > 0$ for all derived constraints $\mathbf{x} \leq \mathbf{x} + a \in \mathcal{D}(\mathcal{E})$ and $\mathbf{x} \leq -\infty \in \mathcal{D}(\mathcal{E})$ implies that $\mathbf{x} = -\infty$ is an equation of $\mathcal{E}$. The greatest solution μ' of a feasible system $\mathcal{E}$ of simple conjunctive equations is feasible.

Assume now that $\mathcal{E}$ denotes a system of *simple* integer equations with least solution μ^*. A $\vee$-strategy π for $\mathcal{E}$ is called *feasible* iff $\mathcal{E}(\pi)$ is feasible. Similar to Lemma 7 it can be shown that algorithm 1 considers feasible strategies, only. For systems of simple equations we have the following property:

Lemma 10. *Let $\mathcal{E}$ be the system $\mathbf{x}_1 = e_1, \ldots, \mathbf{x}_n = e_n$ of simple integer equations and μ a solution of $\mathcal{E}$. Assume that π is a feasible $\vee$-strategy with $e_i\pi = -\infty$ whenever $\mu(\mathbf{x}_i) = -\infty$ for $i = 1, \ldots, n$. Let μ_π be the greatest solution of $\mathcal{E}(\pi)$. Then $\mu_\pi \leq \mu$.*

Proof. Note that μ_π is a feasible solution of $\mathcal{E}(\pi)$ and μ is a post-solution of $\mathcal{E}(\pi)$. Let $\mu^{(0)} := \mu$ and, for $j \in \mathbb{N}$, let $\mu^{(j+1)}$ be defined by $\mu^{(j+1)}(\mathbf{x}_i) = [\![e_i\pi]\!]\mu^{(j)}$. Then $\mu' := \bigwedge_{j \in \mathbb{N}_0} \mu^{(j)} \leq \mu$ is a solution of $\mathcal{E}(\pi)$ and, since $a > 0$ for all derived constraints $\mathbf{x} \leq \mathbf{x} + a \in \mathcal{D}(\mathcal{E}(\pi))$, $\mu'(\mathbf{x}_i) = -\infty$ implies $\mu(\mathbf{x}_i) = -\infty$ which implies $e_i\pi = -\infty$ for $i = 1, \ldots, n$. Thus, μ' is a feasible solution of $\mathcal{E}(\pi)$. Since, by Lemma 8, $\mu_\pi = \mu'$, we get $\mu' \leq \mu$. □

Consider the sequences (μ_j), (μ'_j) and (π_j) which we obtain from algorithm 1 using the $\vee$-strategy improvement operator $P_\vee^M$. We show that there do not exist indexes $j < k$ with $j \geq n$ such that $\pi_k|_{M(\mathcal{E}) \setminus M} = \pi_j|_{M(\mathcal{E}) \setminus M} \neq \pi_{j+1}|_{M(\mathcal{E}) \setminus M}$ (∗). In order to derive a contradiction, assume the opposite. By the definition of $P_\vee^M$, μ_j' is a solution of $\mathcal{E}' := \mathcal{E}(\pi_j|_{M(\mathcal{E})\setminus M})$. Furthermore, μ_k' is the greatest solution of the feasible system $\mathcal{E}(\pi_k) = \mathcal{E}(\pi_k|_{M(\mathcal{E})\setminus M})(\pi_k|_M) = \mathcal{E}(\pi_j|_{M(\mathcal{E})\setminus M})(\pi_k|_M) = \mathcal{E}'(\pi_k|_M)$. Since $k > j \geq n$, we have $e_i\pi_k = -\infty$ whenever $\mu_j'(\mathbf{x}_i) = -\infty$. Thus we can apply Lemma 10 which implies that $\mu_k' \leq \mu_j'$. This contradicts the fact that (μ_j') is strictly ascending.

We use the $\vee$-improvement operator $P_\vee^{M_c(\mathcal{E})}$, i.e., $M = M_c(\mathcal{E})$. The $\vee$-improvement operator $P_\vee^{M_c(\mathcal{E})}$ first tries to improve at expressions $e \vee e' \in M_c(\mathcal{E})$ and only if this is not possible it tries to improve at expressions $e \vee e' \in M_{nc}(\mathcal{E})$. For $M \subseteq M(\mathcal{E})$, we call j an *update index* on M iff $\pi_{j+1}|_M \neq \pi_j|_M$. Assume that $e \vee e' \in M_c(\mathcal{E})$ where w.l.o.g. e' is a constant expression. Then, since μ_j is ascending, if there is a k such that $\pi_k(e \vee e') = e$, then $\pi_j(e \vee e') = e$ for all $j \geq k$. Thus, there are at most $|M_c(\mathcal{E})|$ update indexes on $M_c(\mathcal{E})$ (∗∗).

Let j_i denote the sequence of update indexes on $M_{nc}(\mathcal{E})$. By (∗), these are at most $2^{|M_{nc}(\mathcal{E})|}$. Between two update on $M_{nc}(\mathcal{E})$ there must be updates on $M_c(\mathcal{E})$. By (∗∗) the overall number of updates on $M_c(\mathcal{E})$ is bounded by $|M_c(\mathcal{E})|$, i.e., $\sum_i j_{i+1} - j_i - 1 \leq |M_c(\mathcal{E})|$. Thus, the number of strategies is bounded by $2^{|M_{nc}(\mathcal{E})|} + |M_c(\mathcal{E})|$. We denote the maximal number of updates of strategies on $M_{nc}(\mathcal{E})$ necessary for solving a simple system $\mathcal{E}$ by $\Pi_s(|M_{nc}(\mathcal{E})|)$. We obtain:

Theorem 4. *The least solution of a system $\mathcal{E}$ of simple integer equations can be computed in time $\mathcal{O}(|\mathbf{X}_\mathcal{E}| \cdot |\mathcal{E}| \cdot (\Pi_s(|M_{nc}(\mathcal{E})|) + |M_c(\mathcal{E})|))$.* □

The practical run-time of our algorithm is quite comparable to the discrete strategy improvement algorithm by Vöge and Jurdziński [17]. The number $\Pi_s(|M_{nc}(\mathcal{E})|)$ corresponds to the number of strategy improvements for the parity game. For each improvement-step, we need $\mathcal{O}(n \cdot |\mathcal{E}_G|_{[-m,m]})$ operations where arithmetic operations are on numbers of size $\mathcal{O}(d \cdot \log n)$. The improvement-step of the discrete strategy improvement algorithm by Vöge and Jurdziński [17] uses also $\mathcal{O}(n \cdot |\mathcal{E}_G|_{[-m,m]})$ operations — but arithmetic operations are just on numbers of size $\mathcal{O}(\log n)$.

6 Conclusion

By encoding parity games into integer equations, we have provided a lower complexity bound for precise interval analysis of affine programs. Additionally, we provided a simplified version of the algorithm in [8] for solving integer equations. As in the algorithm of [9] for rational equations, the new version for integers avoids the instrumentation of the underlying lattice. The restriction to integers, on the other hand also allowed to improve on the complicated treatment of conjunctive systems in [9] for rationals.

The methods which we have presented here, can be applied to simplify the algorithm for interval equations from [8] where also multiplication of arbitrary interval expressions is allowed. By modifying the strategy improvement operator, we also have obtained an algorithm for *simple* integer equations where for the complexity estimation only non-constant maxima must be taken into account. By our encoding of parity games into integer systems, we thus obtain a simple but efficient strategy improvement algorithm for computing winning regions and winning strategies of parity games.

References

1. Bordeaux, L., Hamadi, Y., Vardi, M.Y.: An Analysis of Slow Convergence in Interval Propagation. In: Bessière, C. (ed.) CP 2007. LNCS, vol. 4741, pp. 790–797. Springer, Heidelberg (2007)
2. Costan, A., Gaubert, S., Goubault, E., Martel, M., Putot, S.: A Policy Iteration Algorithm for Computing Fixed Points in Static Analysis of Programs. In: Etessami, K., Rajamani, S.K. (eds.) CAV 2005. LNCS, vol. 3576, pp. 462–475. Springer, Heidelberg (2005)
3. Cousot, P., Cousot, R.: Static Determination of Dynamic Properties of Programs. In: Second Int. Symp. on Programming, pp. 106–130. Dunod, Paris, France (1976)
4. Cousot, P., Cousot, R.: Abstract Interpretation: A Unified Lattice Model for Static Analysis of Programs by Construction or Approximation of Fixpoints. In: Proceedings of 4th ACM Symposium on Principles of Programming Languages (POPL), pp. 238–252. ACM Press, New York (1977)
5. Cousot, P., Cousot, R.: Systematic Design of Program Analysis Frameworks. In: 6th ACM Symp. on Principles of Programming Languages (POPL), pp. 238–352 (1979)
6. Emerson, E.A., Jutla, C.S.: Tree automata, mu-calculus and determinacy (extended abstract). In: FOCS, pp. 368–377. IEEE, Los Alamitos (1991)
7. Gawlitza, T., Reineke, J., Seidl, H., Wilhelm, R.: Polynomial Exact Interval Analysis Revisited. Technical report, TU München (2006)
8. Gawlitza, T., Seidl, H.: Precise Fixpoint Computation Through Strategy Iteration. In: De Nicola, R. (ed.) ESOP 2007. LNCS, vol. 4421, pp. 300–315. Springer, Heidelberg (2007)
9. Gawlitza, T., Seidl, H.: Precise Relational Invariants Through Strategy Iteration. In: Duparc, J., Henzinger, T.A. (eds.) CSL 2007. LNCS, vol. 4646, pp. 23–40. Springer, Heidelberg (2007)
10. Jurdziński, M.: Deciding the winner in parity games is in UP ∩ co-UP. Inf. Process. Lett. 68(3), 119–124 (1998)
11. Jurdziński, M., Paterson, M., Zwick, U.: A Deterministic Subexponential Algorithm for Solving Parity Games. In: 17th ACM-SIAM Symp. on Discrete Algorithms (SODA), pp. 117–123 (2006)
12. Karr, M.: Affine Relationships Among Variables of a Program. Acta Informatica 6, 133–151 (1976)
13. Leroux, J., Sutre, G.: Accelerated Data-Flow Analysis. In: Riis Nielson, H., Filé, G. (eds.) SAS 2007. LNCS, vol. 4634, pp. 184–199. Springer, Heidelberg (2007)
14. Puri, A.: Theory of Hybrid and Discrete Systems. PhD thesis, University of California, Berkeley (1995)
15. Su, Z., Wagner, D.: A class of polynomially solvable range constraints for interval analysis without widenings and narrowings. In: Jensen, K., Podelski, A. (eds.) TACAS 2004. LNCS, vol. 2988, pp. 280–295. Springer, Heidelberg (2004)
16. Vöge, J.: Strategiesynthese für Paritätsspiele auf endlichen Graphen. PhD thesis, RWTH Aachen (2000)
17. Vöge, J., Jurdziński, M.: A Discrete Strategy Improvement Algorithm for Solving Parity Games. In: Emerson, E.A., Sistla, A.P. (eds.) CAV 2000. LNCS, vol. 1855, pp. 202–215. Springer, Heidelberg (2000)

Introducing Objects through Refinement

Tim McComb[1] and Graeme Smith[2]

[1] ARC Centre of Excellence in Bioinformatics
Institute for Molecular Bioscience, The University of Queensland, Australia
[2] School of Information Technology and Electrical Engineering
The University of Queensland, Australia

Abstract. We present a strategy for using the existing theory of class refinement in Object-Z to introduce an arbitrary number of object instances into a specification. Since class refinement applies only to a single class, the key part of the strategy is the use of references to objects of the class being refined. Once object instances have been introduced through local class refinements in this way, they can be turned into foreign class instantiations through the application of straight-forward equivalence preserving transformations. We introduce a set of logical classifiers to allow for the precise determination of which parts of the specification logic must be moved into the foreign class.

1 Introduction

Abstract functional specifications are intended to capture high-level requirements. They are not intended to describe any peculiarities of a software system's implementation. Object-oriented software *designs*, on the other hand, necessitate classes that may not exist in an abstract specification (for user-interface specific functionality, internals of data structures, library interfaces, etc.). While design concerns could be included in an initial specification, they may obscure essential system functionality and complicate reasoning. The primary motivation for our work is the need for practical techniques for adding design elements after the initial functional specification has been formulated. In this paper, we provide a mechanism for justifying that a proposed concrete architecture (specified in Object-Z [16]) is a valid implementation of a specification (also in Object-Z) according to the existing refinement theory for Object-Z presented by Derrick and Boiten [3].

The existing refinement theory applies to single classes only. It does not explicitly address the problem of introducing new object instances. In earlier work [9], a specification refactoring rule (adapted from Goldsack and Lano's annealing rule for VDM^{++} [7,8]) was proposed to partially overcome this limitation. This rule is limited, however. It allows the extraction of only one instance of a new class, and consequently does not completely address the challenges of managing object instantiation. In this paper, we present a strategy for using regular class refinement to introduce an arbitrary number of instances. Like the refactoring rule, the strategy works by partitioning the state.

The process involves three distinct stages of data refinement. The first stage is a preparatory stage where the part of the state to be accessed through instantiation is identified and moved into the range of an indexing function. This is followed by another data refinement to split the operations in the class where necessary, so that they distinctly operate over the indexing function or over the rest of the state. The way in which they operate over the indexing function is important, and the identification of this forms part of the process. The final refinement replaces the range of the indexing function with references to the class being refined. These references constitute the new object instances. They can subsequently be made to refer to a new syntactically equivalent class introduced to the specification without changing the specification's meaning. This new class and the original can then be refined individually to reflect their intended roles.

We introduce the above three stages in Sections 2, 3, and 4 respectively. This is followed by concluding remarks and a discussion of related work in Section 5.

2 Indexing Function

In order to refine a class to one which refers to an arbitrary number of object instances, we begin by introducing a non-visible[1] indexing function. The domain of the indexing function is arbitrary, and can be denoted by a given type. The range of the indexing function includes the cross-product of all of the data types that are to form the state of the delegate (instantiated) class.

In [9] we introduced the annealing rule which partitioned the state into those variables that were to stay local to the class and those that were to form the state of the introduced class. The introduction of the indexing function is a general application of this idea. Rather than individual variables being migrated to an instantiated reference, however, with an indexing function we can deal with a plurality of 'instances'. It is a loosely-defined partial function to begin with, but the intention is to eventually have a one-to-one correspondence between the indices and actual instantiation references: this is the final step of the strategy.

The concept is illustrated below where a class A on the left-hand side is refined to a class with an indexing function $index$ on the right-hand side.

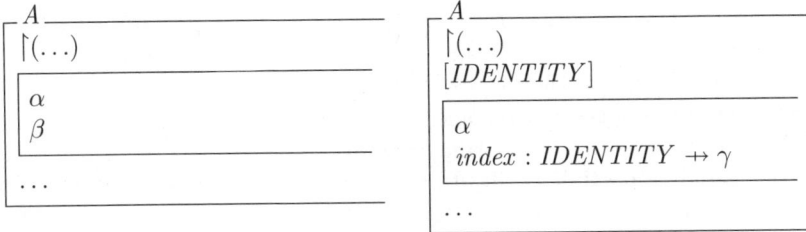

The state of A initially has two sets of variables: α and β. Through the refinement, α remains unchanged, but β is replaced by the new function. The

---

[1] Visibility in Object-Z refers to whether or not a feature is accessible through the class's interface. Visible variables are indicated by their inclusion in a list of the form $\uparrow(\ldots)$ at the top of the class definition [16].

domain of the function is a new given type $IDENTITY$. The range γ captures the state of the objects which we wish to introduce (as a cross-product of data types). The relationship between β and γ is not pre-defined, but must be chosen to ensure the right-hand side refines the left-hand side.

Consider for example the partial specification of an airport shown below. The class *Airport* models queues of a given type $AIRCRAFT$, representing aircraft waiting for clearance to depart from one of the airport's two runways (*runway1* and *runway2*). A variable *holding* keeps a count of the total number of aircraft waiting to depart the airport.

$[AIRCRAFT]$

―― *Airport* ――――――――――――――――――――――
$\lceil (INIT, RequestDeparture)$

    ―― ――――――――――――――――――――――
    $runway1 : \text{seq } AIRCRAFT$
    $runway2 : \text{seq } AIRCRAFT$
    $holding : \mathbb{N}$

    ―― *INIT* ――――――――――――――――――
    $holding = 0$
    $runway1 = runway2 = \langle \rangle$

    ―― *RequestDeparture* ―――――――――――
    $\Delta(runway1, runway2, holding)$
    $a? : AIRCRAFT$

    $((runway1' = runway1 \frown \langle a? \rangle \wedge runway2' = runway2)$
    $\vee$
    $(runway2' = runway2 \frown \langle a? \rangle \wedge runway1' = runway1))$
    $holding' = holding + 1$

The initialisation predicate stipulates that there are initially no aircraft waiting to depart. The operation *RequestDeparture* adds an aircraft $a?$ to a non-deterministically chosen runway and increments *holding*. The *delta-list* of the operation, i.e., the list of the form $\Delta(\ldots)$, indicates that each of the three state variables may be changed by the operation. When a variable does not appear in the delta-list of an operation, its value is unable to be changed by that operation. Since this is only a partial specification, we have not shown any operations that specify departures.

In the following data refinement, the class *Airport* has been structured such that a partial function *index* holds the queues of aircraft. The domain of this function is a new given type $RUNWAY$ which is internal to the class. The fact that there are only two runways is captured by the invariant $\#(\text{dom } index) = 2$. The initial state schema and operation are refined appropriately to accommodate the new representation of the state.

[AIRCRAFT]

┌─ Airport ───
│ ↾(INIT, RequestDeparture)
│ [RUNWAY]
│ ┌──
│ │ holding : $\mathbb{N}$
│ │ index : $RUNWAY \nrightarrow \text{seq}\, AIRCRAFT$
│ ├──
│ │ $\#(\text{dom}\, index) = 2$
│ └──
│
│ ┌─ INIT ───────────────────────────────────────
│ │ holding = 0
│ │ ran index = $\{\langle\rangle\}$
│ └──
│
│ ┌─ RequestDeparture ───────────────────────────
│ │ $\Delta(index, holding)$
│ │ $a? : AIRCRAFT$
│ ├──
│ │ $holding' = holding + 1$
│ │ $(\exists_1 runway : RUNWAY \mid runway \in \text{dom}\, index \bullet$
│ │ $\quad index' = index \oplus \{runway \mapsto (index(runway) \frown \langle a?\rangle)\})$
│ └──

3 Classification and Splitting of Operations

The next stage of our approach involves identifying the operations to remain in the class, and those that will eventually form part of the class of the new object instances. When the indexing function is introduced, the state is effectively separated between the variables that are going to remain local to the class, and those that are going to be accessed via instantiation. Based on this, we identify three general categories of operations:

- the operations that affect the range of *index* (exclusively, no other part of the state is changed);
- the operations that do not affect the range of *index*, but may affect other parts of the state; and
- the operations that do not fit into the former categories.

The operations in the last category must be split into multiple operations, each of which fits into the former two categories. These two categories correspond to *delegate* and *local* operations respectively.

To identify each category we utilise *operation classifiers*. These classifiers are predicates that are implied by the operation if the operation fits the category. We first introduce the local operation classifier, and then the delegate classifier. Following that, we show how operations that imply neither classifier are split.

3.1 Local Operations

If the following property holds for an operation's predicate P, the operation is considered local.

$$P \Rightarrow index \cup index' \in (\_ \nrightarrow \_)$$

The notation $f \in (\_ \nrightarrow \_)$ is used to specify the constraint that f is a partial function. This classifier stipulates that the union of the pre- and post-states of the *index* variable must form a partial function. Since we know that *index* and *index'* are partial functions independently, this classifier is true unless the predicate P specifies the alteration of the range value of an existing domain element in *index* to form *index'*.

In our example, the operation *RequestDeparture* does not satisfy this classifier. For any chosen *runway*, $index(runway) \neq index'(runway)$, thus $index \cup index' \notin (\_ \nrightarrow \_)$.

3.2 Delegate Operations

If an operation predicate P satisfies the following classifier, it is considered a delegate operation.

$$P \Rightarrow \mathbf{delta} = \{index\} \land \operatorname{dom} index = \operatorname{dom} index' \land index \neq index'$$

Here **delta** is a meta-level variable referring to the the set of variables in the delta-list of an operation.

The classifier identifies those operations that exclusively affect *index*, and only modify a mapping in *index* without altering the domain. Our example operation *RequestDeparture* does not satisfy this classifier as $\mathbf{delta} = \{index, holding\}$.

3.3 Unclassified Operations

Unclassified operations, like *RequestDeparture*, need to be split into multiple separate operations where each can be classified independently. This may be achieved in Object-Z by the use of its operation composition operators [16]. There are, in fact, only two general cases of operations that are unclassified. Below we discuss these cases and *how* they must be split.

To derive the two cases, we first realise that an operation can never be classified as both a delegate and a local operation, as the conjunction of those classifiers is contradictory (there does not exist an operation predicate P that could possibly satisfy both). This is because the partial functions *index* and *index'* must have common domains but differing range members to satisfy the delegate classifier, so there must exist at least one member in the common domain that maps to different range members in the respective functions. Thus the union of *index* and *index'* cannot itself be a partial function, which is a requirement of the local classifier.

An unclassified operation P must therefore adhere to neither classifier:

$$P \Rightarrow \neg\,(\mathbf{delta} = \{index\} \land \mathrm{dom}\,index = \mathrm{dom}\,index' \land index \neq index') \land$$
$$\neg\,(index \cup index' \in (\_ \twoheadrightarrow \_))$$
$$\equiv \qquad\qquad\qquad\qquad\qquad\qquad\qquad\qquad\qquad\qquad\text{(de Morgan's law)}$$
$$P \Rightarrow (\mathbf{delta} \neq \{index\} \lor \mathrm{dom}\,index \neq \mathrm{dom}\,index' \lor index = index') \land$$
$$index \cup index' \notin (\_ \twoheadrightarrow \_)$$

If we rewrite this single classifier as a disjunctive series of implications, we derive three potentially overlapping classifiers:

1. $P \Rightarrow \mathbf{delta} \neq \{index\} \land index \cup index' \notin (\_ \twoheadrightarrow \_)$
2. $P \Rightarrow \mathrm{dom}\,index \neq \mathrm{dom}\,index' \land index \cup index' \notin (\_ \twoheadrightarrow \_)$
3. $P \Rightarrow index = index' \land index \cup index' \notin (\_ \twoheadrightarrow \_)$

Refer to the third classifier in this list. Given $index = index'$, then it follows that $index \cup index' = index$. Since $index$ must be in its type, and therefore $index \in (\_ \twoheadrightarrow \_)$, it is a contradiction that $index \cup index' \notin (\_ \twoheadrightarrow \_)$. Consequently, as classifier (3) cannot be satisfied by any operation it is removed.

Both remaining classifiers require the operation to be split. We shall discuss Classifier (1) and Classifier (2) individually, and then discuss the case when both classifiers are satisfied. We refer to Classifiers (1) and (2) as the *delta-list partitioning* and *domain partitioning* classifiers respectively.

Delta-list Partitioning Classifier. The classifier for delta-list partitioning is:

$$P \Rightarrow \mathbf{delta} \neq \{index\} \land index \cup index' \notin (\_ \twoheadrightarrow \_).$$

In this case P is an operation which needs to be a delegate, but it cannot be because other variables are referenced in the delta-list besides $index$. The solution to this is to split the operation. This is generally achieved by promoting logical operators to operation composition operators and introducing communicating variables where necessary (refer to [9]). We will now present an argument that an operation which satisfies this classifier may be split in the general case.

Given that $index \cup index' \notin (\_ \twoheadrightarrow \_)$, it follows that $index \neq index'$, so $index$ must be a member of the delta-list. Since $\mathbf{delta} \neq \{index\}$:

$$P \Rightarrow \mathbf{delta} \supset \{index\} \land index \cup index' \notin (\_ \twoheadrightarrow \_).$$

We define L to be $\mathbf{delta}\setminus\{index\}$ and because of the proper superset relation, we know $L \neq \varnothing$. L represents the local variables that the operation changes excluding the $index$ variable. Part of the operation needs to be delegated (that which changes the range of the $index$ variable), and part must remain local (that which refers to the post-state of any variable in L). Clearly these concerns do not overlap as they apply to different variables, so such operations can be partitioned by the variables they change into one part that satisfies the local classifier, and one part that satisfies the delegated classifier.

The example operation *RequestDeparture* satisfies this classifier, because $\{index, holding\} \supset \{index\}$ and, as established earlier, $index \cup index' \notin (\_ \twoheadrightarrow \_)$. In this case, L is $\{holding\}$, so we create a local operation *IncrementHolding* which applies to *holding*.

$$\begin{array}{|l}\hline \textit{IncrementHolding} \\ \Delta(holding) \\ \hline holding' = holding + 1 \\ \hline \end{array}$$

By promoting conjunction, *RequestDeparture* is split between *IncrementHolding* and the remaining predicate (which we have called *AssignRunway*).

$$\begin{array}{|l}\hline \textit{AssignRunway} \\ \Delta(index) \\ a? : AIRCRAFT \\ \hline \exists_1\, runway : RUNWAY \mid runway \in \mathrm{dom}\, index \bullet \\ \quad index' = index \oplus \{runway \mapsto (index(runway) \frown \langle a? \rangle)\} \\ \hline \end{array}$$

$RequestDeparture \;\widehat{=}\; IncrementHolding \wedge AssignRunway$

The *AssignRunway* operation can be further split to clearly delineate the choice of runway from the joining of the queue (denoted below by *SelectRunway* and *WaitOnRunway* respectively). Naturally, operations may be split in a variety of ways. Our overall aim is to carefully distinguish between those parts of the predicate that apply to the range of *index* and those that do not. In the case of *AssignRunway*, we have illustrated the promotion of logical conjunction to parallel composition ($\parallel$) in Object-Z [16]. This operator unifies the variables *runway!* and *runway?* such that communication occurs across the schema boundary, and then hides these variables so that *AssignRunway* is equivalent to the original version.

$$\begin{array}{|l}\hline \textit{SelectRunway} \\ runway! : RUNWAY \\ \hline \exists_1\, runway : RUNWAY \mid runway \in \mathrm{dom}\, index \bullet runway! = runway \\ \hline \end{array}$$

$$\begin{array}{|l}\hline \textit{WaitOnRunway} \\ \Delta(index) \\ a? : AIRCRAFT \\ runway? : RUNWAY \\ \hline runway? \in \mathrm{dom}\, index \Rightarrow \\ \quad index' = index \oplus \{runway? \mapsto (index(runway?) \frown \langle a? \rangle)\} \\ \hline \end{array}$$

$AssignRunway \cong SelectRunway \parallel WaitOnRunway$

Note that we have introduced the antecedent $runway? \in \text{dom } index$ to the predicate of *WaitOnRunway*. Although this is assured in its context by *SelectRunway*, this predicate would otherwise form part of the precondition (this is implicit in the function application) and thus restrict the further refinement of this operation which is necessary in Section 3.4.

We can now test these three operations against the classifiers, showing that *IncrementHolding* and *SelectRunway* satisfy the local classifier (*index* is unchanged by both operations), and *WaitOnRunway* satisfies the delegate classifier (because only the range of *index* is changed by this operation).

Domain Partitioning Classifier. The classifier for domain partitioning is:

$P \Rightarrow \text{dom } index \neq \text{dom } index' \land index \cup index' \notin (\_ \twoheadrightarrow \_).$

In this case part of the operation needs to be delegated (that which changes a range member such that $index \cup index' \notin (\_ \twoheadrightarrow \_)$), and part must remain local (that which adds or removes mappings such that $\text{dom } index \neq \text{dom } index'$). In a similar fashion to the delta-list partitioning classifier, we present an argument that an operation which satisfies this classifier may be split in the general case.

For the domains to differ, members are either added, removed or both. We refer to the subset of the domain that identifies these added/removed members as δ. It is defined as $\text{dom } index \triangledown \text{dom } index'$ (where $\triangledown$ is symmetric difference: $S \triangledown T = (S \cup T) \setminus (S \cap T)$).

Since $index \cup index' \notin (\_ \twoheadrightarrow \_)$, there must be members in the domain of both *index* and *index'* with different range elements. Let these domain members be represented by ρ. Since they exist in both domains, the following property holds over ρ: $\rho \subset \text{dom } index \cap \text{dom } index'$.

It follows that δ and ρ must be disjoint. This indicates that operations that adhere to this classifier may be split with respect to the domain members they act upon in *index*. The operation dealing with the domain members in δ will satisfy the local classifier. That dealing with the domain members in ρ will satisfy the delegate classifier. No particular domain member will appear in both operations.

Simultaneous Delta-list and Domain Partitioning. Where both classifiers are satisfied by a predicate, the operation can be split as per delta-list partitioning, and then by domain partitioning. That is, the local variables in the delta-list (excluding *index*) may be moved into a separate operation, and then the original operation that includes *index* needs to be split again such that the activity over the domain of *index* is separated into that which is local and that which forms a delegate operation.

3.4 Standard Form of Delegate Operations

Operations that are classified as delegates need to be written to conform to a certain template (via a refinement step). This enables such operations to be changed by the final data refinement stage to use operation composition operators. This template is illustrated below.

$$Op \mathrel{\widehat{=}} \bigl[\, \Delta(index) \mid \forall\, id : \mathrm{dom}\, index \mid G_1(id) \bullet P_1(index(id), index'(id)) \,\bigr]$$
$$\star$$
$$\ldots$$
$$\star$$
$$\bigl[\, \Delta(index) \mid \forall\, id : \mathrm{dom}\, index \mid G_n(id) \bullet P_n(index(id), index'(id)) \,\bigr]$$

We take advantage of the fact that delegate operations exclusively operate over the range of $index$ — this is required to imply the classifier. The operation is rewritten such that predicates $P_1, \ldots, P_n$ are defined according to which part of the range they apply to. In each term, a guard G_i narrows the applicability of a predicate P_i to a subset of domain elements. The asterisk ($\star$) is a placeholder representing any of the Object-Z operation composition operators.

This template can be applied to any operation that satisfies the classifier because $index'$ is the only variable that may change, and only its range can be modified. Since id covers the entire domain of $index$ (and thus $index'$, as the domain must be unchanged to imply the classifier) and each predicate has access to the full state, any constraint over the range of $index'$ can be specified.

Continuing with the airport example, the delegate operation $WaitOnRunway$ could be expressed as such:

$WaitOnRunway \mathrel{\widehat{=}}$
$\quad \bigl[\, \Delta(index)\; a? : AIRCRAFT;\; runway? : RUNWAY \mid$
$\qquad \forall\, id : \mathrm{dom}\, index \mid id = runway? \bullet index'(id) = index(id) \frown \langle a? \rangle \,\bigr]$
$\wedge$
$\quad \bigl[\, \Delta(index)\; a? : AIRCRAFT;\; runway? : RUNWAY \mid$
$\qquad \forall\, id : \mathrm{dom}\, index \mid id \neq runway? \bullet index'(id) = index(id) \,\bigr]$

4 Introducing Object References

Since Object-Z supports recursive class definitions [16], object references can be introduced during the refinement of a single class such that these reference the class being refined.

Our approach uses this to replace the range of the $index$ function with object instances. The data type of the range of $index$ is embedded back into the state as a variable $state$. The concept is illustrated below where a class A on the left-hand side is refined to a class referencing objects of itself on the right-hand side.

```
┌─ A ─────────────────────────┐    ┌─ A ─────────────────────────────┐
│ ↑(...)                      │    │ ↑(...)                          │
│ [IDENTITY]                  │    │ [IDENTITY]                      │
├─────────────────────────────┤    ├─────────────────────────────────┤
│ α                           │    │ α                               │
│ index : IDENTITY ⇸ γ        │    │ index : IDENTITY ⤔ A_©          │
├─────────────────────────────┤    │ state : γ                       │
│ ...                         │    ├─────────────────────────────────┤
└─────────────────────────────┘    │ ...                             │
                                   └─────────────────────────────────┘
```

Letting subscript A identify variables of the abstract class and subscript C identify variables of the concrete, i.e., refined, class, the retrieve relation for this refinement is

$\alpha_A = \alpha_C \wedge$
$\text{dom } index_A = \text{dom } index_C \wedge$
$\forall\, id : \text{dom } index_A \bullet index_A(id) = index_C(id).state_C$

First, note that we have replaced the partial function with a partial injection ($\rightarrowtail$) for the *index* relation. This guarantees that there is no aliasing of objects within the *index* function, i.e., that no object of A is associated with more than one *IDENTITY*. Second, we utilise the *object containment* operator denoted by the subscript © (refer to Smith [16]). The containment of A in this way disallows any object-level recursion, such that an object of class A cannot refer to itself via *index*. In fact, the semantics of the containment operator are more general: it also prevents aliasing of objects contained in the type $A_©$ from all other parts of the system. The combination of the injective partial function and the containment operator ensures that it is safe, from the perspective of object aliasing, to introduce the class type in place of the type γ.

Operations. The operations affected by this refinement are those classified as delegates. These need to be rewritten such that constraints previously specified in terms of $index(id)$ (for some id) are now applied to $index(id).state$. A simple rewriting of the predicates of these operations is not possible since expressions referring to the post-state of a referenced object, e.g., $index(id).state'$, are not legal in Object-Z. Instead, we replace each predicate affecting the post-state of a referenced object by a new operation which acts on the variable *state*. Operations conforming to the template of Section 3.4 are refined as follows.

$Op \,\widehat{=}\, (\forall\, id : \text{dom } index \mid G_1(id) \bullet index(id).Delegate_1)$
$\quad\star$
$\quad\quad ...$
$\quad\star$
$\quad\quad (\forall\, id : \text{dom } index \mid G_n(id) \bullet index(id).Delegate_n)$
$Delegate_1 \,\widehat{=}\, [\,\Delta(state) \mid P_1(state, state')\,]$
$\quad ...$
$Delegate_n \,\widehat{=}\, [\,\Delta(state) \mid P_n(state, state')\,]$

That is, each predicate P_i is embedded within a new operation named $Delegate_i$, and these operations are invoked depending upon the satisfaction of the respective guards. Note that the arguments $index(id)$ and $index'(id)$ to each predicate have been replaced by $state$ and $state'$ respectively.

The proof of this refinement follows by showing that this definition is equivalent to that of Section 3.4 under the retrieve relation above. Starting with the definition from Section 3.4 and using the rules and notation for Object-Z semantics defined in [16]:

$$Op \mathrel{\widehat{=}} \big[\, \Delta(index_A) \mid \forall\, id : \operatorname{dom} index_A \mid G_1(id) \bullet P_1(index_A(id), index'_A(id)) \,\big]$$
$$\star$$
$$\ldots$$
$$\star$$
$$\big[\, \Delta(index_A) \mid \forall\, id : \operatorname{dom} index_A \mid G_n(id) \bullet P_n(index_A(id), index'_A(id)) \,\big]$$

$\equiv$ (applying the retrieve relation and definition of reference semantics to remove delta-list)

$$Op \mathrel{\widehat{=}} \big[\, \forall\, id : \operatorname{dom} index_C \mid G_1(id) \bullet$$
$$P_1(index_C(id).state_C, index_C(id).state'_C) \,\big]$$
$$\star$$
$$\ldots$$
$$\star$$
$$\big[\, \forall\, id : \operatorname{dom} index_C \mid G_n(id) \bullet$$
$$P_n(index_C(id).state_C, index_C(id).state'_C) \,\big]$$

$\equiv$ (definition of dot notation)

$$Op \mathrel{\widehat{=}} \big[\, \forall\, id : \operatorname{dom} index_C \mid G_1(id) \bullet index_C(id).P_1(state_C, state'_C) \,\big]$$
$$\star$$
$$\ldots$$
$$\star$$
$$\big[\, \forall\, id : \operatorname{dom} index_C \mid G_n(id) \bullet index_C(id).P_n(state_C, state'_C) \,\big]$$

$\equiv$ (definition of operation promotion and universal schema quantification ($\forall\!\!\!\forall$))

$$Op \mathrel{\widehat{=}} (\forall\!\!\!\forall\, id : \operatorname{dom} index_C \mid G_1(id) \bullet index_C(id).Delegate_1)$$
$$\star$$
$$\ldots$$
$$\star$$
$$(\forall\!\!\!\forall\, id : \operatorname{dom} index_C \mid G_n(id) \bullet index_C(id).Delegate_n)$$

$$Delegate_1 \mathrel{\widehat{=}} \big[\, \Delta(state) \mid P_1(state_C, state'_C) \,\big]$$
$$\ldots$$
$$Delegate_n \mathrel{\widehat{=}} \big[\, \Delta(state_C) \mid P_n(state_C, state'_C) \,\big] \qquad \Box$$

During this refinement step, it is necessary that the interface to the class through the visibility list has been widened to include the $Delegate_i$ operations. This ensures that the new operations are accessible through the instantiation reference. We take the view that the interface of a class can be widened under refinement [9]. Interface widening is allowable because, prior to the refinement, the context of a class cannot observe a feature that is not exposed by the interface. Since this is the case, and the context is not altered by the refinement, the context cannot observe that the feature is exposed after the refinement.

Returning to our example, the operation *WaitOnRunway* is transformed by this process such that the delegate operations *JoinQueue* and *DoNothing* are introduced.

$$
\begin{array}{l}
WaitOnRunway \ \widehat{=} \\
\quad [\,runway? : RUNWAY\,] \bullet \\
\qquad (\forall\, id : \mathrm{dom}\, index \mid id = runway? \bullet index(id).JoinQueue) \\
\wedge \\
\quad [\,runway? : RUNWAY\,] \bullet \\
\qquad (\forall\, id : \mathrm{dom}\, index \mid id \neq runway? \bullet index(id).DoNothing) \\
JoinQueue \ \widehat{=} \ [\,\Delta(state)\ a? : AIRPORT \mid state' = state \frown \langle a?\rangle\,] \\
DoNothing \ \widehat{=} \ [\,\Delta(state)\ a? : AIRPORT \mid state' = state\,]
\end{array}
$$

However, objects that do not undergo an operation do not change their state in Object-Z [16], so *WaitOnRunway* is more simply expressed as

$$
\begin{array}{l}
WaitOnRunway \ \widehat{=} \\
\quad [\,runway? : RUNWAY\,] \bullet \\
\qquad (\forall\, id : \mathrm{dom}\, index \mid id = runway? \bullet index(id).JoinQueue)
\end{array}
$$

with *DoNothing* removed as it is implied by the language semantics.

Initialisation. The initial state schema is also affected by this refinement. We require that all introduced object instances are initialised. This is achieved by

- adding a predicate $\forall\, id : \mathrm{dom}\, index \bullet index(id).INIT$ to the initialisation predicate[2], and
- rewriting constraints on the values of type γ in the range of *index* in terms of *state*.

This will result in *state* being initialised in the same way that the values in the range of *index* were initialised before the refinement.

After this refinement stage, the airport class will be as follows.

---

[2] The notation *a.INIT* in Object-Z is a predicate that is true precisely when the object *a*'s state satisfies its initialisation predicate [16].

─ Airport ──────────────────────────────────
⌈(INIT, RequestDeparture, JoinQueue)
[RUNWAY]
┌──
│ holding : $\mathbb{N}$
│ index : $RUNWAY \rightarrowtail Airport_{©}$
│ state : seq $AIRCRAFT$
│ ──
│ dom $index = 2$
└──
  ─ INIT ────────────────────────────────────
  │ holding = 0
  │ ($\forall id$: dom $index$ • $index(id).INIT$)
  │ state = $\langle \rangle$
  └──

$RequestDeparture \mathrel{\widehat{=}} IncrementHolding \land AssignRunway$
$IncrementHolding \mathrel{\widehat{=}} [\,\Delta(holding) \mid holding' = holding + 1\,]$
$AssignRunway \mathrel{\widehat{=}} SelectRunway \parallel WaitOnRunway$
  ─ SelectRunway ────────────────────────────
  │ runway! : RUNWAY
  │ ──
  │ $\exists_1 runway : RUNWAY \mid runway \in$ dom $index$ • $runway! = runway$
  └──
$WaitOnRunway \mathrel{\widehat{=}}$
    $[\,runway? : RUNWAY\,]$ •
        ($\forall id$: dom $index \mid id = runway?$ • $index(id).JoinQueue$)
$JoinQueue \mathrel{\widehat{=}} [\,\Delta(state)\; a? : AIRCRAFT \mid state' = state \frown \langle a? \rangle\,]$

4.1 Migrating the References to a Foreign Class

Given the refined class A above, we wish to finally turn the object references to class A into references to objects of a new class. This is accomplished by three equivalence preserving transformations. The first involves introducing a new class B which is syntactically (and hence semantically) equivalent to A above. References from class A to the type $A_{©}$ are replaced by references to the type $B_{©}$. That is, the definition of A above can be replaced by the following.

─ A ─────────────────────── ─ B ───────────────────────
⌈(...)   ⌈(...)
[IDENTITY]   [IDENTITY]
┌──────────────────────── ┌────────────────────────
│ α │ α
│ index : $IDENTITY \rightarrowtail B_{©}$ │ index : $IDENTITY \rightarrowtail A_{©}$
│ state : γ │ state : γ
│ ────────────────────── │ ──────────────────────
│ ...   │ ...

The second transformation involves the visibility list of the class B. Since B is a new class only referenced from A, and A does not refer to any operation other than its $Delegate_i$ operations, all other operations may be removed from its visibility list.

The third transformation involves the visibility list of the class A. Since the operations $Delegate_i$ were introduced by our process, they will not be referenced by any class other than B. As these references are made inaccessible by the previous transformation, the operations will not be referenced at all, and can be removed from the visibility list.

The latter two transformations allow us to perform further data refinements to modify the classes for their intended roles. For example, the airport specification could be refined to the following.

$[AIRCRAFT]$

$\begin{array}{|l}\hline Airport \\ \hline \upharpoonright(INIT, RequestDeparture) \\ [RUNWAY] \\ \begin{array}{|l}\hline holding : \mathbb{N} \\ index : RUNWAY \rightarrowtail Runway_{\copyright} \\ \hline \text{dom } index = 2 \\ \hline \end{array} \\ \begin{array}{|l}\hline INIT \\ \hline holding = 0 \\ (\forall id : \text{dom } index \bullet index(id).INIT) \\ \hline \end{array} \\ RequestDeparture \mathrel{\widehat{=}} IncrementHolding \land AssignRunway \\ IncrementHolding \mathrel{\widehat{=}} [\,\Delta(holding) \mid holding' = holding + 1\,] \\ AssignRunway \mathrel{\widehat{=}} SelectRunway \parallel WaitOnRunway \\ \begin{array}{|l}\hline SelectRunway \\ \hline runway! : RUNWAY \\ \hline \exists_1 runway : RUNWAY \mid runway \in \text{dom } index \bullet runway! = runway \\ \hline \end{array} \\ WaitOnRunway \mathrel{\widehat{=}} \\ \quad [\,runway? : RUNWAY\,] \bullet \\ \qquad (\forall id : \text{dom } index \mid id = runway? \bullet index(id).JoinQueue) \\ \hline \end{array}$

$\begin{array}{|l}\hline Runway \\ \hline \upharpoonright(INIT, JoinQueue) \\ \begin{array}{|l|l|}\hline state : \text{seq } AIRCRAFT & \begin{array}{l} INIT \\ state = \langle\,\rangle \end{array} \\ \hline \end{array} \\ JoinQueue \mathrel{\widehat{=}} [\,\Delta(state)\; a? : AIRCRAFT \mid state' = state \frown \langle a?\rangle\,] \\ \hline \end{array}$

5 Conclusion and Related Work

The *post hoc* extraction of new classes and objects as part of an object-oriented development process in general has been previously addressed in the literature. The Extract Class refactoring rule [6,11] is widely known, but like the annealing rule for VDM^{++} [7,8] (mentioned earlier) it is limited to the extraction of only one object instance. Some other examples exist in the literature that present a formal treatment of class/object extraction but are still restricted to one class and object. These range in application from high-level modelling languages like UML-RT [13] to programming languages (with a formal semantics) such as ROOL [1]. Ruhroth and Wehrheim [15] discuss class extraction in the context of CSP-OZ [4], which is an integration of Object-Z and CSP [14]. However, this work does not address the creation of new object instances (the extracted class is abstract).

There are also examples in the literature of extracting more than one class and instance from an existing specification. As part of a top-down design process, where structure is added after a functional specification is formulated, Cruz *et al.* [2] present a general method in the context of the VDM [5] specification language. Here, structure is inferred as well as manipulated algebraically. As part of a re-engineering process, Periyasamy and Mathew [12] provide a set of heuristics for translating from Z specifications to Object-Z specifications. Unlike the approach in this paper, their approach is not formulated in terms of data refinement.

The use of self-instantiation under data refinement has been presented before by Smith [17]. This work introduced a technique for translating between an older semantics for Object-Z where objects were treated as values, and the current semantics which is reference-based. However, this process does not provide a mechanism for the creation of previously unspecified classes and object instances.

In recent work [10], we have shown that class refinement can be performed compositionally in Object-Z — that is, a class may undergo a data refinement without respect to its context. Given this result, the work presented in this paper can be applied to existing Object-Z specifications without creating system-wide proof obligations.

We suspect that the approach presented in this paper is potentially applicable to other specification frameworks with an object-oriented style (and, particularly, a reference-based object semantics). The investigation of how to adapt this methodology to such frameworks presents an area of possible future work.

To extend the practicality of the method further, other possible future work could explicitly address the case where one wishes to incorporate an existing class into the specification. This would then allow for the targetting of existing library components as part of the overall design process. One means of achieving this using the presented methodology would be to create instances to a new class of which the existing class could be shown to be a refinement. The existing class may then be substituted in place of the introduced class.

Acknowledgements

We would like to thank the anonymous referees for their comments and suggestions, and acknowledge the support of Australian Research Council (ARC) Discovery Grant DP0558408.

References

1. Cornélio, M., Cavalcanti, A., Sampaio, A.: Refactoring by Transformation. Electronic Notes in Theoretical Computer Science 70(3) (2002)
2. Cruz, A.M., Barbosa, L.S., Oliveira, J.N.: From algebras to objects: Generation and composition. J. UCS 11(10), 1580–1612 (2005)
3. Derrick, J., Boiten, E.: Refinement in Z and Object-Z: Foundations and Advanced Applications. FACIT Series. Springer, Heidelberg (2001)
4. Fischer, C.: CSP-OZ – a combination of CSP and Object-Z. In: Bowman, H., Derrick, J. (eds.) FMOODS 1997, pp. 423–438. Chapman and Hall, Boca Raton (1997)
5. Fitzgerald, J., Larsen, P.G.: Modelling Systems: Practical Tools and Techniques for Software Development. Cambridge University Press, Cambridge (1998)
6. Fowler, M.: Refactoring: Improving the Design of Existing Code. Addison–Wesley, Reading (1999)
7. Lano, K.: Formal Object-Oriented Development. Springer, Heidelberg (1995)
8. Lano, K., Goldsack, S.: Refinement of Distributed Object Systems. In: Najm, E., Stefani, J.-B. (eds.) FMOODS 1996, pp. 99–114. Chapman and Hall, Boca Raton (1996)
9. McComb, T.: Refactoring Object-Z Specifications. In: Wermelinger, M., Margaria-Steffen, T. (eds.) FASE 2004. LNCS, vol. 2984, pp. 69–83. Springer, Heidelberg (2004)
10. McComb, T., Smith, G.: Compositional class refinement in Object-Z. In: Misra, J., Nipkow, T., Sekerinski, E. (eds.) FM 2006. LNCS, vol. 4085, pp. 205–220. Springer, Heidelberg (2006)
11. Opdyke, W.F.: Refactoring Object-Oriented Frameworks. PhD thesis, Computer Science Department, Urbana-Champaign, IL, USA (May 1992)
12. Periyasamy, K., Mathew, C.: Mapping a functional specification to an object-oriented specification in software re-engineering. In: ACM Conference on Computer Science, pp. 24–33 (1996)
13. Ramos, R., Sampaio, A., Mota, A.: Transformation laws for UML-RT. In: Gorrieri, R., Wehrheim, H. (eds.) FMOODS 2006. LNCS, vol. 4037, pp. 123–137. Springer, Heidelberg (2006)
14. Roscoe, A.W.: The Theory and Practice of Concurrency. Prentice-Hall, Englewood Cliffs (1998)
15. Ruhroth, T., Wehrheim, H.: Refactoring Object-Oriented Specifications with Data and Processes. In: Bonsangue, M.M., Johnsen, E.B. (eds.) FMOODS 2007. LNCS, vol. 4468, pp. 236–251. Springer, Heidelberg (2007)
16. Smith, G.: The Object-Z Specification Language. Kluwer Academic Publishers, Dordrecht (2000)
17. Smith, G.: Introducing Reference Semantics via Refinement. In: George, C.W., Miao, H. (eds.) ICFEM 2002. LNCS, vol. 2495, pp. 588–599. Springer, Heidelberg (2002)

Masking Faults While Providing Bounded-Time Phased Recovery*

Borzoo Bonakdarpour and Sandeep S. Kulkarni

Department of Computer Science and Engineering
Michigan State University
East Lansing, MI 48824, USA
{borzoo,sandeep}@cse.msu.edu

Abstract. We focus on synthesis techniques for transforming existing fault-intolerant real-time programs to fault-tolerant programs that provide *phased recovery*. A fault-tolerant program is one that satisfies its *safety* and *liveness* specifications as well as *timing constraints* in the presence of faults. We argue that in many commonly considered programs (especially in mission-critical systems), when faults occur, simple recovery to the program's normal behavior is necessary, but not sufficient. For such programs, it is necessary that recovery is accomplished in a sequence of phases, each ensuring that the program satisfies certain properties. In this paper, we show that, in general, synthesizing fault-tolerant real-time programs that provide bounded-time phased recovery is NP-complete. We also characterize a sufficient condition for cases where synthesizing fault-tolerant real-time programs that provide bounded-time phased recovery can be accomplished in polynomial-time in the size of the input program's region graph.

Keywords: Fault-tolerance, Real-time, Bounded-time recovery, Phased recovery, Synthesis, Transformation, Formal methods.

1 Motivation

In this paper, we focus on the problem of automated synthesis for real-time systems that provide bounded-time phased recovery in the presence of faults. To illustrate this problem, first, we provide a motivating example to informally describe the idea of bounded-time phased recovery and the concepts of synthesis and fault-tolerance. We also use this example as a running demonstration throughout the paper.

Consider a one-lane turn-based bridge where cars can travel in only one direction at any time. The bridge is controlled by two traffic signals, say sig_0 and sig_1, at the two ends of the bridge. The signals work as follows. Each signal changes phase from green to yellow and then to red, based on a set of timing constraints. Moreover, if one signal is red, it will turn green some time after the other signal

---

* This work was partially sponsored by NSF CAREER CCR-0092724 and ONR Grant N00014-01-1-0744.

turns red. Thus, at any time, the values of sig_0 and sig_1 show in which direction cars are traveling. The *specification* of this system can be easily characterized by a set $SPEC_{bt}$ of bad transitions that reach states where both signals are not red at the same time. In order to address the correctness of the system, we identify a system *invariant*. Intuitively, the system invariant is a set S of states from where the system behaves correctly. For example, in case of the traffic signals system, one system invariant is the set of states from where the system always reaches states where at least one signal is red and they change phases in time. Obviously, as long the system's state is in S, nothing catastrophic will happen. However, this is not the case when a system is subject to a set of faults.

Let us consider a scenario where the state of the systems is perturbed by occurrence of a fault that causes the system to reach a state, say s, in $\neg S$. Although reaching s may not necessarily violate the system specification, subsequent signal operations can potentially result in execution of a transition in $SPEC_{bt}$. For example, when sig_0 is green and sig_1 is red, if the timer that is responsible for changing sig_1 from red to green is reset due to a circuit problem, sig_1 may turn green within some time while sig_0 is also green. Such a system is called *fault-intolerant*, as it violates its specification in the presence of faults.

In order to transform this system into a *fault-tolerant* one, it is desirable to synthesize a version of the original system, in which even in the presence of faults, the system (1) never executes a transition $SPEC_{bt}$, and (2) always meets the following *bounded-time recovery specification* denoted by $SPEC_{br}$: When the system state is in $\neg S$, the system must reach a state in S within a bounded amount of time. Although such a recovery mechanism is necessary in a fault-tolerant real-time system, it may not be sufficient. In particular, one may require that the system must initially reach a special set of states, say Q, within some time θ, and subsequently recover to S within δ time units. We call the set Q an *intermediate recovery predicate*. The intuition for such *phased recovery* comes from the requirement that the occurrence of faults must be noted (e.g., for scheduling hardware repairs or replacement) *before* normal system operation resumes. Thus, in our example, Q could be the set of states where all signals are red. Such a constraint ensures that the system first goes to a state in which a set of preconditions for final recovery (e.g., via a system reboot or rollback) is fulfilled.

In this paper, we concentrate on the problem of synthesizing real-time systems that provide bounded-time phased recovery in the presence of faults. Intuitively, the problem is as follows. After the occurrence of faults, the system must recover to a state in the set Q within θ and from there, recover to the invariant S within δ time units. The main results in this paper are as follows:

- We formally define the notion of bounded-time phased recovery in the context of fault-tolerant real-time systems.
- We show that, in general (i.e., when $Q \not\subseteq S$ and $S \not\subseteq Q$), the problem of synthesizing fault-tolerant real-time programs that provide phased recovery is NP-complete. An example of such a case is the traffic signals system in which Q includes states where all signals are flashing red.

- We characterize a sufficient condition for cases where the synthesis problem can be solved efficiently. In particular, we show that if $S \subseteq Q$, and, execution of the synthesized system needs to be *closed* in Q (i.e., starting from a state in Q, the state of the system never leaves Q) then there exists a polynomial-time sound and complete synthesis algorithm in the size of time-abstract bisimulation of the input intolerant program. An example of such a case is the traffic signals system in which Q is the set of states where either both signals remain red indefinitely or S holds.

Organization of the paper. In Section 2, we formally define real-time programs and the type specifications that we consider in this paper. In Section 3, we present our fault model and introduce the notions of bounded-time phased recovery and fault-tolerance. We formally state the problem of synthesis of fault-tolerant real-time programs that provide bounded-time phased recovery in Section 4. Then, in Section 5, we present our results on the complexity of the synthesis problem and the sufficient condition for existence of a polynomial-time sound and complete synthesis algorithm. In Section 6, we present the related work. Finally, in Section 7, we make concluding remarks and discuss future work.

2 Real-Time Programs and Specifications

In our framework, real-time programs are specified in terms of their state space and their transitions [AH97, AD94]. The definition of specification is adapted from Alpern and Schneider [AS85] and Henzinger [Hen92].

2.1 Real-Time Program

Let $V = \{v_1, v_2 \cdots v_n\}$, $n \geq 1$, be a finite set of *discrete variables* and $X = \{x_1, x_2 \cdots x_m\}$, $m \geq 0$, be a finite set of *clock variables*. Each discrete variable v_i, $1 \leq i \leq n$, is associated with a finite *domain* D_i of values. Each clock variable x_j, $1 \leq j \leq m$, ranges over nonnegative real numbers (denoted $\mathbb{R}_{\geq 0}$). A *location* is a function that maps discrete variables to a value from their respective domain. A *clock constraint* over the set X of clock variables is a Boolean combination of formulae of the form $x \preceq c$ or $x - y \preceq c$, where $x, y \in X$, $c \in \mathbb{Z}_{\geq 0}$, and $\preceq$ is either $<$ or $\leq$. We denote the set of all clock constraints over X by $\Phi(X)$. A *clock valuation* is a function $\nu : X \to \mathbb{R}_{\geq 0}$ that assigns a real value to each clock variable.

For $\tau \in \mathbb{R}_{\geq 0}$, we write $\nu + \tau$ to denote $\nu(x) + \tau$ for every clock variable x in X. Also, for $\lambda \subseteq X$, $\nu[\lambda := 0]$ denotes the clock valuation that assigns 0 to each $x \in \lambda$ and agrees with ν over the rest of the clock variables in X. A *state* (denoted σ) is a pair (s, ν), where s is a location and ν is a clock valuation for X. Let u be a (discrete or clock) variable and σ be a state. We denote the value of u in state σ by $u(\sigma)$. A *transition* is an ordered pair (σ_0, σ_1), where σ_0 and σ_1 are two states. Transitions are classified into two types:

- *Immediate transitions:* $(s_0, \nu) \to (s_1, \nu[\lambda := 0])$, where s_0 and s_1 are two locations, ν is a clock valuation, and λ is a set of clock variables.

- *Delay transitions:* $(s, \nu) \to (s, \nu + \delta)$, where s is a location, ν is a clock valuation, and $\delta \in \mathbb{R}_{\geq 0}$ is a *time duration*. We denote a delay transition of duration δ at state σ by (σ, δ).

Thus, if ψ is a set of transitions, we let ψ^s and ψ^d denote the set of immediate and delay transitions in ψ, respectively.

Definition 1 (real-time program). A *real-time program* $\mathcal{P}$ is a tuple $\langle S_\mathcal{P}, \psi_\mathcal{P} \rangle$, where $S_\mathcal{P}$ is the *state space* (i.e., the set of all possible states), and $\psi_\mathcal{P}$ is a set of transitions. ∎

Definition 2 (state predicate). A *state predicate* S is any subset of $S_\mathcal{P}$ such that in the corresponding Boolean expression, clock constraints are in $\Phi(X)$, i.e., clock variables are only compared with nonnegative integers. ∎

By *closure* of a state predicate S in a set $\psi_\mathcal{P}$ of transitions, we mean that (1) if an immediate transition originates in S then it must terminate in S, and (2) if a delay transition originates in S then it must remain in S continuously.

Definition 3 (closure). A state predicate S is *closed* in program $\mathcal{P} = \langle S_\mathcal{P}, \psi_\mathcal{P} \rangle$ (or briefly $\psi_\mathcal{P}$) iff
$$(\forall (\sigma_0, \sigma_1) \in \psi_\mathcal{P}^s : ((\sigma_0 \in S) \Rightarrow (\sigma_1 \in S))) \land$$
$$(\forall (\sigma, \delta) \in \psi_\mathcal{P}^d : ((\sigma \in S) \Rightarrow \forall \epsilon \mid ((\epsilon \in \mathbb{R}_{\geq 0}) \land (\epsilon \leq \delta)) : \sigma + \epsilon \in S)). \blacksquare$$

Definition 4 (computation). A *computation* of $\mathcal{P} = \langle S_\mathcal{P}, \psi_\mathcal{P} \rangle$ (or briefly $\psi_\mathcal{P}$) is a finite or infinite timed state sequence of the form:

$$\overline{\sigma} = (\sigma_0, \tau_0) \to (\sigma_1, \tau_1) \to \cdots$$

iff the following conditions are satisfied: (1) $\forall j \in \mathbb{Z}_{\geq 0} : (\sigma_j, \sigma_{j+1}) \in \psi_\mathcal{P}$, (2) if $\overline{\sigma}$ is finite and terminates in (σ_f, τ_f) then there does not exist any state σ such that $(\sigma_f, \sigma) \in \psi_\mathcal{P}^s$, and (3) the sequence $\tau_0, \tau_1, \cdots$ (called the *global time*), where $\tau_i \in \mathbb{R}_{\geq 0}$ for all $i \in \mathbb{Z}_{\geq 0}$, satisfies the following constraints:

1. *(monotonicity)* for all $i \in \mathbb{Z}_{\geq 0}$, $\tau_i \leq \tau_{i+1}$,
2. *(divergence)* if $\overline{\sigma}$ is infinite, for all $t \in \mathbb{R}_{\geq 0}$, there exists $j \in \mathbb{Z}_{\geq 0}$ such that $\tau_j \geq t$, and
3. *(time consistency)* for all $i \in \mathbb{Z}_{\geq 0}$, (1) if (σ_i, σ_{i+1}) is a delay transition (σ_i, δ) in $\psi_\mathcal{P}^d$ then $\tau_{i+1} - \tau_i = \delta$, and (2) if (σ_i, σ_{i+1}) is an immediate transition in $\psi_\mathcal{P}^s$ then $\tau_i = \tau_{i+1}$. ∎

We distinguish between a *terminating* finite computation and a *deadlocked* finite computation. Precisely, when a computation $\overline{\sigma}$ terminates in state σ_f, we include the delay transitions (σ_f, δ) in $\psi_\mathcal{P}^d$ for all $\delta \in \mathbb{R}_{\geq 0}$, i.e., $\overline{\sigma}$ can be extended to an infinite computation by advancing time arbitrarily. On the other hand, if there exists a state σ_d, such that there is no outgoing (delay or immediate) transition from σ_d then σ_d is a *deadlock state*.

2.2 Example

As mentioned in Section 1, we use the one-lane bridge traffic controller as a running example throughout the paper. To concisely write the transitions of a program, we use *timed guarded commands*. A timed guarded command (also called *timed action*) is of the form $L :: g \xrightarrow{\lambda} st$, where L is a label, g is a state predicate, st is a statement that describes how the program state is updated, and λ is a set of clock variables that are reset by execution of L. Thus, L denotes the set of transitions $\{(s_0, \nu) \to (s_1, \nu[\lambda := 0]) \mid g$ is true in state (s_0, ν), and s_1 is obtained by changing s_0 as prescribed by $st\}$. A *guarded wait command* (also called *delay action*) is of the form $L :: g \longrightarrow \mathbf{wait}$, where g identifies the set of states from where delay transitions with arbitrary durations are allowed to be taken as long as g continuously remains true.

The one-lane bridge traffic controller program (TC) has two discrete variables sig_0 and sig_1 with domain $\{G, Y, R\}$ to represent the status of signals. Moreover, for each signal i, $i \in \{0, 1\}$, TC has three clock variables x_i, y_i, and z_i acting as timers to change signal phase. When a signal turns green, it may turn yellow within 10 time units, but not sooner than 1 time unit. Subsequently, the signal may turn red between 1 and 2 time units after it turns yellow. Finally, when the signal is red, it may turn green within 1 time unit after *the other* signal becomes red. Both signals operate identically. Thus, the traffic controller program is as follows. For $i \in \{0, 1\}$:

$$
\begin{aligned}
TC1_i &:: (sig_i = G) \wedge (1 \leq x_i \leq 10) &\xrightarrow{\{y_i\}}& \quad (sig_i := Y); \\
TC2_i &:: (sig_i = Y) \wedge (1 \leq y_i \leq 2) &\xrightarrow{\{z_i\}}& \quad (sig_i := R); \\
TC3_i &:: (sig_i = R) \wedge (z_j \leq 1) &\xrightarrow{\{x_i\}}& \quad (sig_i := G); \\
TC4_i &:: ((sig_i = G) \wedge (x_i \leq 10)) \vee & & \\
      & \quad ((sig_i = Y) \wedge (y_i \leq 2)) \vee & & \\
      & \quad ((sig_i = R) \wedge (z_j \leq 1)) &\longrightarrow& \quad \mathbf{wait};
\end{aligned}
$$

where $j = (i+1) \mod 2$. Notice that the guard of $TC3_i$ depends on z timer of signal j. For simplicity, we assume that once a traffic light turns green, all cars from the opposite direction have already left the bridge.

2.3 Specification

Let $\mathcal{P} = \langle S_\mathcal{P}, \psi_\mathcal{P} \rangle$ be a program. A *specification* (or *property*), denoted $SPEC$, for $\mathcal{P}$ is a set of infinite computations of the form $(\sigma_0, \tau_0) \to (\sigma_1, \tau_1) \to \cdots$ where $\sigma_i \in S_\mathcal{P}$ for all $i \in \mathbb{Z}_{\geq 0}$. Following Henzinger [Hen92], we require that all computations in $SPEC$ satisfy time-monotonicity and divergence. We now define what it means for a program to satisfy a specification.

Definition 5 (satisfies). Let $\mathcal{P} = \langle S_\mathcal{P}, \psi_\mathcal{P} \rangle$ be a program, S be a state predicate, and $SPEC$ be a specification for $\mathcal{P}$. We write $\mathcal{P} \models_S SPEC$ and say that $\mathcal{P}$ *satisfies SPEC from* S iff (1) S is closed in $\psi_\mathcal{P}$, and (2) every computation of $\mathcal{P}$ that starts from S is in $SPEC$. ∎

Definition 6 (invariant). Let $\mathcal{P} = \langle S_\mathcal{P}, \psi_\mathcal{P} \rangle$ be a program, S be a state predicate, and $SPEC$ be a specification for $\mathcal{P}$. If $\mathcal{P} \models_S SPEC$ and $S \neq \{\}$, we say that S is an *invariant of $\mathcal{P}$ for SPEC*. ∎

Whenever the specification is clear from the context, we will omit it; thus, "S is an invariant of $\mathcal{P}$" abbreviates "S is an invariant of $\mathcal{P}$ for $SPEC$". Note that Definition 5 introduces the notion of satisfaction with respect to infinite computations. In case of finite computations, we characterize them by determining whether they can be extended to an infinite computation in the specification.

Definition 7 (maintains). We say that program $\mathcal{P}$ *maintains* $SPEC$ from S iff (1) S is closed in $\psi_\mathcal{P}$, and (2) for all computation prefixes $\overline{\alpha}$ of $\mathcal{P}$, there exists a computation suffix $\overline{\beta}$ such that $\overline{\alpha}\overline{\beta} \in SPEC$. We say that $\mathcal{P}$ *violates* $SPEC$ iff it is not the case that $\mathcal{P}$ maintains $SPEC$. ∎

Specifying timing constraints. In order to express time-related behaviors of real-time programs (e.g., deadlines and recovery time), we focus on a standard property typically used in real-time computing known as the *bounded response property*. A bounded response property, denoted $P \mapsto_{\leq \delta} Q$ where P and Q are two state predicates and $\delta \in \mathbb{Z}_{\geq 0}$, is the set of all computations $(\sigma_0, \tau_0) \to (\sigma_1, \tau_1) \to \cdots$ in which, for all $i \geq 0$, if $\sigma_i \in P$ then there exists j, $j \geq i$, such that (1) $\sigma_j \in Q$, and (2) $\tau_j - \tau_i \leq \delta$, i.e., it is always the case that a state in P is followed by a state in Q within δ time units.

The specifications considered in this paper are an intersection of a *safety* specification and a *liveness* specification [AS85, Hen92]. In this paper, we consider a special case where safety specification is characterized by a set of bad immediate transitions and a set of bounded response properties.

Definition 8 (safety specification). Let $SPEC$ be a specification. The *safety specification* of $SPEC$ is the union of the sets $SPEC_{\overline{bt}}$ and $SPEC_{\overline{br}}$ defined as follows:

1. Let $SPEC_{bt}$ be a set of immediate *bad transitions*. We denote the specification whose computations have no transition in $SPEC_{bt}$ by $SPEC_{\overline{bt}}$.
2. We denote $SPEC_{\overline{br}}$ by the conjunction $\bigwedge_{i=0}^{m}(P_i \mapsto_{\leq \delta_i} Q_i)$, for state predicates P_i and Q_i, and, response times δ_i. ∎

Throughout the paper, $SPEC_{\overline{br}}$ is meant to prescribe how a program should carry out bounded-time phased recovery to its normal behavior after the occurrence of faults. We formally define the notion of recovery in Section 3.

Definition 9 (liveness specification). A liveness specification of $SPEC$ is a set of computations that meets the following condition: for each finite computation $\overline{\alpha} \in SPEC$, there exists a computation $\overline{\beta}$ such that $\overline{\alpha}\overline{\beta} \in SPEC$. ∎

Remark 1. In our synthesis problem in Section 4, we begin with an initial program that satisfies its specification (including the liveness specification). We will show that our synthesis techniques *preserve* the liveness specification. Hence, the liveness specification need not be specified explicitly. ∎

2.4 Example (cont'd)

Following Definition 8, the safety specification of TC comprises of $SPEC_{bt_{TC}}$ and $SPEC_{br_{TC}}$. $SPEC_{bt_{TC}}$ is simply the set of transitions where both signals are not red in their target states:

$$SPEC_{bt_{TC}} = \{(\sigma_0, \sigma_1) \mid (sig_0(\sigma_1) \neq R) \wedge (sig_1(\sigma_1) \neq R)\}.$$

We define $SPEC_{br}$ of TC in Section 3, where we formally define the notion of bounded-time phased recovery.

One invariant for the program TC is the following:

$$\begin{aligned}S_{TC} = \forall i \in \{0,1\} : \;&[(sig_i = G) &\Rightarrow\; &((sig_j = R) \wedge (x_i \leq 10) \wedge (z_i > 1))] \wedge \\ &[(sig_i = Y) &\Rightarrow\; &((sig_j = R) \wedge (y_i \leq 2) \wedge (z_i > 1))] \wedge \\ &[((sig_i = R) \wedge (sig_j = R)) \\ & &\Rightarrow\; &((z_i \leq 1) \oplus (z_j \leq 1))],\end{aligned}$$

where $j = (i+1) \mod 2$ and $\oplus$ denotes the *exclusive or* operator. It is straightforward to see that TC satisfies $SPEC_{\overline{bt_{TC}}}$ from S_{TC}.

3 Fault Model and Fault-Tolerance

3.1 Fault Model

The faults that a program is subject to are systematically represented by transitions. A class of *faults* f for program $\mathcal{P} = \langle S_\mathcal{P}, \psi_\mathcal{P} \rangle$ is a subset of *immediate* and *delay* transitions of the set $S_\mathcal{P} \times S_\mathcal{P}$. We use $\psi_\mathcal{P}[]f$ to denote the transitions obtained by taking the union of the transitions in $\psi_\mathcal{P}$ and the transitions in f.

Definition 10 (fault-span). We say that a state predicate T is an f-span (read as *fault-span*) of $\mathcal{P} = \langle S_\mathcal{P}, \psi_\mathcal{P} \rangle$ from S iff the following conditions are satisfied: (1) $S \subseteq T$, and (2) T is closed in $\psi_\mathcal{P}[]f$. ∎

Example (cont'd). TC is subject to clock reset faults due to circuit malfunctions. In particular, we consider faults that reset either z_0 or z_1 at any state in the invariant S_{TC} (cf. Subsection 2.3), without changing the location of TC:

$$\begin{aligned}F_0 &:: S_{TC} \xrightarrow{\{z_0\}} \text{skip}; \\ F_1 &:: S_{TC} \xrightarrow{\{z_1\}} \text{skip};\end{aligned}$$

It is straightforward to see that in the presence of F_0 and F_1, TC may violate $SPEC_{\overline{bt_{TC}}}$. For instance, if F_1 occurs when TC is in a state of S_{TC} where $(sig_0 = sig_1 = R) \wedge (z_0 \leq 1) \wedge (z_1 > 1)$, in the resulting state, we have $(sig_0 = sig_1 = R) \wedge (z_0 \leq 1) \wedge (z_1 = 0)$. From this state, immediate execution of timed actions $TC3_0$ and then $TC3_1$ results in a state where $(sig_0 = sig_1 = G)$, which is clearly a violation of the safety specification. ∎

3.2 Phased Recovery and Fault-Tolerance

As illustrated in Section 1, preserving safety specification and providing simple recovery to the invariant from the fault-span may not be sufficient and, hence, it may be necessary to complete recovery to the invariant in a sequence of phases where each phase satisfies certain constraints. We formalize the notion of bounded-time phased recovery by a set of bounded response properties inside the safety specification, i.e., by $SPEC_{br}$ (cf. Definition 8). In this paper, in particular, we focus on 2-*phase recovery*.

Definition 11 (2-phase recovery). Let $\mathcal{P} = \langle S_\mathcal{P}, \psi_\mathcal{P} \rangle$ be a real-time program with invariant S, Q be an arbitrary *intermediate recovery predicate*, f be a set of faults, and $SPEC$ be a specification (as defined in Definitions 8 and 9). We say that $\mathcal{P}$ provides 2-phase recovery from S and Q with recovery times $\delta, \theta \in \mathbb{Z}_{\geq 0}$, respectively, iff $\langle S_\mathcal{P}, \psi_\mathcal{P}[]f \rangle$ maintains $SPEC_{\overline{br}}$ from S, where $SPEC_{\overline{br}} \equiv (\neg S \mapsto_{\leq \theta} Q) \wedge (Q \mapsto_{\leq \delta} S)$. ∎

Note that in Definition 11, if S and Q are disjoint then $\mathcal{P}$ has to recover to Q and then S in order, as S is closed in $\mathcal{P}$. On the other hand, if S and Q are not disjoint, $\mathcal{P}$ has the following options: (1) recover to $Q \cap \neg S$ within θ and then S, or (2) directly recover to $S \cap Q$ within $\min(\delta, \theta)$.

We are now ready to define what it means for a program to be fault-tolerant while providing 2-phase recovery. Intuitively, a fault-tolerant program satisfies its safety, liveness, and timing constraints in both absence and presence of faults. In other words, the program *masks* the occurrence of faults in the sense that all program requirements are persistently met in both absence and presence of faults.

Definition 12 (fault-tolerance). Let $\mathcal{P} = \langle S_\mathcal{P}, \psi_\mathcal{P} \rangle$ be a real-time program with invariant S, f be a set of faults, and $SPEC$ be a specification as defined in Definitions 8 and 9. We say that $\mathcal{P}$ is f-*tolerant to* $SPEC$ *from* S, iff (1) $\mathcal{P} \models_S SPEC$, and (2) there exists T such that T is an f-span of $\mathcal{P}$ from S and $\langle S_\mathcal{P}, \psi_\mathcal{P}[]f \rangle$ maintains $SPEC$ from T. ∎

Notation. Whenever the specification $SPEC$ and the invariant S are clear from the context, we omit them; thus, "f-tolerant" abbreviates "f-tolerant to $SPEC$ from S".

Example (cont'd). As described in Section 1, when faults F_0 or F_1 (defined in Subsection 3.1) occur, the program TC has to, first, ensure that nothing catastrophic happens and then recover to its normal behavior. Thus, the fault-tolerant version of TC has to, first, reach a state where both signals remain red indefinitely and subsequently recover to S where exactly one signal turns green. In particular, we let the 2-phase recovery specification of TC be the following:

$$SPEC_{\overline{br}_{TC}} \equiv (\neg S_{TC} \mapsto_{\leq 3} Q_{TC}) \wedge (Q_{TC} \mapsto_{\leq 7} S_{TC}),$$

where $Q_{TC} = \forall i \in \{0, 1\} : (sig_i = R) \wedge (z_i > 1)$. The response times in $SPEC_{br_{TC}}$ (i.e., 3 and 7) are simply two arbitrary numbers to express the duration of the two phases of recovery. ∎

4 Problem Statement

Given are a fault-intolerant real-time program $\mathcal{P} = \langle S_\mathcal{P}, \psi_\mathcal{P} \rangle$, its invariant S, a set f of faults, and a specification $SPEC$ such that $\mathcal{P} \models_S SPEC$. Our goal is to synthesize a real-time program $\mathcal{P}' = \langle S_{\mathcal{P}'}, \psi_{\mathcal{P}'} \rangle$ with invariant S' such that $\mathcal{P}'$ is f-tolerant to $SPEC$ from S'. We require that our synthesis methods obtain $\mathcal{P}'$ from $\mathcal{P}$ by *adding fault-tolerance* to $\mathcal{P}$ without introducing new behaviors in the absence of faults. To this end, we first define the notion of *projection*. Projection of a set $\psi_\mathcal{P}$ of transitions on state predicate S consists of immediate transitions of $\psi_\mathcal{P}^s$ that start in S and end in S, and delay transitions of $\psi_\mathcal{P}^d$ that start and remain in S continuously.

Definition 13 (projection). *Projection* of a set ψ of transitions on a state predicate S (denoted $\psi|S$) is the following set of transitions:

$$\psi|S = \{(\sigma_0, \sigma_1) \in \psi^s \mid \sigma_0, \sigma_1 \in S\} \cup$$
$$\{(\sigma, \delta) \in \psi^d \mid \sigma \in S \wedge (\forall \epsilon \mid ((\epsilon \in \mathbb{R}_{\geq 0}) \wedge (\epsilon \leq \delta)) : \sigma + \epsilon \in S)\}. \blacksquare$$

Since meeting timing constraints in the presence of faults requires time predictability, we let our synthesis methods incorporate a finite set Y of new clock variables. We denote the set of states obtained by abstracting the clock variables in Y from the state predicate U by $U \backslash Y$. Likewise, if ψ is a set of transitions, we denote the set of transitions obtained by abstracting the clock variables in Y by $\psi_\mathcal{P} \backslash Y$. Now, observe that in the absence of faults, if S' contains states that are not in S then $\mathcal{P}'$ may include computations that start outside S. Hence, we require that $(S' \backslash Y) \subseteq S$. Moreover, if $\psi'_\mathcal{P}|S'$ contains a transition that is not in $\psi_\mathcal{P}|S'$ then in the absence of faults, $\mathcal{P}'$ can exhibit computations that do not correspond to computations of $\mathcal{P}$. Therefore, we require that $(\psi_{\mathcal{P}'} \backslash Y)|(S' \backslash Y) \subseteq \psi_\mathcal{P}|(S' \backslash Y)$.

Problem Statement 1. Given a program $\mathcal{P} = \langle S_\mathcal{P}, \psi_\mathcal{P} \rangle$, invariant S, specification $SPEC$, and set of faults f such that $\mathcal{P} \models_S SPEC$, identify $\mathcal{P}' = \langle S_{\mathcal{P}'}, \psi_{\mathcal{P}'} \rangle$ and S' such that:

(C1) $S_{\mathcal{P}'} \backslash Y = S_\mathcal{P}$, where Y is a finite set of new clock variables,
(C2) $(S' \backslash Y) \subseteq S$,
(C3) $((\psi_{\mathcal{P}'} \backslash Y) \mid ((S' \backslash Y)) \subseteq (\psi_\mathcal{P}|(S' \backslash Y))$, and
(C4) $\mathcal{P}'$ is f-tolerant to $SPEC$ from S'. ∎

5 Synthesizing Fault-Tolerant Real-Time Programs with 2-Phase Recovery

5.1 Complexity

In this section, we show that, in general, the problem of synthesizing fault-tolerant real-time programs that provide phased recovery is NP-complete in the size of locations of the given fault-intolerant real-time program.

Instance. A real-time program $\mathcal{P} = \langle S_\mathcal{P}, \psi_\mathcal{P} \rangle$ with invariant S, a set of faults f, and a specification $SPEC$, such that $\mathcal{P} \models_S SPEC$, where $SPEC_{br} \equiv (\neg S \mapsto_{\leq \theta} Q) \wedge (Q \mapsto_{\leq \delta} S)$ for state predicate Q and $\delta, \theta \in \mathbb{Z}_{\geq 0}$.

The decision problem (FTPR). Does there exist an f-tolerant program $\mathcal{P}' = \langle S_{\mathcal{P}'}, \psi_{\mathcal{P}'} \rangle$ with invariant S' such that $\mathcal{P}'$ and S' meet the constraints of Problem Statement 1?

Theorem 1. *The FTPR problem is NP-complete in the size of locations of the fault-intolerant program.* ∎

Example (cont'd). The proof of Theorem 1 particularly implies that if Q and S are disjoint in the problem instance then NP-completeness of the synthesis problem is certain. In the context of TC, notice that according to the definitions of S_{TC} and Q_{TC} in Subsections 2.4 and 3.2, it is the case that $S_{TC} \cap Q_{TC} = \{\}$. Hence, the TC program and specification in their current form exhibit an instance where the synthesis problem is NP-complete. However, in Subsection 5.3, we demonstrate that a slight modification in the specification of TC makes the problem significantly easier to solve. ∎

5.2 A Sufficient Condition for a Polynomial-Time Solution

In this section, we present a sufficient condition under which one can devise a polynomial-time sound and complete solution to the Problem Statement 1 in the size of time-abstract bisimulation of input program.

Claim. Let $\mathcal{P} = \langle S_\mathcal{P}, \psi_\mathcal{P} \rangle$ be a program with invariant S and recovery specification $SPEC_{\overline{br}} \equiv (\neg S \mapsto_{\leq \theta} Q) \wedge (Q \mapsto_{\leq \delta} S)$. There exists a polynomial-time sound and complete solution to Problem Statement 1 in the size of the region graph of $\mathcal{P}$, if $(S \subseteq Q) \wedge (Q \text{ is closed in } \psi_{\mathcal{P}'})$. ∎

In order to validate this claim, we propose the Algorithm Add_BoundedPhasedRecovery.

Algorithm sketch. Intuitively, the algorithm works as follows. In Step 1, we transform the input program into a *region graph* [AD94] (described below). In Step 2, we isolate the set of states from where $SPEC_{\overline{bt}}$ may be violated. In Step 3, we ensure that any computation of $\mathcal{P}'$ that starts from a state in $\neg S' - Q$ (respectively, $Q - S'$) reaches a state in Q (respectively, S') within θ (respectively, δ) time units. In Step 4, we ensure the closure of fault-span and deadlock freedom of invariant. We repeat Steps 3-4 until a fixpoint is reached. Finally, in Step 5, we transform the resultant region graph back into a real-time program.

Assumption 1. Let $\overline{\alpha} = (\sigma_0, \tau_0) \rightarrow (\sigma_1, \tau_1) \rightarrow \cdots (\sigma_n, \tau_n)$ be a computation prefix where $\sigma_0, \sigma_n \in S$ and $\sigma_i \notin S$ for all $i \in \{1..n-1\}$. Only for simplicity of presentation, we assume that the number of occurrence of faults in $\overline{\alpha}$ is one. Precisely, we assume that in $\overline{\alpha}$, only (σ_0, σ_1) is a fault transition and no faults occur outside the program invariant. In our previous work [BK06b], we have shown how to deal with cases where multiple faults occur in a computation when adding bounded response properties. The same technique can be applied while preserving soundness and completeness of the algorithm Add_BoundedPhasedRecovery in this paper. Furthermore, notice that the proof of Theorem 1 in its current form holds with this assumption. ∎

Region Graph. Real-time programs can be analyzed with the help of an equivalence relation of finite index on the set of states [AD94]. Given a real-time program $\mathcal{P}$, for each clock variable $x \in X$, let c_x be the largest constant in clock constraint of transitions of p that involve x, where $c_x = 0$ if x does not occur in any clock constraints of $\mathcal{P}$. We say that two clock valuations ν, μ are *clock equivalent* if (1) for all $x \in X$, either $\lfloor \nu(x) \rfloor = \lfloor \mu(x) \rfloor$ or both $\nu(x), \mu(x) > c_x$, (2) the ordering of the fractional parts of the clock variables in the set $\{x \in X \mid \nu(x) < c_x\}$ is the same in μ and ν, and (3) for all $x \in X$ where $\nu(x) < c_x$, the clock value $\nu(x)$ is an integer iff $\mu(x)$ is an integer. A *clock region* ρ is a clock equivalence class. Two states (s_0, ν_0) and (s_1, ν_1) are region equivalent, written $(s_0, \nu_0) \equiv (s_1, \nu_1)$, if (1) $s_0 = s_1$, and (2) ν_0 and ν_1 are clock equivalent. A *region* $r = (s, \rho)$ is an equivalence class with respect to $\equiv$, where s is a location and ρ is a clock region. We say that a clock region β is a *time-successor* of a clock region α iff for each $\nu \in \alpha$, there exists $\tau \in \mathbb{R}_{\geq 0}$, such that $\nu + \tau \in \beta$, and $\nu + \tau' \in \alpha \cup \beta$ for all $\tau' < \tau$.

Using the region equivalence relation, we construct the *region graph* of $\mathcal{P} = \langle S_\mathcal{P}, \psi_\mathcal{P} \rangle$ (denoted $R(\mathcal{P}) = \langle S_\mathcal{P}^r, \psi_\mathcal{P}^r \rangle$) as follows. Vertices of $R(\mathcal{P})$ (denoted $S_\mathcal{P}^r$) are regions. Edges of $R(\mathcal{P})$ (denoted $\psi_\mathcal{P}^r$) are of the form $(s_0, \rho_0) \to (s_1, \rho_1)$ iff for some clock valuations $\nu_0 \in \rho_0$ and $\nu_1 \in \rho_1$, $(s_0, \nu_0) \to (s_1, \nu_1)$ is a transitions in $\psi_\mathcal{P}$.

We now describe the algorithm Add_BoundedPhasedRecovery in detail:

- (*Step 1*) First, we use the above technique to transform the input program $\mathcal{P} = \langle S_\mathcal{P}, \psi_\mathcal{P} \rangle$ into a region graph $R(\mathcal{P}) = \langle S_\mathcal{P}^r, \psi_\mathcal{P}^r \rangle$. To this end, we invoke the procedure ConstructRegionGraph as a black box (Line 1). We let this procedure convert state predicates and sets of transitions in $\mathcal{P}$ (e.g., S and $\psi_\mathcal{P}$) to their corresponding region predicates and sets of edges in $R(\mathcal{P})$ (e.g., S^r and $\psi_\mathcal{P}^r$). Precisely, a *region predicate* U^r with respect to a state predicate U is the set $U^r = \{(s, \rho) \mid \exists (s, \nu) : ((s, \nu) \in U \land \nu \in \rho)\}$.
- (*Step 2*) In order to ensure that the synthesized program does not violate $SPEC_{\overline{bt}}$, we identify the set ms of regions from where a computation may reach a transition in $SPEC_{bt}$ by taking fault transitions alone (Line 2). Next (Line 3), we compute the set mt of edges, which contains (1) edges that directly violate safety (i.e., $SPEC_{bt}^r$), and (2) edges whose target region is in ms (i.e., edges that lead a computation to a state from where safety may be violated by faults alone). Since the program does not have control over occurrence of faults, we remove the set ms from the region predicate T_1^r, which is our initial estimate of the fault-span (Line 4). Likewise, in Step 3, we will remove mt from the set of program edges $\psi_\mathcal{P}^r$ when recomputing program transitions.

Algorithm 1. Add_BoundedPhasedRecovery

Input: A real-time program $\mathcal{P} = \langle S_\mathcal{P}, \psi_\mathcal{P} \rangle$ with invariant S, fault transitions f, bad transitions $SPEC_{bt}$, intermediate recovery predicate Q s.t. $S \subseteq Q$, recovery time δ, and intermediate recovery time θ.
Output: If successful, a fault-tolerant real-time program $\mathcal{P}' = \langle S_{\mathcal{P}'}, \psi_{\mathcal{P}'} \rangle$.

1: $\langle S_\mathcal{P}^r, \psi_\mathcal{P}^r \rangle$, S_1^r, Q^r, f^r, $SPEC_{bt}^r$:= ConstructRegionGraph($\langle S_\mathcal{P}, \psi_\mathcal{P} \rangle$, S, Q, f, $SPEC_{bt}$);
2: $ms := \{r_0 \mid \exists r_1, r_2 \cdots r_n \;:\; (\forall j \mid 0 \leq j < n : (r_j, r_{j+1}) \in f^r) \;\wedge\; (r_{n-1}, r_n) \in SPEC_{bt}^r\}$;
3: $mt := \{(r_0, r_1) \mid (r_1 \in ms) \vee ((r_0, r_1) \in SPEC_{bt}^r)\}$;
4: $T_1^r := S_\mathcal{P}^r - ms$;
5: **repeat**
6:     $T_2^r, S_2^r := T_1^r, S_1^r$;
7:     $\psi_{\mathcal{P}_1}^r := \psi_\mathcal{P}^r|S_1^r \cup \{((s_0, \rho_0), (s_1, \rho_1)) \mid (s_0, \rho_0) \in (T_1^r - Q^r) \wedge (s_1, \rho_1) \in T_1^r \wedge$
        $\exists \rho_2 \mid \rho_2$ is a time-successor of $\rho_0 \;:\; (\exists \lambda \subseteq X \;:\; \rho_1 = \rho_2[\lambda := 0])\} \;\cup$
        $\{((s_0, \rho_0), (s_1, \rho_1)) \mid (s_0, \rho_0) \in (Q^r - S_1^r) \wedge (s_1, \rho_1) \in Q^r \wedge$
        $\exists \rho_2 \mid \rho_2$ is a time-successor of $\rho_0 \;:\; (\exists \lambda \subseteq X \;:\; \rho_1 = \rho_2[\lambda := 0])\} \;-\; mt$;
8:     $\psi_{\mathcal{P}_1}^r, ns$:= Add_BoundedResponse($\langle S_\mathcal{P}^r, \psi_{\mathcal{P}_1}^r \rangle$, $T_1^r - Q^r$, Q^r, θ);
9:     $T_1^r := T_1^r - ns$;
10:    $\psi_{\mathcal{P}_1}^r, ns$:= Add_BoundedResponse($\langle S_\mathcal{P}^r, \psi_{\mathcal{P}_1}^r \rangle$, $Q^r - S_1^r$, S_1^r, δ);
11:    $T_1^r, Q^r := T_1^r - ns$, $Q^r - ns$;
12:    **while** $(\exists r_0, r_1 : r_0 \in T_1^r \wedge r_1 \notin T_1^r \wedge (r_0, r_1) \in f^r)$ **do**
13:       $T_1^r := T_1^r - \{r_0\}$;
14:    **end while**
15:    **while** $(\exists r_0 \in (S_1^r \cap T_1^r) \;:\; (\forall r_1 \mid (r_1 \neq r_0 \wedge r_1 \in S_1^r) \;:\; (r_0, r_1) \notin \psi_{\mathcal{P}_1}^r))$ **do**
16:       $S_1^r := S_1^r - \{r_0\}$;
17:    **end while**
18:    **if** $(S_1^r = \{\} \vee T_1^r = \{\})$ **then**
19:       **print** ``no fault-tolerant program exists''; **exit**;
20:    **end if**
21: **until** $(T_1 = T_2 \wedge S_1 = S_2)$
22: $\langle S_{\mathcal{P}'}, \psi_{\mathcal{P}'} \rangle$, S', T' := ConstructRealTimeProgram($\langle S_\mathcal{P}^r, \psi_{\mathcal{P}_1}^r \rangle$, S_1^r, T_1^r);
23: **return** $\langle S_{\mathcal{P}'}, \psi_{\mathcal{P}'} \rangle$, S', T';

- *(Step 3)* In this step, we add recovery paths to $R(\mathcal{P})$ so that $R(\mathcal{P})$ satisfies $\neg S' \mapsto_{\leq \theta} Q$ and $Q \mapsto_{\leq \delta} S'$. To this end, we first recompute the set $\psi_{\mathcal{P}_1}$ of program edges (Line 7) by including (1) existing edges that start and end in S_1^r, and (2) new *recovery edges* that originate from regions in $T_1^r - Q^r$ (respectively, $Q^r - S_1^r$) and terminate at regions in T_1^r (respectively, Q) such that the time-monotonicity condition is met. We exclude the set mt from $\psi_{\mathcal{P}_1}^r$ to ensure that these recovery edges do not violate $SPEC_{\overline{bt}}$. Notice that the algorithm allows arbitrary clock resets during recovery. If such clock resets are not desirable, one can rule them out by including them as bad transitions in $SPEC_{bt}$.

After adding recovery edges, we invoke the procedure Add_BoundedResponse (Line 8) with parameters $T_1^r - Q^r$, Q^r, and θ to ensure that $R(\mathcal{P})$ indeed satisfies the bounded response property $\neg S \mapsto_{\leq \theta} Q$. The details of how the procedure Add_BoundedResponse (first proposed in [BK06a]) functions are not provided in this paper, with the exception of the following properties: (1) it adds a clock variable, say t_1, which gets reset when $T_1 - Q$ becomes true, to the set X of clock variables of $\mathcal{P}$, (2) for each state σ in $T_1 - Q$, it includes the set of transitions that participate in forming the computation that starts from σ and reaches a state in Q with smallest possible time delay, if the delay is less than θ, and (3) the regions made unreachable by this procedure (returned as the set ns) cannot be present in any solution that satisfies $\neg S_1 \mapsto_{\leq \theta} Q$. The procedure may optionally include additional computations, provided they preserve the corresponding bounded response property. Thus, since there does not exist a computation prefix that maintains the corresponding bounded response property from the regions in ns, in Line 9, the algorithm removes ns from T_1^r. Likewise, in Line 10, the algorithm adds a clock variable, say t_2, which gets reset when $Q - S_1$ becomes true and ensures that $R(\mathcal{P})$ satisfies $Q \mapsto_{\leq \delta} S_1$.

- (*Step 4*) Since we remove the set ns of regions from T_1^r, we need to ensure that T_1 is closed in f. Thus, we remove regions from where a sequence of fault edges can reach a region in ns (Lines 12-14). Next, due to the possibility of removal of some regions and edges in the previous steps, the algorithm ensures that the region graph $\langle S_{\mathcal{P}}^r, \psi_{\mathcal{P}_1}^r \rangle$ does not have deadlock regions in the region invariant S_1^r (Lines 15-17). Precisely, we say that a region (s_0, ρ_0) of region graph $R(\mathcal{P}) = \langle S_{\mathcal{P}}^r, \psi_{\mathcal{P}}^r \rangle$ is a *deadlock region* in region predicate U^r iff for all regions $(s_1, \rho_1) \in U^r$, there does not exist an edge of the form $(s_0, \rho_0) \rightarrow (s_1, \rho_1) \in \psi_{\mathcal{P}}^r$. Deadlock freedom in the region graph is necessary, as the constraint $C4$ in the Problem Statement 1 does not allow the algorithm to introduce new finite or time-divergent computations to the input program. If the removal of deadlock regions and regions from where the closure of fault-span is violated results in empty invariant or fault-span, the algorithm declares failure (Lines 18-20).

- (*Step 5*) Finally, upon reaching a fixpoint, we transform the resulting region graph $\langle S_{\mathcal{P}}^r, \psi_{\mathcal{P}_1}^r \rangle$ back into a real-time program $\mathcal{P}' = \langle S_{\mathcal{P}'}, \psi_{\mathcal{P}'} \rangle$ by invoking the procedure ConstructRealTimeProgram. In fact, the program $\mathcal{P}'$ is returned as the final synthesized fault-tolerant program. Note that since a region graph is a time-abstract *bisimulation* [AD94], we will not lose any behaviors in the reverse transformation.

Theorem 2. *The Algorithm Add_BoundedPhasedRecovery is sound and complete.* ∎

5.3 Example (cont'd)

We now demonstrate how the algorithm Add_BoundedPhasedRecovery synthesizes a fault-tolerant version of TC, which provides bounded-time recovery. Let the intermediate recovery predicate be:

$$Q_{new} = S_{TC} \cup Q_{TC}.$$

In other words, after the occurrence of faults, the recovery specification requires that either both signals turn red within 3 time units and then return to the normal behavior within 7 time units, or, the system reaches a state in S_{TC} within 3 time units. Since, $S_{TC} \subseteq Q_{new}$, we apply the Algorithm Add_BoundedPhasedRecovery to transform TC into a fault-tolerant program TC'. We note that due to many symmetries in TC and the complex structure of the algorithm, we only present a highlight of the process of synthesizing TC'.

First, observe that in Step 2 of the algorithm, $ms = \{\}$ and $mt = SPEC_{btTC}$. In Step 3, consider a subset of $T_1 - Q_{new}$ where $(sig_0 = sig_1 = R) \wedge (z_0, z_1 \leq 1)$. This predicate is reachable by a single occurrence of (for instance) F_0 from an invariant state where $(sig_0 = sig_1 = R) \wedge (z_0 > 1) \wedge (z_1 \leq 1)$. After adding legitimate recovery transitions (Line 7), the invocation of Add_BoundedResponse (Line 8) results in addition of the following recovery action:

$$TC5_i :: \quad (sig_0 = sig_1 = R) \wedge (z_0, z_1 \leq 2) \wedge (t_1 \leq 2) \quad \longrightarrow \quad \textbf{wait};$$

for all $i \in \{0, 1\}$. This action enforces the program to take delay transitions so that the program reaches a state in Q where $(sig_0 = sig_1 = R) \wedge (z_0, z_1 > 1)$.

Now, consider the case where TC is in a state where $(sig_0 = G) \wedge (sig_1 = R) \wedge (x_0 = 1) \wedge (z_0, z_1 \leq 1)$. In this case, one may argue that TC has the option of executing action $TC3_1$ and reaching a state where $sig_0 = sig_1 = G$, which is clearly a violation of safety specification $SPEC_{\overline{bt}_{TC}}$. However, since we remove the set mt from $\psi_{\mathcal{P}_1}$ (Line 7), action $TC3_i$ would be revised as follows:

$$TC3_i :: \quad (sig_i = R) \wedge (z_j \leq 1) \wedge (sig_j \neq G) \quad \xrightarrow{\{x_i\}} \quad (sig_i := G);$$

for all $i \in \{0, 1\}$ where $j = (i+1) \mod 2$. In other words, the algorithm strengthens the guard of $TC1_i$ such that in the presence of faults, a signal does not turn green while the other one is also green.

In Step 4, consider the state predicate $Q_{new} - S_{1_{TC}} = (sig_0 = sig_1 = R) \wedge (z_0, z_1 > 1)$. Similar to Step 3, the algorithm adds recovery paths with the smallest possible time delay, which is the following action for either $i = 0$ or $i = 1$:

$$TC6_i :: \quad (sig_i = sig_j = R) \wedge (z_i, z_j > 1) \quad \xrightarrow{\{z_i\}} \quad \textbf{skip};$$

It is straightforward to verify that by execution of $TC6_i$, the program reaches the invariant S_{TC} from where the program behaves correctly. Similar to Step 3, the procedure Add_BoundedResponse may include the following additional actions:

$$TC7_i :: \quad (sig_i = sig_j = R) \wedge (z_i, z_j > 1) \wedge (t_2 \leq 7) \quad \xrightarrow{\{x_i\}} \quad (sig_i := G);$$
$$TC8_i :: \quad (sig_i = sig_j = R) \wedge (z_i, z_j > 1) \wedge (t_2 \leq 7) \quad \xrightarrow{\{y_i\}} \quad (sig_i := Y);$$
$$TC9_i :: \quad (sig_i = sig_j = R) \wedge (z_i, z_j > 1) \wedge (t_2 \leq 7) \quad \longrightarrow \quad \textbf{wait};$$

In the context of TC, in Step 5, the algorithm removes states from neither the fault-span nor the invariant, as $ns = \{\}$, and, hence, the algorithm finds the final solution in one iteration of the repeat-until loop.

6 Related Work

Our formulation of the synthesis problem is in spirit close to timed controller synthesis (e.g., [BDMP03, DM02, AM99, AMPS98]), where program and fault transitions may be modeled as controllable and uncontrollable actions, and game theory (e.g., [dAFH+03, FLM02]), where program and fault transitions may be modeled in terms of two players. In controller synthesis (respectively, game theory) the objective is to *restrict* the actions of a *plant* (respectively, an *adversary*) at each state through synthesizing a *controller* (respectively, a *wining strategy*) such that the behavior of the entire system always meets some safety and/or reachability conditions. Notice that the conditions $C1..C3$ in Problem Statement 1 precisely express this notion of restriction (also called *language inclusion*). Moreover, constraint $C4$ implicitly implies that the synthesized program is not allowed to exhibit new finite computations, which is known as the *non-blocking* condition. Note, however, that there are several distinctions. First, in addition to safety and reachability constraints, our notion of fault-tolerance is also concerned with adding new *bounded-time recovery* behaviors to the given program as well, which is normally not a concern in controller synthesis and game theory. Secondly, unlike most game theoretic approaches, we do not consider turns between occurrence of program and fault transitions. Thirdly, in controller synthesis and game theory, a common assumption is that the existing program and/or the given specification must be deterministic which is not the case in our model.

Finally, we concentrate on safety properties typically used in specifying real-time systems (cf. Definition 8). As a result, the complexity of our synthesis techniques is often lower than the related work. For example, synthesis problems presented in [dAFH+03, FLM02, AMPS98, AM99] are EXPTIME-complete and deciding the existence of a controller in [DM02, BDMP03] is 2EXPTIME-complete.

7 Conclusion and Future Work

In this paper, we focused on the problem of synthesizing fault-tolerant real-time programs that mask the occurrence of faults while providing bounded-time phased recovery. We modeled such phased recovery using bounded response properties of the form $(\neg S \mapsto_{\leq \theta} Q) \land (Q \mapsto_{\leq \delta} S)$ where S is an invariant predicate and Q is an intermediate recovery predicate. We showed that in general the problem is NP-complete in the size of locations of the input program. We also showed that if $S \subseteq Q$ and Q is closed in execution of the output program then there exists a polynomial-time solution to the problem in the size of the input program's region graph.

Also, as discussed in Subsection 5.3, the designer can use the contrast between the complexity classes with slightly different problem specifications to determine if system requirements can be slightly modified for permitting automated synthesis. In particular, in Section 6, we argued that the alternate specification (where the problem is in P) for the one-lane bridge problem considered in this paper may be acceptable to many designers. Also, as argued in that section, the modified specification can assist in partial automation of providing fault-tolerance with phased recovery. One of our future works in this area is to develop algorithms that utilize such a partial automation.

We are currently working on other variations of the problem. One such variation is where $S \subseteq Q$, but Q need *not* be closed in the output program. We conjecture that the complexity of this problem is exponential. We also plan to develop symbolic algorithms for synthesizing bounded-time phased recovery. In previous work, we have shown that such techniques are extremely effective in synthesizing distributed programs with state space of size 10^{30} and beyond [BK07].

References

[AD94] Alur, R., Dill, D.: A theory of timed automata. Theoretical Computer Science 126(2), 183–235 (1994)

[AH97] Alur, R., Henzinger, T.A.: Real-Time System = Discrete System + Clock Variables. International Journal on Software Tools for Technology Transfer 1(1-2), 86–109 (1997)

[AM99] Asarin, E., Maler, O.: As soon as possible: Time optimal control for timed automata. In: Hybrid Systems: Computation and Control (HSCC), pp. 19–30 (1999)

[AMPS98] Asarin, E., Maler, O., Pnueli, A., Sifakis, J.: Controller synthesis for timed automata. In: IFAC Symposium on System Structure and Control, pp. 469–474 (1998)

[AS85] Alpern, B., Schneider, F.B.: Defining liveness. Information Processing Letters 21, 181–185 (1985)

[BDMP03] Bouyer, P., D'Souza, D., Madhusudan, P., Petit, A.: Timed control with partial observability. In: Computer Aided Verification (CAV), pp. 180–192 (2003)

[BK06a] Bonakdarpour, B., Kulkarni, S.S.: Automated Incremental Synthesis of Timed Automata. In: Brim, L., Haverkort, B.R., Leucker, M., van de Pol, J. (eds.) FMICS 2006 and PDMC 2006. LNCS, vol. 4346, pp. 261–276. Springer, Heidelberg (2007)

[BK06b] Bonakdarpour, B., Kulkarni, S.S.: Incremental Synthesis of Fault-Tolerant Real-Time Programs. In: Datta, A.K., Gradinariu, M. (eds.) SSS 2006. LNCS, vol. 4280, pp. 122–136. Springer, Heidelberg (2006)

[BK07] Bonakdarpour, B., Kulkarni, S.S.: Exploiting symbolic techniques in automated synthesis of distributed programs with large state space. In: IEEE International Conference on Distributed Computing Systems (ICDCS), pp. 3–10 (2007)

[dAFH+03] de Alfaro, L., Faella, M., Henzinger, T.A., Majumdar, R., Stoelinga, M.: The element of surprise in timed games. In: International Conference on Concurrency Theory (CONCUR) (2003)

[DM02] D'Souza, D., Madhusudan, P.: Timed control synthesis for external specifications. In: Symposium on Theoretical Aspects of Computer Science (STACS), pp. 571–582 (2002)

[FLM02] Faella, M., LaTorre, S., Murano, A.: Dense real-time games. In: Logic in Computer Science (LICS), pp. 167–176 (2002)

[Hen92] Henzinger, T.A.: Sooner is safer than later. Information Processing Letters 43(3), 135–141 (1992)

Towards Consistent Specifications of Product Families*

Alexander Harhurin and Judith Hartmann

Institut für Informatik, TU München,
Boltzmannstr. 3, D-85748, Garching bei München, Germany
{harhurin,hartmanj}@in.tum.de

Abstract. Addressing the challenges faced today during the development of multi-functional system families, we suggest a service-oriented approach to formally specifying the functionality and, in particular, the functional variability already in the requirement engineering phase. In this paper, we precisely define the underlying concepts, such as the notion of individual services, the combination of services, inter-service dependencies, and variability. Thereby, we especially focus on establishing the *consistency* of the overall specification. To that end, we formally define conflicts between requirements and describe how they can be detected and resolved based on the introduced formal concepts.

1 Introduction

Today, in various application domains, e.g. the automotive domain, software plays a dominant role. The rapid increase in the amount and importance of different software-based functions and their extensive interaction as well as a rising number of different product variants are just some of the challenges that are faced during the development of multi-functional system families. As a consequence there is a need for adequate modeling techniques for functional requirements. Prevalent approaches like UML Use Cases or FODA [1] lack a precise semantics in general. However, in order to assure the consistency of a specification, a precise semantics of the modeling techniques is inevitable. Based on a formal foundation, discrepancies between conflicting functionalities can be detected and resolved already in the early phases of the development process. Furthermore, such a formal specification represents the first model in a model-based system development along different abstraction levels as introduced in [2]. It serves as a formal basis for the construction and verification of the models in the consecutive design phase. Consequently, we focus on the formal definitions of functional requirements and relations between them, and show how the upcoming service-oriented paradigm is used to handle the aforementioned functional intricacy.

---

* This work was partially funded by the German Federal Ministry of Education and Research (BMBF) in the framework of the VEIA project under grant 01ISF15A. The responsibility for this article lies with the authors.

Our notation technique, the *Service Diagram*, informally introduced in [3] describes the system as a set of related functional requirements (*services*). Regarding product families, our approach includes concepts which allow for the formal specification of functional variability. Thereby, functional variability means that the specification includes alternative functional requirements. Each variant of the product family is required to satisfy at least one of the alternative requirements. Thus, the denotational semantics of our Service Diagram specifies the behavior of a product family as the behavior that can be delivered by at least one of its variants. Also, we precisely define the meaning of typical dependencies for product families, namely *excludes* and *requires*. These dependencies specify which requirements must and which ones must not be simultaneously satisfied by a variant of a product family.

In this paper, we especially focus on understanding how single services depend on and interfere with each other. Thereby, the main goal of our approach is to ensure the consistency of the specification, i.e. the absence of conflicts between services. Informally, there is a conflict between two services if they impose conflicting requirements on the behavior of a system which can not be simultaneously fulfilled. Giving formal definitions of these concepts, our approach can be used for a tool-supported analysis of the functional requirements and, in particular, for consistency checks between different variants.

1.1 Running Example

The concepts introduced in the remainder of the paper will be illustrated by a simplified example of a cruise control (cp. Figure 1). The cruise control comprises a manual cruise control (MCC) and an adaptive cruise control (ACC). The MCC specifies the acceleration/deceleration of the vehicle triggered by the acceleration/brake pedal (Pedal). Additionally, there is an option to control the speed via buttons on the steering wheel (Steering Wheel). The ACC comprises an automatic speed control (Speed), which controls the vehicle speed for a constant target speed. There exist two alternative variants varying in the way how the target speed is selected by the driver (target speed arbitrarily configurable (Input) or target speed set to the current vehicle speed when the ACC is activated (Save)). Furthermore, the ACC optionally comprises a follow-up control (Follow-Up) to automatically follow a target vehicle and a pre-crash control (Pre-Crash). There exist two variants of the pre-crash control, one which displays a warning (Warning) and one which actively brakes (Brake) as soon as a potential crash is detected. There are several dependencies between these functionalities to assure a correct interplay between them. The dependencies as well as all other relevant details will be described at the appropriate places.

1.2 Outline

The rest of this paper is organized as follows: In Section 2 the semantics of the *Service Diagram* is presented. In particular, we explain the formal specification of functional requirements by means of services, concepts for hierarchically structuring services, variability concepts, and concepts for modeling dependencies between services. In Section 3, we concentrate on the consistency of a service specification. To that end, we formally define conflicts and describe how they can be detected and resolved based on the introduced formal concepts. Contributions of our approach are listed in Section 4. Finally, we compare our service model to related approaches in Section 5 before we conclude the paper in Section 6.

2   Service Diagram

This section introduces the denotational semantics of the *Service Diagram*, a hierarchical model for the specification of the system functionality. This diagram gives a black-box specification of a system, i.e. the system behavior is specified as a causal relation between input and output messages. Thus, an implementation satisfies the specification formalized by a Service Diagram if it shows the same I/O behavior as specified by the diagram. A Service Diagram consists of hierarchically subdivided services and four kinds of relationships between them, namely aggregation, functional dependencies, optional and alternative relations (cp. Figure 1). All these concepts will be introduced in the following subsections. A more detailed description of the basic concepts can be found in [4].

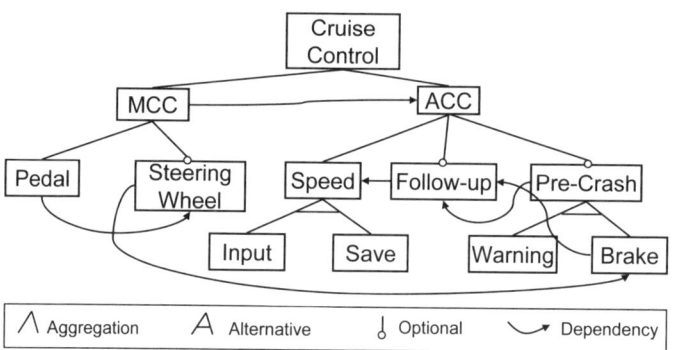

Fig. 1. Service Diagram for the Cruise Control

2.1   Single Service

The Service Diagram is based on the notion of a *service* [5] as the fundamental concept of the model. Intuitively, a service represents a piece of functionality by specifying requirements on the I/O behavior. More precisely, a service specifies a relation between certain inputs and outputs. Hence, the Service Diagram is a restrictive specification, where each service imposes a requirement on the system and, thus, further restricts the valid I/O behavior. Formally, a service is a (partial) stream-processing function which maps streams of input messages to corresponding streams of output messages. Here, a stream s of elements of type Data can be thought of as a function $s : \mathbb{N} \to Data$.

Syntactic Interface. Every service has a *syntactic interface* $(I \blacktriangleright O)$, which consists of a set I of typed input ports and a set O of typed output ports.

Table 1 depicts the syntactical interfaces of the atomar services of our example. Exemplary, the type of the port `currentSpeed` is $\mathbb{N}$ and the type of the port `speed` is $\{accelerate, decelerate, \varepsilon\}$. Note, that if necessary the type of a port includes the empty message ε to explicitly model no interaction.

Table 1. Syntactical Interfaces of the Modular Services of the Cruise Control

Service	I Ports	O Ports
MCC/Pedal	brakePedal, accPedal	speed
MCC/Steering Wheel	brakeButton, accButton	speed
ACC/Speed/Input	currentSpeed, targetSpeed	speed
ACC/Speed/Save	active, currentSpeed	speed
ACC/Follow-Up	objectDetected, objectDistance, currentSpeed	speed
ACC/Pre-Crash/Warning	objectDetected, objectDistance, currentSpeed	warning
ACC/Pre-Crash/Brake	objectDetected, objectDistance, currentSpeed	speed

With each port we associate a set of streams representing the *syntactically correct* communication over this port. Formally, for a given set of ports P, a *port history* is a mapping which associates a concrete stream to each port: $h : P \to (\mathbb{N} \to Data)$. $\mathbb{H}(P)$ denotes the set of all such histories. $\mathbb{H}(I_s) \times \mathbb{H}(O_s)$ specifies the set of all *syntactically correct* I/O history pairs (x, y) for a service s with interface $(I_s \blacktriangleright O_s)$. For a history $h \in \mathbb{H}(P)$, we define its projection $h|P' \in \mathbb{H}(P')$ to be the history containing only streams which are attached to the ports in $P' \subseteq P$. Also, we denote a projection of a history x to the interface of a service s by x_s, i.e. $x_s = x|I_s$. The same goes for an I/O history pair: $(x_s, y_s) = (x|I_s, y|O_s)$. Furthermore, we use $h[p]$ to denote the stream associated with the port p by the history h, i.e. $h[p] = h(p)$. Then, the term $h[p](t)$ denotes the message contained in the stream $h[p]$ on the port p within time interval $t \in \mathbb{N}$.

Semantics. To specify the behavior of a service, we use an assumption/guarantee notation (A/G) which consists of two predicates, namely, an assumption and a guarantee. The assumption specifies the domain of a service[1]. The guarantee characterizes the reaction of a service to its inputs if the inputs are in accordance with the assumption. Formally,

$$A : \mathbb{H}(I) \to \mathbb{B}ool, \qquad G : \mathbb{H}(I) \times \mathbb{H}(O) \to \mathbb{B}ool.$$

By this, a service is a *restrictive* specification which restricts the set of all syntactically correct histories to a subset of *(semantically) valid* histories. An I/O history pair (x, y) is valid for a service if it fulfills the A/G of this service. We

---

[1] We do not require that a service can react to every possible input, i.e. there may be inputs which are not explicitly covered by the service specification.

say, the behavior of a service is the set of all valid history pairs for this service. Formally, a service s with the syntactic interface $(I \blacktriangleright O)$ is defined as a relation from the set of input port histories (according to the assumption) to the powerset of output port histories (according to the guarantee):

$$s : \mathbb{H}(I) \to \mathcal{P}(\mathbb{H}(O)), \qquad s(x) \equiv \{y | A_s(x) \wedge G_s(x,y)\}.$$

In our example, the variant Input of the speed control is specified as follows:

$A(x) \equiv \forall t \in \mathbb{N} : x[currentSpeed](t) \in [20..220] \wedge x[targetSpeed](t) \in [40..200]$
$G(x,y) \equiv \forall t \in \mathbb{N} :$
$x[currentSpeed](t) > x[targetSpeed](t) \Rightarrow y[speed](t+1) = decelerate \wedge$
$x[currentSpeed](t) < x[targetSpeed](t) \Rightarrow y[speed](t+1) = accelerate \wedge$
$x[currentSpeed](t) = x[targetSpeed](t) \Rightarrow y[speed](t+1) = \varepsilon$

The assumption formalizes, that the behavior of the cruise control is only specified for current speed between 20 and 220 km/h and target speed between 40 and 200 km/h. In our terminology, a valid history x must contain a value between 20 and 220 on port currentSpeed and a value between 40 and 200 on targetSpeed within each time interval t. Otherwise, the behavior is not defined. The guarantee requires for each time interval, that the vehicle accelerates if the current vehicle speed is less, decelerates if the current speed is higher, and neither accelerates nor decelerates if the current speed is equal to the target speed.

2.2 Aggregation

The aggregation relation allows to arrange individual services into a service hierarchy. The semantics of a *compound service* (composed of several sub-services) is defined as being a container of all *concurrently* operating sub-services.

The interface of a compound service s_C composed of a set of sub-services S aggregates all I/O ports of all its sub-services. Its behavior is defined as the conjunction of the modular A/Gs of its sub-services. Formally,

$$A_{s_C}(x) \equiv \bigwedge_{s \in S} A_s(x_s), \qquad G_{s_C}(x,y) \equiv \bigwedge_{s \in S} G_s(x_s, y_s). \qquad (1)$$

A more detailed description of the aggregation relation including illustrating examples can be found in [4].

2.3 Variability

The basic concept to model variability are *variation points* (VPs). Intuitively, a VP is a compound service composed of some mandatory, alternative, and/or optional sub-services (the latter two are also called *variants*). In the following, the syntactic interface and the behavior of a VP comprising alternative sub-services are introduced. Subsequently, we explain the semantics of optional services based on the definitions for alternative VPs. To understand the following definitions, it is important to keep in mind that our Service Diagram is a *restrictive* specification. Each service in the Service Diagram imposes a requirement on the I/O behavior which must be fulfilled by any valid I/O history. If a service is absent in a diagram (e.g. the service is not selected in a configuration[2]), the property specified by this service is not required. However, a valid I/O history is not prohibited from fulfilling this property.

Syntactic Interface. An alternative VP comprising a set of alternative services S_V has the *set-valued interface*

$$\mathbb{I}_{VP} \equiv \{(I_s \blacktriangleright O_s) | s \in S_V\}.$$

Herewith, in combination with the aggregation relation, we can specify the interface of a product family. Mandatory and optional ports can be easily identified by means of the set-theoretical operations over the set-valued interface.

We call a history pair (x, y) *syntactically correct* for a VP if it conforms to the interface of one of its variants, i.e. if $\exists (I \blacktriangleright O) \in \mathbb{I}_{VP} : (x, y) \in \mathbb{H}(I) \times \mathbb{H}(O)$.

To be able to aggregate VPs, the definition of the history projection (see Section 2.1) must be adapted for set-valued interfaces. Since a VP comprises a set of interfaces, the projection to the interface of a VP results in a set of histories. For an I/O history pair (x, y) this projection is defined as follows:

$$(x, y) | \mathbb{I}_{VP} \equiv \{(x_s, y_s) | (I_s \blacktriangleright O_s) \in \mathbb{I}_{VP}\}. \quad (2)$$

Semantics. Each alternative VP specifies a set of history pairs which are valid for at least one of its variants. Thereby, for the definition of the semantics, the syntactic interface must be taken into account. A history pair (x, y) defined over the interface $(I \blacktriangleright O)$ is valid if it fulfills the A/G specification of one of the variants with the same interface:

$$\begin{aligned} A_{VP}(x) &\equiv \exists s \in S_V : x \in \mathbb{H}(I_s) \wedge A_s(x) \\ G_{VP}(x, y) &\equiv \exists s \in S_V : (x, y) \in \mathbb{H}(I_s) \times \mathbb{H}(O_s) \wedge (A_s(x) \wedge G_s(x, y)). \end{aligned} \quad (3)$$

The assumption of a VP describes all input histories which are valid for at least one variant, in terms of sets: $\bigcup_{s \in S_V} \{x \in \mathbb{H}(I_s) \mid A_s(x)\}$. The guarantee of a VP describes all I/O history pairs which are valid for at least one variant, in terms of sets: $\bigcup_{s \in S_V} \{(x, y) \in \mathbb{H}(I_s) \times \mathbb{H}(O_s) \mid A_s(x) \wedge G_s(x, y)\}$. Note, according to Definition 1, the projection of a valid history pair of the compound service must fulfill the A/G of a VP if this VP is a sub-service of the compound service. According to Definition 2, the projection of a history pair to the interface of a VP yields a set of history pairs. Thereby, a set of projected history pairs satisfies the specification of a VP if at least one of the pairs fulfills this specification.

---

[2] By *configuration* we mean an instance of a product family specification where all variation points are resolved, i.e. certain variants are selected.

In our example, the speed control Speed is a VP comprising two alternative variants (Input and Save). The specification of Input is given in Section 2.1. The specification of Save differs in the way how the target speed is selected. The target speed is set to the current speed if the speed control is activated. More precisely, let Save be active (value 1 on port active) exactly in the interval $[t_1..t_2]$. Then, in the interval $[t_1+1..t_2+1]$, the target speed for the speed instruction on port speed is equal to the value on port currentSpeed in t_1. The corresponding A/G formulas are similar to those of Input and, therefore, not explicitly specified here. The VP Speed conjoins the behaviors of both variants. So, Speed defines the set of all valid history pairs that fulfills the A/G of Input or Save. The syntactical interface $\mathbb{I}_{Speed}$ is obtained according to the definition of the set-valued interface: $\{(\{currentSpeed, targetSpeed\} \blacktriangleright \{speed\}), (\{currentSpeed, active\} \blacktriangleright \{speed\})\}$. The A/G of Speed is easily derivable according to Definition 3, but due to space limitation not presented here.

Optional Service. Intuitively, an optional service s_o represents an alternative between the presence and the absence of this service within the Service Diagram. Consequently, it can be transferred into an alternative VP. This VP consists of two alternatives, namely the service s_o and *no service*. If the optional service is selected, a valid history must fulfill the requirements specified by the service s_o. If no service is selected, a valid history does not have to fulfill these requirements. Formally, no service is described by a special service s_Ω which has no ports ($I_{s_\Omega} \equiv O_{s_\Omega} \equiv \emptyset$) and is always fulfilled ($A_{s_\Omega}(x) \equiv G_{s_\Omega}(x,y) \equiv true$). Thus, s_Ω imposes no requirement on the I/O behavior of the system. Consequently, s_Ω acts as identity element concerning the aggregation relation, i.e. the aggregation of any service s and s_Ω results in s.

In our example, the service Follow-Up to control the speed based on the distance to a vehicle in front is optional. Thus, it can be transferred into a VP with syntactical interface $\mathbb{I} \equiv \{(\emptyset \blacktriangleright \emptyset), (I_{Follow-Up} \blacktriangleright O_{Follow-Up})\}$. According to Definition 3, this VP (i.e. the optional service Follow-Up) defines the set of history pairs (x,y) with either $(x,y) \in \mathbb{H}(\emptyset) \times \mathbb{H}(\emptyset)$ or $(x,y) \in \mathbb{H}(I_{Follow-Up}) \times \mathbb{H}(O_{Follow-Up})$ and (x,y) in accordance with the specification of Follow-Up.

2.4 Dependencies

By dependencies, we mean relations between services in a way that the behavior of one service influences the behavior of another one. As our approach aims at the specification of the user-visible behavior, only those dependencies are specified which are observable at the overall system boundaries. Dependencies between services can be explicitly given by functional requirements or they are introduced during the aggregation process to solve conflicts between services (see Section 3).

In the following, we introduce two kinds of dependency relations: *dependency predicates* and *dependency functions*. Dependency predicates formalize additional requirements on the I/O behavior and, thus, further restrict the set of valid I/O histories. Dependency functions, however, modify the user observable behavior of the influenced services without explicitly modifying their modular specifications. Having introduced these relations, we show how the behavior of a compound service composed of several sub-services is defined in consideration of the dependencies in-between. To simplify matters, we limit the following formal definitions to dependencies between two services. However, the extension to $m : n$ dependencies is straightforward.

Dependency Predicates. A dependency predicate describes further restrictions on the inputs or outputs of the services. Formally, a predicate between the services s_1 and s_2 specifies a relation between messages on I/O ports of s_1 and s_2 in certain time intervals:

$$dPr : \mathbb{H}(I_{s_1}) \times \mathbb{H}(O_{s_1}) \times \mathbb{H}(I_{s_2}) \times \mathbb{H}(O_{s_2}) \to \mathbb{B}ool.$$

Dependency Functions. A dependency function specifies a mapping from the original output histories (specified by the modular A/G specification) to new ones. This transformation of output histories greatly supports the modularity of our approach since single services can be specified without considering the interaction with other services. This is especially suitable in the context of product families where the context, i.e. the interaction with other services, may differ from variant to variant. Formally, a dependency function $dFct$ between an influencing service s_1 and an influenced service s_2 is a function of the form

$$dFct : \mathbb{H}(I_{s_1}) \times \mathbb{H}(O_{s_1}) \times \mathbb{H}(I_{s_2}) \times \mathbb{H}(O_{s_2}) \to \mathcal{P}(\mathbb{H}(O_{s_2})).$$

In our example, there is a dependency function between the services MCC and ACC. The application of the brake or accelerator (pedal or button) immediately deactivates the ACC. Whenever the MCC requires a nonempty speed instruction on port speed, the speed instruction calculated by the ACC is overwritten by those of MCC. This dependency is formalized as follows:

$$d(x_m, y_m, x_a, y_a) \equiv y'_a : \forall t \in \mathbb{N} : y_m[speed](t) = \varepsilon \Rightarrow y'_a[speed](t) = y_a[speed](t)$$
$$\wedge y_m[speed](t) \neq \varepsilon \Rightarrow y'_a[speed](t) = y_m[speed](t).$$

Analogously, a further dependency between ACC and MCC determines that empty speed instructions of MCC are overwritten by those of ACC. Furthermore, there is a dependency function between the services Pedal and Steering Wheel. This dependency resolves situations where the services require different instructions on the common port speed, e.g. when the driver simultaneously presses a pedal and a button. In this case the output history of Steering Wheel is modified, i.e. Pedal overrules Steering Wheel. Analogously, the Follow-Up control overrules the Speed control. The formalizations of these dependences are very similar to the foregoing one and therefore omitted here due to the limitation of space.

Aggregation with Dependency. For each kind of dependency relation, the behavior of the compound service s_C composed of two sub-services s_1 and s_2 and a dependency d in-between is defined in the following paragraphs.

If d specifies a dependency predicate between s_1 and s_2 which restricts the outputs of the services, the additional predicate must hold in the compound guarantee:

$$G(x,y) \equiv G_{s_1}(x_{s_1}, y_{s_1}) \wedge G_{s_2}(x_{s_2}, y_{s_2}) \wedge d(x_{s_1}, y_{s_1}, x_{s_2}, y_{s_2}). \quad (4)$$

If the dependency predicate affects the input histories, the compound assumption has to be modified analogously.

If d is a dependency function (s_1 influences s_2), the guarantee of the compound service is defined as:

$$G(x,y) \equiv \exists y' \in \mathbb{H}(O_{s_2}) : G_{s_1}(x_{s_1}, y_{s_1}) \wedge G_{s_2}(x_{s_2}, y') \\ \wedge y_{s_2} \in d(x_{s_1}, y_{s_1}, x_{s_2}, y'). \quad (5)$$

In the compound service the assumption and guarantee of the influencing service s_1 must hold. Additionally, there must exist an output history y' which fulfills the guarantee of s_2 and which is transformable to y_{s_2} by the dependency d.

Obviously, if the respective compound services are optional, the dependencies must only be considered if the services are selected. Regarding product family dependencies, the effects on the syntactical set-valued interface must be considered in addition to the effects on the behavior (see the following subsection).

Requires and Excludes Dependencies. Although there are a lot of methodological significant dependencies, here, we focus on typical dependencies for product families, namely *requires* and *excludes*. These dependencies specify that certain services must or must not be selected together in a configuration. Thereby, to select a service means that the valid I/O history pairs must fulfill the requirement formalized by this service. In the following, we introduce precise semantics of these relations by describing the corresponding dependency predicates.

A *requires* dependency between two alternative or optional services (t requires s) means that if t is selected in a configuration, s must be selected, too. Intuitively, a valid history is required to fulfill the requirement specified by the service s whenever it fulfills the requirement specified by t. Formally, a history pair (x,y) of the compound service is valid if its projections to the interfaces of the services t and s satisfy the condition $A_t(x_t) \wedge G_t(x_t, y_t) \Rightarrow A_s(x_s) \wedge G_s(x_s, y_s)$. However, this condition is only sufficient if the sets of valid histories specified by alternative services are disjunct. Otherwise, (x, y) – more precisely, respective projections of (x, y) – could fulfill the specification of more than one variant, e.g. t and t'. Since t' is allowed to be selected without s, a pair (x, y) which fulfills t and t', is valid even if s is not fulfilled. Thus, the correct meaning of *requires* is that all history pairs which *exclusively* fulfill the service t must fulfill the service s. Valid history pairs fulfilling t and another variant of the same VP do not necessarily have to fulfill s. Formally, the definition of t *requires* s is given by:

$$(\nexists t' \in V_T \setminus \{t\} : (x_{t'}, y_{t'}) \in \mathbb{H}(I_{t'}) \times \mathbb{H}(O_{t'}) \wedge A_{t'}(x_{t'}) \wedge G_{t'}(x_{t'}, y_{t'})) \\ \Rightarrow (A_s(x_s) \wedge G_s(x_s, y_s)), \quad (6)$$

where V_T denotes the set of all variants of the VP comprising t. This means, a valid history pair (x, y) that fulfills the A/G of no variant of V_T except for t must fulfill the A/G of s. Although, satisfying t is not explicitly required in this definition, it is implicitly given since any valid history pair must fulfill at least one of the variants according to Definition 3. Here, this variant can only be t.

The dependency t *excludes* s means that the services t and s are not allowed to be selected simultaneously, i.e. if the satisfaction of the service t is required (i.e. t is selected), the satisfaction of the service s must not be required. Since at least one of the alternatives of a VP must be fulfilled, this implies that the satisfaction of one of the other alternatives must be required. Formally, the definition of the dependency t *excludes* s is given by:

$$(\nexists t' \in V_T \setminus \{t\} : (x_{t'}, y_{t'}) \in \mathbb{H}(I_{t'}) \times \mathbb{H}(O_{t'}) \wedge A_{t'}(x_{t'}) \wedge G_{t'}(x_{t'}, y_{t'})) \Rightarrow \\ (\exists s' \in V_S \setminus \{s\} : (x_{s'}, y_{s'}) \in \mathbb{H}(I_{s'}) \times \mathbb{H}(O_{s'}) \wedge (A_{s'}(x_{s'}) \wedge G_{s'}(x_{s'}, y_{s'}))), \quad (7)$$

where V_T and V_S denote the sets of variants of the respective VPs. A valid history pair (x, y) that fulfills the A/Gs of no variant of V_T except for t must fulfill the A/G of a variant $s' \neq s$ of V_S.

Additionally to the behavior, the effects on the syntactical interface must be considered. The set-valued interface of a compound service only comprises interfaces which result from the aggregation including s_1 and s_2 or none of them if there is a *requires* dependency between them. If there is an *excludes* dependency between these services, the set-valued interface of their common compound service does not comprise the interfaces which originated from combinations including s_1 and s_2.

In our example, there is a *requires* dependency between Pre-Crash and Follow-Up which reflects technical prerequisites: the pre-crash control uses the sensors of the follow-up control, which are available in a vehicle only if the latter control is built in. Thus, their common compound service ACC defines a set of valid history pairs which obligatory satisfy Speed and fulfill Follow-Up if they fulfill Pre-Crash. Also, there is an *excludes* dependency between Steering Wheel and the variant Brake of the pre-crash control. If both services would be present in a configuration, there might be a conflict, e.g. if the pre-crash control demands the vehicle to slow down and, simultaneously, the driver presses the acceleration button. Hence, it was a marketing decision (non-functional requirement) to resolve this conflict by means of an *excludes* dependency. Consequently, if Steering Wheel is selected, Warning must be selected, too.

3 Consistency

The basic idea of our approach is that the overall specification is the combination of modularly specified sub-functionalities. Thereby, different services might be defined over the same I/O ports. Thus, the integration of different functions might cause unforeseen conflicts (known as *feature interaction*) and consequently lead to an inconsistent specification of the overall behavior. As a consequence, it becomes a central task during the functional integration to detect and resolve conflicts in order to assure the consistency of the overall specification. In the following sections, we precisely define what we mean by *conflicts* and show how the introduced formal concepts can be used to detect and to resolve conflicts between functional requirements. Regarding product families, we show how the compatibility of different variants can be analyzed.

3.1 Consistency of a Single System

A specification of a single product is *consistent* if there is no conflict neither between different modular services nor between services and dependencies. To allow tool-supported conflict detection and consistency checks we firstly introduce formal definitions of conflicts. Subsequently, we show how these conflicts can be detected and resolved.

Conflict Definitions. We differentiate two kinds of conflicts, namely input and output conflicts. There is an *input conflict* between aggregated services and/or dependencies if there is no history $h \in \mathbb{H}(I_{s_C})$ that fulfills the assumption of their common compound service s_C:

$$\{x \in \mathbb{H}(I_{s_C}) \mid A_{s_C}(x)\} = \emptyset. \tag{8}$$

An input conflict shows that the assumptions of the sub-services of s_C (and potential dependencies between them) are contradictory.

The follow-up control of our example (`Follow-Up`) is designed for city traffic and consequently only defined for target speeds between 40 and 80 km/h. The pre-crash control, however, is designed for motorway traffic, e.g. for target speed between 100 and 200 km/h. Then, the aggregations of these services results in an input conflict as there exists no input history which satisfies the assumptions of both services on their common input port `targetSpeed`.

Analogously, there is an *output conflict* between aggregated services and/or dependencies if the history set defined by the guarantee of their common compound service is empty for a valid input history:

$$\exists x \in \mathbb{H}(I_{s_C}) : A_{s_C}(x) \wedge \{y \in \mathbb{H}(O_{s_C}) \mid G_{s_C}(x, y)\} = \emptyset. \tag{9}$$

An output conflict indicates that the guarantees of the sub-services of s_C (and potential dependencies between them) are not satisfiable simultaneously for at least one valid input.

In our example, the services `MCC` and `ACC` are output-conflicting. There are input histories which cause contradictory output histories, e.g. an input history where the brake pedal is pressed in a time interval in which the current speed is lower than the target speed. In this case, the `MCC` demands the message `decelerate` on the output port `speed`, whereas the service `ACC` requires the message `accelerate` within the same time interval.

The conflicts captured by the introduced definitions can be further classified according to their causes. We differentiate *service-service conflicts*, *dependency-service conflicts*, and *dependency-dependency conflicts*. Thereby, the definitions of I/O conflicts remain the same but the common compound service s_C is obtained in different ways (cp. Definition 1, 4).

Note, there are no conflicts between a dependency function and the service influenced by it. Nevertheless, there might be conflicts between the influenced service and other services or dependency predicates. These conflicts are also covered by the definitions introduced above (cp. Definition 5).

Conflict Detection and Resolution. Obviously, two services are independently combinable if their sets of I/O ports are disjunct. Thus, methodically, we propose to start with an analysis of the syntactical interface to define the set of candidates for conflicting services. These services must be analyzed for service-service conflicts as described above. Subsequently, we take dependency predicates into consideration and check all affected services for dependency-service and dependency-dependency conflicts.

In order to get a consistent specification all detected conflicts have to be resolved. Therefor, we propose two methodical procedures. A conflict can be resolved by changing the modular specification of at least one of the affected services or dependencies respectively. In many cases, conflicts can be resolved easily by introducing nondeterminism in the modular specification. This resolution method is applicable to all kinds of conflicts. Moreover, changing the modular specification is the only way to solve input conflicts.

The input conflict between Follow-Up and Pre-Crash is solved by changing the modular specifications of both services. The assumption of both services is enlarged to target speed between 40 and 200 km/h. However, it is not further specified how the system reacts to the additional input histories, i.e. every output message is valid – both services are nondeterministic. This nondeterminism is resolved in the compound service ACC according to Definition 1.

For most of the output conflicts this procedure is not adequate since changing the modular specification accordingly to the behavior of another service implies a loss of modularity. Therefore, to resolve the source of output conflicts (namely, the service interaction) we propose to introduce additional dependency functions. A new dependency modifies the output histories in such a way that both interacting services always send the same message on the common ports. By this, we preserve the modularity of services and, furthermore, make functional dependencies explicit.

In our example, the output conflict between MCC and ACC is resolved by introducing the dependency function as described in Section 2.4. This dependency specifies that the service MCC overrules the service ACC, i.e. if conflicting the output of the service ACC is substituted by the output of the service MCC.

3.2 Consistency of a System Family

Next, we aim at ensuring the consistency of a product family. The specification of a product family is consistent if there is at least one consistent configuration of this family. In the following, we explain the meaning of conflicts between a service and a VP and sketch the methodology to analyze product families for conflicts.

Conflict Definitions. Obviously, I/O conflicts between services and a certain variant of a VP are covered by the same definitions as conflicts between services of a single product. Based on these definitions, there is no conflict between a service s and a VP comprising a set of variants V if no conflict is detected between s and any variant $v \in V$. Particularly, the service s and the VP are *independently combinable* if s and each variant $v \in V$ are independently combinable.

Conflict Detection and Resolution. In order to reduce the effort of the conflict detection we firstly analyze the syntactical interfaces. If s has no common port with the maximum interface of a VP[3], i.e. s has no common port with any variant of the VP, there is no conflict between s and any variant – no further analysis is necessary. Otherwise, a syntactical analysis of the single variants yields the variants which must be further analyzed (analogously to single services). To resolve conflicts we apply the already introduced procedures. Furthermore, we can eliminate conflicts by introducing *excludes* or *requires* dependencies.

To exemplify the procedure, we analyze the service Follow-Up and the VP Pre-Crash for output conflicts. An output conflict can not be excluded based on the syntactical analysis of the maximum interface of the VP. But the syntactical analysis of the single interfaces yields that Follow-Up and Warning have no common output port – they are independently combinable. Brake and Follow-Up use the common output port speed and a further analysis of their behaviors shows an output conflict between them. To resolve the conflict we introduce a dependency function which states that the service Brake has a higher priority. Note, that introducing an excludes dependency (Brake *excludes* Follow-Up) would also solve this output conflict, but would provoke a new dependency-dependency conflict because of the dependency Pre-Crash *requires* Follow-Up.

3.3 Tool Support

Thanks to the formal definitions of services, dependencies as well as conflicts, we can use a theorem prover (e.g. Isabelle [6]) to assure the consistency of a service specification. Thereby, all services (atomar as well as compound) are transformed into Isabelle functions. Then, for each compound service we have to prove two lemmata that claim that the sets of defined valid histories are not empty (negation of Definitions 8 and 9). However, the transformation to Isabelle is not scope of this paper – it is precisely addressed in [7].

4 Contributions

Having introduced the formal foundation of the underlying concepts in the previous sections, we shortly sketch the potential of our approach in the following.

Formalization of requirements. In contrast to pure informal approaches like FODA, we have introduced a formal model with a well-defined semantics for

---

[3] The maximum interface is the conjunction of the sets of all I/O ports of all variants.

specifying functionality. This has several advantages. Firstly, a formal model which formalizes (functional) requirements allows an analysis of the system already in the early phases of the development process. By this, discrepancies between conflicting requirements can be detected and resolved. Secondly, since implementation models will build upon this functional specification, it supports bridging the formal gap between functional requirements and design models. The Service Diagram provides formal specification of the functional requirements which can be used for a (tool-supported) verification of the subsequent design models.

Functional Variability. Furthermore, we have enlarged our approach to model whole families of related systems instead of single systems only. While traditional approaches mainly focus on structural aspects, we concentrated on the behavior and have precisely defined the behavioral meaning of variability. We especially focused on the consistency of the specification of a product family. By formally reasoning about the behavior conflicts between variants can be detected and resolved by introducing *excludes* and *requires* relations. By this, dependencies between variants which have not been realized during earlier engineering stages can be derived and made explicit.

5 Related Work

Formal Semantics. The definition of a formal semantics for feature models – the main method to formalize variability in product families – is not new. In [8], Batory and O'Malley use grammars to specify feature models. The formalization of feature models with propositional formulas goes back to the work by Mannion [9], in which logical expressions can be developed using propositional connectives to model dependencies between requirements. Further formal semantics are compared in [10]. Another approach to specifying multi-functional systems is introduced by van Lamsweerde et al in [11]. The main deficit of all these approaches is a disregard for the behavior of single features. Moreover, approaches like FODA only provide a two-valued notion of variability, i.e. a functionality might be present or not present in a system. "As a consequence, these approaches focus on the analysis of dependencies, however abstracting away from the causes for these dependencies" [12].

In [13], Czarnecki and Antkiewicz recognize that features in a feature model are "merely symbols". They propose an approach to mapping feature models to other models, such as behavior or data specifications, in order to give them semantics. However, this approach only focuses on assets like software components and architectures. Our approach, however, focuses on formalizing user requirements and their analysis in the early phases of the development process.

Our work is founded on a theoretical framework introduced by Broy [5] where the notion of a service behavior is formally defined. This framework provides several techniques to specify and to combine services based on their behaviors. However, this approach does not cover several relevant issues such as techniques for the specification of functional variability and of inter-service dependencies.

Feature Interaction. Using the formal foundation, a central task of our approach is to detect and resolve conflicts between single requirements (feature interaction) in order to assure the consistency of the overall specification. A large body of research [14] on feature interaction was caused by the the huge amount of software-based functions in telecommunication. The telecommunication-specific approaches to modeling feature interaction, like those by Jackson and Zave [15] or Braithwaite and Atlee [16], consider only telecommunication-specific features (functionality *additional* to the core body of software) and show how they can be combined in telecommunication systems. Thus, they are not directly applicable to other kinds of systems and for this reason can be barely compared to our work.

If we consider "feature" as a synonym of "function", we find further related work, e.g. approaches by Stepien and Logrippo [17] or Klein et al. [18]. All these approaches are comparable in the sense that they aim at explicit specification of feature behavior and at identifying feature interaction on the basis of behavior models. In our terminology, they look for interactions between services of a single product. However, they do not provide any means of variability.

To summarize, to the best of our knowledge, there is no approach to specify a product family, by formally describing the behavioral variability in requirements, and to detect conflicts between variants based on their behavioral specifications.

6 Conclusion and Future Work

In this paper, we have introduced and formally founded the underlying concepts of our service specification, which focuses on the modeling and structuring of functional requirements. Thereby, the concept of a service is used to model functional requirements in a modular fashion. In this paper, we especially concentrated on concepts to explicitly modeling inter-service dependencies. We have integrated the concept of behavioral variability which makes the Service Diagram suitable to formally capture functional requirements of a system family.

The formal specification of the functional requirements, their dependencies, and the behavioral variability already at an early stage of the development process allows to perform a formal (and therefore tool-supported) analysis of the functional requirements for conflicts. Since ensuring the consistency of the specification is one of the main goals of our approach, we have precisely defined the meaning of conflicts in the Service Diagram. Furthermore, we have described the detection and resolution of conflicts from a methodological point of view. Regarding product families, we have shown how the compatibility of different variants can be analyzed.

Since the effort to perform consistency checks separately for all possible combinations of variants grows exponentially, we are currently working on concepts to reduce the effort of consistency checks by extracting commonalities between variants. Beyond this, our future work includes the development of a user-friendly syntax for the semantics introduced in this paper and the transition from the Service Diagram to the consecutive design models.

References

1. Kang, K., Cohen, S., Hess, J., Novak, W., Peterson, A.: Feature-oriented domain analysis (FODA) feasibility study. Technical report, SEI, CMU, Pittsburgh (1990)
2. Gruler, A., Harhurin, A., Hartmann, J.: Modeling the functionality of multifunctional software systems. In: Proceedings of ECBS 2007 (2007)
3. Gruler, A., Harhurin, A., Hartmann, J.: Development and configuration of service-based product lines. In: Proceedings of SPLC 2007 (2007)
4. Harhurin, A., Hartmann, J.: A Formal Approach to Specifying the Functionality of Software System Families. Technical report, Technische Universität München (2007), http://www.in.tum.de/forschung/pub/reports/2007/TUM-I0720.pdf.gz
5. Broy, M.: Service-oriented systems engineering: Modeling services and layered architectures. In: FORTE, pp. 48–61 (2003)
6. Nipkow, T., Paulson, L.C., Wenzel, M.: Isabelle/HOL. LNCS, vol. 2283. Springer, Heidelberg (2002)
7. Spichkova, M.: Specification and Seamless Verification of Embedded Real-Time Systems: FOCUS on Isabelle. PhD thesis, Technische Universität München (2007)
8. Batory, D., O'Malley, S.: The design and implementation of hierarchical software systems with reusable components. ACM Trans. Softw. Eng. Methodol. 1 (1992)
9. Mannion, M.: Using first-order logic for product line model validation. In: SPLC, pp. 176–187 (2002)
10. Trigaux, J.-C., Heymans, P., Schobbens, P.-Y., Classen, A.: Comparative semantics of feature diagrams: Ffd vs. vdfd. CERE 0, 36–47 (2006)
11. van Lamsweerde, A., Letier, E., Darimont, R.: Managing conflicts in goal-driven requirements engineering. IEEE Trans. Softw. Eng. 24, 908–926 (1998)
12. Schätz, B.: Combining product lines and model-based development. In: Proceedings of Formal Aspects of Component Systems (FACS 2006) (2006)
13. Czarnecki, K., Antkiewicz, M.: Mapping features to models: A template approach based on superimposed variants. In: GPCE, pp. 422–437 (2005)
14. Calder, M., Kolberg, M., Magill, E.H., Reiff-Marganiec, S.: Feature interaction: a critical review and considered forecast. Comput. Networks 41, 115–141 (2003)
15. Jackson, M., Zave, P.: Distributed feature composition: A virtual architecture for telecommunications services. IEEE Trans. Softw. Eng. 24, 831–847 (1998)
16. Braithwaite, K.H., Atlee, J.M.: Towards automated detection of feature interactions. In: FIW, pp. 36–59 (1994)
17. Stepien, B., Logrippo, L.: Representing and verifying intentions in telephony features using abstract data types. In: FIW, pp. 141–155 (1995)
18. Klein, C., Prehofer, C., Rumpe, B.: Feature Specification and Refinement with State Transition Diagrams. In: Fourth IEEE Workshop on Feature Interactions in Telecommunications Networks and Distributed Systems (1997)

Formal Methods for Trustworthy Skies: Building Confidence in the Security of Aircraft Assets Distribution

Scott Lintelman, Richard Robinson, Mingyan Li, and Krishna Sampigethaya

Boeing Phantom Works, Bellevue, WA, USA
{scott.a.lintelman,richard.v.robinson,
mingyan.li,radhakrishna.g.sampigethaya}@boeing.com

Abstract. A recent application in commercial aviation is the electronic distribution of loadable software parts and data. Its safe and beneficial use, however, warrants that information security vulnerabilities are analyzed and mitigated at an adequate assurance level. In our prior work, we have identified security threats and assurance requirements for a generic aircraft asset distribution system or AADS. In this paper, we focus on supporting analytical processes to address security vulnerabilities as well as describing our experiences in applying formal methods to AADS.

Keywords: Loadable Software Parts, Safety, Security, Formal Methods.

1 High Assurance for eEnabled Aircraft Assets

Today, commercial aviation is experiencing a revolutionary trend with technological innovations in aircraft manufacturing, operation and maintenance. A resulting concept is the *eEnabled aircraft* that can connect to ground infrastructure via shared networks and use commercial-off-the-shelf (COTS) solutions for onboard components. The benefits of the eEnabled aircraft are significant. A pivotal concern, however, is the impact of information security vulnerabilities from unprecedented features, such as network applications distributing aircraft assets as well as highly integrated COTS hardware/software impacting aircraft operation. Regulatory institutions world-wide have recognized that existing guidance for certification and continued airworthiness must be updated to cover the emerging threats to flight safety and proper functioning of eEnabled aircraft systems [1].

Our research focuses on vulnerabilities in the electronic distribution of eEnabled aircraft information assets, specifically loadable software parts and onboard generated data. We consider a generic model of the large and complex electronic distribution system, referred to as Aircraft Asset Distribution System (AADS), that involves multiple entities with different roles, including avionics suppliers, airframe manufacturer, airline and aircraft [3,4]. The objective of the AADS is to deliver software and data from the original source to the end-destination, referred as the end-to-end distribution.

Our proposed work expresses the need for highly assuring the end-to-end security properties of the AADS based on the following. The safety-critical value of loadable avionics software is established by regulatory guidance mandating classification of such software according to the levels defined in Radio Technical Commission for

Aeronautics (RTCA) DO-178B, along with process controls for assuring that software is correct and complete. Suppliers are required to demonstrate that safety-related loadable software are designed, developed and produced in accordance with the guidance in DO-178B. However, if aircrafts are not able to verify that received software is from the correct source (authenticity) and that the software has not been tampered (integrity), the aviation industry's significant investment in assured software development processes and practices is to some degree devalued. Similarly, the potential safety impact of onboard data, such as health diagnostics and aircraft configuration reports, warrants that they be secured at an adequate assurance level.

Loadable software safety standards are being revised in RTCA/DO-178C to provide guidelines for a formal method based software vulnerability analysis. However, no standardized efforts or guidelines exist to evaluate and mitigate at a high assurance level potential vulnerabilities in the end-to-end distribution of loadable software/data.

2 Securing Electronic Distribution of Aircraft Assets by AADS

Recently, the need to assure authenticity and integrity of aircraft software has been recognized by the FAA and quantified by Aeronautical Radio, Inc. (ARINC), the internationally recognized standardization body responsible for defining interoperability standards for aviation software. ARINC is currently in the process of defining interoperable software part format standards that explicitly include the use of cryptographic signature as the mechanism for assuring parts. However, the mere application of signatures to data does not in itself provide any degree of assurance. To be effective, signature capabilities must be employed within process contexts and application environments that support the required degree of assurance.

Based on the Common Criteria (CC) [2] standard methodology, we have established a security framework to identify threats, requirements and mitigation controls for the AADS. The complete assurance requirements for AADS was developed and documented in the form of a CC Protection Profile [4]. The CC approach was selected because it is the accepted international standard for defining protection needs, security functional requirements, assurance requirements and evaluating product security. For critical systems that call for high assurance levels (EAL 6 and above), the CC require a very rigorous evaluation approach including the use of formal methods.

3 Relevant AADS Challenges for Formal Methods

In developing and deploying an instance of the AADS, we have encountered the following challenges pertinent to the use of Formal Methods (FM).

Lack of regulatory guidance on software development for ground systems. A well established standard, i.e., DO-178B, exists for the development of loadable avionics software, making it possible for integration of formal methods in software specification, design and verification in the upcoming revision of the standard (DO-178C). However, no such guidance is currently available for development of ground systems such as AADS that distributes avionics software from suppliers to aircraft.

Specification of consistent and complete security requirements. Establishment of requirements is the first step towards rigorous system design and assessment. As the AADS is a globally distributed system that involves multiple stakeholders, establishment of adequate security requirements for AADS among multiple entities is a significant challenge. Similarly, establishment of an agreeable level of assurance for determining the formalization level for AADS is also a major challenge.

AADS cost constraints. Another major obstacle is balancing security evaluation effort with assurance needs. While the use of formal methods for rigorous evaluation of components distributing safety-critical parts can significantly increase the confidence in the security of the AADS, it can significantly increase its development costs. These costs can be reduced by developing an architecture that confines the formal analysis to the critical AADS components.

Integration of FM into AADS design and development. It is ideal to incorporate FM into AADS design and development process so we have high confidence in the correctness of the implemented algorithms and protocols. However, there are factors preventing the use of FM in software requirement specification, design and debug, including a lack of understanding on benefits versus cost of FM, a dearth of user-friendly tools for formal modeling and analysis [5], and limited expertise on FM.

Tradeoff between full formalization and light weight FM. AADS is a complex and large scale distributed system. Full formalization of such a system provides completeness and rigor to the analysis, but on the other hand can be overwhelming, time consuming and expensive. Comparatively, lightweight FM, which focuses on partial specification and abstracts away details, is more economically feasible. Therefore, we adopt a light weight FM in our current verification process.

4 Towards Establishing Confidence in the Security of AADS

Our objectives are manifold: Define security requirements necessary to support an appropriate degree of confidence that the assurance of high-value software assets is maintained. Inform the processes for design, development, and deployment of a concrete AADS implementation. Establish a set of processes, corresponding to the "development assurance" recommendations of the DO-178B, that may be recommended to aviation industry stakeholders (namely, avionics suppliers, airframe manufacturers, airlines) to assure that the authenticity and integrity of information assets is preserved during distribution and storage and throughout their post-development life-cycles.

Development of the AADS assurance requirements specification in the CC Protection Profile was accomplished by an analysis of the threats and vulnerabilities to which software assets may be exposed, and validated through a series of interviews and dialogues with a community of software architects and system designers. With the requirements in hand, we prepared a proposal to pursue assessment and evaluation of the implementation architecture and concrete distribution applications under development. Reception to our proposals proved lukewarm, at best. Many questions were raised regarding the need for assessment exercises and the nature and value of formally modeling a software part distribution system. Customers pointed out that existing regulatory guidance for aircraft certification and operational approval carries neither provisions nor requirements for assessment of the kind we proposed.

Overall, we found it very challenging to communicate the need for assessment, and in particular to express the value of developing a formal model of the distribution system for use in performing a model-checking based analysis. In response to the skepticism which met our original proposals, we determined to conduct a small scale case study to demonstrate the value of exploiting formal methods in our business context. We identified a single, discrete component necessary to the end-to-end airplane asset distribution topology, namely the protocol by which an airplane's unique identity is established and initialized.

In the AADS, the aircraft's identity and public key are carried in a certificate which may be validated by ground-based systems to confirm the authenticity of aircraft-generated data. We introduced a protocol for initializing such a certificate, describing the basic protocol and several protection variants. Our analysis provided an informal discussion as well as a precise formal description, pointing out the differences in security properties of the variants. Finally, we documented the results of model-checking our formalizations using the public-domain Automated Validation of Internet Security Protocols and Applications (AVISPA) protocol validation tool.

We were able to make use of the results of our analysis in business and engineering venues, as a concrete example for explaining how we can model, analyze, and discuss the design of critical IT systems and applications. Through this example, we were able to show that our methodology is helpful for exploring requirements and design alternatives, bringing up important issues, for instance making explicit the assumptions and conditions on IT administration and maintenance to be met by the system environment, and giving evidence whether the system architecture meets desired security goals. The analysis provided a concrete example of modeling and analyzing a key component of the security infrastructure needed to support eEnabled aircraft, to verify its security properties. We were able to show unambiguously that a number of non-obvious details may be easily overlooked unless one analyzes variants in a rigorous formal way. Our analysis, as limited and focused as it was, provided definitive evidence that some designs do not afford adequate protection and thus materially influenced the design of the final system.

Our documentation and presentations of these analytical results was received very positively by our business partners. Interviews conducted with architects and developers provided concrete value to our interviewees, giving them an appreciation for the full range of design alternatives available. Demonstrations to management showing how model development and model checking are performed for a real problem effectively communicated the utility of our methodology, the value added by application of FM, and the reasonable level of cost incurred in the context of the importance of the subject software system. We showed that it is possible for formal methods to be understood, if not directly utilized, by system designers, software architects, and management. We have demonstrated to our customers that the value and benefits of modeling go beyond the assurance assessment objective, *per se*, to add concrete value to our organization's software products.

5 Open Problems

Formal methods have the potential for building confidence in the security of a large scale distributed system such as AADS. However, we have not applied FM in its full form into the specification, design, development, and verification of AADS. An open issue is the lack of visual representations of FM with transparent analysis to facilitate the communication of FM benefits to business management. Further, to enable practical use of FM, we need a specification language that is accessible to software architects/developers without substantial training. Such a language, ideally, should be easy for customers to understand so they can contribute to the formal specification. Furthermore, a user-friendly, automatic FM analysis tool that can handle complex systems and generate reliable feedback is needed. Another open research problem is in addressing the complexity and cost issues, such as composing partial formal specification and verification while retaining consistency/correctness.

References

1. Federal Aviation Administration, 14 CFR Part 25, Special Conditions: Boeing Model 787-8 Airplane; Systems and Data Networks Security—Isolation or Protection from Unauthorized Passenger Domain Systems Access, [Docket No. NM365 Special Conditions No. 25-357-SC], Federal Register, Vol 72(248) (2007), http://edocket.access.gpo.gov/2007/pdf/E7-25075.pdf
2. Common Criteria. Version 3.1 (2006), http://www.commoncriteriaportal.org/
3. Robinson, R., Li, M., Lintelman, S., Sampigethaya, K., Poovendran, R., von Oheimb, D., Bußer, J., Cuellar, J.: Electronic Distribution of Airplane Software and the Impact of Information Security on Airplane Safety. In: Reliability and Security (SAFECOMP) (2007)
4. Robinson, R., von Oheimb, D., Li, M., Sampigethaya, K., Poovendran, R.: Security Specification for Distribution and Storage of Airplane-Loadable Software and Airplane-Generated Data, Protection Profile. Available upon request (2006)
5. Heitmeyer, C.: On the Need of Practical Formal Method. In: proc. of the 5th International Symposium on Formal Techniques in Real-Time and Fault-Tolerant Systems (1998)

An Industrial Case: Pitfalls and Benefits of Applying Formal Methods to the Development of a Network-Centric RTOS

Eric Verhulst, Gjalt de Jong, and Vitaliy Mezhuyev

Open License Society, Leuven, Belgium
{eric.verhulst,gjalt.dejong,
vitaliy.mezhuyev}@OpenLicenseSociety.org

Abstract. This paper describes a project to develop a network-centric RTOS from scratch using formal methods. The (initial) purposes of the project was to get acquainted with the use of formal methods for software engineering and to obtain a trustworthy RTOS as a component for building networked embedded systems. The work was done by a small, distributed team that had no prior experience on using formal methods and with a small budget. The outcome is that the use of formal methods is most useful as an architectural design method, perhaps more than as a formal verification of software code. The resulting software has many properties that were not anticipated at the beginning and would likely not have been achieved without the use of Formal Methods.

Keywords: RTOS, Formal Methods, Trustworthy, Safety, Security, Network centric.

1 Problem Statement

Real-Time Operating Systems are an essential component in most embedded systems. They are essential when the application becomes complex and safety critical. They provide a way to organize the application in a set of modules that interact, the scheduler helps in achieving predictable real-time behavior, and they allow to recover from run-time error conditions.

Nevertheless, almost none of the commercial and open-source RTOS-es have been certified according to standards like IEC61508 or DO178. Almost none have been formally verified. Part of the reason is historical: RTOSes are fairly complex and highly concurrent pieces of software that in addition must provide good performance with as little as possible resources. Hence, RTOSes are often developed by very skilled software engineers, but often following a bottom-up approach with little documentation, preventing even certification.

Open License Society undertook the OpenComRTOS project in 2004 with the aim to develop a novel network-centric RTOS. Formal methods were used from the start with much effort going into finding the right architecture and being able to verify that the software is correct.

We also noted related work by Iain D. Craig [11,12] when this project was finished. This work is however rather different. It is mainly concerned with the formal specification and refinement of existing Operating Systems. The author shows that this is viable. Our work has indicated that formal methods provide serious benefits as well when used for designing new architectures from the very beginning, even for non-trivial pieces of software like an RTOS. As a result, formal verification of the final architecture is also a lot more straightforward because it results in a much cleaner architecture.

2 Systems (and Software) Engineering Approach

The Systems Engineering approach developed by Open License Society is a classical one as defined in [4] but adapted to the needs of embedded software development. It is an evolutionary iterative process. In such a process, much attention is paid to an incremental development requiring regular review meetings by several of the stakeholders. On the architectural level, the system or product under development is defined under the paradigm of "Interacting Entities", which maps very well on an RTOS based runtime system. When programming with an RTOS, the application is split over a number of concurrent entities called "Tasks", scheduled in time by the RTOS scheduler. They "interact" through RTOS services, essentially points of synchronization but with a service specific semantic behaviour. In OpenComRTOS these services decouple the tasks completely from each other. Applied on the development of OpenComRTOS, the process was started by elaborating a first set of requirements and specifications. Next an initial architecture was defined. Starting from this point on, two groups started to work in parallel. The first group worked out an architectural model while a second group developed an initial formal model using TLA+/TLC [2]. This model was incrementally refined until the formal model was deemed close enough to the implementation architecture. Next, a simulation model was developed on a PC (using Windows NT as a virtual target). This code was then ported to a real 16bit microcontroller [5]. On this target a few target specific optimizations were performed on the implementation, while fully maintaining the design and architecture. The software was written in ANSI C and verified with a MISRA

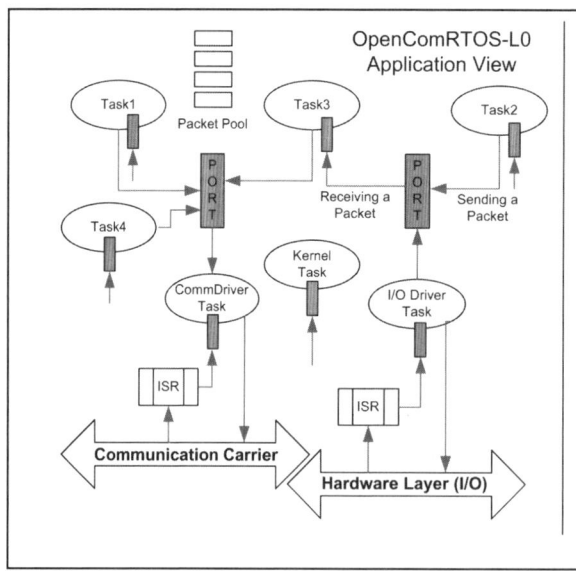

Fig. 1. OpenComRTOS-L0 view

rule checker. [8] Finally the reverse process was undertaken. For each service class a formal model was built matching the implementation and essential properties were verified.

3 Lessons from Using Formal Modeling

3.1 Selecting a Methodology

Formal techniques basically fall into two categories. First we have model checkers: a model of the software is constructed at an abstract level and the model checker will basically verify that specified properties are never violated and if they are a trace of a counter-example will be provided. A second class of formal techniques are so-called proofing systems. They allow to proof by deduction and aided by a computing machine that a certain property holds. Given that the project started with a clean slate and the strong architectural nature of the project we opted to use a model checker. A first observation is that while there are many tools and methods available, most of them are based on the same principles. However, many of the tools we found are academic and suffer from lack of robustness, performance or ease of use, clearly indicating that this is still an emerging discipline. Also when used by commercial vendors, the formal tools are often hidden and do their work in the background. This obliterates the need to be mathematical proficient and user can stay in the problem domain, instead of the math solution domain, but no such integration was found that applied to our project.

While we had an initial bias toward using SPIN [7], in the end it was decided to use TLA/TLC from Leslie Lamport. [2] Although the mathematical notation of the TLA language was first considered a hindrance versus the C-like Promela language of SPIN. In the end this has proven to be a major benefit as it forced to reason in a much more abstract way about the RTOS.

3.2 Why Are There No Errors?

The initial goal of using formal techniques was to be able to prove that the software is correct. This is an often heard statement from the formal techniques community. A first surprise was that each model gave no errors when verified by the TLC model checker. This was due to the iterative nature of the model development process and partly its strength. From an initial rather abstract model, successive models were developed by checking them using the model checker and hence each model is correct when the model checker finds no illegal states. As such, model checkers can't proof that the software is correct. They can only proof that the formal model is correct. For a complete proof of the software the whole programming chain as well as the target hardware should be modeled and verified as well. In the ideal case, the software should even be generated from the formal models. This is today an unachievable result due to its complexity and the resulting state space explosion. The model itself would be many times larger than the software being developed. It indicates however that if we would make use of verified target processors and verified programming language compilers, the model checker becomes practical as limited to modeling the application.

Other issues were discovered in relation to the use of formal modeling. E.g. the TLC model checker declares every action as a critical section, whereas e.g. in the case of a RTOS, many components operate concurrently and real-time performance dictates that on a real target the critical sections are kept as short as possible. While this dictates the avoidance of shared data structures, it would be helpful to have formal model assistance that indicates the required critical sections.

Nevertheless, a major benefit of using the model checker has proven to be its abstraction. The models developed in the beginning of the project had to be discarded after it was clear that they reflected how a programmer would write the software, often by unconsciously taken implementation decisions, resulting in unnecessary complexity. Once this was understood, (re)developing the models was much more straightforward.

The final issue is the well known problem of state space explosion. Just modeling a small OpenComRTOS application, the TLC model checkers has to examine a few million states, exponentially taking more time for every task added to the model. This also requires increasing amounts of memory and limits the model checking to subsets of the whole architecture. However, this was not a real issue as the architecture is generic and based on a message passing protocol that is independent of the size of the system. The algorithmic logic of the RTOS kernel also makes no difference between local or remote services, making it independent of the topology of the target network and hence there was no need to make the network topology explicit.

4 A Thin Boundary between Past Experience, Creativity and Model Checking

For completeness, we need to mention that some of the elements of the OpenComRTOS architecture were inherited from a previous distributed RTOS (Virtuoso [4]) that was developed in a traditional way, and with some inspiration from CSP. The communication layer of this distributed RTOS used packets but the kernel was a large jump table. We had also experienced issues with portability and scalability. Finally, the third generation of the Virtuoso RTOS was loosing performance through what we can call "feature bloating". Nevertheless, it was difficult to see how a better architecture could be found that would at the same time provide improvements in terms of code size, safety, security and scalability properties. In addition we defined as objective that it should be able to run from memory restricted multi-core CPUs to widely distributed processing nodes running legacy software.

Formal modeling has helped a lot in formalizing the problem and as a result we can claim success beyond initial expectations.

5 Novelties in the Architecture

OpenComRTOS has a semantically layered architecture. At the lowest level (L0) the minimum set of entities provides everything that is needed to build a small networked real-time application.

The entities needed are **Tasks** (having a private function and workspace) and an interaction entity we called an L0_Port to synchronize and communicate between the

Tasks. **Ports** act like channels in the tradition of Hoare's CSP but allow multiple waiters and asynchronous communication. One of the tasks is a kernel task scheduling the tasks in order of priority and managing and providing services. Driver tasks handle inter-node communication. Pre-allocated as well as dynamically allocated packets are used as a carrier for all activities in the RTOS such as: service requests to the kernel, synchronization, data-communication, etc. Each Packet has a fixed size header and data payload with a user defined but global data size. This significantly simplifies the management of the Packets, in particular at the communication layer. A router function also transparently forwards packets in order of priority between the nodes in a network.

OpenComRTOS L0 therefore is a distributed, scalable and network-centric operating systems consisting of a packet-switching communication layer with a scheduler and port-based synchronization. This architecture has proven to be very efficient.

In the next semantic level (L1) services and entities were added as found in most RTOS:

Boolean events, counting semaphores, FIFO queues, resources, memory pools, mailboxes, etc. The formal modeling has allowed defining all such entities as semantic variants of a common and generic entity type. We called this generic entity a "**Hub**". In addition, the formal modeling also helped to define "clean" semantics for such services whereas ad-hoc implementations often have side-effects.

As the use of a single generic entity allowed a much greater reuse of code, the resulting code size is about 10 times less than for an RTOS with a more traditional architecture. One could of course remove all such application-oriented services and just use the Hub based services. This has however the drawback that the services loose their specific semantic richness. E.g. resource locking clearly expresses that the task enters a critical section in competition with other tasks. Also erroneous runtime conditions like raising an event twice (with loss of the previous event) are easier to detect at the application level than when using a generic Hub.

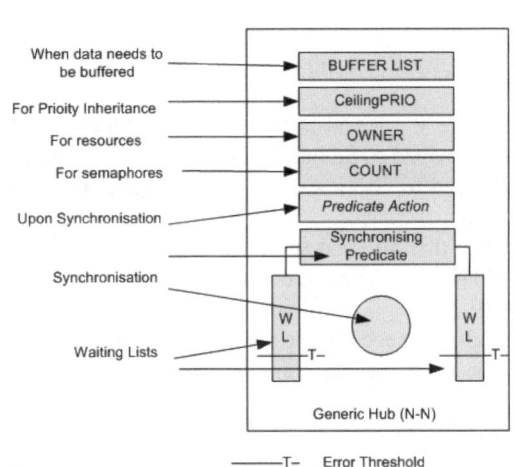

Fig. 2. L1 RTOS generic Hub

An unexpected side-effect of the use of Hub entities is that the set of services can be expanded independently of the kernel itself. A Hub is a generic synchronization entity and the Hub semantics are determined by the synchronization predicate and by the predicate action following successful synchronization. The result is not only that the RTOS can be made application specific, it also provides better performance and more safety as most of the services and the driver code execute in the application domain, leaving the essential RTOS functions to a small kernel function.

In the course of the formal modeling we also discovered weaknesses in the traditional way priority inheritance is implemented in most RTOS and we found a way to reduce the total blocking time. In single processor RTOS systems, this is less of an issue but in multi-processor systems, all nodes can originate service requests and resource locking is a distributed service. Hence the waiting lists can grow much longer and lower priority tasks can block higher priority ones while waiting for the resource. This was solved by postponing the resource assignment till the rescheduling moment.

Finally, by generalization, also memory allocation has been approached like a resource locking service. In combination with the Packet Pool, this opens new possibilities for a safe and secure management of memory. E.g. the OpenComRTOS architecture is free from buffer overflow by design. We shortly summarize the results obtained on a real processing target. Although fully written in ANSI-C (except for the task context switch), the kernel could be reduced to less than 1 Kbytes single processor and 2 Kbytes with multi-processor support (measured on a 16bit Melexis microcontroller). A sample application with two tasks and one Port required just 1230 bytes of program memory and 226 bytes of data memory (static and dynamic). More information is available in [4].

6 Formal Verification

This project would have been incomplete if we had not attempted a formal verification of the source code. In the end this proved to be quite straightforward because the orthogonal and clean architecture allowed to check each service using a similar pattern. Following issues however must be mentioned:

- We did not find tools and methods that allowed to verify our asynchronous and concurrent design (inevitable for a RTOS) at the source code level. Tools only exist for static and synchronous programs [9,10]

- It was practically impossible but also unnecessary to verify the kernel as a whole. Hence we verified the algorithms for each service class independently. Given the orthogonality of protocol based architecture (by using packets), this is sufficient.

- The hardest part remained to find all properties to check for. A lot of these properties look rather trivial at first sight and our human brain has a tendency to overlook them.

- The final issue is related to the programming in C itself. It is clear that this language is a major source of errors. Hence, some errors were found at the programming level that no formal verification would ever find.

- However, the fact that the formal modeling helped a lot in achieving such a clean and orthogonal architecture, verification as well as at the abstract level by using a formal model checker as well as at the language level was a lot easier, because the complexity is minimized and the code size is much smaller than comparable hand written code.

7 Future Developments and Research

Above we already identified the need for the model checkers to detect the minimal critical sections. Another area of research is how to maintain consistency between the formal model and the implementation. This will require that the formal model can be used as a reference and requires that the source is generated rather than written by the software engineer.

Future OpenComRTOS developments will focus on adding more safety and security properties to a SW/HW co-design pair of OpenComRTOS and processor. Formal modeling should contribute in identifying minimum architectures that still are providing safety and security in the resource constrained domain of deeply embedded systems.

Another area of interest is to find a better way to separate orthogonally the priority based scheduling from the logical behavior of the kernel entities. E.g. the use of priority inheritance support results in this code being mixed up in the manipulation of the data structures (e.g. to sort waiting lists). This makes the code more convoluted to read and understand while the impact is only on the timely behavior of the application.

8 Conclusion

The OpenComRTOS project has shown that even for software domains often associated with 'black art' programming, formal modeling works very well. The resulting software is not only very robust and maintainable but also very performing in size and timings and inherently safer than standard implementation architectures. Its use however must be integrated with a global systems engineering approach as the process of incremental development and modeling is as important as using the formal model checker itself and resulting in many improvements of the RTOS properties.

It can not be emphasized enough how many problems in the software world can be avoided by a systematic use from the very beginning.

Acknowledgements

The OpenComRTOS project received funding as an IWT project for the Flemish Government in Belgium. The formal modeling activities are provided by the University of Gent. Melexis was industrial sponsor.

References

1. OpenComRTOS architectural design document on, http://www.OpenLicenseSociety.org
2. TLA+/TLC home page on, http://research.microsoft.com/users/lamport
3. INCOSE, http://www.incose.org
4. http://www.OpenLicenseSociety.org
5. http://www.Melexis.com
6. http://www.verisoft.de

7. http://www.spin.org
8. http://www.misra.org
9. Blanchet, B., Cousot, P., Cousot, R., Feret, J., Mauborgne, L., Miné, A., Monniaux, D., Rival, X.: Design and Implementation of a Special-Purpose Static Program Analyzer for Safety-Critical Real-Time Embedded Software. In: Mogensen, T.Æ., Schmidt, D.A., Sudborough, I.H. (eds.) The Essence of Computation. LNCS, vol. 2566, pp. 85–108. Springer, Heidelberg (2002), http://www.astree.ens.fr/
10. Edmund, C., Daniel, K., Flavio, L.: A Tool for Checking ANSI-C Programs. In: Jensen, K., Podelski, A. (eds.) TACAS 2004. LNCS, vol. 2988, pp. 168–176. Springer, Heidelberg (2004), http://www.cprover.org/cbmc/
11. Craig, I.D.: Formal Models of Operating System Kernels. Springer, Heidelberg (2007)
12. Craig, I.D.: Formal Refinement for Operating System Kernels. Springer, Heidelberg (2007)

Software Engineering with Formal Methods: Experiences with the Development of a Storm Surge Barrier Control System

Klaas Wijbrans[1], Franc Buve[2], Robin Rijkers[2], and Wouter Geurts[2]

[1] Acision, Merweplein 5, 3432GN Nieuwegein
klaas.wijbrans@acision.com
[2] Logica, PO Box 8566, 3009 AN Rotterdam
franc.buve@logica.com, robin.rijkers@logica.com,
wouter.geurts@logica.com

Abstract. This paper revisits the experiences with the use of formal methods in the development of the control system for the *Maeslant Kering*. The *Maeslant Kering* is the movable barrier which has to protect Rotterdam from floodings while, at almost the same time, not restricting shipping traffic to the port of Rotterdam. The control system, called BOS, completely autonomously decides about closing and opening of the barrier and, when necessary, also performs these tasks without human intervention. BOS is a safety-critical software system of the highest Safety Integrity Level according to the IEC 61508 standard. One of the reliability increasing techniques used during its development is *formal methods*. This paper revisits the earlier published experiences with the project after the system is in operation for ten years and has performed its first autonomous barrier operation on November 11th, 2007.

Introduction

BOS is the software system which controls and operates the storm surge barrier in the Nieuwe Waterweg near Rotterdam (figure 1). It is a complex, safety-critical system of medium size, which was developed by CMG Den Haag B.V.[1], commissioned by Rijkswaterstaat (RWS) – the Dutch Ministry of Transport, Public Works and Water Management. The project completed in May 1997 and the system was officially commissioned in October 1998 on time and within budget. CMG used formal methods in the development of the BOS software in addition to a number of other techniques recommended in the IEC 61508 standard [1]. The experiences with formal methods and other techniques were published during and after the project in a number of publications [2][3][4][5][6].

The storm surge barrier control system has been in operation since October 1997 and is each year active during the storm season (the summer period is used for

---

[1] CMG Den Haag BV in 2003 merged with Logica. Acision is the result of the sale of the LogicaCMG Telecoms Products division to private equity.

maintenance on the barrier). In its operational life, there has been a test closing of the barrier each year. On November 11th, 2007 the barrier closed successfully on its own because of a combination of high tide and storm for the first time.

The Barrier and the BOS System

The history of The Netherlands has been shaped by the struggle against the sea. The great flood disaster of 1953 in Zeeland was a rude shock to the Netherlands, demonstrating yet again that the country was vulnerable. It was shortly after this flood that the Delta Plan was drafted, with measures to prevent such calamities from occurring in the future. This Delta Plan involved building a network of dams in Zeeland and upgrading the existing dikes to a failure rate of 10^{-4}, i.e., one flooding every 10,000 years. The realization of the Delta Plan started soon after 1953 and in 1986 the impressive dam network in Zeeland was finished. The weak point in the defence was now the Nieuwe Waterweg, an important shipping route for Rotterdam and the outlet for the Rhine. Being completely open, it is a major risk for flooding of Rotterdam. To protect Rotterdam from flooding a storm surge barrier in the Nieuwe Waterweg was constructed near Hoek van Holland: the *Maeslant Kering*. The geographic map and an impression of the barrier are depicted in the Figures below.

The barrier consists of two hollow floating walls, called sector doors, connected with steel arms to pivot points on both banks. Each of these is as large as the Eiffel Tower. During normal weather conditions the two sector doors rest in their docks. Only when storms are expected with danger of flooding the two sector doors are closed. For more information, we refer to the internet-site of the Dutch Ministry of Transport, Public Works and Water Management about the Delta works where an animation of the moving barrier is provided, see [7].

The main requirement on the barrier is that it must be as reliable as a dike. Careful failure analysis showed that manual control of this barrier would undermine the reliability. Therefore it was considered to be safer to let a computer control the barrier. The control system that decides about opening and closing of the barrier and that also completely autonomously performs these tasks, was baptized *BOS* (Dutch: *Beslis & Ondersteunend Systeem*, i.e., decision and support system). When BOS predicts the expected water level in Rotterdam will be too high, it has the responsibility to close the barrier. Since Rotterdam is a major port, the barrier should be closed only when really necessary and as briefly as possible. An unnecessarily closed barrier will cost millions of Euros because of restricted shipping traffic.

The realization of the BOS system is an effort in linking several distinct disciplines, viz., the organizational and global overview of the system functionality, requirements and decision rules by *Rijkswaterstaat* (RWS), the hydrological knowledge and model-based water level predictions by Delft Hydraulics[2], (independent research institute for water management and control), and the controlling and automation discipline and systems' integration knowledge by CMG. Because of the dangers and costs involved, very strict safety and reliability requirements are imposed on the BOS software. These high safety and reliability requirements make that the BOS is a *mission critical system* (or safety critical system), for which special care, effort and precautions should be taken in order to guarantee its safe, reliable and correct operation. To this extent, the design and development of the BOS software were guided by the IEC 61508 standard [1], which gives guidelines for software development for safety critical systems. One of the "highly recommended" techniques applied in the BOS system development is formal methods. With formal methods, systems are modeled using precise mathematical concepts. Due to their mathematical underpinning these models allow for precise specification and design description, formal (automatic) verification of system behaviour, simulation and animation, derivation and calculation of system properties, and derivation of test cases. In the development of BOS the formal methods PROMELA and Z were used for modelling and specification of the design.

Barrier Reliability Revisited

During 2006 concerns were raised on the actual reliability of the Maeslant barrier. An independent study showed that instead of the required 1 in 1000 probability of failure per closure (one closure every 10 years), the actual probability of failure was 1 in 10 per closure. The news around this study resulted in questions to the Minister on the subject and resulted in an extensive project to re-investigate the reliability and take appropriate measures to improve it [8]. As at that time no public information was available on what actually was the cause for the decreased reliability, it also resulted in a lot of opinion pieces in more popular computer magazines [9] arguing that the software was the problem of the reliability.

However, the actual report sent by the Minister to the House provides a better view on the actual problems [10]. In the report, it can be seen that in terms of probability of failure, the main issue was the lack of pro-active maintenance. Though the barrier was working correctly, some spare parts for the barrier were not available or contracts with guaranteed repair times not in place. As the probability of failure is determined by both the MTTF (Mean Time To Failure) and the MTTR (Mean Time To Repair), the lack of spare parts and guaranteed repair times directly increases the probability of failure. In addition, the change in the water level at which the barrier must close also decreases the probability of failure through a complex relation.

---

[2] Now called Deltares.

With respect to the BOS system, the main changes were stricter guaranteed repair times for specific hardware failures. In 2004, BOS was already extended with more validation logic for the wind and water measurements and hydraulic and meteorological forecasts. Validation of input information was extensively discussed during the initial BOS project. It was required to rely on the external measurements and forecasts as validation might introduce errors (note that the hole in the ozone layer over the south pole was missed because of incorrect validation rules[11]).

Actual Operation of the BOS System

During the life time of the BOS system, one test closure was performed every year. In addition, on November 11th, 2007 BOS closed the barrier for the first time because of a storm surge. In addition, during the storm season BOS was actively monitoring water and weather predictions and measurements. During its operational life of ten years, no critical or major errors that might affect barrier operation were found in the system itself. Minor errors have been found, in the area of incorrect alarm signals at startup et cetera. In the BOS system, a number of change requests were implemented to introduce simple input validation so that blatantly incorrect data from the measurement networks is rejected and an alarm is raised and to allow human intervention in error cases.

Mid-Life Upgrade Project

Currently, the BOS system hardware is end of life and needs to be replaced. The project for creating its successor has started. In it, the formal method Z is used as it was in the original project, i.e., the specifications and designs are still done in Z and the development process is followed as in the original project. Promela is not foreseen to be used as there are no architectural or protocol changes planned that require re-validation. In terms of hardware, again a single, hardware fault-tolerant Stratus server is used. Communications lines are however terminated on standard terminal servers and use standard redundant networking to communicate to the Stratus. The total probability of failure decreases through the introduction of this hardware. With respect to the software, the following changes are being planned:

1. Improved diagnostics to help detect errors in the external environment.
2. De-coupling of the GUI from the actual system to simplify the system and de-couple one of the less critical components onto separate hardware.
3. Support for analysis and data mining to help determine the root cause of errors.

Conclusions

The use of formal methods has helped the project achieve the required software quality goals. As is common with software systems that only have to perform their critical operation incidentally, it is impossible to determine the software reliability itself. However, the following conclusions can be drawn:

- The learning curve for formal methods in the mid-life upgrade is still steep. New engineers still lack a good background in formal methods.
- The combination of formal methods and code reviews/module testing pays off for analyzing subtle behavior. Detailed questions on behavior can be answered within minutes through the formal specification. Also, FM support what-if analysis extremely well.
- In the initial project all of the system was specified in Z and validated in Promela. This could have been optimized by applying it to the critical parts only.

Though the application of formal methods was successful for the BOS system, with respect to the future, there are some remarks to be made:

- Commercially, for LogicaCMG, very few customers are willing to pay the price of a SIL-4 system. Instead, very often the required software reliability is reduced to a lower level through conventional conservative design techniques.
- The learning curve for formal methods, e.g., Z, is still steep for a new team.
- For Acision, a major provider of messaging equipment, the experience over the past period is that the role of formal methods has decreased. Where conventional standards used SDL to specify protocols, both 3GPP and Open Mobile Alliance seem feature driven in the definition of new standards. Bad examples include the Multimedia Messaging Standard and the Diameter based charging standards.

For a future role for formal methods, we therefore think it is necessary to focus on:

- Support for the specification and design phase. As experiences with BOS show and as standardization shows, the majority of the problems are introduced in the specification and design, not the implementation.
- Support for practical methods and tooling that make the use of formal methods simple.
- Standardize on specific formal methods (best of breed) as a part of the standard computer science education.

Fortunately, there seems more focus on practical methods and tooling. However only if all three conditions are fulfilled, formal methods will be a major benefit to software development for critical systems.

References

[1] IEC, Functional Safety: Safety Related Systems, International Standard IEC 61508, International Electrotechnical Commission, Geneva, Switzerland (1996)
[2] Wijbrans, K., Buve, F., Geurts, W.: Practical Experiences in the BOS project. In: Proceedings of the Embedded Systems Symposium, Eindhoven, The Netherlands (1998)
[3] Wijbrans, K., Buve, R.: Software bestuurt de stormvloedkering. Software Release Magazine 50(5) (in Dutch, 1998)
[4] Chaudron, M., Tretmans, J., Wijbrans, K.: Lessons from the Application of Formal Methods to the Design of a Storm Surge Barrier Control System. In: Woodcock, J.C.P., Davies, J., Wing, J.M. (eds.) FM 1999. LNCS, vol. 1709, pp. 1511–1526. Springer, Heidelberg (1999)

[5] Geurts, W., Wijbrans, K., Tretmans, J.: Testing and Formal Methods – BOS project case study. In: EuroSTAR 1998: 6th European Int. Conference on Software Testing, Analysis & Review, Munich, Germany, pp. 215–229 (1998)
[6] Tretmans, G.J., Wijbrans, K.C.J., Chaudron, M.: Software Engineering with Formal Methods: The Development of a Storm Surge Barrier Control System - Revisiting Seven Myths of Formal Methods. Formal Methods in System Design 19(2), 195–215 (2001), ISSN 0925-9856
[7] http://www.deltawerken.com/Maeslant-barrier/330.html
[8] Letter from the minister to the Tweede Kamer, RWS/SDG/NW 2006/332/23875 (February 20, 2006) (in Dutch)
[9] Groote, J.F., Verhoef, C.: Hoe betrouwbaar is de Maeslantkering. Automatiseringsgids 14 (April 7, 2006) (in Dutch)
[10] prof. Horvath, et al.: Second Opinion Faalkans Maeslantkering (June 27, 2006) (in Dutch)
[11] http://catless.ncl.ac.uk/Risks/3.34.html

Application of a Formal Specification Language in the Development of the "Mobile FeliCa" IC Chip Firmware for Embedding in Mobile Phone

Taro Kurita[1], Miki Chiba[2], and Yasumasa Nakatsugawa[2]

[1] FeliCa Networks, Inc.
Taro.Kurita@FeliCaNetworks.co.jp
[2] Sony Corporation

Abstract. We have adopted formal specification language in the development of firmware of "Mobile FeliCa" IC chip and have achieved successful results and confirmed its effectiveness.

1 Outline of Project

"FeliCa" is a contactless IC card technology widely used in Japan, developed and promoted by Sony Corporation. This FeliCa technology is utilized in Mobile FeliCa IC chip which is embedded in a mobile phone. Mobile phones embedded with a FeliCa IC chip are known as "Osaifu Keitai" (means of mobile wallet) by NTT DoCoMo, Inc., and today those chips are embedded in over 50 million mobile phones which can be used as electric money, train tickets, identifications, door keys and so on.

Mobile FeliCa system is comprised of mobile phones with a FeliCa IC chip, FeliCa servers connected to the mobile telecom network and FeliCa reader/writers. The characteristics of the Mobile FeliCa IC chip firmware are as follows:

- Contains the secure file system and the communications protocol, which are the basis of the FeliCa technology;
- Possesses firewall functions that enable the multiple services in the Mobile FeliCa IC chip such as electric money and train tickets;
- Provides the extended functions and performance required to be embedded in a mobile phone while maintaining compatibility with FeliCa IC cards.

For the project, we must ensure the extremely high quality of the software so as to avoid serious problems related to social infrastructure and to ensure that multitude of stakeholders will not be affected.

The project duration was three years and three months. There were 50-60 members affiliated with this project, and the average age was about 30 years old. There were no members who had the knowledge of or the experience with formal methods at the time of project launch.

We employed several chip manufacturers in order to reduce risks in manufacturing and sales. It was necessary that the firmware on the different ASICs and firmware development environments behave exactly the same so that the compatibility was retained.

C/C++ and assembler languages are used in the implementation of the Mobile FeliCa IC chip firmware.

2 Objectives

After an intensive consideration to the characterization of the development of the Mobile FeliCa IC chip, we decided to focus on improvements in upstream processes related to software development and mutual understanding between engineers, and we have taken on the challenge of writing formal specifications.

The objectives of adopting formal methods were as follows:

- Description of precise specifications and defining functions;
- Development and adoption of a scheme and processes for specification development, firmware implementation and testing;
- Enhancing the quality of deliverables in upstream processes;
- Thoroughgoing testing with formal specifications for whole software development processes;
- Improvement of communications between stakeholders.

3 Approach

We have developed and tested external specifications using VDM++[1].

The process of specification development is as follows:

1. Discussed requirements with stakeholders and wrote the general specifications in a natural language with various diagrams based on UML notation, such as state transition diagrams and sequence diagrams;
2. Modeled the FeliCa file system and designed and implemented a framework in VDM++;
3. Described command and security specifications using the framework;
4. Tested developed specifications using a unit test framework.

The main components or functions of the formal specifications are as follows:

- The FeliCa file system specification that defines the basic data structure;
- The framework for describing and testing specifications that are based on the basic data structure;
- Command specifications which are the basis of the FeliCa technology;
- Security specifications.

We have decided to use the formal specification language VDM++ and VDM-Tools, since they support describing and executing of models in large-scale.

Non-functional specifications such as performance and reliability were written in the natural language separately from the formal specification.

In the project, we organized three teams; specification team, firmware implementation team and testing team. There were 5-10 members, 15-20 members and 25-35 members respectively.

4 Test Scheme

Test engineers design black-box test specifications from the formal specifications and then implement test scripts. Executable formal specifications, firmware on development boards and IC chips are tested using the test scripts.

From the results of the tests, we were able to confirm whether the test cases and scripts are consistent with the specifications. In addition, from measuring the coverage of the executable formal specifications we were able to confirm whether the test items cover all the defined specifications. Therefore, executable formal specifications, firmware on development boards and IC chips can be tested at the same time.

5 Results and Considerations

The results related to specifications are as follows:

- 383 pages of a protocol manual written in a natural language (manual for other departments within the company and for outside customers);
- 677 pages of an external specification document written in the formal specification language.

We developed the formal specifications of about 100,000 steps, inclusive of unit testing for formal specifications and comments written in a natural language as a supplement of the formal specifications. Using this specifications, we implemented the C/C++ code of about 110,000 steps, inclusive of comments, as firmware of a single IC chip.

The percentages of errors related to specifications for the overall project are as shown in Table 1.

Table 1. Percentages of the Cause of Errors

Reason for Errors	Percentage
Missing description	0.2%
Erroneous description	0%
Unclear description	1.8%
Oversight	5.6%
Insufficient understanding	10.7%
Insufficient confirmation	0%
Failure of change propagation	0.2%
Others (reasons unrelated to specifications)	81.5%

The formal methods are useful for finding errors in the early stages of development.

From the above results, it can be said that we have successfully described the specifications in precise way. On the other hand, the total percentage of "oversight" errors and "insufficient understanding" errors was 16.3%. This was due to the fact that the separations between the actual specifications and the code required to execute the specifications was unclear.

The average productivity of VDM code for the formal specifications was about 1,900 lines per engineer per month (approximately 160 hours). This number is equal to the firmware implementation. It can be said that there was no particular disadvantage by using the formal specification language.

The line coverage rate of the formal specifications by unit testing was 82%.

We were able to enhance the coverage rate of unit testing cases by coverage analysis. As a result of unit testing, we were able, for example, to discover an incorrect path in postconditions. It is generally difficult to discover this kind of inconsistency in a specification by review.

The line coverage rate of the formal specifications by black-box testing was 100%. This coverage rate is inclusive of visual inspection.

"Random Test" is an aging test; the test tool sends randomly selected commands continuously to the test target and checks whether the test target sends back correct responses.

By carrying out about 7,000 black-box tests and 100 million random tests, the high quality of IC chips was achieved.

We have analyzed all the questions related to the specifications from firmware engineers, test engineers and stakeholders and have divided questions into three categories: "Comprehension," "Intent" and "Error."

As compared with the formal specification, there are more requests for clarification on the general specifications and the manual written in natural language. On the other hand, there are more questions related to comprehension of the formal specification.

This result shows that the specifications in natural language were not precise and for the formal specifications the background of the specifications were unclear to readers. Therefore, it is preferable that the background of the specifications written in natural language are included as comments in the formal specifications.

6 Conclusion

The application of the formal method was highly effective for the success of our project.

The formal method contributes the quality of deliverables in upstream processes, especially in the specification development process and the improvement of communication within a project.

Additionally, the fact that the executable formal specifications are resembled to program codes is an substantial advantage because the know-how accumulated through program development can be applied (for example, configuration management, filter programs, batch programs, object oriented analysis and design technology, unit testing and so on).

It is necessary to pay attention to not only executable features but also the readability of specifications. Since specifications are referred to by all project members, it needs to be a simple specification that can be read without stress.

7 Difficulties

In our project, the capability for abstraction required by formal specification engineers did not go beyond that required by usual programmers.

In the case of VDM++, an engineer who is familiar with the object oriented design and the implementation of C++/Java languages will easily be able to carry out coding and testing of formal specifications after training of about 1 month.

8 Future Issues

Future issues are listed below:

- Validating whether specifications fulfill requirements;
- Negotiating with stakeholders who do not read formal specifications;
- Testing manuals for users that is based on formal specifications;
- Defining effective combinations of formal and informal specifications;
- Description of formal specifications suitable for embedded systems;
- Validation and testing of the formal specification; for example validation of whether the security specification is logically consistent;
- Framework for describing specifications that are easy-to-read and executable.

Acknowledgements

We would like to thank Professor Peter Gorm Larsen of Engineering College of Aarhus, Professor Keijiro Araki of Kyushu University, Shin Sahara of CSK Systems Corporation and Sako Hiroshi of Designers' Den Corporation for their great assistance in the application of the formal method.

Reference

1. Fitzgerald, J., Larsen, P.G., Mukherjee, P., Plat, N., Verhoef, M.: Validated Designs for Object-oriented Systems. Springer, Heidelberg (2005)

Safe and Reliable Metro Platform Screen Doors Control/Command Systems

Thierry Lecomte

ClearSy, Aix en Provence, France
thierry.lecomte@clearsy.com

Abstract. In this article we would like to present some recent applications of the B formal method to the development of safety critical system. These SIL3/SIL4[1] compliant systems have their functional specification based on a formal model. This model has been proved, guaranteeing a correct by construction behaviour of the system in absence of failure of its components. The constructive process used during system specification and design leads to a high quality system which has been qualified[2] by French authorities.

1 Introduction

Historically, the B Method was introduced in the late 80s' to design correctly safe software. Promoted and supported by RATP[3], B and Atelier B, the tool implementing it, have been successfully applied to the industry of transportation. First real success was Meteor line 14 driverless metro in Paris: Over 110 000 lines of B models were written, generating 86 000 lines of Ada. No bugs were detected after the proofs, neither at the functional validation, at the integration validation, at on-site test, nor since the metro lines operate (October 1998). The safety-critical software is still in version 1.0 in year 2007, without any bug detected so far. Today, Alstom Transportation Systems and Siemens Transportation Systems (representing 80% of the worldwide metro market) are the two main actors in the development of B safety-critical software development. Both have a product based strategy and reuse as much as possible existing B models to develop future metros. For the time being, ClearSy has developed for Siemens the biggest B application: the Charles de Gaule airport shuttle automated pilot is a 150 000 lines of code program. On a different domain, Gemplus has developed a smartcard java bytecode verifier [Casset 99].

---

[1] SIL (Safety Integrity Level) is defined as a relative level of risk-reduction provided by a safety function, or to specify a target level of risk reduction. Four SIL levels are defined, with SIL4 being the most dependable and SIL1 being the least. A SIL is determined based on a number of quantitative factors in combination with qualitative factors such as development process and safety life cycle management.
[2] French authorities define Qualified as « Certified and working » while Certified is mainly a verification of conformance to specification (the system produced may or may not work properly).
[3] Régie Autonome des Transports Parisiens : operates bus and metro public transport in Paris.

A more widely scope use of B appeared in the mid '90s, called *Event-B*, to analyze, study and specify systems. One of the outcome of *Event-B* is the proved definition of systems architectures and, more generally, the proved development of, so called, "system studies", which are performed before the specification and design of the software. This enlargement allows one to perform failure studies right from the beginning in a large system development. *Event-B* has been applied in many cases to various fields: certification of smartcard security policies (level EAL5+, Common Criteria), verification of Ariane 5 launcher embedded flight software, generation of proven hardware specification, etc.

In this article, we detail the first platform screen door system which has been modelled in B, details the development process and presents qualitative and quantitative results.

2 COPPILOT: A Platform Screen Door Controller

2.1 Presentation

In France, RATP has used for years platform screen doors (PSD) that prevent customers to enter or to fall on tracks. Such a system was adopted by the METEOR driverless metro, as it dramatically improves trains availability. In order to offer higher quality services and more safety to its customers, RATP was trying to introduce this kind of protection system in several lines, automated or not. For practical reasons, trains and cars could not be modified with the introduction of PSD. Before starting to deploy a new PSD system in an entire line, RATP initiated a project aimed at developing a prototype PSD system for three stations of line 13.

These prototypes would be evaluated during eight months. ClearSy was in charge of developing the SIL3 compliant (probability of system failure less than 10^{-7}), control command controller. This controller is in charge of detecting the arrival, presence at a standstill and departure of trains without direct connection with them (on the contrary, Meteor[4] trains communicate with PSD through dedicated communications lines). Once the train is at standstill, the controller should be able to detect train doors opening and closing, and then issue PSD opening and closing orders. These orders have to be securely issued (failure by elaborating a wrong opening order may lead to customers injury or death), and controller have to be designed, tested and validated in accordance with railway regulations (IEC 50126, 50128, 50129 in particular).

The timescale of this project was quite short as the PSD controller would be installed in only 10 months after the beginning of the project. Given these strong timing constraints, we decided to adopt a secure architecture able to be quickly qualified by regulation authorities, loosely coupled with sensor technology. The final architecture was based on Siemens safety automaton, SIL3 compliant, and ordinary infra-red and radar sensors. In this case, security relies on the safety automaton and on sensor measure redundancy, not on the safety properties of the sensors. This approach leads to a decrease in system costs as usual since non-safety sensors are really cheaper than safety ones, leading to easier provisioning (shorter delay, no dependency towards a unique provider).

---

[4] First driverless metro operated in Paris.

2.2 The Development Process

In order to reach the required safety level during project timescale, we decided to set up a development method aimed at reaching targeted reliability, and also ensuring traceability between the different stages of the projects in order to reduce the validation effort. This method was heavily based on the B formal method, and applied during most phases of the project.

Before any development activity, a formal functional analysis of the system was performed, to evaluate "completeness" and ambiguity freeness of the statement of work. At that time, the solution imagined by RATP was to point two laser telemeters on the platform, and to apply two independent 2D image recognitions in order to detect train arrival and departure, as well as train door opening and closing. The B method was used to:

- Verify on the overall system (PSD + controller) that functional constraints and safety properties were verified (no possibility to establish forbidden connections between train and platform or between train and tracks).
- Lead to the observation of dangerous system behaviour.

Telemeter based solution was then evaluated in order to verify that its compliancy with project constraints. This solution was finally abandoned due to the fact that designing two independent (but concordant) image recognition algorithms was judged too risky during the short lifetime of the project.

A new architecture was then imagined and proposed, making use of usual sensors and processing based on temporal sequence recognition of sensor events. Hyper frequency, infrared and laser sensors help to improve system resistance to various perturbations. Redundancy among sensors using different technology raises measures confidence. These sensors were positioned on the platform and pointed to the tracks in order to measure train position, train speed and train door movements.

System and software specification were then formalized in B by the development team, taking into account only nominal behaviour for the sensors (in absence of perturbation). Models obtained from previous functional analysis (independent from any PSD controller architecture) were directly reused. The proposed architecture was modelled and inserted in these previous models. New architecture was successfully checked by proof to comply with functional specification of the system, including parts of the French underground regulations. Controller functions were then precisely modelled (train arrival, train detection, train departure, train door opening, train door closing, etc). In the meantime, an independent safety case[5] was developed in parallel by the security team, in order to precisely define how external perturbations may influence the behaviour of the PSD controller. Perturbations were given a priori or a posteriori frequencies, depending on availability of such data at RATP, and a mathematical model, independent from the B model, was set up in order to determine quantitatively the security level of the system. A priori frequencies were verified during the eight month experiment. In case these frequencies were not verified and lower system security below SIL3 level, the PSD controllers would have to be redesigned considering this new information.

---

[5] Safety oriented study that provides a convincing and valid argument that a system is adequately safe for a given application in a given environment.

The resulting B model was animated with the Brama animator[6], in order to verify on given scenarios that the model produced was corresponding to the real system we were modelling. This model animator was not part of the validation process, as this would require it to be qualified as a SIL3 software, but it helped us to check models against reality and to internally verify their suitability.

Specification documentation was partly elaborated from the system level models developed during this project. The composys[7] tool helps the modeller to add contextual information (comments, description, component name, etc) in B models that are used to generate in natural language the specification documentation descrybing the complete system. As events are associated to components and as variables are used within events (read/write), Composys computes relationships among components constituting the system being modelled, depending on how variables are read or modified. This document was used to check models with experts of the domain, unable to read and understand formal models.

The development of the software was based on the formal models, as B enables the production of source code, proven to comply with its specification. Siemens automaton can be programmed in the LADDER language but, unfortunately, requires entering program source code via its graphical interface (according to its certificate) to keep its SIL3 accreditation. A dedicated translation schema (from B to LADDER) was elaborated. B to LADDER state diagrams translation is straightforward and some optimisations were introduced in order to verify temporal constraints (cycle time in particular). During validation phase, one can determine which event of the B model corresponds to the path of the LADDER program for a cycle (a LADDER program is defined by logical equations and is analyzed in term of execution path). In case the source code is automatically generated by a qualified translator (as for automatic pilots, by Siemens and Alstom), no unit test is required, this testing phase being covered by the proof of the model. In this project, as the source code was not generated automatically by such a translator, test was required and test specification was elaborated by usual means. Some months after the beginning of the project, we obtained a fully functional, tested and validated application. The process described above has enabled us to produce a 100% tested, error free (against its specification) software when running validation test bench for the first time. A dedicated test bench was designed to simulate major perturbations (sensors were emulated) and run during days, but no faulty behaviour was observed.

Integration testing was performed on a dedicated testing platform installed in the METEOR line. Tracks and sensors being already protected by PSD in the line, measurement campaigns were setup quickly in order to assess as quickly as possible security, availability, response time, etc). Sensor technology choices were validated at that occasion.

2.3 Results

Finally, 4 months after the beginning of the project, the PSD controller was deployed on 3 platforms on line 13, for a 8 month experiment. The following metrics were obtained:

---

[6] http://www.brama.fr
[7] http://www.composys.fr

- equip: a project manager, a developer, a validation engineer, a safety engineer
- initial system level functional specification: 130 page document
- safety case: 300 pages
- development documentation: 600 pages
- formal B models: 3500 lines of code, representing about 1000 proof obligations. 90 % were demonstrated automatically, the remaining proof obligations were discharged in two days with the Atelier B interactive prover.

This system was experimented during 8 months, controlling around 96 000 trains. No fault was observed. Hypotheses made during the safety case were confirmed and made more accurate. System availability conformed to expectations and, after initial setup and tuning, no passenger remained stuck in the train (PSD should open 9999 out of 10000 times when a valid train is at standstill opening its doors).

3 Conclusion

The methodology we have developed appears to be efficient and well suited to address projects requiring high level of safety and short development time. The B formal method was not initially considered by RATP, but is now well accepted. The writing of some extra documents were required to help RATP engineers to fully understand, verify and qualify our deliverables. Reuse of existing models for similar projects proved to be efficient.

The resulting systems are nowadays deployed worlwide.

References

Burdy, L.: Automatic Refinement. In: Proceedings of BUGM at FM 1999 (1996)
Sabatier, D., et al.: Use of the Formal B Method for a SIL3 System Landing Door Commands for line 13 of the Paris subway, Lambda Mu 15 (2006)

Author Index

Aktug, Irem   262
Amtoft, Torben   229
Arvind   12

Bischof, Markus   165
Bonakdarpour, Borzoo   374
Buve, Franc   419

Chalin, Patrice   246
Chang, Felix Sheng-Ho   326
Chetali, Boutheina   198
Chiba, Miki   425

Dam, Mads   262
Darvas, Ádám   68
Dave, Nirav   12
Dovland, Johan   52

Emmi, Michael   116
Engler, Dawson   33

Fitzgerald, John   181
Furia, Carlo A.   132

Gawlitza, Thomas   342
Geurts, Wouter   419
Giannakopoulou, Dimitra   116
Gonzalia, C.   100
Grandy, Holger   165
Greve, David   229
Gurov, Dilian   262

Harhurin, Alexander   390
Hartmann, Judith   390
Hatcliff, John   229
Hoag, Jonathan   229

Jackson, Daniel   326
Johnsen, Einar Broch   52
Jong, Gjalt de   411

Katelman, Michael   12
Katz, Shmuel   1
Khurshid, Sarfraz   310
Kiniry, Joseph R.   214

Kitchen, David   34
Kulkarni, Sandeep S.   374
Kurita, Taro   425

Larsen, Peter Gorm   181
Lecomte, Thierry   430
Li, Mingyan   406
Lintelman, Scott   406

Macedo, Hugo Daniel   181
Mateescu, Radu   148
McComb, Tim   358
McIver, A.K.   100
Mezhuyev, Vitaliy   411
Misra, Jayadev   34
Morgan, C.C.   100
Müller, Peter   68

Nakatsugawa, Yasumasa   425
Nguyen, Quang-Huy   198
Noll, Thomas   84
Norrish, Michael   294

Owe, Olaf   52

Păsăreanu, Corina S.   116
Pnueli, Amir   35
Ponsini, Olivier   278
Powell, Evan   34
Pradella, Matteo   132

Reif, Wolfgang   165
Ridge, Tom   294
Rieger, Stefan   84
Rijkers, Robin   419
Rioux, Frédéric   246
Robby   229
Robinson, Richard   406
Rodríguez, Edwin   229
Rossi, Matteo   132
Rudich, Arsenii   68

Sampigethaya, Krishna   406
Schellhorn, Gerhard   165
Seidl, Helmut   342
Serwe, Wendelin   278

Sewell, Peter 294
Smith, Graeme 358
Steffen, Martin 52
Stenzel, Kurt 165

Thivolle, Damien 148
Torlak, Emina 326

Uzuncaova, Engin 310

Verhulst, Eric 411

Wijbrans, Klaas 419

Zaks, Anna 35
Zimmerman, Daniel M. 214

Lecture Notes in Computer Science

Sublibrary 2: Programming and Software Engineering

For information about Vols. 1– 4346
please contact your bookseller or Springer

Vol. 5030: H. Mei (Ed.), High Confidence Software Reuse in Large Systems. XII, 388 pages. 2008.

Vol. 5020: J. Barnes, Ada 2005 Rationale. IX, 267 pages. 2008.

Vol. 5014: J. Cuellar, T. Maibaum, K. Sere (Eds.), FM 2008: Formal Methods. XIII, 436 pages. 2008.

Vol. 5007: Q. Wang, D. Pfahl, D.M. Raffo (Eds.), Making Globally Distributed Software Development a Success Story. XIV, 422 pages. 2008.

Vol. 4989: J. Garrigue, M.V. Hermenegildo (Eds.), Functional and Logic Programming. XI, 337 pages. 2008.

Vol. 4966: B. Beckert, R. Hähnle (Eds.), Tests and Proofs. X, 193 pages. 2008.

Vol. 4954: C. Pautasso, É. Tanter (Eds.), Software Composition. X, 263 pages. 2008.

Vol. 4951: M. Luck, L. Padgham (Eds.), Agent-Oriented Software Engineering VIII. XIV, 225 pages. 2008.

Vol. 4949: R.M. Hierons, J.P. Bowen, M. Harman (Eds.), Formal Methods and Testing. XIII, 367 pages. 2008.

Vol. 4937: M. Dumas, R. Heckel (Eds.), Web Services and Formal Methods. IX, 169 pages. 2008.

Vol. 4916: P. Merino, S. Leue (Eds.), Formal Methods: Applications and Technology. X, 251 pages. 2008.

Vol. 4906: M. Cebulla (Ed.), Object-Oriented Technology. VIII, 204 pages. 2008.

Vol. 4902: P. Hudak, D.S. Warren (Eds.), Practical Aspects of Declarative Languages. X, 333 pages. 2007.

Vol. 4899: K. Yorav (Ed.), Hardware and Software: Verification and Testing. XII, 267 pages. 2008.

Vol. 4888: F. Kordon, O. Sokolsky (Eds.), Composition of Embedded Systems. XII, 221 pages. 2007.

Vol. 4880: S. Overhage, C.A. Szyperski, R. Reussner, J.A. Stafford (Eds.), Software Architectures, Components, and Applications. X, 249 pages. 2008.

Vol. 4849: M. Winckler, H. Johnson, P. Palanque (Eds.), Task Models and Diagrams for User Interface Design. XIII, 299 pages. 2007.

Vol. 4839: O. Sokolsky, S. Taşıran (Eds.), Runtime Verification. VI, 215 pages. 2007.

Vol. 4834: R. Cerqueira, R.H. Campbell (Eds.), Middleware 2007. XIII, 451 pages. 2007.

Vol. 4829: M. Lumpe, W. Vanderperren (Eds.), Software Composition. VIII, 281 pages. 2007.

Vol. 4824: A. Paschke, Y. Biletskiy (Eds.), Advances in Rule Interchange and Applications. XIII, 243 pages. 2007.

Vol. 4821: J. Bennedsen, M.E. Caspersen, M. Kölling (Eds.), Reflections on the Teaching of Programming. X, 261 pages. 2008.

Vol. 4807: Z. Shao (Ed.), Programming Languages and Systems. XI, 431 pages. 2007.

Vol. 4799: A. Holzinger (Ed.), HCI and Usability for Medicine and Health Care. XVI, 458 pages. 2007.

Vol. 4789: M. Butler, M.G. Hinchey, M.M. Larrondo-Petrie (Eds.), Formal Methods and Software Engineering. VIII, 387 pages. 2007.

Vol. 4767: F. Arbab, M. Sirjani (Eds.), International Symposium on Fundamentals of Software Engineering. XIII, 450 pages. 2007.

Vol. 4765: A. Moreira, J. Grundy (Eds.), Early Aspects: Current Challenges and Future Directions. X, 199 pages. 2007.

Vol. 4764: P. Abrahamsson, N. Baddoo, T. Margaria, R. Messnarz (Eds.), Software Process Improvement. XI, 225 pages. 2007.

Vol. 4762: K.S. Namjoshi, T. Yoneda, T. Higashino, Y. Okamura (Eds.), Automated Technology for Verification and Analysis. XIV, 566 pages. 2007.

Vol. 4758: F. Oquendo (Ed.), Software Architecture. XVI, 340 pages. 2007.

Vol. 4757: F. Cappello, T. Herault, J. Dongarra (Eds.), Recent Advances in Parallel Virtual Machine and Message Passing Interface. XVI, 396 pages. 2007.

Vol. 4753: E. Duval, R. Klamma, M. Wolpers (Eds.), Creating New Learning Experiences on a Global Scale. XII, 518 pages. 2007.

Vol. 4749: B.J. Krämer, K.-J. Lin, P. Narasimhan (Eds.), Service-Oriented Computing – ICSOC 2007. XIX, 629 pages. 2007.

Vol. 4748: K. Wolter (Ed.), Formal Methods and Stochastic Models for Performance Evaluation. X, 301 pages. 2007.

Vol. 4741: C. Bessière (Ed.), Principles and Practice of Constraint Programming – CP 2007. XV, 890 pages. 2007.

Vol. 4735: G. Engels, B. Opdyke, D.C. Schmidt, F. Weil (Eds.), Model Driven Engineering Languages and Systems. XV, 698 pages. 2007.

Vol. 4716: B. Meyer, M. Joseph (Eds.), Software Engineering Approaches for Offshore and Outsourced Development. X, 201 pages. 2007.

Vol. 4709: F.S. de Boer, M.M. Bonsangue, S. Graf, W.-P. de Roever (Eds.), Formal Methods for Components and Objects. VIII, 297 pages. 2007.

Vol. 4680: F. Saglietti, N. Oster (Eds.), Computer Safety, Reliability, and Security. XV, 548 pages. 2007.

Vol. 4670: V. Dahl, I. Niemelä (Eds.), Logic Programming. XII, 470 pages. 2007.

Vol. 4652: D. Georgakopoulos, N. Ritter, B. Benatallah, C. Zirpins, G. Feuerlicht, M. Schoenherr, H.R. Motahari-Nezhad (Eds.), Service-Oriented Computing ICSOC 2006. XVI, 201 pages. 2007.

Vol. 4640: A. Rashid, M. Aksit (Eds.), Transactions on Aspect-Oriented Software Development IV. IX, 191 pages. 2007.

Vol. 4634: H. Riis Nielson, G. Filé (Eds.), Static Analysis. XI, 469 pages. 2007.

Vol. 4620: A. Rashid, M. Aksit (Eds.), Transactions on Aspect-Oriented Software Development III. IX, 201 pages. 2007.

Vol. 4615: R. de Lemos, C. Gacek, A. Romanovsky (Eds.), Architecting Dependable Systems IV. XIV, 435 pages. 2007.

Vol. 4610: B. Xiao, L.T. Yang, J. Ma, C. Muller-Schloer, Y. Hua (Eds.), Autonomic and Trusted Computing. XVIII, 571 pages. 2007.

Vol. 4609: E. Ernst (Ed.), ECOOP 2007 – Object-Oriented Programming. XIII, 625 pages. 2007.

Vol. 4608: H.W. Schmidt, I. Crnković, G.T. Heineman, J.A. Stafford (Eds.), Component-Based Software Engineering. XII, 283 pages. 2007.

Vol. 4591: J. Davies, J. Gibbons (Eds.), Integrated Formal Methods. IX, 660 pages. 2007.

Vol. 4589: J. Münch, P. Abrahamsson (Eds.), Product-Focused Software Process Improvement. XII, 414 pages. 2007.

Vol. 4574: J. Derrick, J. Vain (Eds.), Formal Techniques for Networked and Distributed Systems – FORTE 2007. XI, 375 pages. 2007.

Vol. 4556: C. Stephanidis (Ed.), Universal Access in Human-Computer Interaction, Part III. XXII, 1020 pages. 2007.

Vol. 4555: C. Stephanidis (Ed.), Universal Access in Human-Computer Interaction, Part II. XXII, 1066 pages. 2007.

Vol. 4554: C. Stephanidis (Ed.), Universal Acess in Human Computer Interaction, Part I. XXII, 1054 pages. 2007.

Vol. 4553: J.A. Jacko (Ed.), Human-Computer Interaction, Part IV. XXIV, 1225 pages. 2007.

Vol. 4552: J.A. Jacko (Ed.), Human-Computer Interaction, Part III. XXI, 1038 pages. 2007.

Vol. 4551: J.A. Jacko (Ed.), Human-Computer Interaction, Part II. XXIII, 1253 pages. 2007.

Vol. 4550: J.A. Jacko (Ed.), Human-Computer Interaction, Part I. XXIII, 1240 pages. 2007.

Vol. 4542: P. Sawyer, B. Paech, P. Heymans (Eds.), Requirements Engineering: Foundation for Software Quality. IX, 384 pages. 2007.

Vol. 4536: G. Concas, E. Damiani, M. Scotto, G. Succi (Eds.), Agile Processes in Software Engineering and Extreme Programming. XV, 276 pages. 2007.

Vol. 4530: D.H. Akehurst, R. Vogel, R.F. Paige (Eds.), Model Driven Architecture - Foundations and Applications. X, 219 pages. 2007.

Vol. 4523: Y.-H. Lee, H.-N. Kim, J. Kim, Y.W. Park, L.T. Yang, S.W. Kim (Eds.), Embedded Software and Systems. XIX, 829 pages. 2007.

Vol. 4498: N. Abdennahder, F. Kordon (Eds.), Reliable Software Technologies - Ada-Europe 2007. XII, 247 pages. 2007.

Vol. 4486: M. Bernardo, J. Hillston (Eds.), Formal Methods for Performance Evaluation. VII, 469 pages. 2007.

Vol. 4470: Q. Wang, D. Pfahl, D.M. Raffo (Eds.), Software Process Dynamics and Agility. XI, 346 pages. 2007.

Vol. 4468: M.M. Bonsangue, E.B. Johnsen (Eds.), Formal Methods for Open Object-Based Distributed Systems. X, 317 pages. 2007.

Vol. 4467: A.L. Murphy, J. Vitek (Eds.), Coordination Models and Languages. X, 325 pages. 2007.

Vol. 4454: Y. Gurevich, B. Meyer (Eds.), Tests and Proofs. IX, 217 pages. 2007.

Vol. 4444: T. Reps, M. Sagiv, J. Bauer (Eds.), Program Analysis and Compilation, Theory and Practice. X, 361 pages. 2007.

Vol. 4440: B. Liblit, Cooperative Bug Isolation. XV, 101 pages. 2007.

Vol. 4408: R. Choren, A. Garcia, H. Giese, H.-f. Leung, C. Lucena, A. Romanovsky (Eds.), Software Engineering for Multi-Agent Systems V. XII, 233 pages. 2007.

Vol. 4406: W. De Meuter (Ed.), Advances in Smalltalk. VII, 157 pages. 2007.

Vol. 4405: L. Padgham, F. Zambonelli (Eds.), Agent-Oriented Software Engineering VII. XII, 225 pages. 2007.

Vol. 4401: N. Guelfi, D. Buchs (Eds.), Rapid Integration of Software Engineering Techniques. IX, 177 pages. 2007.

Vol. 4385: K. Coninx, K. Luyten, K.A. Schneider (Eds.), Task Models and Diagrams for Users Interface Design. XI, 355 pages. 2007.

Vol. 4383: E. Bin, A. Ziv, S. Ur (Eds.), Hardware and Software, Verification and Testing. XII, 235 pages. 2007.

Vol. 4379: M. Südholt, C. Consel (Eds.), Object-Oriented Technology. VIII, 157 pages. 2007.

Vol. 4364: T. Kühne (Ed.), Models in Software Engineering. XI, 332 pages. 2007.

Vol. 4355: J. Julliand, O. Kouchnarenko (Eds.), B 2007: Formal Specification and Development in B. XIII, 293 pages. 2007.

Vol. 4354: M. Hanus (Ed.), Practical Aspects of Declarative Languages. X, 335 pages. 2006.

Vol. 4350: M. Clavel, F. Durán, S. Eker, P. Lincoln, N. Martí-Oliet, J. Meseguer, C. Talcott, All About Maude - A High-Performance Logical Framework. XXII, 797 pages. 2007.

Vol. 4348: S. Tucker Taft, R.A. Duff, R.L. Brukardt, E. Plödereder, P. Leroy, Ada 2005 Reference Manual. XXII, 765 pages. 2006.